Tolley's Guide
Share Scheme

GW01465294

Tolley's Guide to Employee Share Schemes

LexisNexis®

Members of the LexisNexis Group worldwide

United Kingdom	LexisNexis, a Division of Reed Elsevier (UK) Ltd, Halsbury House, 35 Chancery Lane, London, WC2A 1EL, and London House, 20–22 East London Street, Edinburgh EH7 4BQ
Australia	LexisNexis Butterworths, Chatswood, New South Wales
Austria	LexisNexis Verlag ARD Orac GmbH & Co KG, Vienna
Benelux	LexisNexis Benelux, Amsterdam
Canada	LexisNexis Canada, Markham, Ontario
China	LexisNexis China, Beijing and Shanghai
France	LexisNexis SA, Paris
Germany	LexisNexis Deutschland GmbH, Munster
Hong Kong	LexisNexis Hong Kong, Hong Kong
India	LexisNexis India, New Delhi
Italy	Giuffrè Editore, Milan
Japan	LexisNexis Japan, Tokyo
Malaysia	Malayan Law Journal Sdn Bhd, Kuala Lumpur
Mexico	LexisNexis Mexico, Mexico
New Zealand	LexisNexis NZ Ltd, Wellington
Poland	Wydawnictwo Prawnicze LexisNexis Sp, Warsaw
Singapore	LexisNexis Singapore, Singapore
South Africa	LexisNexis Butterworths, Durban
USA	LexisNexis, Dayton, Ohio

© Reed Elsevier (UK) Ltd 2009
Published by LexisNexis

This is a Tolley title

A CIP Catalogue record for this book is available from the British Library.

ISBN for this volume

ISBN 978 0 7545 3766 3

Typeset by Letterpart Ltd, Reigate, Surrey
Printed in the United Kingdom by Hobbs the Printers Ltd, Totton, Hampshire
Visit LexisNexis at www.lexisnexis.co.uk

About the Author

David Craddock is an independent consultant specialising in employee share ownership and reward management. Following a successful corporate career during which he established numerous employee share schemes worldwide, he founded his own consultancy services company in 1997 through which he has developed a varied clientele from major public limited companies with international considerations to small and medium-sized private concerns.

David Craddock Consultancy Services addresses all aspects of employee share scheme design, compliance, implementation, communication and administration and has successfully established employee share scheme arrangements across Europe, the Americas, the Far East, Australasia, and Africa. A regular speaker on employee share ownership at conferences, seminars and courses around the world and making occasional television appearances, David Craddock is a recognised authority on employee share ownership and a major contributor to the debate on its relevance to business organisations and employee involvement.

David Craddock has undertaken research on the relationship between employee share ownership and employment levels and the strategic role of employee share ownership in a social market economy, with his work being used for representations to the British Government and the European Commission.

David Craddock is also a member of the Academic Committee of The ESOP Centre and an examiner for the Diploma in Employee Share Ownership Studies, the qualification run by The ESOP Institute.

Acknowledgements

I wish to acknowledge Jane Jevon for her significant contribution to Chapter 30 on Share Schemes for Non-Employees and Chapter 31 on Annual Report Disclosure Guidelines. Additionally, I wish to thank the ESOP Centre for their kind permission to include in Chapters 3, 4 and 5 material that I researched and prepared when developing the course material for the first module of the Diploma in Employee Share Ownership Studies.

Dedication

This book is dedicated to my mother, Marjorie Craddock, who has given to me steadfast and committed support throughout the whole of my professional career.

Contents

Contents

List of abbreviations

Abbreviations

AIM	=	Alternative Investment Market
ABI	=	Association of British Insurers
ASB	=	Accounting Standards Board
AGM	=	Annual General Meeting
BVCA	=	British Venture Capital Association
CEO	=	Chief Executive Officer
CGT	=	Capital Gains Tax
CSOS	=	Company Share Option Scheme
CSR	=	Convertible Securities Regime
CSOP	=	Company Share Option Plan
EAT	=	Employment Appeals Tribunal
EIS	=	Enterprise Investment Scheme
EMI	=	Enterprise Management Incentives
ESC	=	Extra Statutory Concession
ESSU	=	Employees Shares and Securities Unit (HMRC)
ECJ	=	European Court of Justice
EU	=	European Union
ESOP	=	Employee Share Ownership Plan
E/CSOP	=	Executive/Company Share Option Plan/Scheme
FICA	=	Federal Income Tax (social security)
FRS	=	Financial Reporting Standard
FM	=	Fair Market Value
FSMT	=	Financial Services and Markets Tribunal
FSA	=	Financial Services Authority
FRSSE	=	Financial Reporting Standard for Smaller Entities
GAO	=	General Accounting Office (US)
HMRC	=	Her Majesty's Revenue & Customs
IASB	=	International Accounting Standards Board
IFRS	=	International Financial Reporting Standard
IMV	=	Initial Market Value
ISO	=	Incentive Stock Option
IIGs	=	Institutional Investor Guidelines
L-TIP	=	Long-Term Incentive Plan
MV	=	Market Value
MoU	=	Memorandum of Understanding
MGDM	=	Modified Grant Date Method

NAPF	=	National Association of Pension Funds
NCEO	=	National Center for Employee Ownership (US)
NICs	=	National Insurance Contributions
NHS	=	National Health Service
NSO	=	Non-qualified Stock Option
PSOS	=	Phantom Share Option Scheme
PSESS	=	Profit-Sharing Employee Share Scheme
ROA	=	Return on Assets
RSR	=	Restricted Securities Regime
SPA	=	Sale and Purchase Agreement
SSOP	=	Savings-related Share Option Plan/Scheme
SIP	=	Share Incentive Plan
SVD	=	Shares Valuation Division (HMRC)
SCEC	=	Small Company Enterprise Centre
TSR	=	Total Shareholder Return
TPG	=	Transfer Pricing Guidelines
USM	=	Unit of Service Method
QCBs	=	Qualifying Corporate Bonds
QUEST	=	Qualifying Employee Share Trust
VCT	=	Venture Capital Trust
WIP	=	Work In Progress

Legislation

CA 1985	=	Companies Act 1985
CA 2006	=	Companies Act 2006
CA 2006 Order 2006	=	Companies Act 2006 [Commencement No 1, Transitional Provisions and Savings] Order 2006
CJA 1993	=	Criminal Justice Act 1993
CTA 1988	=	Corporation Taxes Act 1988
DDA 1995	=	Disability Discrimination Act 1995
DRRR 2002	=	Directors Remuneration Report Regulations 2002, SI 2002/1986
EE(A) Regs 2006	=	Employment Equality (Age) Regulations 2006, SI 2006/1031
EUITD	=	European Union Insider Trading Directive 89/592/EEC
EUTDDD	=	Transparency Directive and Disclosure Directive 2004
FSMA 2000	=	Financial Services and Markets Act 2000
FA 1980	=	Finance Act 1980
FA 1984	=	Finance Act 1984
FA 1996	=	Finance Act 1996
FA 2003	=	Finance Act 2003

FA 2004	=	Finance Act 2004
FA (No 2) 2005	=	Finance Act (No 2) Act 2005
FA 2009	=	Finance Act 2009
FSA 1986	=	Financial Services Act 1986
FSMA 2000	=	Financial Services and Markets Act 2000
ICTA 1998	=	Income and Corporation Taxes Act 1988
ID(SRM) 1994	=	Insider Dealings (Securities and Regulated Markets) Order 1994
ITA 1984	=	Inheritance Tax Act 1984
ITA 2007	=	Income Tax Act 2007
ITEPA 2003	=	Income Tax (Earnings and Pensions) Act 2003
ITTOIA 2005	=	*Income Tax (Trading and Other Income) Act 2005*
FTE(PLFT) Regs 2002	=	Fixed-Term Employees (Prevention of Less Favourable Treatment) Regulations 2002
LMCG Regs 2008	=	Large and Medium-sized Companies and Groups (Accounts and Reports) Regulations 2008
PTW(PLFT) Regs 2000	=	Part-Time Workers (Prevention of Less Favourable Treatment) Regulations 2000
POS Regs 1995	=	Public Offer of Securities Regulations 1995
TCGA 1992	=	Taxation of Chargeable Gains Act 1992
TMA 1970	=	Taxes Management Act 1970
TUPE Regs 1981	=	Transfer of Undertakings (Protection of Employment) Regulations 1981
UCTA 1977	=	Unfair Contract Terms Act 1977

Chapter 1

Function of employee share schemes

Introduction

1.1 This chapter offers an appreciation of the policy reasons that have motivated successive UK governments since 1978 to introduce employee share ownership initiatives. The explanation is given in the context of the historical dimension since the introduction of the tax-approved profit-sharing employee share scheme in the last full year of James Callaghan's Labour government. The historical dimension offers a subtle insight into the evolution of employee share schemes in the UK together with the developing awareness of the effectiveness of employee share ownership initiatives to achieve particular objectives that have been set as government policy.

Government scheme objectives

1.2 Employee share ownership as a serious policy initiative was begun in its tax-approved form by the 'Lib-Lab' pact in 1978 and then subsequently fostered by the Conservative administrations of Margaret Thatcher and John Major. The accession to power of New Labour in 1997 has seen no abatement in the developing profile of employee share ownership and Gordon Brown, in particular, has embraced the tenets of a shareholding democracy as a means of achieving the economic objectives of New Labour.

After the introduction of the profit-sharing employee share scheme and the election of Margaret Thatcher as Prime Minister, the torch for the development of employee share schemes was taken up by the Conservatives, developing themes that had to a very large degree been researched during their years of opposition.

For the Conservatives, employee share ownership as a government policy initiative was implemented in forms that sought to encourage financial participation of employees in a way that supported two key categories of policy as follows.

Employee financial participation

1.3 The Conservative governments encouraged employee financial participation through two types of mechanism as follows:

- participation in profits; and
- participation in ownership.

Wider share ownership

1.4 In terms of encouraging wider share ownership for the UK public at large, the Conservative governments embarked upon a series of initiatives that were addressed at encouraging wider share ownership within the community at large, irrespective of whether or not the individuals taking up the offers were employees. However, for individuals who were employed and whose companies chose to embrace the opportunities the Conservative governments introduced employee share schemes.

In summary, therefore, the wider share ownership initiatives fell into two categories as follows:

- privatisation issues; and
- employee share schemes.

The use of employee share schemes was, quite clearly, part of the strategy of the Conservative governments to encourage the employees of companies to think in a way that was consistent with governmental policy objectives. However, it was also part of their strategy to encourage the public at large to adopt a similar way of thinking.

At the time, this approach represented a radical departure from the industrial policies that had hitherto been pursued by the Wilson and Callaghan governments throughout the 1960s and 1970s. Indeed, the resolution to introduce wider share ownership, and with it employee share schemes, signalled a colossal change in policy from the old-fashioned and discredited policies of nationalisation that Labour had pursued since the end of the Second World War. The belief that nationalisation represented ownership by the people, albeit through state governance, was exploded as a myth that must give way to effective mechanisms for the real ownership of national business by theUK citizens.

The transition to a share-owning democracy was aided and abetted by the failure of most nationalised businesses to operate efficiently and effectively within financial budgetary constraints for the achievement of business objectives. The openness of Margaret Thatcher to take up the mantel of employee share ownership as an element in the restructuring of UK industry manifested itself in key employee share scheme initiatives that were to be developed and enhanced by successive administrations without any serious opposition from entrenched Labour interests.

The device used to bring employee share schemes to the attention of employer and employee alike had first been used to good effect by the 'Lib-Lab pact' in the introduction of the profit-sharing employee share scheme. This device was the bait of tax relief. It continued to be the bait used by the Conservative governments. Once employee share schemes are active in a company through the holding of shares or the granting of options to purchase shares by employees, then the operation of the schemes develops a power of its own to involve, motivate and incentivise employees. However, the companies could easily have ignored the employee share scheme initiatives as legislative follies, and may well have, without the presence of tax relief. As such, employee share schemes became and continue to be noteworthy items for discussion and analysis in the annual budget statement that is presented to Parliament by the chancellor of the exchequer each spring.

The policy reasons why the Conservative governments gave official support to employee share ownership were linked to addressing the demise of UK industry and can be categorised as follows.

To recognise an identity of interest

1.5 It is a matter of business reality that shareholders, managers and employees all have an interest in the continuing success of the business in which they are involved. The shareholder's or the employer's interest in success in the competitive market of trade in which the business is engaged is to protect and grow the shareholding investment. However, the employee's salary or wages is also dependent on the success of the business in the same competitive market of trade. There is, therefore, an undeniable identity of interest between shareholders and employers on the one hand and managers and employees on the other. Nevertheless, to break down the established divide between employers and employees required a definite policy initiative that had practical manifestation and could be understood by both sides of the industrial divide. It was always recognised that a recognition of identity of interest would evolve and develop. However, the resolve was there on the part of the Conservative governments, with what essentially constituted cross-party support apart from a few dissident parliamentarians, to put the process in motion with the full belief that the evolution and development would happen.

To assist in improving industrial relations

1.6 Recognising an identity of interest contributes greatly towards the development of consensus attitudes expressed in the desire to work together within the workplace.

It is now well recognised that consensus approaches to resolving business problems and tensions within the operation of the business, if properly implemented, have the capacity to achieve the following:

- Stronger motivation and incentive for employees as they develop a stronger sense of participation in the business development and respect for their own business worth.

- Greater understanding amongst employees of the business, indeed everything about the business, including corporate business performance as expressed in recognised parameters such as profitability levels, share prices and price/earnings ratios.

- Better work performance, resulting in enhanced productivity and sustained business growth, particularly where the consensus approaches embrace a range of compatible human resources policies that are designed to encourage employee involvement, such policies being typically meaningful and focused training arrangements, works councils and supportive profit or performance-related pay arrangements as well as employee share schemes.

- Recognition of the need for the business to make profits, particularly if you are sharing in them which for the employees became possible through involvement in profit-sharing and employee share scheme arrangements where by involving employees offered a more progressive and strikingly more commercial approach to involvement in the business.

To promote self-sufficiency and self-reliance

1.7 With the opportunity of financial gain, in some cases significant financial gain, from participation in the schemes, employee share ownership became one of a number of policies promoted by the Conservative governments designed to promote self-sufficiency and self-reliance.

Although this was a defined policy reason for introducing employee share scheme arrangements, it was always recognised to be a long-term consequence of these policy initiatives. Nevertheless, an understanding of the consequences of involvement in employee share schemes does, of course, give an awareness of how such employee involvement can provide an element that contributes to the wider wealth of the individual.

Interestingly, a meaningful understanding of these last two policy reasons operating in combination shows the power of employee share ownership to play a prominent role in encouraging *individual* wealth through promoting self-sufficiency and self-reliance but also assisting *collective* social cohesion through improved industrial relations and a growing national economy.

Objectives of scheme introduction for UK companies

1.8 Increasingly, throughout the 1980s shareholders and employers began to see the merits of the government initiatives on employee share ownership. Although initially the awareness on the part of UK business developed at a slow pace, it became clear that these policy initiatives were taking root in the economic and industrial fabric of the nation.

However, as already mentioned, the bait and, therefore, the attraction to British companies was, and in many ways continues to be, the tax relief. The acid test, of course, is 'Would companies still introduce employee share schemes if the attendant tax reliefs were not available?' The answer to this question is two-fold as follows:

- The withdrawal of tax reliefs for profit-related pay on the basis, according to Kenneth Clarke, that profit-related pay was now an established feature of UK industrial life has led to a withdrawal of profit-related pay arrangements for the reason that without the tax reliefs companies wish to pursue alternatives that are cost-effective, with or without tax reliefs.

- The presence of employee share schemes has become an established feature of British industrial life where employee expectations have developed in line with key social changes that lead employees to expect wider involvement in the business for which they work, where the involvement includes some form of capital stake in the business through either direct shareholding or share option arrangements.

From the outset, back in the early 1980s, it should be recognised that companies have been and continue to be attracted to employee share schemes through the following:

- the flexibility of the legislation; and

- the preferability over cash bonus schemes.

The company response to these two attractive attributes of the schemes is discussed in more detail in the chapter entitled 'Business case for employee share schemes'.

It is immensely encouraging that employee share ownership has continued to command cross-party support in Parliament. In this sense, as a subject and policy initiative, it operates as a unifying force amongst politicians of differing backgrounds and differing political persuasions. It is expected that the New Labour economic strategies will continue to give employee share schemes a pivotal role and that the structures and, indeed, the tax reliefs will continue to evolve in succeeding years to the benefit of UK companies and their employees.

Chapter 2

Concept of tax approval

Introduction

2.1 This chapter introduces the concept of tax approval as the basis for the introduction of the statutory employee share scheme arrangements. Tax approval is the mechanism that enables HMRC to give to companies statutory protection from the tax charges that would otherwise arise under the tax legislation. For a fuller context of the protection afforded by the tax-approved legislation and the statutory references please see the section in the chapter entitled 'Development of the tax legislation'.

The concept of tax approval was introduced in order for the sponsoring company to obtain a clearance from HMRC's employee shares & securities unit (ESSU) that the scheme rules and associated documents comply with the tax legislation that confers the tax reliefs.

The UK governments of the late 1970s and early 1980s introduced three tax-approved employee share schemes as follows:

- Profit-Sharing Employee Share Scheme (1978).

- Savings-Related Share Option Scheme (1980).

- Share Option Scheme (1984).

These tax-approved employee share schemes are designed specifically to assist in achieving the objectives of the government in introducing the schemes. The particular design features that were decided upon in order to achieve government objectives are as follows:

1. *Shares*: the shares must be part of the ordinary share capital of the company that has set up the scheme or the company that controls the company that has set up the scheme. The Ggovernment's intention behind this stipulation is to ensure that companies do not use shares with either restricted rights or alternatively favoured rights. In particular, preference shares, redeemable shares, restricted shares, debentures or loan stocks cannot be used to service the schemes.

2. *Company*: the company must either be quoted on a recognised stock exchange or be the subsidiary of a company that is quoted on a recognised stock exchange, or alternatively, be an unquoted company that is not controlled by another unquoted company.

3. *Tax reliefs*: the tax reliefs are given on income tax for employees and on corporation tax for companies. The capital gains tax regime does

not contain any specific reliefs for employee share schemes. However, a key tax planning point is to utilize as efficiently as possible the capital gains reliefs that are afforded under the CGT legislation. In particular, the CGT annual exemption limit can assist employees in avoiding CGT on the sale of shares that are acquired by virtue of the tax-approved employee share schemes.

4. *Participation*: participation in the scheme is limited to employees including executive directors. In order to qualify for participation neither the executive nor the employee must have a 'material interest' in the company or control of the company.

Where the scheme is an 'all employee' scheme, the distribution of free shares under the profit-sharing employee share scheme or the granting of share options under the savings-related share option scheme must be offered on an all-employee basis. The all-employee basis will usually be subject to a length of service requirement. However, for those employees to whom participation is offered under an all-employee arrangement the offer and indeed all the aspects of their participation must be on a fair or 'similar terms' basis.

5. *Limitations*: the value of the shares for which the tax freedoms are available is limited.

6. *Retention*: the legislation stipulates specified minimum periods for the retention of shares or indeed options over shares if the employees are to secure the tax reliefs.

This stipulation applies as much to shares held within the profit-sharing employee share scheme trust as it does to options granted under either an all-employee savings-related arrangement or alternatively options granted on a discretionary basis.

The New Labour initiatives through FA 2000 are as follows:

• Under New Labour, the first new tax-approved scheme since 1984 has been introduced in the form of the share incentive. It is an all-employee scheme, containing a free shares module that is a company share-gifting scheme, a partnership shares module that is an employee share purchase scheme and a matching shares module that enables the company to match free shares (separate from the free shares module) to partnership shares.

• Enterprise management incentives (EMI), a discretionary share option scheme, although a government-sponsored scheme is not a tax-approved scheme, in that an up-front tax approval is not required as a clearance procedure from the ESSU before introduction. Instead, a notification procedure has to be followed, advising HMRC's small company enterprise centre (SCEC) in Nottingham when grants of option have been made. Despite not being a tax-approved scheme, EMI is the most tax-efficient employee share scheme ever to be introduced in the UK.

Approval process

2.2 Application for approval of a scheme has to be made by the company setting up the scheme. This application must be made in writing to HMRC's ESSU. Where the scheme is a group scheme, the application must be made by the controlling company.

There is no requirement to complete an application form. However, there is a requirement for companies who wish to introduce the scheme to forward certain specified information to HMRC's ESSU as set out below.

Checklist of information required by HMRC

2.3 Checklist of information to be forwarded to HMRC's ESSU:

- the scheme rules (two copies);
- the Memorandum and Articles of Association, together with any amendments, for the company whose shares will be used in the scheme (one copy).
- the documents that are to be issued to eligible/participating employees and shareholders (one copy);
- the resolution adopting the scheme, duly certified with the date of approval by the company clearly stated (one copy);
- a statement of the name and registered office of the company setting up the scheme together with the names of the tax offices and the reference numbers under which the company submits its corporation tax returns and its PAYE returns and, for a group scheme, the information for all participating companies in the scheme (one copy).
- A statement confirming that the scheme extends to all participating companies of which the company that is setting up the scheme is a member and that there are no features of the scheme which would discourage any employees from meeting the conditions for participation set out in the legislation (one copy).
- A declaration on company headed notepaper by the company secretary that the scheme shares satisfy the conditions set out in the schedule of ITEPA 2003 that is appropriate for the scheme in question (one copy).
- A declaration that any directors power to veto the transfer of shares will not be used to discriminate against the transfer of shares which are required on the exercise of the options and included in the declaration should be a statement that the participating employees will be told of this declaration (one copy).
- The resolution adopting the scheme, certified and stating the date of approval of the scheme by the company (one copy).

Chapter 3

Business case for employee share schemes

Introduction

3.1 This chapter explains the response given by UK business to the initiatives of the UK government to encourage employee share involvement in companies through the introduction of the tax-approved schemes. The chapter goes on to explain various studies that have been conducted in the UK and in the USA on the linkage between the introduction of employee share schemes and employee productivity. The chapter then explores the role played by employee share schemes in staff retention, reward and incentive, and in acting as the corporate 'glue' within businesses.

Business response to tax approval

3.2 Throughout the 1980s shareholders and employers in the UK responded to the tax-approved legislation as they began to see the merits of the government initiatives on employee share ownership. Although initially the awareness on the part of UK business developed at a slow pace, it became clear that these policy initiatives were taking root in the economic and industrial fabric of the nation. The main sector to embrace the tax-approved legislation at the outset was the banks with Lloyds Bank as the first to receive HMRC approval for their profit-sharing employee share scheme on 3 April 1979 followed by Midland Bank on 23 April 1979. However, the other sectors soon followed with an avalanche of applications for all the tax-approved schemes as the 1980s progressed and into the early 1990s.

As mentioned in the previous section the bait and, therefore, the attraction to UK companies was and, in many ways, continues to be the tax relief. The acid test, of course, is whether or not companies will still introduce employee share schemes if the attendant tax reliefs were not available. The reality is that the presence of employee share schemes has become an established feature of UK industrial life. Employee expectations have developed in line with key social changes that lead employees to expect recognition of their contribution from management and wider involvement in the decision-making of the company for which they work. That involvement includes some form of capital stake in the business through either direct shareholdings or share option arrangements.

Buttressed by the tax reliefs the attraction of employee share schemes to UK companies, particularly in the quoted sector, has been as follows:

- In spite of the restrictions the *flexibility of the legislation* has been recognised increasingly by UK companies, particularly in the quoted sector, the more so when pointed out to them by the advancing market of professional advisers. The schemes operate at the discretion of the employers, both in terms of when they are operated and the frequency of their operation. By giving to the employers' choices and, indeed, key choices in the design of the schemes, employers, generally speaking, do not view the schemes as rigid monolithic slabs of legislation over which they have no flexibility. Indeed, working with their professional advisers, companies have come to appreciate that the flexibility of the legislation allows them to fine-tune the structure to be appropriate to their particular business. The flexibility allows the creation of a meaningful incentive to support the corporate objectives of the business, maybe or maybe not working alongside a tax-unapproved version. This means that the companies can tailor the use of the schemes to suit their particular human resource needs. As an incentive, an employee share scheme, properly communicated, can contribute greatly to the achievement of the corporate objectives.

- The *preferability over cash bonus schemes* can quite clearly be appreciated once the significance of the tax reliefs is properly understood. It is a matter of historical record that throughout the 1960s and 1970s many UK companies had introduced cash profit-sharing schemes in an attempt to introduce motivation and incentive into UK business. The operation of these schemes had had varying degrees of success. However, the polarisation between management and trade unions had mitigated against their success and the leaders of UK companies had become increasingly frustrated with the failure of their motivation and incentive policies. The structure of the profit-sharing and employee share scheme arrangements offered, and continues to offer, significant advantages over treating the profit share as a cash pay-out. These advantages are as follows:

  — As a non-cash benefit, the shares create a longer and potentially more meaningful memory for the employees of the company, particularly in circumstances where there is the opportunity for an ongoing income return in the form of dividends and where there is the spectre of a capital gain.

  — Where shares are retained, the continuing shareholding contributes towards a lasting relationship of goodwill between the company and its employees who have a greater sense of involvement and with it a stronger sense of identity with the company, its shareholders and its management.

  — The tax reliefs enable shares to deliver greater value into the hands of the employees than would do cash, particularly where there is a rising share price and the employees are educated through meaningful communication processes to understand that their efforts can have a direct effect on productivity, profitability and share value.

Evidence of a linkage to productivity

3.3 In 1988 the United States' general accounting office (GAO) performed a study which concluded that companies that embrace employee share ownership on an all-employee basis show more improvement in productivity where their employee ownership initiative is accompanied by a policy of employee involvement in corporate decision-making through work groups or work committees having the opportunity to make recommendations to management. These findings suggest that employee share ownership pursued as a policy in isolation from general employee involvement policies does not maximise the benefit for the business of the employee share ownership initiative. As a base position, though, the study also concluded that the productivity of companies that have introduced employee share ownership is at least comparable with the productivity of companies that have not introduced employee share ownership, supporting the position that at the very least employee share ownership does not have a detriment effect on productivity.

The studies performed by Michael Quarry and Corey Rosen (*How Well is Employee Ownership Working* (1986 and 1987) provide more substantial support for the productivity benefits of employee share ownership. This key study that is recognised to have been tightly-controlled focused on 45 companies in the US and established their sales growth five years before the introduction of employee share ownership and also five years after the introduction of employee share ownership. The conclusion was that the sales growth in comparison with the competition was an additional 1.9% before the introduction of employee share ownership but 5.3% after the introduction of employee share ownership. However, this study, as with the US GAO study, emphasised general employee participation in corporate decision-making as a major factor in the success of the employee share ownership initiative.

A study performed by Gorm Winther in 1987, also as a before-and-after analysis on employee share ownership, focused on 25 companies in the state of New York and 28 companies in the state of Washington. It also concluded that any positive result from employee share ownership was dependent on wider employee participation generally.

The Hewitt Associates Study (1998) performed by Professor Hamid Mehran of Northwestern University's JL Kellogg Graduate School of Management for Hewitt Associates is regarded as influential in the field, most especially so given the size of the sample of 382 publicly quoted companies, all of which had introduced an executive/company share option scheme (ESOP). However, it is also regarded as being tightly controlled in its measurement of the economic parameters. The study which refers to the companies as ESOP companies considered the financial returns of the companies for two years before implementation and for four years after implementation and compared each company to industry norm return on assets (ROA) positions for both periods.

The performance and productivity conclusions of the study were as follows:

- for the 303 ESOP companies that survived the full four-year ESOP period ROA was 14% higher than the comparator group;

- for the 382 ESOP companies as a group ROA was 6.9% higher in the four-year ESOP period; and

- for the 382 ESOP companies the TSR increased by 12% compared with the peer group over the ESOP period.

Interestingly, the analysis showed that for over 60% of the companies there was an increase in the share price in the two-day period following the introduction of the ESOP. The average increase for all companies in the group was 1.6%. These statistics indicate a positive response from the market to the introduction of an ESOP.

The study also reported on attitudinal responses of executives to matters of ownership culture as follows:

- 82% of executives reported that employee share ownership increased corporate performance;

- 18% of executives reported that employee share ownership improved employee behaviours; and

- 85% of companies reported increased access to company information for employees, including financial information, corporate strategies and customer expectations.

In a study in 2001, *Shared Modes of Compensation and Firm Performance in the United Kingdom,* Professor Richard Freeman of Harvard University and the London School of Economics and Martin Conyon, of Wharton School, University of Pennsylvania, investigated the consequences of introducing employee share ownership in approximately 300 companies, again a substantial sample. The study analysed the productivity of UK companies by measuring their added value before-and-after the introduction of an HMRC tax-approved all-employee free share plan, either in the form of the profit-sharing employee share scheme or subsequently the free shares module of the share incentive plan (SIP). Added value equates in general terms to gross profit which to labour economists is accepted as a fairly accurate indicator of labour productivity. The general conclusion is that the study found a 17% increase in added value following the introduction of the free shares arrangement.

Staff retention and share retention

3.4 The staff retention impact of employee share ownership comes from aligning the self-interest, and often the financial self-preservation, of the employee with continued employment within the business. In Greek philosophy terms, the principles of employee share ownership derive more from the enlightened self-interest approach of Aristotle, rather than Plato's selfless sacrificial approach.

However, as 'The Mondragon Experience' in Spain shows, at the more advanced level of the enlightened co-operative, employee involvement encourages charitable donations and a more holistic awareness of the stewardship of the world's resources. It is where the individual is able to relate to and indeed embrace this wider perception that staff retention is at its highest, where the communal way of life is reflected in the business and vice versa so that the individual sees an indivisibility between himself or herself and the business. In such circumstances, the natural response is to remain with the business. Supporting this employee response is the belief that the company is committed to the individual with no prospect of compulsory redundancy.

In practice, the business outside the world of the co-operative can achieve degrees of this identification, with the consequential effect on staff retention. An example is the success of the 'Palmer's People' where Charlie Palmer introduced a policy of employee financial participation into his famous Aureole Restaurant in New York. The policy was introduced by offering cash bonuses linked to performance. For example, when the ratio between costs and sales fell below the standard 32% a cash bonus of up to 30% was awarded to the chef. Charlie Palmer then gave the employees the option to invest in the business on the same terms as he didhimself. The result was to reduce the labour turnover rate in an industry renowned for percentages as high as 80% to 100% a year to a consistently respectable figure.

In his study with Martin Conyon, Richard Freeman did not provide evidence of staff retention but commented in his conclusions that he felt that there were signs that employee share schemes had a positive impact on staff retention.

Shares retention is, of course, a separate issue from staff retention, with share option schemes and free shares schemes encouraging different behaviours as follows:

- *Share option schemes*: generally speaking assist staff retention, at least during the life of the scheme, whether the scheme is of the discretionary mode or in the form of the savings-related share option scheme (SSOP). This is for the reason that on resignation or dismissal the employee's option lapses. The option contract truly represents 'golden handcuffs'. Share option schemes though are generally not thought to assist shares retention beyond the exercise of the options. However, the company may after exercise make another grant invitation.

- *Free shares schemes*: though, only carry a disincentive to leave the company to the extent that there is normally a tax liability on the employee if they withdraw their shares before the end of the five-year life within the trust. Share ownership can continue beyond the end of the employment. The free shares schemes, therefore, may assist shares retention but make less of a contribution to staff retention than the share option arrangements. Indeed, research conducted by ProShare over 300 companies established that for that sample group 68% of employees kept their shares from free shares models while only 41% of employees kept their shares from Share-Save schemes.

The essence of understanding the linkage between employee share owner-ship and staff retention is again within the context of wider employee involvement where exit behaviour is reduced by giving to employees the opportunities to voice their concerns and resolve problems through participation in the decision-making process.

Rewards and incentives

3.5 The research conducted in 2001 by Richard Freeman and Martin Conyon addresses the extent to which UK businesses have replaced standard wage-employment contracts with *shared modes of compensation* and the impact of any development on the economic fortunes of the businesses.

The conclusions of the research may be summarised as follows:

- United Kingdom companies have responded to the policies of the UK government to encourage shared compensation. The trend is towards an acceleration of corporate interest in shared compensa-tion practices, embraced currently by over 50% of UK businesses and over a third have more than profit-related pay which in its tax relieved form finally became statutorily extinct in 2000.

- Where businesses have embraced shared compensation the research supports the position that those businesses are more likely to establish formal employee communication and consultation channels in the spirit of wider employee involvement in the running in the business.

- Where businesses have embraced shared compensation they tend to establish a better record than businesses that have not embraced shared compensation as measured by the parameters of productivity and financial performance and in general this is reflected in the performance of the share price.

The evidence from Freeman and Conyon and from many other researchers is that the potential reward for employees of shared compensation becomes an incentive when combined with participatory management techniques.

Corporate 'glue'

3.6   The capacity of employee share ownership to contribute to the corporate 'glue' is dependent to a large degree on how the shareholders and even more so the directors, view their workforce. In this regard the work of Thomas Petzinger in his 1999 book, *The Men and Women Who Are Transforming the Workplace and Marketplace* is influential, arguing that the conceptual models of how the world works has to move from the mechanical to the biological and that although science has made this transition business has been slow to follow suit. Petzinger takes the view that the biological or organic model is more appropriate to respond to the colossal and seismic social, and cultural changes that characterised the latter part of the twentieth century. These changes included the development in international markets through globalisation, civil rights and democratisation, the growth of mature inter-relations between cultures and rapid technological development. His approach is to see the business as an organism making its way in a hostile world rather than a machine with many parts. In this context and using this language the organism is processing information from all its sensors, consciously and subconsciously. The business is adopting the characteristics of a human, metaphorically seeing and hearing, smelling and tasting and feeling, the business requirements and processing accordingly. As with the philosophical arguments for retention the arguments for corporate 'glue' find their basis is taking identity of interest to the point of establishing that indivisibility between the business and its employees.

Summary conclusions

3.7   In summary, the evidence through empirical research suggests that employee share ownership can contribute significantly to improving the performance of the business through its influence on productivity levels, retention strategies, remuneration and reward incentives, and by reinforcing the community aspect of the business to create the corporate 'glue'. The potential of the business organism is, therefore, unlimited as the capacity to change becomes unlimited, giving the opportunity for consistently high performance in new and expanding markets.

Chapter 4

Empirical evidence for employee share schemes

Introduction

4.1 This chapter responds to the question that is often asked by company directors about the effectiveness of introducing employee share schemes into businesses. The chapter provides UK statistics that result from research conducted by ProShare into the interest shown by companies in the all-employee tax-approved ShareSave and SIP. The chapter also provides a detailed appreciation of the empirical evidence that derives from research conducted in the US, measuring the effectiveness of employee share schemes against a range of parameters.

Do employee share schemes work?

4.2 The success of employee share schemes is measured, in one sense, by the extent to which they have been embraced by companies that have chosen to introduce them and in turn, embraced by employees who have chosen to accept invitations to participate. To measure the success defined in this sense requires *a statistical analysis of take-up*. However, the ultimate measure of success must be the extent to which the introduction and operation of the schemes have assisted companies in achieving their corporate objectives. Measurement of success in this sense must be by way of *case study analysis* and *research* using credible sampling techniques.

UK statistics

4.3 The all-employee schemes of ShareSave and the SIP were surveyed in the summer of 2003 by ProShare through data collection from the main frontline out-source administrators, 6 for ShareSave and 11 for the SIP.

ShareSave

4.4 The survey focused on the operation of the schemes that were introduced by the client companies of the administrators. The results reveal that ShareSave continues to be a popular all-employee share scheme despite the introduction of the SIP. The number of schemes administered was 1,188, representing a slight downturn on the 1,193 of the previous year. However, the average monthly savings contribution was £67.97, representing an increase of £13.61 on the average monthly savings contribution of the previous year that stood at £54.36. The average take-up for the three-year schemes was nearly 24% that is 10% higher than the take-up of the five-year schemes and 20% higher than the seven-year schemes. The most popular terms were, therefore, three and five years. Other key statistics to emerge were that 80% of schemes offered the full 20% discount and 45% of companies had some of their ShareSave options underwater, ie the current market value (MV) was less than the option price.

The report comments on the low take-up of 24% on three-year schemes that it considers to be disappointing and surprisingly low. The interpretation that the report gives is that this may reflect employees' current concerns about share prices after a bear market of three years, a declining interest in or ability of employees to save regularly and possibly a response to reducing bonus rates. The report also comments on the increase in the average monthly savings contribution which given the low take-up may reflect a reduction in the number of employees saving small amounts per month, and/or an increase in the number of employees saving larger amounts. The implication is that the schemes are possibly being used more by higher-paid employees with more disposable income. The report welcomed the high percentage of companies offering the 20% discount despite the fall in share prices.

Share incentive plan

4.5   The report estimates that the 11 participating administrators in the survey account for two-thirds of the SIPs that have been launched. The survey does not include SIPs that are administered by companies inhouse.

The figures released by HMRC are included in the report, revealing a growing interest in the SIP. As at April 2003, 800 SIP applications had been received of which 502 had been approved, representing 63% of all applications. As a result of these approvals HMRC estimates that 1.5 million employees are able to participate in a SIP.

Regarding the choices of module, the most widely offered module arrangement is the partnership shares module, offered by 95% of the companies covered by the survey. The number of companies offering free shares increased by 8% – from 37% to 45% (between 2001 and 2002) and then fell during 2003 to 40% of the companies. The most popular combination for the year of the survey, 2003, is partnership shares and matching shares, offered by 19% of the companies covered by the survey. This compares with solely partnership shares as the most popular arrangement in the previous year. In the 2003 year of the survey the next most popular is partnership shares combined with matching shares and dividend shares followed by partnership shares operating on its own.

On free shares, 98 out of the 243 companies offered the free shares module, representing 40%. The most popular eligibility period consistently has been 12 months. Of the companies: 78% have forfeiture conditions, and 60% operate the maximum three-year forfeiture period.

Only 11% operate performance conditions. The average take-up is 85% compared with 87% in the previous year.

On partnership shares, 230 out of the 243 companies offered the partnership shares module, representing 95%. The average take-up, covering partnership shares only or in combination with matching shares, is 32% compared with 34% in the previous year and 46% in the year before that. The average monthly savings contribution has risen from £70.70 to £75.56. For those companies that have introduced an eligibility period the most popular period has consistently been three months.

On matching shares, 132 out of the 243 companies offered the matching shares module, representing 54%. If companies offer a combination of partnership shares and matching shares the average take-up figure for the combination is 28.5%, compared with 15% if partnership shares only.

On dividend shares, 106 out of the 243 companies offered the dividend shares module, representing 44%.

Enterprise management incentives (EMI)

4.6 Although no independent survey has been located on enterprise management incentives (EMI) the most up-to-date position available is that at 31 January 2003 when 3,354 companies had introduced EMI and altogether had granted 44,484 options. Company interest, though, in EMI has always been robust and the indications are that the enthusiasm has shown no prospect of waning.

United States statistics

4.7 The strongest source of statistical research in the US is the national center for employee ownership (NCEO) that has published its best available updated position as at December 2003. The figures are derived from a combination of company surveys and government generated data.

The statistics are formidable both in employee and in company terms, as follows:

- *Employee terms*: approximately 25 million US employees own employee shares through: ESOPs, share options, share purchase plans, 401K plans and other sundry scheme arrangements, while 14.6 million Americans hold share options.

- *Company terms:* in 2003 37.8% of for-profit companies provided employee ownership plans for 50% or more of their employees, and 16.3% granted options to a similarly broad group.

The analysis by type of plan is equally impressive as follows:

- *For ESOPS:* share bonus plans and profit-sharing plans mainly for reinvestment into company shares, the number of plans as of 2003 was 11,000 with 8.8 million employee participants with the value of plan assets in excess of $400 billion.

- *For 401K plans*: mainly for reinvestment into company shares, the number of plans as of 2003 was 2,200 with 11 million employee participants with the value of plan assets in excess of $160 billion.

- *For broad-based share option plans*: the number of plans as of 2003 was 4,000 with 8 to 10 million employee participants with the value of plan assets several hundred billion.

- *For share purchase plans*: the number of plans as of 2003 was 4,000 with 15.7 million employee participants, with the value of plan assets not realistic to estimate.

The research shows that the number of ESOPs is growing while the number of employee participants is falling for the following reasons:

- the average size of companies with ESOPs has been shrinking. Generally speaking the closely held ESOP companies do not go public anyway;

- many large companies that introduced ESOPs historically solely to benefit from financial and accounting advantages are gradually terminating the plans; and

- broad-based share option plans and 401K plans are increasingly being introduced for the wider employee population rather than ESOPs.

The percentage of company shares owned by employee ownership plans in the US is illustrated by the results of surveys from Ohio and Michigan in 1984 and 1990, an NCEO survey from 1995 on 401K plans, a 2000 NCEO survey of companies with broad-based share option plans and the general NCEO database. The following table has been derived from this variety of sources by the NCEO:

Category	0 to 10%	11 to 30%	31 to 50%	51 to 100%
Private company ESOP	20%	20%	30%	30%
Public company ESOP	62%	34%	3%	1%
401K plans	85%	10%	5%	0%
Share options	32%	65%	3%	0%

Who benefits from employee share schemes?

4.8 The productivity benefits have already been explained in a separate chapter that refers to a number of studies conducted in the US and the UK. This chapter now seeks to establish the relationship between employee share scheme involvement and a range of economic indicators.

1. Relationship between share options and corporate performance

4.9 The study performed by Douglas Kruse, Joseph Blasi and Jim Sesil of Rutgers University and Maya Krumova of The New York Institute of Technology in 2000 focused on the relationship between share options and corporate performance.

This study provided data for companies that made options available to most or to all employees. The sample of 105 companies contained 91% of companies whose shares were traded through stock exchanges. The study concluded that productivity rates improved once a share option scheme was introduced. The productivity scores for the overall sample for the period before introduction, 1985 to 1987, were compared with the period after introduction. Productivity levels were up 14.8% when the comparison group was all non-option group companies and 16.8% when analysed as paired comparisons with otherwise similar non-option companies. These results were mirrored in returns on assets which showed an improvement of 2.5% relative to the non-option group companies and 2.05% when analysed as paired comparisons with otherwise similar non-option companies. There was no mirror though on TSR which showed no statistically significant difference in the comparators across the pre-introduction and the post-introduction periods. The study concluded that any share dilution caused by the introduction of broad-based share option plans is counterbalanced by enhanced productivity levels.

2. Relationship between share options and specifically corporate growth

4.10 The study performed by Douglas Kruse and Joseph Blasi of Rutgers University also in 2000 focused on the relationship between share options and specifically *corporate growth* measured across a range of parameters.

This study is the largest and most significant study conducted on the performance of the ESOP in closely-held companies. The process was based on 343 companies for the overall sample although there was ultimately missing data that reduced the comparison opportunities. Comparing pre-ESOP performance with post-ESOP performance, annual sales growth was up by 2.4%, annual employment growth was up by 2.3% and annual growth in sales per employee was up by 2.3%.

3. Relationship between broad-based employee share ownership and share price performance

4.11 The study performed by Douglas Kruse, Joseph Blasi and Michael Conte and from 1993 American Capital Strategies, based on data compiled between 1992 and 1998, focused on the relationship between broad-based employee share ownership and *share price performance*.

The study focused on an investment of equal amounts in a basket of shares in public companies with more than 10% broad-based employee share ownership. The study concluded that these companies generated a return of 170% compared with 143% for the Dow and 152% for the S&P 500. To put the results into context the study did not go as far as to conclude a causal link between employee share ownership and share price performance as it accepted that companies that are of a disposition to establish an employee share scheme may possess other characteristics that are conducive to more superior performance that is reflected in the share price.

4. Relationship between employee share ownership in ESOP companies and employee compensation (remuneration)

4.12 The study performed by Peter Kardas and Jim Keogh of the Washington Department of Community, Trade and Economic Development and Adria Scharf of the University of Washington in 1998 focused on the relationship between employee share ownership in ESOP companies and *employee compensation (remuneration)*.

The study, called Wealth and Income Consequences of Employee Ownership concluded that employees in ESOP companies are significantly better remunerated than employees in comparable non-ESOP companies. Using data from the Washington State Employment Security Department, retirement data from companies and from federal income tax forms the study worked on the basis of a comparison between 102 ESOP companies with 499 comparator companies in terms of industrial classification and the size of the workforce. The report stated that on wages the median hourly wage in the ESOP companies was 5% to 12% higher than the median hourly wage in the comparator companies. In the ESOP companies the average corporate contribution per employee per annum was between 9.6% and 10.8% of pay per year compared with between 2.8% and 3.0% for the non-ESOP companies.

5. Relationship between share options and organisational stability

4.13 The study performed by Douglas Kruse, Joseph Blasi and Margaret Blair in 1998 focused on the relationship between share options and *organisational stability*.

The results were based on a study of companies between 1983 to 1996. The study concluded that 74.1% of the ESOP companies remained as independent businesses. In comparison only 37.8% of the comparator non-ESOP companies maintained their independence. The ESOP companies all maintained their solvency whereas in comparison 25% of the comparator companies did not.

6. Comparison between the pure ESOP and the poison pill ESOP

4.14 The 1995 study performed by Donald Collat focused on the comparison between companies that did *not* set up their ESOP in response to a takeover threat and companies whose motivation in setting up the ESOP was to counter a takeover threat.

The study examined the operating margins in the three years before the ESOP introduction and three years after the ESOP introduction. The results for those companies whose ESOP initiative was not motivated by a desire to counter a takeover threat showed improved margins of 2.1% per annum whereas the comparator group showed a reduction in margins of 3.3%. The improved margins may be explained by the presence of a general ownership culture in those companies.

Chapter 5

Employee share schemes: case studies

Introduction

5.1 This chapter presents two case studies, one for an unquoted private company and the other for a quoted public limited company. It uses the case studies to illustrate the methodology that a company needs to follow in order to determine the most appropriate employee share scheme or combination of employee share schemes in order to support the corporate objectives of the business. Always the employee share scheme is a corporate incentive which must be focused on the motivation and incentivisation of employees. The case studies show how it is necessary to work with an understanding of the law alongside an appreciation of the human behaviours within the business.

Case study 1: an unquoted private company

5.2 PC Tech Limited is a private limited company, resident, registered and incorporated in the UK. It is a high-tech company, specialising in the development of Internet communication systems. The company is projecting a period of strong growth for the next two years and anticipates selling out to a third party acquiring company in the next two to five years. The company's constitution limits the opportunity to issue new shares to support employee share scheme arrangements.

There are five shareholders, all individuals. Seventy per cent of the shareholding is concentrated in the hands of the two founder shareholders who each own 35%. The company pays a low dividend. The company has one wholly-owned subsidiary that employs the 25 employees in the UK and another wholly-owned subsidiary that employs 35 employees in the US. The company wishes to involve its two non-executive directors in its share scheme arrangements.

The intention is to grant options to all employees following the completion of the final accounts for the financial year to 31 December 2002 but at a level for each employee that is agreed by the board of directors. The gross assets are £2,500,000 and the share valuation of the group is £7,400,000. This comparatively low share valuation surprised the existing shareholders, particularly when another company that they own, completely separate from the PC Tech Group, a company called Computer Sales Ltd that trades through the purchase and sale of computer equipment, is valued at £15,400,000.

Computer Sales Ltd has promised each of its 30 employees a share incentive over 1% of the issued share capital of the company. The company has paid a healthy dividend for many years but is not regarded as being in strong growth mode. Computer Sales Ltd has a 60% stake in Photocopy Sales Ltd.

The questions that the company directors asked to be addressed were as follows below.

1. What share scheme(s) would be appropriate for PC Tech Ltd?

5.3   The approach is to devise a scheme or schemes that support the corporate objectives and then to introduce the most tax-advantageous schemes possible. The company's objectives are geared to strong growth over a comparatively short period of time. The incentive must encourage strong performance over that concentrated period. By examining the most tax-advantageous scheme first, the company does qualify as a qualifying company and the UK employees do qualify as eligible employees for EMI. The company chose to introduce EMI on an all-employee basis even though statutorily it is a discretionary arrangement. Using EMI, rather than the statutory all-employee schemes of SIP or ShareSave, the company was able to determine the level of share involvement for each employee while at the same time honouring its commitment to all-employee involvement. The exercisable events were linked exclusively to possible exit positions of takeover, stock exchange listing and management buy-out. For the US based employees the company introduced a general tax-unapproved share option scheme that did not qualify the US resident employees for any tax advantages. The company rejected the opportunity to introduce a scheme that was tax-efficient under the US legislation for the US resident employees although the directors did clearly understand that it is the residence of the employees that determines the availability of employee tax reliefs.

2. What share scheme(s) would be appropriate for Computer Sales Ltd?

5.4   Computer Sales Ltd is a standalone company, separate from PC Tech Ltd. The common shareholding with PC Tech Ltd does not cause the company to fail the EMI independence test. However, its 60% ownership of Photocopy Sales Ltd at an ownership of less than 75% causes it to fail the EMI trading subsidiaries requirement which applied at the time but has since been abolished for grants after 16 March 2004. Computer Sales Ltd wanted to grant an option over a value in excess of £100,000 to each employee. If it had passed all the EMI tests it could have operated EMI for each employee up to £100,000 with the excess dealt with under a tax-unapproved version. However, failing as an EMI qualifying company it chose to grant options under a tax-unapproved scheme to all employees with exercisable events linked exclusively to exit positions.

3. Will all the employee share arrangements be 'schemes'?

5.5 All the schemes were bona fide employee share schemes under CA 2006, s 1166 (CA 1985, s 743) thereby allowing exemptions from the legislative requirements for share issues, financial assistance and financial services. The financial assistance exemption was particularly important given that the company had chosen to grant the options over existing shares that were purchased from the existing shareholders by an employee share trust funded by cash contributions from the company.

4. Can the existing shareholders be granted share options?

5.6 The two founder employee shareholders of PC Tech Ltd were not eligible for EMI given that they owned more than 30% of the shares at the date of grant. As it happens, with more than 10% each of the shares they would not have been eligible for CSOP either. The final decision was that they chose not to participate in even a tax-unapproved employee share scheme, even though they would be eligible, taking the view that their remaining shareholding, after the sale of some of their shares to the employee share trust, was to all intents and purposes their share scheme. They took the same view in relation to their shareholding in Computer Sales Ltd.

5. Why is the share valuation of PC Tech Ltd so low?

5.7 The company was projecting a period of strong growth for the next two years. This is exactly the situation in which the HMRC's shares valuation division (SVD) recognises hyper-growth for which they will typically assume a higher cost base for the next two years and mark down the share valuation accordingly. Additionally, PC Tech Ltd had not paid a dividend ever, a factor that will ensure that the dividend-generated premium is not attached to the share value. The share valuation was prepared by an independent share valuer who submitted his workings to the SVD for agreement.

6. Why is the share valuation of Computer Sales Ltd so high?

5.8 This surprised the directors of the two companies as they considered PC Tech Ltd to be the more valuable company. In reality, for share valuation purposes Computer Sales Ltd was the converse of PC Tech Ltd. Its cost base could not be assumed higher for the reason that it was not regarded as being in strong growth mode. It had, though, consistently paid a healthy dividend, enhancing the value of even a small minority share-holding in the business. Again, the share valuation was prepared by an independent share valuer whose share valuation was relied upon for purposes of the grant of options. As a tax-unapproved scheme the SVD would not have given an agreement for the share valuation although HMRC could raise questions about the shareholding on the basis of entries on the self-assessment returns.

7. How will the options be satisfied?

5.9   Although the constitution of PC Tech Ltd did not give the opportunity to issue new shares to support employee share schemes it was the desire of the existing shareholders to realise cash for the sale of some of their shares under the CGT regime that finalised the decision to grant over new issue shares. For this reason it was agreed that the exercise of the options would be satisfied by the transfer of existing shares from the employee share trust to the employees. This transfer would be on the basis of an operating agreement between PC Tech Ltd and the trustees of the employee share trust under which the employee share trust agreed to assist the company in the operation to satisfy the exercise of options. For Computer Sales Ltd there was no such limitation on the use of new issue shares to satisfy the exercise of options and the existing shareholders were prepared to wait until the exit position to realise a cash value for their shares. It was established, therefore, that the exercise of the options would be satisfied through the issue of new issue shares directly to the employees at the time of exercise.

8.Can the existing shareholders have granted to them a put option by the trust?

5.10   The shareholders accepted the advice that to have a put option under which the trust had to buy their PC Tech Ltd shares at their request would undermine the independence of the trust, especially as they controlled the company. The independence of the trust is crucial in establishing that the scheme arrangement does not represent a preordained series of transactions entered into with the express purpose of tax avoidance. If it did then the potential would be there for HMRC to treat the structure as though it had never been established in the first place with the resultant effect of significant tax exposure for the founder shareholders. Rather than enter into a put option arrangement the directors accepted the advice given to them as existing shareholders to grant a call option to the employee share trust, for the trust to have the right to call upon the shareholders for delivery of the shares as and when the trust required them. This call option feature of the arrangement strengthened still further the independence of the trust.

9. What communications are required with HMRC?

5.11   The HMRC's SCEC was notified about the grants of option under EMI. The HMRC's shares valuation division was involved in agreeing the share valuation for purposes of the EMI grants. The HMRC's ESSU was notified of grants under the tax-unapproved share option schemes.

10. What arrangement should be introduced for the non-executive directors?

5.12   Neither the non-executive directors of PC Tech Ltd nor the non-executive directors of Computer Sales Ltd were employees. If they were to be involved in the employee share schemes then the status of the schemes as bona fide employee share schemes would be contaminated. Each of the two companies chose to grant options to the non-executive directors through separate schemes specifically for non-executives.

Case study 2: The quoted plc

5.13 Market Services plc is a company that is quoted on The London Stock Exchange and The New York Stock Exchange and as a multinational company provides marketing services to businesses across 30 countries. The company had developed through ad hoc acquisition and as a consequence the directors wished to introduce some form of all-employee scheme that had the capacity to unite the whole international workforce under the incentive of share growth.

The group had an inspirational leader in the office of chief executive who was supported by a high calibre chairperson who also required an incentive that was linked to shares. However, the company had a plethora of executive share option schemes in place and had, therefore, virtually exhausted its headroom under the institutional investor guidelines (IIGs) on new issue shares. The company needed advice, therefore, on how to service any new schemes with shares.

The operation worldwide had separate country boards and the main link to head office in London was through the local finance directors. There was a clear requirement for local advice on scheme implementation and an equally clear requirement for local communications for the employee populations. Although the stated language of the company worldwide was english there was a multiplicity of languages spoken across the world group and concern, therefore, particularly in the Far East that the detail of any scheme that was introduced may not be fully understood.

The company had a history of high quality in the services that it provided to its clients and a pedigree of outstanding success as a business. The chief executive had set a three-year target for growth and profitability, and communicated freely and regularly with the employees across the world through corporate email messages, and through regular visits to local offices.

Once the scheme had been introduced, the company some years later was acquired by a foreign company that was prepared to see the scheme continue throughout the natural term that had been agreed for the scheme at the original launch. Unless the optionholder wanted to take the cash exit offer from the scheme the option was converted into a new option over shares in the acquiring company. The option price and the number of shares was redefined on the basis of the share-for-share exchange ratio offered by the acquiring company on takeover.

The questions that the company directors asked to be addressed were as follows.

1. What share scheme(s) would be appropriate for the company?

5.14 The company required a scheme that could unify the world group around a common cause and focus employees on the achievement of the three-year plan. This was a key corporate objective. The choice of scheme was influenced to a large degree by the extent to which the scheme could be easily and readily exported to other countries without losing its essential features. The company settled on ShareSave as a tried and tested structure in the UK which it considered to be compatible or at least not incompatible with the cultures to which the group companies were exposed. It gave to the scheme its own internal brand name.

2. Would the scheme structure vary around the world?

5.15 The company was intent initially on offering a 20% discount to all employees around the world group. However, the US advisers explained that for accounting reasons in the US the maximum discount offered there should not exceed 15%. The directors resolved, therefore, to offer 15% universally in order to ensure consistency throughout the group. In essence the UK model was exported with whatever tax exposure prevailed in any country with the exception that if there was a tax exposure at the date of grant then the scheme structure would be amended accordingly.

3. How would shares be made available for the scheme?

5.16 Given that the investor institutional headroom was limited the company established an employee share trust offshore in Jersey to purchase existing shares through the stock exchange. A further motivation to service the scheme with existing shares was to avoid the need to secure shareholder approval in general meeting which would be required for new issue shares. Careful financial modelling was given to the decision on the funding of the trust and eventually it was decided to fund the trust piecemeal over time. The early funding that coincided with the date of grant allowed a hedge on the growth of the share price while the deferred funding enabled the company to allocate the cash on an opportunity cost basis to capital projects that were anticipated to produce a higher financial return to the company.

4. What share scheme(s) would be appropriate for the chairperson?

5.17 The chairperson was offered a straightforward phantom arrangement without, surprisingly, any linkage to performance conditions. The growth in the share price was considered to be an adequate incentive. The same employee share trust was used to purchase shares specifically for hedging purposes. On exercise the trust sold the shares and distributed the cash directly to the chairperson.

5. How would the employee communications operate around the world?

5.18   The link person in each country for the distribution of documents and the transfer of information both ways was identified as the local finance director. This approach used the communication channels that existed for document distribution and information flow in relation to all corporate matters. All employee communication documents were written in English. However, where necessary the local finance director provided a verbal explanation to employees in the local language.

6. Do the savings arrangements have to differ around the world?

5.19   Wherever possible it was decided that the savings would be in sterling that was the currency of the option price. However, in most countries this was not considered practical so the employees in those countries saved through a monthly local currency contribution that was fixed at the outset of the arrangement on the basis of the exchange rate at the date of grant. When the employees came to exercise their options they were allowed to make up any deficiency arising on the exchange of their local funds into sterling. This was done through an additional top-up contribution. Any surplus on exchange at exercise was paid back to the employees in cash as a return of contributions.

7. Will different securities laws and exchange controls complicate matters?

5.20   The employees in the countries of the Far East – China, Malaysia, Thailand and Vietnam – and also India were offered a phantom arrangement that was given the far more attractive name of share appreciation rights. Under this arrangement the employees were required to save through monthly contributions in a local savings account and then at the date of exercise provide evidence of that saving to qualify for a company payment from the employee share trust. The payment was based on the calculation of multiplying the increase in the share price by a notional number of shares that had been calculated at the outset by dividing for each individual the option price into the total expected savings contributions. In this way the phantom arrangement mirrored the real savings-related share option arrangements that operated in the other countries.

Chapter 6

Process of scheme design

Introduction

6.1 This chapter addresses the basic structural model that is chosen by the company for the share incentive arrangement and seeks to address the basic principles in scheme design with a view to meeting the objectives for motivation and retention of the employees.

Company objectives in the design process

6.2 The process of scheme design represents the opportunity for the company directors, working with their advisers, to ensure that the structure of the scheme supports the achievement of the corporate objectives of the business. The corporate objectives will usually be the growth of the company coupled with enhanced profitability. However, there are corporate situations where the definition of the corporate objectives will be somewhat different and, at the outset of the design process, therefore, it is important to challenge the company directors to formulate their corporate objectives in clear and unequivocal terms. If there is a corporate business plan then it should be possible to derive the corporate objectives from that document so that by a combination of studying company documents and engaging in active discussion with the directors it should be possible to agree upon the corporate objectives.

Feeding and supporting the corporate objectives

Corporate Objectives	The Umbilical Cord of the Design Process	Incentive Scheme

This connection, then, between the corporate objectives of the business and the incentive scheme represents the umbilical cord of the share incentive scheme design process. The key principle is this: by introducing an incentive scheme that gives the employees a share of the capital that they create they are motivated and incentivised to achieve the capital growth with enhanced profitability that is the corporate objective. If that umbilical cord is broken and the incentive scheme is not derived from the corporate objectives then the risk is that the incentive scheme becomes like an ornament on a mantelpiece, pleasing to the eye but with no utility purpose to the business whatsoever.

In times past, share incentive schemes operated with a motivation period followed by a retention period so that once the options had been exercised, say, at the maturity of the three-year motivation period they were locked into a further three-year period to secure the retention of the scheme participants. This methodology was discarded long ago and replaced with a methodology that seeks to coincide the motivation period with the retention period so that the two operate simultaneously, and achieve both motivation and retention at the same time. All the models in this chapter are based on the principle of 'the simultaneous period' for motivation and retention and represent designs that give continuity and vibrancy to the share incentive scheme initiative.

It is crucial in the design process to remember that the share scheme is first and foremost an incentive for the employees to deliver value for their own benefit and for the benefit of the shareholders, to secure reward for employee and shareholder alike based on 'the identity of interest' in the share capital of the company. To the extent that it is an investment for the employees, they are investing in their own efforts and in the efforts of their colleagues within the corporate team of the business. This precise point is illustrated to good effect in circumstances where a group of employees, say an executive management team in a private company, are introduced into an employee share purchase scheme having worked together for, say, some five years or more. In these circumstances, they have already been significantly instrumental in building the business and being responsible for its success. The discount in the purchase price should reflect this fact, may be up to 100%; to request that they pay MV would be to ask them to pay a monetary value for something for which they have already paid with their own efforts and endeavours.

Staggered grants and overlap periods

6.3 The approach of annual staggered grants and overlap periods is based upon the structural model that is favoured by the quoted companies. When this approach is linked to a set of performance conditions it is the approach that is favoured by the investment committees of the association of british insurers (ABI) and the national association of pension funds (NAPF). In the case of the private company, there is, of course, no requirement for approval by the ABI or the NAPF. Nevertheless, if the private company has significant external investment and ambitions to grow to a substantial size, it is worth being aware of models that external investors in the quoted sector perceive as having merit in the motivation and the incentive of key executives.

In this model, normally share options are granted each year, after the announcement of the final results for the financial year. Typically, the exercise of the options will be linked to the three-year performance period that commences with the date of grant. The second share option will be granted on the first anniversary of the date of grant of the first share option with its own three-year performance period. The third share option will then be granted on the second anniversary of the date of grant of the first share option, again with its own three-year performance period and so on.

The strength of this model is that it simultaneously acts as a motivational scheme and as a retention scheme. It is a motivational scheme for the reason that the exercise of the options is based upon the achievement of the performance conditions that were set at the date of grant. However, it is also a retention scheme for the reason that when the employee exercises his or her first option at the end of year three, the second and the third options have already accumulated value and, as a consequence, the employee will be reluctant to leave the company without realizing the benefit of subsequent options.

The model: staggered grants and overlap periods					
Year 0	*Year 1*	*Year 2*	*Year 3*	*Year 4*	*Year 5*
Grant			Exercise		
	Grant			Exercise	
		Grant			Exercise

Accumulating right to exercise

6.4   The approach of accumulating the right to exercise also seeks to achieve at the same time and over the same period the dual objectives of motivation and retention. At some point, though, to achieve retention beyond the initial set period a second option will have to be granted. In its 'plain vanilla' form it is aptly suitable for a company that is expected to have a limited life before exit in say, typically, 5 to 6 years' time. Even without the prospect of an exit there is often merit in this approach, particularly where it is possible to anchor the grant into position when the MV is low. With this approach, the grant will usually be a more substantial than each single grant in the staggered grant model and, typically, in percentage terms, be equivalent to the summation of the grants in that model over the agreed set period.

The basis for this approach is to allow the right to exercise to accumulate, linked to service and often also to performance achievement. However, the actual exercise is usually linked either to the expiry of a fixed term or to exit positions, say a flotation on a recognised stock exchange or a sale to either an independent third party or through a management buy-out. When an exit event happens in advance of the fixed term the employee is allowed to exercise over the percentage rights that have accumulated which, depending upon the timing, could be less than 100%.

The model: accumulting right to exercise					
Year 0	Year 1	Year 2	Year 3	Year 4	Year 5
Grant	1 years' 25% rights accumu- lated				
		2 years' 50% rights accumu- lated			
			3 years' 75% rights accumu- lated		
				4 years' 100% rights accumu- lated	
					5 years' 100% rights accumu- lated
Grant					Actual exercise 100% option/ purchase of shares

Early purchase with restrictions

6.5 The early purchase of the shares is often a technique to bring the whole of the increase in value into the CGT regime. Often the way to achieve this objective and, certainly, the way in the UK is for a tax election to be made which instigates a tax charge at unrestricted value at the outset as a condition for all future gain falling into the less punitive CGT regime.

Where the unrestricted value is not income taxed at the outset the restrictions will be lifted either on the sale of the shares or on the basis of the lapse of time, often with staggered lifting based on pre-set time junctures, as indicated in the diagram below. At each lifting of a restriction, usually an income tax liability arises based upon the additional value that has accrued to the employee through the lifting of that restriction. Typically, the amounts that have been subject to income tax over the time period contribute to the base cost for CGT purposes on the ultimate sale of the shares.

The model: Early purchase with restrictions					
Year 0	*Year 1*	*Year 2*	*Year 3*	*Year 4*	*Year 5*
Pur-chase	1 years' restric-tions lifted				
		2 years' restric-tions lifted			
			3 years' restric-tions lifted		
				4 years' restric-tions lifted	
					5 years' restric-tions lifted
Pur-chase					Actual sale of 100% of shares

Summary conclusions

6.6   The design process precedes all the legal work and requires an understanding of the culture of the business, its organizational manage-ment, the mindset of the employees as well as that all-important formula-tion of the corporate objectives. The process should involve the widest consultation possible within the company, including the employees. The design principles set out in this chapter are tried and tested. However, they must always be refined to the precise circumstances of the company if they are to be successful in their application and execution, and facilitate corporate achievement.

Chapter 7

Underwater options and share price volatility

Introduction

7.1 This chapter considers the current challenge that faces companies during the recession in the form of underwater options and examines the approaches that companies can take in response to the challenge. The term underwater options refers to share options for which the option price/the exercise price, which typically will be set at the MV that prevails at the date of grant, is higher than the current MV as a consequence of a general downturn in the market.

Challenge for companies from underwater options

7.2 The challenge that underwater options present to companies is that of maintaining the motivation and incentive of their employee share scheme participants who have entered into the employee share scheme arrangements in anticipation that their quality work efforts and endeavours on behalf of the company will reflect in the upward movement of the share price.

This problem is exacerbated for the public quoted companies for two main reasons:

- *Firstly*: for the reason that the share price is visible on a daily basis through the media transmission of the prices that are quoted on the recognised stock exchange, prices that are easily accessible to the employees.

- *Secondly*: for the reason that the ABI Guidelines do not lend their support to any form of swift corrective action. Indeed, historically during periods of recession it has been the rigidity of the ABI Guidelines that has made it difficult for the public quoted companies to respond with any speed to the challenges posed by underwater options.

For the private unquoted companies, there is a mirror problem in that share valuation work that is performed for these companies in order to set share prices for share scheme purposes uses price/earnings ratios and multiples that are derived from the quoted sector. The difference for the companies in the private sector – the SME sector – is that there is no daily visibility of the share price and there is no requirement for compliance with the ABI Guidelines so there is opportunity for speed of response to be swifter.

As well as the challenge of underwater options there is also the separate challenge of volatile share price movement that injects uncertainty into the share scheme involvement, particularly for the public quoted companies that have the daily visibility of the share price. Where there is share price volatility one day the options may be underwater and the next day back in credit. Just as with the underwater options, though, managing the aspirations of the workforce and maintaining their motivation, and incentive represent a challenge, and potentially a more difficult challenge than with underwater options.

The low share price could, of course, be as a result of the low performance of the company. Alternatively, the company may be performing well, and the low share price is caused by the general malaise of the market. Whatever the cause of the underwater value the matter has to be addressed with positive action. The absence of any action whatsoever by the company is not a credible response.

ABI guidelines on underwater options

7.3 The most recently updated ABI Guidelines, entitled *Executive Remuneration – ABI Guidelines on Policies and Practice*, dated 3 December 2007, remain definitive in clause 6.3 of that document, entitled 'Pricing and Timing', that: 'Re-pricing or surrender and re-grant of awards for "underwater" share options is not appropriate'. Any dialogue with the ABI and its institutional investor members has to overcome the stricture of this statement.

The same document does actually provide a recommendation through clause 3.1 on how to lessen the possible incidence of underwater options. This reccommendation is to follow the Grant Policy of clause 3 that is to adopt a policy of 'regular phasing of share incentive awards and option grants, generally on an annual basis'.

Practical problems

7.4 The problems that arise from underwater options are as follows.

Motivation required in recession

7.5 At the time when companies need their executive and employee share schemes to provide the highest level of motivation and incentive, as a basis for enhancing the competitiveness of the business in time of recession with a view, of course, to emerging from recession, the underwater option position mitigates against that requirement.

Requirements of accounting

7.6 The UK financial reporting standard (FRS 20): Accounting for Share-Based Payment stipulates that all share options are accounted for on the basis of the values that were set at the grant of the options. This principle is enshrined also in the international financial reporting standard (IFRS 2). Any fall in the share values subsequent to the date of grant does not qualify the company to reduce the values that are disclosed in the company's financial statements.

ABI Guidelines dilution limits

7.7 Where it is anticipated that options will be satisfied through the issue of new shares that share allocation will continue to contribute to the headroom calculations for the dilution limits that are set by the ABI Guidelines in their regulatory framework.

Statutory limits for tax-approved and government-sponsored schemes

7.8 Additionally, the tax-approved schemes and EMI have statutory limits for grant and appropriation imposed by the respective statutory provisions that govern their operation. Again, the share requirements are set at the date of grant or appropriation without any facility for correction in the wake of underwater options.

Demand for large quantities of shares

7.9 Although there is the opportunity to introduce new grants and new appropriations in accordance with current year plans for new share scheme participation the low share prices will result in a requirement for large quantities of shares to be allocated to meet particular values that have been allocated to employees, say on the basis of a multiple of salary for each employee share scheme participant. The consequence will inevitably be to place demands upon the ABI Guidelines dilution headroom calculation and, potentially, exhaust the headroom capacity.

Upward pressure on salaries and wages

7.10 The absence of any feel-good factor within the workforce over the employee share scheme participation can cause a demand for upward pressure on salary and wage positions. There will typically be a time-lag before this pressure is brought to bear for the reason that it is the longer the recession persists and the underwater option situation persists the more, the dissatisfaction with the share scheme involvement develops. Although the company's natural response will typically be to resist these pressures, fear over the loss of key employees and fear over not being uncompetitive with the overall reward package can lead to an inflationary response over the salary and wage settings.

Start-up cash-starved businesses

7.11   In companies that are start-up cash-starved businesses where there has been a reliance on the employee share scheme element within the reward package problems can become particularly acute. Typically, in this type of company, substantial employee share scheme involvement has provided the compensatory element in the absence of competitive salaries and wages. Without a commercial market salary and with little prospect of share scheme gain the temptation for employees to leave the company becomes stronger and may prove to be irresistible although any decision will always be predicated upon the availability of alternative jobs in the marketplace.

Solution approaches

7.12   The range of solution approaches are more than may at first be expected and which one is chosen by any particular company will depend upon the precise circumstances of the company at the time as I explained as follows.

Re-pricing and re-granting strategies

7.13   As already indicated, re-pricing and replacement schemes are considered not to be appropriate by the ABI Guidelines. It is, of course, the case that non-compliance with the ABI Guidelines has the potential to cause serious embarrassment at the AGM if the ABI and the investor institutions who they represent have not been consulted in advance with a view to garnering their support. However, it is important to appreciate that the ABI Guidelines are not the law. Rather they represent guidelines that are intended to protect the interests of the institutional investors and in that context an approach to those institutional investors, albeit with an approach at the same time to the ABI, could secure the support that is required to implement the re-pricing or the re-granting strategy, whatever is considered appropriate.

In any approach, the argument that is presented to the institutional investors and the ABI must be that it is in their interest to have an executive team that is motivated and the same applies also to the wider workforce. A vibrant employee share scheme with the potential for capital gain at some point in the future establishes that identity of interest with the institutional investor shareholders, an argument that could well secure that institutional investor support for the repricing or the regranting strategy. The institutional investors together with the ABI must be persuaded that the exceptional circumstances of the current recession and the severe economic climate worldwide require an initiative of this nature and, even if they do not agree to the repricing or regranting of all the current options they may still be persuaded to agree to some form of limited repricing or limited regranting of some of the options.

There are key practical matters that must be addressed when adopting a repricing or a regranting strategy. If the options are to be repriced then that will represent a change in the terms on which the option is granted, a change that goes to the root of the share option contractual arrangement and will require, therefore, the options to be cancelled and new options to be issued in their place. Thankfully, the exchange of an existing employee share option for a new share option is not in the UK an event that is subject to tax. If the company has employee share scheme participants in other countries then it must consult with its overseas advisers in order to check the tax treatment for an exchange of options in those countries.

Before embarking upon a repricing or a regranting strategy the scheme rules and share option contracts must be carefully examined. The scheme rules will usually allow for options to be cancelled or replaced, and provided they do the company should invite the employees to each sign a deed of surrender. Given that the employees are being offered a more motivational arrangement in substitute there should be no difficulty in persuading them to sign. It will normally be the case that the scheme rules provide that cancelled or lapsed options can be taken out of the dilution headroom limit calculation. However, given the potential benefit to the employee share scheme participants it is advisable to ensure that the grant of the replacement options for the public quoted company secures shareholder approval through a general meeting of the company.

At the time that the repricing and regranting strategy is introduced by the company it is worth considering whether or not to introduce a discount into the setting of the option price. Given that the company is seeking to address the underwater problem it may consider that it wishes to have a buffer in place to protect it from sliding back into an underwater situation again. This suggestion needs to be put with great sensitivity to the institutional investors who will be conscious of the fall in value of their own shareholding. However, again it is the case that if the institutional investors can fully appreciate the advantage from having a fully motivated workforce they may agree.

Purchase of existing shares

7.14 The proposals for repricing and regranting strategies to the institutional investors may be better received if they contain a provision for the replacement options to be satisfied on exercise by existing shares that are purchased off the market by an employee share trust funded by the company. The pre-eminent concern of the ABI and its members is the potential dilution of existing shareholdings and to work with existing shares rather than new issue shares acts as a counter to objections that are based on dilution.

The use of existing shares has the advantages of: (1) not diluting existing shareholdings; and (2) not creating additional dividends to be paid in perpetuity. Properly presented to the ABI and the institutional shareholders these arguments represent arguments of substance and at a time when it is imperative that underwater options are addressed it may represent the stance that wins over reluctant shareholders.

In the UK, the clause within the ABI Guidelines that governs the position on dilution, clause 8 entitled 'Dilution' is concerned solely with new issue shares and re-issue of treasury shares. Normally the share scheme rules in their limitations on the use of shares will reflect this approach and not include any limitation on the use of existing shares. It should be possible, therefore, to amend the rules without having to secure shareholder approval for the reason that the shareholders have already approved rules that give to the directors the authority to make that amendment.

Introduction of a long-term incentive plan

7.15 The company may choose to abandon the use of the traditional share option schemes for future executive share scheme participation and introduce, instead, new long-term incentive arrangements, sometimes known as performance share plans. The company would need to establish an employee share trust arrangement and be committed to the purchase and recycling of existing shares purchased from the market. However, the key advantage of this approach is that with a nil option price, the option price/exercise price can never go underwater. The underwater option problem is solved for all-time!

By adopting this approach, the company will have resolved to offer free shares to satisfy its obligations under the new scheme. Interestingly, it is often the case that support for the L-TIP from the institutional investors is easier to secure as they perceive the arrangement as establishing more closely the identity of interest between existing shareholders and employees.

The long-term incentive plan or performance free share approach is also highly efficient in terms of its use of shares. Given that the option price is effectively nil the scheme requires significantly fewer shares than does the traditional option scheme to deliver the same monetary value to the employee. Again, this is another reason why the support from the institutional investors may be more easily forthcoming.

As a long-term incentive scheme, however the scheme is described, named or titled – performance share plan or whatever – if it involves directors or is structured in such a way that involves new shares, it will require shareholder approval.

Settlement through free shares

7.16 There is an unusual approach that some companies have chosen to embrace which is for the company to meet its obligations on exercise of options through enabling the share scheme participants to receive free shares that are equal in value to the net gain. The settlement through these free shares will be without the attachment of further performance conditions. The employees will then have the capacity for further growth in their shares once market conditions are stabilized and a new upward trend in growth is re-established.

The decision on whether to use new issue shares or exiting shares as discussed above has to be made. However, if existing shares are used the approval of shareholders in the general meeting will not be required and, depending on the precise wording of the share scheme rules (ie what the shareholders have already agreed by authorising the rules) approval may not be required for the free shares to come from new issue.

Introduction of personal performance conditions

7.17 The performance conditions for public quoted companies are usually linked to corporate measurement criteria, usually a market-based measure like total shareholder return (TSR) or a profits-based measure like earnings per share or possibly a combination of the two, one acting as the primary measure and the other acting as the secondary measure. However, in the private unquoted sector it is not unusual at all for the share scheme performance conditions to be linked to personal measurement criteria based on a framework of competencies and objectives that are set at the date of grant.

The point is this, even with the L-TIP for which the option price is nil, if the performance conditions are not met the employees cannot benefit from the maturity of the scheme. Yet it may well be the case that they have worked extremely hard and that their work contribution to maintaining the company in recession has been even more substantial than in the days of boom! There are advantages in allowing them to acquire the shares with absolute title so that they can have a continuing holding and have complete identity of interest with the institutional investors and every other shareholder in the company.

In these circumstances, the public quoted company could consider introducing personal performance conditions in the same way as is done for some private company employee share schemes. The exercise of the options by the employees would be dependent on the achievement of the pre-set personal objectives that are assessed on the basis of the competency framework agreed at the date of grant.

Public quoted companies, generally speaking, apply personal performance conditions to determine pay-out under the annual bonus arrangements, albeit often in alongside corporate profitability measures. However, it is not unusual for the annual bonus to be determined solely on the basis of personal performance conditions. The requirement then is to structure the performance conditions for the employee share scheme in similar fashion, and recognise that that provides the basis for long-term reward through shares, as it does for short-term reward through bonuses.

The agreement of the performance conditions in relation to an employee share scheme should, of course, be agreed by the shareholders in the general meeting, particularly where the introduction of personal performance conditions represents a significant departure from how the share scheme performance conditions have been formulated previously.

Amendments to corporate performance conditions

7.18 If the introduction of personal performance conditions is considered too radical then amendments to the corporate performance conditions may prove to be acceptable in the current economic environment. Changes to the corporate performance conditions can provide an effective tool in addressing either underwater options or share price volatility. The concern, of course, that options and awards can lapse as a consequence of failed performance conditions even where the executives and employees have made a quality work contribution to the development of the company.

With a change in the economic outlook the employee share scheme participants, particularly the executives, may take the view that the performance conditions that were introduced at the time of their entry into the scheme are out-of-date and possibly inappropriate in these changed economic times. The problem is exacerbated by the fact that over the five years leading up to the recession companies were introducing increasingly onerous performance conditions. So with the onset of recession the gap between current performance conditions and what would be considered realistic is perceived as wide and in need of redress.

The question, then, to address is how existing performance conditions can be adapted to this changed economic scene. The mature answer to this question is to consider how performance conditions can be constructed with a flexibility that can cope with different market conditions as follows.

A progressive use of two performance conditions

7.19 As already mentioned above, companies often introduce two performance conditions, one primary and the other secondary, but with both applying in whatever market conditions happen to prevail over the performance period. A permutation on this theme is to have two performance conditions, one of which applies in one set of market conditions and the other of which applies in another set of market conditions. For example, the profits-based measurement, say earnings per share, would apply in circumstances where profitability is strong but has not been reflected in the share value. The other measurement would typically be market-based, say TSR, applying where the stock exchange is displaying more buoyancy. Always the need is to fine-tune the structuring of the performance conditions to support the employee motivation and to be consistent with the requirements of clause 4 of the ABI Guidelines for linkage to 'the achievement of challenging and stretching financial performance'.

Composition of the comparator group

7.20 It is possible that the composition of the comparator group is not constructed in a way that registers the strength in the performance of the company and, therefore, requires review. Sometimes it is the case that the comparator group does not properly or adequately reflect the comparison with companies in the same trade. For example, the comparator group for a FTSE 100 company may comprise the whole of the FTSE 100 companies. However, if the comparator group comprised the direct competitors only, then it may be that the performance of the company would register as more effective.

Tthresholds and hurdle positions

7.21 The performance condition may be constructed with a narrow performance range that may be concentrated in the region of high-level performance. In these testing economic times, it is preferable to have a multiplicity of threshold positions that allow the performance condition to register qualification for at least a proportion of the shares at a lower level than may exist currently. Again the structuring of the thresholds and hurdle positions requires fine-tuning in order to ensure that only effective performance is being rewarded. The introduction of multiple positions operates better with profit-based measurements, say earnings per share or profitability levels, and as a general rule of thumb should not be used with TSR as a sole measure.

Extension of the performance period

7.22 The extension of the performance period is a viable approach for companies to consider for existing awards. The advantage that this approach can have is to extend the period over which an averaging calculation can be performed on market-based measures. It will have limited use and potentially no use whatsoever if the market continues in an economic malaise for the long-term. Some companies have approached the institutional investors with a proposal for an open-ended extension with the suggestion to have any rolling period of three financial years going forward.

Substitution of relative for absolute measures

7.23 The use of absolute measures as opposed to measures that operate relative to a peer comparator group should be considered. Although absolute measures have been frowned upon by the institutional investors in recent years they do offer a credible basis for measurement if there are particular challenges in the company that are not mirrored in companies that would comprise the comparator group. They are also appropriate if the company is starting from a low base position whether that is in share value for a market-based measurement or in earnings for a profits-based measurement.

Change of performance condition during the performance period

7.24 The change of the performance condition during the performance period can often be controversial and representations to the institutional investors should be carefully prepared. The compromise is to request that the performance condition is changed for the remainder of the performance period rather than have a retrospective application to the part of the performance period that has already expired. This compromise approach can then be applied to the number of shares that represents a number that is calculated pro rata to the part of the performance period that remains outstanding.

The concluding comment on performance conditions is that each company must assess the opportunities that are open to them and fine-tune a response that is sensitive to the requirements of the company to maintain executive and employee motivation. The best advice must always be to seek the approval of the institutional investors or at the very least consult with them when making change to the performance conditions. Where the changes are for new share schemes then the custom and practice has become for the performance conditions to be disclosed to the shareholders in the general meeting as part of the approval procedure for the schemes. However, for existing schemes the scheme rules will often give authority and the discretion to the remuneration committee to amend existing performance conditions if they are no longer considered to be effective. Any decision on the effectiveness of the performance conditions is bound up with the motivational impact on the employees and the fairness to the employees. However, any replacement or revised performance condition should possess the same level of difficulty to satisfy, an assessment that surely must be made against current market conditions rather than market conditions at the date of the original grant or award.

Introduction of flexible benefits

7.25 The company may choose to allow the performance conditions to fail and the options to lapse or at most introduce a rolling performance period but at the same time augment the benefits package. This objective will typically be achieved through the introduction of flexible benefits linked maybe to enhanced pension contributions, flexible holiday arrangements, flexible working generally and a range of other incidental benefits relating to lifestyle and health, insurances of various kinds and car benefits. There are, of course, businesses in the public sector that cannot introduce share scheme for the reason that they do not have a share capital. The response for purposes primarily of recruitment and retention is to introduce flexible benefits which can become motivational, if the company chooses to link the availability of certain benefits to achievement; defined either in individual terms or department/business unit terms or even corporate terms.

Enhancement of the salary position

7.26 For most companies the enhancement of salary position really would be the last resort. This point is included to illustrate that if a company chooses to abandon its employee share schemes then over time in order to be competitive in recruitment and retention of quality employees it will have to increase its salary positions. There are examples of substantial companies that, in private and for various reasons, family or structural, cannot or will not introduce employee share schemes. – The consequence for these companies has been, certainly at the senior executive and middle management level, to have to increase salaries to positions in excess of market rates.

Chapter 8

Coping with a downturn in the share price

Introduction

8.1 This chapter addresses the matter that is often thought to be tortuous, namely how to cope with a downturn in the share price. The chapter explains how with trust and positivity in the employee communications this sensitive and delicate subject can present opportunities for strengthening corporate trust, educating the employees about wider corporate issues and giving due profile to the full range of employee participation policies within the company.

Severity of the problem

8.2 The severity of the problem that the company can find in communicating with employees at the time of a downturn in the share price is, to a degree, dependent upon the type of scheme that has been introduced. Where the scheme is aSSOP, the cash return parachute will take all the risk away from the employees. Where the scheme is a share purchase scheme, though, with shares already purchased by the employees then it is the employees who face the exposure with the downturn. If viewed in isolation the downturn in the share price can present a major challenge to corporate managers and the size of the challenge will often depend upon the extent of the employee involvement in the shares of the company coupled with the prospects for the future.

All-important trust employee communications

8.3 The key to coping with the share price downturn is to ensure that from the time of the introduction of the scheme the company has sought to establish trusted communication with the employees. It is definitely the case that the company should not seek to hide the truth from its employees or, indeed, assume that employees do not have the ability to understand. Rather, the employees should be treated as partners in the business enterprise of the company and given respect for the commitment that they have shown in engaging in the employee share scheme initiative in the first place.

It is in the context of mutual commitment from the company to the employees and vice versa that the company is in a position to encourage the longer-term view from its employees. This positive approach must be the foundational base for dealing with any downturn in the share price.

Opportunity for employee communication

8.4 Building upon this foundation of trust, the company must use the opportunity and use the following approaches to deal with the problem.

Contextualise the dowturn: as an investment

8.5 The company should put the downturn into context in demonstrating comparisons with other investments in the market and, also, with the performance of other companies in the same peer group.

Explain the business plans to the employees

8.6 The company should explain its business plans to the employees so that the ethos of mutual interest between the company and its employees can be fostered, and the employees can see future opportunities for the success of the company, hopefully reflecting in a future upturn in the share price.

Emphasize the long-term to the employees

8.7 The company should emphasize the long-term nature of the investment and encourage the belief that the employee share scheme involvement is a marathon and not a sprint, requiring patience and fortitude.

Use the opportunity to build trust

8.8 The company should capitalise on the fact that the downturn has captured the attention of the employees and use this opportunity to build loyalty, trust and commitment by educating the employees about belonging to a company that has embraced employee share ownership.

Emphasize the range of employee participation policies

8.9 The company should maintain a mentality of investing in its employees and, where there is a network of employee participation policies, seek to give greater emphasis to them, demonstrating that the employee ownership culture is manifested in a range of policies, not solely the employee share scheme.

Seek to avoid redundancies if possible

8.10 The company should seek, as far as is possible, to avoid redundancies which would send out the most negative of signals to the employee workforce. Conversely, a positive signal is to show that the shareholders are sharing in the distress, maybe through lower dividend levels.

Hold regular meetings with the employees

8.11 The management must give a commitment to hold regular structured meetings with the employees. If, as part of the business culture and organization, there are regular meetings anyway, say weekly or monthly, then management must ensure that time is allocated within the meetings to address points that employees wish to have addressed about the share value.

Keep all channels of communication open

8.12 As well as having the regular communication meetings, employees must be given the assurance that they can raise questions on a one-to-one basis with management or, indeed, by email as not all are comfortable asking questions in an open meeting. Crucial to the coping strategy is the need to ensure that the level of understanding is maximized and that employees have outlets for their thoughts and feelings. Indeed, avoiding pent-up feelings is essential to the health of corporate relations anyway.

Chapter 9

Progressive communication strategies

Introduction

9.1 This chapter appreciates the fact that when all the legal work has been completed the success or failure of the employee share scheme launch will depend upon the quality and the sensitivity of the employee communications. The chapter explains advanced employee communication strategies based on cultural indices that provide an understanding of national cultures and enable bespoke solutions to issues that need to be addressed when formulating employee communications. The chapter also develops an advanced understanding of the role of employee share schemes within the overall context of human resource management.

Developing the global share scheme

9.2 The trend towards introducing global share scheme arrangements has arisen from a belief in the need for corporate unity sustained by a credible form of employee incentivisation. Clearly, the globalisation of world markets has contributed to this belief with a recognition of the interconnectedness of all the disparate elements within and across a world corporate group.

It was Leonardo Da Vinci who famously encouraged his students to study the art of science and the science of art and to recognise that everything is interconnected. Certainly, the world corporate group is a body with a complexity of interconnected parts or elements. However, the concept of interconnectedness is equally applicable to the management of the mechanism that is chosen to oil this complexity, namely the global share scheme itself. The introduction of the global share scheme most certainly requires the tools of science to ensure its logical self-consistency. However, a successful introduction will require the artist's design capability together with the sensitivity of understanding in the communication to peoples from different cultures and backgrounds. Indeed, in its execution, the global share scheme becomes predominantly social-scientific in its need to respond to the different ways in which people think and feel. This is, of course, an attitude of mind necessary for the successful implementation of any human resource management subject and, indeed, for the success of any corporate initiative.

Any business depends for its vibrancy and vigour, its productivity and its performance upon its people, the human resource, and increasingly business leaders are prepared to recognise this intellectually, if not always instinctively. This recognition is, of course, a significant departure from days gone by when business leaders sought to impose their grand design and expected automatic compliance from their employees. Employee involvement has come to have a worldwide credibility. However, there remains a continuing need to assist and coach managers into attitudes and behaviours that are consistent with the belief that employee involvement really does have the capacity to enhance industrial relations and increase productivity. It is not for nothing that the progress of employee involvement and, in particular, the employee share ownership version of employee involvement is known as 'The Quiet Revolution'.

There are clear reasons for a move away from the totalitarian attitude of management imposition and the expectation of automatic employee compliance. Firstly, of course, are the higher expectations on the part of all peoples, certainly in the Western world, for better treatment from their managers. The growth of materialism has led people to believe that much of what they want is within their grasp and, in some cases, their right. Additionally, the expansion of global communications means that people are given, through a variety of media, glimpses of other worlds which in themselves generate aspiration and, indeed, expectation. On top of all this, there is an increasing tendency around the world for governments to be less intrusive and dictatorial with the cultural consequence for business of having to mirror this governmental attitude if their management style is not to be resented by the workforce. People become more conditioned to thinking for themselves with a belief, certainly in part, that they have a capacity to create what they want for themselves. All this leads to the very simple conclusion that employees' expectations are considerably higher than they were even, say, ten years ago. The expectation is for meaningful relationships in the workplace, relationships that have the characteristics of acceptance and mutual respect.

The challenge for corporate business leaders and, in particular, for human resources managers is to reflect these social-scientific trends in the management of the business environment. With employees socially empowered and placing high value on their own freedom, the role of management is to harness the release of energy that comes from all this into the achievement of the corporate aims and objectives. Essentially, the need is for management to retain control of the business whilst, at the same time, working to create an environment that maximises the opportunity for worthwhile contribution from the employees.

In this context, management can choose a purposeful set of policies to create that environment. This thesis is based on a classic cause and effect approach to human behaviour. The causes are the policies and, in particular, the human resource policies. The effects in this causal chain are the environmental characteristics that contribute towards the employees' self-esteem and enhanced business contribution. Typically, the environmental characteristics will be a requirement for accountability coupled with ample opportunity for creativity and learning and a sense of belonging that is true to the spirit of consensus but does not diminish the clarity of focus on business priorities.

It is, of course, the mark of the mature business to be able to combine apparent opposites. The fusion of accountability and creativity is one example. The ability to achieve consensus while maintaining focus represents another.

Exporting the UK model

9.3   It is into this social-scientific and business context that the global share scheme emerges as an appropriate tool for the creation of this environment. Indeed, as a human resource policy it is beautifully equipped to act as a cause initiated by management for the effect of the compatible environment.

The UK and the US have been, and continue to be, the countries in which employee share ownership initiatives are best encouraged by governments. The employee share ownership initiatives in each country have developed different traditions. In the USA, the tradition lies predominantly in succession planning and long-term pension provision. However, in the UK, the government tax incentives have been more geared towards shorter-term incentives and capital gain within the space of three to seven years or, as in the case of the 1984 legislation, or more recently the 2000 EMI legislation, within ten years as a maximum. It is from both the US and the UK traditions that models of employee share ownership have been exported throughout the rest of the world, primarily, of course, in situations where the holding company is resident and registered in either the UK or the US.

Focusing on the UK model, it is the tax reliefs that have brought the schemes to the attention of business managers. However, from a management point of view, this is the sole purpose of the tax reliefs. Once the schemes are introduced, the structure and design of the schemes, the communication and implementation, the strategy and the planning should all be geared towards the human resource objectives of creating the most compatible environment for productivity and working towards the achievement of corporate aims and objectives.

As with any export product, it is essential to refine the product to be suitable for the importing countries. However, at the same time, the essence of the initiative must not loose sight of the international objective of corporate unity and incentive. Certainly, it is important to accommodate, as far as possible, the tax reliefs in the importing companies and, clearly, it would be foolhardy to introduce the schemes without a full due diligence on all relevant statutes and regulations. However, to restrict the international vision to a group of molecular legal structures loses sight of the human resources context that should be the driving force for extending the schemes into the overseas businesses. The reasons behind the corporate entity establishing those businesses overseas in the first place was visionary. The introduction of employee share schemes to service those businesses should be done in the same spirit.

Initial implementation in the UK, though, has provided the opportunity to understand the schemes, indeed to gain some mastery over how the schemes can best be put into effect. With a solid basis of success in the UK, the business can be confident in exporting its product with appropriate refinement. In the interest of international corporate unity, it is necessary to find the balance between having as many common features as possible and structuring the scheme in the localities that allows the employees as many tax advantages as possible.

Sensitising communication by country

9.4 The subtle point is this: the structure of the scheme should be as similar as possible across the world. However, with regard to the communication of the international scheme, certainly the content will be similar although the delivery will be highly sensitised to the different audiences around the world. The factors to be taken into account when preparing for the communication are many and may be found either singularly or in combination in any particular country. The rule of thumb must be to prepare each communication in a way that maximises the opportunity for each person throughout the world group to understand. Given the disparity of culture, tradition and language throughout the world, a sensitised approach to communication becomes a necessity.

Understanding culture is, of course, a very delicate exercise. However, it is possible to create indices for the purpose of identifying the differences between cultures. Essentially these indices can be reduced to five main indexes as follows:

1. *Emotional distance index*: measures the level of emotional distance between managers and the people reporting to them. Emotional distance, or power distance as it is sometimes called, measures the level of trust and affinity between people in authority and the people who are subject to that authority.

2. *Individualism/collectivism index*: measures the extent to which a community is bound by ties of collectivity or is made up of individuals who are pursuing their own personal agendas with or without regard to the collective good of the community.

3. *Gender index*: measures the extent to which the traditional roles of men and women still prevail in a community.

4. *Rrisk index*: measures the inclination of the culture to avoid uncertainty and for people within that culture to accumulate around them benchmarks as points of certainty and inflexibility.

5. *Timescale index*: measures the extent to which the community thinks short-term at the expense of long-term or vice versa.

The following is intended to explain how an understanding of these indices/factors can help to sensitise the communication of the introduction of an employee share scheme.

Immigrant minorities

9.5 It becomes immediately apparent that an understanding of these indices/factors can be very helpful indeed when seeking to bring people from different cultures together. This is especially well-illustrated in the situation where there are immigrant minorities present in the business that is to receive the communication.

The composition of each communication group must strike a balance between the desire for unity across all the disparate elements and the need to ensure that all concerned have a proper and meaningful communication. This consideration is, indeed, no more paramount than in the case of immigrant minorities within a company. Clearly, this will arise most often in countries that have offered a home to immigrant populations. Typically, this will be the US, Australia or Canada where people have emigrated in the hope of creating a better life for themselves. Alternatively, it may be, for example, in the UK, where peoples from the former colonies have sought asylum from war, political upheaval, or poverty.

The extent to which the presence of immigrant minorities presents a communication problem is dependent upon the degree of assimilation. However, to put this matter into context, it should be recognised that the twentieth century saw a greater proportion of the world's population migrate than in any previous century in history!

Research shows that migration can lead to severe culture shock that, in turn, can lead to illness, both physical and mental, homesickness or even suicide. The problem can become exacerbated where migrants are moving to and fro between the cultures of their home country and their new host country, and finding that the clash of cultures makes it impossible to settle. Interesting also, is the research that migrants will settle more easily at work than at home and that an apparent normality at work can actually disguise cultural turmoil back in their domestic-setting.

Clearly, the presence of immigrant minorities must be treated with great sensitivity. Interestingly, the most effective vehicle for cultural transfer is shown to be language. Crucial, therefore, in the communication process is that respect is given to different levels of fluency so as not to undermine the confidence of those who are using the language as a means of assisting in their cultural assimilation.

At the same time, it is important for the communicator not to make the rash assumption that all peoples who speak the same language necessarily receive the message in the same way. This illustrates that culture is determined by other factors besides language, and the accommodation of these factors in the communication process will usually only be made possible by the communicator using intuitive acuity and interactive skills to their full extent.

Linguistic implications

9.6 Different languages and different uses of the same language can often contribute to cultural misunderstandings. The most obvious example in the communication of employee share schemes is the use of the word 'scheme'. Particularly in the US, the word 'scheme' has connotations of Mafia association and manipulative practice. Better, therefore, to christen the initiative with a title that uses the word 'plan' rather than 'scheme'.

Interestingly, the vocabulary that surrounds employee share scheme initiatives includes the words 'share' and 'trust' that can be universally translated and incorporated into phrases that convey the true essence of what the initiative is trying to achieve. Such examples would be 'sharing in success' and 'putting your trust in the trustees'.

Language, important though it is, should be supplemented as necessary with the use of symbols and images to convey the meaning of the scheme. Typically, the brochure may show a cake being cut into a number of pieces, illustrating profit-sharing, or a tree beginning as an acorn and growing into a mighty oak, illustrating the growth in the share price.

Care should also be taken in the use of numbers where, for example, in Chinese communities the number '4' is associated with death and the number '8' is associated with success. The lesson must surely be to pepper your examples with the number '8'! Clearly, cultural issues of this nature can only be dealt with by engaging in a full and proper preparation with local managers before finalising the brochures and delivering the communication.

In working with the communities in the Far East, it becomes apparent that there is a great contrast between the Chinese and the Japanese. The Chinese communities expect a short and pithy but, at the same time, detailed communication. In contrast, presentations in Japan would go on for two or three hours with the Japanese not acknowledging that they understand the scheme until they have understood every minute detail.

One word of special caution must be in the use of interpreters. Very important indeed is the need to ensure that the interpreter understands the scheme and will deliver the interpretation with enthusiasm. It may be necessary to win the support of the interpreter over to the merits of the scheme before feeling confident about giving the presentation via the interpreter.

Allied to this whole subject of linguistics is the tradition of story-telling which holds great credibility in certain countries around the world. Typically, in the rural communities of Ireland, for example, where community has been reluctant to break down, and hearsay, myth and legend have been passed down through generations, the audience will place great value on a story-telling-type presentation of the scheme.

Intelligence levels

9.7 Always, the intention should be to simplify the communication materials and any accompanying presentation. The temptation on the part of the company and their lawyers is often to include detailed legal explanations in order to cover themselves. It is, indeed, an art to distil the legal essence into a form that can be easily communicated and understood. In taking this approach, the problem of catering for different intelligence levels usually evaporates.

However, there are still issues that need to be considered with regard to different intelligence levels within the company. The first and foremost of these issues is to ensure that every employee has an opportunity to put their question to their company/communicator without any fear of embarrassment or humiliation. Supplementing the group presentation meeting, it is advisable to offer the employee the opportunity to ask questions individually at the end of the meeting on a one-to-one basis. Indeed, it can often prove to be a very welcome gesture to give to each employee the opportunity to send in questions by written note, fax or email with the full knowledge that they will receive a personal reply addressed directly and confidentially.

In catering for differing intelligence levels, 'the old chestnut' of the employee mix in the group communication should be given careful attention. Again, the concern is to avoid any potential embarrassment or humiliation and to give all employees the maximum opportunity to feel relaxed and receptive to the communication. Clearly, though, the need to have some degree of mix in the communication group is important; the presence of the mix in itself is a contribution to the sense of corporate unity that the scheme is designed to encourage.

Often, the accusation is that in catering for all intelligence levels, the subject is reduced to a common denominator level that is inconsistent with preserving proper meaning in the explanation. However, this is not necessarily the case if the subject is approached with all the professional tools of the trade. By distilling into simple form, and using symbols, illustrations and presentational aids to support the written employee brochures, the meaning and understanding can actually be enhanced rather than undermined. This is, again in Da Vinci's words: 'the art of science and the science of art'.

Additionally, of course, it should be remembered that intelligence comes in different forms in different people. The ability of a high-flying technocrat to pose a complicated question about the inner workings of the scheme; will often be no more intelligent than the tea lady or the cleaner asking a common sense, down-to-earth question about, for example, the procedures for lodging the application.

Collectivism versus individualism

9.8　The relative strength of individualism versus collectivism is crucial to the preparation of a professional communication on employee share schemes. Interestingly, the expressed intention of the Conservative administrations under Margaret Thatcher and John Major in the 1980s and 1990s that enacted employee share scheme legislation was, in part, individualist and, in part, collectivist. The policy initiative was to recognise the identity of interest between managers, shareholders and all employees in having a continuing interest in the success of the business. Furthermore, it was to assist in the progress of industrial relations, recognising that the identity of interest contributes greatly to the development of consensus attitudes expressed in the desire to work together. However, the employee share scheme legislative initiatives coupled with the privatisation issues were all designed to promote self-sufficiency and self-reliance. The power of employee share ownership is to play a prominent role in encouraging individual wealth whilst, at the same time, assisting collective social cohesion through improving industrial relations and growing the national economy.

An understanding of any national or ethnic culture reveals a natural propensity to a predominant cultural disposition of individualism or collectivism. The majority of societies display a tendency towards the collectivist approach where the interests of the group are given precedence over the interest of the individual. In these cultures, there prevails a sense of national identity and a general sense of loyalty to the group. Often a characteristic of the collective society will be the presence of extended family ties and small self-consistent village communities. However, there are also countries that are predominantly individualist where the individual's identity is defined on the basis of individual characteristics rather than group association. In these countries, the nuclear family tends to predominate with family members leaving home early, often to form their own nuclear family and sometimes severing existing family ties altogether.

Strong individualism tends to be characteristic of nations with an imperialism past such as the UK and the Netherlands, and also nations that are made up primarily of ambitious immigrant populations or the descendants of those populations such as the US, Australia and Canada.

Employees in countries with the individualist predisposition should be able to see the potential personal benefit of entering into an employee share scheme. However, if properly communicated, the scheme can act powerfully as a unifying force, in an environment where individualism may sometimes be expressed to the detriment of the company's collective and overall purpose.

Clearly, the message here is to achieve a balance between individualism and collectivism. The communication of the scheme offers the opportunity to achieve a balance between the two dispositions. Where individualism predominates, high take-up is achieved by appealing to the individualist instinct, but then using their involvement in the scheme through ongoing company communications to strengthen the collective sense of unity behind the growth in the value of the one share. Where collectivism predominates, high take-up is achieved by appealing to the community ethos and company loyalty of the employees and, then, through the ongoing company communications to use the potential growth in the share price to encourage individual effort as a contribution to company profitability.

It is a fascinating observation that research shows a strong correlation between countries that have an individualist predisposition and countries that have a capacity to generate wealth. This offers strong evidence to suggest that individualism should be encouraged. However, the all-important balance with collectivism is what can be achieved through an employee share ownership programme. The approach that employee share ownership initiatives offer is the potential to create a fusion between the positive elements of both individualism and collectivism.

The words 'individualist' and 'collectivist' refer to the natural inclination of a country and not to any enforced approach by a totalitarian government or authority that requires mass manipulation in order to sustain its existence. The identification of natural tendency is absolutely crucial to designing and delivering a communication strategy that appeals to and encourages the best human instincts. Essentially, by asking how people truly think and feel, an honest understanding emerges, that can then be used to fine-tune the employee communication process.

Gender factor

9.9   An understanding of the gender factor lies in a recognition of the predominant gender characteristics of a culture. The concern is not with the innate biology of man and woman but with the gender characteristics of masculinity or femininity. The mark of a mature society is where culture has evolved to display an optimum balance between masculine characteristics and feminine characteristics.

As an example, the roles of men and women in the UK, at least in business, are much more traditional than, say, those of men and women in the Netherlands. Where roles are more traditional, the aggression of the male, either overtly or indeed subtly, will more readily show itself in the workplace, than in a cultural environment where the traditional roles of men and women have, at least to some degree, broken down. As a general rule, the relative breakdown of traditional roles should lead, in time, to a relatively non-aggressive business environment where women do not have to assume the aggressive characteristics that traditionally have been associated with men in order to progress their careers. In the short-term, of course, the nature of society may cause women to assume the gender characteristics of masculinity. However, in the long-term, the mark of cultural maturity is that both men and women can achieve a balance of gender characteristics and be perfectly relaxed in that state in carrying out the duties of their employment and in furthering their careers. In the longer-term, of course, this makes for more mature individuals being more productive in the workplace and being confident that their career aspirations will be more directly related to hard work and effort.

This understanding of gender becomes important in the preparation of the verbal employee communication presentations. For example, in a traditional manufacturing environment with strong trade unions the archetypal cynical aggressive male may be encountered as an obstacle to high take-up. To be forewarned is to be forearmed. Knowing that this may be a problem will lead, at the very least, to trying to determine a strategy to cope with it!

Clearly, in countries where traditional roles have broken down and the roles of men and women are interchangeable the appeal of the schemes lies predominantly in working together for the common good of the business. In the more mature environment, the workforce will have a greater recognition of the merits of co-operation and teamwork. The cultures in which the natural feminine characteristics of compassion, understanding and co-operation prevail are those in which a mature approach to employee share ownership is probably most readily found. Research shows that, in general, the presence of natural feminine instinct brings a more balanced contextual understanding of the activity of work within the overall lifestyle.

Timescale orientation

9.10   When asked about the effects of the 1789 French Revolution, Chou En-lai of China replied: 'It is too early to say'. However, interestingly, during the days of Hong Kong as a British colony, discussion amongst the expatriate community on the subject of pension provision would be at a premium, if you pardon the pun, with the focus on significant short-term gain arising from their efforts.

The benefit of understanding the timescale orientation with respect to employee share schemes is deciding on the length of the scheme. For example, where there is a high turnover of staff, the scheme would be more acceptable with a life of, say, three years rather than, say, seven years. If the expectation is of 'jobs for life' and comparatively long-length of service per individual then the spectre of using an ESOP trust structure for pension provision, or even succession planning, takes on more reality. The concern on timescale comes from an appreciation of the nature of the business with regard to expected length of service and, indeed, the potential volatility of the business. However, it also comes from understanding the national culture or ethnic culture in which the business is operating.

Example 9.1: Using cultural indices with the United States

Compiling a set of cultural indices becomes extremely useful when wanting to construct a cultural profile of the culture in which the business is operating. The availability of data means that inevitably this understanding is restricted to national cultures. This means, quite simply, that indices used in relation to a business will be the indices that relate to the nation in which the business is geographically situated.

As an example, a business situated in the US will work with a profile as follows:

1. Emotional distance

Generally speaking, there will be comparatively little emotional distance between those in authority and those subject to that authority. This reflects a consensus culture and what is historically a sense of working together to achieve a better world.

2. Individualism/collectivism

The United States is primarily an individualist culture where individual achievement is rewarded and, indeed, highly applauded.

3. Gender

There is a reasonable degree of balance in the culture of the US between the gender characteristics across both sexes of masculinity and femininity. Again, this reflects a comparatively, 'consensus-business environment'. If anything, there is a skew towards the gender characteristics of masculinity, displayed by both men and women, reflecting the competitive edge in US business.

4. Risk

Generally speaking, US business is by no means risk-averse. This is reflected in a comparatively high reading on the risk index with a comparatively low reading on the uncertainty avoidance index.

5. Timescale

Generally speaking, the timescale of US business will be to think and plan with long-term visionary strategy but, at the same time, break down this vision into short-term periods of, in some cases, less than a year. These short-term successes are seen as incremental steps towards the realisation of the larger vision.

The fascination, of course, of US business culture is that it is not determined by the indigenous american people. It is determined by a combination of migrant peoples over a period of over 200 years or more, primarily from the UK, Ireland, Continental Europe and Africa. Clearly, there is also a sizeable Hispanic business community not only from Europe but also from Latin America. It is this melting-pot of migrant cultures that makes the US such a fascinating business culture to analyse.

Essentially, the cultural indices represent the relative position of a national culture compared with other national cultures. The indices represent a relative analysis rather than an absolute analysis. In this way, the benchmarks on any index scale for any one national culture reading are all the other national culture readings on that particular scale. The indices provide us, therefore, with a management tool and do not constitute an absolute science. Correlations between different indices are always open to question as there may be other factors at work that have not been brought into the analysis. The test, therefore, of the relevance of the indices lies in matching their interpretation with basic common sense and practical knowledge of the countries concerned.

This explanation focuses on the use of the indices in the development of employee share scheme communication strategy. The indices do, of course, offer themselves for use in other areas of human resource and business management. In particular, they may be used to prepare for expatriate assignments where the expatriate can be forewarned of any potential culture shock. The indices may be used also in determining the suitability of two businesses coming together from different cultures in a merger or take-over situation.

Case study: South East Asia

South East Asia is dominated by two ethnic groups: the Japanese and the Chinese. The success of the Japanese in their post-war, pre-recession rise to economic dominance lies in the homogeneity of the people of the Japanese islands with minimal immigrant influence, except for US instruction on reconstruction; following the devastation of the Second World War. The homogeneity of the Chinese peoples on mainland China offers, interestingly, a similar opportunity for economic expansion in the new millennium. However, the success of the Chinese peoples outside mainland China over the last 20 years is testimony to the innate business skills of the Chinese and the capacity of the Chinese to establish meaningful business leadership in their settled lands.

The application of cultural analysis throughout South East Asia offers an understanding that is, at the same time, both fascinating and complex. Operating with an individualism and short-term orientation, that is probably uncharacteristic of their natural cultural inclination, the peoples of South East Asia have sometimes floundered in an attempt to build economic success without the supporting infrastructure of strong political and social institutions.

The lessons, therefore, for South East Asia, and, indeed, this includes lessons for Japan, are first and foremost to establish institutions of state that operate with the necessary checks and balances to guard against and to expose corruption. Secondly, of course, the lesson is to understand their own culture and, in particular, the need to both plan and operate long-term with a recognition that their success will only be achieved through natural consensus and a meaningful assessment of risk.

The case study on South East Asia is also indicative in revealing the global complexity of world business and the ways in which businesses from different cultures have come together with a view to achieving success. In particular, of course, the lending institutions of the West, operating with their own cultural profile, failed to understand the cultural profile and, more than that, the inherent weakness of many of the South East Asian tiger economies.

The future success of the individual South East Asian economies is best facilitated by the economic momentum of China while drawing

---

upon the considerable bank of professional expertise that exists in Hong Kong and Singapore and, potentially, with a role for the institutional stability of Australia which is, quite clearly, part of the region.

Employee share schemes represent one of many techniques and tools that properly used can assist in the economic success of the region. It must be the case, quite clearly, that cultural understanding is crucial to the success of any employee share scheme initiative and, in this regard, the indices are able to offer great significant assistance in the formulation of successful communication strategies.

Conclusions

9.11 Working without an understanding of the natural inclination or predisposition of a country is often a recipe for failing to achieve maximum benefit from the introduction of an employee share scheme. Indeed, cultural understanding coupled with an understanding of the national economy represents the key to unlocking the potential of the scheme in the country concerned.

Human motivation and awareness is an exceedingly complex phenomenon. To be sure, every human being is uniquely different with his or her own inner motivations for survival and achievement. How to tap into the motivations that will release the potential for optimum business contribution for each individual employee presents a conundrum indeed. However, creating a compatible environment, using cause-and-effect; with policies as causes to create the environmental effects, and developing a matrix of cultural indices linked to cultural and economic understanding will almost certainly assist in arousing those inner motivations. Once aroused, the responsibility of the ongoing corporate team communication throughout the term of the scheme is to nurture, develop and encourage those motivations in the direction of corporate unity, goal congruence, and the achievement of corporate aims and objectives.

Chapter 10

Approved savings-related share option scheme

Introduction

10.1   This chapter explains how the savings-related share option scheme (SSOS) operates together with an appreciation of its advantages and disadvantages. The reason for the continuing popularity of the SSOS is the potential for significant capital gain coupled with the risk-free tax-efficient investment that it offers to employee participants. Even in circumstances where movement in the share price does not generate a gain the employee participants can still benefit from the tax-free cash bonus and at the same time have their savings returned. (The changes that were introduced to the scheme through FA 2003 are explained in detail in a separate chapter.)

Scheme synopsis

The company grants share options to employees on an all-employee basis to purchase shares in the company at a discount of up to 20% of the MV of the shares at the time of grant. The employees save in order to build a fund that is available for the purchase of shares either three or five or seven years later. The increase in the MV of the shares from the date of grant to the date of exercise is income tax-free. The international SSOS mirrors the UK version in its structure with tax reliefs around the world determined by their availability within individual country tax regimes.

The savings-related share option scheme was introduced by the Finance Act 1980 (FA 1980) with legislation that took effect from 1 July 1981. To a large degree this new legislation mirrored the provisions for the introduction of a SSOS that were introduced through FA 1972 but were repealed through FA 1974.

The legislation that governs the operation of the current SSOS is ITEPA 2003, Pt 7, Chap 7, together with Schedule 3 of the same Act.

The tax-approved all-employee SSOS must have the following characteristics:

- Employees *must* have rights under the scheme to acquire shares that meet particular criteria as set out in the legislation.

- Rights that are obtained by employees under the scheme *must* not be transferable except in the circumstances of death when the rights pass to the personal representatives.

- Features that are neither essential nor reasonably incidental to the purpose of providing share benefits to employees in the form of rights *must* not be included. Typically, the rules must not allow for the exercise of an option to be satisfied by the payment of cash instead of the delivery of shares.

Employee eligibility criteria

10.2 The express intention of introducing the SSOS was to encourage wider employee share ownership and employee participation. It is, therefore, designed as an all-employee share scheme arrangement and is definitively *not* a discretionary scheme.

For schemes approved from 1 May 1995, an individual is eligible to participate provided they meet the eligibility criteria as follows:

- The individual must be an employee or a full-time director, where full-time is working 25 hours a week or more, excluding meal breaks, of the company that has established the scheme or, in the case of a group scheme, of a participating company.

- The individual meets a qualifying period that must not exceed five years ending on the date of grant.

- The individual is chargeable to income tax under Schedule E, Case 1 in respect of the office or employment that they hold with the company.

- The individual must meet the material interest test set out in the legislation.

The company has the discretion to reduce the qualifying period to less than five years. Typically, participation is extended to employees with one year's service and increasingly to all employees who are in the employment of the company that has established the scheme or, in the case of a group scheme, a participating company, at the date of grant.

The company has the discretion to extend participation to overseas employees and directors whose emoluments are outside the scope of Schedule E, Case 1.

This eligibility criteria for participation covers the following:

- obtaining rights to acquire the shares through the grant of an option; and

- exercising the right to acquire the shares.

As with all the tax-approved employee share schemes in the UK there are limitations on employee participation as follows:

- The limitation on employee participation in the SSOS is defined by the maximum savings stipulation of £250 per month. This is in relation to all options granted under SSOS arrangements that are live at any point in time.

- The minimum contribution per month in relation to any individual savings-related share option grant is £5.

Similar terms requirement

10.3 As an all-employee scheme the similar terms requirement must be applied as follows:

- through an eligibility to participate on similar terms; and

- all participants must participate on similar terms.

The application of the similar terms requirement requires a definition of eligibility *and* participation in relation to some objective factor such as permanence of employment or length of service.

Material interest test

10.4 Participation in the scheme is not available to an individual who has or has had within the preceding 12 months a material interest in:

- a close company whose shares may be acquired on the exercise of an option granted under the scheme; or

- a company which has control over such a company or as a member of a consortium which owns such a company.

A material interest in a company is defined as:

- beneficial ownership of, or the ability to control, directly or through the medium of other companies, or by any other indirect means, more than 25% of the ordinary share capital of the company; or

- in circumstances where the company is a close company, the possession of or entitlement to acquire such rights as would, in the event of the winding-up of the company or in any other circumstances, give an entitlement to receive more than 25% of the assets that would then be available for distribution among the participators.

The interests of any of the employee's associates are included in the shares of the employee in the determination of material interests where associates are:

- husband or wife, parent or remoter forebear, child or remoter issue, or brother or sister;

- partner;

- trustee of any settlement for which the employee or his or her relative, living or dead, is or was settlor; or

- trustee of a settlement over the shares of the company where the employee has an interest.

Operation of the scheme

10.5 The scheme operates through two contractual arrangements as follows.

A share option contract between the company and the employee

10.6 The share option is granted to the employee by the company as a right to purchase shares in the company at a discount of up to 20% on MV determined in relation to the date of grant.

The scheme rules must exclude any right of voluntary transfer of the option rights, any assignment of the option rights or any charge over the option rights.

A savings contract between the appointed savings carrier and the employee

10.7 The contractual savings scheme arrangement gives to the employee the opportunity to build up savings with which to purchase the shares on the exercise of the option.

The savings contract, sometimes referred to as the Sharesave contract, excludes any right of voluntary transfer of the savings.

The savings contract makes provision for action by the savings carrier in such circumstances as follows:

- Any purported transfer *before* the completion of the savings term is treated as a notice to cease paying contributions and all contributions will be repaid together with any interest that has accrued.

- Any purported transfer *after* the completion of the savings term is treated as an application for repayment of the savings and the bonus.

Both the share option contract and the savings contract are, therefore, personal to the employee optionholder.

Share option

10.8 The main features of the share option contract are as follows.

1. The level of the discount is at the discretion of the directors and must not exceed 20% of the MV of the shares determined in relation to the date of grant.

2. Options are normally exercisable after three, five or seven years, within a window period of six months from the date the bonus is credited to the savings account.

3. The company decides on the following:

    - the term of the scheme that is to be offered to the employees, whether three, five or seven years;

    - the maximum monthly savings amount that each employee will be allowed to save; and

    - whether or not the bonus will be available for the purchase of shares.

4. The scheme usually contains provisions to scale down applicatons where necessary. The scaling down provisions will arise where the total amount of the desired savings contributions for all employees who have applied to participate requires a share allocation that is beyond the limit that the company is either willing or able to sustain. The excess is eliminated by applying a succession of steps that are recommended by HMRC.

5. Depending on the choice offered by the company, each employee must decide at the outset of the arrangement before the option is granted on the term that they wish to accept, although the decision to participate by the employee is totally voluntary.

6. Options are normally granted over newly-issued shares, although shares purchased off the market, which are normally then held in an employee share trust, can be used as the shares over which the options are granted.

7. Options normally lapse if employees leave by reason of resignation or dismissal. However, the scheme *must* provide that options can be exercised within the period of six months following the date of leaving if employees leave for one of the specified reasons as follows::

    - injury or disability;

    - redundancy in accordance with the Employment Rights Act 1996 or the Employment Rights (Northern Ireland) Order 1996; or

    - retirement on reaching a specified age, or any other age at which he or she is bound to retire in accordance with the contractual terms of the contract of employment.

8. The scheme *must* provide that options can be exercised if an employee dies as follows:

    - If the employee dies before the bonus date then the personal representative can exercise the option within 12 months of the date of death.

- If the employee dies within six months after the bonus date then the personal representative can exercise the option within 12 months after the bonus date.

9. The scheme *may* provide that options can be exercised in the following circumstances:

   - If there is a *change of control* of the company whose shares have been used for the grant of options resulting from a general offer then the employees may exercise their options within six months of the change of control subject to all conditions of the offer being satisfied.

   - If there is a *reconstruction* of the company whose shares are used for the grant of options or an *amalgamation* with other companies following a court sanction for compromise of arrangement under CA 2006, s 899 (CA 1985, s 425) or Companies (Northern Ireland) Order 1986, Article 418 then the employees can exercise their options within six months of the court sanction.

   - If any person becomes *bound or entitled to acquire* under CA 2006, ss 974–991 (CA 1985, ss 428–430) or the Companies (Northern Ireland) Order 1986, Articles 421–423 the shares of the company whose shares are used for the grant of options then the employees can exercise their options at any time when that person remains so bound or entitled.

   - If there is *a voluntary winding-up* of the company then the employees can exercise their options within six months of the passing of the resolution.

   - If at the bonus date an employee who has been granted an option *holds an office or employment with a company that is not a participating company* then the employee can exercise the option within six months of the bonus date provided the office or employment is with either an associated company of the grantor or a company of which the grantor has control.

   - If an employee *holds an office or employment in a company over which the grantor ceases to have control or the office or employment relates to a business that is transferred* to a business which is neither an associated company of the grantor or a company of which the grantor has control, then the employee can exercise the option within six months of the office or employment ceasing to be an eligible office or employment.

10. The statute allows tax-approved share option schemes to contain provisions under which an optionholder can exchange approved options in circumstances where another company obtains control of the company or becomes bound or entitled under CA 2006, ss 974–991 (CA 1985, ss 428–430) to acquire the shares. The new options

must be exercisable in the same manner as the old options, and the value and aggregate subscription price of the new options must be exactly the same as the value and aggregate subscription price of the old options.

Savings arrangement

10.9   The main features of the savings arrangement are as follows:

1.   The savings contract is with a savings carrier, which is a savings organisation that is nominated and specified by the sponsoring company.

2.   The employee decides at the outset on a monthly savings contribution level of between £5 and £250.

3.   The contributions accumulate over a three- or a five-year period.

4.   The savings carrier credits bonuses at the end of three years for a three-year scheme, at the end of five years for a five-year scheme and at the end of five years and seven years for a seven-year scheme.

5.   The employees who enter into a seven years' arrangement do not have to make contributions during the sixth and seventh years.

6.   The employee must decide at the time of application between a three-, a five- and a seven-year scheme.

7.   If at any time during the life of the scheme the employee does not wish to complete the savings contract the employee may close their account, withdraw savings and, in these circumstances, the employees' share option will lapse.

8.   The employee is allowed to miss up to six monthly contributions during the savings term. If the employee does miss contributions then the crediting of the bonus, the closure of the account, and the deadline date to exercise the option will be delayed by one month for every missed contribution so that the employee has the opportunity to complete all contributions.

9.   The bonus is credited to the savings account as a lump sum paid in lieu of interest after the completion of the savings arrangement. The bonus is calculated as a number of equivalent contributions as a multiple set by government.

Shares

10.10   The legislation identifies the type of shares that may be used in a savings-related share option scheme. The shares *must* be:

●   fully paid;

●   non-redeemable; and

- not subject to any restrictions other than the restrictions which apply to all shares of the same class although noting the use of the Articles of Association.

The Articles of Association can impose a restriction on the shares. It takes the form of a requirement that all shares held by directors and employees are to be disposed of when they leave the company, and when shares are acquired as a result of options exercised after directors and employees have left the company when the exercise may be by them or by their personal representatives. In these circumstances, the sale of the shares must be for money on the terms laid down by the Articles of Association for the disposal of all shares of the same class.

It is important to recognise that a restriction can be imposed by any contract or agreement or arrangement or condition that will be regarded as a restriction if it does any of the following:

- restricts the freedom to dispose of the shares or any interest in the shares or the proceeds from the sale of the shares; or

- restricts the freedom to exercise any right conferred by the shares; or

- causes a disadvantage to the participant or a connected person if the shares are disposed of or any right conferred by them is exercised.

If the period between the exercise of the option and the allotment of the shares exceeds 30 days then this will be deemed to be imposing a restriction on the shares. Consequently, the period of time between the exercise of the option and the allotment of the shares cannot exceed 30 days.

The shares *must* form part of the ordinary share capital of:

- the company that has set up the scheme; or

- the company that controls the company that has set up the scheme; or

- the company which is or has control of the company which is a member of a consortium owning either the company which has set up the scheme or the company which has control of the company which has set up the scheme.

Company

10.11 The legislation identifies the characteristics that a company must have in order to operate a SSOS as follows:

The company *must* be:

- a company whose scheme shares are quoted on a recognised stock exchange;

- a company that is under the control of a company whose scheme shares are quoted on a recognised stock exchange; or

- an unquoted company that is not controlled by another unquoted company.

Option price

10.12 The legislation stipulates the rules that determine the setting of the option price as follows:

- the option price *must* be stated at the time the rights are obtained by the employees under the grant of the option;

- the option price *must* be 80% or more of the MV of the shares of the same class at the time the option is granted;

- the option price *must* be set precisely in accordance with the rules of the scheme which is approved by HMRC's ESSU, otherwise it will not qualify for income tax relief;

- the option price *may* be set on the basis of the average MV over a period of time that must commence no more than 30 days before the date of grant; and

- the scheme *may* provide for adjustments to the option price to account for any variations in the share capital.

Share rights

10.13 The employees do not have the statutory rights of shareholders during the savings period for the reason that they are only optionholders until they have exercised their option to purchase the shares.

The employees do, however, have a legal interest in the shares of the company through the rights that are conferred upon them through the option arrangement.

Even though as optionholders the employees are not shareholders, the company may choose to provide them with annual and interim reports in order to encourage the sense of involvement that the introduction of an employee share scheme is designed to achieve.

The ultimate success of any employee share scheme arrangement for the motivation of the employees relies upon the communication that the company has with the employees and the sense of worth that the communication conveys.

Tax reliefs

10.14 The application of the tax-approved legislation gives income tax relief to the employee and corporation tax relief to the company. Additionally, the general legislation offers CGT relieving opportunities to the employees.

Income tax

10.15   The key advantage of the scheme for UK taxpayers is that, provided the share options are granted and exercised according to the rules of the scheme which have been approved by the HMRC's ESSU under ITEPA 2003, Sch 3 the employee is able to take advantage of income tax relief as follows:

- a charge to income tax will *not* normally arise when the option is granted, even where the option price is granted at a discount on the MV of the underlying shares; and

- a charge to income tax will *not* normally arise when the option is exercised, provided that the exercise is within the six months window period that is stipulated by the legislation.

Income tax relief is not available on the exercise of options within three years of grant where the right to exercise is allowed under the provisions that the company has at its discretion included in the rules of the scheme and which are set out as item 9 under the description of the share option above.

Capital gains tax

10.16   On the subsequent sale of the shares, the difference between the sale proceeds and the option price represents a chargeable gain for CGT purposes, subject to the CGT annual exemption limit and any other available CGT reliefs that the employee may choose to use.

There are no special CGTreliefs given under the legislation that governs the SSOS. The rules that apply to the calculation of gains and losses arising on the sale of shares acquired by the exercise of a SSOS are the ordinary CGTrules that are set out in Taxation of Chargeable Gains Act 1992 (TCGA 1992).

Corporation tax

10.17   The company benefits from corporation tax relief on the costs incurred in setting up a SSOS that is approved by HMRC's ESSU. This relief is available on costs that are incurred for this purpose from 1 April 2001.

The corporation tax relief is available as an allowable deduction for the period of account for which the expenditure is incurred. The exception to this is in circumstances where the scheme is approved more than nine months after the end of that period of account, in which case the corporation tax relief is given as an allowable deduction for the period of account in which the ESSU gives the approval.

In order to secure the corporation tax relief it is imperative to ensure that the options are not granted before the scheme has been approved by the ESSU.

Finance Act 2009

10.18 Under Finance Act 2009 (FA 2009), with effect from 29 April 2009, the following changes will be operative:

- The process of specifying new bonus and interest rates applicable to SAYE savings contracts that are linked to the tax-approved SSOS will be transferred from HM Treasury to HMRC.

- When the notification of a change of rate is published, HMRC may specify that savings contracts entered into within a period following the date of the rate change, in response to invitations issued just before the rate change was announced, will be subject to the old rates prevailing at the time when the invitations were issued.

- The period of notice that HMRC gives of rate and interest changes is to be reduced from 28 to 15 days.

- The notification of future changes will be made by HMRC to the banks, building societies and European savings institutions by email.

Advantages of the savings–related share option scheme

Risk–free investment

10.19 Employees have participation in a risk-free investment as:

- their contributions are always protected in the savings contract that they have with the specified savings carrier; and

- the bonuses that will be credited to their savings account are guaranteed and offer a return even in the absence of a rise in the share price.

Discounted option prices

10.20 Discounted option prices establish unrealised gains for the employees at the date of grant given that the discount is applied to the MV of the underlying shares determined in relation to the date of grant. Once a discounted option price has been set, the MV of the underlying shares, as expressed in the share price for a company that is quoted on a recognised stock exchange, can fall to the value of the discount without creating a capital loss.

Employee retention

10.21 Positive assistance is provided for the company in retaining employees for the reason that employees who leave by way of resignation or dismissal will lose their option rights. As an employee retention tool, the grant of an option under a SSOS represents 'a golden handcuff'.

No company funding

10.22 If the options are granted over shares that are to be newly issued following the exercise of the options there will be no funding requirement by the company for the purchase of existing shares.

Powerful communication tool

10.23 The power of the option based upon the intrinsic structural strength of the SSOS arrangement is to focus the minds of the employees for a concentrated period of time between the grant of the option and the exercise of the option. Realising this power and intrinsic strength for enhanced employee productivity, and performance depends upon the company engaging in meaningful employee communications that are directed towards employee motivation and incentive.

Tax reliefs

10.24 The supporting tax-approved legislation secures a full set of income tax reliefs in all normal circumstances for the employees at both the grant, and the exercise of the option, and a corporation tax deduction for setting up costs for the company. Additionally, the CGT legislation can be used to the advantage of the employees.

Employee financial commitment

10.25 The structure of the scheme requires monthly savings contributions from the employees. The reward in the form of a gain on exercise and the bonus return on the savings offers, therefore, a reward for employee financial commitment to the savings contract.

Employee sense of value

10.26 The requirement for the employees to make a financial commitment encourages the employees to attach value to the share options that are granted to them under the scheme.

Flexibility in design

10.27 The company has significant flexibility in the design of the scheme. Provided the company makes its decisions before the options are granted, it can limit the monthly contribution, it can choose which savings term periods are to be offered to the employees, it can determine the extent of the discount (if any) and it can decide whether or not bonuses are to be available for employee share purchase.

Disadvantages of the savings-related share option scheme

Employee shareholders only at exercise

10.28 The employees are optionholders throughout the term of the savings and do not become shareholders until they exercise their options.

However, the share option represents, through the legally binding share option contract, a legal right in relation to the ordinary share capital of the company, a fact that should be communicated to the employees by the company. Even though the employees are not shareholders until they exercise their options they can be treated as shareholders through the issue of annual and interim reports, supported by a powerful communication exercise.

Employee affordability

10.29 Typically, different employees within a company will be able to afford different levels of monthly saving or, in some cases, not be able to afford saving at all. Potentially, there is the danger of discrimination arising through different levels of saving. However, it is a purely voluntary matter as to at what level employees choose to save and whether or not they wish to save at all. If employee affordability is a concern to the company, then the company may choose to reduce the maximum savings contribution from £250 to something less in order to mitigate against potential disparity in savings levels.

Not performance linked

10.30 Grants of option cannot be linked to performance, either of the individual employee or of the business as a whole. However, a rise in the share price will typically represent the enhanced productivity and performance of the company, and it is the rise in the share price that will generate the gain on exercise for the employees. With the opportunity for the employees to benefit in this way the rise in the share price represents an overall company team incentive although for companies that are quoted on a recognised stock exchange other factors besides company productivity, and performance will affect the share price. Indeed, for companies that are not quoted on a recognised stock exchange other factors could affect the share valuation.

Example 10.1: What the SSOS means for the employee

Suppose a SSOS is granted to an employee who chooses to save the maximum £250 per month.

Assume that the savings contract is for 36 months and that although the tax-free cash bonus will be credited at the completion of the savings contract it is only the savings contributions that are available for the purchase of the shares.

The total savings contributions after 36 months are, therefore, £9,000. The market value of the shares at date of grant is £5. However, with a maximum 20% discount the option price is set at £4.

The option is granted over 2,250 shares calculated by dividing £9,000 by £4.

Some years later, the employee exercises the option to purchase the shares at £4 each using the savings of £9,000. The market value of the shares is now £10. Some years later still, the employee sells the shares when the share price has reached £20.

The tax consequences for the employee are summarised as follows:

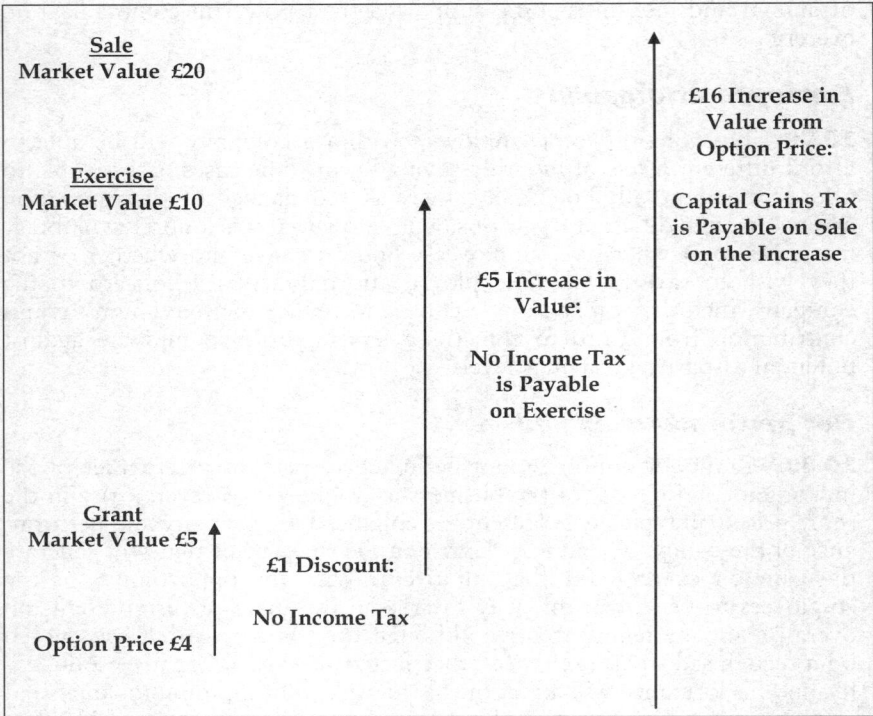

Sale
Market Value £20

£16 Increase in Value from Option Price:

Capital Gains Tax is Payable on Sale on the Increase

Exercise
Market Value £10

£5 Increase in Value:

No Income Tax is Payable on Exercise

Grant
Market Value £5

£1 Discount:

No Income Tax

Option Price £4

List of savings carriers

10.31

Barclays Wealth
Barclays Share Plans Team
12th Floor
1 Churchill Place
London
E14 5HP
Contact name: Tony Carter
Tel: 020 7114 8528
Tony.Carter2@barclayswealth.com

Capita Share Plan Services
Ibex
2nd Floor
42–47 The Minories
London
EC3N 1DX
Contact name: David Kilmartin
Tel: 020 954 9773
david.kilmartin@capita.co.uk

Computershare
Share Plans
68 Upper Thames Street
London
EC4V 3BJ
Contact name: Iain Wilson
Tel: 0870 703 6257
iain.wilson@computershare.com

Equiniti
Aspect House
Spencer Road
Lancing
West Sussex
Contact name: Phil Ainsley
Tel: 01903 833447
phil.ainsley@equiniti.com

HBSOS
HBSOS Employee Equity Solutions
1st Floor
62/64 Cornhill
London
EC3V 3PL
Contact name: Paul Stoddart
Tel: 07836 660733
paulstoddart@hbosplc.com

Yorkshire Building Society
Corporate Business Department
1 Filey Street
Bradford
Yorkshire
BD1 5AT
Contact name: Louise Drake
Tel: 01274 263101
lndrake@ybs.co.uk

Chapter 11

Approved executive/company share option scheme

Introduction

11.1 This chapter explains how the tax-approved share option scheme operates together with an appreciation of its advantages and disadvantages. The chapter also includes guidelines for determining the date of exercise. When the scheme was first introduced it quickly became known as the 'executive' share option scheme. However, after the reduction in tax relief in 1996 it became known as the 'company' share option scheme although in some companies it continued to be used solely for senior executives. Nevertheless, since 1996 it has had an increasing use as an all-employee arrangement even though this is not a statutory requirement. (The changes that have been introduced to the scheme through FA 2003 are explained in detail in a separate chapter.)

Scheme synopsis

The company grants share options to selected employees to purchase shares in the company at the MV at the time of grant. The employees can exercise their options between the third and the tenth anniversaries of the date of grant. The increase in the value of the shares from the date of grant to the date of exercise is income tax-free on the condition that the initial MV of the underlying shares over which the option is granted does not exceed £30,000.

The share option scheme in its tax-approved form was introduced by the Finance Act 1984 (FA 1984). The legislation that governs the operation of the share option scheme is ITEPA 2003, Pt 7, Chap 8, together with Schedule 4 of the same Act.

The tax-approved discretionary share option scheme must have the following characteristics:

- employees *must* have rights under the scheme to acquire shares which meet particular criteria as set out in the legislation;

- rights that are obtained by employees under the scheme *must* not be transferable except in the circumstances of death when the rights pass to the personal representatives; and

- features that are neither essential nor reasonably incidental to the purpose of providing share benefits to employees in the form of rights *must* not be included. Typically, the rules must not allow for the exercise of an option to be satisfied by the payment of cash instead of the delivery of shares.

Performance conditions or performance targets or other additional conditions can be included if the company so decides, with the employee's rights to acquire the shares dependent upon the conditions or targets being met. It must be made clear that the inclusion of performance conditions or performance targets is not a requirement for tax-approval. However, it is an expectation of the institutional investment committees for the quoted company, particularly where the company has significant institutional shareholdings.

Director and employee eligibility criteria

11.2 The express intention of the UK government in introducing the share option scheme was to provide an incentive for directors and senior executives of companies at a time when the economy was recovering from recession in 1984.

An individual is eligible to participate in the scheme provided he or she meets the eligibility criteria as follows:

- the individual must be a full-time director or a qualifying employee of the company that has established the scheme or, in the case of a group scheme, of a participating company; and

- the individual must meet the material interest test set out in the legislation.

To be eligible as a full-time director, the following principles are applied:

- the individual must devote at least 25 hours a week, excluding meal breaks, to the duties of his or her office of director; and

- in the case of a group scheme, the individual may aggregate the hours that he or she works for all participating companies in the group.

To be eligible as a qualifying employee, the individual must be a full-time or part-time employee who is not also a director of the company or, in the case of a group scheme, a participating company.

Specifically in relation to the eligibility requirements, the scheme *may* include the following provisions:

- for an individual to exercise his or her option even though at the time of exercise he or she has ceased to be an employee; and

- for the option of an individual who dies without exercising his or her option to be exercised by the personal representative(s) within 12 months of the date of death.

Material interest test

11.3 Participation in the scheme is not available to an individual who has or has had within the preceding 12 months a material interest in:

- a close company whose shares may be acquired on the exercise of an option granted under the scheme; or

- a company which has control over such a company or as a member of a consortium which owns such a company.

A material interest in a company is defined as:

- beneficial ownership of, or the ability to control, directly or through the medium of other companies or by any other indirect means, more than 25% of the ordinary share capital of the company; or

- in circumstances where the company is a close company, the possession of or entitlement to acquire such rights as would, in the event of the winding-up of the company or in any other circumstances, give an entitlement to receive more than 25% of the assets that would then be available for distribution among the participators.

The interests of any of the employee's associates are included in the shares of the employee in the determination of material interests where associates are:

- husband or wife, parent or remoter forebear, child or remoter issue, or brother or sister;

- partner;

- trustee of any settlement for which the employee or his or her relative, living or dead, is or was settlor; or

- trustee of a settlement over the shares of the company where the employee has an interest.

Operation of the scheme

11.4 The scheme operates as a straightforward share option scheme as follows:

1. The share option is granted as an option to purchase shares in the company at an option price that is not less than the MV of the underlying shares at the date of grant.

2. If the employee is to secure income tax relief on the exercise of the option the employee must exercise the option between the third and the tenth anniversaries of the date of grant.

3.   Options normally lapse if employees leave by way of resignation or dismissal. However, the scheme *may* provide that options can be exercised if employees leave for one of any specified reasons that are set out in the rules of the scheme. Usually the rules will distinguish between 'good leavers' as a term to describe leavers who are eligible to exercise their options on leaving the company and 'bad leavers' as a term to describe leavers who are not eligible to exercise their options on leaving the company

The funding of the exercise and the sale of the shares does not constitute part of the share option scheme. However, the next steps followed by the employee are typically as follows:

4.   The employee exercises the option using either funds that are provided from his or her own resources or, alternatively, takes out a loan equal to the funds that are required to exercise the option.

5.   In circumstances where the optionholder takes out a loan, he or she will typically sell at least as many shares as is necessary in order to realise cash for the repayment of the loan on the settlement date that follows the sale of the shares.

6.   In practice, the company that is quoted on a recognised stock exchange will usually ask the appointed stockbroker to set up an arrangement which will appear to the employee as a seamless transaction whereby 'tail-swallowing' allows the loan to be repaid from the share sale proceeds. The term 'tail-swallowing' derives from this practice of paying for the initial cost of the shares through the subsequent sale of the same shares.

7.   A minimal interest cost arises on the loan that is outstanding for the settlement period only. This interest charge is also usually paid out of the share sale proceeds.

8.   The appointed stockbroker pays the share sale proceeds net of commission charges, the loan repayment and the loan interest to the company for deduction of income tax and accounting to HMRC for income tax and NICs.

Share option

11.5   The main features of the share option contract are as follows:

1.   The tax-approved discretionary share option scheme was first introduced through FA 1984 and became known as the executive share option =scheme (ESOP) as it was used primarily to incentivise directors and senior executives, particularly in the quoted sector although statutorily it can be applied with equal effectiveness and vigour in the private quoted company.

2.   On individual participation limits for options granted before 17 July 1995, the value of the shares over which the options could be

granted was restricted by the statute to the greater of 'four times relevant emoluments' or £100,000 where 'relevant emoluments' included earnings and bonuses paid in the current or preceding tax year, whichever was the greater. This restriction was significantly tightened by a reduction to £30,000 imposed by FA 1996. It is the belief of many tax and share scheme practitioners that this initiative from the then Chancellor of the Exchequer, Kenneth Clarke, primarily in response to his anticipation of the Greenbury recommendations, has enabled the scheme to survive a change of government to New Labour where initially (although he later appeared to change his mind with the introduction of EMI). The new Chancellor of the Exchequer, Gordon Brown, appeared to be hostile to the concept of share option and favoured immediate ownership through share purchase or share-gifting arrangements.

3. Specific rules were introduced for the operation of this tax-approved discretionary share option scheme in order to cater for this reduction in tax relief.

    (*a*)   For options granted before 17 July 1995, the tax relief afforded to share options is not affected by the changes enacted in FA 1996 provided certain conditions are met as follows:

    - the options are exercised within the statutory limits, namely between the third and tenth anniversaries of the date of grant; and

    - the company did not elect before the end of 1996 for the scheme to become unapproved.

    (*b*)   For options granted on or after 17th July 1995 but before 29th April 1996 there will be no income tax arising at the date of grant or at the date of exercise provided certain conditions are met as follows:

    - the option is not granted at a discount; and

    - the total value of unexercised options does not exceed £30,000 and unexercised options granted before 17th July 1995 count towards this £30,000 limit.

    If an option is granted under a tax-approved discretionary share option scheme during this period over shares with an initial value that would cause the £30,000 limitation to be exceeded or further exceeded then the approved status of the scheme remains unaffected. However, the whole of that option is deemed for tax purposes to have been granted on a tax-unapproved basis.

    The significance of 29 April 1996 is that it is the day that FA 1996 was passed.

    (*c*)   For options granted on or after 29 April 1996, the tax relief is limited to £30,000. Again, unexercised options granted before

29 April 1996 count towards this £30,000 limit and an option granted that causes the £30,000 limit to be exceeded, is deemed to have been granted on a tax-unapproved basis.

The £30,000 limitation is deemed by the Finance Act 1996 (FA 1996) to apply to all schemes that were approved by HMRC before 29 April 1996 unless the company elected before the end of 1996 for the scheme to become unapproved. If the company did make such an election then the scheme will have become a tax-unapproved scheme with the result that all options, including those granted before 17 July 1995, will be subject to income tax at the date of exercise.

4.　The scheme operates the 'three-year rule' that is designed to avoid participants receiving a preponderance of their executive reward in the form of share options rather than in the form of cash. The operation of the 'three-year rule' is as follows:

(*a*)　Relief from income tax on option gains made under the tax–approved discretionary share option scheme shall not apply where an option is exercised within three years of grant or, for options exercised up to and including 8 April 2003, within three years of a previous exercise by the same option-holder under the same scheme or under a different tax-approved discretionary share option scheme where that previous exercise enjoyed an exemption from income tax.

(*b*)　When this rule is applied the exercise of more than one option on the same day is treated as a single option exercise that is not subject to income tax.

(*c*)　When the exercise of an option does not benefit from the relief it will subsequently be disregarded in determining whether or not the 'three-year rule' applies to a subsequent option exercise.

(*d*)　Unlike the SSOS, the company will not give the employee a choice on, say, a three- or a five- or a seven-year period over which the option subsists. Rather, the company will set the period over which the option can be exercised or, for that matter, a set date, which will be after three years from the date of grant in order to allow the employee to benefit from the income tax relief. The company may choose to set exercisable events which when they happen, allow the employee to exercise the option. Indeed, if the company so decides at the date of grant, the exercise of the option may be restricted to the set exercisable events that are typically flotation on a recognised stock exchange, takeover or trade sale.

5.　Options can be granted over newly-issued shares, that is shares issued specifically for the purposes of satisfying the exercise of the options, or shares that are already in existence and are purchased off the market by an employee share trust.

6. The statute allows tax-approved discretionary share option schemes to contain provisions under which an optionholder can exchange approved options in circumstances where another company obtains control of the company or becomes bound or entitled under CA 2006, ss 974–991 (CA 1985, ss 428–430) to acquire the shares. The new options must be exercisable in the same manner as the old options and the value, and aggregate subscription price of the new options must be exactly the same as the value and aggregate subscription price of the old options.

7. The statute does not require options granted under tax-approved discretionary share option schemes to be subject to performance conditions or performance targets. However, the HMRC Guide on the tax-approved discretionary share option scheme allows additional conditions of exercise to be included if that is the choice of the company. If this is the case, the additional conditions must either be clearly specified in the rules of the scheme or the rules of the scheme must contain clear and objective guidelines by which those additional conditions will be determined.

Shares

11.6 The legislation identifies the type of shares that may be used in a company share option scheme. The shares must be fully paid; non-redeemable; and not subject to any restrictions other than the restrictions which apply to all shares of the same class although noting the use of the Articles of Association.

The Articles of Association can impose a restriction on the shares. It takes the form of a requirement that all shares held by directors and employees are to be disposed of when they leave the company and when shares are acquired as a result of options exercised after directors and employees have left the company when the exercise may be by them or by their personal representatives. In these circumstances, the sale of the shares must be for money on the terms laid down by the Articles of Association for the disposal of all shares of the same class.

It is important to recognise that a restriction can be imposed by any contract, or agreement, or arrangement, or condition that will be regarded as a restriction if it does any of the following:

● restricts the freedom to dispose of the shares or any interest in the shares or the proceeds from the sale of the shares; or

● restricts the freedom to exercise any right conferred by the shares; or

● causes a disadvantage to the participant or a connected person if the shares are disposed of or any right conferred by them is exercised.

If the period between the exercise of the option and the allotment of the shares exceeds 30 days then this will be deemed to be imposing a restriction on the shares. Consequently, the period of time between the exercise of the option and the allotment of the shares cannot exceed 30 days.

The shares *must* form part of the ordinary share capital of:

- the company that has set up the scheme; or

- the company that controls the company that has set up the scheme; or

- the company which is or has control of the company which is a member of a consortium owning either the company that has set up the scheme or the company that has control of the company that has set up the scheme.

Company

11.7 The legislation identifies the characteristics that a company must have in order to operate a company share option scheme as follows. The company must have:

- scheme shares that are quoted on a recognised stock exchange; or

- be under the control of a company that has scheme shares quoted on a recognised stock exchange; or

- be an unquoted company that is not controlled by another unquoted company.

Option price

11.8 The legislation stipulates the rules that determine the setting of the option price as follows:

- The option price *must* be stated at the time the rights are obtained by the employees under the grant of option.

- The option price *must not* be less than the MV of the shares of the same class at a time that HMRC calls 'the material time' that is the time at which the employees obtain the rights to purchase the shares or, alternatively, an earlier time that is agreed between HMRC'c ESSU and the company that has established the scheme.

- The determination of MV is prepared in exactly the same way as it is for CGT purposes.

- The option price *must* be set precisely in accordance with the rules of the scheme that is approved by HMRC's ESSU; otherwise it will not qualify for income tax relief.

- The option price *may* be set on the basis of the average MV over a period of time that must commence no more than 30 days before the date of grant.

- The scheme *may* provide for adjustments to the option price to account for any variations in the share capital.

Share rights

11.9 The employees do not have the statutory rights of shareholders during the period during which the option subsists for the reason that they are only optionholders until they have exercised their option to purchase the shares.

The employees do, however, have a legal interest of the shares of the company through the rights that are conferred upon them through the option arrangement.

Even though as optionholders the employees are not shareholders, the company may choose to provide them with annual and interim reports in order to encourage the sense of involvement that the introduction of an employee share scheme is designed to achieve.

The ultimate success of any employee share scheme arrangement for the motivation of the employees relies upon the communication that the company has with the employees and the sense of worth that the communication conveys.

Tax reliefs

11.10 The application of the tax-approved legislation gives income tax relief to the employee and corporation tax relief to the company. Additionally, the general legislation offers CGT relieving opportunities to the employees.

Income tax

11.11 The key advantage of the scheme for UK taxpayers is that, provided the share options are granted and exercised according to the rules of the scheme that have been approved by HMRC's ESSU under ITEPA 2003, Sch 4 the employee is able to take advantage of income tax relief as follows:

1. A charge to income tax will not normally arise when the option is granted.

2. A charge to income tax will not normally arise when the option is exercised, provided that the exercise is between the third and tenth anniversaries of the date of grant.

For options exercised up to and including 8 April 2003, tax relief is not available on the exercise of an option if exercised within three years of the last exercise of option under the same scheme or same type of scheme in circumstances where that last exercise qualified for tax-relief. For options exercised on or after 9 April 2003, this 'second three-year rule' does not apply.

Capital gains tax

11.12   On the sale of the shares, the difference between the sale proceeds and the option price represents a chargeable gain for CGT purposes, subject to the CGT annual exemption limit and any other CGT reliefs that the employee may choose to use.

Corporation tax

11.13   The company benefits from corporation tax relief on the costs incurred in setting up a share option scheme that is approved by HMRC's ESSU. This relief is available on costs that are incurred for this purpose from 1 April 2001.

The corporation tax relief is available as an allowable deduction for the period of account for which the expenditure is incurred. The exception to this is in circumstances where the scheme is approved more than nine months after the end of that period of account, in which case the corporation tax relief is given as an allowable deduction for the period of account in which the ESSU gives the approval.

In order to secure the corporation tax relief it is imperative to ensure that the options are not granted before the scheme has been approved by the ESSU.

Advantages of the executive/company share option scheme

Discretionary choice

11.14   The company has the freedom to decide which employees are granted options and the terms on which the options are granted. The scheme is truly a discretionary arrangement with the selection conducted either by the board of directors or, alternatively, a remuneration committee with powers that are delegated by the board of directors or, in some cases, maybe the CEO or the chairperson.

Performance measures

11.15   Options are often linked to performance measures that take the form of performance conditions or performance targets. This is allowed under the scheme although it is not a prerequisite for its operation. However, if the scheme is to include performance measures then the HMRC stipulation that they must be objective offers an effective selling point to the employees.

Widespread participation

11.16   The implementation of the scheme encourages widespread participation as there is no requirement for the employees to do anything to be granted the options. This contrasts with the SSoS where there is a requirement for financial commitment in the form of monthly savings contributions. The employees are unlikely to reject an option that does not cost them anything, has the potential for significant gain in the event of share price rise but ultimately lapses if an option gain can never be achieved by exercise.

Tax reliefs

11.17   The supporting tax-approved legislation offers, in all normal circumstances, a full infrastructure of income tax reliefs for the employees at both the grant of the option and the exercise of the option and a corporation tax deduction for setting up costs for the company. Additionally, the CGT legislation with its array of reliefs and exemptions can be used to the advantage of the employees.

Employee retention

11.18   The scheme offers a positive help to the company in retaining key employees for the reason that employees who leave usually lose their option rights. Like theSSOS, the grant of the option represents 'a golden handcuff' that the employees will be reluctant to lose until the scheme has delivered the share benefits. As a retention tool, the scheme is potentially more powerful than the SSOS in that the selection criteria targets key employees and the option levels can be significantly higher.

Disadvantages of the executive/company share option scheme

Employee shareholders only at exercise

11.19   The employees are optionholders from the date of grant and throughout the period during which the option subsists. They do not become shareholders until they have exercised their options. Nevertheless, the share option represents, through the legally binding share option contract, a legal right in relation to the ordinary share capital of the company. The nature of the interest should be given prominence in the communication that is linked to the grant of the option. The company is seeking to register worth in the minds of the employees by granting them share options in the interest of enhanced productivity. The company may well choose, therefore, to treat the optionholders as though they are shareholders through the issue of annual and interim reports, supported by timely communication.

Absence of employee value

11.20 Although the options may have immense potential value, the employees may not attach value at the outset as, unlike the operation of theSSOS, they are not required to make a financial commitment. Some companies do choose to require their employees to perform to certain levels before granting them their share options. This is part of the selection process. However, it is also part of a desire on the part of the company to encourage the employees to value the options that are granted to them. In a sense, they are being asked to earn the right to be granted an option. In legal form, any earning of the right should be separate from the rules of the scheme that should simply include a general discretionary selection provision.

Tax reliefs

11.21 The operation of the 'three-year rule' restricts the opportunity for tax relief although tax relief is, of course, available. Prior to FA 2003, the 'second three-year rule' also had the effect of limiting, to some extent, the design of the scheme by precluding the opportunity for year-on-year tax-free exercises, and the benefit to moral and motivation that this design may give to employees. Finance Act 2003 abolished the 'second three-year rule' for exercises on or after 9th April 2003.

Immediate sale

11.22 Evidence shows that most optionholders under this type of scheme sell their shares immediately on exercise, usually for the reason that they need to repay the loan that they have taken out to fund the purchase or to recover their outlay from their own personal resources. However, all investments become perceived as worthwhile when they give the opportunity for financial return. The share option arrangement is no exception to this general rule. If the employees benefit from a sale immediately following exercise then they will usually feel positive about the company in whose employment they have been given this opportunity to make a profit. Surely the best thing for the company to do next is to grant another option with another opportunity for profit arising from employment with the company.

Example 11.1: What the CSOP means for the employee

Suppose a tax-approved CSOP option is granted to an employee over 5000 shares at an option price of £5.

The £5 in this example represents the MV of the shares at the time the option is granted.

Some years later the employee exercises the option when the MV of the shares has reached £10. The employee uses a short-term loan facility over the settlement period to fund the purchase of the shares at exercise. This loan facility is arranged by the stockbrokers who have been nominated by the company to arrange the exercises for employees. The employee sells just enough shares to repay the loan. This is 2,500 shares calculated by dividing the option value/purchase cost of £25,000 by the sale price at exercise of £10. The employee pays the loan interest and the commission costs from his own resources.

Some years later, still the employee sells his remaining 2500 shares when the share price has reached £20.

The tax consequences for the employee are as follows:

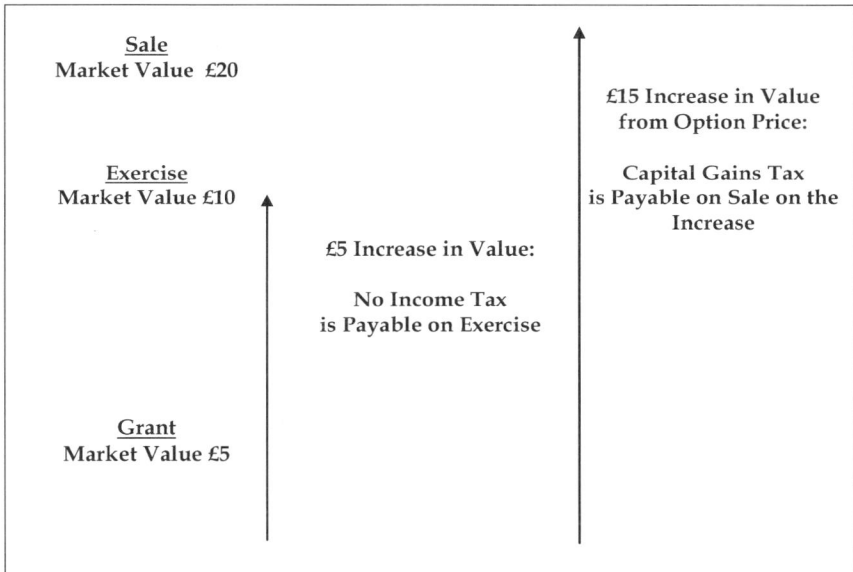

Sale
Market Value £20

£15 Increase in Value
from Option Price:

Capital Gains Tax
is Payable on Sale on the
Increase

Exercise
Market Value £10

£5 Increase in Value:

No Income Tax
is Payable on Exercise

Grant
Market Value £5

Guidelines for determining the date of exercise

11.23   Although the formula for determining the date of grant is usually prescribed by the rules of the scheme it is not always clear how to determine the date of exercise.

The guidelines for determining the date of exercise of share options are as follows:

- The rules must be examined to determine the date of exercise.

- The savings-related share option scheme rules usually require the receipt of the notice of exercise together with the receipt of the exercise (savings) monies.

  In these circumstances, where the employee is obliged to provide both the notice and the monies the date of exercise is usually taken as the later of the two receipts.

- The discretionary share option scheme does not require the payment of exercise monies by the employee where the exercise monies are paid out of the proceeds of sale on 'a tail-swallowing' basis.

  In these circumstances, the date of exercise is usually determined by the delivery date of the notice of exercise where the exercise becomes unconditional. This is the case even though no exercise monies have been received by the company and no shares have been issued to the employee.

  The company then has a separate obligation to deliver the shares to the employee.

- The company may choose to waive certain conditions for exercise.

- In these circumstances, the company treats the individual employee as having exercised from the point at which the remaining conditions are waived.

- The exercise cannot usually be taken as valid later than the date on which the company gives an instruction to the registrars to issue the shares to the employee.

Chapter 12

Approved share incentive plan

Introduction

12.1 This chapter sets out an appreciation of the way in which New Labour has developed its understanding of employee share schemes and embraced the concept of employee share ownership in a way that is central to its approach of fairness and enterprise in the implementation of its economic strategy and policies. The chapter goes on to explain how this tax-approved employee share scheme operates at the choice of the company either: (1) as a share-gifting scheme; or (2) as a share purchase scheme; or (3) as both with the two elements operating alongside each other. As well as explaining the income tax benefits for employees and the corporation tax benefits for companies, the chapter explains how the share incentive plan (SIP) is the first tax-approved scheme to build a highly tax-advantageous CGT relief for employees into the fabric of the legislation. (The changes introduced through FA 2003 are explained in a separate chapter on changes to the tax-approved schemes introduced through that Act.)

Scheme synopsis

Under SIP, the company chooses which modules it wishes to introduce as follows:

1. Free shares module

The company supplies funds to a trust for the purchase of shares that are then allocated free to individual employee accounts. The beneficial ownership of the shares is vested in the individual employees. After five years the shares are transferred out of the trust to the individual employees, income tax-free.

2. Partnership shares module

The employee supplies funds to a trust for the purchase of shares through a pre-tax salary deduction administered through the payroll. The employee enjoys beneficial ownership of the shares whilst they are held by the trust for a period of five years at the end of which they are transferred by the trust to the employee, income tax-free.

> **3. Matching shares module**
>
> The company supplies funds to a trust for the purchase of shares that are matched on an agreed ratio that cannot exceed 2:1 to the shares that have been purchased by the employees under the partnership module.

Finance Act 2000 initiative

12.2 The share incentive plan was introduced as FA 2000, Sch 8. It is not a share option scheme. It is a share-gifting scheme and it is a share purchase scheme.

The enterprise management incentives legislation is now contained in ITEPA 2003, Pt 7, Chap 6 and in Schedule 2 of that Act. This replaces FA 2000, Sch 8. The ITEPA 2003 came into force on 6 April 2003 as part of the Tax Law Rewrite Project, the project established with the objective of making the tax legislation clearer and easier to use.

The tax reform programme of the then Chancellor of the Exchequer, Gordon Brown, involved the requirement to combine enterprise with welfare. The share incentive plan is designed to give significant tax advantages that are aimed at encouraging long-term employee shareholdings. This is consistent with Gordon Brown's desire to have employees with real shareholdings rather than share option scheme arrangements. His drive is, therefore, aimed at share retention.

Gordon Brown states explicitly in his booklet entitled *Consultation on Employee Share Ownership*:

> I want, through targeted reform, to reward long-term commitment of employees. I want to encourage the new enterprise culture of teamwork in which everyone contributes and everyone benefits from success. And I want to double the number of companies in which all employees have the opportunity to hold shares.

Gordon Brown explained his wish to extend employee share ownership into the small- to medium-sized sector of the economy and recognised that in order to do this he needs to respond to the concerns of the smaller businesses. He sought, therefore, to respond to the specific concerns of the smaller businesses by introducing forfeiture arrangements and performance conditions.

In *Consultation on Employee Share Ownership* the Gordon Brown further states:

> Today only a fraction of British employees and even a smaller minority of those outside senior management own shares in the companies that they work in. Yet the evidence is that employee commitment is a vital strength for companies competing and succeeding in the global economy.

The scheme is, therefore, an all-employee scheme, encouraging employee share ownership throughout the whole company. However, the scheme is structured in a way that enables some employees to have access to more shares than other employees have. Again, this appears to be a response to the smaller business requirement to operate discretion as to which employees are to participate in the employee share scheme arrangements.

Country models

12.3   The Chancellor's initiative is based on actual country models, the US and France, and the research that supports the success of employee share ownership in those countries. In *Consultation on Employee Share Ownership* he states:

> ... the economic case that employee share ownership can play a part in enhancing company performance is borne out by research evidence. Many UK companies have already recognised the potential of employee share ownership in setting up such schemes.

The Chancellor does recognise, therefore, that there are examples of employee share ownership success in the UK. However, his concern is that the US and France have embraced employee share ownership in a way that is more finely-tuned to enhancing company productivity.

Experience of the United States

12.4   In the US there is a widespread implementation of employee share ownership plans (ESOP). The popularity of ESOP in the US arises from the use of employee share ownership to facilitate pension provision for retirement. In this capacity, the ESOP take on the role of a savings vehicle. The Chancellor was keen to bring to the attention of the consultation during 1998/99 that there are approximately 11,000 ESOP in the US in which approximately 10 million US employees participate. This represents 10% of the US workforce.

Experience of France

12.5   In France there is a legal obligation on all companies with at least 50 employees to set up a company savings scheme. In practice, the employee makes an individual decision as to whether or not they wish to participate. However, in 1998/1999, approximately 23% of the workforce in France, representing 6 million employees, actually participated in company share schemes. The Chancellor alerted the consultation to the fact that on 1994 figures there were almost 16,000 such agreements in France covering over 19,000 companies.

> The features that the then Chancellor appeared to find attractive from these country models are as follows:
>
> * the encouragement through the US model to participate for the longer term;

- the US requirement for contributions to be paid out of pre-tax salary into an investment fund;

- the company top-up that is so often characteristic of US arrangements; and

- the French use of a five-year term as a requirement for tax exemptions.

Purpose test

12.6 The legislation is explicit about the purpose of the plan arrangement and offers its own definition of the purpose test.

The purpose test is that: 'The purpose of the plan must be to provide benefits to employees in the nature of shares in the company which give them a continuing stake in that company.'

The application of this test is, therefore, entirely consistent with Gordon Brown's aims of retention and long-term commitment.

The statement of purpose is followed in the legislation by a requirement that: 'The plan must not contain, and the operation of the plan must not involve features which are neither essential nor reasonably incidental to that purpose.'

The Chancellor is, therefore, encouraging for employees an arrangement that is focused on the purpose as defined in the legislation.

Similar terms requirement

12.7 The operation of all-employee share schemes on a similar terms basis is a principle that has previously been applied and, indeed, continues to be applied in relation to the SSOS and, of course, to the profit-sharing employee share scheme (up to its phasing out) through FA 2000.

The share incentive plan legislation refers to this requirement as 'participation on same terms'. By definition, the requirement is, therefore, that every employee who is invited to participate in an award must be invited to participate on the same terms and those who actually do participate must do so on the same terms.

Where free shares are awarded, the requirement is that the award should be made by reference to one or a combination of the following three factors:

- the employee's remuneration;

- the employee's length of service with the company; and

- the employee's hours worked, usually expressed as hours worked per week.

Where more than one of the factors is used, each factor must give rise to a separate entitlement and the total entitlement is the sum of the separate entitlements.

Where the award of free shares is linked to performance conditions or, as the legislation calls them 'performance allowances', there are special provisions for giving effect to this requirement for participation on the same terms.

No preferential treatment

12.8   There must be no feature of the SIP that has the effect of conferring benefits wholly or mainly on the following:

- directors; or
- employees receiving higher levels of remuneration

No loan arrangements

12.9   There must be no arrangements for the provision of loans to employees for use in association with the operation of the scheme.

Eligibility of the participants

12.10   The key principle that emerges from the legislation is that if employees meet the eligibility requirements then they must be invited to participate. This is not a discretionary scheme.

The eligibility criteria are as follows:

- Companies that choose to introduce the scheme must offer the version that they have chosen to introduce to all employees who are taxable under Schedule E, Case 1, on the emoluments from the employment that represents the basis for their qualification to participate.
- Participants must be employees of the company or, where there is a group, of a participating company.
- Employees may have to comply with the minimum qualifying period in order to be participants.
- Employees must meet the special material interest criteria set out in the legislation.
- Participation in an award of free shares is not available to employees in any tax year if in that tax year they have participated in another of these schemes, or an approved profit-sharing employee share scheme established by the company or a connected company, except in circumstances where there is a move to a new employment within the group.

Minimum qualifying period

12.11 Companies can require employees to have completed a minimum qualifying period of employment before they are allowed to participate in the scheme. If this is a requirement for scheme participation, the employee must have been an employee throughout the qualifying period. The minimum qualifying period cannot exceed 18 months.

For free shares, the qualifying period must be a period of not more than 18 months ending with the date on which the award is made.

For partnership shares or matching shares, where there is no accumulation period, the qualifying period must be a period of not more than 18 months ending with the deduction of partnership share money relating to the award.

For partnership shares or matching shares, where there is an accumulation period, the qualifying period must be not more than six months ending with the start of the accumulation period relating to the award.

For any award of shares all employees must be subject to the same qualifying period. However, the scheme rules can authorise the company to specify different qualifying periods in respect of different awards of shares.

Material interest test

12.12 Participation is not available to employees who have or have had within the preceding 12 months a material interest in:

- a close company whose shares may be appropriated or acquired under the scheme; or
- a company which has control over such a company or is a member of a consortium which owns such a company.

A material interest in a company is defined as:

- beneficial ownership of, or the ability to control, directly or through the medium of other companies or by any other indirect means, more than 25% of the ordinary share capital of the company; or
- in circumstances where the company is a closed company, the possession of or entitlement to acquire such rights as would, in the event of the winding-up of the company or in any other circumstances give an entitlement to receive more than 25% of the assets that would then be available for distribution among the participators.

The interests of any of the employees' associates are included in the shares of the employee in the determination of material interest where associates are:

- husband or wife, parent or remoter forebear, child or remoter issue, or brother or sister;

- partner;

- trustee of any settlement for which the employee, or his or her relative, living or dead, is or was a settlor; or

- trustee of a settlement over the shares of the company where the employee has an interest.

When interpreting the meaning of 'material interest' the right to acquire shares is treated as having the right to control them. In this regard, the shares that are attributed to an individual are the shares which he or she has a right to acquire and if on the exercise of that right the shares acquired were previously unissued then in determining at any time prior to the exercise of that right whether or not the number of shares attributed to the individual exceeds a certain percentage of the ordinary share capital of the company, the ordinary share capital shall be increased by the number of unissued shares.

Type of share that may be used

12.13　The legislation identifies the type of shares that may be gifted or purchased in a SIP as follows:

- If the shares are to be eligible shares for purposes of the legislation then they must be ordinary shares. The shares must form part of the ordinary share capital of the company, or a company that has control of the company, or a company that either is or has control of a company which is a member of a consortium owning either the company or a company having control of the company.

- The shares must be of a class listed on a recognised stock exchange, or the shares in a company which is not under the control of another company, or the shares in a company which is under the control of a company (which is not a close company) whose shares are listed on a recognised stock exchange.

- The shares must be fully paid up and not redeemable.

- The shares must not be subject to special restrictions except as to:

  - voting rights;

  - provision for forfeiture; and

  - pre-emption conditions.

- The shares can be a special class of shares.

- The shares do not necessarily have to be the shares of a company that is either incorporated or resident in the UK.

- The shares must not be the shares of a prohibited company where the prohibition is on non-independent service companies whose business consists substantially in the provision of services of persons employed by it where the majority of their services are provided to a connected company or person. This provision would typically prevent an accountancy or law practice that operates as a partnership from transferring its employees to a company solely for purposes of benefiting from a SIP arrangement.

The legislation seeks to describe the use to which the ordinary share capital can be put by giving shares the following names:

- free shares (module 1);

- partnership shares (module 2);

- matching shares (module 3); and

- dividend shares.

However, please note that these shares are all drawn from the same ordinary share capital. The titles that the legislation gives to them are purely for distinguishing the purposes of their use.

All these shares are held in a trust for the life of the scheme arrangement.

The modules of the three main types of share usage are illustrated as three segments of a triangle. Additionally, dividend shares are depicted as a fourth usage. All four types of share are held in the trust that is illustrated by the circle below.

Remember: the SIP is not a share option scheme

12.14 The free shares approach uses company money usually through cash contributions to fund the trust for the purchase of shares that are then appropriated to employees.

- The partnership shares approach uses employee money through payroll deductions to fund the trust for the purchase of shares on behalf of employees.

- The matching shares approach is another form of 'free shares', using company money usually through cash contributions to fund the trust for the purchase of shares that are then appropriated to employees.

Free shares represents a gifting of shares by the company.

Partnership shares represents the purchase of shares by employees.

Matching shares also represents a gifting of shares by the company.

A meaningful way to understand the legislation for 'free shares' and for 'partnership shares' is to identify the compulsory and the discretionary elements for each. This approach provides a framework in which to understand the operation of the scheme.

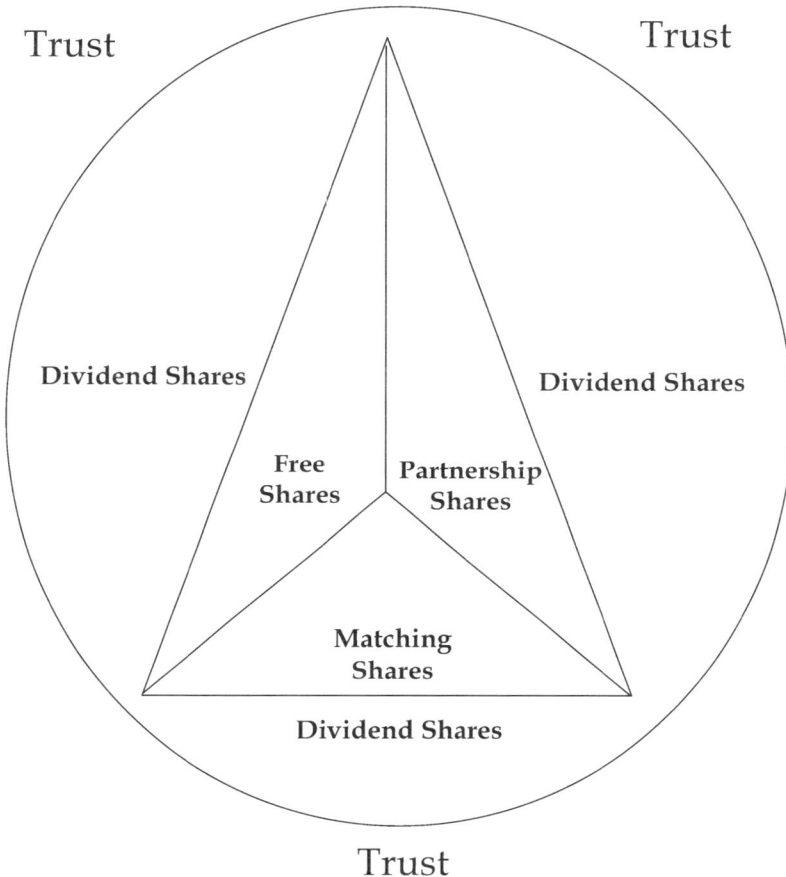

Module 1: free shares

12.15   This is the part of the scheme that in its structure most closely resembles the profit-sharing employee share scheme. It is in order to avoid duplication of the same scheme structure in the legislation that the profit-sharing employee share scheme represents the only casualty among the existing employee share schemes following the consultation period that is culminated in FAct 2000.

This part of the scheme is best understood by examining its different elements as follows.

Compulsory elements

The £3,000 limit

12.16   Up to £3000 initial MV of 'free shares' can be awarded to each employee in a tax year. The initial MV is a reference to the MV of the shares on the date on which they are awarded.

This £3000 limit contrasts with the profit-sharing employee share scheme where the limit is defined as not greater than the higher of £3000, or 10% of earnings that are subject to PAYE, with an overriding ceiling on the 10% of £8,000.

Holding period

12.17 The holding period cannot be less than three years but cannot be more than five years from the date the shares are awarded. The purpose of the holding period is to ensure that employees cannot sell or withdraw their shares immediately.

The requirement is for the company to specify in relation to each award of free shares a holding period. The participant is bound by contract with the company to allow his or her free shares to remain in the trust for the duration of the holding period and not to assign, to charge or otherwise to dispose of his or her beneficial interest in the shares.

Once a holding period has been specified in relation to a particular award of free shares it cannot be increased. However, it can be prematurely ended if the employee's employment ceases, in which case the employee's obligations in respect of the holding period also come to an end.

Tax treatment of leavers

12.18 The trust must transfer scheme shares to those employees who leave their employment for whatever reason.

The charge to income tax and NICs depends on the time period that has elapsed between the date on which the shares were awarded and the date on which the shares are withdrawn from the scheme as follows:

- Where the employment ends before the shares have been held for more than three years the employee will have to pay income tax and NICs on the MV of the shares at the date of leaving.

- Where the shares are withdrawn between three and five years after they have been awarded the employee will have to pay income tax and NICs on the lower of the initial MV of the shares when they were first awarded and the MV of the shares at the date of leaving;

- Where the shares are kept in the trust for the full five-year period employees do not pay either income tax or NICs.

- Where employees forfeit shares on leaving, in accordance with forfeiture restrictions that were imposed at the time of the award of the shares, they do not have to pay income tax or NICs in respect of the forfeited shares.

- The shares can be withdrawn tax-free where the employment ends for one of the specified reasons, the 'good leaver' reasons, as follows:

    – injury or disability;

- redundancy in accordance with the Employments Rights Act 1996 or the Employment Rights (Northern Ireland) Order 1996;

- transfer where the Transfer of Undertakings (Protection of Employment) Regulations 1981 (TUPE Regs 1981) apply;

- change of control or other circumstances ending the associated company status of the company in which the employee is employed;

- retirement on or after the retirement age specified by the scheme which must be the same for men and women and cannot be less than 50; and

- death.

• The presence of forfeiture provisions in the rules cannot prevent the application of the good leaver provisions. If the rules include forfeiture provisions then the rules must also include the good leaver provisions. If the rules do not include forfeiture provisions then the rules do not have to include the good leaver provisions that apply anyway under the legislation. The rules must always include the retirement age.

Discretionary elements

Performance allowances

12.19   The legislation allows for the introduction of 'performance allowances' as the basis for making an award of shares. These provisions allow the number or value of free shares awarded, or indeed whether or not free shares will be awarded at all to a participant, to be conditional on the meeting of performance targets.

For the operation of the scheme where performance allowances are introduced, it is important to be clear about the following:

• the period over which the performance allowances are set to be achieved is at the choice of the company;

• the shares are awarded only once the performance allowances have been achieved. It is from the date of the award that the five-year period of beneficial ownership commences. It is at the end of the five-year period that the shares are transferred from the trust to the employees; and

• where performance allowances are introduced they must apply to all qualifying employees in relation to that particular award of free shares.

The performance allowances have three components as follows:

- *Performance measures*: which must be based on criteria that can be demonstrated to be objective, typically an objective measure of business results, and be fair and objective in relation to the performance units to which they are being applied.

- *Performance targets*: which must be set for performance units.

- *Performance units*: each of which comprises one or more employees on the condition that no employee must be a member of one performance unit.

Where performance allowances are introduced the company must engage in a proper employee communication by notifying each participating employee of the performance measures and performance targets. Any information that would prejudice commercial confidentiality can be excluded from this disclosure. However, the notification must be made on a timely basis as soon as reasonably practicable.

There are two alternatives for awarding shares on the basis of performance.

1. Method 1: is to link up to 80% of the shares that are awarded to performance so that at least 20% of the shares are awarded without the attachment of performance allowances in accordance with the participation on same terms requirement. The highest performance award to any employee cannot be more than four times greater than the highest award made to an employee on the basis of the participation on same terms requirement. The participation on same terms requirement does not apply to any award of shares that is made on the basis of performance allowances.

2. Method 2: is to award some or all shares by reference to performance. The awards made to employees within each performance unit must be made in accordance with the participation on same terms requirement to all employees within that performance unit. There can be different performance measures for different performance units, as long as all performance units have a broadly comparable chance of achieving their performance targets.

Forfeiture

12.20 The forfeiture period cannot exceed three years from the award of the shares. The company can specify a shorter period if they so wish.

Where the company chooses to introduce forfeiture provisions they must apply identically to all free shares and, as it happens, all matching shares that are included in the same award.

Under these forfeiture provisions participants will cease to be beneficially entitled to shares on the occasion of certain events happening. However, forfeiture cannot be linked to individual personal performance.

Dividend reinvestment

12.21 The legislation allows the reinvestment of cash dividends in that the scheme may provide that the company can make a direction with regard to the treatment of cash dividends as follows:

- that all cash dividends must be applied in acquiring further shares on behalf of participants; and

- that all cash dividends must be applied in acquiring further shares on behalf of participants who elect to reinvest their cash dividends.

The legislation refers to these shares as dividend shares and provides for the reinvestment of cash dividends tax-free into the shares within specified limits.

The conditions on the reinvestment of cash dividends are as follows:

- the total dividend reinvestment for any participant cannot exceed £1500 in any tax year;

- 'dividend shares' are subject to a holding period of three years during which employees are not permitted to sell unless they leave the employment;

- if employees leave the employment during the holding period then the shares are transferred out of the scheme and income tax is payable on the original dividend as if it had been received in the year in which the employment ceased;

- 'dividend shares' must be of the same class and carry the same rights as the shares which provide the basis for the dividend;

- 'dividend shares' must not be subject to forfeiture provisions; and

- the number of 'dividend shares' is determined on the basis of the MV of the shares on the set acquisition date which must be within 30 days after the dividend is received by the participants.

Module 2: partnership shares

Compulsory elements

Pre-tax salary

12.22 The scheme must provide for a partnership share agreement that is put into practice by deductions from salary. The partnership share agreement must specify what amounts are to be deducted and at what intervals the amounts are to be deducted although by agreement the company and the employee can vary either the amounts or the intervals or both.

'Partnership shares' offer the opportunity for individual employees to purchase shares out of pre-tax salary up to a maximum of £1500's worth of salary that can be allocated in this way, in any one tax year. Pre-Finance Act 2003, this was subject to a maximum limit of the lower of £125 per month, or 10% of the employee's salary in the deduction period. Post-Finance Act 2003, the maximum limit is defined as the lower of £1500 a year or 10% of annual salary. The change in the legislation allows a bulk purchase of shares in the month in which the employee receives a bonus from the company.

Finance Act 2003 also allows for the company to provide for a lower percentage of employee's salary than the limit of 10% and a description of earnings that leaves out certain earnings which must then be identified. This change is in the interest of greater ease of administration, particularly for schemes whose participants have an element of variable earnings.

The 10% rule needs to be carefully administered. Where there is an accumulation period it is 10% of the total of the employee's salary payments over the accumulation period. However, where there is no accumulation period it is 10% of the salary payment from which the deduction is made.

In practice, the opportunity to discriminate between different employees for 'partnership shares' is less than for 'free shares'. Although employers will be able to set a lower limit for the maximum percentage of salary that can be allocated under 'partnership shares' the same maximum limit must be applied to all employees.

The minimum deduction that is specified in the scheme cannot be greater than £10.

Tax treatment

12.23 Employees can withdraw 'partnership shares' from the scheme at any time.

The amount of any income tax charge reduces the longer the 'partnership shares' are held in the scheme.

The charge to income tax and NICs depends on the time period that has elapsed between the acquisition date of the shares and the date on which the shares are withdrawn from the scheme as follows:

- Where 'partnership shares' are held in the scheme for less than three years employees will have to pay income tax and NICs on the MV of the shares at the time they are transferred out of the scheme.

- Where the 'partnership shares' are held in the scheme for at least three years but less than five years, employees will have to pay income tax and NICs on the lower of the salary used to buy the shares and the MV of the shares at the time they are transferred out of the scheme.

- Where the 'partnership shares' are held in the scheme for at least five years employees will be able to transfer the shares out of the scheme at any time without paying income tax or NICs.

- The shares can be withdrawn tax-free where the employment ends for one of the specified reasons which are exactly the same as for 'free shares'.

Holding period

12.24 There is no holding period for 'partnership shares'.

Forfeiture

12.25 There is no forfeiture allowed for 'partnership shares'.

Discretionary elements

Where there is an accumulation period

12.26 The accumulation period is to all intents and purposes a savings period. It allows salary that is deducted for purposes of purchasing 'partnership shares' to be accumulated for a period of up to 12 months. If the company chooses to operate an accumulation period the shares must be bought within 30 days of the end of the accumulation period.

The partnership share agreement must specify the start date and the end date of the accumulation period. For any award of 'partnership shares' the accumulation period must be the same for all participating employees. The partnership share agreement may specify that the occurrence of a specified event will bring the accumulation period to a premature end.

Where there is an accumulation eriod the purchase price of the shares is the lower of the MV of the shares at the beginning of the accumulation period and the MV of the shares on the acquisition date following the end of the accumulation period. This determines the number of shares that are awarded to each employee.

Where there is no accumulation period

12.27 The alternative to an accumulation period is for the shares to be purchased out of weekly or monthly deductions as and when those deductions arise. The shares must then be purchased within 30 days of the deduction of pay.

Where there is no accumulation period the purchase price of the shares is the MV of the shares to the trustees on the acquisition date. This determines the number of shares that are awarded to each employee.

Dividend reinvestment

12.28 Dividend reinvestment operates in the same way as for 'free shares'.

Module 3: matching shares

12.29   Employers are able to provide additional free 'matching shares' to employees. The matching is to 'partnership shares'. However, it must be recognised for a proper understanding of the scheme that 'matching shares' represent another species of 'free shares'. Like 'free shares', they are purchased with company money whereas 'partnership shares' are purchased with employee money.

The characteristics of the 'matching shares' are as follows:

- 'Matching shares' must be of the same class and carry the same rights as the 'partnership shares' to which they relate.

- 'Matching shares' must be appropriated to the employees on the same day as the 'partnership shares' are acquired.

- 'Matching shares' must be appropriated to all employees on the same basis.

- The ratio of 'matching shares' to 'partnership shares' cannot exceed 2:1.

- Where employees enter into agreement to purchase 'partnership shares' they must be informed whether or not they are to be offered 'matching shares' and the precise ratio that will apply.

- 'Matching shares' have the same holding period rules as 'free shares'.

- Companies can make 'matching shares' subject to forfeiture if the employee leaves the employment other than for a specified reason (eg disability, redundancy) or the corresponding 'partnership shares' are withdrawn within three years of purchase.

- The income tax treatment is the same as for 'free shares'.

Capital gains tax implications for employees

12.30   Capital gains tax is only payable on the extent to which the shares increase in value following their withdrawal from the scheme. The base cost for CGT purposes is the MV of the shares at the date of withdrawal from the scheme. There is, therefore, no charge to CGT at the point at which the shares are taken out of the scheme.

This offers a key planning point to the employees for the avoidance of CGT. If the employees remain in the employment of the company beyond the five-year term of the scheme they can still allow the shares to remain in the trust. If they withdraw the shares only at the time they wish to sell then no CGT will arise on sale for the reason that the base cost for the CGT computation is the MV at date of withdrawal.

Corporation tax relief

12.31 Companies are able to claim corporation tax relief on the following:

- the company cost of setting-up the scheme;

- the company contributions to the expenses of the trustees in operating the scheme;

- the gross salary allocated for the purchase of 'partnership shares';

- the market value of 'free shares' and 'matching shares' at the time they have been acquired by the trustees, with the relief afforded in the period in which the shares are awarded;

- the provisions of the Employee Share Schemes Act 2002, which are explained at the end of this chapter, offer a more advantageous tax relief provided certain specified conditions prevail.

PAYE and NICs

12.32 When income tax charge arises and the shares are readily convertible assets companies must operate PAYE and account for NICs.

Tax reliefs for trustees

12.33 The tax reliefs available for trustees of the trust that is holding the shares are as follows:

- No charge to income tax on dividends arising on unallocated shares provided those shares are awarded to employees within two years of their acquisition.

- The period of two years is extended to five years where the shares are not readily convertible assets or within two years of the date at which they become readily convertible assets if that is earlier.

Trust structure

12.34 The trust structure must be a UK resident trust.

The trust structure will be similar to that used for the existing tax-approved profit-sharing employee share scheme with:

- the power to acquire shares; and

- the power to appropriate shares.

The trust structure *differs* from that used for the existing tax-approved profit-sharing employee share scheme in that this new structure has:

- the power to borrow; and

- the power to buy 'partnership shares'.

Other points

12.35   Unless the scheme is regarded as a long-term incentive plan (L-TIP) shareholder approval will not be required where the scheme is serviced by existing shares.

The procedure for the application of tax-approval will be similar to the procedure for the current tax-approved employee share schemes.

Employee Share Schemes Act 2002

12.36   The provisions of the Employee Share Schemes Act 2002 came into force on 6 April 2003 with the express intention of encouraging a more extensive use of the SIP.

Corporation tax deduction

12.37   The bait used by the legislation to provide this encouragement is a more advantageous provision for claiming the corporation tax deduction on an up-front basis as follows:

- The corporation tax deduction is given on the company's payments to the SIP trust for the acquisition of the shares that are to constitute the basis of the employee incentive under the SIP.

- The previous arrangement was that the corporation tax deduction was not allowed until the shares that were held in the trust were awarded to the employee participants.

- The effect of this provision is that depending on the timing of the payment and the award the corporation tax deduction could be given in an earlier accounting period than previously.

The conditions that must prevail for the corporation tax deduction to be given in the accounting period of the payment are as follows:

- The payment to the SIP trust can be used to purchase shares from any person other than a company.

- The purpose to which the trustees must put the funds received from the company must be the purchase of shares as defined under the SIP legislation.

- The trust must at the end of the 12-month period following the acquisition of the shares hold at least 10% of the ordinary share capital of the company with rights to at least 10% of the distribut-able profits and to at least 10% of the distributable assets in the event of a winding-up.

HMRC has the power to withdraw the benefit that the company has derived from the corporation tax deduction in either of the following circumstances:

- Where at least 30% of the shares that have been acquired from the company payment have not been awarded under the SIP rules within five years of the date of the acquisition.

- Where not all of the shares that have been acquired from the company payment have been awarded within ten years of the date of acquisition.

In applying this rule on withdrawal, it is important to recognise that the corporation tax deduction may subsequently be allowed in circumstances when the shares are then awarded.

Income tax and capital gains tax exemptions

12.38 Provided the conditions for the upfront corporation tax deduction are met, the following two exemptions are available for the trustees of the SIP trust as follows:

- The period during which they are exempt from CGT on a transfer of shares to employee participants is extended.

- The 25% CGT charge on dividends on SIP shares received by the trustees of the SIP trust will not apply and in its place the standard 10% rate would apply with the advantage of being covered by the tax credit.

The exemptions are available for a total period of ten years from the date of the acquisition of the shares by the trustees. This contrasts significantly with the position that prevailed previously, namely two years for shares for which there is a ready market and five for shares for which there is not a ready market.

Employee trustees

12.39 The legislation allows the company to stipulate that the SIP trust must include representatives who are employees of the company. It is neither compulsory nor mandatory to include this provision and does not in essence provide anything new as the company even prior to this legislation could structure the arrangement in this way if it so chose.

Chapter 13

Enterprise management incentives

Introduction

13.1 The arrangement known as enterprise management incentives (EMI) represents the most tax-advantageous employee share scheme incentive ever introduced in the UK. It is an arrangement that does not require tax approval before introduction. It does, however, only relate to the smaller independent company whose gross assets do not exceed £30 million. Instead of a tax approval arrangement there is a notification arrangement under which the employing company must inform HMRC when options have been granted.

This chapter explains how EMI operates. It includes a structural comparison with the other discretionary share option scheme arrangements and includes an explanation of how to prepare an employee communication document, the general approach to which could be applied to any of the scheme arrangements.

Scheme synopsis

Under EMI, the qualifying company grants share options to selected employees to purchase shares in the company at a value that can be less than the MV of the shares at the date of grant. The employees can exercise their options on an income tax-free basis up to the tenth anniversary of the date of grant. The increase in the value of the shares from the MV at the date of grant to the MV at the date of exercise is income tax-free on the condition that the initial MV of the underlying shares over which the option is granted does not exceed £120,000. Instead, the increase in value from the MV at the date of grant to the MV at the date of sale is subject to the less punitive CGT regime.

Finance Act 2000 initiative

13.2 This Government EMI initiative was introduced by FA 2000, Sch 14 as an arrangement that operates on a discretionary selective basis and is designed to help smaller higher-risk companies attract and retain key people.

Although companies do sometimes introduce EMI on an all-employee basis, it is not a statutory requirement to introduce EMI on an all-employee basis. The reasons for a company choosing EMI for the all-employee scheme rather than the schemes that are statutorily all-employee, ie the SIP and the SSOS, are two-fold, firstly the strength of the tax reliefs, and secondly the control that EMI gives to the company to set the number of shares over which the option is granted.

In order to qualify as an EMI option, the arrangement must satisfy a number of statutory requirements relating to the qualifying company requirements for the sponsoring company and the eligible employee requirements for the participating employees. Fundamentally, the arrangement must satisfy the purpose test. Under the purpose test, an option is an EMI option only if it is granted:

> ... for commercial reasons in order to recruit or retain an employee in a company, and not as part of a scheme or arrangement the main purpose, or one of the main purposes, of which is the avoidance of tax.

To qualify for the tax reliefs, therefore, the scheme must be established for commercial reasons, defined as recruitment or retention. Once established for these reasons then the scheme has met the purpose test.

In the early days following the granting of Royal Assent to FA 2000, where possible, companies wished to transfer the employee share scheme involvement for their employees from the Company Share option plan (CSOP) to EMI. Particular case studies that illustrate the application of the purpose test in these transfer arrangements are as follows:

Case study 1: A company operating an all-employee scheme arrangement

A company had already introduced CSOP on an all-employee basis before the advent of EMI. With EMI on the statute book, the company wanted to grant new options to employees who were newly qualified under its eligibility criteria and at the same time wanted to arrange for the surrender of existing CSOP options in favour of granting replacement EMI options. In this particular case, HMRC agreed this approach on the basis that the company was proposing an arrangement that was designed to avoid discrimination between longer-serving employees and shorter serving employees, and therefore seeking to treat all its employees on an equal basis. This approach was deemed by HMRC to be consistent with the requirements of the purpose test.

Case study 2: A company operating a discretionary scheme arrangement

A company had already introduced CSOP on a discretionary basis for its senior directors and executive team members before the

---

advent of EMI. Once it became possible for companies to introduce EMI the company was concerned that it may lose some of its key executives to competitors who were introducing EMI. The company, therefore, wanted to replace existing CSOP options with EMI options. In this particular case, HMRC agreed this approach on the basis that the company was proposing an arrangement that sought to retain its senior director and executive team members. As a retention strategy, therefore, the proposal was thoroughly consistent with the application of the purpose test.

Finance Act 2001 enhancement

13.3   Under FA 2001, the limit of 15 employees in each company who can hold EMI options at any time was removed and a company headroom limit was introduced based on total unrestricted MV.

Under FA 2000, companies could grant an option to each of the 15 nominated employees with an unrestricted MV that does not exceed £100,000 at the date of grant. Under FA 2001, companies became empowered to grant options over a maximum new unrestricted MV company headroom of £3,000,000 worth of shares spread across, however, many employees they choose as long as the £100,000 MV for each nominated employee is not exceeded. As a consequence of FA 2001, the purposes test no longer restricts involvement to 'key employees'.

Finance Act 2002 enhancement

13.4   The Finance Act 2002 doubled the EMI asset limit to £30 million from the existing £15 million that was set by FA 2000.

Income Tax (Earnings and Pensions) Act 2003 (ITEPA 2003)

13.5   The EMI legislation is now contained in ITEPA 2003, Chap 9, Pt 7 and in Schedule 5 of that Act. This replaces FA 2000, Sch 14. The ITEPA 2003 came into force on 6 April 2003 as part of the Tax Law Rewrite Project, the project established with the objective of making the tax legislation clearer and easier to use.

A discussion point: A scheme or a bilateral agreement?

13.6   Under EMI, scheme rules are not required by the HMRC's ESSU in London for approval in advance in order to secure the tax reliefs. Instead, the employer company simply has to notify HMRC once EMI options have been granted.

However, even if scheme rules are not introduced and the company enters into a bilateral agreement with the employee optionholder that bilateral agreement must include all the terms of the option together with the details of any restrictions or risk of forfeiture that attaches to the shares over which the options have been granted.

Whereas for CSOP or unapproved options there is 'long rules and short option certificate', there is by contrast for EMI 'short rules and long agreement'.

The company will have to introduce a scheme anyway if the exercise of options is to be satisfied by the transfer of existing shares where financial assistance is involved through company funding of a trust to purchase the shares. There is a general prohibition under CA 2006, ss 678–680 (CA 1985, s 151) on financial assistance by the company for the purchase of its own shares. However, there is an exception to Companies Act 2006, ss 678–680 (CA 1985, s 151) under CA 2006, s 682(2)(c) (CA 1985, s 153(4)(b)) where the financial assistance is provided in good faith in the interests of the company for the purposes of an employee share scheme where 'scheme' is defined under CA 2006, s 1166 (CA 1985, s 743).

The definition of the all-important section 1166 (section 743) is explained in the chapter entitled 'The Employer's Statutory Framework', in section 3.

Comparison with the company share option plan (CSOP)

13.7 Enterprise management incentives are best understood when viewed in comparison with the CSOP legislation, the tax-approved discretionary share option scheme that has been in place in its amended form since FA 2006.

The enterprise management incentives options differ from the current CSOP options as follows:

- The maximum initial MV of shares over which the EMI options may be held by an employee is £120,000. This contrasts with £30,000 under the CSOP.

- Surprisingly, an EMI option does not have to wait for a period of three years for exercise in order to qualify for income tax relief. The EMI option could be exercised as early as is considered to be appropriate after the date of grant provided that waiting time for exercise is determined at the date of grant, and included in the terms under which the option is granted. The terms must, of course, be consistent with the purpose test;

- The enterprise management incentives option can be granted at an option price that is less than the MV of the shares at the date of grant. This contrasts with the CSOP option that cannot be granted at an option price that is less than the MV of the shares at the date of grant. Provided the option is granted over existing shares it can be granted as a nil-cost option at 100% discount on the MV of the shares at the date of grant. However, if the option is granted over shares that will be created as new issue shares to satisfy the exercise of the option then the option cannot be granted at less than the nominal value as under CA 2006, s 580 (CA 1985, s 100) shares cannot be issued at less than their nominal value.

- Shares acquired upon the exercise of an EMI option may qualify for favourable CGT treatment with a flat rate of 18% and the availability of the CGT exemption limit. Taper relief from the date of grant at business asset rates is not available on disposals of shares after 5th April 2008.

- The shares over which EMI options are granted can be subject to restrictions or made subject to a risk of forfeiture. This contrasts starkly with CSOP options that are subject to limitations of restrictions under ITEPA 2003, Pt 4, Sch 4, para 19.

- Enterprise management incentives options may be granted over shares of a specially-created class. Again, this is a stark contrast with CSOP options that are subject to the limitations imposed by a requirement for the majority of shares to be either employee-controlled shares or open market shares under ITEPA 2003, Pt 4, Sch 4, para 20.

However, much of the initial due diligence will be the same for EMI as for CSOP. In particular, the Memorandum and Articles of Association must be studied carefully with regard to key questions as follows:

- Is there any prohibition within the constitution of the company on the introduction of employee share scheme arrangements?

- Are there any relevant clauses on pre-emption or transfer restrictions?

- Where will the shares come from to satisfy the exercise of the EMI options?

- Are there any supplementary shareholder agreements?

At a glance comparison between EMI, CSOP and unapproved options

Structural comparison

Elements for consideration	Discretionary HMRC approved (CSOP)	Discretionary tax-unapproved	EMI under ITEPA 2003, Sch 5
Option price calculation	Current MV at the date of grant	Any value not less than nominal value where the option is granted over new issue shares (Note: CA 2006, s 580)	Any value with the opportunity for nil cost options although not less than nominal value where the option is granted over new issue shares (Note: CA 2006, s 580)
Participation	Selected employees and full-time directors working at least 25 hours a week excluding those with a material interest (25%)	Selected employees and directors	Selected employees and directors working at least 25 hours a week or, if less, for at least 75% of their working time, excluding those with a material interest (30%)

Elements for consideration	Discretionary HMRC approved (CSOP)	Discretionary tax-unapproved	EMI under ITEPA 2003, Sch 5
Limitations	Option value for any employee at any time cannot exceed £30,000 if it is to be tax-free at the date of exercise	Option value for any employee at any time is unlimited but none is tax-free at the date of exercise	Option value for any employee at any time cannot exceed £120,000 and any discount on MV at the date of grant is taxed at the date of exercise
Performance criteria	Expected by institutional investors if a quoted company	Expected by institutional investors if a quoted company	Optional but if introduced must be included in the share option contract
Minimum period for option to exist before exercise	Three years	None	None
Period available for exercise	From the third anniversary of the date of grant to the tenth anniversary of the date of grant	At the design of the company although the institutional investors expect options not to be exercisable after the tenth anniversary of the date of grant	At the design of the company up to the tenth anniversary of the date of grant

Elements for consideration	Discretionary HMRC approved (CSOP)	Discretionary tax-unapproved	EMI under ITEPA 2003, Sch 5
Share rights	No statutory shareholder rights until the options have been exercised although a legally binding agreement through the share option contract	No statutory shareholder rights until the options have been exercised although a legally binding agreement through the share option contract	No statutory shareholder rights until the options have been exercised although a legally binding agreement through the share option contract

At a glance comparison between EMI, CSOP and unapproved options

Taxation comparison

Elements for consideration	Discretionary HMRC approved (CSOP)	Discretionary tax-unapproved	EMI under ITEPA 2003, Sch 5
Income tax at the date of grant	None	None	None provided not capable of being exercised more than ten years after the date of grant
Income tax at the date of exercise	None	Yes, calculated on the difference between MV at the date of exercise and the original option price	Yes, calculated on the difference between MV at the date of grant and the original option price
NICs at the date of grant	None	None	None

Elements for consideration	Discretionary HMRC approved (CSOP)	Discretionary tax-unapproved	EMI under ITEPA 2003, Sch 5
NICs at the date of exercise (if readily convertible assets)	None	Yes, calculated on the difference between MV at the date of exercise and the original option price	Yes, on any taxable amount resulting from discount given at the date of grant and/or a disqualifying event
CGT at the date of sale	Sale represents a chargeable event and may result in a CGT liability but a range of CGT reliefs and exemptions are available	Sale represents a chargeable event and may result in a CGT liability but a range of CGT reliefs and exemptions are available	Sale represents a chargeable event and may result in a CGT liability but a range of CGT reliefs and exemptions are available

Tax treatment

13.8   An enterprise management incentives option arrangement offers to the employee to whom the option is granted a high level of tax-efficiency.

In summary, the EMI tax benefits to the employee are as follows:

At the grant of the option

13.9   There is no charge to income tax or NICs arising upon the grant of an EMI option.

At the exercise of the option

13.10   Upon the exercise of an EMI option there is a charge to income tax (and NICs if the shares are 'readily convertible assets') on any discount on restricted MV that had been given at the date of grant in the calculation of the option price.

If, upon the exercise of the option, the MV at the date of exercise is less than the MV of the shares at the date of grant the charge to income tax (and NICs if the shares are 'readily convertible assets') arises on the excess of the restricted MV at the date of exercise over the option price.

At the sale of the shares

13.11 Shares acquired upon the exercise of an EMI option may qualify for favourable CGT treatment with a flat rate of 18% and the availability of the CGT annual exemption limit. Taper relief from the date of grant at business assets rates is not available on disposals of shares after 5 April 2008.

The following diagram illustrates the basic principle for the application of CGT under the respective schemes.

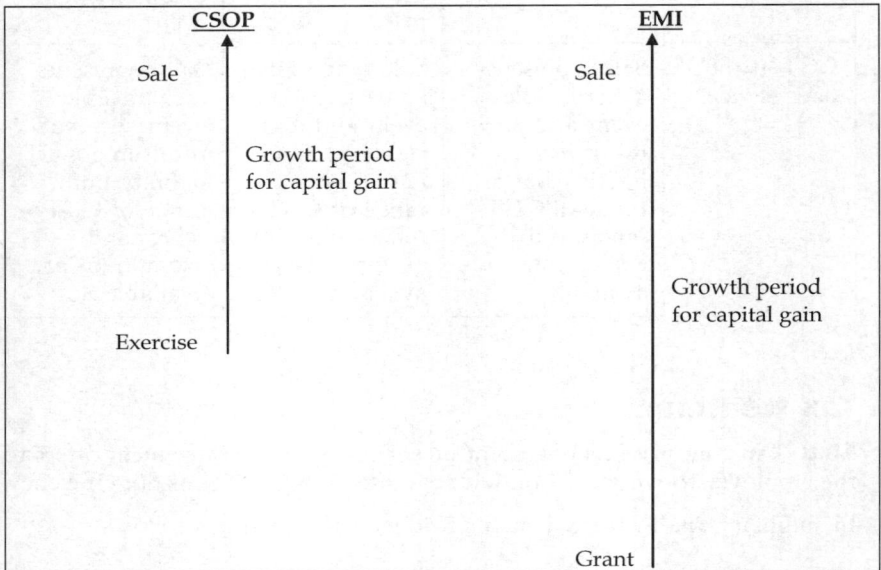

The following example illustrates the tax treatment and can be used as an illustrative example for purposes of inclusion in an employee communication document.

Example 13.1:– How does the scheme work

Let us suppose that you are granted an option in August 2009 over 10,000 Shares in PC Tech Ltd and that the option price is £0.01 per share.

The market value at date of grant is £1.00. The option price is, therefore, set at a discount of £0.99 per share.

The market value per share has been independently determined and agreed with HMRC's shares valuation division (SVD) and reflects the current valuation of the business.

Remember: the option price is the acquisition price that you pay for the shares at the time you exercise the option. The term 'exercising your option' simply means that you choose to buy the shares over which you have the option.

Suppose that the share price has risen to £2 per share at a time when, under the rules of the scheme, you are allowed to exercise your option.

In these circumstances, you will make a gain on the exercise of the option calculated as follows:

Value of the shares at the date of
exercise
= number of shares × new value
per share
= 10,000 × £2
= £20,000   £20,000

Less:
option price of shares
= number of shares × option price
= 10,000 × £0.01
= £100   £100

option gain before tax
= £20,000 – £100
= £19,900   £19,900

In these circumstances, at the date of exercise an income tax liability arises on the discount that was set at the date of grant. The discount is calculated as follows:

Market value of shares at the date
of grant
= number of shares × MV
= 10,000 × £1.00
= £10,000   £10,000

Less
Option price of shares
= number of shares × option price
= 10,000 × £0.01
= £100   £100

Discount at the date of grant
= £10,000 – £100
= £9,900   £9,900

Special notes

The enterprise management incentives tax benefits of the scheme have key consequences for the optionholders as follows.

The exercise of the option does not produce an income tax liability on the increase in value from the MV at the date of grant to the MV at the date of exercise. Rather a CGT regime applies to the increase in the MV from the date of grant to the date of sale, provided that the statutory conditions for EMI continue to be met.

A further item that is useful for inclusion in an employee communication document in relation to tax implications is as follows.

What are the tax implications for me?

The company cannot take responsibility for the impact of the scheme on your own personal tax circumstances. If in doubt you should consult your own personal tax adviser.

However, the scheme has been constructed in such a way as to give you significant tax advantages provided certain conditions are met.

Income tax

The above example shows the calculation of a gain arising on the exercise of your option and assumes that the option price is set at a level that is less than the MV at the date of grant. If you are a UK-resident for tax purposes, you will not, in normal circumstances, have to pay income tax on the increase in value from the MV at the date of grant to the MV at the date of exercise, provided that the statutory conditions for EMI continue to be met.

Note

Under enterprise management incentives, if the option price is set at a discount on the MV at the date of grant then the discount is subject to income tax at the date of exercise, not at the date of grant. Any increase in value from the MV at the date of grant to the MV at the date of exercise is, in normal circumstances, free of income tax.

Capital gains tax

If you are a UK-resident for tax purposes, the gain that arises on the exercise of your option above the MV at the date of grant is subject to the CGT regime, again provided that the statutory conditions for EMI continue to be met. The capital gain is the difference between the disposal proceeds that arise on the sale of your shares and the market value at the date of grant.

Special note on capital gains tax

There are various ways of reducing or eliminating CGT, depending on the circumstances of each individual. In particular, you will be able to set off the CGT annual exemption limit against your capital gain.

You may wish to consult your personal tax adviser with regard to opportunities for your own personal tax planning, involving utilizing the CGT annual exemption limit of a marital or civil partner in any given tax year and potentially staggering sales in order to utilize your CGT annual exemption limit over more than one tax year.

At the disqualifying events

13.12 The income tax treatment is complicated if a disqualifying event occurs before an EMI option is exercised. In these circumstances, unless exercised within 40 days of the disqualifying event, income tax will be charged at the time the option is exercised on any increase in MV from the MV of the shares at the time of the disqualifying event to the MV of the shares at the ultimate date of exercise.

Suppose that an EMI option is granted at MV and suppose also that a disqualifying event subsequently occurs before the expected exercise date. The tax consequences are illustrated as follows:

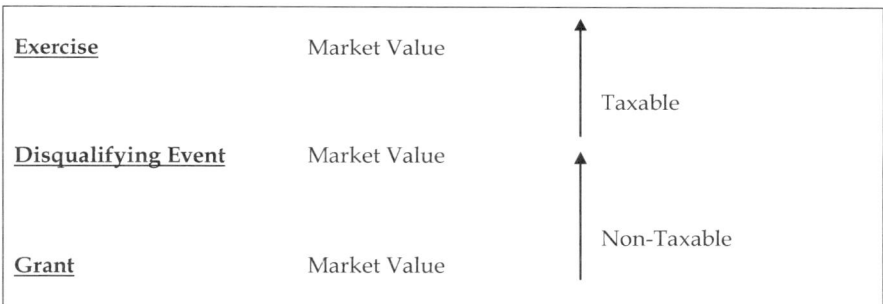

Exercise	Market Value	
		Taxable
Disqualifying Event	Market Value	
		Non-Taxable
Grant	Market Value	

Suppose that an EMI option is granted at an option price that is discounted to MV at the date of grant and suppose also that a disqualifying event subsequently occurs before the expected exercise date. The tax consequences are illustrated below.

Ten-year rules

13.13 Under the EMI legislation, there are two 'ten-year rules' that must be complied with as follows.

● If the income tax reliefs of an EMI option are to be realised the option must be exercised within ten years of the date of grant.

● If the option is not capable of being exercised within the period of ten years beginning with the date on which it is granted then it will not qualify as an EMI option anyway. It is important to note that the period for exercise can be less than ten years as any period of less than ten years would be within ten years.

Exercise	Market Value	
		Taxable
Disqualifying Event	Market Value	
		Non-Taxable
Grant	Market Value	
	Discount	Taxable
Grant	Option Price	

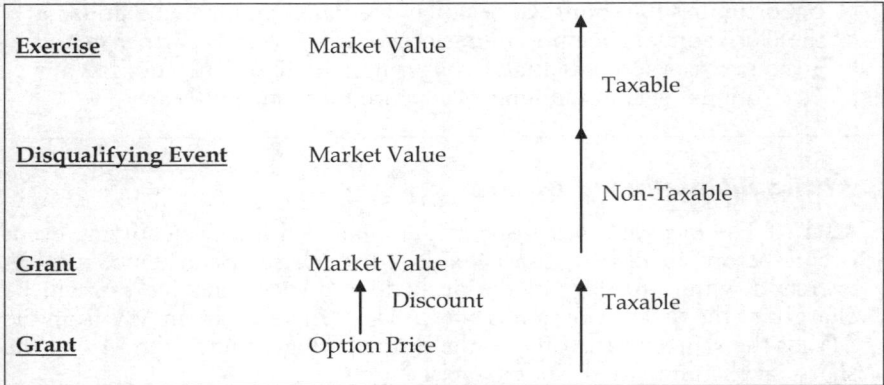

Readily convertible asset status of the shares

13.14 If the shares are readily convertible assets in that there is a market or potential market for the shares at the time of exercise and the EMI reliefs are not available then income tax and NICs are payable and accountable under the PAYE procedures. It is the employer company that must operate the PAYE procedures.

Interaction with other tax charges

13.15 There is no special relief from any income tax charge that might arise under the following:

- charges for the removable or the variation of a restriction, or conditional acquisition of shares under ITEPA 2003, Pt 7, Chap 2; or

- charges for special benefits under ITEPA 2003, Pt 7, Chap 4.

Corporation tax deduction at a change of control

13.16 The concern is to ensure that the company whose shares are being acquired by the employees can claim the corporation tax deduction under FA 2003, Sch 23 following the exercise of the options such that the corporation tax deduction is based on theMV of the shares at the date of exercise less the option price.

Under FA 2003, Sch 23, para 4(3)(b) the shares acquired by the employee on the exercise of the option must be 'shares in a company that is not under the control of another company'. In essence, the requirement is to ensure that the exercise of the options by the employees and, therefore, the acquisition of the shares by the employees must take place before the takeover and, therefore, before the change of control to the acquiring company.

Typical wording that should be used to meet this statutory requirement is to allow the options to be exercised 'within seven days immediately prior to the change of control' so that the full clause within the share option contract should read as follows:

> If the Company becomes aware of an offer being made to any of the shareholders of the Company which, if accepted, would result in a change of control, the company shall immediately give notice of such offer to the optionholder giving him a period of not less than 7 calendar days immediately prior to the change of control in which to exercise the Option.

Shares

13.17 Part 5 of Schedule 5, para 35 identifies the type of shares over which an EMI option may be granted as follows.

The shares must be:

- shares that form part of the ordinary share capital of a qualifying company;
- are fully paid; and
- are non-redeemable.

The shares may:

- form part of a separate class of shares which are subject to restrictions and/or a risk of forfeiture; and
- although the existence of any such restrictions or risk of forfeiture are to be disregarded in determining the initial MV of such shares for purposes of applying the £120,000 limit.

In understanding the nature of the share that is available for EMI purposes the best interpretation of paragraph 35 is set out below.

Ordinary share capital

13.18 Paragraph 35 is explicit that the right to acquire shares must be over shares that form part of the ordinary share capital of the company. It is definitively the case, therefore, that the option cannot be over loan notes which are not covered by the EMI definition of shares.

Fully paid status of the shares

13.19 Where shares are classified as not fully paid up there is an arrangement to pay cash for them at a future date after the date of purchase. The shares that are used for EMI purposes must be fully paid up shares.

Non-redeemable status of the shares

13.20 Where shares are classified as redeemable shares they are issued with an agreement that the company will buy them back at the option of the company or the shareholder after a certain period or on a fixed date. The shares that are used for EMI purposes must not be redeemable shares. However, the non-redeemable status does not preclude the inclusion of a provision whereby the shares have to be sold or forfeited by the employee on leaving the company.

Deferred-selling arrangements

13.21 The absence of restrictions on the type of shares THAT may be put under an EMI option means that it is possible to impose a contractual obligation on the optionholder not to sell any shares acquired for a given period. This is a feature that can be very useful in circumstances where options are exercisable only on a flotation or sale, and the company wishes to include provisions under which shares cannot be cashed in until a given time period has elapsed.

Statutory requirements

13.22 The checklist for ensuring that all the statutory requirements are met is as follows:

- purpose test;
- Individual £120,000 limit;
- eligibility of the grantees:
  - employee status;
  - commitment of working time; and
  - material Interest test.
- terms of the option;
- conditions of a qualifying company;
  - independence test;
  - gross assets test;
  - qualifying subsidiary requirement (only for options granted up to 16 March 2004); and
  - trading activities requirement.

Purpose test

13.23 The Purpose Test allows an option to be a qualifying option:

> only if granted for commercial reasons in order to recruit or retain an employee in a company, and not as part of a scheme or arrangement the main purpose, or one of the main purposes, of which is the avoidance of tax.

This definition becomes particularly pertinent in the circumstances where an EMI option is granted to replace an existing option.

Technically, the replacement of a less tax favourable option, by a more tax favourable option could provide a basis for contending that the granting of the EMI option 'is for the avoidance of tax'. HMRC may well have a strong case here, particularly if there is no or little evidence that the employee would not have been retained as an employee had he or she not been granted the replacement EMI option.

However, please note the following case study situations.

Case study 3: A company operating an all-employee scheme arrangement

A company had already introduced CSOP on an all-employee basis before the advent of EMI. With EMI on the statute book, the company wanted to grant new options to employees who were newly qualified under its eligibility criteria and at the same time wanted to arrange for the surrender of existing CSOP options in favour of granting replacement EMI options. In this particular case, HMRC agreed this approach on the basis that the company was proposing an arrangement that was designed to avoid discrimination between longer-serving employees and shorter-serving employees, and therefore seeking to treat all its employees on an equal basis. This approach was deemed by HMRC to be consistent with the requirements of the purpose test.

Case study 4: A company operating a discretionary scheme arrangement

A company had already introduced CSOP on a discretionary basis for its senior directors and executive team members before the advent of EMI. Once it became possible for companies to introduce EMI the company was concerned that it may lose some of its key executives to competitors who were introducing EMI. The company, therefore, wanted to replace existing CSOP options with EMI options. In this particular case, HMRC agreed this approach on the basis that the company was proposing an arrangement that sought to retain its senior director and executive team members. As a retention strategy, therefore, the proposal was thoroughly consistent with the application of the purpose test.

Grantor

13.24 The grantor is usually the company. However, the grantor could be an employee share trust or even an individual shareholder. If the grantor is other than the company then there should be an operating agreement between the company and the grantor and, in any event, the instigator of the scheme will always be the company.

Individual £120,000 limit

13.25 The maximum initial MV of shares over which an employee may hold unexercised EMI options is £120,000.

Although the share option contract normally states the precise number of shares over which the option is granted the inclusion of a formula in the share option contract for the determination of the number of shares is acceptable. Typically the formula would state 'such number of shares that at the date of grant gives a value not exceeding £120,000' or indeed any other value that the company chooses as long as it does not exceed £120,000.

In applying the £120,000 limit, a series of legislative requirements must be met:

- the option will not qualify as an EMI option if the £120,000 limit has already been exceeded at the date of grant;

- the £120,000 limit is reduced by the initial MV of shares over which the employee at that time holds unexercised CSOPs at the date of grant;

  — this means that the combined initial MV of unexercised CSOP options and unexercised EMI options at the date of grant cannot exceed £120,000.

- whatever discount is set on MV in determining the option price the £120,000 limit is set by reference to the unrestricted MV at the date of grant;

- any restriction or risk of forfeiture that is attached to the shares over which the EMI options are to be granted must be ignored for purposes of applying the £120,000 limit;

  — any restriction or risk of forfeiture is not ignored for purposes of calculating any discount in the determination of the EMI option price; and

  — any restriction or risk of forfeiture is not ignored for purposes of calculating MV as the basis for the CSOP option price;

- an option that is granted to an employee within three years of the last EMI option granted to him or her where that last EMI option has taken him or her to the £120,000 limit will not qualify as an EMI option, whether or not the £120,000 EMI option(s) have been exercised or released;

- a option that is granted with an option value that exceeds £120,000 (under the EMI definition of £120,000) will qualify up to the limit of the £120,000 only and the value in excess of the £120,000 limit will not qualify as an EMI option; and

- an individual can be a participant in an EMI arrangement in more than one company at the same time up to the maximum limit of

£120,000 for each company provided the individual qualifies separately in relation to each company through meeting the eligibility conditions.

Conditions for an eligible employee

13.26   The conditions are as follows:

- *employment status*: this condition has to hold throughout the life of the option;

- *commitment of working time*: this condition has to hold throughout the life of the option; and

- *material interest test*: this condition has to hold at the date of grant only.

Eligibility of the grantees

13.27   The legislation is definitive about the conditions for employee eligibility as follows:

- the individual is an employee of the company or an employee of a qualifying subsidiary of the company;

- the individual satisfies the requirement as to commitment of working time; and

- the individual does not have a material interest in the company or, if the company is a parent company, in any company within the group.

Employment status

13.28   There must be an employment relationship between the individual and either the company or a qualifying subsidiary of the company. It is definitively the case that EMI is not open or available to non-employees in any circumstances whatsoever. The employment relationship should be evidenced either through a contract of employment/terms and conditions of employment or through an aggregate of factors which indicate an employment status rather than a self-employment status.

Commitment of working time

13.29   An employee is a qualifying employee only if his or her 'committed time' amounts to at least 25 hours a week or, if less, for at least 75% of his 'working time'.

'Committed time' means the time that the employee is required to spend on the business of the company or, if the company is a parent company, on the business of any company within the group.

Committed time includes time that the employee would have been required to spend but for:

- injury, ill-health or disability;

- pregnancy, childbirth, maternity or paternity leave or parental leave;
- reasonable holiday entitlement; or
- not being required to work during a period of termination of employment (eg 'garden leave').

'Working time' means the time spent on remunerative work in either employment, the income from which is taxable under Schedule E, Case I, or self-employment, the income from which is taxable under Schedule D, Case I or Case II or would be so chargeable if the employee were resident or ordinarily resident in the UK.

Working time includes time that the employee would have been required to spend but for:

- injury, ill-health or disability;
- pregnancy, childbirth, maternity or paternity leave or parental leave;
- reasonable holiday entitlement; or
- not being required to work during a period of termination of employment (eg 'garden leave').

Note: unpaid leave

13.30 It is not possible to interpret unpaid leave as either 'committed time' or 'working time' given that 'committed time' is time required to spend on the business of the company and 'working time' is time spent on remunerative work.

Material interest test

13.31 An employee is not eligible to be granted an enterprise management incentives option if at the time of grant he or she has a material interest in the company or, if the company is a parent company, a material interest in any company within the group.

The material interest test applies whether or not the company is a close company. In this regard, the application of a material interest test differs from the application test in the case of CSOP and Sharesave options and SIP arrangements.

For enterprise management incentives arrangements:

- Material interest means beneficial ownership of, or the ability to control, as defined under ICTA1988, s 840, directly, or indirectly through the medium of other companies, more than 30% of the ordinary share capital of the company, or, if the company is a close company, possession of, or entitlement to acquire, rights to 30% of the assets that would be available for distribution among the participators in any circumstances.
- The shares over which the EMI option is granted are disregarded for purposes of the material interest calculation.

- The material interest test applies at date of grant only and does not have to be applied when the option is exercised, unlike in the case of CSOP and Sharesave options.

- Where the employee holds other options over shares in the company then those shares must be counted in the determination of material interest but if it is an option to subscribe for new shares then the ordinary share capital of the company is grossed up to include this number of shares for purposes of the determination of material interest;

- Where shares are held in a profit-sharing employee share scheme trust or an SIP trust then they will not be included in the shares of the employee in the determination of material interest provided they have not been appropriated to or acquired on behalf of the employee.

- The interests of any of the employee's associates are included in the shares of the employee in the determination of material interest where associates are:

  — husband or wife, parent or remoter forbear, child or remoter issue but not brother or sister;

  — partner;

  — trustee of a settlement for which the employee or his or her relative, living or dead, is or was a settlor; or

  — trustee of a settlement over the shares of the company where the employee has an interest.

Terms of the option

13.32 Under the legislation, the EMI option must take the form of a written agreement between the grantor of the option and the employee to whom the option is granted.

Part 5, Schedule 5, para 37 lists the items that must be included in the written agreement as follows:

- date on which the option is granted;

- fact that the option is granted under the provisions of Schedule 5;

- number, or maximum number of shares that may be acquired through the exercise of the option;

- price (if any) that is payable by the employee to acquire the shares, or the method by which that price is to be determined; and

- when and how the option may be exercised.

Part 5, Schedule 5, para 37 also states the following:

- Conditions, such as performance conditions, that affect the terms or the extent of the employee's entitlement must be set out in the agreement.

  Note: Linkage of exercise to performance conditions

  The company has complete freedom on whether or not to link the exercise of EMI options to performance conditions, and on the nature of the performance conditions. However, where there are performance conditions they must be treated as part of the terms on which the option is granted.

- Restrictions, indeed the details of any restrictions that attach to the shares, must be set out in the agreement.

  In practice, if the restrictions are contained within the provisions of the Articles of Association then HMRC will accept the inclusion of the Articles of Association as a Schedule or Appendix to the written agreement.

- Forfeiture, or more precisely risk of forfeiture arrangements to which the shares are subject, must be set out in the agreement.

Part 5, Schedule 5, para 38 states that the option will not be regarded as qualifying for EMI purposes unless:

- the terms on which the option is granted prohibit the transfer of any of the rights that are given to the employee under the option; and

- if the rights permit the exercise of the option after the death of the employee then they do not permit such exercise more than one year after the date of death.

The written agreement that includes these terms must be a legally binding document and, therefore, must be either:

- executed as a deed; or

- for consideration that is given for the option (even if only for a nominal £1).

Where the document is executed as a deed then the company must be signed for the company, by either two directors, or a director and the company secretary. The optionholder must sign on his or her own account; with the optionholder's signature duly witnessed. If the option-holder is a director or the company secretary, the director can also sign for the company, although such duplication is not considered best practice, as it gives the appearance of a conflict of interest.

Once the option has been granted, any change to the terms on which the option has been granted will have the effect of cancelling the right created by the grant. In these circumstances, if the employee is to continue as a participator in the scheme, new grants would be required with new market values and new option prices established on the basis of new share valuations. In order to understand the view of the courts on this matter, it is useful to read the case of *CIR v Reed International plc* (CA) [1995], 67 TC 552; [1995] STC 889.

Conditions of a qualifying company

13.33 The company can be either a quoted company or an unquoted company.

The company must satisfy a series of tests if it is to be a 'qualifying company' for purposes of granting EMI options.

These tests are as follows:

- Independence test: this test must hold throughout the life of the option;
- Gross assets test: this test has to hold at the date of grant only;
- Qualifying subsidiary requirement: (for EMI options granted up to 16 March 2004 only) – this test has to hold at the date of grant only.
- Trading activities requirement: this test must hold throughout the life of the option.

Independence test

13.34 The focus of EMI is specifically on independent companies that meet certain specified conditions. The target company for the legislation is the smaller, higher-risk, trading company that needs to improve ability to recruit and retain high calibre management.

In order to satisfy the independence test for EMI purposes, the company must not be:

- a 51% subsidiary of another company; or
- under the control (as defined under ICTA 1988, s 840) of another company (or of another company and any other person connected with that other company), without being a 51% subsidiary of that other company.

In applying the independence test, it is important to recognise the following:

- A company is a 51% subsidiary of another company if, and for so long as, more than 50% of its subsidiary company share capital is beneficially owned, directly or indirectly, by that other company.
- There must not be any arrangements in place by virtue of which independence might be lost.
- Where a company is directly wholly-owned by an individual (or typically jointly-owned by husband and wife) the requirements of the independence test will be met. However, if a controlling individual transfers any part of the share capital, however small, to a corporate

trustee or to an investment holding company, with which the individual is connected then the independence test will not be met. Even if the individual still has control of the company it will still be the case that the independence test is not met.

- If a non-controlling corporate shareholder, not owning either directly or indirectly more than 50% of the ordinary share capital, is not connected with any other person who has an interest in the EMI company then the independence test will be met.

- If there exists 'step-in rights' or 'rainy-day provisions' under which a venture capital company or a venture capital trust can exercise these rights to save the company from liquidation or, alternatively, to ensure an orderly liquidation then the existence of these rights will not be regarded as establishing control for purposes of compromising the independence test. Normally these rights would be triggered by default on loan repayments by the company.

- For the period up to 5 April 2006, HMRC contended that control by a corporate trustee caused the company to fail the independence test. However, from 6 April 2006, HMRC takes the view that control by a corporate trustee will not cause the company to fail the independence test. The introduction of section 685E into ICTA 1988 by FA 2006, effective from 6 April 2006, means that the trustees of a settlement are treated as if they are a single person distinct from the persons who are trustees of the settlement from time to time. The consequences of this legislative change are that, in the case of a corporate trustee, assets held by trustees are not treated as held by the trustee company but by the trustees as a distinct body. A company that is controlled by a corporate trustee of a settlement is controlled, therefore, by the trustees of the settlement and not by a corporate body.

Gross assets test

13.35 The application of the gross assets test is strictly in accordance with a £30,000,000 threshold as follows:

- the gross assets of the company, where the company is not part of a group, must not exceed £30,000,000 at the date of grant; and

- if the company is a parent company of a group of companies then the gross assets of the whole of the group must not exceed £30,000,000 at the date of grant.

There is guidance on how to apply the gross assets test is applied although it is not in the legislation. Instead the guidance is found in Statement of Practice 2/00. The approach that is generally taken by HMRC is that the value of a company's gross assets at any time is the aggregate of the values of the company's gross assets as shown in its balance sheet if the company were to draw up a balance sheet at that time.

It is important, in particular, to be aware of the following:

- the formula is applied without any deduction in respect of liabilities;

- the balance sheet will be drawn up on a basis consistent with that used in the accounts for preceding periods;

- if options are granted at times other than dates at which balance sheets are made up for statutory purposes then the values will initially be based on values given in the company's latest available balance sheet, but with updating as precisely as is practical taking into account all the relevant information available to the company;

- where the test is applied to group assets, the consolidated value of the group assets must exclude any assets that represent shares in rights against another company in the group. The gross assets position should be neutralized, therefore, for assets that are part of the intercompany balances;

- the gross assets should include goodwill as the aggregation of the goodwill from all the individual companies in a group. This is not the consolidated goodwill from the group balance sheet;

- if the gross assets level has a tendency to move above and below £30,000,000, care must be taken to ensure that the gross assets level does not exceed £30,000,000 in UK currency at the actual date of grant. Where the gross assets are denominated in a non-UK currency particular care is required, through the application an appropriate exchange rate at the date of grant; and

- where the company is holding monies on behalf of other persons then the treatment for EMI will follow the accountancy treatment. If the recognised accountancy principles exclude the monies that are held on behalf of others then the EMI definition of gross assets will exclude those monies and vice versa.

Qualifying subsidiary requirement

For EMI options granted up to 16 March 2004 only

13.36 Under FA 2004, for EMI options granted on or after 17 March 2004, it is no longer necessary for all subsidiaries of the holding company to be 75% owned and controlled by the qualifying company. Any subsidiary company of the holding company need only be 51% owned and controlled. The exception is property subsidiaries. If the holding company has any subsidiary which owns or manages property then the holding company must own at least 90% of its issued share capital, have 90% of the voting power, and be entitled to 90% of the profits available for distribution, and 90% of the assets on a winding-up.

If the company that is granting the EMI options has control of any other company then that other company must meet certain conditions. For purposes of applying this requirement, control is as defined in ICTA 1988, s 416. These control provisions apply if the company that is granting the

EMI options has control either alone or when taken together with any other person, connected with the company that is granting the EMI options.

The conditions that each of the subsidiary companies must fulfil are as follows:

- The company must be a 75% subsidiary of the company granting the EMI options in that the company granting the EMI options or a qualifying subsidiary of that company must possess 75% of the issued share capital and have 75% of the voting power.

- The company that is granting the EMI options or a qualifying subsidiary must be beneficially entitled to 75% of the profits available for distribution to the holders of ordinary shares, and 75% of the assets available for distribution to the holders of ordinary shares upon the winding-up of the company or in any other circumstances.

- The subsidiary company must not be under the control of any other company, as defined under ICTA 1988, s 840.

- There must be no arrangement in existence under which any of the above conditions would cease to be met.

Special rules for winding-up or sale of qualifying subsidiaries

13.37 There is a special set of rules that applies to subsidiaries that are wound up, or sold where the company granting the EMI options ceases to have beneficial ownership although the company continues to remain under the control of the group. These special rules prevent these circumstances from giving rise to a disqualifying event.

Provided that the winding-up or the sale is for bona fide commercial reasons, and not part of a scheme or arrangement for the avoidance of tax, the company does not lose its qualifying subsidiary status if it would have remained a qualifying subsidiary except for the winding-up or sale.

Trading activities requirement

13.38 The rules for the single company and the group situation respectively are as follows.

If the company is a single company without subsidiaries then it must exist wholly for the purpose of carrying on one or more 'qualifying trades', disregarding 'incidental purposes'.

If a company is a parent company of a group then it is the activities of the group taken together that:

- must not consist, as to a substantial part, in the carrying on of 'non-qualifying activities'; and

- at least one group company must, disregarding incidental purposes, exist wholly for the purpose of carrying on one or more qualifying trades, or be preparing to do so.

The treatment of companies where there are non-UK activities is as follows.

A company which has no qualifying subsidiaries but nevertheless has employees in the UK must carry on a qualifying trade wholly or mainly in the UK. The company does not have to be either resident or incorporated in the UK.

For a group of companies, it is only necessary for one group company to carry on a qualifying trade in the UK. Provided one group company carries on a qualifying trade of which over one-half of its aggregate activities are carried on in the UK it does not matter that all the other activities of the group are carried on overseas, as long as, taking the business as a whole, the activities do not consist wholly, or to a substantial part, in the carrying on of non-qualifying activities. Neither the company that is carrying on the qualifying activities, nor the holding company has to be resident or incorporated in the UK.

Key definitions

Qualifying trade

13.39   A 'qualifying trade' is a trade carried on wholly or mainly in the UK, is conducted on a commercial basis with a view to the realisation of profits and does not consist wholly or as to 'a substantial part' in the carrying on of excluded activities.

The phrase 'carried on wholly or mainly in the UK' refers to an activities-based test and is definitively not a customer-based test. The company may at any given time carry on some of the activities of the trade outside the UK and at the same time satisfy the activities-based test if at least 50% of its trading activity is at that time carried on in the UK.

Where HMRC is requested or chooses to determine whether or not this activities-based test is met, it will consider the totality of the activities of the company and ask key questions: (1) Where is the business base of the company? (2) Where are the majority of the company's employees based? (3) Where are the capital assets of the company held? (4) What is the base for the purchasing, processing, manufacturing and selling?

In emphasising that this is an activities-based test it is important to be aware that HMRC will not regard a company's activities as not being carried on in the UK solely because: (1) the company exports or supplies its goods or services to overseas customers; or (2) the company goods or services from overseas suppliers; or (3) the company stores raw materials, work-in-progress (WIP) or finished products overseas. In making its decision, HMRC will take into account all relevant factors and generally speaking, it is difficult to single out one factor as decisive in the decision.

Example 13.2

Suppose that the company has a UK manufacturing base and a UK-based sales force. However, all the customers are based in China and India. The trade will qualify as a qualifying trade.

Incidental purposes

13.40   The 'incidental purposes' are those purposes that have no significant effect on the company's activities.

Substantial part

13.41   A 'substantial part' is a matter of fact, to be considered in the light of all the relevant circumstances, using a measure that is reasonable in the circumstances such as turnover or capital employed, and should account for less than 20% of the activities of the trade as a whole.

Excluded activities

13.42   The 'excluded activities' are the activities set out in Schedule 5 as follows:

- dealing in land, in commodities or futures or in shares, securities or other financial instruments;

- dealing in goods otherwise than in the course of an ordinary trade of wholesale or retail distribution;

- banking, insurance, money-lending, debt-factoring, hire purchase financing or other financial activities;

- leasing (including letting ships on charter or other assets on hire) or receiving royalties or licence fees;

- providing legal or accountancy services;

- property development;

- farming or market gardening;

- holding, managing or occupying woodlands, any other forestry activities or timber production;

- operating or managing hotels or comparable establishments, or managing property used as a hotel or comparable establishment;

- operating or managing nursing homes or residential care homes, or managing property used as a nursing home or residential care home; and

- shipbuilding, coal and steel production.

For interpretation of the 'excluded activities' rules it is important to be aware of the following:

- 'dealing in goods otherwise than in the course of an ordinary trade of wholesale or retail distribution' would exclude the purchase and sale of goods for speculative purposes, say, in minerals or commodities;

- 'banking, insurance, money-lending, debt-factoring, hire purchase financing or other financial activities' applies where the company is taking financial risk in say the lending of money or the underwriting of insurance and not the provision of services that are typically associated with a broker;

- 'leasing (including letting ships on charter, or other assets on hire) or receiving royalties or licence fees' does not exclude companies in receipt of royalties or licence fees that result from the exploitation of assets for which the company is the creator.

  Where the intangible asset that gives rise to the royalties, has been created by the company or, alternatively, the company is the source of the greater part of its value, then the receipt of the royalties will not represent excluded activities for purposes of EMI. The receiving of royalties or licence fees is first listed in the EMI list of excluded activities in paragraph 16(e) that refers to paragraph 19 for the full statutory position. Paragraph 19(2) states that the receipt of royalties and licence fees will not be regarded as excluded activities provided the requirement of paragraph 19(3) is met. This requirement is that the receipt of royalties of the licence fees is attributable to relevant intangible assets where a relevant intangible asset is defined in paragraph 19(4) as an intangible asset the whole of whose value or the greater part of whose value has been created by the company.

- 'Providing legal or accountancy services' would exclude services customarily provided by members of the legal profession or the accountancy profession but would not exclude business consultancy that does not fall into either of these two categories.

- 'Property development' refers to the development of land by a company that has, or has at the time had, an interest in the land and with the sole or main object of realising a gain from the disposal of an interest in the land when it is developed. In applying this underlying principle based on an interest in land it is not possible to separate the property that is constructed on the land from the land itself.

If there is genuinely no interest in the land as defined above then it is unlikely that the activities will be excluded activities for purposes of EMI.

Example 13.3

Suppose that a company provides contracting services with another company to build houses on land in which the other company has a direct interest through titled possession and, therefore, an interest in the land. The company that is providing the contracting services has no interest in the land.

In these circumstances, the company providing the contracting services will not be involved in excluded activities provided the income that it receives is payment for contracting services and it is not receiving income from the sale of the properties.

How to apply the trading activities requirement

13.43 The practical application of the trading activities requirement requires a careful implementation of ITEPA 2003, Pt 7, Sch 5, paras 14 and 15 as follows.

Part 3, Schedule 5, para 14 requires the following:

- At least one group company exists wholly for the purpose of carrying on one or more qualifying trades and is carrying on a qualifying trade or is preparing to do so.

- The business of the group does not consist either wholly, or as to a substantial part, in the carrying on of non-qualifying activities.

Part 3, Schedule 5, para 15 requires the following:

A trade is a qualifying trade if:

- it is carried on wholly or mainly in the UK;

- it is conducted on a commercial basis and with a view to the realization of profits; and

- it does not consist either wholly or to a substantial part in the carrying of excluded activities.

The methodical step approach that must be carefully followed is as follows:

- *Step 1*: Identify at least one group company under paragraph 14 (which does not have to be a UKresident company) that exists wholly for the purpose of carrying on a qualifying trade.

- *Step 2*: Ensure that the trade of the one group company that has been identified meets the qualifying trade requirements under paragraph 15.

- *Step 3*: Consider the business of the group as a whole under paragraph 14 and ensure that the test is met for the business of the group as a whole.

Disqualifying events

13.44 If a disqualifying event occurs and the EMI option has not been exercised the employee must exercise his or her option within 40 days of the disqualifying event if the relief from income tax and NICs is not to be curtailed.

The terms of the option as set out in the share option contract may state (and this is often the case) that the option lapses after the 40 days anyway. If the option does not lapse after the expiry of the period of 40 days but remains exercisable under the share option contract then the effects are as follows:

- relief is given only in respect of any increase in MV from the MV at date of grant to the MV at the time the disqualifying event occurs; and

- any subsequent increase in MV after the date of the disqualifying event to the eventual date of exercise is subject to income tax under ITEPA 2003, ss 471–487.

The following are classified as disqualifying events.

Loss of company independence

13.45 This is the situation where the company comes under the control of another company or another company together with its connected persons or arrangements are made under which the company could fall under such control.

Important: The loss of independence by the company is not a disqualifying event if it occurs as a result of either:

- a takeover; or

- the interposition of a new holding company.

    and there is a rollover of the EMI option into a corresponding right to acquire shares in the acquiring company.

Variation in the terms of the EMI option

13.46 This is a disqualifying event to the extent that the requirements of ITEPA 2003, Sch 5 are no longer met.

Alteration to the share capital, impacting on share valuation

13.47 This is a disqualifying event to the extent that it affects the value of the shares under option and where HMRC has not approved the alteration in advance.

Conversion of shares into a different class

13.48   There is an exception to conversion of shares into a different class under which a disqualifying event will not arise. This is where the conversion of the shares is from one class only into shares of one other class only, and all the shares of the original class are converted in this way and either immediately before the conversion the majority of the shares of the class were held otherwise than by directors and employees, or the EMI company was employee controlled by virtue of holdings of that class.

Changes in qualifying trades

13.49   The company ceases to meet the trading activities requirement.

Changes in the employee status

13.50   The employee ceases to be an eligible employee through no longer being an employee of the company or one of its qualifying subsidiaries or for the reason that he or she ceases to meet 'the commitment of working time' requirement.

Particular care should be taken where the scheme rules continue to allow exercise after the expiry of the period of 40 days, say, for example, within six months of leaving as will typically be the provision contained within the scheme rules. In these circumstances, only an exercise within the 40-day period following the cessation of the employment is eligible for the full relief from income tax and NICs.

It is important to recognise that where cessation of employment arises as a consequence of death the 40-day period can effectively be extended to one year. It is the combination of the following that leads to this conclusion:

● if the terms on which the option is granted allow the option to be exercised after death they must not allow it to be exercised more than one year after the date of the death; and

● death is not included in the list of disqualifying events in the legislation.

Granting of CSOP options

13.51   The interaction between EMI options and CSOP options is best illustrated in a number of examples as follows:

Example 13.4

Suppose an employee has a £120,000 EMI option and is subsequently granted a £30,000, say, CSOP option.

In these circumstances, the grant of the CSOP option disqualifies the EMI option for the reason that the combined £120,000 limit under Schedule 5 has been breached. In these circumstances, the new CSOP option of £30,000 remains alive even though the existing EMI option is disqualified.

Example 13.5

Suppose an employee has a £30,000 CSOP option.

In these circumstances, the employee can be granted an EMI option up to £90,000 only if the £120,000 limit under Schedule 5 is not to be breached.

Example 13.6

Suppose an employee has an £100,000 EMI option and is subsequently granted a £30,000, say, CSOP option.

In these circumstances, the grant of the CSOP option disqualifies the EMI option for the reason that the combined £120,000 limit under Schedule 5 has been breached. In these circumstances, the new CSOP option remains alive even though the existing EMI option is disqualified.

Restricted securities

13.52 Under FA 2004, s 88 for shares purchased on or after 18 June 2004 as a consequence of the exercise of MV non-discounted EMI options, there is no requirement to make a tax election under ITEPA 2003, s 431(1) to avoid charges to income tax when the option shares are sold or a chargeable event otherwise occurs. Under FA 2004, the tax election will have been deemed as having been made.

In contrast, where the shares are purchased as a consequence of the exercise of non-MV discounted options there may still be a requirement to make a tax election under ITEPA 2003, s 431(1) at the time the shares are purchased following the exercise of the option. Each situation must be examined on its own merits. However, the tax elections will normally be required in the event that the MV of the shares has increased since the date of grant.

Treatment of EMI share options in the event of a takeover

Situation 1

13.53 At the time of the takeover the EMI option has not been exercised and the new company does not have an EMI scheme.

The option can be exercised within 40 days of the taking of control by the new holding company.

In these circumstances, please note:

- the full set of tax reliefs from income tax and NICs apply; and

- the more friendly CGT regime applies to the gain from the grant of the option to the sale of the shares.

Situation 2

13.54 At the time of the takeover the EMI option has not been exercised and the new company does have an EMI scheme.

This is the situation in which the optionholder releases his or her EMI option in exchange for the grant of an EMI option in the new holding company.

In these circumstances, please note that the replacement option is treated for income tax, for NICs and for CGT purposes as if it were the original EMI option provided:

● relevant time limits are adhered to; and

● relevant requirements are met.

The relevant time limits are as follows:

● If it is a takeover as a result of a general offer being made, six months from when control passes and any condition subject to which the offer is made is satisfied.

● If control passes as a result of a scheme of arrangement sanctioned by the court for the interposition of a new holding company, six months from when control passes.

● If the acquiring company becomes bound or entitled to acquire outstanding minority interests, the period during which the acquiring company remains so bound or entitled.

The relevant requirements are in the form of meeting the following tests:

● purpose test;

● limit on the maximum number of employees holding EMI options;

● independence test;

● trading activities requirement;

● option terms requirement; and

● optionholder is an eligible employee in relation to the holding company.

But not: the £30 million gross assets test.

There are two additional requirements as follows:

● That the total MV, immediately before the exchange of options, of the shares under the old option is equal to the total MV, immediately after the grant, of the shares in respect of which the new option is granted.

● That the total amount payable upon the exercise of the new option is equal to the total amount that would have been payable upon the exercise of the old option.

Situation 3

13.55   At the time of the takeover the EMI option has been exercised.

This is the situation in which the optionholder has become a shareholder as a result of exercising an EMI option, and the shares acquired upon exercise of the EMI option are exchanged for shares in the new holding company.

In these circumstances, please note that the replacement shares are treated for CGT purposes as if they had been acquired as a result of exercising the original EMI option provided:

- the replacement shares are fully paid, non-redeemable shares which form part of the ordinary share capital of a qualifying company; and

- the replacement shares are treated for CGT purposes under TCGA 1992 as explained in the one page explanation entitled 'Exchange of sShares on a Reorganisation'.

Share valuation

13.56   For enterprise management incentives purposes, the MV of the shares must be determined on each of the following events:

- at the time the option is granted;

- at the time a disqualifying event occurs;

- at the time the option is exercised, if the exercise triggers a charge to income tax; and

- at the time of an exchange of options following a 'qualifying exchange of shares', ie the 'rollover situation'.

The market value of the shares is 'the market value' as defined in TCGA 1992, Pt VIII and must be agreed by HMRC's SVD, the address of which, is as follows:

HMRC shares valuation division (share schemes)
Ferrers House
PO Box 38
Castle Meadow Road
Nottingham
NG2 1BB

The HMRC's SVD will agree a valuation that will be applicable for a period of 30 to 60 days, and is subject to the usual condition that they must be informed if any changes in the company's circumstances occur before the options are granted.

The steps for preparing the share valuation are as follows:

- determine an appropriate price/earnings ratio by reference to the quoted sector;

- establish current pre-tax and post-tax profits;

- calculate an initial value by multiplying the price/earnings ratio by the earnings;

- deduct an appropriate discount percentage in order to account for the size of the company, its diversity compared with the quoted comparator, the lack of a market quotation and any other relevant factors;

- deduct a further appropriate discount percentage in order to represent a minority interest; and

- recognise that dividend payments in recent years may act as a contributory factor towards strengthening value.

An example of determining a value before the deduction of the appropriate percentage discounts is as follows.

Example 13.7: Share valuation

Suppose an appropriate price earnings ratio, p/e, is 10.

Suppose also that current post-tax earnings or profits, e, are £240,000.

In these circumstances:

p = 10 × £240,000

p = £2,400,000

Value is represented in p.

Value = £2,400,000

The appropriate discount percentages, determined on the basis of established share valuation methodologies, then needs to be applied to produce a meaningful valuation for the company.

Cautionary note

It will usually be preferable to enlist the support of a professional share valuer in preparing the application to HMRC's SVD.

The HMRC share valuation form Val231 can be accessed at: www.hmrc.gov.uk/shareschemes.

Procedures for operation

13.57 Enterprise management incentives are a statutory arrangement that confers significant tax benefits on employees who are granted and exercise EMI options. However, it does not follow a tax approval process where the company submits rules to HMRC's ESSU, that then produces a letter giving notification of the tax approval status. Rather than have an approval process EMI follows a grant notification process.

Notice of option to be given to HMRC

13.58 The notice that an EMI option has been granted must be sent to HMRC by the employer company. It should be noted that the employer company would not necessarily be the company that has granted the option, the 'EMI company'.

The HMRC notice, together with the accompanying documents, must be sent to the following address:

Small company enterprise centre
HMRC
1 Floor
Ferrers House
Castle Meadow Road
Nottingham
NG2 1BB

The notice must be received by HMRC within 92 days of the date on which the EMI option has been granted and must be in a form that is required or authorised by HMRC and [is included for your reference at the back of this document]. The notice must contain or be supported by information that may be required for HMRC to determine whether or not the requirements of Schedule 5 have been met.

For each employee a separate notice must be prepared for signature by the following:

- a director or the company secretary on behalf of the employer company; or

- the employee.

The notice does not have to be accompanied in the submission by any other documents. However, the following documents must be available for inspection by HMRC if it is the case that HMRC requests them:

- share option contract (the agreement between the company and the employee);

- the rules of the scheme;

- the articles of association of the company; and

- any shareholders' agreements that are in place.

An appropriate wording for inclusion in the share option contract may be as follows::

> This Option Agreement is subject to restrictions that are set out in the Articles of Association dated .... and the Shareholders' Agreement dated ....

It is important not to refer to Articles of Association and shareholders' agreements that are in place 'from time to time' as this will affect the terms of the option.

Correction of notice by HMRC

13.59 HMRC may amend the notice in order to correct obvious errors and omissions, and notify the employer company accordingly that such amendments have been made.

HMRC has nine months to make such corrections from the day on which the notice was given to them.

The employer company can reject the correction within three months from the date that HMRC issues the notice of correction. If the employer company does reject the correction then the correction will have no effect.

Right of enquiry by HMRC

13.60 HMRC has a period of 12 months, beginning with the end of the period of 30 days (the end of the notification period) to issue a notice of enquiry to the employer company.

HMRC may enquire as to whether the 'commitment of working time' test is met by giving notice of its intention to do so to the employee, with a copy of the communication sent to the employer company.

HMRC may also give notice of an enquiry at any time, if it discovers that any of the information that has been submitted is materially false or misleading.

HMRC must notify the employer company when an enquiry is completed through the issue of a closure notice. Through this communication, HMRC gives its decision as to whether the requirements of Schedule 5 are met. If the enquiry is into the status of the optionholder, HMRC will notify both the optionholder and the employer company.

The employer company may apply to HMRC for the closure of its enquiry within a specified period. As appropriate, the employee can also make such an application.

If HMRC does not issue a notice of enquiry then the employer company can assume that the requirements of Schedule 5 are met.

Right of appeal to HMRC

13.61 The employer company does have the right to appeal against a decision of HMRC within 30 days after the closure notice is given to the employer company.

The appeal by the employer company would be against the decision of HMRC in respect of the following:

- that the notice that the EMI option had been granted was not given in accordance with the requirements of Schedule 5; or

- that the requirements of Schedule 5 are not met in relation to the option.

The employee also has the right to appeal against the decision of HMRC within the same period of 30 days if HMRC has decided that the employee does not meet the 'commitment of working time' test.

The right of appeal is normally to the General Commissioners of HMRC. However, if the employer company or the employee so chooses and makes the appropriate election it will be heard by the HMRC's Special Commissioners

Annual returns

13.62   The company who has granted an EMI option and whose shares are subject to an EMI option at any time during the tax year must make an annual return to HMRC within three months of the end of the tax year to which it relates.

The annual return will require details of grants and exercises of the EMI options.

Practitioner checklist

13.63   A suggested checklist for items to be covered by an EMI share option contract as required as terms under Schedule 5 is as follows:

1.   name and address of the grantor;

2.   name and address of the employee;

3.   date of grant, usually coinciding with the date of execution of the contract;

4.   a statement that the option is granted under the provisions of Schedule 5 and by reason of the optionholder's employment;

5.   details of the type of shares over which the EMI is granted;

6.   maximum number of shares that may be acquired on exercise of the EMI option or a formula for determining the maximum number of shares;

7.   option price or the method by which the option price is determined;

8.   when the EMI option may be exercised;

9.   a statement that the option must be capable of exercise, if at all, within ten years of the grant;

10.   how the EMI option may be exercised;

11.   conditions on the employee's right to exercise the EMI option;

12.   restrictions attaching to the shares over which the EMI option has been granted;

13.   a statement that the option is non-transferable except to the personal representatives of the employee upon death; and

14. a statement that if the option can be exercised following death then it will lapse if not exercised within one year of the date of death.

HMRC checklist

13.64 The checklist that is used by HMRC in Nottingham on the receipt of the notification from the Inland Revenue is as follows:

1. agreement is in a legally binding form;

2. notification has been submitted by the employer company;

3. notification has been received within 92 days of date of grant;

4. notification includes a declaration from the company secretary that the information given is correct and complete;

5. notification includes a declaration from the employee that the working hours or working-time commitment is satisfied;

6. agreement specifies the date of grant;

7. agreement specifies that the option has been granted under the EMI provisions;

8. agreement specifies the type of shares over which the option has been granted;

9. agreement specifies the maximum number of shares that can be acquired or the formula for determining the maximum number of shares that can be acquired;

10. agreement specifies the option price or the formula for determining the option price;

11. agreement specifies how and when the option is exercisable, and that the option must be capable of exercise within ten years of the date of grant;

12. agreement specifies that the option is not transferable;

13. if the agreement specifies that the option can be exercised on death, the agreement must also specify that the option, if it is to be exercised at all, must be exercised within one year of death; and

14. no optionholder can have an EMI option or EMI options with a MV or a combined MV that exceeds £120,000 at the date of grant(s).

Construction of the rules and share option contract for EMI – pro forma list of clauses

13.65 A suggested list of clauses to be included in the rules is as follows:

1. definitions;

2. grant of options;

3. option price;

4. overall limit on the granting of options;

5. individual limit on the granting of options;

6. ton-transferability of options;

7. tights attaching to shares;

8. alterations to the scheme; and

9. miscellaneous.

Construction of the rules and share option contract for EMI – pro forma list of clauses

13.66 A suggested list of clauses to be included in the share option contract is as follows:

1. grant of option;

2. definitions and interpretation;

3. status of an EMI option;

4. relationship with contract of employment;

5. non-transferability of this option;

6. exercise of this option – general provisions;

7. manner of exercise of options;

8. optionholder to bear cost of employer's NICs on option gains;

9. optionholder's tax indemnity and recovery of employer's NICs;

10. winding-up;

11. sale;

12. takeover in consequence of a general offer;

13. takeover other than in consequence of a general offer;

14. exchange of options following reconstruction;

15. statutory reconstruction of the company;

16. variation of share capital;

17. amendment of this share option contract;

18. service of documents; and

19. eiscellaneous.

Schedule: articles of Association of the company

Appendix: notice of exercise of option

Construction of employee communication document

13.67 A suggested list of items, to be included in an EMI employee communication document, are as follows:

1. Why is the company introducing the scheme?

2. What are share options?

3. Who is eligible to participate in the scheme?

4. Who grants the option to me?

5. How often will grants of option be made to me?

6. Do all optionholders have options over the same number of shares?

7. What is the option price?

8. Will my shares be different from the shares of the principal shareholders?

9. How does the scheme work?

10. When can I exercise my option?

11. What are the tax implications for me?

12. Do any taxes arise for me at the time the option is granted?

13. Will I ever be forced to exercise my EMI option?

14. What happens if I leave the company before I have exercised my option?

15. What happens if I die before I have exercised my option?

16. What happens if I leave the company and have already exercised my option?

17. What happens if I die and have already exercised my option?

18. Am I allowed to transfer my option?

19. When is the last time that I can exercise my option with EMI benefits?

20. How will my option be evidenced?

21. When can I sell my shares?

22. Who will buy my shares when I wish to sell them?

23. Once I exercise my option what are my responsibilities as a shareholder?

24. Once I own my shares will I be eligible to receive dividends?

25. Is this option contract, part of my terms and conditions of employment?

26. Who do I contact if I have any further questions?

Chapter 14

Finance Act 2003 changes to the tax-approved schemes

Introduction

14.1 This chapter considers the changes to the tax-approved schemes that have been introduced by FA 2003. The chapter explains the changes to the tax-approved company share option scheme (CSOS), the tax-approved savings-related share option scheme (SSOS) and the tax-approved share incentive plan (SIP). For each change, the precise date of implementation is identified.

Finance Act 2003 introduced key changes to the operation of the HMRC tax-approved employee share schemes. In many ways, these changes can be regarded as tidying-up provisions. However, in their practical application, these measures enhance the overall tax and administrative efficiency of the schemes.

Approved company share option scheme

Abolition of 'the second three-year rule'

14.2 The abolition of 'the second three-year rule' has the effect of allowing the exercise of an option under the tax-approved discretionary share option scheme to be free of income tax even where the exercise takes place within three years of the previous income tax-free exercise under the scheme.

'The second three-year rule' no longer applies to options exercised on or after 9 April 2003, even where they are granted before that date. The option that is exercised on or after 9 April 2003 is required to comply with 'the first three-year rule' only in order to secure freedom from income tax, namely that it is exercised on or after the third anniversary of the grant of the option.

Where options were exercised before 9 April 2003, income tax relief could be obtained on the exercise of the option only if the exercise met the following two conditions:

- 'The first three-year rule' under which the option must be exercised on or after the third anniversary of grant.

- 'The second three-year rule' under which the option must not be exercised at least three years after the last occasion on which the optionholder exercised a tax-approved discretionary share option in circumstances in which income tax relief is secured.

As a company option-planning tool within its overall employee share scheme strategy, if tax-approved discretionary share options have been granted annually, this abolition will allow such options to be exercised each year as they mature without loss of income tax relief.

Exercise of options within three years of grant

14.3 The change extends the treatment of 'good leavers' that operates for the tax-approved SSOS and the tax-approved SIP to the tax-approved discretionary share option scheme where the options are exercised within three years of the date of grant.

It had always been inconsistent to operate a more punitive arrangement than for the other tax-approved schemes. This change is effective for all tax-approved discretionary share options exercised on or after 9 April 2003.

The consequences of this change are significant. In circumstances where employee optionholders cease employment with the company through injury, disability, redundancy or retirement they are now in a position to exercise their tax-approved discretionary share options before the third anniversary of the date of grant, without being subject to an income tax charge on the gain.

In order to secure this relief, the options must be exercised within six months of the termination of the employment. This six months' window period is crucial to obtaining the relief. For options that are exercised at a date that is later than six months after the termination of the employment, the gain will not be free of income tax unless they are exercised on or after the third anniversary of the date of grant.

Where the reason for leaving is retirement the income tax relief is available only if the employees retire on or after an age that is specified. This age must not be less than 55. It is preferable to identify the age in the rules although HMRC has indicated that in certain circumstances it may accept an age that is specified in the employment contract.

Extension of the material interest test

14.4 The tax-approved discretionary share option scheme now operates with a threshold level for the material interest test of 25%. Previously the threshold level was 10%. This change is effective for determining the material interest test in relation to an employee on or after 10 July 2003, the date of Royal Assent.

This increase in the threshold level at which an employee is debarred from participation in the scheme establishes the material interest threshold level at the same level as for the all-employeeSSOS. The new threshold level does, of course, reflect a more relaxed position in relation to the material interest test for the tax-approved discretionary share option scheme.

Procedure for amendments to 'key features' in the rules

14.5 This legislative provision stipulates that only those amendments to the scheme rules that constitute 'key features' require approval from HMRC. The term 'key features' is defined explicitly as the provisions of the scheme that are necessary in order to meet the requirements of the relevant tax legislation.

Previously it was the case that any changes to the scheme rules, including any minor changes, required approval from HMRC.

If the company wishes to take advantage of this provision or anticipates that it may wish to take advantage of this provision in the future then it should take steps to change the amendment rules within the scheme rules. This is a prerequisite to applying this simplified amendment procedure.

This change is effective from 10 July 2003, the date of Royal Assent.

Determination of market value

14.6 The company is now allowed to specify in the scheme rules the term 'market value' (MV) by reference to published prices on recognised investment exchanges in terms similar to those for shares that are listed on either the London Stock Exchange or the New York Stock Exchange.

This provision is available from 9 April 2003 and will have the effect of considerably speeding up the agreement on the share valuation for purposes of operating the scheme. In particular, it will assist greatly in determining the MV of a share for purposes of setting at the date of grant the option price that is payable on the exercise of the option and in applying the individual £30,000 limit at the date of grant for the total MV of the shares over which the option is granted.

In practice, this provision will have the effect of avoiding the need to agree with HMRC the MV of the shares that are quoted on recognised investment exchanges.

Generally speaking, for shares that are quoted on the London Stock Exchange and whose prices are published in the Daily Official List HMRC have always accepted a rule that takes the market value to be:

- either the middle MV of a share in the company as derived from the Daily Official List for the day on which the MV is to be determined; or

- the lower of the two prices shown for the shares on that day plus one-quarter of the difference between them; or

- the average of the values as indicated by the two prices over a period of up to five consecutive dealing days.

For shares that are quoted on the New York Stock Exchange, HMRC have always accepted the prices that are published in the Wall Street Journal as the basis for the share valuation, providing the information for a similar process to the use of published prices from the Daily Official List for shares that are quoted on the London Stock Exchange.

Changes to PAYE and NI Cs

14.7   The company now has an obligation to account for income tax and NICs arising on the exercise of a tax-approved discretionary share option through the PAYE system in circumstances where:

- the option is exercised within three years of the date of grant and not available for the 'good leaver' relief provisions or, alternatively, more than ten years after the date of grant; and
- the shares are readily convertible assets.

This change is effective for all tax-approved discretionary share options exercised on or after 9 April 2003. Notably it will impact in relation to employee optionholders who have a right to an early exercise at the time of a corporate transaction.

Previously HMRC has been reluctant to allow companies to include provisions in the scheme rules for the withholding of tax. The reason for this reluctance was quite simply that it was considered to be an unnecessary provision given that PAYE did not apply to the exercise of tax-approved discretionary share options.

If the rules do not cater for withholding tax the following amendments are required:

- the insertion of a new rule giving the company the authority to withhold tax, then an amendment is required in order to include a withholding tax provision. The rule should be suitably drafted to cover both income tax and NICs; and
- the insertion of a new rule establishing an indemnity mechanism to enable the employing company to recover from the employee optionholder any amount due under the PAYE system. The importance of this indemnity mechanism is highlighted by the fact that HMRC will not permit the grantor to unilaterally sell in the market, shares purchased by the employee on exercise to cover the amount of withholding tax due.

Any amendments will require the approval of HMRC and, potentially, the approval of the employee optionholders to whom options have already been granted.

Approved savings-related share option scheme

Procedure for amendments to 'key features' in the rules

14.8   The procedure for amendments to 'key features' in the rules is exactly the same as for the tax-approved discretionary share option scheme, the detail of which is explained in section A.4. above.

This change is effective from 10 July 2003, the date of Royal Assent.

End of scheme-related employment

14.9 Where the sale of a subsidiary or a business results in the end of scheme-related employment and the transfer of an employee optionholder's employment to a non-associated company the scheme rules may now provide for the following:

- either the employee may exercise the option within six months of the transfer of the employment and if not exercised in that six months will lapse; or

- the employee may retain the option and exercise within six months after the employment is subsequently terminated by reason of injury, disability, redundancy or retirement.

In these circumstances, if the stricture of the legislation is understood correctly, the employee optionholder cannot retain and exercise after the bonus date. In other words, the opportunity to exercise is limited to these two situations. It is difficult to see how the company would see any advantage in drafting the scheme rules to allow the second situation for exercise. The situation represents the opportunity that prevailed in advance of FA 2003 anyway and has always been included routinely in scheme rules.

This change is effective from 10 July 2003, the date of Royal Assent.

Approved share incentive plan

Redefinition of individual limits for partnership shares

14.10 Under the partnership shares module, the specification of the individual limits for the employee who wishes to fund the purchase of partnership shares has changed to a total of £1,500 a year or 10% of annual salary.

This change is effective from 10 July 2003, the date of Royal Assent, and has the positive effect of allowing employees to use their bonuses to fund the purchase of partnership shares. As a result of this change to the legislation, the purchase can actually be as a bulk purchase in the month in which the employee receives the bonus from the company.

Previously the limits were defined as £125 per month, paid as a monthly contribution, or 10% of monthly salary where monthly salary is not limited to basic salary.

If companies wish to offer this new flexibility to employees then existing scheme rules must be amended to allow the opportunity, and new rules drafted to allow the opportunity in the first place.

Redefinition of earnings for partnership shares

14.11   Under the partnership shares module, the scheme rules may, if the company so decides, provide for the following:

- a lower percentage of employee's salary than the limit of 10%; and

- a description of earnings that leaves out certain earnings which must be identified.

The thinking behind this change is to provide for companies' greater ease of administration, particularly for schemes whose participants have an element of variable PAYE earnings.

This change is effective from 6 April 2003, namely the beginning of the tax year to 5 April, 2004, and then for subsequent years.

If companies wish to offer this new flexibility to employees then existing scheme rules must be amended in order to allow the opportunity and new rules drafted in order to allow the opportunity in the first place. Companies can amend to existing scheme rules and/or establish new scheme rules from 10 July 2003, the date of Royal Assent.

Move to a new employment within a group

14.12   The company can now invite its employees to participate in more than one tax-approved SIP operated by the group in the same tax year in circumstances where the employment of employee participants is moved from one group company, to another group company. It is important to stress that the limits on participation for any given employee will apply to both tax-approved SIPs in which the employee participates in the tax year.

This provision caters for the situation where within a group of companies, different tax-approved SIPs are established for employees within different subsidiaries or different subgroups. The provision facilitates a continuity of employee participation in SIP arrangements. Previously when employees moved between group companies into the jurisdiction of another tax-approved SIP they were prevented from participating in the tax-approved SIP of the new employer by the legislative rule that an employee cannot participate in more than one tax-approved SIP in any given tax year.

If companies wish to make use of these new flexibility existing scheme rules, must be amended in order to allow the opportunity, and new rules drafted in order to allow the opportunity in the first place. Companies can amend to existing scheme rules and/or establish new scheme rules from 10 July 2003, the date of Royal Assent.

Chapter 15

Tax-unapproved share option scheme

Introduction

15.1 This chapter explains how a share option scheme can be constructed from the general legislation together with an appreciation of its advantages and disadvantages. The model for this scheme arrangement is the tax-approved executive/company share option scheme (E/CSOP) but without the income tax relief at the time the option is exercised.

Scheme synopsis

The company grants share options to selected employees to purchase shares in the company at a value that can be less than the MV of the shares at the date of grant. The employees can exercise their options in accordance with exercise conditions that are set out in the rules of the scheme. The increase in the MV of the shares from the date of grant to the date of exercise is subject to income tax and NICs.

The structure of the scheme mirrors the approved executive company discretionary share option version without the tax relief at the date of exercise and there is no £30,000 limitation for this tax-unapproved version on the MV of the underlying shares over which the option is granted. It is possible to compensate for the absence of tax relief at the date of exercise by granting the option at a discount. This feature may be viable in the private company but would be highly unlikely in the publicly-quoted company in view of the position taken by the institutional investment committees.

The standard share option scheme without the support of the tax-approved infrastructure operates as a discretionary selective arrangement. Participation in the scheme is determined by the board of directors or the remuneration committee appointed by the board of directors or maybe the CEO or the chairperson.

It is important to note, in particular, the implications of the scheme having a tax-unapproved status as follows:

- The discretionary nature of the scheme means that it can be used to discriminate in favour of particular employees. There are no restrictions either on which employees are granted options or the basis on which employees are granted options.

- Without a tax-approved status, employees can be granted options over shares that have a MV greater than £30,000 under a tax-unapproved share option arrangement.

- Although there is no restriction on the value of the shares over which the options are granted for a tax-unapproved share option arrangement under UK tax legislation, care should be taken to comply with the limitations that are set by the IIGs. These guidelines are explained in detail in the chapter entitled 'The Institutional investor guidelines'.

Operation of the scheme

15.2 The scheme operates typically in the same way as the tax-approved discretionary share option scheme except for two key features as follows:

- The share option can be granted at below the MV of the shares at the date of grant provided that where the exercise will be satisfied through the issue of new shares the option price is set at a value that is not less than the par value, or the nominal value of the shares. Where the exercise will be satisfied through the transfer of existing shares the option price can be set at a value that is less than the nominal value of the shares.

  Under CA 2006, s 580 (CA 1985, s 100), the issue price of the shares must amount to at least the nominal value of the shares. If the shares are issued for a sum that exceeds the nominal value of the shares the excess is credited to the share premium account. It is possible for the company to make a contribution to an employee share trust which in turn can subscribe for new shares and then transfer the shares to the employees in order to satisfy the exercise of the options. In these circumstances, the option price can be less than the nominal value of the shares for the reason that the option is not being satisfied directly through the issue of new shares.

- For the share options granted prior to FA 2003 the options could not be capable of being exercised more than ten years after the date of grant. This was a condition that must be complied with in order to avoid an income tax liability at the date of grant.

  Under FA 2003, from 1 September 2003, the rules changed in relation to the tax charge on option grants for tax-unapproved share option schemes. The option no longer has to be capable of exercise only within the period of ten years from the date of grant in order to avoid income tax on any discount given at grant in the calculation of the option price. The legislation effectively abolishes the charge to income tax that would previously have arisen at the date of grant where the option was classified as a 'long option', capable of exercise more than ten years after the date of grant. It is now the case that a charge to income tax does not arise on the grant of the option regardless of when the option may be exercised or the level at which the option price is set.

To put this change in context, the number of years in the condition had already been increased from seven to ten with effect from 6 April 1998. Finance Act 2003 establishes the opportunity for a truly 'long option' without any penalty at the date of grant in the form of a tax charge.

It is, of course, important to recognise that quite apart from the more lenient position taken by HMRC, courtesy of FA 2003, the institutional investor committees still contend that options should not be exercisable more than ten years from the date of grant. Although this is not a statutory requirement publicly quoted companies with institutional shareholders would be wise to follow the guidelines set by the Association of British Insurers. For the private company the guideline will not usually present a constraint.

Tax position at the date of grant

15.3 In order to ensure that the employee will not be liable to income tax at the time the option is granted the option must be granted by virtue of an office or employment whose emoluments are taxed under Schedule E, Case I.

For purposes of meeting this condition, the office or employment is considered to be within the scope of Schedule E, Case I in circumstances where:

- the director or the employee is resident and ordinarily resident in the UK; and

- the emoluments from the employment are not foreign emoluments from an office or employment where the duties were performed wholly outside the UK.

For options granted prior to FA 2003, where income tax arose at the date of grant the basis for calculating the income tax charge was as follows:

- the amount that is subject to income tax is usually the extent to which the MV of the shares at the date of grant exceeds the option price;

- the market value of the option can never be less than the MV of the shares, although HMRC may determine it to be more than the MV of the shares. If this is the case, the amount that is subject to income tax at the date of grant is whatever HMRC deems to be the MV of the option less the option price;

- when the option is exercised the income tax that then arises is calculated on the extent to which the MV of the shares at the date of exercise exceeds the MV of the shares at the date of grant.

Significance of the case law

15.4 The significance of the case law was initially in establishing the date at which the emolument arises for income tax purposes. This principle has subsequently been enshrined in statute. It is important, though, to understand how the principle first developed through the case of *Abbott v Philbin*.

Abbott v Philbin

15.5 *Abbott v Philbin* (HL) [1960] 2 All ER 763 contended that the grant of a share option gave rise to a taxable emolument in the year in which it was granted.

The circumstances of the case concerned the acquisition in October 1954 by a company secretary of a non-transferable option for £20. Under the option arrangement 2000 shares could be issued to the company secretary at their then market price of 68s 6d. The company secretary eventually acquired 250 shares under this option arrangement in March 1956 when the market price of the shares had risen to 82s.

HMRC raised an assessment under Schedule E on the extent to which the market price of the shares at the date of exercise exceeded their cost and deducted also an appropriate proportion of the cost of the option.

The House of Lords heard an appeal and by a majority of 3 to 2 decided the following:

- 'relevant perquisite', by which they were referring to the emolument, was represented in the grant of the option in October, 1954; and

- the increase in the price of the shares between October 1954 and March 1956 did not represent a 'relevant perquisite' of his office.

The key principle that is established by this case is that the emolument for purposes of income tax arises at the date of grant.

The decision in this case has subsequently been overridden by a statutory provision which became represented in I CT A 1988, s 135 and subsequently in ITE PA 2003, ss 471–487. This enables the taxpayer to avoid a charge to income tax at the date of grant.

For the record, it is important to state the following:

- Income Tax (Earnings and Pensions) Act 2003, ss 471–487 holds for employees whose UK income tax position is governed by Schedule E, Case I.

- The House of Lords decision in the case of *Abbott v Philbin* continues to hold for employees to whom options are granted and whose UK income tax position is governed by Schedule E, Case II and Case III. This has special implications for employees who are non-UK resident. These implications are explained in the chapter 'Overseas implications for employee share schemes'.

Tax position at the date of exercise

15.6   The tax charge under a tax-unapproved share option scheme is triggered by the date of exercise.

The amount which is subject to income tax, the option gain, is calculated by deducting from the MV of the shares that is relevant to the date of exercise the two items' cost as follows:

- the amount actually paid for the shares; and

- any amount paid as consideration for the grant of the option.

In order to determine the precise amount of income tax which is payable to HMRC following the date of exercise it is necessary to deduct from the tax charge so calculated any tax which has been paid already in relation to the grant of the option.

It is absolutely crucially important to recognise that the charge to income tax arises following the exercise of the option whether or not the shares are sold. The implication of this is as follows: if the employee does not sell the shares and there is subsequently a fall in the value of the shares there is no income tax relief from the tax charge that has been exacted under ITE PA 2003, ss 471–487 formerly I CTA 1988, s 135. In these circumstances the employee will have paid income tax on a gain that may never realise actual cash in the hands of the employee!

Timing of the tax on option exercises

15.7   Under FA 2003, from 1 September 2003, the rules changed in relation to the timing of the tax charge on option exercises.

The position prior to FA 2003 was that the charge to income tax on the employee was based on the MV of the shares at the date of exercise and this was the position that prevailed whether the company satisfied the exercise of the options through the issue of new shares or through the transfer of existing market-purchased shares. However, FA 2003 stipulates that the exercise of the option triggers a charge to income tax on the employee at the time the shares are acquired where the term 'acquired' refers to the acquisition of a beneficial interest in the shares.

The strict legal implications of this change are as follows.

Where new shares are issued

15.8   The shares will only be acquired once they exist to be acquired and they can only exist once they are issued. If there is a delay between the date of exercise of the option and the date of allotment of the shares there will be a delay between the date of exercise, and the date of acquisition and the MV for income tax purposes will be the date of acquisition.

Where existing market-purchased shares are transferred

15.9   The date of acquisition of the shares will coincide with the date of exercise of the option. This is for the reason that the shares already exist at the point at which the option is exercised. In these circumstances, as soon as the option is exercised the employee has a beneficial interest in the shares and is regarded as acquiring them. The market value for income tax purposes is the date of exercise.

Where there is a mixture of issued shares and existing market-purchased shares

15.10   There is a need for the company to obtain an agreement with HMRC, probably based upon the majority of shares over which the option is granted. If the option is satisfied primarily through the issue of new shares then the case could be put to take the MV for income tax purposes at the date of allotment of the shares. However, if the option is satisfied primarily through the transfer of existing market-purchased shares then the case could be put to take the MV for income tax purposes at the date of exercise of the option.

Where there is a cashless exercise facility

15.11   A cashless facility is where the employee chooses to sell enough shares to pay the option price and the resultant PAYE and NIC liabilities that arise from the exercise. The indications from HMRC are that in these circumstances the MV at the date of exercise should provide the basis for the tax charge. This is logical and will generally speaking coincide with the actual sale price achieved for the sale of the shares.

Depending upon the circumstances of any particular company situation, there may be opportunity to obtain an agreement with HMRC in order to deal with practical difficulties that may arise from this change in the legislation.

The main causes for concern are as follows:

- where new shares are issued, the delay between the date of exercise and the date of the allotment could result in a lower income tax liability for the employee if the share price falls but a higher income tax liability for the employee if the share price rises;

- where new shares are issued, the delay between the date of exercise and the date of the allotment could result in a lower corporation tax deduction for the company if the share price falls but a higher corporation tax deduction for the company if the share price rises; and

- there is an express need to ensure that the PAYE and NIC liabilities are calculated in relation to the correct market value.

Tax position of the sale of the shares

15.12   On the sale of the shares, the CGT liability is calculated on any subsequent increase in value of the shares from the date of exercise. The calculation for determining the amount that is subject to a CGT charge is the difference between the sale proceeds and the MV that provided the basis for the income tax charge at the date of exercise.

In preparing the CGT computation, it is important to recognise the significance of the decision in *Mansworth (Inspector of Taxes) v Jelley* [2002] All ER (D) 156(CA), the statement from HMRC on 8 January 2003 and the subsequent corrective action that was taken through FA 2003.

Mansworth (Inspector of Taxes) v Jelley

15.13   This case was concerned with whether or not an acquisition of shares should be treated as deemed to be for a consideration equal to the MV of the shares at the date of acquisition in accordance with TCGA 1992, s 17(1).

The facts of the case were as follows:

- The employee was granted an option in his employer's parent company at a time when he was not resident for tax purposes in the UK. It was the non-UK-resident status at the date of grant that ensured that income tax did not arise at the date of exercise.

- At the time he exercised his option and sold his shares he had become UK-resident. HMRC determined that for CGT purposes the base cost of the shares was the sum of the option price and the MV of the shares at the date of grant (which was treated as nil) and raised assessments accordingly. The employee appealed on the basis that the base cost was the MV of the shares at the date of exercise.

- The Special Commissioners allowed the appeal and subsequently the decision of the Special Commissioners was upheld by the Chancery Division and the Court of Appeal.

The decision reached in this case was as follows:

- The case ruled that consistent with T CGAt 1992, s 17(1) the purchase cost on the exercise of an share option by an employee was deemed to be for a consideration equal to the MV of the shares at the date of exercise.

- The basis of this decision was that the acquisition of the shares was not an arm's length transaction. It was 'an incident of the taxpayer's employment' and, therefore, arose at least in part by virtue of the employee's employment.

- The final tax position for the employee was that no income tax had arisen at the date of exercise nor had a CGT arisen at the date of sale. The employee had sold his shares immediately after exercise so the base cost of the MV at the date of exercise reduced the capital gain to nil. The employee exercised his option and sold his shares free of any UK taxes.

On 8 January 2003, HMRC announced that following the decision in *Mansworth v Jelley* , it had decided not to appeal against the decision in that case. However, HMRC took a position that appeared to go beyond the decision in the case and effectively established for the exercise of tax-unapproved share options the following position:

- The consequences for employees are that on the sale of the shares, the CGT computation takes as a deduction from sales proceeds the MV of the shares at the date of exercise and the amount subject to income tax. The application of these consequences to give double tax relief is illustrated in Example 15.1 below. Prior to this announcement, the deduction was the option price and the amount subject to income tax.

- The consequences for onshore employee share trusts was that on the transfer of shares the CGT disposal proceeds was increased to the MV of the shares at the date of transfer.

Under FA 2003, the tax treatment of the acquisition of shares arising on the exercise of a share option has been reinstated for the exercise of options on or after 10 April 2003 to the position that was understood prior to the case of *Mansworth v Jelley* as follows:

- The deduction in the CGT computation is limited as before to the option price and the amount subject to income tax.

- The reinstatement is achieved through the insertion of section 144Z into CGA 1992.

  — For the person exercising the option, the market value rule in T CGA 1992, s 17(1) does not apply for determining the cost of acquiring the shares.

  — For the transferor of the shares, the market value rule in *TCGA 1992, s 17(1)* does not apply for determining the consideration received on the sale of the shares.

Example 15.1: Application of HMRC statement following the decision in Mansworth v Jelley

Suppose the circumstances for an employee optionholder to whom an unapproved share option has been granted are as follows:

- option is granted over 1000 shares;
- exercise price/option price as set at the date of grant is £2 per share;
- market value at the date of exercise is £5 per share; and
- shares are sold later at £5.60 per share.

The calculations are set out below.

Income tax arising on the exercise of the option (this remains unchanged)

Market value at the date of exercise (1000 shares × £5)	£5000
Less: Exercise price (1000 shares × £2)	£2000
Amount subject to income tax	£3000

Capital gains tax arising on the sale of the shares pre-IR announcement

Sales proceeds (1,000 shares × £5.60)	£5,600
Less: exercise price (1,000 shares × £2)	£2,000
Subtotal	£3,600
Less: Amount subject to income tax	£3,000
Capital gain subject to CGT regime	£600

Capital gains tax arising on the sale of the shares post-IR announcement

Sales proceeds (1000 shares × £5.60)	£5,600
Less: MV at the date of exercise (1000 shares × £5)	£5,000
Subtotal	£600
Less: Amount subject to income tax	£3,000
Capital loss subject to CGT regime	£2,400

Alternatives to exercise

15.14 It is important to recognise the tax consequences of the alternatives to exercising the option as follows.

Release of an option

15.15 Where an employee releases an option that has been granted to him under Schedule E, Case I an income tax charge can arise under Schedule E.

The amount that is subject to income tax is the difference between the amount received by the individual for release and any amount that was paid as consideration for the grant of the option.

The unusual situation may arise where the individual is granted another option for releasing the first option. In these circumstances, if an income tax charge is to arise at all it will be on the exercise of the second option.

Assignment of an option

15.16 Where an employee assigns an option that has been granted to him under Schedule E, Case I an income tax charge can arise under Schedule E.

The principles that apply on assignment are exactly the same principles that apply on release.

Omission to exercise an option

15.17   Where an employee omits to exercise an option that has been granted to him under Schedule E, Case I an income tax charge can arise under Schedule E where money or money's worth is received for omitting to exercise.

The amount that is subject to income tax is the difference between the money or money's worth received by the individual for omission and any amount that was paid as consideration for the grant of the option.

The statute covers situations where money or money's worth is received for any of the following:

- omission to exercise the right that is represented in the option;

- undertaking to omit to exercise the right that is represented in the option; and

- grant by the director or the employee of a right to acquire the shares over which the option was granted.

Death of the optionholder

15.18   Where the optionholder dies and the option is transferred to the personal representatives, no income tax will be charged on the exercise of the option.

Share rights

15.19   The employees do not have the statutory rights of shareholders during the period during which the option subsists for the reason that they are only optionholders until they have exercised their option to purchase the shares.

The employees do, however, have a legal interest of the shares of the company through the rights that are conferred upon them through the option arrangement.

Even though as optionholders the employees are not shareholders, the company may choose to provide them with annual and interim reports in order to encourage the sense of involvement that the introduction of an employee share scheme is designed to achieve.

The ultimate success of any employee share scheme arrangement for the motivation of the employees relies upon the communication that the company has with the employees and the sense of worth that the communication conveys.

Corporate governance under the Sarbannes-Oxley Act 2002

15.20   It is important to be aware of the implications of the Sarbannes-Oxley Act – legislation that was passed through the US Congress in July 2002. The express purpose of the legislation is to address corporate governance matters. It was not concerned prima facie with employee share scheme arrangements. However, it does impact in its implementation on the design and the administration of employee share schemes and although directed towards US Listed Companies non-US-listed companies are increasingly recognising the Sarbannes-Oxley Act as a benchmark for their own corporate governance.

The main areas that require focus from company secretaries and employee share scheme administrators are as follows.

Prohibition on the provision of loans to company executives

15.21   This prohibition extends also to organising the provision of loans. Where the company is listed in the US specific advice should be obtained from the company's advisers on whether the exercise procedures for administering executive share option scheme arrangements require amendment.

Alternative exercise procedures that should be considered are as follows:

- if the exercise is to be satisfied through the issue of new shares then the gain could potentially be paid out in new shares;

- the company could potentially invite the optionholder to surrender in part a cash bonus to pay the option price on exercise together with the income tax that arises on exercise; and

- the company could arrange a cashless exercise using deferred payment terms rather than the immediate 'tail-swallowing' arrangement.

Management of risk by the company

15.22   Under the legislation the directors must undertake a review of the company's internal controls with a view to identifying areas of risk in the business. In practice, the work is carried out by the auditors on behalf of the directors. The key implications for employee share schemes are as follows:

- The mismanagement of the employee share scheme administration generates exposure to risk. If proper processes are not in place, say, a leaver who is not eligible to exercise on leaving could potentially exercise his or her option, resulting in the issue of shares. Risks of this nature need to be quantified and processes must be put in place to prevent such occurrences from happening.

- The legislation emphasises the need to have all processes and procedures in written form as a demonstration that processes and procedures are properly in place. The application of this approach should extend to employee share schemes with records that can be passed down on a generational basis to successors in the role.

Advantages of the tax-unapproved share option scheme

Discretionary choice

15.23   The company has the freedom to decide which employees are granted options and the terms on which the options are granted. The scheme is truly a discretionary arrangement with the selection conducted either by the board of directors or, alternatively, a remuneration committee with powers that are delegated by the board of directors or, in some cases, maybe the CEO or the chairperson.

Performance measures

15.24   Options are often linked to performance measures that take the form of performance conditions or performance targets. In framing its performance measures, the company, particularly if it is a publicly-quoted company, should give full recognition to the guidelines issued by the institutional investment committees.

Widespread participation

15.25   The implementation of the scheme encourages widespread participation as there is no requirement for the employees to do anything to be granted the options. This contrasts with the SSOS where there is a requirement for financial commitment in the form of monthly savings contributions. The employees are unlikely to reject an option that does not cost them anything, has the potential for significant gain in the event of share price rise but ultimately lapses if an option gain can never be achieved by exercise.

Tax reliefs, albeit limited

15.26   The tax reliefs are available to avoid an income tax charge at the date of grant. Provided the legislation is complied with, the company can grant options at an option price that is less than the MV of the shares at the date of grant and not trigger an income tax liability on the employees even though the employees have benefited from a discount in the calculation of the option price. The introduction of a discount would be unlikely for a publicly-quoted company. The capital gains tax legislation with its array of reliefs and exemptions can be used to the advantage of the employees on the sale of their shares.

Employee retention

15.27 The scheme offers a positive help to the company in retaining key employees for the reason that employees who leave usually lose their option rights. Like the savings-related share option scheme and the tax-approved discretionary share option scheme, the grant of the option represents 'a golden handcuff' that the employees will be reluctant to lose until the scheme has delivered the share benefits. As a retention tool, the scheme is potentially more powerful than the SSOS in that the selection criteria targets key employees and the option levels can be significantly higher.

Disadvantages of the tax-unapproved share option scheme

Employee shareholders only at exercise

15.28 The employees are optionholders from the date of grant and throughout the period during which the option subsists. They do not become shareholders until they have exercised their options. Nevertheless, the share option represents, through the legally binding share option contract, a legal right in relation to the ordinary share capital of the company. The nature of the interest should be given prominence in the communication that is linked to the grant of the option. The company is seeking to register worth in the minds of the employees by granting them share options in the interest of enhanced productivity. The company may well choose, therefore, to treat the optionholders as though they are shareholders through the issue of annual and interim reports, supported by timely communication.

Absence of employee value

15.29 Although the options may have immense potential value, the employees may not attach value at the outset as (unlike the operation of the SSOS) they are not required to make a financial commitment. Some companies do choose to require their employees to perform to certain levels before granting them their share options. This is part of the selection process. However, it is also part of a desire on the part of the company to encourage the employees to value the options that are granted to them. In a sense, they are being asked to earn the right to be granted an option. In legal form, any earning of the right should be separate from the rules of the scheme that should simply include a general discretionary selection provision.

Tax reliefs

15.30 There is no tax relief given at the date of exercise. However, the loss of value for the employees arising from the requirement to pay tax can be anticipated at the outset of the arrangement and potentially compensated for by granting the option at a discount that is not subject to income tax at the date of grant.

There is the disadvantage that once the income tax charge has crystallised it cannot be reduced by any subsequent fall in the MV of the shares between the date of exercise and the date of sale. If there is a fall in the share price after exercise and the employees have not sold their shares it is possible, depending on the subsequent share values, that they may not be able to realise cash from share sale proceeds to pay the income tax charge. It is this possibility that may lead to the sale of the shares immediately after the exercise of the options.

Immediate sale

15.31 Evidence shows that most optionholders under this type of scheme sell their shares immediately on exercise, usually for the reason that they need to repay the loan that they have taken out to fund the purchase or to recover their outlay from their own personal resources. However, all investments become perceived as worthwhile when they give the opportunity for financial return. The share option arrangement is no exception to this general rule. If the employees benefit from a sale immediately following exercise then they will usually feel positive about the company in whose employment they have been given this opportunity to make a profit. Surely the best action for the company to take next is to grant another option with another opportunity for profit arising from employment with the company.

Example 15.2

This example is designed to illustrate how the introduction of a discount in the calculation of the option price at the time the option is granted can compensate for income tax that is subsequently payable on the exercise of the option.

Suppose that a tax-approved CSOP option is granted at an option price of £5.

The £5 in this example represents the MV of the shares at the time the option is granted.

Suppose that a tax-unapproved share option is granted at an option price of £1.

The £1 in this example represents the MV of the shares at the time the option is granted less a discount of £4.

Some years later the employee exercises both options.

The gain that arises at exercise is gross/net of £5 under the tax-approved CSOP arrangement and a net of £5.40 under the tax-unapproved share option arrangement.

In this example the discount at grant has more than compensated for the anticipated income tax charge arising at exercise.

Tax-Approved CSOP				Tax-Unapproved Share Option

Exercise
£10 ◄———— Market Value = £10 ————► £10

Gross Gain = £5	Net Gain = £5		Net Gain = £5.40	Gross Gain = £9

Grant
£5   £1
At Market Value   At Market Value Less
                                                 Discount of £4

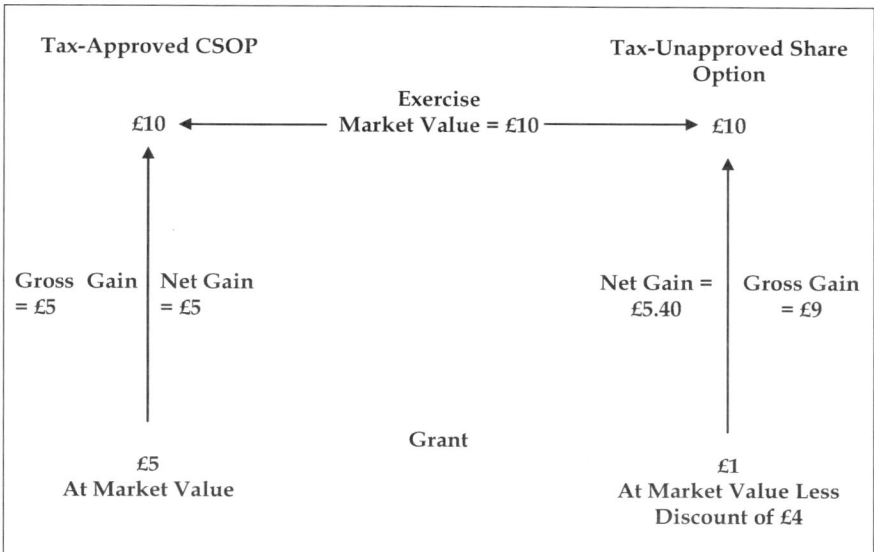

Although this example illustrates the tax-unapproved share option as an alternative to the tax-approved CSOP option, it is common indeed for companies to grant two options, one of each type under their respective schemes at the same time.

Suppose that the company wishes to grant an option over the shares with a MV of £80,000.

Instead of granting one tax-unapproved share option the company might choose to grant a tax-approved CSOP option over shares with a MV of £30,000 coupled with a tax-unapproved share option over shares with a MV of £50,000.

Chapter 16

Phantom share option scheme

Introduction

16.1 This chapter explains how the phantom share option scheme (PSOS) operates in a way that links a deferred cash bonus arrangement to the growth of the share value of the business. Share value is expressed for the publicly quoted company in the share price and for the private company in the share value that is determined on the basis of applying established share valuation techniques.

The chapter seeks to remove the mystique surrounding the implementation of PSOS arrangements and shows that the principles that underpin the concept are easy to understand, easy to communicate, and comparatively easy to implement. The chapter presents the PSOS as an arrangement that can work alongside bona fide employee share schemes in order to meet a particular incentive requirement or, alternatively, be implemented instead of bona fide employee share schemes.

Scheme synopsis

This scheme carries all the features of the real share option scheme with the exception that the employees do not actually take title to the shares. However, they have a right to benefit from the increase in the share value. The amount paid on the exercise of the phantom option comes out of company funds and is subject to PAYE and NICs. It is calculated by reference to the growth in the share price over the period of the option multiplied by a notional number of shares that has been agreed at the outset of the arrangement.

The phantom share option scheme operates as a discretionary selective arrangement with participation determined by the board of directors or the remuneration committee appointed by the board of directors or maybe the chief executive or the chairperson. The phantom share option scheme is sometimes referred to as the share appreciation rights scheme.

It is important to note the freedom that the company has in introducing the PSOS as follows:

- There are no restrictions whatsoever either on which employees are granted phantom share options, or the basis on which employees receive phantom share options. The company can operate the scheme by discriminating in favour of particular employees in the selection procedure for participation.

- There are no statutory limitations on the value of phantom share options. It is, after all, a deferred cash bonus arrangement. Additionally, the value of phantom share options is not limited by an institutional investor headroom calculation. In practice, one of the reasons for introducing a PSOS is to circumvent the need to issue new shares that would cause dilution and/or the need to use existing shares that would require a cash contribution from the company for their purchase.

Definition of a phantom arrangement

16.2 A phantom share option scheme is a deferred cash bonus arrangement. The amount paid as the cash bonus to the employee participant is calculated by reference to the growth in the share value over a period of time that is usually set at the outset of the arrangement. There is no legal stipulation on the minimum or maximum period that is set for this purpose.

The phantom share option scheme offers an incentive that is linked to a right that the employee participant can exercise. By exercising this right the employee participant is asking the company to confer upon him or her a benefit that is linked to the appreciation of the share value. This is why share appreciation rights scheme is sometimes considered to be a more appropriate name to give to the scheme. It does also succeed in removing the vacuous connotations of the word 'phantom'.

In defining the PSOS, it is important to be aware, in particular, of the following:

- The employee participant is not given a right at any stage to purchase shares. The scheme does not seek to deliver real shares into the hands of the employee participants.

- The only involvement for the shares in the arrangement is in using the growth in the share value to calculate the bonus entitlement. The scheme is intended to generate a reward for the employee participant that is linked to a potential upward movement in the share value.

Operation of the scheme

16.3 The scheme operates in a fairly straightforward way as follows:

1. Employee participant is granted the 'right to call' upon the company for a cash sum that may or may not be dependent upon the meeting of conditions that take the form of performance measures or otherwise.

2. Calculation of the cash sum is prepared by the company; at the time the employee participant exercises the 'right to call'. The basis of the calculation is the difference between the option price that is agreed at the outset of the arrangement and the MV of the shares at the time the employee participant exercises the 'right to call'.

3. The share option price can be less than the MV of the shares at the date of the grant. In practice, the share option price can be set at any value at the discretion of the board of directors.

4. At the time the employee participant exercises the 'right to call', the company pays, subject to any pre-set conditions being met, the calculated value as taxable emoluments. In practice, the amount paid by the company is a bonus entitlement.

Tax treatment

16.4 The phantom share option scheme operates without the support of any tax-approved infrastructure. It is actually difficult indeed to introduce any form of tax-efficiency whatsoever into the PSOS for the employee participant. As a cash remuneration scheme, rather than a real employee share scheme, there are no tax reliefs available for the employee although for the company any payments made to the employee on exercise are corporation tax deductible as is the case with any taxable emoluments.

When the cash sum is eventually paid by the company, to the employee participant, it is treated for income tax purposes as part of taxable emoluments of the employee participant for the tax year in which it is paid. As taxable emoluments, the cash sum is subject to the following:

- income tax at the highest rate that is paid by the employee participant; and

- NICs.

The employing company must account to HMRC for income tax on the cash sum that is due when the employee first becomes entitled to receive that cash sum. This point of entitlement must be distinguished from the date the sum is actually paid, which may be later.

The tax planning point on entitlement and payment is to ensure that the scheme rules stipulate that there is no entitlement for the employee participant to receive a cash payment from the company unless and until such time as the employee participant exercises the 'right to call' by serving a notice of exercise on the company.

In executing the tax planning, if the employee participant is a director then the requirement to account for income tax through PAYE can arise earlier at the time the amount due is credited in the company's accounts or alternatively the company's supporting accounting records. This is the case even where the director is not allowed to draw upon the money to which he or she has become entitled.

In designing the scheme for the involvement of directors and subsequently in operating the rules concerning entitlement, the meeting of conditions and the introduction of fetters, it is important to distinguish between the following:

- *conditions*: that must be satisfied before the director is entitled to the payment; and

- *fetters*: on delivering cash to the director where there is a delay on the actual payment to which the director is entitled.

Scheme refinements

16.5 There are two key refinements that might be considered worthwhile as follows:

- To include in the scheme rules a discretion for the directors to use the amount of the option gain to purchase on behalf of the employee participant shares at the MV that prevails at the time the participant exercises the 'right to call'. The directors will typically activate this clause within the scheme rules where there is not a reservoir of cash available to the company to support the cash payment to the employee participant.

- To allocate within an employee share trust a number of shares that equals the number of notional shares that will be used to calculate the cash payments at the time the employee participants exercise their 'rights to call'. At the time the phantom options are exercised, the employee share trust will sell the shares in order to generate cash for transfer to the employee participants as beneficiaries of the employee share trust.

Implications of *Abbott v Philbin*, House of Lords 1960

16.6 A strict application of the House of Lords decision in the case of *Abbott v Philbin* HL [1960] 2 ALL ER 763 could result in contending that the grant of the 'right to call' represents a taxable benefit, generating a tax charge at the date of grant. If this is the case, then no further income tax charge would arise at the date of exercise when the employee participant exercises the 'right to call' upon the company for a cash payment.

The conditions that should be in place if this argument is to have any strength whatsoever are as follows:

- the rights are capable of immediate exercise; and

- the rights are transferable.

However, the generally accepted counter argument to this is that participation in the PSOS does not really make any sense or have any purpose unless it is linked to the continuing employment of the employee participant. If this is the case, as it will almost always be, then a charge to income tax will not arise until the date of exercise when the employee participant exercises the 'right to call' upon the company for a cash payment.

Share rights

16.7 The employee participants do not have the statutory rights of shareholders. In practice, the scheme does not confer upon them any rights whatsoever to ever actually become shareholders.

The employees do not even have a legal interest in the shares of the company through their participation in the scheme and, furthermore, the scheme does not have the capacity to confer upon them a legal interest in the shares of the company.

The employee participants are invited to become phantom share optionholders with the 'right to call' upon the company for a sum of money; at which point cash is delivered into the hands of the employees rather than actual shares. However, the company may choose to provide the phantom share optionholders with annual and interim reports, in order to encourage the sense of involvement; that involvement in a conventional share scheme arrangement is designed to achieve.

As with any employee share scheme or, for that matter, any cash incentive scheme, the motivation of the employees relies upon the communication that the company has with the employees and the sense of worth that the communication conveys.

Advantages of the phantom share option scheme

16.8 The advantages of the PSOS compared with a conventional share option arrangement are as follows.

Avoids dilution

16.9 The absence of any requirement to issue new shares ensures that the implementation of the scheme does not dilute the value of the shares that are currently in issue. The institutional investor headroom calculation is unaffected by phantom share option arrangements.

Easy to understand

16.10 The concept that supports the PSOS is relatively easy for the employee participants to understand. The implementation of the scheme requires a relatively simple communication by the company.

Implementation costs

16.11 The development of a PSOS is not usually as costly as the development of a conventional share option scheme. However, the PSOS can be operated at different levels of sophistication, particularly in relation to performance conditions.

Subsidiary companies

16.12 The phantom share option scheme is often an acceptable alternative in circumstances where it is not possible for the company to introduce the conventional share option scheme. This will be the case where the company is a subsidiary company and there is either a statutory prohibition, or an institutional prohibition, or simply a company reluctance to allow the possibility of minority interest shareholdings in the subsidiary company.

Disadvantages of the phantom share option scheme

16.13 The disadvantages of the PSOS compared with a conventional share option arrangement are as follows.

Tax-inefficient

16.14 Any gains that accrue to the employee participant as a result of exercising the 'right to call' are taxed like any other emoluments without the tax reliefs that are associated with the tax-approved share option schemes.

Absence of identification

16.15 The phantom share option scheme is not a genuine employee share scheme arrangement. Without the opportunity for the delivery of real shares, either through new issue or transfer, the employee participant may not feel the same sense of identification with the company. However, the reward to the employee participant is linked to the growth in the share value. Additionally, a carefully prepared company communication, potentially without the use of the word 'phantom', can provide the basis for a meaningful and motivating implementation, and ongoing operation of the scheme.

Example 16.1: What the PSOS means for the employee

Suppose a phantom option is granted over a notional number of 5000 shares and suppose also that the option price is set at £1.

The £1 in this example represents the MV of the shares at the time the option is granted.

Some years later the employee exercises the option, or more precisely exercises the 'right to call' upon the company for a sum of money that is calculated on the basis of the rise in the share price from the date of grant to the date of exercise.

The market value of the shares at the time of exercise is £5.

The gross sum of money that the employee is entitled to is calculated as follows:

5000 shares × (£5 − £1) = £20,000

The £20,000 is subject to income tax and NICs, payable through the PAYE system.

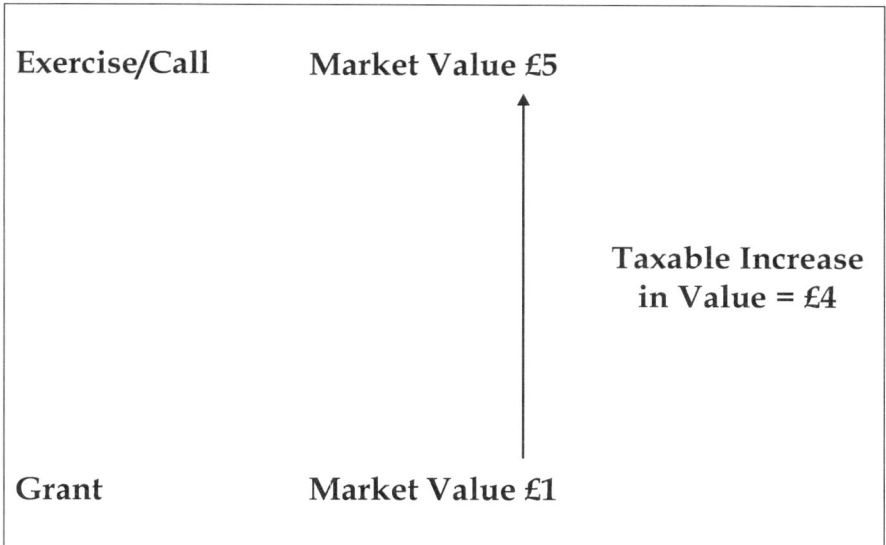

Exercise/Call	**Market Value £5**
	↑
	Taxable Increase in Value = £4
Grant	**Market Value £1**

Chapter 17

Inheritance tax

by Toby Harris, Tax Consultant

Introduction

17.1 The most significant problems with inheritance tax (IHT) on property are these:

- it is a 'dry' tax charge, ie one that may arise even though the occasion of charge generates no cash to fund the tax;

- it can easily affect 'ordinary' people, ie those without significant wealth, or certainly without high net liquid wealth;

- valuation may not be straightforward; and

- the availability of relief is capricious and now increasingly of doubtful logical basis.

Owners of property are much less willing to employ advisers, especially in the context of administration of family property, than 25 years ago, perhaps through the predilection of professionals to charge a value element which may not always have been truly earned; but in this area that can lead to serious difficulties, as will be seen.

IHT on death

Reporting requirements

17.2 An academic knowledge of IHT is of little use without the procedural knowledge of how to report transactions affecting property. IHTA 1984, s 4 treats death as the occasion of transfer and the majority of IHT charges on property will arise on death.

Use the right form

17.3 A full discussion of the rules as to excepted estates is outside the scope of this book but reference should be made to the Inheritance Tax (Delivery of Accounts) (Excepted Estates) Regulations 2004 (SI 2004/2543) as amended by Regulations in 2006 (SI 2006/2141), which identified three categories of excepted estate. Broadly, the first of these categories is for estates that are small in themselves, ie within the IHT thresholds. The second category is for larger estates, up to £1m, where the net estate passes to an exempt beneficiary such as spouse, civil partner or a charity. The third category applies where the deceased was neither domiciled nor deemed to be domiciled in the UK and the estate is small.

This chapter concerns those estates that fall outside the excepted categories, either because they are large in themselves and chargeable or because, when seen in the context of lifetime giving, the chargeable gift comes from a donor with a substantial estate and is itself over the current limits (as to which see below).

There are two reasons to use whichever form is appropriate to the transfer, ie IHT200 in respect of transfers on death or IHT100 for lifetime transfers, with supporting schedules. The first is basic competence. Form IHT200 is regularly updated. This is partly for legal reasons such as formal changes in the law and partly for administrative reasons such as the need to combat fraud or negligence. An example of the latter is the development of the forms that relate respectively to chattels and to lifetime gifts. In each case it appeared to HMRC that there was a risk of under-declaration that might be moderate in relation to any one case but could be widespread. For example, instead of simply showing one item for the value of the contents of a house it is now necessary to supply details of each vehicle that the deceased owned, giving registration number, condition and the like.

The use of a slightly out of date form is not fatal, but shows that you are not up to date. In recent years form IHT200 has been redrawn so as to elicit details of occupation which may be particularly relevant where the property used to be, but is no longer, owned by the deceased but which was nevertheless still occupied by him, possibly alone, at the date of death: see paragraph **17.4** below. A new series of forms, IHT 400, has been developed and tested and will be launched soon; see HMRC IHT and Trusts Newsletter August 2008.

There is another, more sinister reason for using the correct form. There is a story, possibly apocryphal, concerning a long-running enquiry into the affairs of the deceased and certain lifetime transactions. Evidence was called for and was eventually supplied which elicited a reply along the following lines (names naturally changed):

'Dear Sirs

Q J Swindels deceased

Thank you for your letter of 17th November last enclosing the copy holdover claim signed by the Deceased and supporting papers. What particularly interests us is how the Deceased was able to sign a form, the first edition of which was not printed until three months after his death.'

Although ownership of a share in property will be shown on form D4 that accompanies IHT200, the main form for property is D12. This requires detail, naturally, of the address of the property but also the tenure, any lettings or leases, the value of any element in respect of which it is claimed that there is agricultural relief, woodland relief or heritage relief and the open market value. As will be seen in section **17.4** below, the value for agricultural purposes may be very different from the open market value. There is space to show whether there is any 'damage' to any of the property that may affect its value, such as structural failure. There is also space on the form to show whether it is the intention of the personal representatives, or trustees as appropriate, to sell any property within 12 months. That affects the valuation issues described below.

Valuation issues, both lifetime transfers and on death

17.4 The value to be shown in IHT200 and D12 is (see IHTA 1984, s 160), 'the price which the property might reasonably be expected to fetch if sold in the open market at [the date of death]; but that price shall not be assumed to be reduced on the ground that the whole property is to placed on the market at one and the same time'. There is no such thing as 'probate value' in the sense of a value that is markedly lower than open market value.

Low values

17.5 The use of an artificially low value has two drawbacks, one short term and one long term. The short term drawback is quite simply that an account that might have been passed without enquiry is subjected to more detailed scrutiny, perhaps on the basis that if people are 'pushing the envelope' on valuation issues they may have taken a cavalier attitude to other aspects of compliance. (For insight into HMRC view, see the article by Charles McNichol in Christie's Bulletin for Professional Advisers, vol 6 no 2 p 10. This is currently an issue that HMRC are considering with representatives of the professional bodies.)

A gloss on IHTA 1984, s 160 is found in the judgment of Ungoed-Thomas J in *Re Hayes Will Trust [1971] 1 WLR 758* at page 768:

> 'It has been established time and time again in these courts, as it was in our case that there is a range of price, in some circumstances wide, which competent valuers would recognise as the price which property would fetch if sold in the open market.
>
> Neither the section nor [the judgment of] Sankey J [in *Earl of Ellesmere v Inland Revenue Commissioners [1918] 2 KB 735*] requires that the top price of that range should be the price fixed for Estate Duty. That price, together with the lowest price in the range, may be expected to be the least likely price within the range, to be obtained from the open market. The most likely price, in the absence of consultation between valuers representing competing interested, would presumably be the mean price. The habitual well-recognised process for arriving at that price is for the executors to put in the lowest price within the range and then to confer with the District Valuer who acts to safeguard the Revenue.'

The suggestion of Mr McNichol in the article referred to was that choosing the lowest price in a range makes it most likely that the account will be selected for enquiry. It might be more worthwhile for the taxpayer to adopt a less adversarial stance and to put in the account a figure which is nearer the middle of the possible range of values.

'Amateur' valuations and the interaction of IHT and CGT

17.6 In a 'domestic' case, ie the common situation of the death of the survivor of a married couple where the estate exceeds the nil-rate band and passes to chargeable beneficiaries such as close family, it is increasingly common for the family to seek to dispense both with the services of a solicitor and with the formalities of a valuation. This may, at least in regard to the valuation, be false economy. What happens, all too frequently, is that the family speak to three estate agents who each put forward a figure which is actually not a valuation at all. It is no more than a bid to get the job of selling the house. It is very common for the letter to include a phrase such as 'Asking price £395,000 but for probate put in a figure of £345,000'.

The long term reason that it may be false economy not to have a more formal valuation is the burden of CGT on later sale of the house. In the domestic situation, especially where the executors have no training in tax law, it is widely known that main residence relief shelters the proceeds of sale of the family home from CGT. What is not appreciated is that usually main residence relief under TCGA 1992, s 222 or 225A or, in the case of an ongoing trust, under s 225 will be available only where the strict requirements of those sections is satisfied.

In the more normal case, where the house stands empty after Granny's death whilst the children obtain a grant of probate and agree the division of chattels, main residence relief will not be available. If, as is assumed in this chapter, the estate is taxable and the value of the property has been 'ascertained' for the purposes of IHT, the value so ascertained will be the value for CGT also: see TCGA 1992, s 274. Thus if that value had been put forward by an experienced valuer, who could back up his opinion with comparisons to other prices achieved in the market at that time, it is likely that the value would 'stick' for IHT.

Example 1

At his death on 23 October 2007 Cedric, a widower, was sole owner of The Grange. His late wife had used her nil rate band. He was survived by a son and two daughters, one of whom, Alice, practised as a solicitor nearby and dealt with the estate. Alice obtained a formal (but inexpensive) valuation of the house from an estate agent colleague who would later be selling the house. It was detailed: there had been a problem of flooding some time before which may have affected the foundations; and Cedric had long resisted his daughters' suggestion that the kitchen be modernised. The value was assessed at £450,000 and IHT assessed on the estate as a whole.

Alice had difficulties with the estate. Cedric had been a Name at Lloyd's who had losses going back to 1992 and the recent 'takeover' of Equitas by Berkshire Hathaway gave rise to interesting questions as to whether Alice could still use the simplified procedures derived from the case of re Yorke; so many months passed before Alice had all the details she needed to prove the Will so as to be able to sell The Grange.

The family did not mind. They agreed other matters, such as division of the furniture and antiques, and knew that, contrary to the general trend property of this particular type was holding its value, even rising. The Grange sold to a builder, who was not frightened by its condition, for £525,000 in March 2008, having first been appropriated out to Alice and her siblings so that there were three capital gains by the beneficiaries, rather than one by the executor. Alice had no difficulty with the Valuation Office: the District Valuer had had an opportunity of inspecting the Grange back in August 2007, before Alice had the place tidied up, and had agreed the probate value with the estate agent, who had produced comparables in support of his figure.

The example also illustrates the interaction between IHT and CGT. The marginal rate of IHT is 40% but that is no longer the rate for CGT. The rate is now 18%. Moreover, if the value of property rises from the date of death to the date of sale and if the value has been fully fixed as described above, the gain that arises will not all be taxable. On the one hand, there is available to the executors for the year of death and for the two following years, the annual exempt amount for an individual. Second, personal representatives may set against the gain arising on sale the allowances described in Statement of Practice 2/04. Finally, as was the case in the example, if the combination of those factors is not sufficient to shelter the gain, the executors can consider whether it is they who should be selling the property or whether they should instead be transferring it to beneficiaries who may, between them, be able to fragment the gain by relying on TCGA 1992, ss 62 and 64.

None of this planning is as easy if there has not been a proper valuation at the outset. The personal representatives described in the earlier brief illustration, faced with a difference between their original guess of the value at, say £350,000 and eventually gross sale proceeds of £390,000 are in a weak position if the District Valuer argues that the value at date of death should be, say, £380,000. Unlike Alice, they simply do not have the evidence to contradict him.

Flooding the market

17.7   This aspect of IHTA 1984, s 160 does not affect domestic cases but is more relevant to landed estates. Here the valuation has to be upon the basis that the seller would market the property in the way that would produce the best price. That could involve dividing it into lots or it could require assembly of various items of land which, taken together, would be more attractive. That issue of assembly raises difficulties where the land is not all owned in the same title, ie where part of it was the personal estate of the deceased and part was land in which the deceased had a lesser interest or a trust interest. The leading case, already referred to, is *Earl of Ellesmere v IRC [1918] 2 KB 735*. After wide advertisement the estate was sold as a single entity. The purchaser of the estate kept part of the land but then sold the rest on, making a profit of around 19%. This caused the Revenue to challenge the original sale price by assessing estate duty at more. The court eventually reduced the figure to about 111% of the figure achieved on the sale of the estate as a whole.

'Natural units'

17.8 In *Duke of Buccleuch v IRC [1967] 1 AC 506* the estate was more complicated. The Revenue divided it into 532 separate lots, and on that basis arrived at a valuation of £868,129. Whilst the trustees did not challenge the methodology they considered that after the readily saleable lots had been taken out, which were about 9% of the whole, the rest should be valued at what an individual buyer would pay expecting a 'turn' of 20% for taking on all of the different parcels in that way. That concept was acceptable to the House of Lords, by comparison with the valuation of the example of a library. It was considered, taking the example suggested by Wynn LJ, that, if a library were graded so as to lot out the best items, the remaining mixed lot would have a lower value:

> 'Suppose, however, that the Deceased had bought a miscellaneous and mixed lot of surplus stores intending to sort out and arrange them in saleable lots. That might involve a great deal of work, time and expense, and I see no justification for requiring the supposition that that had been done and then valuing the saleable lots that would have emerged.'

The result is this: there should be lotting of a landed estate into what the court described as 'natural units' provided that that does not involve undue expenditure of time or effort.

Mixed interests

17.9 The difficulty was noted above of the situation where land is not all held under the same title. In *Gray (Surviving Executor of Lady Fox) v IRC [1994] STC 360* the Lands Tribunal had to consider the value of both a parcel of land and the interest of a partnership in the same land. The partnership had an agricultural tenancy of the land and Lady Fox was entitled to 92.5% of partnership profits. The Revenue wanted the land itself and the partnership share to be valued together, with the vacant possession of the value being discounted. The result was a much higher value than would apply merely taking the investment value of the land and disregarding the partnership share.

It had been agreed that the vacant possession value of the land was £6,125,000 from which the District Valuer had deducted an estimate of the price that the partners (other than Lady Fox) would take for their share of the tenancy, ie £100,000. It had already been agreed that the tenanted value of the land was £2,751,000, so the District Valuer took 45% of the difference between tenanted value and vacant possession value. He then applied a discount of 7.5% of the vacant possession value to compensate for the risk and delay in obtaining possession of the whole. Adding these interests together he arrived at a value of £5,565,000.

The Tribunal reviewed these figures. They were not helped by the fact that there was no better valuation evidence than that of the District Valuer. They thought the discount of 7.5% was on the low side but, for want of evidence, did not dispute it.

The effect of a tenancy on value

17.10 A different issue arose in *Baird's Executors v IRC [1991] SLT (Lands Tr9)*. George Baird had given up the tenancy of an agricultural holding in favour of his daughter-in-law and grandson. The transfer of the tenancy, which dated back to July 1921, took place in 1977, the landlord consenting. Mr Baird died in 1985. The Revenue claimed CTT on the transfer and the Lands Tribunal had to decide whether the interest of a tenant in these circumstances was capable of valuation.

It tried to determine the price which the interest might reasonably be expected to fetch if sold on the open market at the date of transfer, disregarding the fact that the tenancy could not be assigned but assuming that any purchaser would be subject to the same restrictions. The District Valuer, applying these principles, arrived at a valuation figure of 25% of the vacant possession value of the land itself. He considered:

- what a landlord might pay to get the land back;

- what a prospective tenant might accept from a prospective landlord in a sale and leaseback transaction;

- the compensation that is paid to a tenant on compulsory acquisition of agricultural land; and

- rents on equivalent land holdings in the open market on terms similar to the lease in question.

The Valuer said that the value could be as high as 50% of vacant possession value but for the uncertainties of the four factors just described. The Tribunal was satisfied. As a result the right of a tenant in an agricultural lease is an asset that can have a value. The value is not necessarily 25% of the vacant possession value of the land.

Valuation of shares in land

17.11 As a general rule, an undivided share of land will be worth less than the appropriate proportion of the entirety. The actual discount will vary according to the circumstances. Thus *Wight v IRC [1982] 264 EG 935* is authority for the proposition that a discount of 15% is allowable for certain residential properties where a view can be taken on how likely it is that the court would exercise its discretion and order a sale at the request of a joint owner.

Charkham v IRC, a decision of the Lands Tribunal, concerned the valuation for IHT of undivided shares in a portfolio of investment properties. The interests had to be valued at various dates and the size of the share of the taxpayer in the portfolio, and thus in the underlying properties, differed from one date to another. The taxpayer had an interest that at best was 24% and at least 6%. For the taxpayer it was argued that one should look at the income produced by the share in question and that a minority owner could less easily obtain an order for the sale of the properties than a majority owner and that that should influence the value.

The Tribunal disagreed, holding that the correct approach was to consider how likely it was, at any given time, that a minority owner of property might get an order for sale. The size of the minority share was not as important as the purpose for which the property was held. An order for sale was more likely where the purpose of the trust which held the properties had come to an end. The Tribunal held that a purchaser of a minority interest would know that it was difficult to get an order for sale and would discount the open market value of the property because he would not be able to get his money back. That would be the same whether the interest purchased was 6 or 24%. What was more important was whether, for example, it was likely that planning permission could be obtained for a property making it more likely that the owners as a group would want to sell. The result of these principles was a discount of 15% in respect of some of the properties and of between 20 and 22.5% on others.

Commonly, for example in the domestic situation where only one half of the property is in the estate and where the related property rules (see below) do not apply, the parties settle on a discount of 10%. The valuation principles are especially important in connection with lifetime transfers and the 'loss to the estate' principle.

Example 2: Gift of a share

Rachel was the owner of an investment property in Hendon that she wished to give to her son Leonard. The property had risen substantially in value during Rachel's ownership and a simple transfer of it would trigger a substantial chargeable gain. On 16 October 2006, Rachel was advised by her solicitors that any settlement of the property would be treated as a chargeable transfer, with the result that hold-over relief would apply for CGT. Rachel wanted to set up a lifetime trust for Leonard for life, with remainder to his children absolutely. At that time the value of the property was £600,000 and Rachel had imagined that a gift of one half of the property would be within the nil-rate band, which at that point was £285,000, because a half share would be discounted somewhat. However, IHTA 1984, s (1) defines the transfer by reference to the fall in the value of the estate of the transferor. The half share that would be retained by Rachel after applying a discount of 10% would be worth £270,000 so the fall in value would be £330,000.

Matters dragged on until 7 April 2007 though the value of the property did not increase meanwhile. On completion of the transfer the value for IHT was the fall in value of £330,000, less annual exemptions available for that year and the previous one of £6,000 and less the nil-rate band, leaving £24,000 in charge to tax at 20%, yielding tax of £4,800. The expenses of the transaction would have been relevant to the issue of the gain, if not held over; they were not deducted from the transfer itself, but (since Rachel paid them) they did reduce her estate.

Related property

17.12 IHTA 1984, s 161 applies a statutory fiction that overrides the principles just discussed so as to value an interest in property which, on it own, might qualify for a discount, in the context of other 'related' property so that, in that fictional context, the share is more valuable and is taxed higher. Section 161(2) provides that property is 'related' if:

- it is comprised in the estate of the taxpayer's spouse or civil partner; or

- it is, or has within the last five years, been either

  - the property of a charity or held on charitable trusts only; or

  - the property of a 'public benefit' body such as a political party, housing association or a 'Schedule 3' body, i e one that exists for national purposes.

Where the related property rules apply it is necessary first to value all the related property and then to fix the proportion that is attributable to the taxed property as part of that aggregable value, in other words, ignoring the discount.

There is a similar rule that relates to trust property, though the conclusion is arrived at by a different fiction. If the taxpayer, for example, owns part of a farm in his own right but is life tenant of a family settlement that owns the remainder there is actually no need for IHTA 1984, s 161. Section 49(1) treats the taxpayer as if he were the owner of the settled property so it may be valued as a whole. Naturally, following FA 2006, the number of 'old-style' interests in possession may reduce. Whilst it will still be possible to create an immediate post-death interest, which will fall within this valuation rule, and whilst it will be possible until 5 April 2008 to create transitional serial interests which will be taxed the same as old-style interests in possession, in general it will no longer be possible to create interests in possession by way of lifetime settlement except for special categories of beneficiaries such as the disabled.

Thus in future, and this is a point that may be exploited in other ways, it may be possible to create a lifetime settlement for a beneficiary for life in circumstances where the tenant for life enjoys all the rights to income as hitherto but which is a 'relevant property' settlement such that the IHT charge is on the ten-yearly basis and not by reference to his death. CGT is the subject of a separate chapter but it may be seen that relief for a main residence under TCGA 1992, s 225 can now be available in respect of a dwelling which forms no part of the estate of the tenant for life on death.

IHTA 1984, s 171 provides that valuation for transfers on death is on the basis that changes in the value of the estate which occur by reason of the death are to be taken into account as if they occurred just before death unless those changes fall within s 171(2). Section 171(2) is concerned with changes as follows:

- an addition to the property comprised in the estate;

- an increase or decrease of value of the property in the estate; but not a decrease that arises on capital reconstruction of a company arising on death (which does not concern us here); but

- termination on the death of any interest is excluded as is the passing of any interest by survivorship.

The interaction of IHTA 1984, ss 161 and 171 was considered in *Arkwright v IRC [2004] STI 147*. Mr and Mrs Williams had owned Ashland Farm as tenants in common in equal shares. He was 83, she 79 and in good health. He left her a life interest in his half of the farm. His Will was varied so as to give his share to the daughters. The case concerned the value of the share of the house as at the date of the death of Mr Williams.

The property as a whole was worth £550,000, so IRCT valued the half share at £275,000. IRCT noted that s 171(1) was disapplied on the termination on death of any interest or the passing of any interest by the survivorship (as noted above) and applied s 161.

The executors disagreed. Any purchaser of the interest of Mr Williams before his death would have taken account of the fact that Mrs Williams was fit, well, and had a right of occupation of the property. The purchaser would realise that he could not sell the property without the consent of Mrs Williams and that would reduce the price that a purchaser would pay for the share of Mr Williams.

The hearing before the Special Commissioner went perhaps further than was ideal. The Special Commissioner reviewed the legislation and held that the interest of Mr Williams did not pass by survivorship. It went under the terms of the Deed of Variation. The value of his interest in the house would change on the occasion of his death. As a result of his death there would then be a certainty, and not merely a possibility, that he would die first. That decrease in the value of his share occurred by reason of his death and should be taken into account in valuing his interest. When considering s 161 the Commissioner held that one must first value the whole and then value each share as a proportion of that whole but that did not necessarily mean, in the present situation, that each share was necessarily one half. Thus, as far as the Commissioner was concerned, the value of the share of Mr Williams in the house was not necessarily one-half.

On appeal to the High Court, Gloster J in part agreed with the Revenue argument that the Special Commissioner had gone a little too far in deciding the basis of valuation. The Special Commissioner had been entitled to conclude that the value of the interest of Mr Williams was not necessarily one-half but had gone too far in determining that, as a matter of fact, the value of the interest was less than one-half. That was a matter for the Lands Tribunal. That view was upheld by the Court of Appeal.

Development value

17.13 A house with a large garden enjoying road access may be attractive to a builder or developer. If so, that should be reflected in the probate value, say HMRC in their IHT Newsletter of 28 April 2006. This will also be true if new information emerges that enhances the value of the land. This principle was explored in *Prosser v IRC (DET/1/2000)*, where a plot of land had hope value at the date of death. The Lands Tribunal put its value at 25% of development value.

Fall in value relief

17.14   At para 17.6 above the situation was examined where property had risen in value following the death. It has not happened much until the last few months, but clearly values can go the other way and when they do it would be harsh for the taxpayer to have to pay tax on a greater value than he can actually recover on sale of the property. IHTA 1984, ss 190–198 provide relief. Essentially, if land is sold at arm's length within four years of the date of death it may, subject to various qualifications, be possible to substitute the gross sale proceeds for the probate value.

De minimis

17.15   No relief is available where the difference between the gross sale proceeds and the probate value is less than £1,000 or 5% of the value, whichever is lower.

Arm's length transactions

17.16   There is no relief if the sale of the property is by a personal representative, not to a stranger, but to a person who has an interest in the property. More specifically there is no relief on the sale to:

- someone entitled to an interest in possession in the property being sold; or
- the spouse of such a person; or
- the civil partner of such a person; or
- the child of such a person; or
- any remoter descendent of such a person; or
- trustees of a settlement under which such a person has an interest in possession in the property; or
- a sale in connection with which the vendor or any person such as is described in the bullets above obtains a right to acquire the interest.

Identity of the claimant

17.17   The legislation refers to 'the appropriate person' meaning the person who is liable for the IHT attributable to the value of the interest sold. Personal representatives and the trustees of the settlement are each treated as a single and continuing body of persons as distinct from the persons who may at any time hold that office.

'Cherry-picking'

17.18   Where an estate comprises several properties which are sold during the administration period, naturally some may sell for more, and some for less, than probate value. If any claim to relief is made under IHTA 1984, s 191 it must take account of all the sales. It is therefore not possible, except with some ingenuity, to 'cherry pick' the sales where the result has been disappointing and claim a reduction of the IHT on those sales in isolation.

Ingenuity in this context is moderate only. If the value of a particular property is not actually required by the personal representatives to meet liabilities of the estate, such that they can, without difficulty, place it unreservedly at the disposal of the beneficiaries, they may do just that. The beneficiaries take advantage of TCGA 1992, ss 62 and 64 to acquire the property at probate value and sell it themselves. They are not the 'appropriate person' for the purposes of the relief and the personal representatives may restrict their claim to relief to the properties that they sell in their own right.

This facility will not be readily available where estate properties are sold at auction, since the hammer price cannot be forecast with certainty. The executors will have to guess which properties will sell well and appropriate them well before the date of the auction, selling as mere agents for the beneficiaries. Practitioners who choose this course must get all the paperwork right beforehand.

The nature of the interest transferred

17.19   It might at first sight seem quite obvious what is the property that is being taxed in any transaction but cases, in particular concerning the family home on death, highlight the importance of identifying exactly what is being transferred. The difficulty of establishing the exact interest of a person in a trust was highlighted recently in *Stow and others v Stow and others [2008] EWHC 495 (Ch)*. A widow claimed under the Inheritance (Provision for Family and Dependants) Act 1975 that her late husband had personally owned Nigerian assets in some trusts. HMRC issued notices of determination charging IHT on the basis that the deceased had been settlor of the trusts. The trustees, instead of appealing to the Special Commissioners, went to the High Court for a declaration that the deceased was not beneficially interested in the trust funds, which had belonged to a Nigerian business associate. The High Court dismissed the HMRC application to strike out the proceedings: the issue of ownership of the funds affected not only IHT but also income tax which had been assesed on the deceased. Where a dispute affects more than just what is in issue in a notice of determination, the Special Commissioners do not have exclusive jurisdiction.

Personal estate

17.20   The simplest case is the transfer by the taxpayer, in lifetime or on death, of the whole of what he or she owns. Matters become more complicated where the taxpayer does not own the entirety. First there are the valuation issues of shares in land already discussed. The second issue is the examination of whether the transferor has an interest in the share of land only or in a greater entity.

Example 3: Eating your cake and still having it

Doreen and Ernest were married for many years and from the 1960s onwards owned their properties jointly as joint tenants. Doreen died in 2000 leaving her estate to Ernest. On advice, Ernest entered into a Deed of Variation of Doreen's Will under which the joint tenancy in the property was severed and Doreen was treated as leaving her half share in the family home to her daughter Frances and her savings to her granddaughter Gemma. The gift in the Deed to Frances was a simple and absolute gift, without any kind of restriction on the ability of Frances to deal with the half share.

In 2006 Ernest died, by his Will leaving his half of the family home to Gemma. The issue for the executors to decide on completing the Inland Revenue Account in Ernest's estate was the extent of his interest. The simple answer might be that at his death Ernest had an interest in one half only of the family home and that interest should be discounted, say, 10% because the other half at that point was owned by his daughter and was therefore not related property. The alternative view would be that, from Doreen's death until the death of Ernest, Frances had not really had any benefit at all from her inheritance. She had not lived at the property, merely visiting it occasionally to keep an eye on her father. She had not mortgaged her interest in order to raise capital for her husband's business. She had not really had any advantage at all. It could therefore be argued that, to all intents and purposes, the entire benefit of Doreen's share in the house actually rested with Ernest during widowhood such that in effect he had a life interest in the half of the house, with remainder to Frances.

In the light of FA 2008, s 10 and Sch 4 and the new rules as to the transferable nil-rate band, any such argument should be pursued. The terms of the Deed of Variation did not impose the 'elaborate provisions' that applied in *IRC v Lloyds Private Banking Ltd [1998] STC 559*. However, Frances actually did nothing with her share of the house. If her business had failed, her creditors could have claimed against her interest in the house; but in the event nothing of the kind occurred. The way that IHT200 is now formulated will force Ernest's executors to disclose the situation. They should claim that Ernest had an interest in possession under Doreen's will and that, to that extent, she had not used her nil rate band so it is available now to Ernest's executors.

'Old' interest in possession trusts

17.21   FA 2006 changed the landscape of trusts, preserving the position of interests in possession that existed prior to 22 March 2006, allowing some transitional relief until 5 April 2008. As will be seen in connection with Agricultural Property Relief (APR) at paragraph **17.30** below, the linkage between outright ownership of land and holding an interest in possession can be important to securing the relief. From 23 March 2006 onwards it is still possible for interests in possession to arise, in relation for example to disabled trusts or deemed interests in possession that arise under Statement of Practice 10/79, or as noted below, immediate post-death interests; but many of the situations in which an interest in possession could have been created, for example accumulation and maintenance trusts and interest in possession trusts created in lifetime, are no longer possible.

The present Government does not much like the structure of a long-running trust. With, perhaps, more emotion than accuracy, the structure of the trust was roundly criticised in the debates on Finance Bill 2006 as a situation in which an interest 'disappears into the labyrinth'. Given that attitude, it is as surprising as it is important that transitional relief was allowed. The basic structure is that the termination of old interests in possession can still be a PET where the fund in which the interest in possession subsisted becomes the absolute property of another individual but, with the one exception next described, it will no longer generally be possible to maintain a succession of life interests. The relevance of this can be seen in an example.

Example 4: Generation skipping

Hugo, a successful businessman, left his estate to his wife Ingrid for life with remainder on such trusts, for such of his children and further issue, as Ingrid should by Deed or Will appoint. Ingrid's income from her own savings and from Hugo's pension plan was sufficient for her needs and she was happy to give away her interest in Hugo's estate. Her son, John, was well provided for, so Ingrid wanted to benefit her teenage grandchildren Kylie and Liam (though their aspirations were to a lifestyle epitomised by better known holders of those names).

On advice, Ingrid created transitional serial interests under IHTA 1984, s 49C for Kylie and for Liam for life, with powers to advance capital and with remainders over. This should all have been done well before the deadline of 5 April 2008 but there were delays. Ingrid was mightily relieved (as were her advisers!) to learn that FA 2008, s 141 had extended the deadline to 5 October 2008. What Ingrid had in mind was that the capital of the trust fund was effectively safe from dissipation because it remained in the hands of the trustees. Should her grandchildren ever settle down and marry or form civil partnerships, exemptions would be available to them under IHTA 1984, s 18.

There would be no immediate charge to IHT. If Ingrid survived seven years there would be no charge at all. There would be no charge to CGT because the fund remained with the trustees. The trustees could advance capital if it should be needed but if it was not, Kylie and Liam would actually have old-style interests in possession. They would be able, if they wished, to terminate their interest in the trust fund wholly or in part in favour of a spouse or civil partner. By this means, even if the fund was from time to time equal to four nil-rate bands, it might not be taxed for many years to come.

Immediate post death interests (IPDIs)

17.22   The requirements for such interests is that they comply with IHTA 1984, s 49A, being trusts that are created on death under which a beneficiary is immediately entitled to an interest in possession. The interest can be created either by a Will or under the provisions as to intestacy but either way it must come into being on the death of the testator or the intestate. There are two further conditions to be satisfied. One of these is to distinguish this kind of interest from other interests that do qualify as interest in possession. It is condition 3, set out in s 49A(4), and excludes from the category of IPDI both bereaved minors' trusts under IHTA 1984, s 71A and trusts for disabled persons.

The final qualification, condition 4, is that the requirements of condition 3 have been satisfied throughout the time from which the beneficiary holding the IPDI became entitled to an interest in possession. The intention of Parliament, as expressed in the debate on the Finance Bill 2006, was to leave as an interest in possession only the simplest form of family provision and as far as possible to reduce the scope for creating ongoing trusts with successive interests.

Relevant property trusts

17.23   Except for trusts with preferred status such as immediate post-death interests, transitional serial interests, trusts for bereaved minors, 18–25 trusts, and trusts for disabled persons, most trusts now created will be relevant property trusts and, unless they qualify for an exemption such as for charity, their creation will be an immediately chargeable transfer. This produces the result, which at first seemed anomalous, that the creation of a lifetime settlement for a spouse is a relevant property trust and is a chargeable transfer.

IHT on lifetime transfers

Reporting requirements

17.24   Before FA 2006 there were relatively few transfers that required reporting. For example the establishment of a pilot trust was and still is excepted under the Inheritance Tax (Delivery of Accounts) (Excepted Settlements) Regulations 2002 (SI 2002/1732) ie one

- which is of cash only;

- which receives no further property from the settlor after its initial creation;

- where the trustees are resident in the UK;

- where the gross value of the property initially settled does not exceed £1,000; and

- where there are no related settlements.

Apart from that, the establishment of 'small' settlements benefited from reduced requirements under the Inheritance Tax (Delivery of Accounts) (Excepted Transfers and Excepted Terminations) Regulations 2002 (SI 2002/1731) 'the 2002 Regulations', so that, broadly, a transfer of less than £10,000 did not require reporting provided that it and other chargeable transfers by the same transferor in the ten years before did not exceed £40,000.

FA 2006 had the result that many family gifts which would previously have been potentially exempt became chargeable, although, if within the nil-rate band, would generate no tax charge either on creation or, possibly, later. If no action had been taken this would have greatly increased the burden of processing transfers without actually yielding any tax (at least in the early stages of such trusts). To address this, the Inheritance Tax (Delivery of Accounts) (Excepted Transfers and Excepted Terminations) Regulations 2008 (SI 2008/605) and the Inheritance Tax (Delivery of Accounts) (Excepted Settlements) Regulations 2008 (SI 2008/606) were laid before Parliament on 6 March 2008.

The regulations as to excepted transfers and excepted terminations come into force on 6 April 2008 and, in relation to the transactions covered by the regulations, remove the obligation to deliver an account unless HMRC serve a notice requiring one. For some purposes they are retrospective to 6 April 2007. Trustees must still file an account in respect of failed PETs. Both trustees and others must file an account on the termination of a settlement which would have been a PET, but fails under the seven-year rule. Similarly, there is a duty to file a return where the parties thought that the transfer was excepted within the new rules and it turns out not to be.

Excepted transfers

17.25 An excepted transfer under the new rules is one made by an individual and is an actual transfer, not a deemed transfer. There are two categories, according to whether the value of the transfer can be identified when made. Where the transfer is either cash or quoted shares or securities the transfer will be excepted if the value transferred, together with values of chargeable transfers by that transferor in the preceding seven years, do not exceed the current nil rate band.

Where, however, the transfer includes assets other than cash or quoted shares or securities it is exempt where:

- its value, together with other transfers by that transferor in the preceding seven years do not exceed 80% of the nil-rate band; and

- the value transferred by this particular transfer does not exceed the nil rate band after deducting the value of all the previous chargeable transfers.

For this purpose neither BPR nor APR is to be taken into account, so to be excepted the entire value must be within the limits prescribed.

Example 5: Gift of a share in a flat

Sylvia, who has available to her this year's annual exemption but not that for last year, wishes to give her two nieces a one-quarter interest each in a flat in

London which is let. The flat is worth £500,000. She settles the interest, which might seem to be a gift of £247,000 (£250,000 – £3,000) but for the loss to estate rule. Before the transfer her estate includes the full value; after, she has 50%, which should be discounted, say 15%, and is therefore worth £212,500. The loss to her estate is £284,500 (£287,500 – £300).

At a time when the nil rate band is £312,000, the limit above which the transfer must be reported is 80% of that, £249,600. Sylvia's transfer to the girls must be reported: it is not £247,000, which would have been within the limit, but £284,500.

Example 6

Doting uncle

Jim, having used his annual exemptions, put cash into a series of small discretionary trusts for his nieces totalling £37,500 in the years 2002–06. That was all below the old filing rules. He has used his annual exemption for this year but now proposes to settle another £215,000 which will bring his cumulative total to £252,500, well over the limit under the old 2002 Regulations.

The limit is now the nil rate band of £312,000 for this year and, since Jim has £274,500 of the nil-rate band left he will not have to file an IHT100.

Transactions during the currency of a trust

17.26 Where a chargeable event affects a trust but no tax is immediately in issue, the intention of the new rules is that there should be no duty to deliver an account. Note that the use of a power of appointment within two years of death, which relates back to the death under s 144, need not be reported.

The rules as to excepted terminations apply only to 'specified' trusts, ie:

- interest in possession trusts that existed before Budget Day 2006;

- trusts for bereaved minors under s 71A(c);

- IPDI trusts within s 49A;

- disabled persons trusts; or

- TSI trusts within ss 49B–49E.

The termination of an interest in possession in a trust can be a chargeable transfer, but it need not be reported in one of three circumstances:

- The transfer may be small, for example within the annual exemption, and the life tenant may have served notice under s 57(3) that an exemption is available. If the amount of the transfer is within the specified exemption, there is no need for a return.

- Where the trust property is cash or quoted securities and the value of the fund in respect of which the termination takes place, and the value of transfers by the tenant for life of any other kind together are within the nil rate band, there is no need for an account.

- Where the trust fund does not consist wholly of cash or quoted securities there is still no need to file a return if the value of the 'termination fund' and of previous chargeable transfers by the life tenant in the previous seven years do not exceed 80% of the nil rate band.

These termination rules, like those for excepted settlements, take no account of APR or of BPR. The 2008 regulations replace those made in 2002 in relation to lifetime transfers made on or after 6 April 2007.

Pilot trusts

17.27 The new rules reduce the filing requirements for pilot trusts and small settlements. There is no need to file a return in respect of a pilot trust, ie a settlement made to UK trustees who stay in the UK of cash of £1,000 or less where there are no related settlements. Apart from that, the new Excepted Settlements Regulations dispense with filing of a return in respect of:

- UK trusts (which remain in the UK); by

- settlors domiciled in the UK at the time the settlement is made;

- who remain domiciled here until either the chargeable event or the death of the settlor whichever first happens, where

  - there are no related settlements; and

  - one of the following conditions is met.

Extra condition 1: to avoid filing for a ten-year charge. The trust is excepted where the value in the trust at the anniversary is not more than 80% of the nil rate band (disregarding liabilities or reliefs such as APR or BPR).

Extra condition 2: to avoid filing for the exit charge in the first ten years of the trust. The language of reg 4(5) is somewhat obscure, but it concerns the value that is transferred by the notional chargeable transfer which is one element of calculating the exit charge in the first ten years of the relevant property trust. Take no account of liabilities or reliefs such as APR and BPR. On an exit charge in the first ten years of a relevant property trust, there is no need for a return if the value released from the trust does not exceed 80% of the nil rate band.

Extra condition 3: to avoid filing for an exit charge after the first ten-year anniversary. There is no need to file a return if the value of the transfer does not exceed 80% of the nil rate band.

Extra condition 4: to avoid filing for an exit charge from an 18-to-25 trust. There is no need for a return where the chargeable transfer is within 80% of the nil rate band.

Death of transferor

17.28 Trustees may have received sums which are well within the nil rate band and may have appointed funds out, again well within the levels that are now exempt from reporting. If the settlor had made other transfers, such as PETs, in the seven years before death those PETs will fail on his death. There will be a 'knock-on' effect on the trust because, when seen in the context of the failed PETs, the transfers that were previously exempt from reporting must now be shown in an account. Depending on the value there might not be any extra tax to pay, but the return must be filed.

There is draft guidance, with illustrations, IHTM 06100 to 06130; or see http://www.hmrc.gov.uk/cto/iht/ets-draft-guidance.pdf and, for example, the detailed guidance there on discounted gift schemes and their valuation at IHTM 06105. A duty to file may arise on discovery within six months, if the amount of discount claimed was wrong.

Under the new regulations, there is no duty to file a return if the transfers are covered by the rules as to the nil rate band; but if greater, even if within another exemption such as IHTA 1984, s 21 (normal expenditure out of income) the transfers are assumed for this purpose to be chargeable, and reportable, because HMRC have not been satisfied that the exemption applies.

A taxpayer may have thought that a transfer was outside the filing rules and realise the error later. If so, as with the discount situation mentioned above, he has six months to put things right.

Bare trusts

17.29 Few taxpayers or their advisers want the complication or the immediate tax charge that follow the creation of a relevant property trust, yet they want to start the seven-year period running on a gift of, say, land or shares to a child under 18. Many have resorted to creating bare trusts; but have included administrative powers in the document, in particular in relation to Trustee Act 1925, s 31.

HMRC raised the issue that in certain circumstances such trusts were substantive, and not bare, trusts, because the trustees had active duties to perform and the arrangement might be 'a trust to accumulate the income'. Even if Trustee Act 1925, s 31 had been excluded, the trustees would, really, have to accumulate because they would not pay to the child.

The professional bodies have strenuously resisted the argument (see the websites of CIOT (The Chartered Institute of Taxation) at http://www.tax.org.uk/ and STEP (The Society of Trust and Estate Practitioners) at http://www.step.org/) but the position remains unclear. It may have to be litigated.

Reliefs from IHT

Agricultural property relief

17.30   This relief has been considered in detail in **Chapter 11** at paragraph **11.13**. From the point of view of the practitioner there is an important distinction between agricultural relief and business relief, discussed at **17.32** below. Agricultural relief is available in respect of the categories of property enumerated in IHTA 1984, s 115 and in many instances there need be no connection between the ownership of the asset and the carrying on of the activity upon which relief is based. That is in sharp contrast to the treatment of land and interests in land for the purposes of business relief, where the connection between the ownership of the land or interest and the running of a business is close.

In relation to bare land it must be shown either that the land was occupied by the transferor for the purposes of agriculture throughout the two years preceding the transfer; or that it was owned by the transferor for seven years prior to the transfer and was throughout that period occupied (by him or another) for agricultural purposes: see IHTA 1984, s 117.

Doubt persists as to what is a sufficient agricultural purpose. To take an extreme example, *Dixon v IRC (SpC 297) [2002] SWTI 43* tells us that a rural cottage enjoying a reasonable sized garden that was intermittently used for purposes recognisable by any devotee of The Good Life did not constitute agricultural property.

A more common situation, in relation to marginal land, is specifically covered by IHTA 1984, s 142C so that land within a habitat scheme is regarded as agricultural land. Land that was formerly farmed but which is now largely left fallow because its owner relies upon the Single Farm Payment for his only income from the land is probably still treated as occupied for the purposes of agriculture.

IHTA 1984, s 115(4) provides that the use of land as a stud farm is agricultural use. This includes the breeding and rearing of horses and grazing them in connection with those activities. The loose boxes and other buildings used in connection with the stud farm are treated as farm buildings.

Farming need not be profitable. Many agricultural communities will appreciate that. There are few cases directly in point, and HMRC have in the IHT manual to Inspectors at paragraph 24049 put forward the argument that stud farming must be viable to qualify for the relief, but actually that assertion is without direct authority in the statute. This again is an example of the distinction between agricultural relief and business relief. Business relief (see IHTA 1984, s 103(3)) is not available in respect of a business that is 'carried on otherwise than for gain'.

Woodlands

17.31   This relief has been explored extensively in **Chapter 12**. It is seldom encountered in practice. There are good reasons. First, it is essentially a relief of deferral only. Second, the basis of charge on disposal is excessively complicated, requiring much detail to calculate the deduction of expenses or credit for tax charged on an earlier occasion and, for example, the 50% reduction under IHTA 1984, s 127 is little known and complicated to establish. Third, where it can be shown that there is commercial occupation of woodlands and where the requirements for business relief can be established, business relief is infinitely preferable. As a result, in many respects woodlands relief is not worth having.

Business property relief

17.32 Chapter 2 examined some of the issues that divide investment in property from dealing and the same distinctions, and others, must be addressed when formulating a claim to Business Property Relief (BPR) under IHTA 1984, s 104. There are six categories of the relief but few are of interest to the land owner. We may therefore ignore for most practical purposes the categories of business property that comprise company securities and shares.

Property as a business: the 100% claim

17.33 It was widely thought until recently that, whilst property that consists of a business or an interest in a business could qualify for relief at 100% under IHTA 1984, s 105(1)(a), the underlying land was not in itself a business: something had to be done with it. That view was successfully challenged in the *Nelson Dance* case examined below, which may be subject to appeal. The closest to a 'pure property play' qualifying for the relief to come before the courts was the Hertford case. In *Seymour 9th Marquis of Hertford and others (executors of Marquis of Hertford deceased) v IRC (2004) SPC 444* the Special Commissioner had to consider Ragley Hall, a grade I listed historic house. The whole of the outside of the building was accessible to the public view and by volume 78% of the interior was also open, the remainder being occupied by the taxpayer, his son and their families as living quarters.

In 1991 the taxpayer gave his son a business: the opening of a historic house to the public, Ragley Hall itself, its contents, the goodwill of the opening business, copyrights in the catalogues and brochures, book debts, cash in hand and at the bank and the benefit of all contracts, motor vehicles, foodstuffs, beverages and other chattels used in the business. The taxpayer died within seven years of the gift triggering the clawback provisions for BPR in IHTA 1984, s 113A.

The executors claimed 100% relief on the whole gift: the whole of the Hall qualified for 100% relief because the whole of the building was one of the assets that was used in the business. It was part of the net value of the business for the purposes of establishing relief under IHTA 1984, s 110(b). IRCT (as they then were) argued for restriction of relief to the part of the building that was open to the public. This was not, as one might have thought, a case turning on IHTA 1984, s 112 (which excludes from relief the value of excepted assets).

It was held that, if an asset was wholly or mainly used for the purposes of the business concerned, there was actually no procedure for proportioning relief. It was not appropriate to divide Ragley Hall into two assets. There was no separate business of showing only the exterior of the building. The brochure showed the whole building. It was difficult to draw the line between the area that the public could see and the private quarters. The Hall was, in the normal sense of the word, a single asset and it was simply not possible to divide the Hall in any sensible way so as to exclude part from relief. It was plainly important as a single structure and the whole building was a vital backdrop to the business carried on.

Farmland enjoys valuable relief as such but where it has development value the taxpayer will hope to avoid the restriction to relief on agricultural value only and will seek BPR, which can exempt the full market value. That was at the heart of two recent cases. In *Dance Family Settlement (Trustees of the) v Revenue and Customs Cormrs [2008] SWTI 1394, SpC 682* Mr Dance, a farmer, transferred land to a settlement. Agricultural relief was not in issue: the taxpayer wanted business relief, because the land had development value. HMRC denied relief on the basis that what Mr Dance transferred was not an interest in his farming business but a 'mere asset'.

He successfully argued that we must look, not at the asset transferred, but at the transfer of value and apply the 'loss to the estate' principle. His estate was reduced by the transfer: what was reduced was the value of his farming business; he had been in farming for many years; so the transfer of value fell to be reduced by business relief. The Special Commissioner could see a distinction between those cases, such as spouse relief, where the recipient is important, and the present situation, where the basis of relief is the transfer, not the underlying asset, commenting (at para 16):

> 'All these form part of an overall scheme. Everything turns on the loss in value to the donor's estate, rather than what is given or how the loss to the estate arises, except where the identity of the recipient is crucial to a particular exemption.'

If it should still be necessary to say whether a particular asset is a business or a 'mere asset' we must refer to the line of old cases that used to be relevant to the old CGT Retirement Relief, then fell into disuse but which may now enjoy a revival of interest in applying the new CGT Entrepreneurs' Relief, for example *McGregor (Inspector of Taxes) v Adcock [1977] STC 206; Mannion (Inspector of Taxes) v Johnston [1988] STC 758; Atkinson v Dancer [1988] STC 758* and *Pepper (Inspector of Taxes) v Daffurn [1993] STC 466.*

The second recent case was *McCall (personal representatives of McClean, decd) v Revenue and Customs Comrs [2008] STC (SCD) 752, [2008] SWTI 1256,* where a parcel of land had an agricultural value, at the date of death, of £165,000 but a market value of £5,800,000. It was clearly important for the executors to show that there was, at the date of death, a business qualifying for BPR rather than an agricultural interest.

The evidence, though not entirely convincing, showed that the son-in-law of the deceased had spent time looking after the land. It lay on the edge of a town in Northern Ireland. Neighbours were a problem: a van was driven into the fields and abandoned, resulting in a claim for compensation for criminal damage. The son in law walked the land, repaired fencing, cleaned drinking troughs, cleared the drains, cut and sprayed weeds, probably working no more than 100 hours per year. Some work was contracted out. The grazier fertilised the fields.

It was held that the son in law's activity 'was, just, enough to constitute a business'. The deceased had lost her mental faculties, though that was not relevant to the issue as to whether the business should qualify for relief. The business was more than just the ownership of the land and receipt of its income. The deceased, despite her disability, owned the business constituted by the activities of her son-in-law and the letting of the land.

However, it was 'the wrong kind of business': it consisted wholly or mainly of holding investments, within s 105(3). The management activities related to letting the land; it was unlike a 'pick your own' fruit farm, where after months of weeding, fertilising, spraying and pruning, customers could enter to take the produce and pay by the pound for what they take away. In the taxpayer's business 'there was less preparatory work, the fields were let for the accommodation of the cattle as well as for the grazing, and the rent was paid by the acre rather than by the ton of grass eaten'.

The right kind of business was however noted in *Executors of Piercy (deceased) v R & C Comrs SpC 687 [2008] SWTI 1647*, where HMRC claimed that the business of a property company was mainly investment but the Special Commissioner agreed with the executors that it continued to hold its land as trading stock that it wished to develop. The only type of land-dealing company that fails the 'wholly or mainly' test of s 105(3) is a dealing or speculative trading company that does not actively develop or build. To be an investment company, it must actually have some investments. This decision may prove very useful in future, though it has only the authority of a low tribunal.

Land used in a business: the 5% claim

17.34 Where land is used as part of the business, as is more normal and less contentious, the relief will not be under IHTA 1984, s 105(1)(a) but will be under s 105(1)(d) or (e) and in either case the relief will be at 50% only. These last categories relate to land or buildings (and other assets not the subject of this book) which, immediately before the relevant transfer, were used wholly or mainly for certain business purposes. Under s 105(1)(d) the business is one carried on by a company controlled by the transferor or by a partnership of which the transferor was a member. Section 105(1)(e) allows the relief where the land was used for a business carried on by the transferor himself but where the land was settled property in which the transferor had an interest in possession. A common example of the category might be farmland in a family settlement where the tenant for life is the farmer.

Business relief will not be available where the business itself is carried on otherwise than for gain. In practical terms this means that the practitioner can expect HMRC to call for the accounts of the business to be satisfied that it is a 'proper' viable business and not merely a property-related hobby. This may be the theoretical basis for the HMRC argument already noted at **17.30** in connection with stud farms, ie that a 'farm must be a viable business': but that argument is weak.

The 'wholly or mainly' test

17.35 IHTA 1984, s 105(3) excludes investments from business relief so the property portfolio of an investor will generally not qualify. This issue was addressed in detail in *Clark (executors of Clark decd) v Revenue and Customs Comrs (2005) SPC 502 2005*. The case concerned relief in respect of the shares in a company but is equally relevant to the ownership by a sole trader of a property portfolio. A partnership, established in 1895, was later incorporated. In the 1920s it built many homes. In hard times the company bought back many of the properties and leased them to the former purchasers. The company had its own work force to deal with the substantial amount of maintenance and refurbishment required. At the date of the taxpayer's death the company owned 92 dwellings, 4 shops, 4 offices, 2 industrial units and 20 lock-up garages. The taxpayer's family owned another 141 properties, all requiring active management. The company managed its own properties and Clark family properties. The directors spent about three-quarters of their time in managing the rental activity and the remainder on building works.

The executors, in a direct challenge to earlier cases, argued that the letting of property was no mere investment activity. It was so time-consuming that it constituted a business. The shares of the company should qualify for business relief. HMRC argued that activities that produce a rent are necessarily investment. There was a distinction between managing properties for third parties, such as members of the Clark family, and managing the properties that were still owned by the company. A management fee was not the same as rent.

It was held that the business of the company consisted 'mainly' of holding investments. The Commissioner looked at the business in the round, reviewing profit, the overall context, capital employed, time spent by the directors and the turnover. The profit on building and management activities was too small to bear the proportion of management time that was spent on it. The rental activity subsidised the other activity. Investment activity produced more turnover and profit but took less time. The main asset shown in the accounts related to the investment activity.

This decision confirmed the earlier cases of *Moore v IRC* and *Burkingyoung v IRC [1995] STC (SCD) 29*. The test, in respect of property, is the nature of income that is received. If the income is mainly rent it matters not how diligent the landlord is in managing his estate: if his work is referable to the drawing in of rents his is an investment activity.

The caravan park cases

17.36 There is a string of authority, mainly concerning caravan parks, which reinforces this principle. Thus in *Hall (executors of Hall deceased) v IRC [1997] STC (SCD) 126* a caravan park was refused relief even though much work was done on it. Part of the site contained wooden chalets that were let on 45-year leases. It was not a touring caravan park. The caravans were static. There was no right to occupy them during the winter. On balance the commissioner regarded the caravan park as being mainly a business which consisted of the making or holding of investments. 84% of the total income came from rents and from standing charges, which was enough to deny BPR.

Powell (personal representatives of Pearce deceased and IRC [1997] STC (SCD) 181 also concerned a caravan park with pitches for long term and short term lettings and again there was evidence of the work that the family did in looking after the residents many of whom were long term and retired. Few of the sites were on short term lets. The income came from pitch fees.

Brendan Peter James Furness (SPC202) went in favour of the taxpayer. This was a very different set-up, with evidence that the park was licensed both for static and for touring caravans. There were rallies at the weekend. No permanent residence was allowed. 80% of the taxpayer's time was spent in looking after the welfare of the residents at the caravan park, maintaining it and its structures, with three people employed full time to help. Less than half the net rent for the business came from pitch fees. There was much income from caravan sales. Even without the evidence of the source of profit, which might have been enough to sway the Commissioner, the very considerable amount of work done persuaded the Commissioner to allow relief. The work was not what one would normally find in a business that was concerned wholly or mainly with holding of investments.

Caravan owners have however suffered a setback in the decision in *Weston (executor of Weston) deceased v IRC [2001] STC 1064*, but that was not a holiday park. It lay near the M25 and was residential, for people aged 50 or over. There was no shop nor social club, just a laundry and storeroom. Pitch fees usually exceeded the fees from sales and there were few sales anyway. In every year but one from 1988–1994 pitch fees exceeded the income from sales.

The most detailed examination of the issue was in *Stedman's executors v IRC [2002] STC (SCD) 358*, later *IRC v George and another [2003] EWCA Civ 1763, [2004] STC 147*, which concerned a substantial business comprising a residential homes park, a club for residents, caravan storage and other property. Whilst some of the income was clearly investment income, taking the business in the round only 40% of turnover came from 'investment type' income. The decision of the Special Commissioner was overturned by the High Court but restored by the Court of Appeal which recognised this to be a hybrid business. The holding of property as an investment was only one part of the business and, on the findings of fact of the Commissioner, not the main part. It was difficult to see why an active family business such as that comprised in this case should fail to qualify for BPR simply because one necessary component of the making of profits was the use of land.

One case much relied upon by taxpayers is *Farmer (executors of Farmer deceased) v IRC [1999] STC SCD (321)* where the taxpayer both farmed and let surplus property, making no distinction in his accounts between the two activities. The holding was 449 acres of which farmland and woodland accounted for 441. Eight acres was either tracks or let properties. There were 23 tenancies, mainly shorthold or licenses. The landlord was responsible for repairs and supplied water to the tenants. The farmhouse, farm buildings and farmland were a very significant proportion of the whole and the let property amounted to a little more than a third.

The Special Commissioner, considering all relevant factors, did not rely exclusively on the way in which profits were earned. The business was that of a landed estate. Most of the land was used for farming. The let properties were subsidiary not only because they occupied a relatively small proportion of the total area but also because they were sited towards the centre of the land and would not have existed but for their connection with the farm. The business consisted mainly of farming and the let property was not an excluded asset under IHTA 1984, s 112. Applying the principle that we have seen in the later case of *Hertford*, discussed as 17.33 above, once it had been decided that there was a single business for the purposes of IHTA 1984, s 105, all the relevant assets qualified for that relief.

Unwise gifts of land

17.37 Since the availability of relief under IHTA 1984, s 105(1)(d) rests on control of a company or membership of a partnership, care must be taken not to jeopardise relief by unwise action.

Example 7: Tardy conveyancing

Michael owned, with his sons Nigel and Oliver, a printing business. Michael held 60% of the shares and his sons 20% each. He also owned the premises from which the company traded and wished to reduce the value of his estate by lifetime gifts. He therefore proposed to give Nigel and Oliver the premises and most of his shares. He gave instructions to his solicitors and accountants, hoping the work could be completed by a date that was significant for family purposes. The accountant duly prepared the stock transfers which were ready on the appointed day but there were difficulties with the conveyancing because of rights of way and other environmental matters, as well as defects in the title.

Anxious to make progress, on the due day Michael executed the transfers of the shares, retaining a nominal 20% holding. The conveyancing was completed two months later.

The result of this delay was that, at the time of the transfer of the property, relief was no longer available under the precise terms of IHTA 1984, s 105(1)(d) because by then Michael no longer controlled the company. There is no relief at all on the transfer of a 'mere asset' even though it may be used for business purposes. Thus the family were on risk of a charge to IHT if Michael should die within seven years which, as to 50%, might have been sheltered by relief (if not clawed back under IHTA 1984, s 113A). The lawyer ended up finding, out of his own pocket, the cost of term assurance on Michael's life for 40% of one-half of the value of the transfer.

Example 8: Clawback conundrum

Percy owned, with his sons Quentin and Richard, a business of running health clubs and saunas. He held 46% of the shares, his sons 23% each. Like Michael in the previous example he wished to hand on the business and the land from which it traded. His advisers were better organised than Michael's and the transfer from Percy's sole name of the freehold to Quentin and Richard in equal shares was done whilst Percy still owned 54% of the company. As a result, the gift of the land qualified for BPR at 50% under IHTA 1984, s 105(1)(d).

There were no 'lazy' assets in the company: there was nothing that fell foul of IHTA 1984, s 112 as an 'excepted asset'. When Percy transferred his shares to Quentin and Richard in equal shares he believed that he had done everything that he possibly could to help his sons and to mitigate the burden of IHT on his estate. As it happened, 50% of the value of the land came to less than the nil-rate band available to Percy and the transfer of the shares qualified in every respect for relief at 100% under IHTA 1984, s 105(1)(bb). The whole transaction appeared to be entirely within the spirit of relief for business property from IHT. What could go wrong?

Sadly, Percy died less than seven years after the gifts. It became necessary to re-examine the gifts in the light of IHTA 1984, s 113A. It then appeared that Quentin and Richard had, as they thought, done everything correctly. They had not sold the land. They continued to run the business and to sweat its assets. They were dismayed to learn of a possible charge to IHT on the transfer to them of the land because of the operation of s 113A(3). The clawback provisions for BPR are no doubt intended to deny relief where the taxpayer no longer 'deserves' the relief, because the business no longer continues or the taxpayer has sold it or other similar events have occurred; but that is not how the legislation works. It operates by examining an imaginary transfer by the transferee of the relevant asset at the date of the enquiry. In this case it will be seen that Quentin and Richard both own the land but, since they are equal shareholders in the company, neither of them satisfies the requirements of s 105(1)(d) because neither of them controls the company. This seems both illogical and unfair.

Heritage relief

Practical problems: timing the claim

17.38 This relief is a specialised topic and reference should be made to the relatively few published works for detailed analysis. One area where it may arise is as a 'default' relief in respect of substantial landed houses. A claim may have been made that the residence in question is a farmhouse qualifying for relief under IHTA 1984, s 115(2). However, such claims are resisted firmly, as the taxpayer was to learn in *Arnander, Lloyd and Villiers (Executors of McKenna) v Revenue and Customs Comrs [2006] STC (SCD) 800, SpC 565* concerning Rosteague House, Cornwall, which seemed in many respects to satisfy the test of a farmhouse. The house had medieval origins and its title deeds went back to the thirteenth century, the present building being part Elizabethan and part eighteenth century. It was listed Grade II*. In the event, and for the reasons which are described more fully in **Chapter 11**, the building was denied agricultural relief.

It does, however, appear, from the report, that the building was outstanding. It had many period details including 12-pane sash windows, mullioned windows and intricate plastered ceilings. The principal rooms faced south over lawns and had sea views. Its music room could be used for concerts. It failed to qualify as a farmhouse, in part because it was 'larger, grander, more elaborate and more expensive than was required for the reduced farming purposes for which it was in fact used' and, by comparison with other farmhouses – many also listed Grade I, Grade II or Grade II*, it was 'at the very top end of the size of a farmhouse in Cornwall'.

This particular property is an example of the difficulties faced by executors of landed estates. Depending on the location of the property and the circumstances of the family of the taxpayer, the executors may have to consider an application for conditional exemption from IHT as a 'fallback' position if the claim for agricultural relief fails. The difficulty lies in the procedures for heritage relief. Any claim to heritage relief must (see IHTA 1984, s 30(3A)), be made no more than two years after the date of the transfer of value. It took over three years for the case to reach the Special Commissioners in *McKenna* and many practitioners will be aware of negotiations with HMRC that last longer than that. If allowing public access to the family home is acceptable to the family and if there is any real doubt that agricultural relief will be available, executors should not delay to consider the procedures for heritage relief.

The same issue arises in connection with other decisions made by personal representatives in the administration of an estate, such as entering into a deed of variation in reliance on IHTA 1984, s 142. Executors would really like to know where they stand as far as IHT liability is concerned well inside the two year time limit, but that will not always be possible.

All may not be lost. IHT Newsletter, issued to practitioners about twice per year, contained in the issue for April 2001 the point that HMRC have a discretion to allow a longer time than two years. That is clear (for diligent readers of this somewhat specialised legislation) from the wording of IHTA 1984, s 30(3BA). However, as is common with much of the law and practice relating to heritage relief, there are few decided cases and the practitioner is left with a rather difficult situation that the Revenue will consider a late claim on its merits. The best course is probably to make a protective claim though it should be noted that such a claim, made without any realistic prospect of success, could attract the imposition of penalties just as easily as the making of a claim to any other relief where it cannot, in truth, be supported by the circumstances of the case.

The introduction of the transferable nil-rate band between spouses and civil partners in FA 2008 is greatly complicated by the need to take account of the extent to which, on an earlier death, the nil rate band was in fact used. It will be noted, below, that occasionally there is a choice for HMRC, in imposing clawback, as to which former holder of the heritage property to tax. That choice has just become more complicated for both HMRC and the adviser.

The scope of the relief

17.39 As far as land is concerned the main categories of heritage property are:

- land of outstanding scenic or historic of scientific interest;

- a building for the preservation of which special steps should be taken because of its outstanding historic or architectural interest; and

- land essential for the protection of the character and amenities of a building that falls within one of the two categories just mentioned.

It is interesting to note that land that falls within this last category, which might be called 'amenity land', need not be in the same ownership as the other land that it protects. This may be very useful where land is held partly in a trust and partly by a member of the family. There has been debate in recent years, in particular since the overhaul of heritage relief by FA 1998 in respect of transfers of value on or after 17 March in that year, as to what quality of property qualifies, but most of that debate centres upon chattels rather than land.

Public access

17.40 Fundamental to the availability of heritage relief is the extent of public access. IHTA 1984, s 31(2)(b) requires steps to be agreed between the taxpayer and the Treasury for the preservation of the property and for securing 'reasonable access' to the public. The taxpayer must give an undertaking as to the maintenance of the land and the preservation of its character, which in practice will incorporate a detailed plan, the 'Heritage Maintenance Plan' for the management of the land. That does not necessarily mean free right to roam over the entire estate. It will usually be limited to existing and any new permissive rights of way but with appropriate extension to those rights so as to meet the needs of riders and cyclists. HMRC have issued revised guidance at www.hmrc.gov.uk/manuals/ihtmanual/annex.htm which reflects help from National Archives, the Heritage Lawyers' Group and Historic Houses Association. It addresses security issues such as requiring proof of identity from visitors. It may be too much to ask for the documents to be sent in advance, but they may be requested at the time of the visit.

Any application for conditional exemption must include provisions that secure reasonable access to the public including such details as the publication of the terms of the undertaking itself and other information relating to the property. What actually amounts to reasonable access will depend on the nature of the property. The Revenue will seek a certain minimum number of days of access per year and in this the situation of the land is a relevant factor. Less will be demanded of a remote location than might be appropriate for heathland adjoining a conurbation. Generally, the minimum number of days per year for amenity land and exempt buildings will be 25 and may commonly be as much as 156.

For bare land it is likely that access will have to be available all the year round though there may be agreed periods of temporary closure for the purposes of land management or nature conservation. Equally, an outside event such as swine vesicular disease or foot and mouth disease and the attendant restrictions on movement of animals and access to land will override what might otherwise have been a breach of undertakings.

The level of publicity for access that is appropriate will depend on the land itself. Tourist Boards need to know and owners will commonly have to advertise the opening arrangements on one or more suitable publications with national circulation. Commonly the owner will have to display a notice outside the property giving details of the opening arrangements and to agree such other publicity as may be appropriate, including advertisement in some public place in the locality. The actual level of disclosure in respect of land is less demanding than for chattels. The requirements are to show:

- where the land is – for example the name of the estate and the nearest town or village; and

- the name, address and telephone number of the person whom can give further details on respect.

In future, HMRC will not agree conditional exemption until an agreed Heritage Maintenance Plan is in place, but will give a reasonable time for it to be drawn up.

Breach of undertaking

17.41 If the taxpayer fails to observe the terms of the undertaking given in respect of the heritage property, a chargeable event arises. The Tax Bulletin of May 2001 addressing issues raised by foot and mouth disease showed that it would not be regarded as a breach of undertaking for the owner of land to decide, after judging the risks, that access or visits should be suspended. Equally, where there is a commitment to allow visits on a number of pre-arranged days in each year, the Revenue will not normally insist, for tax compliance purposes, that any days missed should be made up later in the year.

The death of the owner of heritage property also triggers a chargeable event, as does the sale of the property itself. Matters become quite complicated where the land concerned is 'associated property' within IHTA 1984, s 32A. These rules apply where heritage property is held by several different persons, perhaps all members of the same family, and relief in respect of assets held by one person rest in part on ownership and appropriate undertakings given by the owner of other property. However, these issues will most often arise where relief is also being claimed in respect of chattels and as such are outside the scope of this work.

The loss or destruction of heritage property is not as such a chargeable event. This will be so even where the owner receives insurance money. It will be different if the taxpayer had clearly done something in breach of an undertaking which in turn caused the loss. Assuming, however, that the damage to the building is partial only, its sale (other than to an approved heritage body) thereafter will be a chargeable event like any other sale. There can be a knock-on effect. If the principal heritage property loses its relief ancillary land also loses its relief because it is not heritage property in its own right.

Clawback charges of heritage relief

17.42 The charge to tax is specialised and complex. In a simple case where there has been only one conditionally exempt transfer of the property before the chargeable event, the relevant person for the purposes of the legislation is the person who made the transfer.

Often, however, heritage property lies within family ownership for generations and in these more complex cases it is necessary to consider the ownership of the heritage property for the period of 30 years leading up to the chargeable event. Where the most recent transfer of the property as more than 30 years ago, the person who made that transfer is the relevant person. Where there have been several transfers, but one only within the last 30 years, that last transferor is the relevant person.

Where, within the last 30 years, there have been two or more transfers, HMRC place the taxpayer in an unenviable position because they may choose whichever of the transfers they please as the 'relevant person'. This is to prevent avoidance of tax by channelling heritage property through impecunious relatives so as to mitigate the clawback charge.

The tax charge is calculated by reference to the relevant person. If alive at the time of the chargeable event, lifetime rates apply, as where an immediately chargeable transfer was made after 17 March 1986. Whilst the nil-rate band may be available to reduce the charge to tax there are no other allowances. In particular neither APR nor BPR is available to reduce the clawback charge; nor is taper relief under IHTA 1984, s 7 available to reduce it.

Where the relevant person has died the rules become more complicated. If the conditionally exempt transfer was made in that person's lifetime the tax is charged at lifetime rates. Where the conditionally exempt transfer was made on the death of the relevant person special rules apply as if the conditionally exempt transfer was also a gift with reservation. By virtue of

IHTA 1984, s 33(2) the lifetime transfer rules apply but the tax is charged at the death rates as the top slice of the estate of the transferor.

Matters are also made more complicated by the fact that, over time, the rates for IHT have changed. It can be imagined that, where one of the deaths occurred at a time when rates were particularly high, that person may be selected as the 'relevant person' for the purposes of the tax if the statute so allows. The changes introduced in FA 2008 add to the complication: see IHTA 1984, s 8C(1)(b) as inserted by FA 2008, Sch 4 and the quite complicated formulae to determine the residual nil-rate band that may be claimed.

The family home

The use of the nil-rate band prior to October 2007

17.43 A problem frequently encountered in practice, but which has been addressed by FA 2008 is the family that is 'asset rich' but not necessarily 'awash with cash', mainly through poor asset allocation. People spend too much on housing. They have poor liquidity. There may be assets of considerable value in overall terms but most of that value cannot be spent, and tax cannot be paid from it because it is represented by the family home. People want to provide for the next generation without suffering hardship now. Although the changes introduced in FA 2008, s 10 and Sch 4 will probably render the established practice unnecessary an illustration is set out below because some understanding of the rules will remain relevant for a time. A number of variations on this scenario may be imagined. The tax rates are those in force for 2007/08.

Example 9A

Jack, aged 69, retired a few years ago. He is the joint owner with his wife, Gill, aged 64, of their house currently valued at £400,000. During their marriage, they have shared their income. There has never been a major gift from one to the other. Jack invested his retirement lump sum. The securities are now worth £140,000. Gill has cash savings of £90,000. Their son Roger is currently embroiled in divorce proceedings. He has two children. Their daughter Mary is a single mother with one daughter.

Jack and Gill originally had straightforward Wills leaving the whole of their estate to the survivor, with a gift over to their children in equal shares and had been advised, under the law as it then stood, that there would be no IHT on the death of the first of them to die but that, on the second death, the combined assets will fall to be taxed as one estate. Ignoring inflation, therefore, and assuming that Jack died first, Gill's estate for taxation would amount to £630,000 (before expenses) of which £300,000 will be taxed at 0% and the balance of £330,000 at 40% – a tax burden of £132,000.

Jack and Gill saw that, the way their Wills had been drawn under the then law, the nil rate band of the first of them to die had effectively been thrown away. (This has been addressed by FA 2008, Sch 4 allowing transfer between spouses of the unused portion of the nil-rate band, but this example illustrates the law pending enactment of that change.) The first to die could have left to the next generation the sum of £300,000 free of tax. The tax on Gill's estate would have been only £12,000, a saving of £120,000. There were however several difficulties. Neither Jack nor Gill had liquid assets amounting to £300,000. They do not wish to put family money at risk by establishing a legacy for Roger. They naturally hoped that they both had some years to live.

Consider a gift by Will of half the house

17.44   We must remember that whilst the rules as to transferable nil-rate band will be of considerable value to the vast majority of the population of the UK, there are still pockets of affluence where two nil-rate bands do not go very far and where the need is to shelter a large residence, worth £2,000,000 or more, from IHT. In the situation outlined above, but substituting higher values, it might seem quite simple for each of Jack and Gill to leave one half of the family home to the next generation. The survivor could go on living in the half of the house that he or she had always owned. However, that kind of arrangement was considered in *IRC v Lloyds Private Banking [1998] STC 559*. On the particular facts it was there held that the Will effectively gave to the surviving spouse such a high degree of security that he had, in effect, a life interest in the part of the property not already owned. As a result the whole of the house fell to be taxed on the death of the surviving spouse – precisely the result which the family had hoped to avoid.

It is argued that, if the Will makes a simple gift to the next generation and gives the surviving spouse absolutely no security, the *Lloyds* case will not apply. That is fair enough, but there are three problems.

- First, many couples will want to give the surviving spouse some security and will not be happy with the idea that a child or child in law might have control over part of the family home.

- Second, if the only case directly in point went against the taxpayer, is it safe to risk a further challenge by HMRC?

- Third, unless the recipient of the share of the house lives there, CGT may become payable on final sale of his share.

The 'debt or charge' scheme

17.45   Until 9 October 2007 the most effective way of addressing this particular problem was to establish the 'debt or charge' scheme. In outline, the will provided for a legacy of the nil rate band. The Will contained provision not only for the nil rate band legacy to be held for the benefit of the family as a whole but also that the amount of the legacy need not be paid immediately in cash. Instead, the trustees of the nil rate band legacy could be required to accept, instead of immediate payment, a promise of payment from the surviving spouse. Generally, the surviving spouse is the beneficiary of the residue of the estate. To see how the scheme used to work in practice we can return to the example of Jack and Gill:

Example 9B

They make Wills incorporating the scheme set out above. They sever their joint tenancy in the house so that one half of the house can pass under the terms of the will and not by survivorship. Their solicitors, mindful of the Court of Appeal decision in *Carr-Glyn v Frearsons [1998] 4 All ER 225*, insist that this is done before the Wills are signed.

Jack dies first. His will leaves the nil rate band to trustees to hold on discretionary trusts. The potential beneficiaries are Gill, Roger, Mary and the grandchildren. Jack's Will leaves the rest of his estate to Gill. The executors, to avoid a SDLT charge, first place a charge on the half share of the house that Jack owned for £285,000 (or such sum as cannot be found in cash from the estate) then, subject to that charge, pass the half share over to Gill.

Jack's estate is administered. There is no IHT because the £300,000 uses up the nil rate band (Jack not having made any chargeable transfers in his lifetime) and the rest of the estate, passing as it does to Gill, is exempt. The residue comprises half the house (£200,000, charged to secure the promise), and probably some of the cash. £100,000 of the cash goes to the trustees.

Gill later reviews her lifestyle. She still has her own savings of £90,000 to which may have been added about £40,000 cash from Jack's estate. The family home is no longer suitable. She 'trades down' to a less expensive property to be closer to Mary, so that she can lend a hand with her granddaughter whilst Mary is at work.

CGT is not a problem: under the scheme Gill is the sole owner of the house, so main residence relief applies to the whole gain she makes. (As already noted, that would not have been the case, had a share of the house been held on discretionary trust. In such a case, either there would have been a deemed life interest under the rule in *Sansom v Peay [1976] 3 All ER 375*, exempting the gain from CGT but putting it squarely within IHT, or there would have been a true discretion, saving IHT but making the gain taxable: an unsatisfactory and uncertain situation.) At the time of the sale, the charge on Jack's half share is called in.

The new property costs £230,000. Gill asks the trustees to lend her some of the money that they received when the house was sold. They review the needs of all the beneficiaries and agree. They take a new mortgage (for a smaller amount) over the new house, which is less expensive to run. Gill can manage on her pension and investment income. Roger's position is now more settled. Gill therefore feels that it is wrong for her still to owe the trustees so much, even though by this time the actual debt is smaller than it was originally. The trustees agree. She repays them part of the sum and asks the trustees to continue to lend her the remainder. She says that, if all goes well, she will pay more later.

The trustees, after they have received the money, again review the needs of the whole family. They decide to keep some of the fund in reserve. Gill is a beneficiary and, if she ever needed to go into a nursing home, there might come a time when her own funds were exhausted. Having made that reserve, they make capital payments to Roger, who is heavily indebted following his divorce, to ease his situation. The trustees also begin to fund some education costs for Mary's daughter, who lives in an area where state educational provision is not as good as might be hoped.

Finally, at a time when the nil rate band is, say, £360,000, Gill dies. Her estate comprises:

Her estate comprises:	£	£
Her house, now worth		380,000
Savings		100,000
		480,000
Debts due at death are:		
Funeral	2,000	
Balance owed to trustees, say	98,000	
		100,000
Net estate thus		380,000

Under the rules in force before October 2007, Gill's executors would pay IHT at 40% on £20,000, being the excess of Gill's estate over the (assumed) nil rate band: they would pay £8,000 only. There would be no IHT on the discretionary fund because she did not have an interest in possession in it.

On sale of the house, the trustees recover £98,000. They still have funds from the earlier repayment of the IOU. There is no IHT charge on the fund resulting from the death of Gill. The trustees appoint all the funds out, the trust having served its purpose and the trustees being keen to avoid the periodic and exit charges that could result if they retained a fund that appreciated in value.

Jack and Gill have both used the allowances available to them.

Practical issues and advice for existing schemes

17.46 For many families, the debt or charge scheme represented an intellectual challenge. It was important that the structure was understood, to avoid the difficulties illustrated in *Wolff v Wolff and Wolff [2004] STC 1633*.

The principle of the 'debt or charge' scheme was challenged by Inland Revenue Capital Taxes in *Phizackerley v IRC*, as described below, on a specific point. The parties must be careful to avoid 'sham'. That is the situation where the documents describe a transaction but the parties intend something different. It was fundamental that the trustees should understand that they had powers and discretions, and where appropriate should use them. For example, there must be no tacit agreement 'never to call in the IOU', since that would effectively make the surviving spouse the owner of the asset, nullifying the scheme. There must at all times exist the possibility of calling in the debt. Equally, the surviving spouse must not be treated as the only possible beneficiary. When the trustees came to exercise their discretion, they must consider the needs of all the beneficiaries.

It did initially seem that the changes in the 2006 Budget would affect the debt or charge scheme. In the event, the introduction of the immediate post-death interest (IPDI) on more generous terms than originally proposed has left much of the original thinking intact. A sophisticated arrangement became available under which a half share of a house can sit within a Will trust in such a way that it is not subject to the burden of CGT and yet not automatically subject to IHT on the death of the surviving spouse because it is not an IPDI. However, this arrangement involves supervision of the administration of the estate for a period of more than two years from the date of death. As a result, it may be more complicated than some people wish to use.

A problem, illustrated in *Phizackerley v HMRC [2007] SpC 00591,* had been known to practitioners for some time but the case gave cause for concern. It relates to the operation of FA 1986, s 103. The mischief to remedy which s 103 was probably enacted is the situation where a person tries in effect to reserve a benefit out of a gift. A gives Blackacre to B and, then or later, B lends £10,000 to A. If at A's death the £10,000 loan is still outstanding it is not deductible in calculating the value of his estate to the extent that Blackacre exceeds £10,000 in value. As will be seen, the effect of this is to prevent A from deriving a £10,000 'cash back' benefit to himself by reference to the gift of Blackacre.

Dr Phizackerley, a consultant biochemist, had lived in tied accommodation until his retirement in 1992 when he and his wife purchased, for £150,000, a small house which was put in their names as joint tenants. A mortgage taken out initially for £30,000 was repaid two years later. The agreed Statement of Facts was that *'Mrs Phizackerley did not work during her marriage, and the funds must have been provided by the Deceased.'* In 1996 Dr Phizackerley severed the joint tenancy so that he and Mrs Phizackerley held the property that they had purchased as tenants in common. The same week Mrs Phizackerley made a Will which left the nil rate sum on discretionary trusts and gave the (relatively small) residue of her estate to her husband (and this was crucial) absolutely. Mrs Phizackerley died early in 2000. Pursuant to the terms of the Will, Mrs Phizackerley's half share in the house was assented to Dr Phizackerley, who promised to pay the trustees of the nil rate sum £150,000 (index-linked). On Dr Phizackerley's death two years later his estate, ignoring the promise of payment to the trustees, was valued at just under £530,000.

Dr John Avery-Jones as Special Commissioner was asked to decide whether the liability, which had meanwhile increased to £153,222.99, was deductible from the estate of Dr Phizackerley or whether that deduction was prevented by FA 1986, s 103.

FA 1986, s 103 prevents the deduction of the debt where, and to the extent that, the consideration given for the debt or encumbrance consists of 'property derived from the Deceased'. The Special Commissioner said that on the face of it, the half share in the house was indeed derived from the deceased. It was the subject matter of a disposition made by the deceased, so the debt incurred by the deceased in favour of the trustees of the nil-rate band was not deductible.

The taxpayer argued that FA 1986, s 103(4) should apply, which would save the situation by disapplying the provisions of s 103(1) because in certain circumstances the initial disposition, the gift, may be left out of account. Those circumstances are that the first disposition was neither:

- a transfer of value; nor

- part of associated operations that included a disposition by the transferor or by anyone else to reduce the value of the estate of the transferor.

The taxpayer, argued that IHTA 1984, s 11 should apply, under which a disposition is not a transfer of value if made by one party to a marriage in favour of another or of a child of either party and for the maintenance of the other party. The most basic requirement 'maintenance' is a roof over one's head.

That argument was rejected by the Revenue. The circumstances of the transfer were 'maintenance'. Dr Phizackerley could provide Mrs Phizackerley with somewhere to live without giving her a half share in the house. IHTA 1984, s 11 is not relevant to transfers between spouses because they are exempt under s 18. Section 11 is needed in cases of divorce or separation. The transaction was a gift, not maintenance.

The Special Commissioner concluded that maintenance ordinarily 'has a flavour of meeting recurring expenses' and that whilst it is wide enough to cover the transfer of an interest in a house that would apply 'only if it relieves the recipient from income expenditure, for example on rent'. The Special Commissioner rejected the maintenance argument and dismissed the appeal.

The introduction of the transferable nil-rate band will make the *Phizackerley* issue relevant only to existing debt or charge schemes, so the commentary, in an earlier edition of this work and elsewhere, will become academic.

It was important, in the implementation of the scheme, that there must always be the 'frisson' of uncertainty that the trustees could at any time call in the loan. Where, following the first death, the surviving spouse decided to 'trade down' in property terms, it was always important for the trustees to call in all or practically all of their debt and to force the surviving spouse to use his or her own resources to purchase the replacement property; and only to help when those resources are used up. Equally, the simple version of the debt or charge scheme, ie the one that is exemplified by the Will of Mrs Phizackerley, remained effective where there had been no substantial gift or disposition between the spouses that fell within FA 1986, s 103(1).

It is probably increasingly common that, at some time during a marriage, particularly in the early years, both husband and wife will work. Most wives will be able to claim, as a matter of simple mathematics and disregarding the attitudes of the courts on divorce, that they have actually made a contribution to the cost of the house and that the purchase of the house in joint names does not lead to the automatic conclusion that '*the funds must have been provided by the Deceased*'. Many families will be able to show that both husband and wife directly or indirectly contributed to the cost of one home after another; and that the family home that is in their joint ownership at the time of the death of the first of them to die is truly owned by them equally and that, for them, the facts of *Phizackerley* can be distinguished.

In cases that are left undisturbed by FA 2008, there is another more serious issue to address. FA 1986, s 103 contains no time limit. The debt which the executors seek to deduct from the estate of the second spouse to die is (see s 103(1)):

'subject to abatement to an extent proportionate to the value of any of the consideration for the debt or encumbrance which consisted of –

(a)   property derived from the Deceased; or

(b)   consideration (not being property derived from the Deceased) given by any person who was at any time entitled to, or amongst whose resources there was at any time included, any property derived from the Deceased.'

It does not matter how long ago the property passed from one spouse to the other, it could still be caught. Clearly, these are matters of proof. Some executors will take a more cavalier approach to their duties in delivering accounts under IHTA 1984, s 216 than they should. If there is any clear link between the debt which is to be deducted from the estate of the surviving spouse and a gift made, however long ago, by that spouse to the first spouse to die, it would seem that *Phizackerley* can apply. This case increases the burden on executors and their advisers, and the risk of the penalty for failure to make proper enquiries.

The practical implications of FA 2008 for existing Wills that incorporate nil-rate band discretionary trusts

17.47   FA 2008, Sch 4 now addresses the problem that the use of nil-rate band trusts was designed to solve. The executors of the surviving spouse or civil partner can claim the benefit of the unused portion of the nil-rate band of the first spouse to die. If part of the then available band was used, only a part of the band, at the rates in force on the second death will be available. 'Serial marriers' may benefit from no more than one unused nil-rate band.

In its simplest form, the change will avoid the tax penalty that used to apply on the aggregation of the estates of spouses who had left everything to each other. It renders the Debt or Charge scheme unnecessary, though many practitioners currently recommend leaving that structure in place in relation to business or agricultural property and to achieve a shelter from care fees.

Example 10

Jonathan and Margaret own a house worth £700,000 but have few other assets save their pensions, which they spend. They sign simple wills leaving everything to each other, remainder on the second death to their children. They have made no lifetime gifts.

On Jonathan's death the whole house becomes Margaret's and she dies still owning it, at a time when the nil-rate band is £325,000. The IHT charge on her death is:

Estate	700,000
Less Jonathan's unused nil-rate band	325,000
Less Margaret's unused nil-rate band	325,000
	50,000
IHT at 40%	20,000

The maximum transferable nil rate band is 100% of that rate at the current rate.

Example 11

'Enery was the eighth husband of Sylvia, who had over the years inherited from his predecessors, in particular Hal, who left her £300,000, and Harry, who set aside £400,000 in an interest in possession trust for her prior to 22 March 2006. 'Enery made no lifetime gifts and left everything to Sylvia. Harry did not use his nil-rate band but Hal had in his Will left £130,900 to his children at a time when the nil-rate band was £154,000; so he had used 90% of the band.

Sylvia dies at a time when the nil-rate band is £375,000. The maximum transferable relief is £375,000 even though £37,500 might be transferable in respect of Hal and £375,000 from each of Harry and 'Enery.

17.48   A claim to transferable band must be made within two years or such longer period as HMRC allow. It does not matter when the first spouse died. This is both sensible and kind. Many who are bereaved need a long time to put their affairs in order. Hitherto, the surviving spouse, who might well be infirm, must take action within two years of death to put in place a deed of variation to introduce the debt or charge scheme for the benefit of the next generation. From now on, there is no pressure on the surviving spouse. All that the family need do, after the second death, is assemble the documents to make a claim, which will be seen as merely part of the process of completing IHT200. However, it seems that many claims are defective and do not include the relevant evidence, even where it is already in the possession of the personal representatives.

Interesting choices become available to families.

Example 12

James left his estate on discretionary trusts for Liz, his wife, and their children and grandchildren. His estate was £400,000 when he died in May 2007. Liz has assets of £300,000 being half the family home, owned as tenants in common with James, and savings. Liz wants her children to have some money now. How should the trustees exercise their discretion?

For convenience perhaps Liz should own the entire house anyway, avoiding the problems of capital gains tax that could arise on a sale by trustees. If she is in good health she may also feel that it will be best for her to inherit as much as possible under James' Will, because that uses as little as possible of his nil-rate band. Subject to waiting three months from his death, an appointment to her of an absolute interest will be read back to the date of his death and will thus be an exempt transfer.

Liz makes the gifts to her children out of her own resources as PETs, hoping to survive seven years. If she does so survive, and if at her death the nil-rate band is much larger than it was in May 2007, and if none of it was used in the distributions from James' trust, there will be two much larger bands available than would otherwise have been the case.

17.49 What action should people take? The answer seems, in nearly all circumstances, to do nothing at all for the time being. This is for several reasons, according to the circumstances:

- *Existing Wills incorporating nil-rate discretionary trusts where both spouses are still alive:* There is no immediate need to change the Will. The trustees can appoint the entire discretionary fund to the surviving spouse, taking care to comply with the difficulties of IHTA 1984 s 144 as illustrated above. Note that the three-month rule does not apply if the interest appointed is an IPDI.

- *Existing Wills as above where a spouse has died within the last two years:* Appoint as above.

- *Existing Wills as above where the trust has been in place for two years or more:* do nothing, and in particular do not increase the estate of the surviving spouse, because it is not now possible to 'un-use' the nil-rate band of the deceased.

- *Existing Wills that do not include nil-rate trusts:* do nothing, because that structure is no longer necessary.

- *Existing Wills that were drawn partly with an eye to sheltering assets from the burden of care fees:* do nothing and use the power of appointment according to the circumstances at the time that it is needed.

- *Existing Wills* that aim to 're-cycle' APR and BPR: do not change the Wills. Use the structure to pass valuable assets free of IHT into the trust. Later, encourage the surviving spouse (who inherits any cash) to buy the relieved assets from the nil-rate trust and to hold them, hoping to survive two years.

17.50 Changes may be appropriate where the nil-rate band was left, not on discretionary trusts for the family as a whole, including the spouse, but to the younger generation only. If this was done because there was ample for the survivor, well and good; but if the Wills were drawn that way only to use the nil rate band, where a trust was perceived to be artificial, or too expensive, some revision may now be warranted. Whilst the beneficiaries could disclaim their share of the nil-rate band, it might be unwise to rely on them to do so.

Chapter 18

Origins of the employee share trust

Introduction

18.1 This chapter describes the origins of the employee share trust as a support mechanism for the efficient operation of employee share schemes, particularly where existing shares are recycled as part of the employee share scheme arrangement. The chapter explains the ingenious economic model that was devised by Louis Kelso for Peninsula Newspapers in Palo Alto, California, US, during the 1950s, and how the concept was given statutory form in the US by Senator Russell Long, and eventually exported to the UK through the work of The ESOP Centre in London. The chapter concludes with a brief explanation of the history of the trust from early Anglo-Saxon times to the present day.

Louis Kelso and Peninsula Newspapers

18.2 The United States' tradition fostered the use of employee share ownership for solutions to longer-term industrial problems, particularly in relation to succession, and in relation to pension provision. In contrast, the development of employee share ownership in the UK since 1978 has been in the context of short-term incentive and motivation, sometimes for all employees and sometimes for target groups of senior executives.

This longer-term perspective from the US is well-illustrated in the work of Louis Kelso, a West Coast lawyer who developed economic theories about the requirement for a modern capitalist state to share its wealth within the wider population. The work of Louis Kelso is set out in his two books, *The Capitalist Manifesto* (1958) and *Two-factor Theory: The Economics of Reality* (1967).

Louis Kelso is widely credited with having invented 'the ESOP structural concept' – a trust mechanism in which to hold the company shares and to receive company profits for the express purpose of enabling the trust to pay the existing owner for the shares.

Indeed, the case to which Louis Kelso applied his theory in 1956 involved the payment of all the company profits into the trust for a period of five to seven years. This was a successful Californian newspaper company, Peninsula Newspapers, based in Palo Alto, whose founder and sole shareholder had decided to retire. However, he did not want to sell the company to one of the large newspaper chains. He wanted to offer the business to his employees. The problem that Louis Kelso's solution addressed was that the employees, despite their willingness to buy the company, did not have the cash to enter into the transaction. The sole shareholder had to prepare for his retirement and so was in a position to gift the business to his employees. Louis Kelso was consulted to provide the solution and duly obliged by producing the ESOP concept.

Wages of capital

18.3 The natural consequence of Louis Kelso's theories is a belief that every employee should receive a return from his or her ownership of capital assets as well as from his or her labour and so was born the economic model known as the 'wages of capital' – the sharing of the business rewards through employee share ownership. Under this economic model it is important to recognise that success depends on the contribution of the 'factors of production', which are required for that particular business. Traditionally, each factor of production is rewarded for its contribution to the business with each factor and its associated reward clearly defined as follows.

Factor of production	Reward
Labour	Wages or salary
Capital	Dividends and capital gains
Entrepreneurship	Profits

This list of factors is not intended to be exhaustive. However, it is intended to be illustrative of the role that employee share ownership plays in extending the base of reward to the factor of production known as 'labour'. By means of employee share ownership initiatives, the reward to 'labour' under the 'wages of capital' is widened to include the rewards that are traditionally associated with the other factors of production, namely 'capital' and 'Entrepreneurship' as follows.

Factor of Production	Reward	Mechanism for reward
Labour	Wages or salary	Payroll
	Dividends and capital gains	Employees share schemes
	Profits	Cash profit-sharing schemes and profit-sharing employee share schemes
Capital	Dividends and capital gains	Shareholdings
Entrepreneurship	Profits	Profit margins

The consequences of rewarding labour with the rewards that would traditionally be associated with 'cCapital' and 'entrepreneurship' are tendencies towards the following:

- closer identification for the employees with the owners and the employers of the business through a stronger identity of mutual interest;

- greater opportunities to vary the mix of remuneration and reward to employees or different groups of employees; and

- stronger interest from the employees in understanding the corporate objectives of the business, particularly if supported by a meaningful communications strategy.

Russell Long and the ESOP concept in statutory form

18.4 The work of Louis Kelso and his theories were championed at governmental level by Senator Russell Long, the chairman of the powerful US Senate Finance Committee. Russell Long was the son of a famous father, Senator Huey Long who as a populist politician was remembered for his phrase, 'every man a king'. The application of Louis Kelso's theories to employee enfranchisement; was promoted by Russell Long as a policy that was entirely consistent with his father's avowed aim to make every man a king.

Russell Long began to win support for this policy of employee enfranchisement through 'The ESOP concept'. In particular, he was keen to institute fiscal encouragement for the introduction of ESOPS in companies. The legislative success was the Employee Retirement Income Security Act ofin1974, known as ERISA under which ESOPS, in the Louis Kelso form, were recognised as a special form of defined contribution pension plan that as well as receiving contributions had the power to borrow money.

The crowning achievement of Russell Long's career in employee share ownership was to secure fiscal advantages for the ESOP as follows:

- the sponsoring company could repay capital as well as interest on loans taken out by the ESOP trust from its own pre-tax profits (rather than post-tax profits);

- the sponsoring company could pay dividends to the ESOP trust as the owner of its shares out of pre-tax profits (again as opposed to post-tax profits);

- the existing shareholders of the sponsoring company who sell their shares to the ESOP trust could defer their CGT by reinvesting the sale proceeds into US quoted stock; and

- the funding bank did not pay tax on half of the interest that it received on loans made to the ESOP trust, an enormous encouragement for lending institutions to fund ESOP trust arrangements.

Role of Malcolm Hurlston and The ESOP Centre

18.5 The ESOP concept was imported into the UK by Malcolm Hurlston, the Chairman of The Employee Share Ownership Centre (The ESOP Centre), and given a UK application and perspective. Malcolm Hurlston, who founded the Centre in 1986, was alert to the opportunities for the employee share trust when coupled with bona fide employee share schemes, having visited the US on behalf of Unity, the Trade Union bank, in 1985. His lobbying through The ESOP Centre resulted in the Qualifying Employee Share Ownership Trust legislation, the 'QUEST arrangement', in 1989. This gave a statutory status in the UK to the corporation tax deduction for contributions made by the sponsoring company to the employee share trust, providing certain specified conditions were met, notably: (1) a linkage to an all-employee tax approved employee share scheme; (2) the trust being resident in the UK; and (3) employee trustee representation. Changes were also made in CA 1991 to accommodate this arrangement.

Subsequently, The ESOP Centre has played a major lobbying role for the share schemes industry in the UK and among its successes has been the preservation of the popular SSOS (Sharesave), which at one time was threatened by the appearance of the SIP. The ESOP Centre, which is subscription-based, has strong membership among practitioner and employee share scheme-user companies, whom it puts in touch with each other. The ESOP Centre runs an annual programme of conferences for both quoted and unlisted companies, and publishes a monthly newsletter of employee share developments for its members.

Malcolm Hurlston set up a European arm of The ESOP Centre – The European Centre for Employee Ownership – which holds annual forums in Davos and Cannes and which has carried out major research projects for the European Commission to which the author of this book, David Craddock, has been a contributor.

Why use a trust?

18.6 The definition of a trust taken from Underhill and Hayton, *Law Relating to Trusts and Trustees* is as follows:

> A trust is an equitable obligation, binding a person (who is called a trustee) to deal with property over which he has control (which is called trust property), for the benefit of persons (who are called beneficiaries), of whom he himself may be one, and any one of whom may enforce the obligation.

Thus trustees are the legal owners of the trust property. They are legally bound to look after the property of the trust in a particular way and for a particular purpose. Trustees administer the trust and in certain circumstances make decisions about how the property in the trust is to be used. The property of a trust can include money, shares, land or buildings, and other valuable assets, such as paintings. The beneficiaries of the all-employee share scheme trust are the employees, who can benefit from the capital of the trust (by selling their shares) as well as the income (the shares may produce dividends). In the US, the model evolved through the work of Louis Kelso as a trust arrangement.

The trust has its origin, though, in England as a creation of the Anglo-Saxon legal system, and as a result of the parallel development of common law and equity. The trustee has the legal ownership of the trust property, whilst the beneficiary has an equitable interest in that property. The forerunner of the modern day trusts were known as 'uses' and were created for similar reasons as the trusts of today, notably: (1) to preserve confidentiality; (2) to assist in estate planning; and (3) to act as a tax mitigation vehicle.

On the passing of the UK Public Trustee Act 1906, legislative recognition was given to the management of trusts as a business although by this time other common law jurisdictions had identified the commercial opportunities. For example, by the end of the nineteenth century, there were almost 300 trust companies in operation in the US.

A further important step in the globalisation of trust business was made in 1987 with the advent of the Hague Convention on the Law Applicable to Trusts and their Recognition, which provides civil law jurisdictions with rules enabling them to recognise and give effect to the intention of a trust. Fixed interest, discretionary, protective, charitable, pension fund trusts, unit trusts and employee benefit structures are just a few of the examples of the work undertaken by trustees in the twenty-first century. Not quite as traditional, are some of the more 'exotic' trusts created by offshore financial centres e g the 'Star Trust' regime of the Cayman, and the 'Vista Trust' of the British Virgin Islands.

Today the beneficiary may be one of thousands on the payroll of a public company and a beneficiary of the company's employee benefit trust or the life tenant of a fixed interest trust. No matter what the nature of the trust, the trustee will have the same obligations simply described in the quotation from Underhill and Hayton: *Law Relating to Trusts and Trustees*: 'to deal with the property over which he has control, for the benefit of the beneficiaries'. In today's complex and increasingly litigious world the trustee ignores his or her duties and obligations to the beneficiary at his or her peril.

Under the ERISA in the US, the ESOP trust is part of the pension provision that the company facilitates for its employees. In practice the employees never take personal title to the shares of the company. When the employee retires, a lump sum is paid to the employee equal to the value of the shares that are held by the ESOP trust on his or her behalf. It is the recycling process of the company shares that requires the trust vehicle for the holding of shares in perpetuity. The key difference between the US ESOP and its UK counterpart is that the UK version, whether in the QUEST form (now reformed in line with FA 2003) or in the more general offshore ESOP form, actually enables employees to hold shares at some stage.

Chapter 19

Operation of the employee share trust

Why operate an employee share trust?

19.1 Below is a list of 20 reasons why companies and their advisers should consider the introduction of an employee share trust arrangement.

Please note that none of these reasons are mutually exclusive of each other. The company can choose to operate an employee share trust for all, or any combination of these reasons.

1.   To create a market for the shares in the absence of a recognised stock exchange.

2.   To support the operation of employee share scheme arrangements.

3.   To avoid dilution by recycling existing shares for employee share schemes.

4.   To secure the CGT treatment on the sale of shares.

5.   To enable shareholders to diversify their investment portfolio.

6.   To hedge on the purchase of shares when share prices are low.

7.   To warehouse shares in a secure and safe environment.

8.   To budget for the cost of share purchases for employee share schemes.

9.   To cap the initial outlay required to fund phantom liabilities.

10.   To support long-term incentive arrangements.

11.   To create a market for subsidiary company shares.

12.   To facilitate a management buy-out.

13.   To assist in succession planning when a proprietor is planning retirement.

14.   To buy-out dissident shareholders.

15.   To enable outside investors to withdraw their investment.

16.   To enable the personal representative of an estate to dispose of shares.

17. To allow flexibility in share pricing for sales, provided not above MV.

18. To operate a share market offshore with a view to achieving tax-efficiencies.

19. To operate a share scheme as part of a pension arrangement.

20. To give employees security that their scheme shares are ring-fenced for employees.

This chapter explains how employee share trusts operate and their uses. It identifies the advantages including treasury advantages that companies seek to achieve through the operation of an employee share trust. It addresses the commercial basis for employee share trust arrangements, the management of employee share trusts and updates the position of the corporation tax deduction which is now no longer dependent on the existence of an employee share trust.

Employee share trusts have an appeal for both public-quoted companies and for private companies as follows:

• For the public quoted companies, the main advantages are to hedge against share price rises.

• For the private companies, there is the additional advantage of establishing a market for the shares in the absence of a recognised stock exchange for the trading of the shares.

Whether sponsored by either a public-quoted company or a private company the employee share trust has the opportunity to develop as a commercial entity in its own right as it acquires and sells the shares of the company.

The areas that need to be addressed and given careful thought as follows:

1. Definition of an employee share trust

2. Structure of an employee share trust

3. Beneficiaries of an employee share trust

4. Powers and duties of the trustees of an employee share trust

5. Treasury efficiencies of an employee share trust

6. Commercial basis for transactions with the employee share trust

7. Management of the employee share trust

8. Onshore/offshore decision for the employee share trust

9. Illustrative examples for the classic use of the employee share trust

Definition of an employee share trust

19.2 An employee share trust, often referred to in its case law form as the employee share ownership plan (ESOP) is:

- a discretionary trust;

- which has the power to borrow for purposes of investing in the company's shares; and

- which uses one or more bona fide employee share schemes to distribute to employees the shares that it has purchased.

Step structure of an employee share trust

19.3 The step structure of how an employee share trust arrangement operates is as follows:

Step 1   The sponsoring company, as the settlor company, establishes an employee share trust.

Step 2   The employee share trust is funded by either:
— the company making cash contributions to the employee share trust, or
— the company making loans to the employee share trust; or
— the company providing a bank guarantee for a bank loan to be made directly to the employee share trust.

Step 3   The employee share trust purchases company shares from the market.

Step 4   The company grants options over trust shares or makes appropriations of trust shares.

Step 5   The company makes gifts to the employee share trust to fund the interest.

Step 6   The employee share trust repays any loans through the receipt of funds at the time the options are exercised by the employees.

Important: As a general rule of thumb, MV share options are funded in the first instance by loan arrangements with the expectation that the exercise of the share options will provide the funds to extinguish the loans while free share arrangements are funded by direct contributions.

Where the company makes a loan to the employee share trust or provides a bank guarantee for a bank loan to be made directly to the employee share trust the company must make a full disclosure in its annual report and accounts.

Beneficiaries of an employee share trust

19.4 The trust deed should be drafted in order to comply with two key legislative definitions as follows:

- the definition of 'an employee benefit trust' in ITA 1984, s 84;

- the definition of 'an employee share scheme' in *CA 2006, s 1166* (*CA 1985, s 743*).

The beneficiaries of the trust derive from these legislative provisions.

Inheritance Tax Act 1984, section 86

19.5   Under ITA 1984, s 86 the beneficiaries of the trust are:

(a) persons of class defined by reference to employment in a particular trade or profession, or employment by, or office with, a body carrying on a trade, profession or undertaking; or

(b) persons of a class defined by reference to marriage or relationship to, or dependent upon, persons of a class defined as mentioned in paragraph (a) above ...

Specifically, the trust must not permit any of the settled property to be applied for the benefit of persons other than those included in this definition.

The compliance with this section 86 is important for two key reasons as follows:

- It is a requirement if the value of assets held by the trust is not to be subject to the charge to inheritance tax that would otherwise arise every ten years.

- It is a requirement if the property becoming held by and passing out of, a discretionary trust settlement, is to qualify for reliefs under the CGT and inheritance tax regimes.

Companies Act 2006, section 1166 (Companies Act 1985, s 743)

19.6   Under CA 2006, s 1166 (CA 1985, s 74), if the trust is to be a bona fide employee share scheme then the trust must be:

a scheme for encouraging or facilitating the holding of shares or debentures in a company by or for the benefit of:

(a) the bona fide employees or former employees of the company, the company's subsidiary or holding company or a subsidiary of the company's holding company, or

(b) the wives, husbands, widows, widowers or children or step-children under the age of 18 of such employees or former employees.'

Unlike the section 86 definition, the section 1166 definition covers the employees of a holding company or the subsidiary of a holding company.

The compliance with the *CAt 2006, s 1166* (CA 1985, s 743) is important for three key reasons as follows:

- To claim the exception/exemption from the general prohibition imposed by CA 2006, ss 768–680 (CA 1985, s 151) on the giving of financial assistance by a company or its subsidiaries for the purpose of purchasing shares in that company.

- To claim the exemption from communicating financial promotions under FS MA 2000.

- To ensure that CA 2006, s 549 (CA 1985, s 80) and C A 2006, ss 561 and 566 (CA 1985, s 89) on the authority for share issues do not apply to grants of options to subscribe for shares and issues of shares under an employee share scheme.

In deciding upon the class of beneficiaries the sponsoring company should bear in mind a number of additional points as follows:

- The trust deed should provide for a residual beneficiary. This caters for the circumstances in which there is no employee who qualifies to be a beneficiary and there is no desire by the trustee to allow former employees or their dependants to derive a benefit from the trust.

- The trust deed should not identify the sponsoring company as a beneficiary. By excluding itself from the class of beneficiaries the sponsoring company is not creating for itself an asset or indeed an advantage of a capital nature. This is essential if the company is to claim a corporation tax deduction on cash contributions that it makes to the trust although under UK arrangements that opportunity for a corporation tax deduction is no longer available.

Powers and duties of the trustees of an employee share trust

19.7 The trustees' powers and duties derive from the nature of the employee share trust as a discretionary trust as follows:

- to apply at their total discretion the capital and income of the trust settlement for the benefit of any of the beneficiaries; and

- to distribute at their total discretion at the end of the trust period the remaining fund to the beneficiaries.

The trustees normally operate in accordance with the operating agreement that the trust has with the sponsoring company to purchase the shares of the sponsoring company for distribution to employee beneficiaries in order to satisfy the obligations that the company has under the bona fide employee share schemes that it has introduced.

Additionally, though, the trustees usually have their own express powers in relation to the shares that constitute the property of the trust. In particular, these powers extend to the gifting of shares, granting options over the shares and transferring the shares to another employee share trust. Where a transfer is made to another trust the class of beneficiaries of the other trust must be no more extensive than the class of beneficiaries of the trust that is making the transfer.

The main powers of the trustees are primarily as follows:

* to receive funding;

* to invest in the shares of the sponsoring company; and

* to distribute the shares of the sponsoring company to employee beneficiaries.

The additional powers of the trustees that support the execution of these main powers are as follows:

* To pay ancillary expenses, trustees will normally receive additional contributions from the sponsoring company. These expenses will include taxes, management fees, interest costs and trustee expenses.

* To amend the terms of the trust deed, usually in agreement with the sponsoring company. Any such amendment must not endanger the compliance of the trust with either the definition of 'an employee benefit trust' in ITA 1984, s 86 or the definition of 'an employee share scheme' in CA 2006, s 1166 (CA 1985, s 743).

Treasury efficiencies of an employee share trust

19.8 The basic principle from which any treasury-efficiency arises from the use of an employee share trust is that the employee share trust effectively allows the company to purchase its own shares lawfully. It is also important to be aware that the opportunity to hold treasury shares does not extend to unquoted private companies although these companies can purchase and cancel their own shares under existing procedures.

The treasury-efficiency advantages that flow from the arrangement are as follows.

To hedge against share price rises

Hedging and warehousing

19.9 The employee share trust can be used as a hedging device by purchasing and warehousing the shares of the sponsoring company at a time when the share price is comparatively low. This is an approach that is employed to particularly good effect by the public-quoted companies in their purchasing strategy for the purchase of the shares through the recognised stock exchange. However, the approach is equally applicable to the private-unquoted companies, particularly where shares are of low value through whatever reason, maybe as a consequence of a share reclassification or maybe through the reflection of the quoted comparators' stock exchange trading in the shares of the private unquoted company.

Budgeting for employee costs

19.10   By enabling the company to quantify and budget at the outset the cost of funding the employee share schemes, the employee share trust enables the sponsoring company to treat the cost of funding as a profit and loss account cost that is under the control of the board of directors. The cost of funding the employee share scheme is treated, therefore, in the same way as other employee costs, notably salaries, and cash bonuses, and their associated on-costs which are also quantified, and budgeted at the beginning of the financial year as costs under the control of the board of directors. Where the dilution cost of newly-issued shares is unknown and may be nil if, for example, options are not exercised the employee share trust in purchasing the shares at the outset replaces that uncertainty with a cost that is quantified at the outset.

Capping phantom liabilities

19.11   The employee share trust can also be used to hedge amounts which may become payable under phantom share option schemes. In accordance with the terms of a phantom share option scheme the shares will never be transferred into the ownership of the employee. However, by capping the company liability, where the arrangement is a promise by the company to pay the employee a cash payment equal to the rise in value of a number of shares but with the employee having no right to buy the shares the cost of the arrangement is estimable at the outset. The capping is on the initial outlay required by the company to fund the purchase of the shares by the trust. Once purchased and warehoused in the employee share trust the rise in the share value funds the cash payment to the employee at exercise of the phantom option. This capped arrangement replaces the unquantified cost of an open-ended arrangement.

To reduce the corporation tax liability

19.12   Prior to FA 2003, where the corporation tax deduction is not available under a statutory provision it is necessary to establish a case law basis for the corporation tax deduction. The corporation tax deduction is now available only under statutory rules as explained in the chapter on the subject. However, it is important to understand the principles that operated before the enactment of the full statutory corporation tax deduction when there was reliance upon case law principles in order to establish the relief.

Prior to FA 2003, the case law which would support a corporation tax deduction for cash contributions that are made to the trust had as its basis the decisions in three cases as follows.

Heather (HM Inspector of Taxes) v P-E Consulting Group Ltd

19.13   In *Heather (HM Inspector of Taxes) v P-E Consulting Group Ltd* [1973] 1 All ER 8, a trust was established by a company that carried on the business of management consulting engineering. The reason for the trust was to enable the employees to purchase the shares of the company with a view to preventing the company from coming under the control of outside shareholders. The company decided to fund the trust with contributions derived from 10% of its annual profits, subject to a minimum of £5,000.

At the meeting of the Special Commissioners, evidence was given by an accountant that the cost to a company in securing and retaining the services of employees was usually treated as revenue expenditure. The accountant presented the subtle argument that 'employee goodwill' could not be evaluated and, therefore, expenditure for that purpose was normally written off.

The Special Commissioners accepted the evidence of the accountant and held that the payments to the trust were allowable deductions for corporation tax purposes as they had been made for the purpose of the trade. The payments were to be treated as revenue expenditure rather than capital expenditure. This decision has always been regarded as important in establishing the authority of accountancy principles.

The Court of Appeal upheld the decision of the Special Commissioners and recognised that the nature of the expenditure as either revenue or capital was a matter of law for the court to decide.

Jeffs v Ringtons Ltd

19.14 In *Jeffs v Ringtons Ltd* [1986] 1 All ER 144 in 1978 the company set up a trust fund for a class of beneficiaries defined to benefit older employees for whom it believed the current pension provision might fall short of the requirement. The intention was for the company to contribute 5% of its profits to the trust fund and for the trustee, a trustee company, to invest the monies received in the shares of the sponsoring company. In 1980, the trust fund received £35,000 as one of a series of payments.

The Commissioners decided that the payment represented revenue expenditure and was an allowable deduction for corporation tax purposes.

The Court of Appeal upheld the decision and recognised the payment as one of a series of payments. The payment was seen neither as a one-off payment nor as an instalment of a larger amount. Furthermore, although there was an advantage to the company in setting up the trust fund the payment had not created an asset for the company or purchased an enduring advantage of an enduring nature.

E Bott Ltd v Price

19.15 In *E Bott Ltd v Price* [1987] STC 100, 59 TC 437, a trust was established by a company that traded as a fishmongers' business and was owned by two elderly directors and their wives. The reason for setting up the trust was to allay the fears of the employees that the company would cease trading when the directors died. The contributions made to the trust were an initial payment of £2,500 followed by two further payments of £2,224 and £1,000. These payments funded the purchase by the trust of 5% of the share capital from the director shareholders.

The Chancery Division listened to an appeal against the corporation tax assessments that the amounts should represent allowable deductions for corporation tax purposes. The decision was that the payments had been incurred wholly and exclusively for the purposes of the company's trade. The corporation tax deduction was, therefore, allowed.

Lessons from this case

19.16 Prior to FA 2003, this case law established the basis for a full corporation tax deduction on cash contributions made to an employee share trust. The key justifications that emerged from these cases were as follows:

- Any contribution that is made as a payment to an employee share trust should be made on a voluntary basis by the sponsoring company. The contribution should be a gift made to the employee share trust at the discretion of the board of directors without any contractual commitment as to how the employee share trust should use the monies.

- The payment is wholly and exclusively for the benefit and the purposes of the company's trade. In these circumstances, the benefit of the employees and the satisfaction of the employees are regarded as prima facie for the benefit and the purposes of the trade.

- The payment is of a revenue nature rather than a capital nature by which is meant revenue from the point of view of the sponsoring company. To benefit employees (as opposed to building up funds) would be regarded as revenue from the point of view of the company even though from the point of view of the trust the payments may be used, for example, to fund the repayment of the loan principal capital.

The corporation tax deduction for the repayment for the loan principal as well as for the payment of interest is in practice obtaining funds for the benefit of the business in an extremely treasury-efficient or 'cheap' way, namely net of tax at the appropriate rate of corporation tax.

In the years leading up to FA 2003, there was significant debate in relation to the corporation tax deductibility of contributions made from a sponsoring company to an employee share trust where there was no statutory justification for the corporation tax deduction and there was a reliance on case law.

Mawsley Machinery Ltd v Robinson

19.17 In 1998, there was a case, *Mawsley Machinery Ltd v Robinson* [1998] STC (SCD) 236, in which the Special Commissioners decided against the corporation tax deductibility. It is generally thought, though, by practitioners that the *Mawsley* case supports non-deductibility only in the specific circumstances that applied in that case.

In the *Mawsley* case an employee trust was set up by a company to purchase the shares that were owned by the controlling shareholder on his retirement that was planned for 1998.

The Inland Revenue rejected the company's contention that the payments made to the trust should be treated as allowable deductions for corporation tax purposes.

The Special Commissioners dismissed the appeals of the company.

Given the publicity that this case has attracted in the professional press it is important to understand precisely why the sponsoring company failed to achieve a corporation tax deduction.

The Special Commissioners contended that the payments were of a capital nature and stated quite categorically that the:

> purpose was to build up a fund with the view of making a capital purchase of [the controlling shareholder's] shares on his retirement.

The Special Commissioners took the view also that:

> the money was not laid out wholly and exclusively to provide a smooth succession on [the controlling shareholder's] retirement. The primary object was to enable [the controlling shareholder] to sell his shares without trouble when he retired.

The main problem for the company in the *Mawsley* Ccase was that the predominant motive behind the contribution by the sponsoring company and, indeed, the setting up of the whole structure was perceived by the Special Commissioners as giving benefit to the controlling shareholder and the employing company by reducing their tax liabilities. The perception was one of duality of purpose, to serve the purposes of the employer and also to serve the purposes of the employer's trade. It is this duality of purpose that appears to have precluded the corporation tax deduction in the specific circumstances of the case.

Inland Revenue Interpretation, RI 167

19.18   In February 1997, the Inland Revenue issued a Revenue Interpretation RI 167, in order to give some clarification to the corporation tax treatment of contributions into an employee share trust by a sponsoring company.

RI167 was concerned with situations that arise in seeking to determine a corporation tax deduction in relation to the following:

- where there is not an automatic statutory right to a corporation tax deduction;

- where contributions are of a revenue nature rather than a capital nature and the intention is to apply ordinary Schedule D, Case I/II principles; and

- where normal accounting practice requires the application of Urgent Issues Task Force Abstract 13 (UITF 13).

The wording used in RI 167 in relation to a case law employee share trust is as follows:

> Unless therefore, the treatment in the accounts is overridden by such a tax rule, it [the accounting treatment] is followed in computing taxable profit. The point at issue here is whether the time at which contributions to "non-statutory" ESOTs [ESOPs] are charged against profits under UITF 13 is overridden by some general tax principle.

RI 167 goes on to refer to the effect of recent cases by stating:

> Recent cases show that the courts are nowadays reluctant to discern general tax principles which override the time when income and expenses are recognised in accounts drawn up in accordance with normal commercial practice.

RI 167 supports this assertion with two cases as follows:

Threlfall v Jones

19.19 *Threlfall v Jones* (CA) [1993] STC 537. concerned with a leasing arrangement and not with an employee share scheme structure.

The Special Commissioners were clear that the profits and losses of a business were ascertained by applying the accepted principles of commercial accountancy.

The Special Commissioners took the view in particular that expenditure that had been incurred in a particular period was not necessarily available for a corporation tax deduction in that same period.

Johnston v Britannia Airways

19.20 Again, *Johnston v Britannia Airways* CHD [1994] STC 763 was not concerned with an employee share scheme structure. The accounting point under dispute was how best to make provisions in the financial statements for the future overhaul of jet aircraft. The Inland Revenue disputed the accounting procedures that had been adopted and refused to recognise the provision as the basis for the corporation tax deduction.

The Special Commissioners heard the appeal from the company and determined that the trading position of the company was best represented by the inclusion of the provision. The provision was allowed for corporation tax purposes on the basis that there was no rule of law that prevented the deduction.

The Chancery Division upheld the decision of the Special Commissioners by recognising that the accepted principles of commercial accountancy had been applied in the preparation of the financial statements.

The conclusions of RI 167 are as follows:

- Relying to a large extent on the *Threlfall* case, it takes the view that UITF 13 should not be 'overridden for timing purposes on the grounds that it strays too far from the legal form of the transactions'.

- A corporation tax deduction could still be available where a provision that is included in the financial statements is properly calculated and it relates to future contributions to an ESOP based on employee benefit entitlement for that period that has been determined in accordance with the accruals concept.

Updating the legal position on the corporation tax deduction

19.21   The tax position on the corporation tax deduction has, of course, subsequently been clarified and simplified through FA 2003 and the accounting treatment now follows the fair value approach under FRS 20, Accounting for Share-Based Payments.

The key principle to be aware of is that, as a consequence of FA 2003. The corporation tax deduction in the UK in now no longer dependent upon the existence of a trust arrangement. Nevertheless, the employee share trust continues to be a very useful and convenient commercial vehicle for the operation of employee share schemes.

In the pre-FA 2003 days, although RI 167 represented an Inland Revenue pronouncement of authority and there was widespread application of UITF 13 it was still possible under certain circumstances to achieve the corporation tax deduction. From a strict legal point of view, the decided case law should have had precedence over both RI 167 and UITF 13. However, from a practical point of view RI 167 would have had to have been challenged through the judicial system of the English courts. The best approach was to recognise that RI 167 and UITF 13 were recognised by the Inland Revenue. Rather than challenge their position on these pronouncements it was advisable to work with their contents to achieve the corporation tax deduction.

Commercial basis for transactions with the employee share trust

19.22   Any arrangement that involves an employee share trust must have a commercial basis with the transactions between the sponsoring company and the employee share trust grounded in commercial reality. If this is not the case then there is the possibility for a challenge from HMRC on the grounds of the scheme arrangement being of an artificial nature introduced solely for purposes of tax avoidance.

In this regard, there are two key cases of relevance as follows.

WT Ramsey Ltd v CIR

19.23 *WT Ramsey Ltd v CIR* (HL) [1982] AC 300 concerned a scheme (not involving an employee share scheme) that consisted of a circular series of transactions. The culmination of this series of transactions was to generate an allowable loss for CGT purposes. Other than the allowable loss the taxpayer was in exactly the same position as before he had entered into the series of transactions. However, if the allowable loss was allowed to stand it could be offset against a substantial gain arising on the sale of the farm.

The House of Lords considered an appeal against the Court of Appeal's decision that the series of transactions failed and the Inland Revenue advanced the new argument that the series of transactions should be treated as a fiscal nullity under which there was neither gain nor loss arising. The House of Lords accepted this approach and regarded the *Ramsey* transactions as a whole rather than on a step-by-step basis. No tax advantage was allowed to accrue to the taxpayer.

The House of Lords recognised that the scheme was for tax avoidance purposes and that there was no commercial justification for entering into the series of transactions. It identified an intention to allow the scheme to proceed through all its stages to completion and it was on this basis that is chose not to consider each individual step in isolation but to consider the series of transactions as a whole. Recognising the transactions as a series it concluded that the intention had not been commercially driven and had been entered into solely for tax avoidance purposes.

Furniss v Dawson

19.24   In *Furniss v Dawson* HL [1984] 1 All ER 530 the shares in two family companies were to be sold by the Dawson family to Wood Bastow Ltd. The shares were exchanged for shares in Greenjacket Ltd, a company resident and registered in the Isle of Man. Greenjacket Ltd immediately resold the shares to Wood Bastow Ltd, allowing the gain to be rolled over. This ensured that the gain would only crystallise once the shares in Greenjacket Ltd were sold. The purpose of the scheme was, therefore, to defer the CGT liability on the sale of the shares by the Dawson family.

The Court of Appeal allowed the appeal by the taxpayer against the charge made by HMRC for CGT on the basis that the Dawson family had sold the shares to Wood Bastow Ltd.

The House of Lords allowed the appeal by the Inland Revenue by contending that the principle established in *Ramsey* was not confined to self-cancelling schemes. The House of Lords sought to apply the law to the substance of what had actually happened regardless of the formalities that had appeared to govern the transactions.

This case was important in applying *Ramsey* subject to the following:

- there must be what is essentially a single composite transaction, albeit comprised of a pre-ordained series of transactions;

- the series of transactions must include steps that exist solely for tax avoidance and have no commercial basis; and

- it is no consequence that the steps have enduring legal consequences.

There are many other cases that have applied the decisions made in these two cases. It is, therefore, important to examine the commercial reality of transactions before proceeding with any scheme. The purpose for introducing an employee share trust must not be prima facie for the avoidance of tax.

There was a key case in 2002 that was concerned with employee benefit trusts not involving shares, the case of *Dextra Accessories Ltd and others v MacDonald* (*HM Inspector of Taxes*) Sp C 2002. However the *Dextra* case did result in a number of pertinent comments from the Special Commissioners on the role of independent trustees in contributing to the commercial status of transactions involving an employee trusts as a whole.

Dextra Accessories Ltd and others v MacDonald (HM Inspector of Taxes)

19.25   In *Dextra Accessories Ltd and others v MacDonald* (*HM Inspector of Taxes*) 2002 SpC 331, in December 1998, the parent company, Caudwell Holdings Ltd, set up a discretionary employee benefit trust with the express purpose of providing benefits to the employees of the group of companies over which Caudwell Holdings Ltd presided. Cash contributions were made to the trust by various group companies. In January 1999, the group companies informed the trustees that they wished to make awards to three employees for their past performance and also to three of those employees' relatives. In March 1999, six revocable subtrusts in favour of the beneficiaries were created. Funds were allocated to the subtrusts and were held on trust for those beneficiaries. In the ensuing months, various loans were made to the three employees out of the subfunds.

The Inland Revenue contended that the *Ramsay* doctrine applied and the trust should be regarded as a pretence. This argument was based on the contention that the true purpose of the trust was to allocate bonuses to the recipients and obtain a corporation tax deduction while at the same time avoiding Schedule E income tax on emoluments and NICs on earnings.

The Special Commissioners agreed with the counsel for the Inland Revenue that a commercial approach should be adopted in construing the relevant legislation as set out by the House of Lords in the case of *MacNiven v Westmoreland Investments Ltd* [2001] STC 273, All ER (D) 93. However, on the facts of the *Dextra* case the Special Commissioners held the following:

> In our view it is material that the trustees imposed some restraints on the type of investments in which funds could be invested, and that the trustee was not prepared to advance by way of loan the whole of an allocated fund. In order

for the funds to be in the unfettered control of (the director shareholders), the trustee must exercise its discretion and take the further action of appointing those funds absolutely to them as beneficiaries. The highest the case can be put is that the trustee is likely to comply with any reasonable request that is for the benefit of the beneficiaries, which is hardly surprising in the context of a trust established for the benefit of employees. This falls far short of saying that the trustee is a cipher who will do what it is told ...

The Special Commissioners decided that the trust had been established for a bona fide commercial purpose with trustees who were not ciphers of potential beneficiaries. It was the independence of the trustees that the Special Commissioners recognised in coming to their judgment.

Management of an employee share trust

19.26   These management issues are key to unlocking the benefits of the efficiencies that can be derived from the employee share trust arrangement.

Funding of the employee share trust

19.27   The funding of the employee share trust will typically be from one or a combination of means, as follows:

- contributions from the sponsoring company or a subsidiary company of the sponsoring company;
- loans from the sponsoring company or a subsidiary company of the sponsoring company; and/or
- loans from an external third party that are guaranteed by the sponsoring company or a subsidiary company of the sponsoring company.

Return of monies by the employee share trust

19.28   The return of monies to the sponsoring company or a subsidiary company of the sponsoring company is achieved through one of two means, as follows:

- the repayment of loans if, indeed, the employee share trust has been funded through loan arrangements; and/or
- the subscription for new shares by the employee share trust in the sponsoring company.

Notes:

- neither the sponsoring company nor the subsidiary company can be a beneficiary of the employee share trust; and
- where the employee share trust is funded through cash contributions the employee share trust receives those cash contributions without any contractual commitment on how the cash contributions are to be used.

Achievement of commercial efficiency for the employee share trust

19.29   The achievement of trust treasury and tax efficiency for the operation of the employee share trust arises through the efficient and timely movement of the following:

- shares; and

- cash.

Onshore/offshore decision for the employee share trust

19.30   The decision on the residence of the employee share trust and the trustee company/trustees is dictated by two key factors as follows:

- The requirement for the trust to be onshore in order to achieve a statutory corporation tax deduction which is, of course, a stipulation for operating the SIP.

- The advantage of the general administration of the trust being offshore for the trustees to be outside the scope of the charge to CGT.

The decision to establish onshore will have to be the case if the company chooses to introduce one of the following employee share scheme arrangements:

- the SIP;

- the profit-sharing employee share scheme (PSESS) (now being phased out); or

- the qualifying employee share trust (QUEST) (now superseded by the provisions of FA 2003).

The reason for the establishment onshore is to meet a statutory requirement. However, the exposure will remain to UK CGT for which there is no exemption.

In the absence of a need to establish onshore, the decision will usually be to establish offshore an employee trust arrangement that is not restrictive in the variety of bona fide employee share schemes to which it can be linked.

The statutory right to corporation tax relief is now available under FA 2003 whether the trust is established onshore or offshore, and indeed whether or not there is a trust at all.

The corporation tax deduction in the UK is no longer dependent upon the existence of an employee share trust. Outside the UK, careful planning is still required in order to secure the corporation tax deduction. Example 19.2 below illustrates a structure that may succeed in achieving this result for a subsidiary company operating in an overseas country.

Additionally, of course, the offshore status ensures exemption from UK CGT as the trust is neither resident nor ordinarily resident in the UK.

The decision to establish the employee share trust arrangement either onshore or offshore is expressed in diagram form as follows:

Onshore	Offshore
Profit-sharing employee share scheme (PSESS) Qualifying employee share trust (QUEST) Share incentive plan (SIP)	General employee share ownership plan trust (ESOP Trust)
Statutory corporation tax deduction	Statutory corporation tax deduction (no longer case law reliant)
No exemption from UK CGT	Exemption from UK CGT

This diagram should be studied in association with the preceding explanation.

Illustrative examples of the use of the employee share trust

19.31 The opportunity to use trusts in association with employee share schemes is extensive.

The following two examples are designed to illustrate inventive uses of an employee share trust to achieve key tax advantages.

It must be emphasised that these examples are for illustrative purposes only. When introducing an employee share scheme trust detailed and expert professional advice must be obtained before finalising the scheme design and implementing the arrangements.

Example 19.1: Tax-efficient movements of cash and shares

This example is designed to illustrate the movement of cash and the movement of shares in as tax-efficient a way as possible within an employee share scheme arrangement.

The diagram below illustrates the following steps:

1. The company makes a cash contribution to the trust.

2. The trust uses the cash to purchase shares from the existing shareholders.

3. The trust transfers the shares to the employees, either to satisfy the exercise of options or to meet some other obligation arising from employee rights to shares or the company's resolve to dispense free shares to the employees.

This structure allows for cash to be transferred from the company to existing shareholders via the trust and for shares to be transferred from existing shareholders to employees via the trust.

The consequences of this arrangement are as follows:

- The arrangement will offer the possibility of CGT relief for the existing shareholders.

- Through FA 2003, the corporation tax deduction is available for the company independent of the employee share trust arrangement.

- Through the tax-approved and government-sponsored legislation, the income tax and NI reliefs are available for the employees, again independent of the employee share trust arrangement.

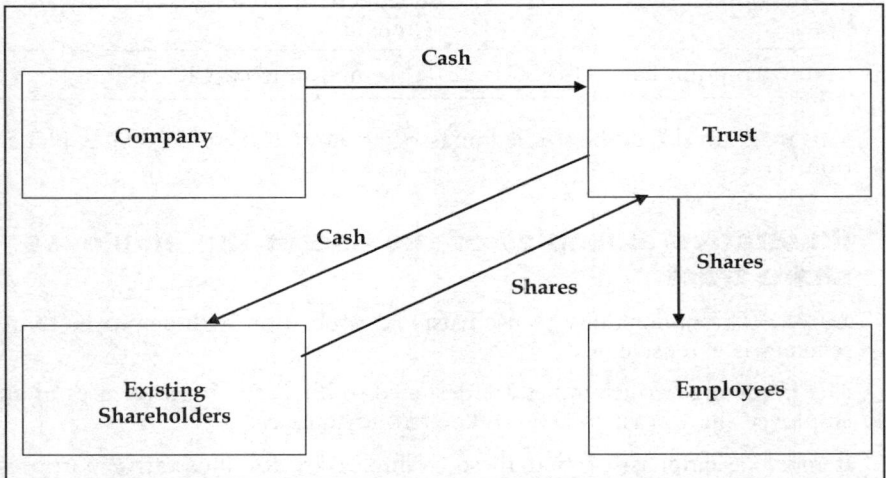

Example 19.2: Tax-efficient use of matching options for overseas subsidiary companies

This example is designed to illustrate the use of matching options designed to achieve a corporation tax deduction in an overseas subsidiary company following the exercise of a share option by an employee.

The diagram set out below illustrates the following steps:

1. The company grants an option to the trust at £5 per share.

2. The trust grants a matching option to the employees of £5 per share.

3. At exercise the employee pays £1 per share to the trust and, on the basis of a preset agreement, the subsidiary company pays £4 per share to the trust.

Note: The £4 per share is taxable on the employee.

4.   The trust now has a total of £5 per share to pay to the company as the option price payable on the exercise of the option that the company has granted to the trust.

5.   The company satisfies the exercise of the option by the trust by transferring shares to the trust and the trust satisfies the exercise of the option by the employee by transferring the same shares to the employee.

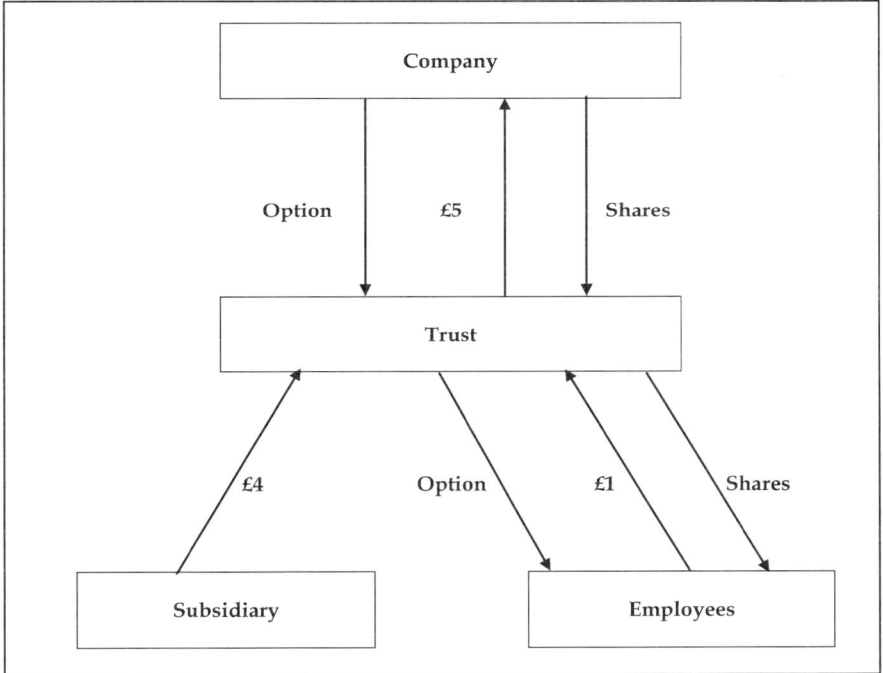

Chapter 20

Employer's responsibilities in operating employee share trust

Introduction

20.1   This chapter discusses the neglected subject of the practical responsibilities that the company has in relation to the employee share trust and to the trustee company once the employee share trust has been established. The chapter also illustrates the subtle and sophisticated mechanisms that underpin the efficient and effective operation of the employee share trust and the network of relationships between the company as the employer, the company's employees and the trustee company.

It is the share schemes administrator who lies at the centre of these relationships with a fulcrum role in managing the network of contacts in the interests of effectiveness and efficiency for the share scheme operations.

Derivation of the employer's responsibilities

20.2   The responsibilities of the company as the employer in relation to the activities of an employee share trust and the trustee company derive from two sources:

- The company is the settlor of the employee share trust.

- The employee share trust is an employee benefits arrangement for the employees where the company as the employer continues to employ the beneficiaries of the employee share trust. The employees are then both employees of the company *and* beneficiaries of the employee share trust.

Under trust law, once the property has been settled on the employee share trust the company is no longer the legal owner of that property. It is the settled property of the employee share trust. Neither is the company able to direct or instruct the trustee as to how it should act. However, the responsibilities which the company continues to have in relation to the employee share trust are substantial and significant. The company should be fully aware of these responsibilities and often it falls to the directors of the professional trustee company to explain these responsibilities to the employer.

It is sometimes observed that the company and the trustee company view this same vehicle, namely the employee share trust, in a different way, an observation that can best be explained as follows:

- *For the company*: its directors and company officials will view the relationship with the trustee company as *substance over legal form* for the reason that the trustee company will (barring some very unusual happenings) respond positively to the recommendations received from the company's remuneration committee and implement those recommendations, even though they are not, in the technical sense, instructions.

- *For the trustee company:* its directors will view the relationship with the company as *legal form over substance* for the reason that the independence of the employee share trust and the trustee company is protected by a substantial body of trust law that is definitive in the powers that are bestowed through a trust deed for the trustee company to exert its independence.

The responsibilities of the company as the employer trust's beneficiaries fall into the following categories:

- communication with the trustee company;

- funding of the employee share trust;

- granting of the options to the employees; and

- removal or the replacement of the trustee.

Communication with the trustee company

20.3 It is incumbent upon the trustee company to satisfy very high standards of care and conduct. The trustee company will, therefore, need to obtain information from the company as the employer in order to be in a position where it can meet these requirements.

It is very particularly important for the trustee company to be aware of the recommendations that the employer wishes the trustee company to consider. The emphasis here must be on the company as the employer asking the trustee to consider the recommendations rather than be directed or instructed by the recommendations. The mechanism that is used to deliver these messages to the trustee company is that of the remuneration committee.

The company should have an exchange of letters in place with the trustee company that identifies the following:

- *Routine matters:* for example, changes to the database of beneficiaries, should be on the authorisation of the share schemes administrator.

- *Substantive matters:* for example, the use to which the company funds are to be put, should require a letter from the company's remuneration committee signed by either the company secretary or a duly authorised director.

Funding of the employee share trust

20.4 The funding of the employee share trust can be through either contributions or loans and the company should have a policy that identifies when funding will be through contributions and when funding will be through loans as follows:

- Usually the funding will be through loans so that if at any time there are excess funds in the employee share trust then there is a mechanism through the loan agreement for those funds to be transferred from the employee share trust back to the company.

- If the funding is through contributions then the company will not have any right to recover any contributions or gifts that are made under these arrangements. However, contributions will on occasions be made to the employee share trust to enable the employee share trust to pay off loans with a circular movement of cash back to the company.

The funding agreement between the company and the trustee company should explain the following:

- the method by which funds can be drawn down by the trustee company;

- whether interest will be payable on loan or alternatively waived; and

- the basis of repayment for any loans.

Although continuing to be separate from the trustee company the company may be called upon to guarantee the obligations of the trustee company.

It is particularly important to ensure that any funding from the company does not contravene the financial assistance provisions of the Companies Act 1985 (CA 1985). The Companies Act 2006 (CA 2006), ss 678–680 (CA 1985, s 151) make it a criminal offence for a company to give financial assistance in connection with the purchase of its own shares. However, CA 2006, s 682(2)(c) (CA 1985, s 153(4)(b)) gives an exception in allowing the provision by a company, in good faith and in the interests of the company, of financial assistance for the purposes of a bona fide employee share scheme, defined under CA 2006, s 1166 (CA 1985, s 743). Protection from the financial assistance provisions can, therefore, usually be achieved by setting up the employee share trust in association with a bona fide employee share scheme in order to ensure that advantage is taken of the exception for employee share schemes under the legislation.

Once the company has provided funds to the employee share trust, the share schemes administrator must ensure that there is timely and accurate reporting from the trustee company on the activity of the trustee company and, in particular, the purposes to which the funds have been put.

Granting of the options to the employees

20.5 It is important to establish who is to grant the options, whether it is the company or the trustee company, for the following reasons:

- If the company is to grant the options then there is a contractual responsibility between the company as the employer and the employees to whom the options have been granted.

- If the trustee company is to grant the options then the trustee company has a contractual responsibility to both the company as the employer and also to the employees as its grantees and beneficiaries.

The usual arrangement is that the agreement stipulates that in all cases the company (and not the trustee company) will grant the options. However, in these circumstances, under the operating agreement, the trustee company agrees to assist the company in meeting its obligations to the share scheme participants and in satisfying the exercise of options on the understanding that the employer provides an adequate level of funding to make it possible for the trustee company to buy the shares and be in a position to honour its agreement.

Whatever the content of the funding agreement and the operating agreement, both the company and the trustee company must be aware of their responsibilities under the agreements and both the company and the trustee company should take responsibility for ensuring that there is no confusion in these responsibilities.

Removal or the replacement of the trustee

20.6 The company, although separate from both the employee share trust and the trustee company, has the responsibility to remove the trustee and appoint a new trustee as long as this is done in accordance with the provisions of the trust deed. A retiring trustee would normally be required to give a notice period, not to the other trustees but to the company. Given that the company has appointed the trustee in the first place it is not incongruence that it has this power of removal and right to be notified of retirement.

Chapter 21

Checklist for an employee share trust

Introduction

21.1 This chapter identifies the procedural items that need to be dealt with when setting up an employee share trust. It is drawn from a real case example of setting up an employee share trust on an offshore basis in Jersey in the Channel Islands.

Source of funding

21.2 For ease of administration and the achievement of corporate tax deductibility, wherever possible, it is preferable to fund particular schemes from the country whose employees are to benefit from that funding. Given that corporation tax regimes differ around the world, this is certainly best practice if corporation tax deductions are to be maximised around the world in the different tax jurisdictions on the most tax-efficient basis.

In this context, although the funding of the employee share trust may be financed in the first instance from a central source it should be the policy of the company to recharge the cost to the companies whose employees are nominated to benefit.

For this purpose the trustee company must keep full records of: (1) the share purchase; and (2) the beneficiaries who are to benefit. The keeping of these records is a necessary requirement to maximising the corporation tax deduction opportunities.

Flexibility of the operation

21.3 Structures that facilitate flexibility of operation are absolutely central to ensuring the effectiveness and the efficiency of the relationship between the company and the trustee company.

To facilitate this flexibility of operation, the information requirements of the trustee company can be distilled into the following:

- the details of the beneficiaries; and

- the rules of the schemes and the trust deed.

Any additional or other activity that is to be performed by the trustee company will be at the requirement of the company. Additional or other activity would involve, typically, the keeping of the records in a way that would easily provide the information to achieve corporation tax deductions around the world in the different tax jurisdictions.

Status of the trustee company

21.4 The trustee company should be independent of the employing group in order to avoid any conflict of interest and in order to act as an element that supports the case that the transactions with the trust are not part of a pre-ordained series of transactions for tax avoidance.

Location of the employee share trust

21.5 It is always preferable for the employee share trust and the trustee company to be located outside the UK in an offshore jurisdiction, for example, the Channel Islands or the Isle of Man. The advantage of this approach is to mitigate any charge to UK CGT on the transfer, sale or gift of the shares out of the employee share trust given that the expectation is for the shares to appreciate in value. Where the trust may have significant amounts of source income or chargeable gains it has been better historically to establish the employee share trust offshore in a low tax/no tax jurisdiction.

For an employee share trust to be resident outside the UK, the directors of the trustee company must be non-UK resident.

However, for a trustee company based in Jersey there is no limited liability for the directors. Any breach of trust carries with it a liability on the part of the directors which is joint, several, unlimited and personal.

Role of the Advisory Committee

21.6 The company will usually register to the trustee company its recommendations for the use of the funding that it provides. This is equivalent to a letter of wishes for a family trust. The message from the company, via the advisory committee (usually the remuneration committee) must in no way whatsoever represent instructions. The message is definitively in the form of recommendations and it must be emphasised that recommendations can never be binding for a discretionary trust, whether it is offshore or onshore. For the smaller private company, usually the recommendations will come from the board of directors.

Additionally, HMRC is keen to see evidence of the independence of the trustee company if the position is to be sustained that the employee share trust is managed and controlled outside the UK. The use of recommendations rather than instructions assists in establishing this independence.

However, although the recommendations are not binding there are usually very definite limits on what the trustee company can do with the funds that are supplied to the trust:

- The trust deed is usually very restrictive on the use to which the funds can be applied. Usually the funds can only be used to purchase shares in the sponsoring company. It would usually be appropriate for the trustee company to have the authority to purchase shares in other companies.

- Any loan agreement between the sponsoring company and the trustee company can state that the loan will be made on specific terms. In these circumstances, the residue will be put on deposit and only used for the acquisition of shares in the sponsoring company.

Contributions which are made to the employee share trust as gifts from the company will be regarded as settled funds and cannot be transferred to the employee share trust on the basis of conditions that are stipulated by the company.

Requirement to avoid insider dealing

21.7 The trustee company would normally be able to buy in a close period in circumstances where the directors are not beneficiaries and there is no record of the company giving recommendations to the trustee company to buy in a close period.

However, in practice the trustee company will usually not buy in a close period for the reason that recommendations are usually given by the company via the advisory committee. Where the committee includes directors of the company and there is a movement in the share price considerable embarrassment could potentially be caused for the directors. It may be possible to avoid this problem by ensuring that the trustee company has been given a generic-type recommendation before the close period has started.

Generally speaking, the trustee company will be prepared to buy at any time other than during a close period with one exception. This exception is where there is price-sensitive information in the hands of the directors, which itself creates a self-imposed close period.

Acquisition of the shares

21.8 The trustee company normally works with the stockbroker to determine a best purchasing strategy. The prime concern is to ensure that any purchases have a minimal effect on the share price. The most important factor in determining the best purchasing strategy will usually be the rate at which shares are turned over. It is absolutely crucial that the company never ever gives any instruction whatsoever to a stockbroker with regard to either the use of the funds which are being or have been transferred to the employee share trust or any shares that the employee share trust is holding.

Every time the trustee company buys or sells shares it should notify the company. The responsibility for stock exchange disclosure continues to lie with the company and, therefore, the company must always have timely information on this matter.

Insurance arrangements

21.9 The trustee company will usually be managed by a highly credible professional trustee and administration company that will almost certainly have a substantial indemnity cover for all its worldwide operations. In these circumstances, the company is not usually required to make any insurance arrangements.

Any suits would be made against the professional trustee and administration company in relation to its management of the trustee company and/or the employee share trust:

* From the beneficiaries where there is a breach of trust.

* From the employer, in its capacity as settlor, for negligence in the administration of the arrangement.

Role of the nominee company

21.10 The purpose of the nominee company is to enable the non-UK-based trustee company to meet its settlement requirements. If there is delay in mail from the offshore jurisdiction then the trustee company will not be able to meet the time requirement for settlement.

As a general rule of thumb, the practicalities will usually dictate that the trustee company has a selling arrangement through the stockbroker's nominee company. The trustee company would normally have a nominee agreement with the nominee company under which the nominee company holds the shares to the order of the trustee company. The nominee company will then sell on the receipt of a letter of instruction from the trustee company.

Provided there is an appropriate agreement between the nominee company and the trustee company the shares can be held on an ongoing basis by the nominee company. The nominee company would not have legal ownership of the shares. The role of the nominee company would be to arrange the receipt and the delivery of the shares, not the acquisition or the disposal. The directors of the nominee company would normally be the partners/directors of the sponsoring stockbroking firm.

Chapter 22

Employee share trust for management buy-outs

Introduction

22.1 This chapter explores how the management buy-out initiative can be enhanced with tax-efficiency and cost-effectiveness through the use of employee share schemes, usually supported by employee share trust arrangements. The chapter explores the opportunities that exist to reinforce the commerciality of the management buy-out with tax structures that are tried and tested, and deliver the value that the company is seeking. The chapter recognizes that these are structures that provide for future tax efficiencies as well as immediate benefit and so the opportunity is there for meaningful tax planning right from the start of the management buy-out initiative.

Opportunity for management buy-outs using employee share schemes

22.2 Although the management buy-out initiative is a frequent and regular feature of corporate life, many director shareholders, outgoing and incoming, and their advisers, are unaware of the tax-efficiencies that can be built into the arrangement through the use of employee share schemes. At the time of the management buy-out the need to secure cost-efficiencies is paramount. With often a requirement from the banks for incoming shareholders to mortgage their private residences and the banks seeking to maximize their return from interest payments it is ironical that minimal attention is given to the tax-efficiencies that can be obtained through incorporating a constructive use of employee share scheme arrangements into the management buy-out process.

Indeed, what is a management buy-out initiative if it is not a major employee share scheme initiative? The incoming shareholder directors are employees and it is employee involvement at any level within the business, whether at director level or at general employee level, that the government-sponsored tax-approved schemes are specifically designed by statute to assist. It is the case that the tax-approved employee share schemes should not in any circumstances be underestimated for their flexibility and versatility, and they will usually have a role to play in the progressive management buy-out arrangement that seeks to utilize the tax advantages of employee share schemes.

Often for purposes of the new shareholder managers and provided the company qualifies enterprise management incentives (EMI) will have a contribution to make as, indeed, will the company share option plan (CSOP). Additionally, the use of the all-employee savings-related share option scheme (sharesave), and the all-employee share incentive plan (SIP) can bring the wider employee workforce into the motivation for growth with a contribution, usually comparatively minor but sometimes substantial, from them to the overall buy-out funding requirement.

However, it is through introducing the plethora of tax-unapproved arrangements that the employee share structures come into their own in supporting the management buy-out. Central to these arrangements is the employee share trust which has the capacity to deliver seriously tax-efficient CGT benefits to the outgoing shareholders and a whole range of tax-efficient share benefits and, indeed, cost-savings measures for the new incoming shareholders. The employee share trust will typically be resident offshore with a recognised trust administrator in the Channel Islands, say Jersey or Guernsey, which have the advantage of offering serious tax-efficiencies while at the same time being subject to regulation which for the management buy-out team gives the security and peace of mind that are so essential.

Interestingly, when exploration is given to the tax-unapproved schemes it is often the case that these schemes can deliver tax advantages that are as beneficial as the tax-approved schemes and sometimes even more beneficial than the tax-approved schemes, and involving higher percentages of shares. Courtesy of ITEPA 2003 the UK now has the full armoury of tax elections, notional loan arrangements and structures involving restricted securities, all of which can be combined with share reclassifications, and new classes of shares as necessary to construct the tax-efficient infrastructure on a bespoke basis to service the management buy-out needs. Furthermore, the new CA 2006 abolishes the prohibition on loans to directors; instead, for director loans there is a shareholder approval regime that opens up significant opportunities for share loan schemes that have the potential in certain circumstances to make a management buy-out possible where otherwise the possibility could easily fade away into the realm of the pipe dream.

So, in summary, the constructive use of the Taxes Acts, the Companies Acts and Trust Law, both from the UK and the Channel Islands, can deliver the management buy-out in a seriously tax-efficient form using employee share scheme arrangements.

Counter to tax avoidance

Clearances under ICTA 1988, section 70 and ITA 2007, section 685

22.3 Income Tax Act 2007, s 685 – within Chapter 1, Transactions in Securities, of Part 13 on Tax Avoidance – provides an exception to ITA

2007, s 684 in circumstances where the transaction is for genuine commercial reasons, and the enabling of income tax advantages is not the main object or one of the main objects of the securities transaction.

In this context it is crucial to apply the commercial test of intention. If there is a linkage between the securities transaction and the establishment, and the operation of a bona fide employee share scheme then there is the basis for genuine commercial reasons. The argument is that the securities transaction has been entered into in order to facilitate a bona fide employee share scheme in that the company has resolved to establish a bona fide employee share scheme and in wishing to avoid dilution chooses to facilitate the bona fide employee share scheme through the use of an employee share trust for the recycling of existing shares.

The clearances under ICTA 1988, s 707 and ITA 2007, s 685 then pertain to the sale of the shares to the employee share trust. It is important to reinforce the basis for genuine commercial reasons as substantially as possible. Coupled with the linkage to the bona fide employee share scheme is the fact that this transaction involves the outright sale of all the shares. This gives both appearance and substance to the capital nature of the transaction. In essence there is no retaining interest intended within the planning arrangements. Further reinforcement to the basis for genuine commercial reasons would be the contention that in the current circumstances, however defined, no alternative exit opportunities are available for the exiting shareholders and that in facilitating shareholder succession the linkage to the bona fide employee share scheme is secure. An overriding argument would then be that the planning arrangements are designed to protect and enhance shareholder value, both in the short-term and in the long-term.

Alternative to purchase of own shares

Procedure under ICTA 1988, section 219

22.4 The employee share trust offers a CGT treatment to the outgoing shareholder and, therefore, an alternative to the purchase of own shares by the company.

Under the purchase of own shares rules, if a company buys its own shares for more than the amount originally subscribed then there is a distribution on the excess and recipients of such distributions are treated in the same way as recipients of ordinary dividends which means that basic rate taxpayers have no further income tax to pay and higher rate taxpayers must pay the additional 22.5%.

However, under the purchase of own shares rules, a CGT disposal will occur automatically rather than an income distribution when an unquoted company or the unquoted parent company of a trading company buys back its own shares in order to benefit its trade, and certain other conditions are satisfied. The trade must not consist of dealing in shares, securities, land or futures. The company may be quoted on the alternative investment market (AIM). The CGT treatment is not given if the main objective is tax avoidance.

The 'benefit to the trade' test for the CGT treatment will be satisfied, subject to the meeting of various conditions, in any one of the following circumstances:

- A dissident and disruptive shareholder who is bought out.

- The proprietor who wishes to retire to make way for new management.

- An outside investor who provided equity, wishes to withdraw his or her investment.

- A shareholder dies and his or her personal representative does not wish to retain shares.

For the 'benefit to the trade' test to prevail, the conditions to be satisfied by the vendor shareholder are as follows:

- He or she must be resident and ordinarily resident in the UK when the purchase is made.

- The shares must have been owned by the vendor, or the vendor's spouse, throughout the five years preceding the purchase. This is reduced to three years if the vendor is the personal representative or the heir of a deceased member, and previous ownership by the deceased will count towards the qualifying period.

- The vendor and his associates must as a result of the purchase have their interest in the company's share capital reduced to 75% or less of their interest before the disposal.

- The vendor must not after the transaction be connected with the company or any company in the same 51% group. A person is connected with a company if he or she can control more than 30% of the ordinary share capital, the issued share capital and loan capital or the voting rights of the company.

Real life case study

Objectives

The objectives that the company has established and communicated to its advisers are, *firstly*, to provide a means by which current shareholders can exit the company to facilitate the future development of the company's business in the hands of successors and, *secondly*, to facilitate at the same time a means through which shares can be dispensed to the employees of its group companies.

Solution

The solution is predicated upon the fact that the transaction for the sale of the shares is for the genuine commercial reasons of establishing and operating bona fide employee share scheme arrangements as the basis for a management buy-out, which is itself seen as the best and only means of ensuring the future growth and development of the business under new management.

The proposed order of events is as follows:

Step 1

The company settles an employee share trust in a compatible offshore jurisdiction, typically Jersey in the Channel Islands, in order to ensure that any transfers, sales or gifts of shares by the trustees to beneficiaries are outside the scope of UK CGT. The trustees are appointed from persons who are independent from the company but who seek from the company recommendations on which to act. The company appoints the trustees on the recommendation of its advisers and retains the right to dismiss the trustees at any time at its own discretion and appoint new trustees. In practice, the employee share trust has one trustee in the form of a trustee company with Jersey-based directors.

Step 2

The company initiates arrangements to place the employee share trust in funds through a combination of contributions and loans either from the company or from a subsidiary of the company or from third party sources to buy *the whole* of the issued share capital of the company. The trust deed can contain waivers for voting rights and for dividend participation, if these waivers are considered appropriate.

Step 3

The existing shareholders sell all their shares to the employee share trust at market value (MV). Any clearances that are applied for from HMRC are on the basis that the outright sale of the shares to the trust is a one-off capital transaction with no retaining interest and that in the current circumstances, however defined, no alternative exit opportunities are available for the exiting shareholders and that in facilitating shareholder succession the linkage to bona fide employee share schemes for all the shares is secure. An overriding argument is that the arrangements are designed to protect and enhance shareholder value, both in the short-term and in the long-term.

Step 4

The employee share trust receives recommendations from the company, typically from a remuneration committee of the board of directors, duly constituted as part of the company's internal corporate governance arrangements. The independence of the trustees in choosing to act upon these recommendations secures immunity from any charge that the arrangements are based on a pre-ordained series of transactions.

Step 5

The remaining family members who are to lead the management of the company purchase their shares from the employee share trust under a general employee share purchase scheme operating as a bona fide employee share scheme.

Step 6

The company settles a separate SIP employee trust (SIP trust) under the tax-approved employee share scheme legislation with a view to dispensing shares to employees through profit-sharing in shares. The settlement funds may derive from the ongoing profitability and liquidity of the business or, alternatively, from funds retained from the original funding arrangement. The SIP trust is based in the UK as this is a requirement of the legislation in order to facilitate a corporation tax deduction on cash contributions made by the company or a nominated subsidiary directly to the SIP trust.

Step 7

The SIP trust purchases shares from the offshore employee share trust in order to have the supply of shares that is required for allocation of shares to all employees (possibly subject to a length of service criterion) under the profit-sharing arrangements. Although the company can choose which modules to operate, it is recommended that full use is made of the three SIP modules which are as follows:

1. Free shares module

As a share-gifting scheme, shares are allocated to employees free of any contribution from the employees up to a maximum £3,000 MV for each employee in any given tax year.

2. Partnership shares module

As a share purchase scheme, shares are purchased by employees through payroll deductions from gross pay up to a maximum of £1,500 worth of salary for each employee in any given tax year.

3. Matching shares module

As a true matching arrangement, the company can allocate further free shares as a matching to partnership shares in a ratio of up to two matching shares for every one partnership share.

Step 8

The employees sell their SIP shares after five years holding by the SIP trust and so avoid all exposure to income tax and NICs. The market for the purchase of their shares is the offshore employee share trust, acting as a surrogate market in the absence of a recognised stock exchange for the trading of the shares. The employees avoid CGT on the principle that the base cost for the CGT computation is the MV of the shares at the time the shares are transferred out of the SIP trust for sale by the employees.

Step 9

Additionally, shares can be dispensed to the employees over time from the employee share trust in order to satisfy exercises of options by employees, managers and others, who have been granted options under the tax-approved company share option plan (CSOP) and any tax-unapproved share option schemes that have been established. The exercise of these options can, if it is deemed appropriate, be linked to the achievement of performance conditions, a feature that is, generally speaking, considered desirable and, particularly so on a management buy-out and is not prohibited by the employment-related securities legislation. For these share option schemes, the corporation tax deduction is available in the employing company on the gain realised by the employee at the date of exercise, whether the scheme is the CSOP or the tax-unapproved scheme.

Additional point: the family trust

The family trust could in its simplest form be UK resident although consideration could be given to the more sensitive arrangement of being settled by a non-group standalone offshore company.

The family trust could facilitate its purchase of shares through loans which enable purchase at MV and which can be paid off through the sale of shares at appropriate junctures to the employee share trust, again acting as the surrogate market in the absence a recognised stock exchange. Alternatively, the majority shareholders could gift shares to the family trust. Detailed tax planning is required in these circumstances.

Chapter 23

Tax issues for employee share trusts established by close companies

Introduction

23.1 This chapter sets out the principal tax charges that are likely to arise where an employee share trust which complies with the provisions of Inheritance Tax Act 1984 (ITA 1984), s 86 is established by a company which is close for tax purposes under Income and Corporation Taxes Act 1988 (ICTA 1988), s 414. The chapter deals only with those aspects that are peculiar to employee share trusts with close settlors and assumes that both the settlor, and the beneficiaries are UK-resident for tax purposes. It is important to recognise that for the close company there is the potential for charges to corporation tax, CGT and inheritance tax.

Funding of the employee share trust by the close company

23.2 An employee share trust will, typically, be funded either by way of loan or by way of direct contribution. If the funds are provided by way of loan then the provisions of ICTA 1988, s 419 need to be considered. This provides that where a loan is made by a close company to a participator then unless it is repaid or waived within nine months following the end of the accounting period in which the loan is advanced a charge equal to 25% of the loan becomes due and is payable as a form of 'shadow advanced corporation tax'. The company can in due course recover this amount as and when the loan is repaid by means of a claim for relief from corporation tax. Similarly, relief can be claimed at the point that the loan is written off although other tax charges might then arise under the inheritance tax provisions. However, the liability to pay this amount can cause a cash flow disadvantage for the company since it could be several years before the loan is eventually repaid or released.

The charge to tax arises only in circumstances where the recipient of the loan is a participator. If, therefore, the employee share trust does not have any shares in the company or has a stake of less than 5% it will not rank as a participator for these purposes. Even where it is explicitly the case that the funds are intended for use in the acquisition of shares some advisors would argue that the employee share trust is not a participator when it receives the loan although it becomes one as soon as it uses the loan to acquire a substantial shareholding. It is important to be aware that HMRC will usually contend that the employee share trust is a participator where loan funds are provided from the company for the acquisition of shares.

If the employee share trust is funded by direct contribution of funds from a company (and not by way of loan) then no section 419 charge will arise although there could be a charge to inheritance tax under ITA 1984, ss 13 or 28. The potential for the inheritance tax charge is explained below.

Capital gains tax implications

23.3 If the employee share trust is established offshore as non-UK resident then UK CGT will not normally be a concern for the trust, regardless of whether or not the company is a close company.

If, on the other hand, the employee share trust is UK resident then there is a risk of double taxation on any capital gain that arises within the employee share trust by which the trustees have to account for CGT. The reason for this risk is that the same gain will be treated as subject to income tax in the hands of the beneficiary. It is in these circumstances that extra statutory concession (ESC) D35 entitled *Employee trusts: transfers of assets to beneficiaries* provides a form of double taxation relief although the concession is not available if participators in a close company are able to receive benefits from the employee share trust in a form which would not be income in their hands for tax purposes. The test for this refers to the relevant inheritance tax legislation and is, therefore, discussed below.

The full text of the ESC D35 is as follows:

ESC D35. Employee trusts: Transfers of assets to beneficiaries

If the trustees of an employee trust transfer assets to a beneficiary for no payment there is normally a charge to CGT on the trustees. There may also be a charge under Schedule E on the employee.

Where in such circumstances the employee is liable to income tax on the full market value of the assets transferred the trustees will not be charged to CGT on any gain arising on the transfer of those assets.

In this context, 'employee trust' means a trust within IHTA 1984, s 86 but without the restriction in subsection (3), and provided that the employee in question is not a person of the kind described in IHTA 1984, s 28(4) and not excluded by subsection (5).

This concession does not apply where on a transfer of assets from the trustees to a beneficiary special statutory rules restrict either the liability to CGT or the Schedule E liability.

Inheritance tax implications

23.4 The principal tax concern in relation to an employee share trust with a close company settlor is in relation to inheritance tax. As a general rule, an employee share trust that complies with ITA 1984, s 86 will not be subject to the usual discretionary trust inheritance tax regime. Relief from the ten-year anniversary charge on the value of the assets held within the employee share trust is provided by ITA 1984, s 86 whilst ITA 1984, s 13 deals with disposals by close companies to the employee share trust, ITA 1984, s 28 covers transfers by individuals to the employee share trust and I TA 1984, s 72 deals with property leaving an employee share trust.

The benefit of the tax reliefs afforded by ITA 1984, ss 13 and 28 on payments into the employee share trust can, however, be lost unless participators are prevented from taking any benefit from the employee share trust other than one 'which is the income of the participator for the purposes of income tax'. It does not matter whether any participator is intended to or does in fact receive a benefit from the employee share trust, ie it is the mere ability of the participator to benefit that is sufficient to cause the reliefs to be lost.

Cash payments out of an employee share trust do not cause the benefit of the reliefs to be lost. However, most other types of benefit, including loans on favourable terms or the grant of share option rights which could be exercised at the time when the exercise price is at a discount to market value would not be acceptable. This is for the reason that although any such benefits would generate income tax charges on the recipients the amounts on which the charges are generated are not themselves considered to be income for tax purposes.

The effects of falling outside the reliefs in ITA 1984, ss 13 and 28 are that any contributions made to the employee share trust are treated as though they were chargeable transfers by the contributor, or, where the contribution comes from the company, all of the participators pro rata to their individual shareholdings. Although the quantum of any resultant inheritance tax charge may be small or non-existent, depending on the circumstances of the participators, the charges are fiddly to calculate and cause added administrative complexity. In order to avoid these difficulties, then, providing it is commercially acceptable it is advisable to limit the ability of participators to take benefits from the employee share trust to those matters that would be treated as income in their hands.

The employee trust deed should contain the following clause:

> if a disposition of property is made to the Trustees by a company which is at that time a Close Company and the property is to be held in addition to the

Trust Fund then no part of such property may be applied at any time for the benefit of persons referred to in Sub-Section (2) Section 13 Inheritance Tax Act 1984 construing that section in accordance with Sub-Sections 13(3) and 13(5), but subject to Sub-Section 13(4) of that Act.

A close company should be defined in the employee trust deed as 'having the meaning given in Section 102(1) Inheritance Tax Act 1984'. This clause is regarded as effective in restricting participators to receiving income benefits only.

It should also be remembered that there is no tax difficulty arising from any third party transactions or transactions between the employee share trust and participators conducted on arm's length basis. If, for example, the employee share trust is to be used as a warehouse for shares that may be sold to it or purchased from it by participators at MV that will not create any additional inheritance tax charges.

When property leaves the employee share trust and is transferred to a participator, an exit charge will arise which again is calculated in accordance with the usual inheritance tax discretionary trust tax regime. As with charges on payments into an employee share trust, the quantum of tax due will usually be small, but the inheritance tax paid cannot be set off against the income tax liability of the recipient in respect of that payment.

Summary position

23.5   An employee share trust established by a close company does have additional tax complications that need to be considered. Most of these can be avoided by careful drafting that provide that participators are willing to have restricted access to the assets in the employee share trust. The commercial situation should always be paramount, however, and there will be occasions on which it is preferable to suffer cash flow delays with extended loan payments to an employee share trust or inheritance tax charges on transfers into and out of the employee share trust in order to better achieve the commercial objectives of the settlor.

Special note: Participator's transactions with the employee share trust

If a participator engages in an arm's-length transaction for the sale of shares to the employee share trust then that is treated in the same way as any other party would be in selling shares to the employee share trust. The requirement should still be to have an exclusion clause which establishes exclusion for the participator to receive a gratuitous benefit from the employee share trust. If there is no gratuitous benefit then there is no inheritance tax charge arising.

Additional note: Planning for an employee trust, whether for shares or general benefits

In planning for an effective employee benefit trust arrangement that avoids the creation of a transfer of value under section 13(1) it is imperative that the trust deed contains a valid exclusion clause for the exclusion of participators in accordance with section 13(2)(a). The participators cannot, therefore, receive any benefit from the trust unless, in accordance with section 12, it is income which is assessable to income tax and here lies a key opportunity for planning. Indeed, the legislative sections that are used in the defence for dispositions made to participators are section 12 (Dispositions allowable for income tax) and section 10 (Dispositions not intended to confer gratuitous benefit). In practice, though, a defence under section 10 is difficult to establish as it appears strange to contend that a gratuitous benefit has not been conferred. However, section 12 is accepted by HMRC as establishing a credible defence as long as it is cash that is received by the participator and an income tax liability is created as a consequence of the transfer.

The position that HMRC has historically taken on beneficial loans to participators is to contend that they do not create income. The capital value of the loan is quite clearly not income. However, the interest on the loan will be subject to income tax and it appears to be for this reason that HMRC has in recent years been at least open to the contention in certain cases that beneficial loans to participators can be defended under section 12. It is the case, though, that the advance of beneficial loans to participators remains a vulnerable area and it is interesting to compare the HMRC treatment of beneficial loans with the HMRC treatment of tax-unapproved share options which when taken to represent in essence deferred cash is recognised by HMRC as having a defence under section 12.

In contrast to the treatment of beneficial loans by HMRC, the treatment of loans made on a commercial basis is thoroughly acceptable as it does not represent a benefit to the participators and, indeed, no defence under section 12 is required. It remains important to ensure, though, that the trust deed contains a valid exclusion clause and, indeed, this is always an imperative for any employee benefit trust arrangement for a close company. The commercial loan must possess the characteristics of a commercial loan, notably in relation to a repayment schedule and to a rate of interest that should not be less than the official rate of 4.75%. Typically, the rate of interest would be fixed in order to hedge against any future rise in the official rate. The trustees will not necessarily require security and in this regard it is important to mirror arrangements for commercial loans generally which will often be made on an unsecured basis without any request whatsoever from the trustees for security.

It is also worth noting that in circumstances where inheritance tax charges do arise for beneficial loans they may not be substantial.

However, commercial loans represent the most effective mechanism for an efficient advance of funds from the trust to participators.

Chapter 24

The diagrammatical representation of key trust principles

Introduction

24.1 This chapter depicts the key trust principles diagrammatically. The main parties in these diagrams are the company, the trust, the existing shareholders and the employees. These four parties are always shown in the same place in the diagrams for a consistency that is designed to assist understanding. There is, in addition, a fifth party, namely the bank, where the trust is funded by an external financial institution.

Diagram 1: Company funding through contributions/loans

24.2 If the company, rather than an external financial institution, is to fund the trust then the alternatives available are either funding through contributions or funding through loans. Where loans are advanced by the company to the trust, it is, of course, possible at a later stage for the company to make contributions to the trust so that with a circular movement of cash the trust can pay off the loans.

Diagram 2: Bank funding through company guarantees

24.3 If the company is 'cash poor but asset rich' it may be necessary and possible for an external financial institution to fund the trust on the basis of guarantees given by the company. In these circumstances, both the company and the trust are parties to the agreement with the external financial institution.

Diagram 1: Company funding through contributions/loans

<u>How to Fund Free Shares: Company Contributions</u>

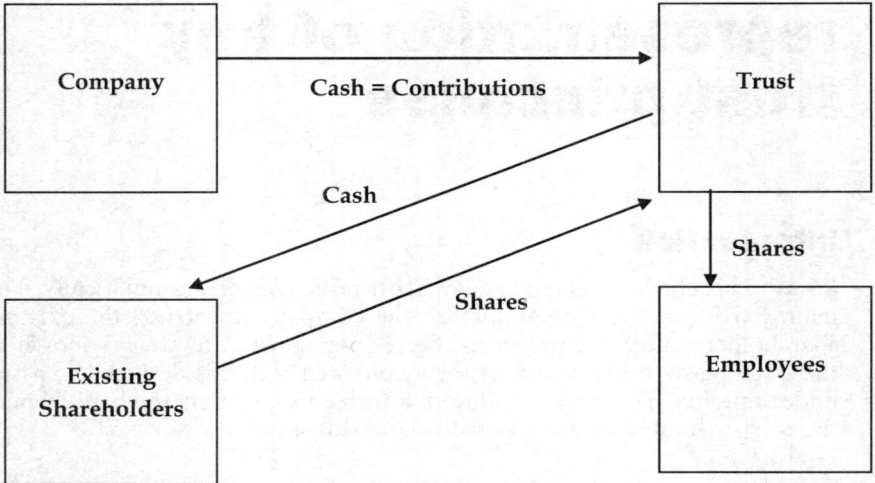

<u>How to Fund Option Shares: Company Loans</u>

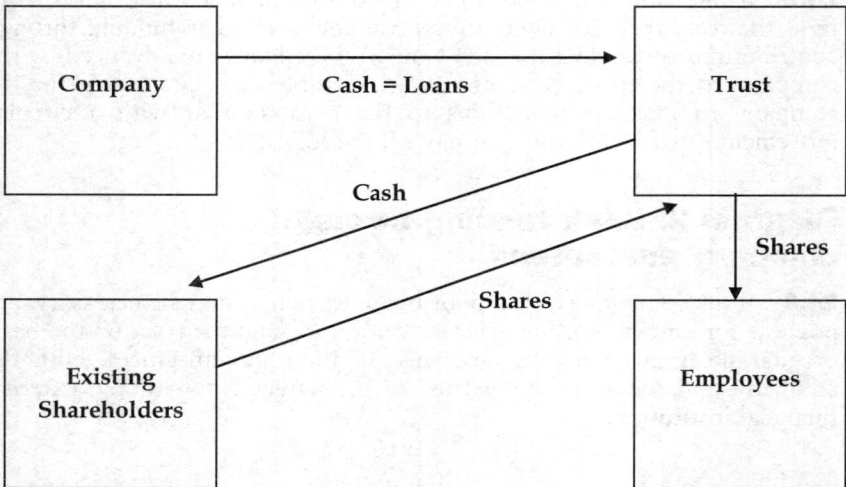

Diagram 2: Bank funding through company guarantees

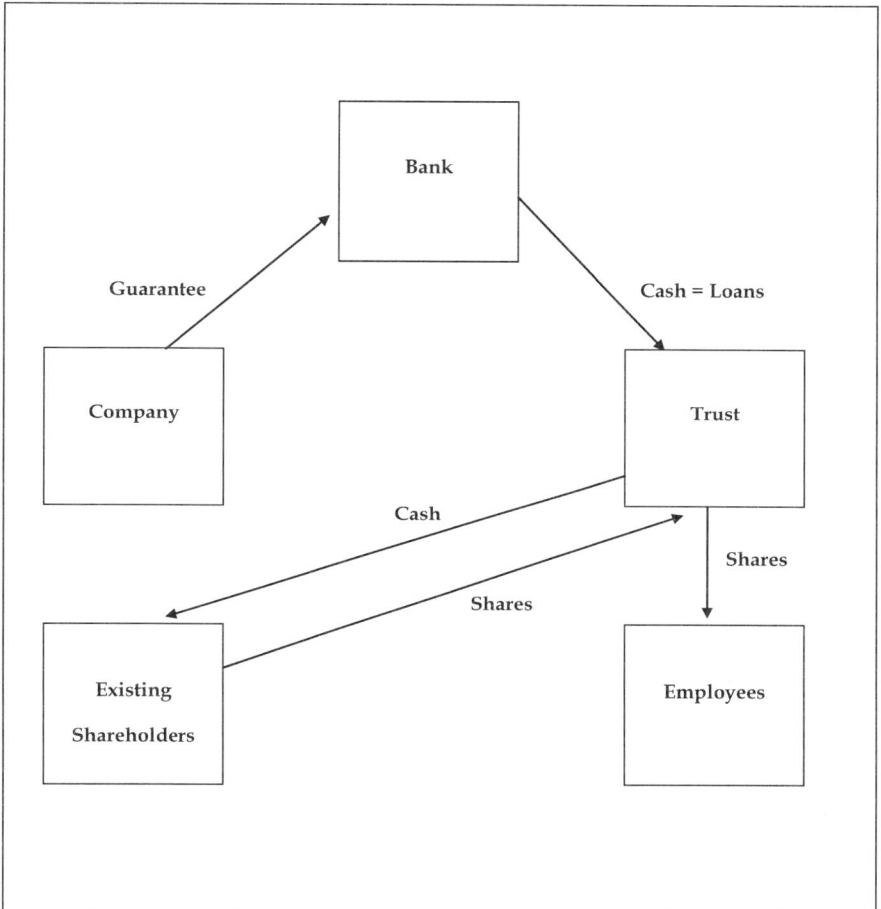

Diagram 3: Funding the loan repayments and interest charges

24.4   Where funding is obtained from an external financial institution, the trust will have to pay interest charges to the external financial institution. In these circumstances, the trust deed will usually not contain a dividend waiver so that dividends received on shares can contribute to the payment of the interest charges. The rest of the funding for the loan repayments and the payment of interest charges will derive from company contributions to the trust.

Diagram 3: Funding the loan repayments and interest charges

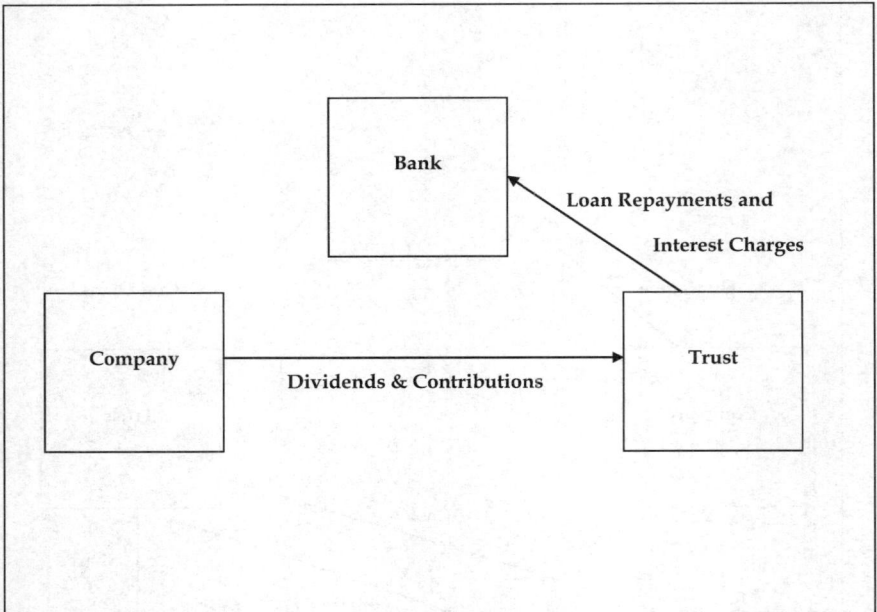

Diagram 4: Employees become shareholders through the transfer of shares

24.5 Once the employees become shareholders through, typically, either the exercise of share options or an award of shares they then, for purposes of selling their shares, move in the diagrammatic representation from the bottom right-hand box to the bottom left-hand box. This illustrates the principle of how the shares are recycled from one generation of shareholders to the next generation of shareholders.

Diagram 4: Employees became shareholders through the transfer of trust shares

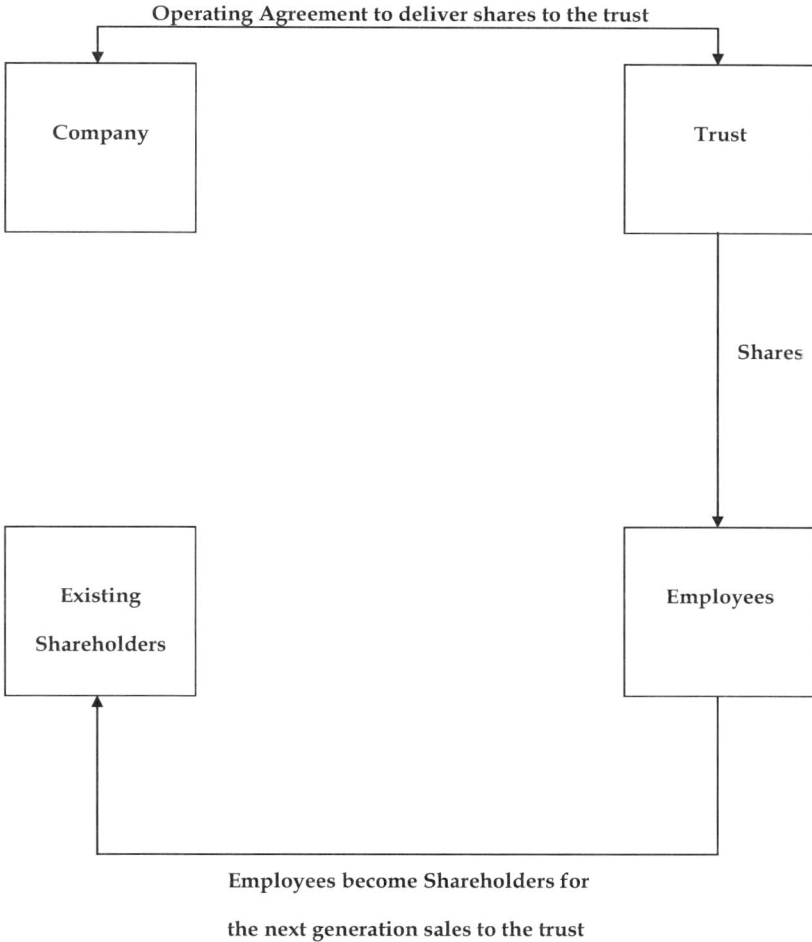

Operating Agreement to deliver shares to the trust

Company		Trust

Shares

Existing Shareholders		Employees

Employees become Shareholders for

the next generation sales to the trust

Diagram 5: Identity of interest

24.6   Although the term 'identity of Interest' is not a legal term of art, it is a well-established term in employee share scheme parlance. It is based on the principle that existing shareholders, through their shareholdings, and employees, through their share scheme involvement, unite around the totem of the share price/value in the interest of both parties wanting to see the capital growth of the company for the reason that both parties do, indeed, have an express interest in that growth. The employees are more likely to work towards the capital development of the company if they have an interest in that growth.

Diagram 5: Identity of interest

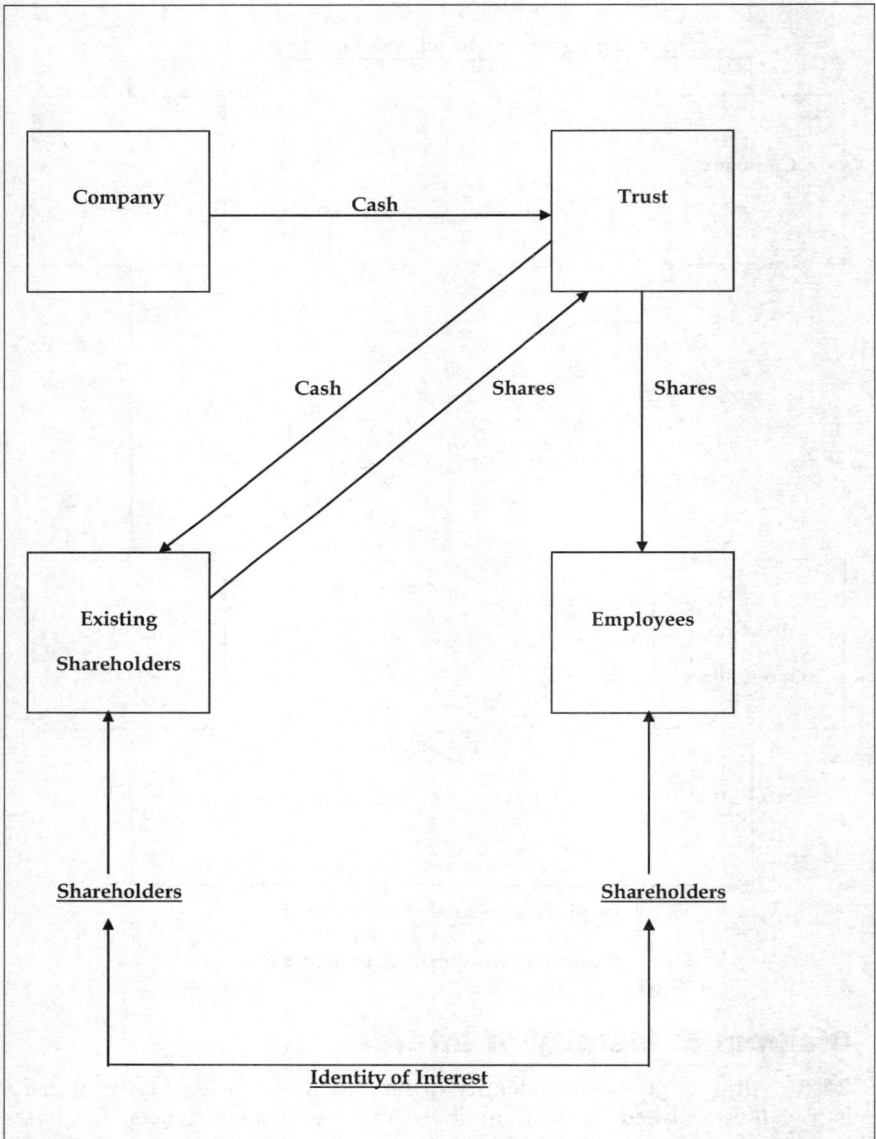

Diagram 6: The operating agreement

24.7 The operating agreement (as distinct from the trust deed) governs the operating relationship between the company and the trust. Under the operating agreement, the trust agrees to dispense shares from the employees on the recommendation of the company, provided the company has arranged for cash to be supplied to the trust so that the trust is in a position to first buy shares that it will subsequently dispense.

Diagram 7: The relationship with the trust structure

24.8   The company can provide recommendations to the trustees for use of trust property. However, these recommendations are not instructions and the trustees must operate as independent trustees, acting in the best interests of the beneficiaries. However, the company, as the settlor of the trust and the employer of the beneficiaries, must continue to be acutely aware of the decisions and the activities of the trustees.

Diagram 6: The operating agreement

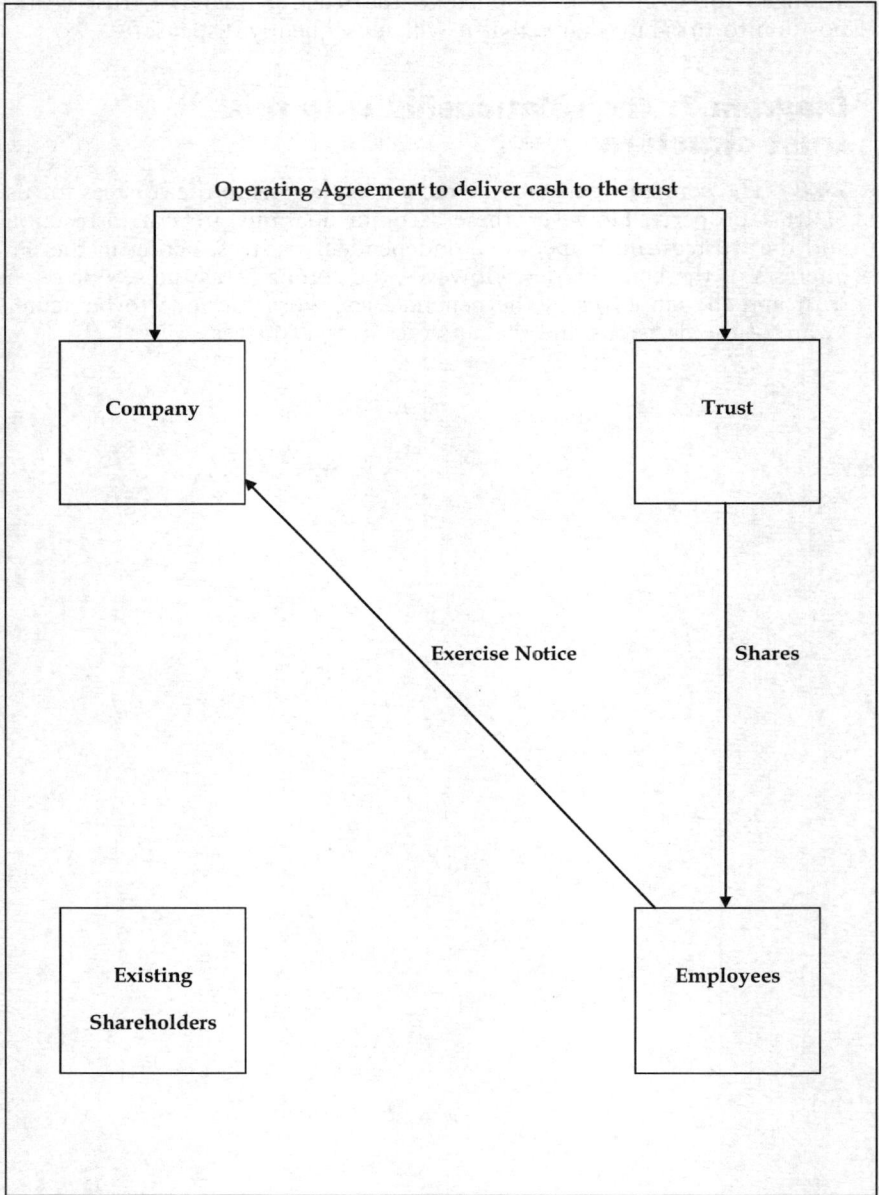

Operating Agreement to deliver cash to the trust

Company

Trust

Exercise Notice

Shares

Existing

Shareholders

Employees

Diagram 7: The relationship with the trust structure

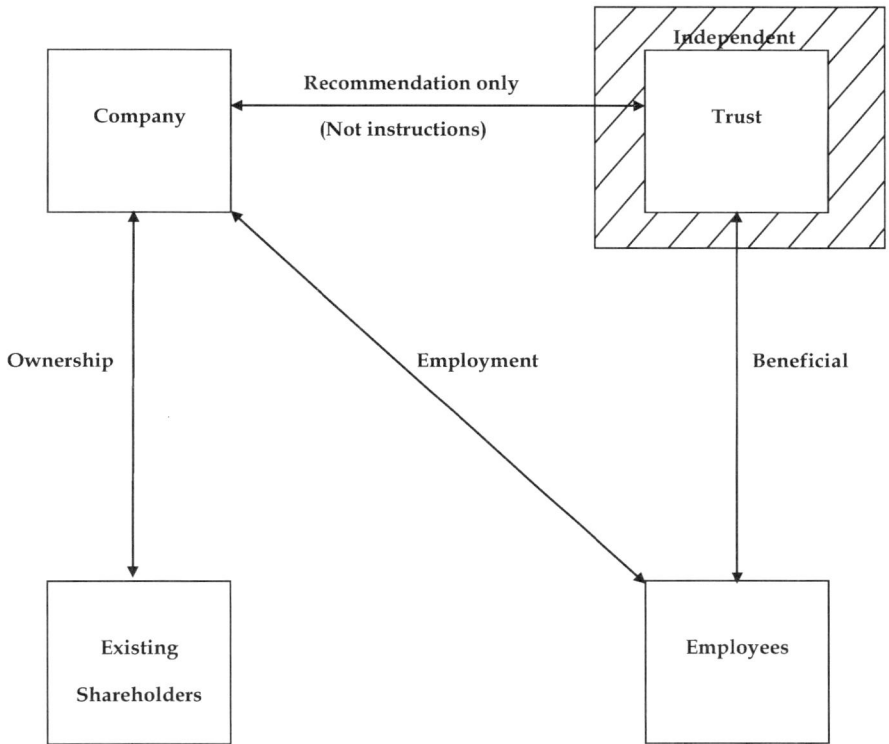

Company

Independent Trust

Recommendation only

(Not instructions)

Ownership

Employment

Beneficial

Existing

Shareholders

Employees

Chapter 25

Securities law

Introduction

25.1 This chapter explains the securities laws and regulations that are relevant to the management and development of employee share scheme arrangements.

Company authority

25.2 When a company is planning for the introduction of an employee share scheme, the directors, working with their advisers, must examine the company's Memorandum and Articles of Association meticulously with regard to key questions as follows:

- Is there any prohibition within the constitution of the company on the introduction of employee share scheme arrangements?

- Is there sufficient authority within the constitution of the company to establish and operate employee share scheme arrangements?

- Does the constitution of the company regulate the extent to which the directors can participate in employee share scheme arrangements?

- Does the constitution of the company regulate the extent to which directors can participate in board meetings in relation to matters in which they have an interest?

- Do the Articles of Association require amendment to allow the ordinary share capital to be used for employee share scheme arrangements?

- Is there sufficient authorised ordinary share capital to satisfy the exercise of options?

- Are there pre-emption conditions or transfer restrictions in the Articles of Association that require shares that are to be sold to be offered to existing shareholders first?

- Are there any supplementary shareholder agreements that need to be studied in relation to any of these items and in particular pre-emption conditions or transfer restrictions?

If the Memorandum and Articles of Association do not give the necessary authorities for the implementation and operation of the employee share scheme then the appropriate resolutions must be passed to amend accordingly.

When introducing the employee share scheme, and attending to all the matters that are required for that introduction and launch, it is very important also to ensure that when maturity happens there will be structures in place to facilitate the delivery of the shares to the employees and to enable the employees to realise a cash return.

Scheme status as an employee share scheme

25.3 The employee share scheme arrangement should be an employees' share scheme as defined by CA 2006, s 1166 (CA 1985, s 743). This is the statutory definition of an employees' share scheme.

This statutory definition requires that the arrangement must be:

> ... a scheme for encouraging or facilitating the holding of shares in or debentures of a company by or for the benefit of –

(a)   the bona fide employees or former employees of –

    (i) the company,

    (ii)   any subsidiary of the company, or

    (iii)   the company's holding company or any subsidiary of the company's holding company, or

(b)   the spouses, civil partners, surviving spouses, surviving civil partners, or minor children or step-children of such employees or former employees.

The importance of ensuring that the scheme is a bona fide employee share scheme is as follows:

- To ensure that CA 2006, s 549 (C A 1985, s 80) and CA 2006, ss 561 and 566 (CA 1985, s 89) on the authority for share issues do not apply to grants of options to subscribe for shares, and issues of shares under an employee share scheme.

- To claim the exemption for the scheme from the general prohibition imposed by CA 2006, ss 678–680 (CA 1985, s 151) on the giving of financial assistance by a company or its subsidiaries for the purpose of purchasing shares in the company.

- To claim the exception from certain requirements within the Financial Services and Markets Act 2000 (FSMA 2000). The definition of employees' share scheme in FSMA 2000 which provides the basis for the exemption is similarly worded to the definition in CA 2006.

This statutory definition applies to all employee share schemes whether they are tax-approved schemes or non-tax approved schemes, and whether they are all-employee schemes or discretionary schemes.

Care must be taken not to taint the status of the scheme as a bona fide employee share scheme through the inclusion of persons who are not covered by the definition. For example, a scheme that is established for the benefit of employees should not be used for the benefit of non-executive directors.

Security laws

25.4 The analysis of security laws must distinguish between offers of shares which are already listed and offers of securities which are not already listed as follows:

Offers of shares which are already listed

25.5 The advantage of having the shares already listed on the Official List is that there is no requirement for the company to produce a prospectus for publication where the shares are offered to persons in the UK

The Prospectus Rules Instrument 2005 applies to the UK effective from 1 July 2005 to govern the offer of securities in both quoted companies and in unquoted companies. For quoted companies that are listed on an EU market, an exemption is available from the obligation to produce a prospectus. These companies will be required instead to produce a short summary document which sets out the details of the shares.

Offers of securities which are not already listed

25.6 For unquoted companies, the Public Offer of Securities Regulations 1995 (POS Regs 1995) cease to apply. Instead, for unquoted companies also The Prospectus Rules Instrument 2005 applies from 1 July 2005, through which there are exemptions available.

Offers by private companies

25.7 Under CA 2006, s 755 (CA 1985, s 81), private companies are prohibited from making offers to the public.

Shareholder approval

25.8 For shareholder approval, it is important to distinguish between listed companies and non-listed companies as follows:

For Listed Companies

25.9 Rule 9.4.1 of The Listing Rules requires that any employee share scheme of a listed company that is incorporated in the UK (and of any of its major subsidiary undertakings, even if incorporated or operating overseas) must be approved by ordinary resolution of shareholders in general meeting prior to its adoption if:

- an employees' share scheme, if the scheme involves, or may involve, the issue of new shares or the transfer of treasury shares; or

- the scheme is a long-term incentive scheme in which one or more directors of the listed company are eligible to participate with the following two exceptions:

  — an arrangement under which participation is offered on similar terms to all, or substantially all, employees of the listed company or any of its subsidiary undertakings whose employees are eligible to participate in the arrangement (provided that all, or substantially all, employees are not directors of the company); and

  — an arrangement, for a single director or prospective director of the company, which is to be established specifically to facilitate, 'in unusual circumstances', the recruitment or retention of the relevant individual.

The definitions upon which Rule 9.4.1 of The Listing Rules rely are as follows:

Definition 1: Long-term incentive scheme

A *long-term incentive scheme:* for purposes of The Listing Rules, is any arrangement (other than a retirement benefit plan, a deferred bonus or any other arrangement that is an element of an executive director's remuneration package) that may involve the receipt of any asset (*including* cash or any security) by a director or employee of a group:

- which includes one or more conditions in respect of service and/or performance to be satisfied *over more than one financial year*; and

- pursuant to which the group may incur (other than in relation to the establishment and administration of the arrangement) either cost or liability, whether actual or contingent.

Definition 2: Deferred bonus scheme

A *deferred bonus scheme:* for purposes of The Listing Rules, is any arrangement pursuant to the terms of which the participants(s) may receive an award of any asset (including cash or any security) in respect of service and/or performance in *a period not exceeding the length of the relevant financial year* notwithstanding that any such asset may, subject only to the participant(s) remaining a director or employee of the group, be receivable by the participant(s) after the end of the period to which the award relates.

Points to remember

- A long-term incentive scheme that excludes directors of the listed company from participation *and* which does not involve the issue of new shares or the transfer of treasury shares is not required under The Listing Rules to obtain shareholder approval.

- The Listing Rules apply to any of the subsidiaries of the company that is listed in the UK even when the subsidiary is incorporated or operates overseas.

- A long-term incentive scheme is any form of executive incentive that can be a share option scheme, a long-term incentive plan or a cash bonus scheme in which the directors of the listed company can participate subject to certain exceptions as follows:

  — Certain bonus conversion plans and schemes which do not involve performance conditions of less than one year.

  — Certain all-employee share schemes and one-off arrangements for directors.

- The shareholders circular must contain either the full text of the scheme or a summary of its principal features. If the scheme is not circulated to shareholders the circular must include a statement that the scheme will be made available for inspection.

- The Listing Rules do not require employee share schemes to meet any requirements with regard to design except that certain amendments must obtain shareholder approval.

Non-Listed Companies

25.10 If a company that is not listed requires shareholder approval to introduce an employee share scheme then it will only be under the provisions of either the Articles of Association of the company or any shareholders' agreement that may be in place at the time.

Share issues

Directors' powers to allot new shares

25.11 The issue of shares must be in accordance with CA 2006, ss 549–551 (CA 1985, s 80) for the authority of the company that is required for certain allotments.

Exemption for employee share schemes

The exemption is given under Companies Act 2006, s 549(2) that reads as follows:

Subsection (1) does not apply –

(a) to the allotment of shares in pursuance of an employees' share scheme, or

(b) to the grant of a right to subscribe for, or to convert any security into, shares so allotted.

Pre-emption rights

25.12 The issue of shares must be in accordance with CA 2006, ss 561–566 (Companies Act 1985, s 89) for offers to shareholders to be on a pre-empted basis.

Exemption for employee share schemes

The exemption is given under CA 2006, s 566 that reads as follows:

> Section 561 (existing shareholders' right of pre-emption) does not apply to the allotment of securities that would, apart from any renunciation or assignment of the right to their allotment, to be held under an employees' share scheme.

In summary, then, for purposes of an issue of shares pursuant to an employee share scheme, the following are exempt:

- Allotment of shares pursuant to an employee share scheme.

- Grants of options over shares pursuant to an employee share scheme.

- Exercise of options over shares pursuant to an employee share scheme.

The exemption is only available if the employee share scheme complies with the definition of 'employees' share scheme' in CA 2006, s 1166 (CA 1985, s 743).

Issue of shares at a discount

25.13 Under CA 2006, s 580 (CA 1985, s 100) it is unlawful to issue shares for a consideration that is less than the nominal value of the shares. Shares can, though, be issued for a consideration that is less than their MV at the date of issue.

Financial assistance

25.14 Financial assistance arises in relation to the funding of a scheme.

Statutory provisions

25.15 The relevant statutory provisions are as follows:

(a) *General statutory prohibition*

Under CA 2006, ss 678–680 (C A 1985, s 151) there is a general prohibition, subject to certain exceptions, on the giving of financial assistance by a company or its subsidiaries for purposes of acquiring shares in that company.

(b) *Statutory exceptions*

The exceptions (which are exemptions) to CA 2006, ss 678–680 (Companies Act 1985, s 151) are as follows:

(*i*)   For *employee share schemes*

Employees' share scheme, under CA 2006, s 682(2)(b) (CA 1985, s 153(4)(b)):

— the provision of financial assistance in good faith'

— in the interests of the company that is providing the financial assistance; and

— for the purposes of an employees' share scheme.

(*ii*)   For *employee loans*

Employee loans, under CA 2006, s 682(2)(c) (CA 1985, s 153(4)(c)).

— the making of loans by the company to employees in good faith;

— to enable those employees to acquire fully paid shares in the company or holding company to be held by them by way of beneficial ownership.

Note: Employee loans under this section are not available to directors.

(*iii*)   For *market-making for employees*

Market-making for employees, under CA 2006, s 682(2)(c); (CA 1985; s 153(4)(bb)).

— the provision of financial assistance by a company or any of its subsidiaries;

— to enable or to facilitate transactions in shares in the first-mentioned company;

— the acquisition of beneficial ownership of those shares; and

— by any of the persons included in the subsection.

Note: This is especially useful for unlisted companies where there is no ready market.

(*iv*)   For public companies

For public companies, under CA 2006, s 682(1), (3)–(4) (CA 1985, s 154), the exceptions will only apply if the company's net assets are not reduced or if they are reduced then the financial assistance is provided out of distributable reserves.

Particular exposure areas

25.16 There are particular exposure areas relating to the following:

(a) *Long-term incentive plans and the share incentive plan*

Where free shares are purchased by an employee share trust the company is arranging for shares to be bought with a view to gifting them to its employees. This is financial assistance. However, with proper structuring of the scheme rules, all of these arrangements will fall within the definition of an 'employees' share scheme'.

(b) *Employee share trusts*

The employee share trust arrangement will be funded only by the company or its subsidiaries or by a third-party financial institution on the basis of guarantees given by the company. This is financial assistance. However, with proper structuring of the relevant documents an employee share trust will fall within the definition of an 'employees' share scheme'.

(c) *Share dealing facilities*

Companies often introduce share-dealing facilities in order to assist employees in the buying and selling of their shares. This does raise complications for the reason that the definition of an 'employees' share scheme' relates only to the holding of shares. These share-dealing facilities usually comprise cashless exercise facility arrangements for options and reduced share dealing charges. This will probably be financial assistance. Each arrangement must be studied in its own right at the time.

(d) *Non-executive director arrangements*

Typically, non-executive directors are not employees of the company in which they hold a directorship. If this is the case, they will not fall within the definition of an 'employees' share scheme' unless the non-executive was formerly a bona fide employee of a group company. Indeed, a scheme which benefits a non-executive director who does not comply with this definition will not be an 'employees' share scheme' under CA 2006, s 1166.

Public limited company and the employee share trust

25.17 The application of CA 2006, Section 682(1), (3)–(4) (CA 1985, s 154) requires particular care as follows:

(a) If a company is a public limited company then any funding arrangement for the trust must satisfy the requirements of section 682(1), (3)–(4).

In these circumstances the funding must be made from distributable profits.

Note: The express purpose of section 682(1), (3)–(4) is to ensure that the public limited company does not bear the cost of the funding where the profits are not available to bear the cost.

(*b*)   If the trust is funded by a subsidiary company of the public limited company from the funds of the subsidiary company then the requirements of section 154 do not apply.

(*c*)   If the funds that the subsidiary company uses to fund the trust are first provided to the subsidiary company by its parent public limited company then the requirements of section 682(1), (3)–(4) will continue to apply, subject to the circumstances set out in (*e*) below.

(*d*)   If the trust is funded by an overseas subsidiary, namely a subsidiary company that is resident and registered outside the UK, then the requirements of section 682(1), (3)–(4) do not apply.

Note: The overseas subsidiary company is outside the scope of the financial assistance sections of the CA 2006.

(*e*)   In certain circumstances the public limited company will initially supply the funds to the trust but then recharge the cost of the funding to one or more of its subsidiary companies so that the subsidiary company is able to achieve a corporate tax deduction.

  • Where there is a recharge to the subsidiary company and the subsidiary company is taken as bearing the cost of the funding, the funding is not regarded as funding from the public limited company and the requirements of section 682(1), (3)–(4) will not apply.

  • Minutes must be in place for the subsidiary company prior to any payment being made by the parent company. In particular, the minutes must make clear the following:

  — the subsidiary company agrees to bear the cost of the funding; and

  — the parent company is authorised to make the payment on behalf of the subsidiary company.

  • In these circumstances it is important to emphasise that the parent company is acting simply as a mechanism for payment rather than actually providing the assistance.

  • Additionally, care must be taken to ensure that the test set out in section 682 (4)(b) holds, namely that the expense is in the interest of the subsidiary company.

Note: An expense for the benefit of the employees of the subsidiary company is regarded as an expense in the interest of the subsidiary company.

Repeal of the financial assistance rules for private companies

25.18 With effect from 1 October 2008, the prohibition on financial assistance from private companies to acquire shares in the company or shares in the company's private parent company was repealed.

A private company can now give financial assistance for the following:

● the acquisition of its own shares; and

● the acquisition of shares in a private parent company.

Despite this repeal, directors must continue to exercise their statutory duty in determining whether the giving of financial assistance is appropriate in any given set of circumstances.

As a consequence of this repeal, there is, therefore, no further requirement for 'the whitewash procedure' that had been contained within CA 1985, s 155. This procedure does not survive, therefore, the introduction of CA 2006 and there is no corresponding section reference.

Director issues

Loans to directors

25.19 Under CA 2006, s 197(1) with effect from 1 October 2007, the general prohibition on loans to directors under CA 1985, s 330 is abolished and replaced with a shareholder approval for all companies which allows loans, quasi-loans and guarantees to directors and connected persons.

Under CA 2006, s 197(2), (4) a written memorandum with the details of the loan must be made available to shareholders before approval is given. Additionally, under CA 2006, s 198 all companies can enter into credit transactions with their directors if shareholder approval has been obtained.

Under CA 2006, s 213 if shareholder approval is not obtained and there is a breach of the requirements then the transaction is voidable.

There are exemptions available under CA 2006 as follows:

● under CA 2006, s 207(1) for loans up to £10,000;

● under CA 2006, s 204(2) for expense accounts up to £50,000; and

● under Companies Act 2006, s 205 for an advance for defence costs (including regulatory proceedings).

Directors' fiduciary duties

25.20 Under CA 2006, ss 171–177 directors have general duties that they owe to the company. These duties extend to being fully aware and giving full consideration to their fiduciary duties in relation to the following:

- the implementation of employee share scheme arrangements;
- the operation of employee share scheme arrangements; and
- the funding of employee share trusts.

This is a general set of duties that requires a general awareness on the part of the director who should take care to ensure that advice given on these matters is accurate and timely.

The general duties of directors as set out in CA 2006 are as follows:

Section 171: Duty to act within powers

Section 172: Duty to promote the success of the company

Section 173: Duty to exercise independent judgement

Section 174: Duty to exercise reasonable care, skill and diligence

Section 175: Duty to avoid conflicts of interest

Section 176: Duty not to accept benefits from third parties

Section 177: Duty to declare interest in proposed transaction or arrangement

Directors' conflicts of interest

25.21 These depend on whether the company is private or public:

(*i*) For *private companies*

For private companies, the conflict in relation to any director can be authorised through a quorum of non-conflicted directors provided there is no alternative provision in the articles of association.

(*ii*) For *public companies*

For public companies, the conflict in relation to any director can be authorised through a quorum of non-conflicted directors provided the authority given to them under the articles of association.

Disclosure of directors' interests

25.22 The Companies Act 2006 establishes the disclosure requirements for directors as follows:

- either under CA 2006, s 177 in advance of a transaction; or
- under CA 2006, s 182 in relation to an existing transaction.

Previously there was general disclosure under CA 1985, s 317.

A declaration under CA 2006, s 182 is not required if the director had made a declaration previously under CA 2006, s 177.

Under CA 2006, s 182 the director can declare an interest in an existing transaction either orally at a board meeting, by notice in writing or by general notice.

Related-party transactions

25.23 Chapter 11 of the Listing Rules stipulates that shareholder approval is required in relation to transactions with a related party.

A transaction with a related party is a transaction (other than one of a revenue nature in the ordinary course of business) between a company, or any of its subsidiary undertakings, and either a substantial shareholder, a director or an associate as defined in Chapter 11 of the Listing Rules.

By strict definition, Chapter 11 of the Listing Rules catches the following:

- grants of options and allocation of shares under employee share schemes; and

- the funding of employee trusts.

However, there are exceptions (exemptions) as follows:

- most transactions affected in accordance with an employee share scheme or a long-term incentive scheme including the grant of options.

- most transactions with employee share trusts for the reason that an employee share trust is neither a related party nor an associate of a related party;

- a transaction of a revenue nature, in the ordinary course of business; and

- certain small transactions.

Chapter 26

Financial services law

Introduction

26.1 This chapter explains the financial services laws and regulations that are relevant to the management and development of employee share scheme arrangements. The legislation that provides the basis for this exploration is the Financial Services and Markets Act 2000 (FSMA 2000) together with the Financial Services and Markets Act 2000 (Regulated Activities) Order 2001, SI 2001/544 (FSMA Order 2001).

The chapter addresses the two prohibitions, firstly on regulated activity and, secondly, on financial promotions, and the exemptions attached to each. The chapter then addresses implications for contract and negligence and for market abuse.

Regulated activity

26.2

> *Regulated activity regulation*
>
> Under FSMA 2000, s 19 it is a criminal offence for a person to carry on a regulated activity in the UK unless he or she is either authorised or is covered by an exemption.
>
> Under FSMA 2000, s 22 a regulated activity is of a specified kind carried on as a business and which relates to an investment of a specified kind.
>
> Where a company establishes an employee share scheme, and an employee share trust is operated in conjunction with that employee share scheme, it is probably the case, depending upon the precise facts that the company is carrying on a regulated activity.

In this regard, the FSMA Order 2001 is particularly relevant in identifying the following:

- the specified activities that are listed in Articles 5–65; and

- the specified investments that are listed in Articles 73–89.

The FSMA Order 2001 is concerned with the following specified activities:

- dealing in investments (which includes dealing in shares as principal or agent);

- arranging deals in investments;

- managing investments;

- safeguarding and administering investments;

- establishing and operating a collective investment scheme;

- advising on buying, selling, subscribing for or underwriting investments; and

- advising on the exercise of rights conferred by investments to sell, subscribe for or underwrite such investments.

Regulated activity exemption

Under FSMA Order 2001, Article 71 there is an exemption for the following:

- For group companies, carrying on activities with regard to the issue and allotment of shares under employee share schemes.

- For relevant trustees, carrying on activities with regard to operation of employee share trusts, including SIP trust arrangements.

The precise detail of the exemption is that it is for group companies and relevant trustees carrying on activities by entering into, as principal, transactions for the purpose of enabling or facilitating transactions in acquiring or holding shares or debentures in connection with employees, or former employees, of that or another group company (or their spouses or dependents).

Financial promotion

26.3 The conduct of financial services and, in particular for employee share schemes, the use of communications is governed by FMSA 2000, under which what was called 'investment advertisements; under the predecessor legislation, Financial Services Act 1986 (FSA 1986), is now called 'financial promotions'.

Financial promotion prohibition

Under FSMA 2000, s 21 only authorised persons are allowed to communicate in the course of business an invitation or an inducement to engage in an investment activity unless the contents of the communication have been approved by a person who is authorised so to do under FSMA 2000.

The international implications of this dictate are as follows:

- If the communication originates inside the UK, then this restriction prevails.

- If the communication originates outside the UK, then the restriction will only apply if it is capable of having an effect in the UK.

- If the communication is made from the UK to persons outside the UK, then it is not covered by the restriction.

In this regard, there are important definitions for the following:

- 'to communicate'; and

- 'to engage in an investment activity'.

"To communicate" includes the causing of a communication to be made.

"To engage in an investment activity" means the following:

- To enter or to offer to enter into; an agreement the making or performance of which; by either party constitutes a 'controlled activity'.

- To exercise any rights conferred by a 'controlled investment' to acquire, dispose of, underwrite or convert a controlled investment.

FSMA Order 2001 defines the following:

- *'Controlled activity'* – falls within FSMA Order 2001, Sch 1 paras 1–11.

- *'Controlled investment'* falls within FSMA Order 2001, Sch 1 paras 12–22.

Schedule 1 to the FSMA Order 2001 is concerned with dealing or arranging deal in shares, rights to subscribe for shares and options to acquire shares.

Depending on their contents the following will probably represent an invitation or inducement to engage in an *'investment activity'*:

- invitations to employees to participate;

- explanatory booklets;

- option certificates and notices of exercise;

- video presentations; and

- verbal presentations.

If FSMA 2000, s 21 is not complied with in relation to a communication to which it applies then the consequences are as follows:

- The person responsible for the contravention has committed a criminal offence.

- The obligations that have been entered into in connection with the contravention are not enforceable against the recipient of the communication.

- An action can be brought for compensation for loss incurred in relation to acting on the communication with an opportunity to recover any other money paid out.

Financial promotion exemption

Under FSMA Order 2001, Article 60 there is an exemption from FSMA 2000, s 21, for employee share scheme arrangements. The prohibition in section 21 does not apply to communications made by a company or a group company or a connected trustee where:

- the communication is for the purposes of an employee share scheme; and

- the communication relates to the shares in the company.

In using this exemption, an employee share scheme is an arrangement made or to be made by the company or by a person in the same group as the company to enable or to facilitate the following:

- Transactions in an investment in that company between or for the benefit, of a defined group of persons.

- The holding of investments in that company by or for the benefit of the same defined group of persons.

The defined group of persons is the following:

- bona fide employees or former employees of the company or a company within the same group; or

- their wives, husbands, widows, widowers or children or stepchildren under 18.

'Group' has a special meaning for these purposes. However, it does include the company whose shares are the subject of the communication and its subsidiaries.

Contract and negligence

FSMA 2000, section 397

26.4 Under FSMA 2000, s 397 any person who:

- makes a statement, promise or forecast that he knows to be misleading, false or deceptive or dishonestly conceals any material facts; or

- recklessly makes (dishonestly or otherwise) a statement, promise or forecast that is misleading, false or deceptive;

  is guilty of an offence if, amongst other things, he makes a statement, promise or forecast or conceals the facts for the purpose of inducing another person to enter into or refrain from entering into an agreement relating to investments, which would include shares and options.

The maximum penalty is seven years' imprisonment.

Tort of negligence

Independent of FSMA 2000 and FSMA Order 2001

26.5 Under the tort of negligence, a person may be able to sue for damages for breach of contract if a negligent misstatement is made to that person that causes that person loss. A person may also be able to sue on the basis, that the person making the statement, was negligent.

Example 26.1

A typical example would be where a person had relied upon a misstatement in an employee booklet and, as a consequence, incurred losses.

Market abuse

26.6 The market abuse regime was introduced through FMSA 2000, s 118. A new Market Abuse Directive 2005 was introduced with effect from 1 July 2005, which is reflected in amendments to FSMA 2000. The market abuse regime supports rather than replaces the insider dealing regime and is intended to catch behaviour which is damaging to markets without being criminal offence.

The relevance to employee share schemes is when directors and employees deal in the quoted shares of their employer or disseminate information about shares of their employer. It is important to understand that the application of the market abuse regime is not limited to companies and individuals who are regulated by the Financial Services Authority (FSA). It can apply to anybody and it is possible to be liable for market abuse without purposely committing the offence.

As a consequence of the Market Abuse Directive 2005, market abuse behaviour falls into seven categories as follows:

- insider dealing;
- improper disclosure of inside information;
- misuse of information;
- manipulating transactions;
- manipulating devices;

- disseminating information to give false or misleading impressions; and

- market distortion.

The powers accorded to the FSA are as follows:

- to impose an unlimited civil fine;

- to publish a statement that the person has engaged in market abuse; and

- to order the payment of compensation to victims.

There is a right of appeal to the Financial Services and Markets Tribunal (FSMT) and if necessary on to the Court of Appeal.

The Code of Market Conduct sets out the views of the FSA on the practical application of the market abuse regime as follows:

- The position of the hypothetical reasonable person who is familiar with the market in question must be considered in the context of the behaviour that is acceptable in the light of all the circumstances.

- In considering the position of the hypothetical reasonable person, the full range of relevant factors should be taken into account, including the following:

  — characteristics of the market in question;

  — investments traded on the market;

  — users of the market;

  — rules of the market and market practice;

  — position and experience of the person in question; and

  — the need for market users not to compromise the fair and efficient operations of the market.

- Any dealings in options (including the exercise of options) is included within the jurisdiction of the market abuse regime.

- Certain behaviour does not fall within the market abuse regime for the reason that under the Code it is protected by a 'safe harbour' that relate to behaviour that conforms with particular rules of the FSA or with certain provisions of The Listing Rules or the Takeover Code.

Chapter 27

Model Code and insider dealing

Introduction

27.1 This chapter explains how the Model Code and the insider dealing regulations are relevant to the management and the development of employee share scheme arrangements.

It is the case that a substantial set of exceptions (exemptions) are available for employee share schemes under the Model Code and that for the insider dealing provisions to apply there must be dealings on a regulated market or through a professional intermediary. As a general principle, if the company is properly complying with the Model Code then there should be limited vulnerability under the insider dealing provisions. Nevertheless, both the Model Code and the insider dealing provisions rely for their execution upon a precise set of definitions and care should always be taken to determine that where the company is relying upon the exceptions for employee share schemes that the conditions that are required for the exceptions are met.

Model Code

27.2 The Model Code on directors' dealings in securities is found in an annex to Chapter 9 of The Listing Rules. It applies, therefore, to listed companies only and represents a code of share dealing. The company must require all 'restricted persons' to comply with a code of dealing that is no less stringent than the Model Code.

The purpose of the Model Code is to impose prohibitions on share dealing in certain periods and operates in addition (and not as an alternative) to the insider dealing regulations. The application of the Model Code is wider than the insider dealing regulations and places a direct responsibility on the listed company to require certain defined to comply with its contents and take all proper and reasonable steps to secure compliance.

The individuals who are subject to the provisions of the Model Code are called 'restricted persons', a term which encompasses the following:

- *Company managers:* every person discharging managerial responsibilities, the directors of the listed company.

- *Employee insiders:* every employee of the company or any group company with access to inside information about the company.

The information that is described as 'inside information' in the Model Code means in relation to the shares of a listed company information which meets the following criteria:

- generally not available;

- relates directly or indirectly to the listed company or to its shares; and

- would have a significant effect on price if generally available.

The term 'dealing' in the Model Code includes the following:

- Any acquisition or disposal, or agreement to acquire or dispose, any securities of the company.

- Any grant, acceptance, acquisition, disposal, exercise or discharge of an option or other right or obligation to acquire or dispose of securities or any interest in securities on the company.

Under the Model Code, 'restricted persons' must not deal in any securities of the listed company during a 'prohibited period' that includes the following:

- A close period which is the period of 60 days or other relevant period before an announcement of results.

- Any other time when there exists unpublished, price sensitive inside information about the company.

Under the Model Code, there is an advance clearance procedure for dealing in the securities of the company as follows:

- As a general rule of thumb, a restricted person must not deal without obtaining clearance in advance from the person designated for that purpose.

- For a director (other than the chairperson or the chief executive) or the company secretary, clearance must be obtained from the chairperson or another designated director.

- The chairperson should seek clearance from the chief executive and the chief executive should seek clearance from the chairperson.

Under the Model Code, directors and all persons discharging managerial responsibilities have responsibilities in relation to connected persons as follows:

- To seek to prohibit any dealing by persons connected to him or her, or by investment managers acting for him or her during a close period.

- To advise all connected persons and investment managers of the following:

  — the name of the listed company;

  — the close periods which are prohibited periods; and

— the requirement for them to advise the company immediately after dealing.

The Model Code contains exceptions from the basic prohibitions on 'dealing' in a 'prohibited period' as follows:

- Under paragraph 12, for the grant of options by the board of directors under an employees' share scheme during a prohibited period to individuals *who are not restricted persons* in circumstances where the grant could not reasonably be made at another time and failure to make the grant would indicate that the company is in a prohibited period.

- Under paragraph 13, for the award of securities and the grant of options by the board of directors under an employees' share scheme during a prohibited period to individuals *who are restricted persons* if made in accordance with the terms as to timing and value set out in the employees' share scheme and failure to make the award would indicate that the company is in a prohibited period; the exceptions to this permission are as follows:

    — Discretionary awards or grants that would not otherwise have been made other than for the event that led to the commencement of the prohibited period.

    — Awards or grants which are made in a prohibited period during which the relevant scheme was introduced or altered.

- Under paragraph 14, for the exercise of options by the company's employees under an employees' share scheme in circumstances where the final date for the exercise of the option falls in an exceptionally long prohibited period and the restricted person could not reasonably have been expected to exercise it at an earlier time when he or she was free to deal.

- Under paragraph 2, it is the case that certain dealings are expressly excluded from the provisions of the Model Code:

    — Under paragraph 2(h), a transfer of shares into a savings scheme that invests in the securities of the company where the shares have been acquired by the employee either through the exercise of an option under a savings-related share option scheme or through a release of shares from a SIP trust; an example would be the transfer of shares to an ISA.

    — Under paragraph 2(i), for certain dealings in connection with a tax-approved savings-related share option scheme of a tax-approved SIP or any other scheme similar to either of the aforementioned on which participation is extended on similar terms and but which do not have the tax-approved status; the exception does not extend to the disposal of shares acquired under the scheme by a restricted person.

—   Under paragraph 2(j), the surrender of an option or the cancellation of an option under an employees' share scheme.

—   Under paragraph 2(l), the transfer of shares by an independent trustee of an employees' share scheme to a beneficiary who is not a restricted person.

● A restricted person may give an instruction to an independent third party to deal on his or her behalf in a prohibited period provided the restricted person enters into arrangements outside a prohibited period, and the arrangements have been approved by the company. Examples of where this exception would be useful are as follows:

—   where a restricted person has set a share price position at which he or she wishes to exercise the option and sell the shares; and

—   where a restricted person needs to sell shares in order to raise funds for the payment of a tax liability arising from participation in the scheme.

● A restricted person may enter into a regular commitment for share purchase arrangements through standing order, direct debit, salary deduction or dividend reinvestment instructions. This exception would be applicable to the partnership shares module, the matching shares module and the dividend reinvestment schemes under the SIP and to contributions to ISAs. However, this exception is subject to the following conditions being met:

—   The restricted person does not enter into the arrangement during a prohibited period.

—   The restricted person does not make the initial purchase of the shares during a prohibited period unless there is a specific requirement in the scheme rules.

—   The restricted person does not cancel or vary his or her participation or carry out the sale of the shares during a prohibited period.

—   The restricted person must obtain clearance to deal before entering into or cancelling or varying the terms of his or her participation in the savings scheme or carrying out the sale of the scheme shares.

Recognition should also be given to The Listing Rules, Chapter 11, *Transactions with related parties*, which imposes requirements on related-party transactions and then provides exceptions as follows:

● The requirement is that where a related-party transaction is proposed with a listed company or any of its subsidiaries then a circular should be issued to the shareholders and prior approval obtained in general meeting. The related party is not permitted to vote at the meeting. A related party is any person who is or has been within the last 12 months a substantial shareholder, any person who is or has been in the last 12 months a director or a shadow director of the company or any group company, any person who exercises significant influence over the listed company and any associate of a related party which includes family trustees.

- By way of exception, this requirement does not apply to any transaction in accordance with an employees' share scheme or a long-term incentive scheme that involves the following:

  — The receipt of any asset including cash or shares of the company or any of its subsidiaries.

  — The grant of an option to acquire such an asset to a director of the company, its holding company or any of its subsidiaries.

  — The provision of a gift or loan to an employee benefits trust in order to finance such a receipt or grant.

- Under Chapter 11, Annex 1R, paragraph 1, the exception for small transactions covers transactions equal to or less than 0.25% in terms of each of the accounting profits, turnover, market capitalization or gross capital of the company.

- The effect of the exceptions for Chapter 11 is to exclude from *Transactions with related parties* most incentive-type arrangements and most employee benefit trusts as an employee benefit trust is neither a related party nor an associate of a related party.

Insider dealing

27.3 The insider dealing regulations are found in the Criminal Justice Act 1993 (CJA 1993), Pt V, supplemented by the Insider Dealings (Securities and Regulated Markets) Order 1994, SI 1994/187. These provisions are drafted to comply with the European Union Insider Trading Directive 89/592/EEC that was promulgated on 13 November 1989.

The criminal offence of insider trading can only be committed by individuals although a company can be guilty of a conspiracy or an incitement to commit such an offence.

Under CJA 1993, s 52, the criminal offences are as follows:

- dealing as an insider;

- encouragement of a third party to deal on the basis of insider information; and

- disclosure of inside information to a third party otherwise and than in the proper performance of the employment, office or profession.

The dealings that are caught are as follows:

- dealings on a regulated market;

- dealings effected in reliance of a professional intermediary; and
- all dealings by a professional intermediary.

A regulated market is a market that is designated by Treasury Order to be one. The definition includes all the major stock trading markets in the European Union (EU) and also the market in the US market, NASDAQ.

To be caught, the dealing or disclosure must involve inside information in relation to securities defined as follows:

- Under CJA 1993, s 57 a person has inside information only if the information is and he or she knows it is inside information and he or she has it and knows that he has it from an inside source defined as follows:

  — he or she has the information through being a director or an employee or a shareholder of an issuer of securities which will be the company; or

  — he or she has the information through having access to the information by virtue of his or her employment, office or profession; or

  — the source is a person as defined in either of the two aforementioned categories.

- Under CJA 1993, s 56 information is inside information if it meets the following criteria:

  — The information must relate to particular securities, to a particular issuer or to particular issuers of securities. It is not sufficient to refer securities generally or issuers generally.

  — The information must be specific or precise.

  — The information must not have been made public but if it were made public it would be likely to have a significant effect on the price of any securities; the securities are, therefore, price-affected securities in relation to the information.

  — The information is not restricted to information about the company itself but extends to information which may affect a company's business prospects.

- Under CJA 1993, s 58 the determination of whether or not the information has been made public and, therefore, what is meant by 'made public' is as follows:

  — the information is published in accordance with the rules of a regulated market for the purpose of informing investors and their professional advisers; or

  — the information is contained in records that are open to the public by virtue of a statutory provision like the records kept at Companies House; or

— the information can be readily acquired by those likely to deal in the securities to which it relates or of the company to which it relates; or

— the information is derived from information that has been made public.

Information can also be treated as made public even though it is communicated only to a section of the public or it can be acquired only by observation or it is communicated only on payment of a fee or it is published only outside the UK or it can be acquired only by persons exercising diligence or expertise.

Under CJA 1993, s 62 there can only be an offence within defined geographical boundaries as follows:

- the individual must have been in the UK at the time; or

- the dealing must have been on a UK regulated market; or

- where a professional intermediary is involved, he or she must have been within the UK at the time of the offence.

The implications for employee share schemes are as follows:

- Although the CJA 1993 offers general and specific defences, it is unlikely that they will be needed in relation to employee share schemes. The insider dealing provisions are restricted to dealings on a regulated market or through a professional intermediary.

  — The grant and exercise of options or the allotment of shares under employee share schemes are not usually affected by insider dealing provisions for the reason that although they constitute dealings they do not normally occur on a regulated market or through or by a professional intermediary.

  — Any subsequent dealing on a regulated market has the potential depending on the application of the insider trading definitions to be caught by Part V.

- The areas of vulnerability are as follows:

  — Where the grantor of the option or the body allotting the shares is a professional intermediary, such as a bank, then the insider dealer provisions need to be considered.

  — Where there are purchases and sales of shares on a stock exchange as a regulated market then the insider dealer provisions need to be considered.

  — The funding of employee trusts to buy shares from the market may constitute encouragement of a third party to deal on the basis of insider information.

  — The penalties, if found guilty under the insider trading provisions are: (1) on summary conviction, a fine not exceeding the statutory maximum or imprisonment for up to six months or both fine and imprisonment can be imposed; and (2) on indictment, a fine or up to seven years' imprisonment or, again, both fine and imprisonment can be imposed.

Chapter 28

Employment law

Introduction

28.1 This chapter explains the employment laws and regulations that are relevant to the management of employee share scheme arrangements. The chapter is concerned explicitly with areas of discrimination, other than age discrimination that is dealt with in a separate chapter, and matters pertaining to the termination of employment.

Status of the contract of employment

28.2 In applying these laws and regulations it is important to appreciate that the benefits that an employee enjoys or has the potential to enjoy from involvement in an employee share scheme do not derive from the contract of employment. They derive from a separate contractual arrangement that has been contracted on the basis of the rules of the employee share scheme. Typically, this contractual arrangement will go under any one of a series of names (share participation contract or share option contract or share agreement, etc) and will usually contain a clause that explicitly separates it from the contract of employment. It may state, for example, that the employee has no compensation rights for employee share scheme benefits foregone in the event of a dismissal and that the share scheme rules do not affect in any way whatsoever the employee's right under the contract of employment.

Sex discrimination

28.3 If participation is not offered to all the employees in the company on an all-employee share basis as opposed to a discretionary basis then sex discrimination may arise if as a consequence of the discretionary participation policy a greater percentage of either male employees or female employees take part.

Sex discrimination with age discrimination

28.4 The case of significance is *Barber v Guardian Royal Exchange* [1990] ECI 1989 (*Barber Judgment*). Under this ruling, there should be no discrimination on the grounds of sex, either directly or indirectly, in the scheme rules for current scheme participants or for future scheme participants. This is an area where sex discrimination interacts with age discrimination in that any reference to retirement in the scheme rules must not discriminate between male employees and female employees on the basis of age. The tax-approved schemes are now required to set a specified date for retirement as explained in the chapter on age discrimination.

Sex discrimination and part-time working

28.5 The case of significance is *R v Secretary of State for Employment ex p Equal Opportunities Commission* [1994] IRLR 176, HL. As a consequence of this case, if the scheme's participation policy limits participation to full-time employees then they may by discriminating unlawfully against part-time employees.

Any exclusion of part-time workers is, in fact, contrary to the Part-Time Workers (Prevention of Less Favourable Treatment) Regulations 2000 (PTW(PLFT) Regs 2000) unless exclusion can be justified on objective grounds. This is a UK employment law initiative that implements EU Directive 97/81/EC and forms part of the programme initiated by the EU to combat discrimination of atypical workers. The Regulations require employers to give individuals on part-time contracts equal pay to individuals on full-time contracts provided they do the same jobs. The interaction with sex discrimination arises from the fact that large numbers of part-time workers are female so, in this context, the Regulations represent an important attempt to combat sex discrimination. Furthermore, the PTW(PLFT) (Amendment) Regs 2002, effective from 1 October 2002, amend the 2000 Regulations by removing the distinction between fixed-term and permanent contracts for the purpose of ascertaining what are different types of contract for purposes of the 2000 Regulations.

Sex discrimination and qualifying service periods

28.6 The Sex Discrimination Act 1976 (SDA 1976) has a wide jurisdiction and, depending on the circumstances, a requirement for a qualifying service period could be construed as indirect sex discrimination.

Fixed-term employee discrimination

28.7 There are mirror regulations to the part-time workers for fixed-term employees that operate on the basis of the Fixed-Term Employees (Prevention of Less Favourable Treatment) Regulations 2002 (FTE(PLFT) Regs 2002) – a UK employment law initiative implementing EU Directive 97/70/EC. The principle of the Directive on which the Regulations are based is that an individual with a fixed-term contract should not be treated less favourably than a comparable permanent co-worker. The effect of these Regulations is that exclusion from an employee share scheme is contrary to the requirements of the legislation unless it can be justified on an objective basis.

Works councils

28.8 If works councils exist then it will usually be expedient for the company to consult them on the introduction of employee share schemes or on amendments to existing employee share schemes. A works council is a committee that represents workers and functions at the local level as a complement to national labour negotiations. They are not compulsory in the UK and even where they are established may not view their remit as inclusive of employee share schemes. However, where there are positive interactions between the company and the works council the opportunity exists for garnering employee support for the introduction of the employee share scheme.

Exclusion of rights in dismissal

28.9 Employee share schemes are usually structured in a way that excludes them from an employee's contractual benefits and entitlements under the contract of employment. The circumstances in which this separation becomes particularly relevant arise at termination where the employee may seek to claim damages for loss of share benefits, current and future, in the event of a wrongful dismissal by the company, arising where there is a breach of contract.

It is important to recognise that share benefits cannot, as a matter of principle, be excluded from a loss that an employee could seek in compensation for a successful statutory claim of unfair dismissal. Remember that, depending on the facts of the case, it is possible for the employee to claim for both wrongful dismissal and unfair dismissal in the same case.

Wrongful dismissal

Micklefield v SAC Technology Ltd

28.10 The case of *Micklefield v SAC Technology Ltd* [1990] 1 WLR 1002; [1990] IRLR 218; [1991] 1 All ER 275 ('Micklefield') illustrates the need to include a carefully structured term in the employment contract specifically to exclude the employee from contractual benefits for which a claim could be sought on dismissal. This exclusion clause has become known as 'The Micklefield Clause'.

In the *Micklefield case*, the scheme rules included a specific provision under which the optionholder was deemed to have waived entitlement to compensation for loss of any benefit of any rights under the scheme as part of his or her compensation for loss of office.

The court's decision established the position under which Mr Micklefield was not entitled to compensation for loss of the option. The basis for this position was as follows:

- The share option contract had included a provision that expressly exempted the company from the part of its liability for wrongful dismissal that related to the option arrangement.

- The relationship between the employer and the employee had ended when Mr Micklefield was dismissed and the option was granted on terms that included the opportunity to exercise the option only to the extent that Mr Micklefield had remained an employee of the company.

The court held that it was a rule of construction rather than a principle of law that a person could not take advantage of his of her own wrong. As a rule of construction, therefore, the court held that it was possible to exclude as the company had sought to so by the express terms of the option contract.

The lessons from the *Micklefield* case are as follows:

- The decision in the *Micklefield* case would seem to imply that in the absence of an exclusion clause it is possible for an employee who was wrongfully or unfairly dismissed to claim compensation for any loss of benefits under the scheme and to exercise his or her option regardless of the fact that he or she had been wrongfully dismissed.

- Interestingly, it was the *Micklefield case* that decided that the Unfair Contract Terms Act 1977 (UCTA 1977) could not be used as a basis for ignoring an exclusion clause as unreasonable. Under UCTA 1977, s 3 it is not possible for a party to a contract with a consumer to exclude or restrict his or her liability for breach of contract. However, with reference to U CTA 1977, Sch 1 para 1 this provision does not apply to 'any contract so far as it relates to the creation or transfer of securities or of any right or interest in securities'. It would seem to follow that the protection cannot apply to an employee share option contract. However, in the case of *Commerzbank AG v Keen* [2006] EWCA Civ 1536, [2006] All ER (D) 239 (Nov) at the Court of Appeal it was held that UCTA 1977, s 3 does not apply to term in a contract for an employee's remuneration. The reason that was given for this conclusion is that an employee does not deal as a consumer with his or her employer with regard to remuneration.

- If the employer and the grantor of the option are different then the *Micklefield Clause* should be repeated in the contract of employment.

- The decision in the *Micklefield case* was later upheld in the leading case of *Clark v BET plc* [1997] IRLR 348 (QBD) HC.

Levett v Biotrace International plc

28.11 A challenge to the position that was understood as a result of the *Micklefield* case came in a later case – *Levett v Biotrace International plc* [1999] ICR 818 (CA), [1999] IRLR 375 ('Levett') in which an employee who had been dismissed tried to exercise share options after he had been dismissed from the employment.

The *Levett* case involved some very valuable share option rights that were held by a managing director who was dismissed from his employment.

Although the dismissal followed the disciplinary hearing, the company did actually concede that the dismissal was in breach of contract and that, indeed, in its own view, there were no grounds to justify a summary dismissal. Nevertheless, the company continued to argue that the share option rights lapsed at the termination of the employment.

The scheme rules did actually contain the exclusion clause designed specifically to exclude liability to compensation for loss of share option rights arising on termination. However, the court decided that the relevant clause could only apply if the dismissal was lawful. In the *Levett* case the dismissal was considered unlawful.

The lessons from the *Levett* case are as follows:

- The court decision needs to be interpreted specifically in the context of the particular facts of each case. The drafting in the scheme rules should make it clear whether the lapse applies in both lawful and unlawful terminations. Again, the requirement is to examine the content of the exclusion clause and to be aware as in the *Micklefield* case that the rule that a party cannot benefit from his or her own wrong is one of construction rather than one of public policy.

- Exclusion clauses and lapse provisions should be drafted very carefully and in particular the scheme rules should refer specifically to unlawful termination of employment and that the rights and discretions that arise under the scheme rules will not be varied in a given case by the provisions of the employment contract, the contents of a side letter or an agreement in any other form that has been established between employer and employee.

Unfair dismissal

28.12 In situations of unfair dismissal, the provisions of the Employment Rights Act 1996 (ERA 1996) prevent employers from contracting out of their obligations to provide compensation for loss of share incentive rights. Where there is demonstrably unfair dismissal, therefore, exclusion clauses cannot be relied upon to assist the company in limiting its liability in relation to the loss of share incentive rights.

The Employment Rights Act 1996 contains provisions that set out the basis for any compensation awards as follows:

- *'Basic award'*: calculated on a scale according to length of service, age and salary.

- *'ompensatory award'*: defined as 'such an amount as the tribunal considers just and equitable in all the circumstances having regard for the loss sustained by the complainant in consequence of the dismissal insofar as that loss is attributable to action taken by the employer'. The current maximum level of a compensatory award is £60,600 unless a claim is brought on the grounds of discrimination in which case if upheld there is no limit on the compensatory award.

In addition to the compensatory award, an employee will also be paid a statutory redundancy payment at the rates ruling at the time.

Casey v Texas Homecare Ltd

28.13 With regard to unfair dismissal, an interesting approach was taken by the Employment Appeals Tribunal (EAT) in the case of *Casey v Texas Homecare Limited* [1988] EAT 632/87 ('*Texas Homecare*') and, indeed, this case established a number of positions that should be given serious consideration as follows:

- The tribunal refused to give an award for the expectation of future grants at some time in the future.

- The tribunal assessed a loss of benefit arising from the lapse of an existing option at £1,000 and declared that the tribunal would be wrong to take the view that an assessment arising from the loss of a share option would be 'too speculative or indefinite'.

The lessons from the *Texas Homecare* case are as follows:

- The rules on unfair dismissal do not prevent scheme rules from containing exclusion clauses. However, the principle is that an employer cannot in normal circumstances use these exclusion clauses to negate the employee's right to make a claim for unfair dismissal.

- Where there is a claim for compensation arising from unfair dismissal, it will be made on totally different principles than the claim for compensation arising from wrongful dismissal. The statutory position in ERA 1996, s 203 establishes that an exclusion clause in a contract cannot circumvent an employee's right to a claim for unfair dismissal.

TUPE Regulations

Pitney Bowes Management Services Ltd v French & Others

28.14 The *Pitney Bowes Management Services Ltd v French & Others* [2002] EAT 408/00, [2002] All ER (D) 51 (Apr) ('*Pitney Bowes*') case gave some much needed guidance on whether or not the Transfer of Undertakings (Protection of Employment) Regulations 1981 ('TUPE Regs') that implement the EU Acquired Rights Directive, applied to employee share scheme arrangements.

The employees, originally employed by Sainsburys Supermarket Ltd, argued that The TUPE Regulations should be strictly interpreted, on the basis that their purpose was to protect workers and to safeguard their rights when a change of employer occurred and that this could only be achieved by ensuring that all the employees' rights were actually transferred. The employees argued further that if the TUPE Regs had intended to exclude employee share schemes then it would have done so explicitly in same way as pension schemes are explicitly excluded.

The new employer argued in reply that the employees were merely entitled to a comparable scheme rather than literally the scheme and that, as Pitney Bowes could not deliver Sainsbury shares, any employee entitlement to remain in the scheme would be impossible.

The importance of this case was that the EAT, identified specifically in its ruling that where a buyer purchases a business out of a group through the acquisition of the assets that comprise the business rather than through purchasing the share capital of the company then the new employer has obligations to deliver an alternative scheme arrangement to the employees. The tribunal did not agree with the strict interpretation of the TUPE Regs for which the employees had argued but agreed with the position that had been put forward by the employer.

The implications of the *Pitney Bowes* case are as follows:

- The transferring employees who were participants of an employee share scheme operated by their employing company before the sale must be offered an employee share scheme participation by the new employing company. Taking the wording of the ruling by the tribunal, the scheme that is offered by the new employing company must provide 'participation in a scheme of substantial equivalence, but one which is free from unjust, absurd or impossible features.'

- The tribunal agreed with the employer that there is no right under the TUPE Regs to continue to participate in the previous employer's profit sharing scheme but that employees do have a right to a comparable scheme. Even if the employment contract does not refer to the employer's profit sharing scheme, the existence of a scheme in which the employee is or may become eligible to participate may be considered to form part of that employee's contract.

- Following the facts of this case, where there is an asset purchase by a company from a transferor company that has an employee share scheme the company must be aware that it may have an obligation under the TUPE Regs to provide an employee share scheme which is substantially comparable to that in place in the transferor company.

Exercise of discretion by the employer

28.15   A series of cases illustrate the success of employees in suing for significant sums of money in circumstances where their employers have in the exercise of discretion not paid bonuses. The bonus clauses in the employees' contracts had traditionally been drafted widely with the express purpose of giving to the employer complete discretion on the level of the bonus that would be awarded.

Clark v BET plc

28.16   In *Clark v BET* plc [1997] IRLR 348 HC Mr Clark was dismissed from the company and claimed that he was entitled to compensation relating to salary increases and bonus payments that he contended, he would have earned during his notice period of three years duration. His contract had provided that he would 'participate in a bonus arrangement providing a maximum of 60% basic salary in any year'.

Mr Clark's employers contended in court that they had complete discretion on how they interpreted the contract for purposes of determining the bonus payment and that they were, therefore, entitled to award no bonus whatsoever.

The court disagreed with the position taken by the employers and held that if the directors had exercised their discretion either capriciously or in bad faith then that represented breach of contract. In making its ruling, the court was mindful of the content of the contract that conferred a right to participate in a bonus scheme with an obligation on the employer to provide a bonus scheme. The court assessed the loss by determining what would have been the position had the employer performed its obligations properly. In particular, the court stated that it should not be assumed that any discretion would have been exercised to give Mr Clark the least possible benefit if that result was on the basis of unrealistic assumptions. Additionally, in making its ruling, the court looked at previous bonuses that had been paid to Mr Clark and at bonuses paid to employees who were adjudged to be comparable to Mr Clark. The award of damages was around £3.25 million, a record for common law damages.

Clark v Nomura International plc

28.17   In *Clark v Nomura International plc* [2000] IRLR 766 Mr Clark, who was a senior equities trader, operated under a contract that secured him a basic salary only together with a discretionary bonus that was 'not guaranteed in any way'. Although he had achieved substantial profits for the company, he was dismissed and paid his basic salary for his notice period of three months. He received no payment for his annual bonus even though he was still in the employment of the company at what would have been the date of the bonus payment.

The court, in making its ruling, sought to make a judgment on whether the employer had acted rationally in the exercise of its discretion. This approach represented the application of a wider test than that of capriciousness that had been applied in the case of *Clark v BET plc* [1997]. The court held that an employer can breach the employment contract if it exercises its discretion, which appears to be unfettered and absolute, in a way that no reasonable employer would have done and ruled that, in this case, the employer's discretion should be dismissed on the grounds of 'perversity'.

The court assessed the loss by considering the level of the bonus payments made to Mr Clark in previous years before he had been dismissed and also the payments made to other employees in the company both before and after his dismissal. The award of damages was £1.35 million, based on what would have been paid had the employer complied with its contractual obligations.

Horkulak v Cantor Fitzgerald International

28.18   The significance of *Horkulak v Cantor Fitzgerald International* [2004] IRLR 942, [2004] All ER (D) 170 (Oct) in the first place, was that it was the first discretionary bonus case to be heard by the Court of Appeal since the case of *Lavarack v Woods of Colchester* [1966] 3 All ER 683 in 1967.

In the case, Mr Horkulak, who was a senior managing director, operated under a contract that provided that the company 'may at its discretion pay you an annual discretionary bonus'. Mr Horkulak resigned which allowed him to bring a case for constructive dismissal, contending that there had been a repudiatory breach of his contract by the chief executive officer (CEO) who he claimed had subjected him to insult and humiliation.

The Court of Appeal upheld the decision of the High Court in awarding significant damages for wrongful dismissal and then went on to consider whether or not the High Court had been correct in assessing those damages on the basis that Mr Horkulak would have received discretionary bonus payments of £630,000.

The Court of Appeal held that an unlimited discretion in a contract will be regarded as subject to an implied term that it will be exercised genuinely and rationally.

The lessons from the *Clark* cases and the *Horkulak* case are as follows:

- These three decisions from 1997 to 2004 indicate a strengthening of the position taken by the courts. In 1997 in *Clark v BET plc* the position taken was somewhat narrow in identifying capricious exercise as a basis for breach of contract. By contrast, in 2004 at the *Horkulak case*, the court identified in more positive mode the wider duty on the employer to exercise the discretion rationally and in good faith.

- In the *Horkulak case*, the court was aware that Mr Horkulak was working in a high-earning environment and that his perception was, quite clearly, that the payment of discretionary bonuses was part of the remuneration structure. Also in the *Horkulak case* the court's identification of the bonus as a contractual benefit was in part based on the fact that Mr Horkulak should not have given his notice and should, therefore, still have been in the employment of the company.

Tesco Stores Ltd v Pook

28.19   In *Tesco Stores Ltd v Pook* [2003] EWHC 823 (Ch), [2004] IRLR 618, [2003] All ER (D) 233 (Apr) case, Mr Pook, the defendant was a senior employee who had committed fraud and was subsequently convicted.

The High Court declared that although there may be no relevant express term in the share option contract it is an implied term of the scheme that an option is not exercisable if the employee has committed a breach of contract that would entitle the employer to terminate the employee's contract of employment.

Mallone v BPB Industries plc

28.20 In *Mallone v BPB Industries plc* [2002] EWCA Civ 126, [2002] ICR 1045, [2002] IRLR 452, [2002] All ER (D) 242 (Feb) Mr Mallone who as a senior employee was a member of the senior executive share option scheme. The scheme rules stated that options could be exercised after three years but lapsed in the event that the employee was dismissed on 'fault' grounds at which point the employee could purchase an 'appropriate number of shares' calculated by taking into account the length of service and the appropriate multiplier, subject to the absolute discretion of the directors.

Mallone left the employment of the company in 1995 on 'no fault' grounds and on the day after leaving the directors cancelled the options, without informing Mr Mallone and calculated that the 'appropriate number of shares' was zero. It was not until 1997 that Mr Mallone tried to exercise his options, only to learn that the directors had cancelled them.

The High Court determined that the cancellation of the options was unlawful under the terms of the scheme and that the directors had acted irrationally. When BPB Industries plc appealed the Court of Appeal upheld the decision of the High Court. The options had been granted for past performance and in anticipation of future loyalty and were vested property rights. The Court of Appeal ruled that although the directors had absolute discretion they had exercised that discretion irrationally and their decision was one that no reasonable employer could have reached.

Role of the remuneration committee

28.21 Provided the company has constituted a remuneration committee, usually as a subcommittee of the Board, all these matters pertaining to the exercise of discretion should be reserved for the remuneration committee. This approach should act as a strong contributor to securing consistency in decision-making. Care must be taken, therefore, to ensure that decision-making does not trickle down to individual directors or maybe, even, the human resources manager, for example, and it become custom and practice in the company for the discretion to be exercised at a lower level in the company. There is no case law that can be cited on this specific point although it is recognised best practice.

Enforceability of restrictive covenants in incentive schemes

Duarte v Black and Decker

28.22 In *Duarte v Black and Decker* [2007] EWHC 2720 (QB), [2007] All ER (D) 378 (Nov) the High Court considered the enforceability of a two-year non-competition covenant in a cash long-term incentive plan which had a Maryland governing law clause although there were no restrictive covenants in his contract of employment.

Duarte, a senior employee with Black and Decker in the UK, resigned his employment to take up a position with a competitor. During the employment he agreed to a number of restrictive covenants which were subject to the laws of Maryland in USA. After the employment had ended, Black and Decker tried to prevent Mr Duarte from taking up the new position with the competitor, citing the restrictive covenants as the basis for their position. Duarte then sought to establish that the restrictive covenants were unenforceable and applied for a declaration to that effect.

Under the Rome Convention, Article 6 the chosen governing law prevails unless it is contrary to mandatory provisions of employment law affording protection to employees. However, under the Rome Convention, Article 16 Maryland law would be subject to any overriding UK public policy on restrictive covenants.

The High Court held that the law on covenants is part of the general law on restraint of trade that is part of the general law on contract. It follows that Maryland law could not displace English law in enforcing the restrictive covenants and that Maryland law would be subject to English law on covenants. If covenants were valid and enforceable under Maryland law but unenforceable under English law, then English law would prevail.

Forfeiture of compulsorily deferred bonuses

Finnegan v J & E Davy

28.23 In *Finnegan v J & E Davy* [2007] IEHC 18 Finnegan, an employee with a firm of stockbrokers in the Republic of Ireland from 1990 to 2000, the company recognised that the possibility of bonus payments comprised a part of his remuneration. Without any consultation with Finnegan, in 1997 the company changed the terms of the bonus arrangement so that part of the bonus would be compulsorily deferred for one year and if Mr Finnegan left within the deferral period he would forfeit the amount. As it happened, Mr Finnegan left the company in 2000 and when he asked for payment of the deferred amount he was told that through the act of leaving he had forfeited the payment.

The specific point that the court considered was whether or not Mr Finnegan could be deemed to have accepted the change in the terms of his bonus arrangement and on the facts of the case, it ruled that he had not accepted the changes and, therefore, was entitled to receive the deferred amount on leaving. The court also considered whether or not forfeiture provisions in relation to deferred bonuses could be deemed to be a restraint of trade for the scheme participant. On this wider point, the court concluded that the forfeiture provision did constitute restraint of trade as it was intended to prevent the individual from accepting any other employment in the same trade.

The lessons from the *Finnegan* case are as follows:

- The case illustrates that for any change in a contractual arrangement the company must secure the consent of the employee, that the company must engage with the employee with a clear and meaningful communication and that the company should secure consent in writing from the employee.

- Whether or not the attachment of forfeiture provisions to contractual benefits can be deemed to be restraint of trade will be depend on the facts of each case, notably the size of the deferred amount and the proportion of the deferred amount within the individual's total remuneration.

Construction of the rules and share scheme contract

McCarthy v McCarthy & Stone plc

28.24 The case of *McCarthy v McCarthy & Stone plc* [2006] EWHC 1851 (Ch), [2006] 4 All ER 1127, [2006] All ER (D) 273 (Jul) concerned the share option entitlements of a former director who had left the company after a failed management buy-out initiative in which he had been involved.

The case revolved around the wording from the share option scheme rules:

> Where an option-holder ceases to hold office or employment, the remuneration committee shall in its absolute discretion determine whether the option will be exercisable having considered the extent to which the performance condition has been achieved at the date of termination. If the remuneration committee so decides, the option-holder may exercise all or a proportion of his option ... such proportion being determined by the remuneration committee pro rata to the achievement of the performance condition.

The rules had been drafted to give discretion to the remuneration committee as a two-stage decision process: the *first stage* required a discretion on whether or not the employee could exercise the option while the *second stage* required a decision on the vesting level, based on actual performance achieved. In the case of Mr McCarthy, although the performance condition had been fully satisfied, the remuneration committee decided that the option could be exercised to purchase only 75% of the shares over which the option had been exercised.

The court overturned the decision of the remuneration committee and agreed with Mr McCarthy that he should be allowed on the exercise of the option to purchase 100% of the shares over which the option had been granted. The basis for the judgment was that, in accordance with the scheme rules, the one and only factor that the remuneration committee could take into account in deciding the extent to which the option would be exercisable was the extent to which the performance condition had been satisfied.

The lessons from the *McCarthy* case are as follows:

- Where rights have already vested and performance conditions have already been satisfied, it requires careful drafting in the construction of the rules and share option to deny the employee participant the entitlement to the shares.

- If the remuneration committee is given an overtly subjective and extensive discretion it may impact on the employee participant's 'right to acquire' the shares which could result in additional exposure to income tax and NICs.

Chapter 29

Age discrimination

Introduction

29.1   This chapter addresses the implications for employee share schemes of the Employment Equality (Age) Regulations 2006 (EE(A) Regs 2006), SI 2006/1031 that came into effect from 1 October 2006. Although similar age discrimination provisions are operating in other countries throughout the EU, it cannot be assumed that they will be applied in the same way in each or those countries. There is also equivalent-type age discrimination legislation that has operated in the USA for many years.

At the time of writing, the age discrimination legislation in the UK has been applied in relation to pensions and redundancy. However, there are features of employee share scheme arrangements that are potentially vulnerable to the Regulations and it is these features that are explored in this chapter.

For a case to be brought to court, an employee would have to take the appropriate action. Unless the employee takes this initiative, no action will be taken in an age discrimination situation, even though it may be a clear case of age discrimination against the individual.

Application of the Regulations

29.2

The overriding key principle is that the company must ensure that there is *objective justification* and *consistent application* with regard to the following:

- any references to age in the employee share scheme rules; and

- any decisions that are based partly or wholly on age.

From the effective date, any discrimination that is age-related may be unlawful. However, this does not necessarily mean that it will not be permissible in circumstances where an objective justification can be established. The vulnerability in relation to employee share schemes is in relation to the provisions in scheme rules that relate to time. In this context, particular care must be given to the framing of the following:

- Any service-related eligibility criteria that is applied by the company; whether or not enshrined in the scheme rules.

- Any early leaver provisions in the scheme rules, particularly where the reason for the early leaving is retirement.

There is a direct impact of the Regulations on all new share options granted and new share awards made on or after 1 October 2006. With regard to existent outstanding options and awards any actions that have already been taken in relation will not be affected although any future discretionary decisions taken by the directors in relation to these options should be with regard to the Regulations.

Concept of retirement and the Regulations

29.3 When retirement is the reason for the early leaving, it could be contended that the provision within the scheme rules establishes a discrimination in favour of older employees, particularly where the early leaver provision operates automatically. As a general principle, it is preferable to deal with retirement on a discretionary rather than an automatic basis although care must be taken to avoid indirect age discrimination when using the discretion.

Under the Regulations, discrimination is unlawful unless it can be objectively justified. If the early leaving provision cannot be objectively justified then the risk is that the retirement rule will have to be applied to younger leavers also in order to avoid discrimination. The principle of objective justification in Regulation 3 is interpreted in the context of 'proportionate means of achieving a legitimate aim'. In order to establish objective justification, it is important, if at all possible, to have supporting contemporaneous evidence.

Service-related eligibility criteria

29.4 Where eligibility to receive an option or an award is dependent on working for a certain length of time or having reached a certain level within the company then there is potential for a case of age discrimination on the basis that employees who are younger may not be in a position to meet the criteria.

However, in applying these rules, there is *a statutory exemption* that allows any requirement up to five years' service as the basis of eligibility not to be unlawful.

Example 29.1

The most obvious examples of cases that will qualify for this statutory exemption are:

- the maximum qualifying period under the tax-approved savings-related share option scheme of five years maximum; and

- the maximum qualifying period under the tax-approved SIP of 18 months.

So although these are clearly examples of service-related criteria they are protected by the statutory exemption.

Where existing scheme rules include a prohibition on the grant of options or the making of awards to individuals who are close to retirement those scheme rules must be changed. For new scheme rules, they must not include any restrictions on eligibility on the basis for the retirement date.

Exercise arrangements

29.5 The concerns over the application of the Regulations to exercise arrangements arise specifically in relation to retirement and the comparison of treatment between *contractual retirement* and *early retirement*. It is the case that in most scheme rules contractual retirement is treated as a good leaver reason. However, early retirement is sometimes treated as a good leaver and sometimes treated as a bad leaver and sometimes the directors have complete discretion on how the retiring employee is to be treated on retirement.

In addressing retirement, first and foremost, any discretionary decision that is made by the directors (or maybe the remuneration committee) must be made in a way that does not discriminate on the basis of age. Additionally, as a general rule of thumb, unless there is an objective justification, if an employee who retires early will always be in a less favourable position than an employee who retires at the contractual retirement age then the provision will most probably be unlawful under the Regulations.

Specified age for retirement

29.6 The specific implications of the specified age for retirement are set out in the sections on each of the schemes respectively. It is important to be clear that any change to the rules of a tax-approved scheme will require specific approval from HMRC. HMRC will allow the lowering of the specified age, but not the highering of the specified age. Indeed, HMRC will allow lowering for existing options as well as new options. However, lowering the age can raise further complications as it can be considered discrimination.

Example 29.2

Suppose that two employees leave the company but one either side of the lowering of the age. In these circumstances, the employee who left before the change may have to forfeit his shares whereas the employee who after the change may not, depending, of course, for each of them on whether or not they had attained the specified age.

Tax-approved savings-related share option scheme ('Sharesave')

29.7 The implications for the tax-approved savings-related share option scheme are as follows:

- *Service-related eligibility criteria:* The scheme's service-related eligibility criterion of up to five years is protected by the statutory exemption.

- *Specified age:* This scheme requires that a specified age is included. It follows that any reference to age is not unlawful as it is required to comply with other statutory requirements. For Sharesave, the specified age is set at any age from 60 to 75. So the question that arises is: What age should be set as the specified age? There would be a good case for adopting the minimum age as the specified age if the company had no other share schemes in place. However, the company may want to encourage older employees to stay in its employment, in which case there would be an objective justification for setting the specified age at a higher age. Also, the company may have other share schemes in place, in which case the objective justification may be to set the specified age for all schemes at the same level.

Tax-approved company share option scheme (CSOP)

29.8 The implications for the tax-approved company share option (CSOP) scheme are as follows:

(a) *Service-related eligibility criteria:* The scheme can have a service-related eligibility requirement as long as it is structured in a form that gives it protection under the statutory exemption of up to five years service. In particular, it must contain no reference to retirement age.

(b) *Specified age:* The legislation that supports this scheme does not require an age to be specified. However, the only way an employee can claim favourable tax treatment on the early exercise of an option as a result of retirement is if the scheme rules do actually include a specified age. So the question arises: Should an age limit be inserted in the rules? Given that it is not a compulsory requirement under the legislation, it would not be automatically justified. However, an objective justification could be that an age must be inserted to ensure that the best tax treatment is secured. The permitted age range is 55 to 70. If, for example, the company also had a savings-related share option scheme it may choose to establish age that is common to the two schemes at between 60 and 70. Additionally, for the CSOP, there will often be included in the scheme rules a discretion in relation to employees who retire at less than the specified age.

Tax-approved share incentive plan (SIP)

29.9 The implications for the tax-approved share incentive plan (SIP) are as follows:

(*a*)   *Service-related eligibility criteria: The* scheme's service-related eligibility criterion of up to 18 months is protected by the statutory exemption.

(*b*)   *Specified age:* This scheme requires that a specified age is included. It follows that any reference to age is not unlawful as it is required to comply with other statutory requirements. For SIP, the specified age has a minimum age of 50 and there is no maximum age. So the question that arises is: What age should be set as the specified age? There would be a good case for adopting the minimum age as the specified age if the company had no other share schemes in place. However, the company may want to encourage older employees to stay in its employment, in which case there would be an objective justification for setting the specified age at a higher age. Also, the company may have other share schemes in place, in which case the objective justification may be to set the specified age for all schemes at the same level.

Non-tax approved employee share schemes

29.10 The implications for the non-tax-approved employee share schemes are as follows:

- Remember that the two aspects of the scheme rules and scheme management that require scrutiny are: (1) service-related eligibility criteria; and (2) early leaver provisions. The fact is that for the non-tax-approved schemes, there are no statutory provisions that impact specifically on any service-related eligibility requirement and there is no requirement to insert a retirement date, the so-called specified date.

- Often the company operates tax-approved schemes alongside the non-tax approved schemes. In these circumstances, it could be argued that the inclusion of these rights in the tax-approved schemes is an objectively justifiable reason in the interests of consistency for including them in the non-tax-approved schemes.

Shareholder approval

29.11 The decision about seeking shareholder approval for the changes will depend on the gravity of the proposed amendments. It could be argued that a Board resolution only is required for changes that are being made to comply with the law. However, sometimes, the scheme rules require shareholder approval for the authorisation of changes.

Chapter 30

Share schemes for non-employees

Introduction

30.1 The chapter explores the considerations that apply to the involvement in company share schemes of individuals who are not employees or executive directors of the company.

Status of potential scheme participants

30.2 The non-employees to whom options are to be granted may be the company's non-executive directors. If they carry out additional work for the company beyond that covered by their directors' fees, but receive payment for those additional services without the company deducting PAYE or NICs then they will not be employees for share schemes purposes. This is so even though any directors' fees paid to them will need to be subject to PAYE and NICs.

Any UK resident non-executive directors who receive options will be treated as having acquired 'employment related securities' for the purposes of tax legislation. It is, unfortunately, possible for a director or other officer to be taxed on option gains as employment income whilst at the same time not being treated as an employee for tax purposes.

Where a UK resident individual who is neither an employee nor an officeholder of the company or any subsidiary receives an option, the tax treatment will depend upon their personal circumstances. If they provide their services through a service company, they may be taxed on any shares they receive as employment-related securities, even though their employment relates to the service company rather than the company itself. In that case, the obligation to account for the tax will rest on the service company and the individual rather than the company.

Some other self-employed consultants may benefit from a more favourable tax regime. In the past, HMRC have been prepared to accept that the grant of a MV or premium priced option to a non-employee will not cause any tax charge at that point. This is on the basis that such an option has no intrinsic value. When the option is subsequently exercised, tax will fall to be charged on the gain made in the same way as the rest of the individual's business profits. Treating a MV option as having no intrinsic value is, quite clearly, contrary to the current share-based payments accounting rules, and the attitude of HMRC in other areas such as transfer pricing, but as it appears to date, this interpretation has not yet been changed.

UK corporate law considerations

Allotment of shares

30.3 Normally, a company may only allot shares to the extent that shareholders have given authority so to do in accordance with CA 2006, ss 549–551 (CA 1985, s 80) and CA 2006, ss 561–566 (CA 1985, s 89). There is an exemption from this requirement for allotments pursuant to an employees' share scheme, but any option grant to non-employees would need to be covered by a separate authority.

Financial assistance

30.4 There is a general prohibition on the provision of financial assistance by a company or its subsidiary for the acquisition of shares in the company. Contravention of these rules is a criminal offence with the company's directors being personally liable. Granting someone an option to subscribe shares at a price which may turn out to be a discount to MV at the time the option is exercised is not in itself financial assistance; however, the provision of any funds, for example, to buy shares into an employees' trust in connection with the satisfaction of such options, would amount to financial assistance.

Prospectus Directive

30.5 If shares or options to acquire shares are being granted, it is always necessary to check whether a prospectus is required to be issued. Preparation of such a prospectus is time-consuming and lengthy. However, various exemptions are available. In particular, if shares are offered to less than 100 individuals, this will not constitute 'an offer to the public' whilst the grant of non-transferable options (at least in the UK) is not considered to be the grant of a 'transferable security'. As a prospectus is only required where there is an offer to the public of transferable securities, the company should not have to issue a prospectus where fewer than 100 grants are to be made.

Regulated activities

30.6 Under the Financial Services and Markets Act 2000 (FSMA 2000), there is a general prohibition on any non-authorised person engaging in regulated activities in the UK. Regulated activities include such matters as dealing in investments as principal (which includes the grant of options and the issue of shares in satisfaction of the exercise of options) and making arrangements for others to deal in shares. It does not matter where the person carrying out the activity is based. If the person on whose behalf the activities are carried out lives in the UK, then the rules apply. Again, contravention of the prohibition carries criminal penalties.

There is a general employees' share schemes exemption, which is not available in relation to options granted to or exercised by non-employees. The company should, however, be able to rely on Articles 15 and 28 of FS MA 2000 (Regulated Activities) Order 2001. Article 15 is an exemption for companies that do not hold themselves out as willing to grant options at prices determined by such companies generally and continuously, and does not regularly solicit members of the public for the purpose of inducing them to enter into options. On the basis that the company is not in the habit of offering to grant options to members of the public in the UK, then this exemption should apply.

Article 28 gives an exemption to the prohibition against making arrangements for others to deal in shares, provided that the person making the arrangements is also a party to them. This exemption should apply, provided that all communications sent to the non-employees are sent out in the name of the company itself rather than any other company in the group or any administrator or third party.

Financial promotion

30.7 Under FSMA 2000, there is also a general prohibition on the making of communications that induce or invite the individual to enter into a transaction which involves a regulated activity or investment. The prohibition does not apply (amongst other exemptions) to communications that are:

- one-off non-real time communications;

- communications to high net-worth individuals; and

- communications to sophisticated investors.

One-off non-real time communications

30.8 The Financial Services and Markets Act 2000 (Financial Promotion) Order 2001, Article 28 defines a 'one-off non-real time' communication. Such communications are limited to written communications that are tailored to the individual circumstances of the recipient, and are individual in nature.

It is possible to argue that non-employee option contracts are personal to the individual circumstances of the non-employee (for example, the differences as to the number of shares under option, the conditions of exercise and the vesting schedule would make such contracts personal to each individual) and that this should fit within the exemption even if each contract is not completely individual. This is, however, only one possible interpretation of the exemption and, if the company wishes to be absolutely certain, the contracts should be signed-off by an adviser with appropriate authorisation under FSMA 2000. In any event, it is important to document the fact that the existence and possible application of the exemption has been discussed and the best place for this is probably in the minutes of the board or the board committee that actually grants the options.

It is important to note that this exemption does not cover all communications and will only apply to a one-off communication without any follow-up discussions in relation to an option. This means that the company must include all the necessary information in a single written document and that any follow-up discussions must be purely factual (ie communications which do not invite or induce the individual to accept the grant of or to exercise an option) in order to fall within the scope of the exemption.

The fact that similar grants may be made in subsequent years to the same or other non-employees should not prejudice the company's ability to use this exemption. The 'one-off' element relates to the individual rather than the number of times a communication is made to that individual (ie if each communication is a 'one-off', the fact that there may be a series of one-off communications should not be problematic).

There are also exemptions available if the optionholder is a 'high net-worth individual' or a 'sophisticated investor'.

Overseas considerations

30.9 Before options are granted in any jurisdiction other than the UK, country-specific advice must be obtained.

Summary position

30.10 With care, it is possible to grant options to non-employees without falling foul of the applicable UK laws, but it is extremely important to ensure that all the documentation is in the correct form, and emanates from the correct source, ie the company rather than any subsidiary or third party.

Chapter 31

Annual report disclosure requirements

General requirements

Applies to all companies

31.1 The requirements include the following:

- The Companies Act 1985, Sch 7 used to contain various provisions requiring the inclusion, either in the Directors' Report or the Notes to the Accounts, of detailed information on the interests of directors in the companies' shares. Based on the information in the company's register of directors' interests it was necessary to include the extent of the interests at the start of the year and at the end of the year together with any grants of option and exercises of option in the year.

- All of the relevant provisions were repealed by the Companies Act 2006 [Commencement No 1, Transitional Provisions and Savings] Order 2006 (CA 2006 Order 2006) with effect from 6 April 2007. This was on the basis that many of the provisions were duplicating the requirements contained in the new EU Transparency Directive and Disclosure Directive, 2004/109/EC.

- There are still extensive disclosure requirements in the case of companies whose shares are quoted on the Official List of the London Stock Exchange and lesser requirements for AIM companies, but as these are in the Listing Rules or in regulations which do not apply to smaller unquoted companies many smaller companies no longer have any statutory obligation to disclose directors' interests in shares.

Directors Remuneration Report Regulations 2002, SI 2002/1986

Applies to quoted companies but not alternative investment market companies

31.2 For financial years ending on or after 31 December 2002, but relating to accounting periods beginning before 6 April 2008 quoted companies are required to disclose in greater detail as part of the annual report their directors remuneration packages in accordance with CA 1985, Sch 7A (now repealed) including involvement in share option schemes and long-term incentive plans.

The regulations apply to fully listed companies and UK incorporated companies that are officially listed in a EEA state or on the New York Stock Exchange or on NASDAQ.

The regulations do not apply to companies that are listed on the AIM.

The key requirements can be summarised as follows:

- The preparation of a detailed annual remuneration report that is signed-off by the Board of directors.

- Details must be provided of directors individual pay packages together with additional graphical information on performance.

- Full disclosure must be made of the names and addresses of the members of the remuneration committee together with details of its significant advisers.

- An advisory shareholder vote should be sought on the report to each annual general meeting (AGM).

The detailed requirements for inclusion in the statutory directors remuneration report are as follows:

- A statement of the company's policy on directors' remuneration for the period under review and subsequent periods for each director in office, from the end of the period under review to the date of the AGM. This section of the report should include the following:

  — The performance conditions to which director entitlement under share option and long-term incentive plan involvement is subject.

  — The reasons for particular performance conditions being chosen.

  — The methods chosen for assessing the fulfilment of the performance conditions and the reasons for choosing those methods.

  — The factors used in making external comparisons on performance conditions and to the extent that the factors relate to the performance of another company *or* of two or more companies, *or* of an index on which securities of a company or companies are listed, the identity of that company or companies or of the index.

  — The description of and reasons for any proposed significant changes to the terms and conditions of any entitlement that a director has under a share option scheme or a long-term incentive plan.

— The reasons why any director entitlement under a share option scheme or a long-term incentive plan is not subject to performance conditions if indeed that is the case for any of the directors.

— The explanation of the relative importance of the performance-related elements and the non-performance-related elements of the remuneration arrangements for each of the directors.

• The total shareholder return on the company's ordinary shares in each of the five years up to and including the period under review, depicted in line graph form and showing a comparison with a named broad equity index.

• The director involvement for each director, shown in table form, in share option arrangements with the company as follows:

— number of shares under option at the beginning of the period, or at the date of appointment if later;

— number of shares under option at the end of the period, or at the date of cessation if earlier;

— awards, exercises or lapses in the period together with options where there have been variations in the terms or conditions in the period;

— description of any variations in the terms or conditions in the period;

— cost of the options to the extent that it is applicable;

— option prices;

— exercisable periods, identifying the dates on which the options first become exercisable and the expiry dates;

— performance conditions to which share option exercises or share awards are subject;

— market price of the shares at the date of exercise for options exercised during the period; and

— market price of the share at the end of the period together with the highest and lowest prices during the period.

The requirement is to differentiate wherever practical between options that have different terms and conditions. However, where differentiation between options with different terms and conditions would produce a report of excessive length then disclosure may be made through weighted average prices and/or a range of dates. Under no circumstances, though should there be any aggregation between options where the option price is below the market price at the end of the period under review with options where the option price is equal to or below the market price at the end of the review period.

- Information on interests under share option schemes and long-term incentive plans *for each director* in table form, identifying the following:

  — interests of the director at the beginning of the period, or at the date of appointment if later;

  — interests of the director at the end of the period, or at the date of cessation if earlier;

  — interests awarded during the period including the number of shares that may become receivable in respect of those interests, the market price of the shares at the date of the award and details of any performance conditions;

  — interests vested in the period, the monies or other assets receivable, the number of shares, the date of the award, the market price at the date of the award, the market price at the date of vesting and the details of any performance conditions; and

  — end of the period over which performance conditions for the interests have to be fulfilled.

Directors' remuneration reports – current requirements

Applies to quoted companies but not alternative investment market companies

31.3 For financial years beginning on or after 6 April 2008 the new legislation contained in CA 2006, Pt 15 is in force. This largely restates the previous provisions for remuneration reports but also introduces a requirement for a shareholder vote (section 439).

The vote is advisory only. An ordinary resolution must be put to shareholders to approve the remuneration report, but if they vote against it the directors can still be paid and the company can still press ahead with the measures set out in the report, although in practice they will often choose to modify them to take account of the wishes of shareholders.

The Large and Medium-sized Companies and Groups (Accounts and Reports) Regulations 2008, SI 2008/410, Schedule 8

Applies to quoted companies but not alternative investment market companies

31.4 For financial years beginning on or after 6 April 2008 these regulations set out the detail required to be included in the directors' remuneration report.

The information to be included is essentially the same as that required under the 2002 regulations discussed above.

Listing Rules requirements

Applies to quoted companies but not alternative investment market companies

31.5 Under Listing Rules, LR9.8.8R, there is a requirement for a company that is listed on the Official List to include in its annual report and accounts a report from its board setting out the details of its directors' remuneration.

The regulations do not apply to companies that are listed on the AIM.

The requirement extends to the inclusion of a statement on the company's policy of granting share options and making share awards together with information on the involvement of each director in the company's share options and long-term incentive plans. The statement should explain any departure from the policy in the period under review and any change from the previous year.

The information for each director should be presented in table form together with explanatory notes as necessary and cover the following:

- number of shares under option at the beginning of the year, or at the date of appointment if later;

- number of shares under option at the end of the year;

- number of options granted, exercised or lapsed as unexercised during the year;

- the option prices;

- exercisable periods, identifying the dates on which the options first become exercisable and the expiry dates;

- cost of the options to the extent that it is applicable;

- market price of the shares at the date of exercise where options are exercised during the year;

- performance conditions to which share option exercises or share awards are subject; and

- market price of the share at the end of the period together with the highest and lowest prices during the period.

In circumstances where the options are exercised at different prices and/or different times this list of information items should be disclosed for each option price and/or exercise date combination. It may be that the information, if provided in this way, would be excessive in which case the company is permitted to meet its disclosure requirements through weighted average prices.

Any long-term incentive scheme involvement not covered by the above should be included in the report of the directors' remuneration committee as follows:

- The interests of each director, by name, at the beginning of the financial year.

- The entitlements or awards granted and commitments made during the year, identifying those that crystallise in the year and in subsequent years.

- The benefits received by each director in the year in the form of shares or cash payments.

- The interests of each director, by name, at the end of the financial year.

General requirements for quoted companies

Applies to quoted companies and alternative investment market companies

31.6 For financial years ending on or after 31 December 2002, but relation to accounting periods beginning before 6 April 2008 quoted companies *and* companies that are quoted on the AIM are required to disclose in accordance with CA 1985, Sch 6 (since repealed) and the Directors Remuneration Report Regulations 2002, SI 2002/1986 (DRRR 2002), there are specific requirements for disclosure in the annual accounts as follows:

- The amount of all gains, shown in aggregate, made by directors on the exercise of share options.

- The aggregate of monies paid to directors or payable to directors under long-term incentive schemes *and* the net value of assets other than monies and share options paid to directors or payable to directors.

For financial years beginning on or after 6 April 2008, the same requirements apply, but the relevant provisions can now be found in the Large and Medium-sized Companies and Groups (Accounts and Reports) Regulations 2008, SI 2008/410 (LMCG Regs 2008), Sch 7, para 10.

General requirements for unquoted companies

31.7 For financial years ending on or after 31 December 2002, but relating to accounting periods beginning before 6 April 2008, companies which are neither quoted companies or companies that are quoted on the

AIM are required to disclose in accordance with CA 1985, Sch 6 (now repealed) and the D RR Regs 2002, SI 2002/1986, there are specific requirements for disclosure in the annual accounts as follows:

- The aggregate of monies paid to directors or payable to directors under long-term incentive schemes *and* the net value of assets other than monies and share options paid to directors or payable to directors.

- The number of directors who exercised share options and for whose services shares were received or are receivable, under long-term incentive schemes.

Where the total of directors emoluments and the amounts disclosed under the above formula exceed £200,000 the following disclosure is required:

- The amount that is attributable to the highest paid director.

- The exercise behaviour of the highest paid director in the period under review and whether any shares were received or receivable by that director in the period.

For financial years beginning on or after 6 April 2008 this information only has to be provided by those unquoted companies large enough to be subject to the provisions of the LMCG Regs 2008, SI 2008/410. There are no longer any applicable requirements for smaller quoted companies.

Chapter 32

Institutional investor guidelines

Introduction

32.1 This chapter appreciates that for the publicly-quoted company or, indeed, for the private company with significant institutional shareholdings, the institutional investor guidelines (IIGs) must be given very careful consideration. The chapter offers an up-to-date understanding of the position currently taken by the relevant investment committees. By explaining the development of the IIGs from the 1960s, the chapter puts into context the status of the pronouncements that are currently operative and provides a detailed understanding of their contents.

Purpose of the institutional investor guidelines

32.2 The Institutional Investor Guidelines exist to protect the interests of the institutions who invest as shareholders in companies. They do not represent statute. However, they should be treated with immense respect by companies who have substantial institutional shareholdings.

In particular, the companies that should seek to apply the IIGs are as follows:

- a company whose shares are listed;

- a company whose shares are traded on the AIM; and

- any private company with significant institutional shareholdings.

The major institutional shareholder investors are represented by the investment committees of the association of british insurers (ABI) and the national association of pension funds (NAPF).

From the pronouncements that the investment committees have made over the years it is clear that the institutional investors are keen to link the size of the rewards that can flow from either share option schemes or long-term incentive plans (L-TIPs) with suitable performance targets which must possess a due degree of challenge.

The guidelines of these investment committees are narrower than the framework which is set by legislation.

The practical application of these guidelines arises from the fact that when a listed company introduces an employee share scheme involving the issue of new shares or introduces certain types of long-term incentive plan it will need to obtain shareholders' approval. It is at this juncture that the institutional investors have the opportunity to vote against a scheme that does not comply with their guidelines.

The latest ABI guidelines are set out in a document first published in 1999 with the latest update revision in December 2007. The framework of the 1999 Guidelines has continued to be used with the aim to refresh its contents for publication each December.

Summary of the main guidelines

Section III: Guidance for Share-Based Incentive Schemes

32.3   The main guidelines are as follows.

Limits on dilution

32.4   Clause 8 sets out the three key principles that are designed to prevent the shareholdings of institutional investors from being diluted by large employee shareholdings as follows:

- In any ten-year period, not more than 10% of a company's issued equity share capital and the re-issue of any treasury shares should be issued pursuant to employee share schemes.

  The Guidelines state that:

  > Remuneration Committees should ensure that appropriate policies regarding flow-rates exist in order to spread the potential issue of new shares over the life of relevant schemes in order to ensure that the limit is not breached.

- In any ten-year period, the equity share capital that is issued or issuable together with the re-issue of any treasury shares in relation to employee discretionary share schemes where participation is restricted to executives must not exceed 5% of the total issued share capital.

- The Guidelines state that: 'This may be exceeded where vesting is dependent on the achievement of significantly more stretching performance criteria'.

- For small companies up to 10% of the ordinary share capital may be utilised for executive discretionary schemes, provided that the total MV of the capital utilised for the scheme at the time of grant does not exceed £1,000,000.

Limits on executive options

32.5   The Guidelines require the following policy positions in setting the limits on individual executive participation in the company's employee share schemes:

- *Under Clause 4.4:* where the exercise of an option is dependent on meeting basic performance it would expect the annual individual limit on the value of shares placed under option to an individual not to exceed one-times annual salary.

- *Under Clause 3.1:* the phased vesting of awards in specific tranches following the minimum three-year performance measurement period is not an alternative to phased grants although it can help to enhance the linkage of vesting of awards to sustained performance and maintain incentivisation.

The Guidelines, through Clause 3.1, encourage the regular phasing approach for the following reasons:

- to reduce the risk of unanticipated outcomes that arise out of share price volatility and cyclical factors;

- to eliminate the perceived problem that a limit on subsisting options encourages early exercise;

- to allow the adoption of a single performance measurement period; and

- to lessen the possible incidence of so-called 'underwater options' where the share price falls to below the option price.

The Guidelines introduced in March 2001 this new principle that options are granted on a phased annual basis and that there is no total limit beyond the limit set for the annual position. Prior to March 2001, the guideline that was operative for many years was that options should not be granted to any individual over shares with a value exceeding four times the annual remuneration of the individual in any ten-year period.

Timing of grants

32.6 The Guidelines, through Clause 6.4, require that options should normally be granted within the 42-day period following the announcement of the company's results.

In practice, separate from the Guidelines, it is the case that, in exceptional circumstances, companies may make grants of options at any time although it must be stressed that justifiable criteria must be established for grants outside the 42-day period.

Performance conditions in executive schemes

32.7 The vesting of executive options and awards should be subject to performance conditions.

The Guidelines, through Clause 4.1, recognise that the alignment between executive and shareholder interests is best achieved through the vesting of awards being conditional upon the satisfaction of performance criteria.

The Guidelines state, through Clause 4.2, that:

These (performance conditions) should demonstrate the achievement of a level of financial performance that is demanding and stretching in the context of the prospects for the company and the prevailing economic environment in which it operates.

The Guidelines, through Clause 4.2, identify the factors that the ABI considers should be characterise challenging performance conditions as follows:

- relate to overall corporate performance;

- be demanding in the context of company prospects and prevailing economic environment in which the company operates;

- be a measured relative to an appropriately defined peer group or other relative benchmark; and

- be disclosed and transparent.

The Guidelines state, through Clause 4.4, that: 'The vesting of awards with high potential value should be linked to commensurately higher levels of performance.'

The Guidelines, through Clause 4.5, strongly encourage the use of sliding scales to correlate the reward potential with a performance scale that incorporates the provisions of the Guidelines. The use of 'sliding scales' is identified as a clear preference to the application of a 'single hurdle'.

The most common performance criteria are as follows:

- increase in earnings per share; and

- increase in total shareholder value, defined as increase in share price plus reinvested dividends.

Typically, these performance conditions are compared to a comparator group.

The Guidelines , through Clause 4.8, refer to total shareholder return (TSR) as 'one of a number of generally acceptable performance criteria'. However, the same Clause 4.8 goes on to state that: 'Remuneration Committees should satisfy themselves prior to vesting that the recorded TSR or other criterion is a genuine reflection of the company's underlying financial performance, and explain its reasoning'.

The ABI does appear now to favour the use of TSR. In practice, it is sometimes difficult to obtain meaningful TSR data. However, there are databases available on the market which enable TSR data to be more readily and cheaply available than they were even a few years ago. It is actually now possible to obtain specialist reports prepared and produced for peer groups and specialist sector indices.

The Guidelines state, through Clause 3.1, that performance conditions should be measured over a minimum of three years. However, strong encouragement is given to longer performance measurement periods and deferred vesting schedules in order to motivate the achievement of sustained improvements in financial performance.

Remuneration committees

32.8 The Guidelines identify clearly the way in which remuneration committees are expected to operate as follows:

- they should conduct a regular review of the share incentive schemes to ensure their continued effectiveness; and

- they should obtain shareholder authorisation for substantive amendments to scheme rules and practice. In particular, shareholder authorisation should be obtained for substantive amendments relating to changes in limits and performance targets.

The Guidelines state in Section I that the *Main Provisions for Remuneration Committees and their Responsibilities* are as follows:

- Remuneration committees are responsible for ensuring that the mix of incentives reflects the company's needs, establishes an appropriate balance between fixed and variable remuneration, and is based on targets that are stretching, verifiable and relevant. They should satisfy themselves as to the accuracy of recorded performance measures that govern vesting of variable and share-based remuneration.

- Remuneration committees should establish effective procedures for disclosure and communication of strategic objectives, which enable shareholders to take an informed and considered view of remuneration policy and its implementation. Where appropriate, account should be taken of the ABI Guidelines on *Responsible Investment Disclosure*.

- Remuneration committees should ensure that remuneration levels properly reflect the contribution of executives and be rigorous in selecting an appropriate comparator group. They should guard against unjustified windfalls and inappropriate gains arising from the operation of share incentive schemes and other associated incentives.

- Where performance achievements are subsequently found to have been significantly misstated so that bonuses and other incentives should not have been paid, effective avenues of redress should be considered.

- Remuneration committees should also pay particular attention to arrangements for senior executives who are not board members but have a significant influence over the company's ability to meet its strategic objectives.

Employee share ownership trusts

32.9 The Guidelines requirements on employee share ownership trusts, stated through Clause 10, reflect the widespread use of such a vehicle to support employee share scheme arrangements and are as follows:

- At any point in time, the employee share ownership trust should hold no more shares that would be required to meet all outstanding liabilities. Additionally, the employee share ownership should not purchase shares simply to act as an anti-takeover device.

- The company should seek the approval of shareholders in advance before the employee share ownership trust can take steps to hold at any time 5% or more of the company's shares.

- The company should disclose the number of shares held in the employee share ownership trust to assist shareholders in evaluating the number of shares that are used for remuneration purposes and explain its strategy on this matter.

- The trust deed should provide that any unvested shares held in the trust shall not be voted at shareholders' meetings.

Letter to chairperson of the Renumeration Committee:

Chairperson of the Remuneration Committee 19 September 2008

Dear Remuneration Committee Chairperson

Executive Remuneration – ABI Guidelines on Policies and Practices

I am writing to advise you in good time that the ABI has decided not to make any changes this year to the Guidelines published in December 2007. This reflects our view that the Guidelines remain relevant at this time. We would encourage Remuneration Committees to satisfy themselves that the Principles of the Guidelines are fully reflected in the remuneration policies and practices of companies.

In addition, we would like to use this opportunity to draw attention to the following points, which we consider to be pertinent in the current economic climate.

The remuneration policy should be fully explained and justified, particularly when changes are proposed. Members will carefully scrutinise remuneration uplifts, particularly increases in salaries or annual bonus levels.

Where a company has underperformed and seen a significant fall in its share price, this should be taken into account when determining the level of awards under share incentive schemes. In such circumstances, it is not appropriate for executives to receive awards of such a size that they are perceived as rewards for failure.

Shareholders are generally not in favour of additional remuneration being paid in relation to succession or retention, particularly where no performance conditions are attached.

In the context of the consultation process for share incentive schemes, Remuneration Committees should ensure that shareholders have adequate time to consider the proposal and that their views are carefully considered. Relevant information related to the consultation should be clearly and fully disclosed.

The ABI and its members are always available to discuss issues relating to executive remuneration and the Guidelines since we strongly believe that good communication between companies and their shareholders is an essential part of the corporate governance process.

For your reference enclosed is a copy of the Guidelines, they are also available on our IVIS website (www.ivis.co.uk) together with the ABI/NAPF Joint Statement on Executive Contracts and Severance.

Yours sincerely

Peter Montagnon

Director of Investment Affairs

Principles and guidelines on remuneration

(The Update Published December 2004)

32.10   It is the responsibility of companies to implement the changes that are required by the update. In this context, companies should be aware of increased shareholder scrutiny and note in particular the warning that is contained in the Guidelines for companies to:

> ensure that an appropriate policy is in place and followed, rather than risk controversy when remuneration outcomes are disclosed in the Annual Report.

The main changes that are included in the latest update are as follows.

Chairperson and the non-executive directors

32.11   The Guidelines state that the chairperson and the non-executive directors should not be granted share incentives that are linked to the performance of the share price. However, if the company considers that a policy of the nature is appropriate the Guidelines state it should ensure:

- the agreement of shareholders in advance of implementing the policy; and

- the shares should be held by the recipient for the duration of the term in office.

Transparency of bonuses

32.12   The Guidelines identify the overall requirement for greater transparency of bonuses through the mechanism of the remuneration report. The Guidelines set out ways in which this requirement can be achieved as follows:

- For short-term bonuses, the basic parameters that have been adopted in the financial year that is being reported should be disclosed although it is acknowledged that commercial sensitivity may prevent companies from disclosing specific short-term targets.

- The expectation on companies is for the remuneration report to include an analysis of the extent to which relevant targets were actually met once the bonuses have been paid.

- Any increase in maximum participation levels in bonus scheme arrangements year-on-year should be explained.

- The schemes that govern the cash bonus arrangements should be tightly drafted, bearing in mind increased scrutiny from shareholders.

- There is a particular encouragement for part of the bonus to be deferred with the payout taking the form of shares.

Change of control provisions

32.13 The Guidelines have recognised and responded to the public concern over payments, sometimes referred to as 'windfall payouts', that are paid to directors following a change of control. The requirements are as follows:

- The performance conditions should not be automatically waived in the event of a change of control.

- The remuneration committee should use its best endeavours to quantify and disclose the payments that would arise on a change of control.

- The remuneration committee should check that the performance conditions contained in the scheme rules genuinely reflect a robust measure of underlying financial performance over any shorter time period. Their reasoning should be explained in relevant shareholder communications, in particular the remuneration report.

- Where there is a change of control share incentive awards should vest on a pro rata basis to reflect the proportion of the vesting period that has elapsed at the time of the change of control.

Companies should respond to these requirements by giving strong consideration to amending scheme rules to be consistent with the Guidelines. Although the amendments could apply to future awards it is unlikely that existing participants would agree to amendments in relation to existing awards.

Employee share ownership trusts

32.14 The Guidelines introduce an additional requirement for employee share ownership trusts as follows:

The trust deed should provide that any unvested shares held in the trust shall not be voted at shareholders' meetings.

Companies should respond to these requirements by giving strong consideration to amending scheme rules to be consistent with the Guidelines in relation to the non-voting requirement to unvested shares.

Vesting of awards and dividend accruals

32.15   The Guidelines address the contended need for dividend accruals on awards made under long-term incentive plans in order to achieve a better alignment on interest between shareholders and executives. The requirements are as follows:

- Long-term incentive plans should be structured to allow for the accrual of dividends that are payable on shares that are subject to awards. The technique for the accrual should be the roll-up of dividends from the date of grant to the date on which the award vests and the participants benefit. Regardless of now the long-term incentive plan is structured, where shares that are awarded on a conditional basis do not vest, any scrip or cash amounts that represent the rolled-up dividends should not vest either.

- When the remuneration committee is determining the size of grants it should be mindful of expected dividend stream over the period to vesting. The expected dividend stream will be represented in the expected dividend yield. Once the expected dividend yield has been calculated and the facility for rolled-up dividends has been introduced the remuneration committee can smaller grant sizes in order to target a similar level of value on the conditional share award.

Companies should respond to these requirements by giving strong consideration to amending scheme rules to be consistent with the Guidelines in relation to ensuring that the scheme rules allow a roll-up facility.

Adjustment to performance conditions

32.16   Under the new international financial reporting standard (IFRS) earnings measures such as earnings per share will be more volatile than under UK GAAP. The company may need to adjust its performance measures in order to reflect this increased volatility. The Guidelines seek to reflect this change as follows:

- The remuneration committee should ensure that its next report explains the policy that the company has adopted to achieve a consistent measurement of performance during the transition to IFRS.

The approach taken by companies will in practice be one of the following:

- To continue to measure earnings per share on the previous UK GAAP basis from the base point until the end of the performance measurement period.

- To restate earnings per share under the new IFRS from the base point.

It is important to note that where the company uses total shareholder return as its performance measure it will be unaffected by the changes.

Impending changes to pensions taxation

32.17   The Guidelines state that: 'We are also encouraging disclosure of any structural changes in remuneration that may be recognised as appropriate in the context of impending changes to pensions taxation.'

The concern of the ABI is to ensure that any changes and their basis together with their implications for shareholder value creation are explained in the remuneration report.

History of the institutional investor guidelines

ABI Guidelines of the 1960s

32.18   The Institutional Investor Guidelines have evolved and developed over the years since they were first published in the 1960s. The first three recommendations that have provided the foundation for the evolution and development were as follows:

- only full-time employees should participate;

- the number of shares made available under share option schemes should not exceed 5% of the company's issued equity share capital in any period of ten years; and

- options should not be granted at less than the MV of the shares at the date of grant.

ABI Guidelines of the 1970s

32.19   In the 1970s the limit of 'four times earnings' was introduced for the first time and at the same time a further limit was introduced that share option schemes should not exceed 3% of the company's issued equity share capital in any period of three years.

As the 1970s drew to a close the stricture was introduced that share option schemes should not exceed 10% of the company's issued equity share capital in any period of ten years. This represents the overall scheme limit that continues to hold today.

ABI Guidelines (1987)

32.20   It was the ABI Guidelines in 1987 that first introduced the concept of performance targets in executive share option schemes. The recommendation was to grant options exercisable on the achievement of a real growth on earnings per share over a three-year period. The economic reality of the time led to this recommendation being largely ignored on practical grounds.

Joint ABI/NAPF Statement (1993)

32.21   It was the ABI and NAPF joint statement on performance targets in executive share option schemes issued in 1993 that required that whatever criteria is chosen as a condition for the exercise of options: the formula should be supported by or give clear evidence of, sustained improvement in the underlying financial performance of the group in question'.

Interestingly, this 1993 joint statement did not impose a particular performance measure but required that individual companies should establish tests that were supported by this formula.

The examples offered by this joint statement fall into two categories as follows.

Absolute measures and targets

32.22   The key example for the ABI and the NAPF in this category is normalised earnings per share.

Where normalised earnings per share is used it should be measured by reference to a percentage margin in excess of inflation over a three-year period. Typically, this percentage margin will be 2% per annum growth. Inflation would normally be measured by the percentage increase in the retail price index over the appropriate period.

Specifically, the ABI and the NAPF require that the earnings figure used in the earnings per share calculation is adjusted or smoothed to avoid distortions arising from extraordinary or exceptional items.

Comparative measures

32.23   Comparative measures are concerned out-performance of an index or the median or weighted average of a pre-defined peer group.

The examples that are offered are as follows.

Normalised earnings per share

32.24   Out-performance of the median or weighted average rate of increase in normalised earnings per share of a peer group.

Net asset value per share

32.25   Net asset value per share measured against a pre-defined peer group or index.

Total shareholder return

32.26   In using TSR the formula should account for two elements, namely, share price performance and gross dividend per share. Where total shareholder return is used it should be based on exceeding a relevant benchmark within a pre-defined period. The ABI and NAPF emphasise that if TSR is used they also expect what they call 'defined secondary criterion validating sustained and significant improvement in the underlying financial performance'.

Comparative share price

32.27 Comparative share price is a relatively simple measure to use. It must be applied relative to a pre-defined peer group and similar to TSR it must have a defined secondary criterion. Where comparative share price is used it should be averaged over a number of weeks to eradicate the influence of short-term market fluctuations.

ABI Guidelines framework (1999) and subsequent updates

32.28 The document entitled *Guidelines for Share Incentive Schemes* replaced the February 1995 Guidelines and the July 1999 Supplement.

The Guidelines covered all share schemes including phantom schemes. Technically, these guidelines only apply to UK listed companies although unlisted companies are expected to give due regard. Observance continues to be voluntary with no legal force available to secure implementation although the institutions might consider sanctions if observance is not maintained.

The latest update on the 1999 framework is the refreshment document of December 2004. The document is now entitled *Principles and Guidelines on Remuneration*.

As before, when implementing the ABI Guidelines it is important for a company to give full consideration to the constituent elements of its shareholder base and the extent to which they are sensitive to compliance with the pronouncements of the investment committees.

The ABI continues to support schemes that fulfil the following objectives:

- the link between remuneration and performance; and
- the alignment of executive interests with shareholder interests.

In supporting schemes that fulfil these objectives, the ABI requires safeguards against the following:

- with regard to shares, the dilution of shareholders' equity; and
- with regard to cash, the commitment of shareholder funds.

The ABI continues to have as its main areas of concern the following:

- limits on dilution;
- limits on executive options;
- timing of grants;
- performance conditions in executive schemes;
- remuneration committees;

- employee share ownership trusts; and
- top of form.

Chapter 33

European Prospectus Directive

Introduction

33.1 The chapter investigates the relevance for employee share schemes of this new European Union Directive, explains the requirements of the Directive and explores the considerations that companies should be aware of in their planning for the introduction of employee share scheme arrangements.

The approach taken in this chapter is, in the first instance, to explain the specific UK interpretation of the Directive and then, secondly, to provide an explanation of the wider canvass of the Directive as the basis from which the UK interpretation has been derived.

Implementation of the Directive

33.2 The European Prospectus Directive, 2001/71/EC came into force on 31 December 2003, when it was published in the *Official Journal of the European Union*. Member states had until 1 July 2005 to implement the Directive into domestic law.

The aim of the Prospectus Directive is to harmonise the public offer and listing regimes across the EU by creating common standards for the offering and listing of securities. It is this harmonization that is designed to ensure that once approval has been obtained in one member state that single prospectus can be used for all offerings and listings in all other member states. This so-called 'passporting' process facilitates the use of the single prospectus to be valid for a public offer or admission to trading on a regulated market in any other country in the EU based on a fairly straightforward notification procedure.

Paragraphs **33.3** to **33.11** cover the specific UK interpretation of the Directive.

Position in the UK

33.3 The Prospectus Directive has been implemented in the UK by amendment to FSMA 2000, the making of the Prospectus Regulations 2005 and the introduction of the FSA Prospectus Rules.

In the UK, under FSMA 2000, s 85(1), there is a prohibition against offering transferable securities without the issue of a prospectus as follows:

> It is unlawful for transferable securities to which this sub-section applies to be offered to the public in the United Kingdom, unless an approved prospectus has been made available to the public before the offer is made.

For the purposes of FSMA 2000, s 85(1) the terms that require definition are as follows:

- The term 'transferable securities' refers to securities for which there are dealings on a recognized stock exchange except for those securities that are identified in FSMA 2000, s 85(5) and Schedule 11A.

- The term 'offered to the public in the United Kingdom' refers to an offer to the public as a result of any communication in any form and by any means that presents sufficient information on the terms of the offer and the securities to enable an investor in any EU country to subscribe for or acquire.

Under FSMA 2000, s 86, section 85(1) will not be contravened for the following:

- the offer is made to or directed at qualified investors only, where the term 'qualified investors' is duly defined;

- the offer is made to or directed at fewer than 100 persons in each EEA state, other than qualified investors, and for this purpose the making of an offer of transferable securities to trustees of a trust or to members of a partnership or to two or more persons jointly will be treated as a offer to a single person;

- the minimum consideration which may be paid by any person for the transferable securities being offered is at least €50,000, or the equivalent amount in another currency or unit of account;

- the transferable securities being offered are denominated in amounts of at least €50,000, or the equivalent amount in another currency or unit of account; and

- the total consideration for the transferable securities being offered cannot exceed €100,000, or the equivalent amount in another currency or unit of account.

Transferable securities offered to the public for UK law

33.4 Under FSMA 2000, s 102A, the definition of 'transferable securities' is referenced to The Investment Services Directive, 93/22/EEC of 10 May 1993 that defines 'transferable securities' as follows:

- shares in companies (and other securities equivalent to shares in companies) which are negotiable on the capital market; and

- any other securities normally dealt in giving the right to acquire transferable securities by subscription or exchange or giving rise to a cash settlement.

Under FSMA 2000, s 102B the definition of 'offered to the public' with regard to transferable securities has the following characteristics:

- a communication in any form or by any means to any person which presents sufficient information on the following:

  — the transferable securities that are being offered; and

  — the terms on which the securities are being offered;

- the communication is designed to enable an investor to decide to buy or subscribe for the securities.

The definitions of 'transferable securities' and 'offered to the public' have a direct bearing on employee share schemes in the following ways.

Grant of share options

33.5 Where the option that is granted is a non-transferable share option and there is no offer of a transferable security, it will be treated as outside the scope of FS MA 2000, s 85(1) and, therefore, also the Directive. This position is accepted by the FSA in the UK and the EU Commission.

Exercise of share options

33.6 When the option is exercised and the transferable securities are acquired, neither the exercise nor the acquisition is treated constituting an offer to the public. Rather, both the exercise of the option and the acquisition of the shares as transferable securities are to be regarded as the exercise of rights pursuant to a contract. Again, it is understood that this is the position accepted by the FSA and the EU Commission.

The regulators take the view that in certain circumstances companies may structure the purchase of shares through the grant and exercise of non-transferable options solely for the purpose of avoiding the requirement to prepare a prospectus in which case they may still request that a prospectus is prepared. Despite this stance, the EC Commission has indicated that the structuring of a share purchase through an option arrangement represents an acceptable commercial reason for structuring the share purchase. The vulnerability arises where the exercise of the option follows in a very short time after the grant of the option.

Award of free shares

33.7 The fact that the award of free shares does not create a situation that requires the employee to buy or to subscribe for the shares establishes the position that free shares are outside the scope of the definition of an offer of transferable securities to the public. The requirement to buy or to subscribe for the shares indicates that monetary consideration is necessary to bring the shares, the transferable securities within the definition.

This interpretation is, of course, pertinent to the free shares module of the tax-approved share incentive plan. It is, though, equally relevant to any other form of free shares arrangement, including the traditional way in which a nil cost long-term incentive scheme is arranged.

Additionally, the FSA and the EU Commission take the view that free shares are outside the scope of the Directive on the basis of the €2.5 million and the €100,000 exemptions. This position relies upon the references to 'consideration' and 'amounts' in each of these exemptions being based on actual payments rather than value.

Award of partnership shares

33.8   The employee supplies funds for the purchase of partnership shares under the tax-approved share incentive plan, an indication that there is monetary consideration paid by the employee for the shares. Like any share purchase scheme, this will be within the scope of the definition of an offer of transferable securities to the public.

Shares in private companies

33.9   The position taken by the EU Commission is that shares in private companies are not by their nature of a kind that restricts them from being negotiable on a capital market and, as a consequence, they could, at least potentially, be subject to the requirements of Directive. However, there is uncertainty over whether or not shares that are restricted by their terms have the capacity for being negotiable in the capital market and, as a case in point, the EU Commission has stated that even where there is an internal market for the shares through an employee share trust this would not represent trading on a capital market.

The defence position would be that, analogous to an option, which is recognised as non-transferable, shares that are not freely transferable should be outside the scope of the Directive.

Employee offer exemption for Listed Companies in UK law

33.10   Under FSMA 2000, s 85(5) the prohibition in FSMA 2000, s 85(1) does not apply to such other transferable securities that may be 'specified in prospectus rules'. In this regard, and specifically for the employee offer exemption, 'the prospectus rules', which literally are entitled *The Prospectus Rules* by the FSA, and which mirror the provisions of EU Prospectus Directive, Article 4(1)(e), provided through Rule 12.2. that FSMA 2000, s 85(1) does not apply to the following:

> transferable securities offered, allotted or to be allotted to existing or former directors or employees by their employer, which has transferable securities already admitted to trading [on a regulated market as defined in the Prospectus

Rules] or by an affiliated undertaking, if a document is made available containing information on the number and nature of the transferable securities and the reasons for and details of the offer.

Even though the class of shares that is traded on the regulated market is a different class of shares from the class that is used for purposes of the employee share scheme, the FSA will still recognise that the exemption applies. The EU Commission has confirmed that it is prepared to accept this interpretation despite the fact that it would appear to be different from their previous pronouncements on this specific point.

For the purposes of the employee offer exemption for Listed Companies, it is important to be aware that the AIM is not a regulated market for the application of the Prospectus Rules. The employee offer exemption will, therefore, not apply so recourse must be made to the other exemptions. If those other exemptions do not apply then a prospectus is required for the offer of shares by the company.

For the employee offer exemption to apply, the company must prepare for inclusion in the employee communication 'an information document' that contains information that is consistent with the guidance given by the Committee of European Securities Regulators. These documents will typically and, indeed, usually include the following information:

- the name of the issuer with references to the website;

- the nature of the securities and their rights;

- the explanation of the reasons for the offer; and

- the details of the offer:

  — the eligibility criteria for participation in the scheme;

  — whether to subscribe for new securities or to acquire existing securities;

  — the price of the securities;

  — the method of payment of the securities;

  — the opening and closing dates for the offer;

  — the minimum and maximum numbers of shares on offer for the individual;

  — the minimum and maximum numbers of shares on offer in total; and

  — the mechanism for operating any scaling back provisions.

There are plans to extend the employee offer exemption with a view to assisting companies that are not listed on a regulated market in the EEA. These proposals represent a response to the situation where a company has to produce a prospectus purely for purposes of an employee share scheme. The Committee of European Securities Regulators has, therefore, updated the document entitled *Frequently asked questions regarding*

Prospectuses: Common positions agreed by CESR Members. There is a new section numbered 71 and entitled *Employee Share Scheme Prospectuses: Short-form disclosure regime for offers to the employees in those cases where a prospectus is required (application of Article 23.4 of the Prospectus Regulations).* Section 71 applies in circumstances where the only reason why a prospectus is required is because the company is introducing an employee share scheme and offers are being made to employees. The short-form disclosure regime is designed to restrict the information provided to matters that are of interest to the employees and to recognise that employees already have information about the company and so are in a different position from the position of external investors.

In January 2009, the EU Commission announced that it will review the scope of the employee share schemes exemption. This consultation process will consider the extension of the exemption to share offers to EU employees from companies that are Listed on third country exchanges or in EU exchange-regulated markets and to non-Listed companies.

The €2.5m exemption

33.11 Under FSMA 2000, Sch 11A para 9, there is a reference relating to an exemption that mirrors the wording in Article 1(2)(h) of the Directive as follows: 'transferable securities included in an offer where the total consideration of the offer is less than €2,500,000 (or an equivalent amount).'

The prohibition does not apply where the total consideration is less than €2,500,000, referring to the aggregate amount of the consideration payable for the shares under the terms of the offer. The €2,500,000 limit is definitively not calculated by reference to the MV of the shares.

When applying this exemption, and solely for purposes of the calculation, an offer is to be combined with any other offer of transferable securities of the same class which was open at any time in the last 12 months and had already satisfied the test for the €2,500,000 exemption.

The €2,500,000 total limit for the exemption is applied by aggregating all consideration for the securities included in the offer in all EEA states so where the offer is extended to other EU states the exemption must be applied on the same basis as it has been applied in the UK.

Paragraphs **33.13** to **33.16** explain the wider canvas of the Directive.

Content of the Directive

33.12 The contents of the prospectus, in the event that a prospectus is required and exemptions are not available, are as follows:

• depending on what the issuing company is offering, the requirement is to provide all information that is considered necessary to allow investors to make an informed investment decision;

- a summary of the key points and risks, for example, the assets and liabilities of the issuing company, its profit and loss account, the prospects of the issuer, the rights attaching to the shares and the timetable that has been agreed for the offer; and

- the prospectus must be in a language that is accepted by the authority in the home member state. A summary must be translated into local languages where offers are made to employees in other member states.

Key implications of the Directive

33.13 The key implications of the Directive for companies are as follows:

- Once a member state has implemented the Directive, an offer of securities cannot be made to the public within its territory, subject to certain exemptions, unless a prospectus has first been published. The prospectus must be made available to the public at the company's registered office or on its website.

- The content of the prospectus across all member states of the EU will be standard and a prospectus approved in one member state will be valid in all other member states. Regulation should, therefore, be the same throughout the EU, the 'passport system'.

- The regulator of the member state must approve the prospectus before it is published. The approval time depends upon whether the issuer already has securities listed on a stock exchange in the EU or has previously offered securities to the public in the EU. However, approval is expected to take between 10 and 20 days and once approval has been given the prospectus will be valid for 12 months.

- For most UK companies, from 1 July 2005 they will simply have to file an Information Document whereas previously there was no such requirement.

The position prior to the implementation of the Directive can be summarised as follows:

- The operation of employee share schemes was classified as an offer of securities although it may be that the company qualified for an exemption, whether as a general exemption or maybe as a specific employee share scheme exemption. The Listing Rules governed offers of securities that were already listed on the London Stock Exchange. The POS Regulations governed offers of securities that were not listed on the London Stock Exchange.

- Across the EU, securities laws applied to offers to the public with the application of different laws giving complexity to the operation of employee share schemes. As a consequence, when preparing to introduce an employee share schemes there was a need to check the position in each country and incur costs on filings and translations.

- The overall effect of the disparity across the EU is that the level of investor protection could vary significantly between countries. There appeared to be a need to implement policy and procedure that achieved a level playing field and encouraged pan-EU offers.

Scope of the Directive

33.14 The scope of the Directive is as follows:

- The Directive is designed to apply to an 'offer of shares to the public' by quoted companies and by unquoted private companies.

- The actual definition of an 'offer of securities to the public' is restricted to an offer to purchase or subscribe for securities, defined widely to include shares. The precise definition is 'a communication to persons presenting sufficient information on the terms of the offer and the securities to be offered, so as to enable an investor to decide to purchase or subscribe to these securities …'. The relevance and, indeed, the application for employee share schemes is that when the employee share scheme is operated the company will normally introduce an employee communication, usually as a document augmented by a verbal presentation.

- The strict technical application of this definition would exclude the grant of rights to purchase free market-purchased shares as happens in the case of a long-term incentive plan arrangement. However, this exclusion is not thought to be deliberate on the part of the EU legislators. The application is very broad and it is not possible to agree a narrower pan-EU definition. In order to establish 'maximum harmonisation', individual member states cannot impose additional requirements.

- The wording of the Directive appears to be deliberately loose in order to allow the application within individual member states of the EU. It is to be regarded as 'framework legislation' to be implemented by local laws. In the UK the application has been facilitated by amendments and additions to FS MA 2000.

Exemption provisions of the Directive

33.15 The opportunity for companies to operate exemption provisions is as follows:

- The scope of the Directive is limited by the exemption provisions under which it will not apply to offers made in the EU where the total consideration, excluding offers made outside the EU, is less than €2.5 million in any 12-month period. Given that this limit relates to the offer price, namely the actual amount paid for the securities and not the MV of the shares, even if local facilitating legislation were to catch the long-term incentive plan this exemption would apply. The intention behind the exemption is, though, to help smaller companies to raise capital for their development without the cost of producing a prospectus.

- There is available to all companies a blanket employee share scheme exemption that covers offers to existing and former employees or directors of the issuing company or its affiliated undertakings. It must be stressed, though, that this blanket exemption is only available if the company has securities that are already admitted to trading on a regulated EU market. It is not available, therefore, to quoted companies that do not have a EU listing, as will be the case with many US incorporated companies and unquoted private companies.

- Where the exemption applies, the issuing company must produce an information document that sets out the name of the issuer and where to find information on the issuer, the number and nature of the securities, the reasons for the offer and the details of the offer. The information document must be approved by the issuing company's home member state.

- There are other non-employee share scheme specific exemptions that can be applied separately or in conjunction with each other as follows:

  — where the offer of securities is addressed to fewer than 100 persons in each member state in any 12-month period;

  — where the offer of securities is addressed to persons who are registered as 'qualified investors', defined narrowly by reference to investment experience or the value of their investments; and

  — where the total consideration for shares acquired by all participants in any 12-month period is less than €100,000.

The domestic laws of the home member state apply as follows:

- It is crucial to the operation of the Directive that the issuing company's member state must be properly identified as it is the member state whose domestic law applies.

- For companies that have a listing in the EU, this is the member state in which the issuing company has situated its registered office.

- For companies that do not have a registered office situated in the EU – non-EU issuers – the home member state is the state in which the state in which the first offer to the public is intended to be made after 31 December 2003 or the state in which the first application for the listing of its securities on a EU stock exchange is made after 31 December 2003.

- The planning opportunity for the 'non-EU issuers' that wish to make offers of securities in several member states at the same time is to decide which state is to be chosen as the home member state for purposes of the Directive and to make the offer of securities in the chosen home member state first.

- The 'non-EU' issuing company could, of course, unwittingly have established by accident home member state status soon after the Directive has been published by making an offer in a EU state even though under the local laws of that member state the Directive has yet to be enforced. Great care is required, therefore, in the planning for the 'non-EU issuers' in order to avoid pitfalls of this nature. The risk is increased by the fact that the term 'offer' in the definition has a wide interpretation. Having established a home member state, either purposely or by accident the 'non-EU' issuing company can only change its home member state if it subsequently arranges for its securities to be listed on a EU regulated market.

- The decision on choosing a home member state will be influenced by a range of factors including the application of the accounting standards in that member state, the ease of language, familiarity with the customs and practices and the convenience for other listings for debt arrangements maybe.

Summary conclusions

33.16 The conclusions that can be made in relation to the Directive are as follows:

- Where there is actually a requirement for a prospectus the process will be simplified as it will only be required in one member state rather than in all the member states in which the company proposes to operate the employee share scheme.

- For companies that are quoted in the EU, the Directive eases the operation of employee share schemes within EU member states through the application of a single-blanket employee share scheme exemption. Previously there was a requirement to examine the securities laws in each member state and file accordingly within each member state.

- Where the company is UK quoted, operating employee share schemes only in the UK, the exemption that previously applied are no longer available. If no exemptions are available under the Directive then the production of a prospectus is required.

- For companies that are non-EU incorporated companies, the individual filings in a range of countries with all the checking that is involved will no longer be necessary. By choosing a home member state, the filing of one document fulfils the requirement.

Chapter 34

Accounting rules

Financial Reporting Standard 20: Accounting for Share-Based Payment

Introduction of FRS 20

34.1   On 7 November, 2002 the IASB issued ED 2 and simultaneously the accounting standards board (ASB) in the UK published FRED 31 with similar proposals to those contained within ED2.

The international financial reporting standard 2 (IFRS 2) and the UK financial reporting standard 20 (FRS 20) entitled *Accounting for Share-Based Payment* apply to all share options and share awards that are granted on or after 7 November 2002 that have not vested by the time that the standard applies. The standard also applies to share options and share awards that were made before 7 November 2002 and which are subsequently modified.

IFRS 2 and FRS 20 came into effect for accounting periods beginning on or after 1 January 2005 for Listed Companies and for accounting periods beginning on or after 1 January 2006 for Unlisted Companies.

It is explicitly the case that companies reporting under the financial reporting standard for smaller entities (FRSSE) will not have to adopt the standard. The UK standard, FRS 20, implements IFRS 2 which was published by the international accounting standards (IASB) board on 19 February 2004.

Principles of FRS 20

34.2   The key principle to understanding the standard is that it is seeking to measure the services that the employees give to the company in return for a reward that for purposes of the standard is reward in the form of a legal interest in the share capital of the company. It works on the premise that employee involvement in employee share schemes is offering a reward for employee services and must be quantified for inclusion as a cost in the profit and loss account.

A summary of the principles upon which the standard is based is as follows:

- the standard replaces the historic cost basis for accounting with an economic or market basis for accounting as a basis for measuring the value of employee services to the company;

- the standard establishes an expense in the accounts for options based on the value of options at the date of grant using an option pricing valuation method;

- the impact of this standard is that companies will have to deduct the calculated cost of share options and other forms of equity remuneration from their reported profits in order to reflect the cost of employee services provided;

- the specific requirement of the standard is that the deduction must represent the fair value of the payments;

- the standard covers all forms of share-based payment and is not limited to executive share options; and

- there is no exemption for all-employee share schemes including the Sharesave scheme. This position contrasts with the exemption under the previous regime for Sharesave under which options may be granted to employees at up to a 20% discount without a charge to the profit and loss account.

Implications for accounting

34.3 The implications for accounting are as follows:

- the profit and loss account must show a charge for the fair value of share options that are granted to employees with the charge spread over the vesting period from the date of grant to the date of vesting;

- the option pricing model that is used to determine the fair value should take into account any performance conditions, the expected life of the options and the volatility of the share price. The binomial and Black-Scholes methods are examples of option pricing models that would be appropriate for this purpose. The flexibility of the binomial model can take into account factors that influence whether options will be exercised sooner or later, for example, accounting for close periods during which options cannot be exercised thereby reducing the charge to the profit and loss account;

- the company will no longer recognise in its profit and loss account the gains and losses that it makes on own company shares; and

- the key assumptions that are used must be disclosed. These will include the main terms of the options, the volatility of the share price, the dividend yield and the risk-free interest rate.

Position prior to IFRS 2 and FRS 20

34.4 It is important to appreciate the position prior to IFRS 2 and FRS 20 as follows:

- where market value options are granted over new issue shares there is no charge to the profit and loss account;

- where discounted options are granted over new issue shares the discount is charged to the profit and loss account with the exception of Sharesave; and

- where options are granted over existing shares that are bought in the market the cost of the shares is charged to the profit and loss account.

Approach of IFRS 2 and FRS 20

34.5 In contrast, under IFRS 2 and FRS 20, share options and share awards will always create a charge in the profit and loss account.

The approach to applying IFRS 2 and FRS 20 should be as follows:

- to calculate the value of the option at the date of grant in order to reflect the value of services that are to be provided over the expected life as opposed to the contracted life; and

- to calculate the charge each year to the profit and loss account on the basis of employee contribution to the company.

Disclosure requirements

34.6 The company is required to disclose the weighted fair value of the share options granted and the share awards given and also information on how the company has measured their fair value.

Specifically, the company must disclose the following information:

- description of each scheme;
- number and class of participants;
- service and performance conditions;
- separate details of grants, exercises and lapses;
- option prices; and
- remaining expected life and contractual life.

Additionally, the company is required to disclose sensitive and confidential information; such as the following:

- probability of meeting the performance conditions;
- expected future dividend stream;

- probability of employees leaving; and
- volatility of the share price used for the option valuation.

Types of share-based payment

34.7 IFRS 2 requires an entity to recognise share-based payment transactions in its financial statements, including transactions with employees or other parties to be settled in cash, other assets, or equity instruments of the entity. There are no exceptions to IFRS 2, other than for transactions to which other Standards apply.

IFRS 2 sets out measurement principles and specific requirements for three types of share-based payment transactions as follows:

- Equity-settled share-based payment transactions, in which the entity receives goods or services as consideration for equity instruments of the entity (including shares or share options).

- Cash-settled, share-based payment transactions, in which the entity acquires goods or services by incurring liabilities to the supplier of those goods or services for amounts that are based on the price (or value) of the entity's shares or other equity instruments of the entity.

- Transactions in which the entity receives or acquires goods or services and the terms of the arrangement provide either the entity or the supplier of those goods or services with a choice of whether the entity settles the transaction in cash or by issuing equity instruments.

Direct and indirect measurement

34.8 The requirement for direct or indirect measurement as appropriate is set out in IFRS 2 as follows:

- For equity-settled share-based payment transactions, IFRS 2 requires an entity to measure the goods or services received, and the corresponding increase in equity, directly, at the fair value of the goods or services received, unless that fair value cannot be estimated reliably. If the entity cannot estimate reliably the fair value of the goods or services received, the entity is required to measure their value, and the corresponding increase in equity, indirectly, by reference to the fair value of the equity instruments granted.

- For transactions with employees and others providing similar services, the entity is required to measure the fair value of the equity instruments granted, because it is typically not possible to estimate reliably the fair value of employee services received. The fair value of the equity instruments granted is measured at grant date.

- For transactions with parties other than employees (and those providing similar services), there is a rebuttable presumption that the fair value of the goods or services received can be estimated reliably.

That fair value is measured at the date the entity obtains the goods or the counterparty renders service. In rare cases, if the presumption is rebutted, the transaction is measured by reference to the fair value of the equity instruments granted, measured at the date the entity obtains the goods or the counterparty renders service.

Modified grant date method

34.9 The modified grant date method (MGDM), which is also applied in the US in FAS 123, provides the basis of the specification in IFRS 2 for differentiating between market and non-market conditions.

For goods or services measured by reference to the fair value of the equity instruments granted, the IFRS specifies that vesting conditions, other than market conditions, are not taken into account when estimating the fair value of the shares or options at the relevant measurement date.

The approach which is adopted is for vesting conditions to be taken into account by adjusting the number of equity instruments included in the measurement of the transaction amount so that, ultimately, the amount recognised for goods or services received as consideration for the equity instruments granted is based on the number of equity instruments that eventually vest.

The consequence is that no amount is recognised on a cumulative basis for goods or services received if through the failure to satisfy a vesting condition, other than a market condition, the equity instruments granted do not vest.

Unit of service method

34.10 The unit of service method (USM), suggested in ED 2 as the preferred approach of the ASB, requires a treatment under which amounts are recognised for goods or services received even if through a failure to satisfy a vesting condition the equity instruments granted do not vest.

The Accounting Standards Board accepted the practical implications of operating the UM and decided to opt instead for the MGDM as applied in the US standard FAS 123. The main practical constraint in the use of the U SM is that if a different number of options are granted to each employee then a fair value per unit of service would have to be calculated for each employee.

The objections to the U SM that were rejected by the AS B are as follows:

• The objection is that the fair value of the services received should not be the accounting focus. The Unit of Service is the period of time that the employee has to work in return for the equity instrument. The Unit of Service is, therefore, the standard measure of the services received or expected to be received.

- The objection is that under the USM where the employee completes the required service period but the performance conditions are not satisfied and as a consequence equity instruments do not vest there is no reversal of amounts recognised during the vesting period.

Application to the different types of employee share scheme

34.11 The best interpretation of the required treatment for schemes is to determine a fair value at the date of grant as follows.

For the long-term incentive plan (L-TIP)

34.12 Whether the L-TIP is 'a nil-cost option' or an arrangement under which the company is committed to deliver to an employee the full cost of a share the economic status of the arrangement is the same. The input into the option-pricing model for the option price is nil. However, the input for the share price at the date of grant will be the MV of the share. The value of the option under the option-pricing model will approximate to the MV of the share.

Where there are performance conditions the value should be adjusted by a discount based on the probability of the performance conditions being achieved. Where there are no performance conditions then there will simply be a subsequent adjustment for leavers.

The cash contribution to the employee share trust that is supporting the L-TIP arrangement where the employee share trust is de facto under the control of the company does not represent a profit and loss account item. The employee share trust for accounting purposes should be treated as a division of the company with the corresponding debit to the cash credit being internal debtors.

The application of IFRS 2 makes the L-TIP arrangement slightly more favourable than the share option arrangement for the reason that the share option arrangement becomes less favourable whereas the L-TIP arrangement in essence becomes neither more favourable nor less favourable than before IFRS 2.

For the phantom scheme

34.13 The phantom share option scheme is a deferred bonus scheme linked to the rise in the share price. It is a cash scheme based on share appreciation rights. For this scheme, the economic equivalent of the real option is the share appreciation right based on the cash liability measurement.

Under IFRS 2 there is a requirement to perform a calculation of the theoretical option value at the end of each financial year based upon the chosen option-pricing model. The final profit and loss position once the employee has exercised the phantom option by exercising the right to call upon the company for the funds must be to charge to the profit and loss account the full cost of the payout, subject to PAYE and NICs, accounted for through the payroll in the normal way.

Different from the equity-settled share-based payment transaction, the corresponding credit entry to the profit and loss account charge is creditors and not equity.

For the share purchase scheme

34.14 For the share purchase dcheme, the full charge should arise on allocation with a discount determined for any lock-up requirement.

For the share incentive plan (SIP)

34.15 The treatment for the share incentive plan (SIP) depends upon the module as follows:

* *Free shares module:* the full charge should arise on allocation with a discount determined for any lock-up requirement and with an appropriate adjustment for any forfeiture provisions.

* *Partnership shares module:* the shares are purchased with the employee's own funds. There will normally, therefore, not be an expense charge to the profit and loss account under IFRS 2. Potentially there could be an expense charge in the event that the module operates with an accumulation period in that there may be a contention that such an arrangement constitutes a quasi-option scheme. However, every arrangement involving an accumulation period requires examination on its own merits.

* Matching shares module: there would generally speaking be an expense charge calculated on a same or a similar basis to the expense charge calculated for the free shares module, given that matching shares are in essence another form of free shares, funded as they are with company rather than employee funds.

Worked examples

34.16 All the examples are based on the illustrative examples found in IFRS 2.

Example 34.1

Situation

An entity grants 100 share options to each of its 500 employees. Each grant is conditional upon the employee working for the entity over the next three years.

The entity estimates that the fair value of each share option is £15.

The entity estimates that 20% of the employees, ie 100 employees, leave over the three years and forfeit their rights to the share options.

Calculation

The cumulative expense for the three years

= (500 – 100) employees × 100 share options per employee × £15 per share option

= £600,000

The annual charge to the profit and loss account

= £600,000 divided by three years

= £200,000

Note

In this situation, given that the options have an intrinsic value of zero, there would have been no profit and loss charge under UITF 17.

Example 34.2

Situation

An entity grants 100 share options to each of its 500 employees. Each grant is conditional upon the employee working for the entity over the next three years.

The entity estimates that the fair value of each share option is £15.

During year 1: 20 employees leave and the entity estimates that over the three years 75 employees will leave, representing 15% of all employees.

During year 2: 22 employees leave and the entity estimates that over the three years 60 employees will leave, representing 12% of all employees.

During year 3: 15 employees leave and, therefore, over the three years 57 employees leave and forfeit their rights to the share options.

Calculation

The cumulative expense for the three years

= (500 – 57) employees × 100 share options per employee × £15 per share option

= £664,500

The annual charge to the profit and loss account in year 1

= [(500 employees × 85%) × 100 share options × £15] divided by three years

= £212,500

The annual charge to the profit and loss account in year 2

= {[(£500 employees × 88%) × 100 share options × £15] × 2/3 years} – £212,500

= £227,500

The annual charge to the profit and loss account in year 3

= [(£500 employees – 57 employees) × 100 share options × £15] – [£212,500 + £227,500]

= £224,500

Note

In the event that all 500 employees leave over the three years, the cumulative expense over the three years would be nil, ie 0 employees × 100 share options × £15 per share option value. Under the U SM a charge would still be recognised in respect of the service provided by each employee before their departure.

Example 34.3

Situation

An entity grants 100 share options to each of its 500 employees. Each grant is conditional upon the employee working for the entity over the next three years.

The entity estimates that the fair value of each share option is £15.

The entity estimates that 20% of the employees, ie 100 employees, leave over the three years and forfeit their rights to the share options.

There is a market condition that at the end of the three-year period the share price must exceed £50.

Calculation

(Where the market condition is met.)

The cumulative expense for the three years

= (500 – 100) employees × 100 share options per employee × £15 per share option

= £600,000

The annual charge to the profit and loss account

= £600,000 divided by three years

= £200,000

(Where the market condition is NOT met.)

The cumulative expense for the three years

= (500 – 100) employees × 100 share options per employee × £15 per share option

= £600,000

The annual charge to the profit and loss account

= £600,000 divided by three years

= £200,000

Note

Where there is a market condition, the charge is the same whether or not the market condition is satisfied.

Example 34.4

Situation

An entity grants 100 share options to each of its 500 employees. Each grant is conditional upon the employee working for the entity over the next three years.

The entity estimates that the fair value of each share option is £15.

The entity estimates that 20% of the employees, ie 100 employees, leave over the three years and forfeit their rights to the share options.

There is a non-market condition that over the three-year period pre-tax profits must exceed an average of £50 million each year.

Calculation

(Where the non-market condition (profit target) is met.)

The cumulative expense for the three years

= (500 – 100) employees × 100 share options per employee × £15 per share option

× 100%

= £600,000

The annual charge to the profit and loss account

= £600,000 divided by three years

= £200,000

(Where the non-market condition (profit target) is NOT met.)

The cumulative expense for the three years

= (500 – 100) employees × 100 share options per employee × £15 per share option

× 0%

= £0

The annual charge to the profit and loss account

= £0

Note

Where there is a non-market condition that is not satisfied, the charge is reduced to zero.

Option pricing models

For employee share schemes

34.17 The option-pricing model provides the basis for the value that is to be disclosed through the financial statements. Although option-pricing models are widely used in the financial markets it is important to recognise that there is a fundamental difference between traded share options and employee share options.

The features that distinguish employee share options from traded share options are as follows:

- For employee share options: there is a period during which the options have a non-exercisable status (see below).

- For employee share options: the options are non-transferable and not, therefore, capable of being traded (see below).

- For employee share options: the exercise of the options can be subject to vesting conditions and if these conditions are not met the options will usually lapse (see below).

- For employee share options, the option term is longer (see below).

The Accounting Standards Board has given assurances that these differences have been taken into account in the development of its standard.

Choice of option pricing formula

34.18 The objective and the requirement of the Standard is to approximate the expectations that would be reflected in a current market or negotiated exchange price for the option. These expectations are reflected in the choice of option pricing formula and in the choice of inputs into the option pricing formula.

The approach is to make reliable estimates based on expectations. When estimating the effects of early exercise the objective is to approximate the expectations that an outside party with access to detailed information about employees exercise behaviour would develop based on information available at the date of grant.

Delay in exercising the options

34.19 Employee share options are exercisable only with the payment of the option price at the date of exercise. The Accounting Standards Board sees this enforced delay between the date of grant and the date of exercise as establishing the period during which the employees provide their services to the company as the payment for their options.

Employee share options are often called *Bermudian options* that accommodate some of the features of the European option and some of the features of the American option. The opportunity to exercise the European option arises only at the end of the life of the option, whereas in contrast for the American option there is usually an opportunity to exercise the option at any time during the life of the option. The freedom to exercise the option earlier and without the enforced delay attaches more value to the American option than to the European option. The employee share option as a hybrid of these two models is more valuable than a European option, but not as valuable as an American option.

The Black-Scholes-Merton formula and the Binomial formula have both been suggested as the basis for valuing employee share options. The Black-Scholes-Merton formula is a formula that values European options. Whereas the Binomial formula is a formula that values American options. It follows that if the Black-Scholes-Merton formula is used there is no need to adjust the model for the enforced delay in exercising the options as this feature will already be an assumption within the model. By contrast, if the Binomial formula is used there will be a need to adjust for the enforced delay in exercising the options as this feature will not be an assumption within the model.

In reality the enforced delay in exercising the options or the inability to exercise the option does not have a significant effect on the value of the option. However, the ASB has stated that where the Black-Scholes-Merton formula is used no adjustment for the enforced delay should be made but where the Binomial formula is used an adjustment should be made for the enforced delay. This treatment is consistent with the technical distinction between the two formulae.

Non-transferability of employee share options

34.20 The feature of non-transferability limits the value-realising opportunities for the employee. Where the transferability is allowed, as is the case with a normal traded share option, the optionholder can realise through the sale of the option the intrinsic value of the share option and the remaining time value of the option. Whereas for the employee share option holder value can be realised only by exercising the option that allows for the realisation of the intrinsic value only. For the employee share optionholder, the exercising of the option usually leads automatically to the foregoing of the remaining time value.

The feature of non-transferability for the company may seem irrelevant. Surely, the reality is that with or without transferability there is a requirement to supply shares in satisfaction of the option by whoever exercises the option, before or after the option being sold. However, the feature of non-transferability will often lead to early exercise as the only opportunity that the employee has to realise value. The employee loses the remaining time value of the option and the company receives the option price earlier than it would by transferability that would allow a later exercise by another person.

The Accounting Standards Board deals with the matter of early exercise by requiring that the option valuation accommodates the expected life of the non-transferable option rather than the contractual option term. In establishing an estimate of the expected life, account must be taken of the life of the option, the average length of time that similar options have remained outstanding and the expected volatility of the underlying shares.

Black-Scholes-Merton formula

34.21 The initial comments made about the Black-Scholes-Merton formula in the Standard highlight the disadvantages as follows:

- the formula requires the use of a single expected life as an input into the option valuation, an assumption that may be unrealistic in practice;

- the formula has a limited capacity to reflect the correlation between the share price and early exercise; and

- the formula does not accommodate the possibility of the option being exercised at a date later than the end of the expected life.

The disadvantages of the Black-Scholes-Merton formula lie in its comparative inflexibility and in particular that it cannot account for either performance conditions or early exercises. However, the Standard does not prohibit the use of the Black-Scholes-Merton formula and appreciates that where there are few option grants or relatively short contractual lives or a requirement for exercise shortly after the vesting date the result may not be materially different from the more flexible formula.

Binomial formula

34.22 The comments made about the Binomial formula in the Standard highlight its flexibility and are on balance more favourable. The comments are as follows:

- The formula uses the option's contractual life as an input and takes into account the possibility of early exercises on a range of different dates in the life of the option.

- The formula allows for the correlation between the share price and early exercise and expected employee turnover.

- The formula permits the inputs into the model to vary over the life of the option.

- The formula allows for the possibility that the volatility of the share price might change over the life of the option, particularly useful where the company experiences a higher than usual volatility.

Operation of the option-pricing model

34.23 A slighter more indepth appreciation of the Black-Scholes-Merton formula illustrates both the application and the limitations of the option-pricing formula approach to valuing options. The Black-Scholes-Merton formula's required inputs illustrate that it is only credible for the company whose shares are quoted. The application distils down to inputting into a formula the following information:

- share price;

- option price;

- assumed risk-free interest rate;

- expected length of time of the options or option term;

- volatility of the share price; and

- dividend yield.

The apparent simplicity of its application through inputting a set of variables disguises the complexity of its mathematical origins and derivation and indeed the extent of its credible usage.

Although the formula can be applied with comparative ease for a quoted company this is not necessarily so for the unquoted or private company. Whereas the absence of a quoted share price can potentially be overcome through determining the share value through the well-established share valuation procedures the determination of share price volatility presents considerable economic and logistical issues. Typically the resort would be to a sector average for the private company concerned.

In relation to the variables that are included in the Black-Scholes option-pricing valuation model, the best understanding of their effect is as follows:

- For the share price: any increase will increase the value of the option.

- For the option price: any decrease will increase the value of the option as the bestowing of a discount raises the value of the option.

- For the risk-free interest rate: at current rates that are low and vary little between long-term and short-term, the variable has the least effect on the option value. The understanding is that the higher the rate, the lower the cost of paying the option price and, therefore, the higher the value of the option. It is the only variable in the model to be determined independently of the company.

- For the option term: the longer the option term the greater is the opportunity to benefit from the rise in the share price so the longer the option term the higher the value of the option.

- For the volatility of the share price: the higher the volatility the greater the opportunity for higher gains in shorter time. However, by the nature of 'volatility' the variable can vary considerably and the difference between say three-year volatility and five-year volatility can be significant.

- For dividend yield: dividends are built into the share price so for option schemes the price has to be neutralised for dividends, given that options do not pay dividends. Higher dividends result in a lower value for the option for the reason that there is a lost benefit and maybe an opportunity cost from being an optionholder rather than a shareholder.

Vesting conditions

34.24 The vesting conditions, whether in the form of a service period or in the form of performance conditions, represent the basis for enabling the employee optionholders to pay for their share options through the services that they render to the company. This contention is supported by the fact that a service period is established to retain staff and a performance condition is established as an incentive for the employees through their services to work towards specified performance targets.

The Standard requires that the company should estimate the expected vesting and revise the estimate as necessary if subsequent information indicates that actual forfeitures are likely to be different from estimates that have been calculated at the date of grant.

Source of the shares

34.25 Shares are sourced for employee share scheme purposes through an issue of new shares by the company, or by the purchase by the company of existing shares from the market.

It is worth noting that where share options are granted and/or share awards are made over a significant percentage of a company's share capital and they relate to new issue shares then the potentially dilutive effect on the share price may reduce the charge to the profit and loss account.

Impact of vesting conditions

34.26 It is usually the case that the opportunity to exercise the share options or to receive the share awards is dependent upon certain specified vesting conditions such as the achievement of pre-set performance conditions or maybe simply still being in the employment of the company at the date of exercise or maturity. The valuation under the standard could be influenced by the presence or absence of these vesting conditions. This will depend on whether or not the vesting conditions are so-called 'market conditions'.

A market condition is a condition that is based on the share price. Where the performance condition is based on a comparison of the company's TSR with the TSR of a comparator group of companies this will almost certainly be a market condition for the reason that the TSR is based on the share price. Market conditions must be taken into account when estimating the fair value. It is important to recognise that it is not possible to introduce a write-back where the market conditions are not met.

Where vesting conditions are non-market conditions, as is the case where linked to continued employment or earnings per share then the treatment under the standard is very different. In these circumstances, the vesting conditions are not based upon the share price. The requirement is to estimate at the date of grant the number of shares that are expected to vest on the basis of the non-market conditions and then to revise the estimate if subsequent information indicates that actual vesting levels will be different. This revision will usually take the form of a write-back from the position that was calculated as the expectation at the date of grant. For non-market conditions and the opportunity for a write-back in the event that the share options or share awards fail to vest a charge to the profit and loss account will only be incurred if the employees receive value under their share options or share awards.

Impact of performance conditions

34.27   Where the vesting conditions are market conditions this may result in a discount on the valuation at the date of grant, particularly where the performance condition is the key determinant in vesting. However, if the condition does not come to fruition the charge cannot be written-back. The company has to decide between the discount at the outset for certain market conditions and the write-back opportunities for certain non-market conditions. The main influences on this decision will be the company's own individual circumstances and the nature of the share scheme.

Option term

34.28   In comparing employee share options with traded share options, the traded version will often have a shorter life whereas the employee share option will usually although not always have a much longer life.

It is much more difficult to estimate the inputs, in relation to the share price volatility and in relation to the risk-free interest rate and in relation to the dividend yield, where the option term is represented in a longer period. The potential for estimation error is, therefore, greater where there is a longer option term.

It is where there is a longer option term that the Binomial formula offers an advantage for the reason that it can mitigate the estimation error by allowing for changes in the model's inputs over the life of the option and by accommodating the effects of early exercises.

Putting share-based payment into an international context

Move towards market values

34.29 The Financial ASB in the US has shown a growing predilection towards using market values for the assets and liabilities that are shown in the company's balance sheet.

If this approach of 'fair value accounting' is to prevail then there will be a need to determine values for items that are included in the profit and loss account that are consistent with the values that are included in the balance sheet. The assumptions that support the auditor's true and fair view will, therefore, be determined on the basis of their capacity to produce current values for inclusion in the financial statements.

Abandonment of historic cost

34.30 At first sight, therefore, this would seem to herald the abandonment of historic cost in favour of a current value basis for accounting. However, further consideration leads to the conclusion that both the balance sheet and the profit and loss account will require statements in both current values and historic cost if the requirements of the regulatory authorities are to be met. The expectation would be, for example, that the tax authorities would continue to require historic cost as the basis for issuing tax assessments.

Nevertheless, the drive towards fair value accounting or current value accounting or economic value accounting will continue to have momentum as long as there is the empirically quantifiable divergence between the historic cost book values that appear in the financial statements of companies and their market capitalisations as determined by the recognised stock exchanges on which their shares are quoted.

Historic cost – preferable?

34.31 The arguments against historic cost are well-documented, notably that it appears ludicrous to show balance sheet positions that are based on the amounts that were paid at the time of purchase which will typically have been different for each of the items that are shown in the accounts.

Over the last 15 years or so with comparatively low rates of inflation the argument against historic cost has been rarely employed in discussions on improving the credibility of the true and fair view.

The arguments for historic cost are consistency of treatment between companies and between years, coupled usually with the absence of significant volatility year-on-year.

Market or current values – preferable?

34.32 The main argument against market or current values, then, in circumstances where the annual depreciation charge to historic cost positions is abandoned, must be the propensity towards significant changes in real values year-on-year with the consequential volatility to the bottom-line profit.

The volatility in the markets as reflected in the performance of the recognised stock exchanges will in turn be reflected in the financial statements that are prepared by companies.

In relation to the impact on particular companies, therefore, the companies that would be most affected would be the companies that have the greatest proportion of financial assets to total assets, namely the banking organisations and the pension and life assurance companies.

Need for circumspection

34.33 If the momentum towards current values continues then MV treatment will gradually become the defining theme within all accounting standards. However, enthusiasm must give way to circumspection at some stage if perspective is to be preserved and catastrophe is to be avoided.

As well as becoming more volatile, financial statements will inevitably become more difficult to understand and potentially more subjective in the assumptions that are used to generate the current values. There is, of course, potential for the spectre of financial statements being reflective of current values at the time of preparation, only to be out-of-date by the time of the voting at the AGM.

The very group that the current value approach is designed to serve, the investors, could become confused within a mass of information and competing concepts, and be ill-served by supposedly accurate information soon becoming untimely.

Preoccupation with employee share schemes

34.34 The accounting bodies have increasingly over the last ten years been preoccupied with employee share schemes. This has culminated in employee share schemes becoming the prime candidate for the exploration of the appropriateness of using current values. It arises in the quest to measure the true cost of employee service and to include an appropriate valuation as an expense item in the profit and loss account.

The first initiative from the US Financial ASB to treat the cost of share options as an expense in the profit and loss account, came in 1994. However, the US Congress responded forthrightly to the Financial ASB, with a direct challenge to remove its powers to determine accounting standards if it did not rescind on its attempts to institute its expensing proposals. This second initiative, though, did not meet with a similar response given the disquiet engendered over the financial scandals of recent years, notably Enron.

Pension scheme reporting

34.35 Success for the accounting bodies over employee share schemes will open the sluice gates for further reform of the accounting standards. Interestingly, the FRS in the UK on accounting for pensions, FRS 17, requires pension assets to be shown at MV. The consequence of this is that the company is required to show in its balance sheet any shortfall of pension fund assets to pension fund liabilities.

This economic value approach is not the approach commonly adopted outside the UK where companies may still account on the basis that their pension schemes are generating profits whereas in reality the pension schemes are in deficit, and sometimes significantly in deficit. The US Financial ASB has already addressed accounting for employee pension schemes as a priority with a view to the introduction of pension scheme accounting on an economic value basis in the US.

Revenue recognition

34.36 Further edicts can be expected on such subjects as revenue recognition and the accounting for off-balance sheet vehicles.

The date of revenue recognition is the case in point with the question being one of determining cut-off. Is accounting in the profit and loss account required when the invoice is issued or should it be before, say when the order is received from the customer or maybe it should be sometime after the invoice has been issued, say, for example, when payment is received?

This matter is to a large degree dealt with by the application of the fundamental accounting concepts of accruals and consistency. It is, then, a sign of the accounting bodies determination to address these issues that it has chosen to focus on producing more refined standards for these matters rather than leave the matter to the integrity of company directors operating within the confines of existing custom and practice.

Off-balance sheet vehicles

34.37 On off-balance sheet vehicles, the US Financial ASB has issued some guidance. It is an issue brought to light by the Enron scandal with their operation of 'special-purpose entities'.

The one factor that the guidance on off-balance sheet vehicles and the expected proposals on revenue recognition have in common is that without regulatory dictates the company directors working with their auditors have the opportunity to exercise subjective criteria in manipulating the balance sheet net asset value of their companies and the sales turnover income and profits as disclosed in their profit and loss accounts.

Accounting irony

34.38 The real irony is that the fair value accounting approach taken by the accounting bodies is a response to many highly regarded economic commentators on either side of the Atlantic who contend that the downturn in the stock markets is to a large degree attributable to lack of confidence in financial statements that have disguised the financial scandals within the companies whose activities they purport to reflect.

Surely, the irony is that in resorting to fair value accounting the accounting bodies may be applying principles that do not only defy economic sense for the user of the financial statements but defy the logic upon which they so pride themselves.

Feline/canine fallacy

34.39 Let us look at this in the context of employee share schemes, our subject for purposes of today's seminar.

The feline/canine fallacy states the following:

'A cat has four legs,

a dog has four legs;

therefore, a cat is a dog;.

The conclusion from the information given is patently wrong. The fact that the two animals each have four legs does not make a cat a dog. Each has other characteristics that define them as separate animals.

The feline/canine fallacy applies to the accounting bodies approach to share-based payments for employee share schemes as follows:

'Salaries and wages are a cost,

share options and share awards are a cost;

therefore, both are costs to the company and should be expensed in the profit and loss account forthwith.'

Again the conclusion from the information is wrong. Share options and share awards should not be given the same financial treatment simply by virtue of the fact that they are costs. The feline/canine fallacy applies. Just as the cat and the dog are different species; so there is a distinct difference in kind between 'salaries and wages' on the one hand, and 'share options and share awards' on the other. It is true that each represents a cost. However, 'salaries and wages' represents a cost to the company whereas all-importantly 'share options and share awards' do not represent a cost to the company. 'Share options and share awards' do actually represent a cost to the shareholders whose personal shareholding suffers from a dilution in value.

By failing to recognise that the company is a separate persona at law and in substance from its shareholders the accounting bodies have committed the feline/canine fallacy.

Potential solution

34.40 Companies trade in international markets with international customers, international suppliers and, of course, international competitors. The solution, therefore, must be capable of international application if meaningful and comparable financial statements are to be produced that serve their main audience of the investing public. However, a remorseless drive towards the use of market or current values must be severely tested in the laboratory if this approach is ultimately to survive as a credible accounting standard.

Better as an interim measure at least, would be to remain with the historic cost approach for the presentation of the balance sheet and the profit and loss account, but to provide a significant body of supporting information in the financial statements for purposes of further explanation.

Although accounting for employee share schemes is being subjected to this current value scrutiny it should be recognised that this is in the context of an initiative by Sir David Tweedie, the Chairman of the IASB, to apply these principles to all accounting standards.

In seeking to account more effectively for employee share schemes, though, the fallacy must be exposed. The proposed treatment has the capacity to detract from the truth and the fairness of the financial statements although it seems extremely unlikely at this late stage that that there will be any reversal of the decision to introduce some form of expense accounting for share-based payments.

The essential need is to return to the drawing board in order to review how it is possible to measure the true cost of service, which we must always remember, is the fundamental objective of the exercise.

Abstracts of the urgent issues task force

34.41 In addition to IFRS 2 and FRS 20, it is important to be aware that the Urgent Issues Task Force of the ASB periodically makes pronouncements in the form UITF Abstracts.

The UITF Abstracts that are included in the Appendices are as follows:

*   *UITF Abstract 25: National Insurance Contributions on Share Option Gains;*

*   *UITF Abstract 32: Employee Benefit Trusts and Other Intermediate Payment Arrangements;* and

*   *UITF Abstract 38: Accounting for ESOP Trusts.*

Chapter 35

Treasury shares

Introduction

35.1 This chapter explains what treasury shares are, how they operate, the tax treatment and the accounting rules. The chapter then provides a comprehensive comparison between the use of treasury shares and an employee share trust as the supplier of the shares.

Shares that function as treasury shares

35.2 A company is, from 1 December 2003, allowed to buy its own shares from existing shareholders and hold those shares as treasury shares provided the company is a company whose shares fall into one of the following categories:

- the shares are quoted on the London Stock Exchange with an official listing in accordance with FSMA 2000, Pt 6;

- the shares are quoted on the AIM of the London Stock Exchange; and

- the shares are quoted on one of the equivalent exchanges in the European Economic Area (EEC) with an official listing, or on a market that is regulated under the Directive 93/22/EEC, Art 16.

The opportunity to hold treasury shares does not extend to unquoted private companies although these companies can continue to purchase their shares under the existing procedures. They do, of course, have to cancel them immediately, again under the existing procedures.

Implications of using treasury shares

35.3 The implications of the introduction of treasury shares are that for the first time the company whose shares qualify can choose warehouse rather than cancel shares that it buys from existing shareholders.

The new definition of 'qualifying shares' is found in CA 2006, s 724(2), (CA 1985, s 162(4)). The amendment to the CA 1985 was facilitated through a combination of the Companies (Acquisition of Own Shares) (Treasury Shares) Regs 2003, SI 2003/1116 and the Companies (Acquisition of Own Shares) (Treasury Shares) No 2 Regs 2003, SI 2003/3031. The previous position under company law was that when a company bought its own shares it was required to cancel them immediately.

Treasury shares are by definition held 'in treasury' by the company. It is a warehousing arrangement. The company is the registered owner of the shares for the whole of the time that they are held in treasury during which they will have neither voting rights nor dividend rights attached to them. The shares do, of course, remain in existence for their time in treasury and, indeed, retain any Official List status that they have at the point at which they enter treasury. They do not, therefore, need to apply for listing on coming out of treasury. At the point at which the shares do come out of treasury, the shares once again assume their voting rights and dividend rights and rank on the same basis with the other shares in the same class.

At any time after purchasing the shares the company is empowered to opt for any of the following courses of action:

- To transfer treasury shares 'for the purposes of or pursuant to an employees share scheme' to assist the company in meeting its obligations to employees in respect of shares. In this context, 'employees share scheme' is as defined in CA 2006, s 1166 (CA 1985, s 743), the normal bona fide employee share scheme definition.

- To sell the treasury shares for cash. The term 'cash' has a broad definition, including the release of a debt for a known sum and an undertaking to pay cash within 90 days. However, the company's right to sell is subject to first offering the treasury shares to all existing shareholders in proportion to their existing shareholdings, analogous to the way in which a rights issue would be administered. Additionally, the sale must be within the 5% limit that shareholders approve for new issues of shares and the Listing Rules will not allow the cash sale price to be discounted to less than 90% of the MV of the shares.

- To cancel the treasury shares, in the same way as previously, such that they cease to have an existence.

The company must obtain shareholder approval to acquire shares that are to be held in treasury, a position that is analogous to the position that prevails in relation to share buy-backs, subject to the following:

- the shareholders can give to the company a standing authority that is valid for a period up to 18 months to buy shares into treasury;

- the total nominal value of shares that are held in treasury may not at any one time exceed 10% of the nominal value of any one class of the issued share capital of the company; and

- if the company exceeds this limit, either purposely or indeed inadvertently, then the company has a period of up to 12 months to bring the number back to within the 10% limit by disposing of shares through the methods that are allowed.

Tax treatment of treasury shares

35.4   The tax treatment of treasury shares is dealt with through FA 2003 and is designed to ensure that there is no tax liability arising for shares that are held in treasury as follows: Treasury shares cannot carry dividend rights so the matter of the income tax treatment of dividends does not arise. In reality, income cannot arise in relation to treasury shares and, therefore, income tax cannot arise either.

Under FA 2003, s 195, any sale or transfer of treasury shares is treated as a new issue of shares which for the company is tax neutral in that it is deemed that neither a capital gain nor an allowable loss arises at the time of the sale or the transfer. There will, for purposes of the transferee's CGT computation on any subsequent sale or transferee by the transferee, be a purchase cost as the base cost in the calculation.

There is a fixed charge for stamp duty of £5 on each transfer of treasury shares at the time they come out of treasury at the time of sale or transfer. Stamp duty also arises when the company buys the shares into treasury, based on the price paid by the company.

Accounting treatment for treasury shares

35.5   The accounting treatment for treasury shares is as follows:

- There must be distributable reserves available as the basis for shares to be bought in by the company to be held as treasury shares. This is the only basis for supporting the purchase as an explicit purchase of shares, for holding in treasury cannot be funded by the proceeds of a new issue of shares or a purchase out of capital. It is important to recognise that the only basis available for the funding of the shares is distributable reserves and that the buying in of shares to be held as treasury shares will reduce the overall capacity of the company to pay dividends.

- Any reduction in the issued share capital of the company that arises as a result of cancelling shares must be transferred to a capital redemption reserve account. There are strict limitations on the use of the capital redemption reserve, namely that it is treated in the same way as capital and can only be used for bonus issues on existing shares.

The special accounting rules for the treatment of treasury shares when applied to employee share schemes or sold for cash are as follows:

- where the company receives a price for the shares that is less than the amount originally paid by the company the amount received is credited to distributable reserves; and

- where the company receives a price for the shares that is more than the amount originally paid by the company the amount received is credited to distributable reserves up to the level of the amount that was originally paid by the company and the excess is credited to share premium account.

The accounting rules that are established by FRS 20, Accounting for Share-Based Payment, are as follows:

- the company's balance sheet should show treasury shares as a deduction from shareholders funds;

- the company's profit and loss account should not show any gains or losses when shares are bought, transferred or cancelled;

- the reconciliation of movements in shareholders funds should show the amounts paid and received for treasury shares as separate amounts; and

- separate disclosures are required for the reduction in shareholders' funds and the number of treasury shares held.

The use of treasury shares for purposes of employee share schemes arises from the fact that they present an alternative to using an employee share trust arrangement in circumstances where the company wishes to use existing shares to satisfy employee rights under employee share schemes arrangements.

Treasury shares can be transferred to employees to meet company obligations and to satisfy employee rights under any other employee share scheme arrangement.

Contrast with the employee share trust

35.6 The use of treasury shares contrasts with the use of an employee share trust as follows.

Shareholder approval

Treasury shares

35.7 The approval of shareholders is required in general meeting as part of the procedure for the purchase of own shares.

Employee share trust

35.8 There will usually be no need to secure shareholder approval for an employee share trust to be used for employee share scheme purposes.

Earnings per share

Treasury shares

35.9 Given that there are no voting rights or dividend rights attached to treasury shares, current recognised best practice, in the absence of further clarification from the authorities, is to exclude from the denominator shares number and, therefore, increase earnings per share.

Employee share trust

35.10 Shares held in the employee share trust do not count as additional shares in the earnings per share calculation which shows, therefore, an increase in earnings per share.

Distributable reserves

Treasury shares

35.11 Under company law there is a deduction from distributable reserves for the cost of acquisition of the shares.

Employee share trust

35.12 There is a possible deduction from distributable reserves.

Shareholding limits

Treasury shares

35.13 The limitation of 10% is stipulated by statute.

Employee Share Trust

35.14 The limitation of 5% is stipulated by the regulatory guidelines.

Dilution limits

Treasury shares

35.15 Treasury shares must be included in the dilution limits that are set by the Association of British Insurers.

Employee share trust

35.16 Shares held in the employee share trust are excluded from the limits that are set by the Association of British Insurers.

Source of shares

Treasury shares

35.17 The source of shares is restricted to existing shares only in that new issue into treasury is prohibited.

Employee share trust

35.18 The source of the shares may be existing shares, or new issue shares issued directly into the trust.

Transfer pricing

Treasury shares

35.19 Where share awards are made from treasury shares, they are probably treated as outside the scope of the UK transfer pricing rules.

Employee share trust

35.20 Where the trust transfers shares to employees, the company loses the capital exemption from the UK transfer pricing rules.

Administration costs

Treasury shares

35.21 There are no independent trustee or nominee costs.

Employee share trust

35.22 There are external trustee and administration costs.

Tax treatment

Treasury shares

35.23 Transfers out of treasury do not generate taxable gains or losses.

Employee share trust

35.24 Where there are offshore trustees, the tax treatment is favourable.

Type of companies

Treasury shares

35.25 The limitation is to quoted companies and AIM companies.

Employee share trust

35.26 The trust can hold the shares of either listed or unquoted private companies.

Share rights

Treasury shares

35.27 The shares cannot carry either voting or dividend rights.

Employee share trust

35.28 The shares can carry voting rights and dividend rights.

Chapter 36

Transfer pricing and recharge arrangements

Including the *Waterloo* case and new legislation

Introduction

36.1   The relevance of transfer pricing to employee share schemes came to prominence through the Special Commissioners case of *Waterloo Plc, Euston & Paddington v IRC*, 24 October 2001.

Prior to the *Waterloo* case, transfer pricing did not appear to have any application to employee share schemes. However, the concerns for employee share schemes that arise from Waterloo are that although the initial interpretation of the decision appeared to be narrow a much wider set of implications have emerged. HMRC subsequently produced a formal response in February 2003 followed by the release of comprehensive guidance in October 2003.

What is transfer pricing?

36.2   The subject matter for issues that arise over transfer pricing are the prices at which goods and services are transferred between associated businesses where the absence of arm's length negotiation could result in taxable profits being transferred from one associated business in one country to an associated business in another country.

Transfer pricing is, therefore, concerned with the expatriation of profits across national boundaries on the basis of non-commercial terms in a way that minimises the tax liability of a company in the country in which it is subject to tax. In view of this concern, it is not surprising that governments around the world enact legislation that is specifically directed at preventing companies with international operations from artificially setting transfer prices with the express intention of minimising the tax charge.

Waterloo case

36.3   The name *Waterloo* is a code name as the taxpayer in the case requested and was granted anonymity. Although the current UK transfer pricing legislation is found in FAt 1998, Sch 28AA, the *Waterloo* case was brought under the earlier legislation in ICTA 1988, s 770 et seq under which it was contended that the parent company had provided a 'business facility'.

The facts of the case are that Waterloo, a UK resident company, operated as the parent company of a large multinational group of companies whose employees had been granted share options through the mechanism of employee share trusts. The funding for the employee share trusts came exclusively from the parent company through interest-free loans, with the subsidiaries not contributing to the funding whatsoever. When the employees exercised their options, the company fulfilled its obligations to the employees primarily through shares that had been purchased by the employee share trusts.

The central issue to emerge from *Waterloo* was in respect of the funding of the remuneration for another company's employees in the sense of whether a company is required to charge the other company for granting options to the employees of that other company, albeit within a group arrangement.

The position taken by HMRC in *Waterloo* was as follows:

* Under ICTA 1988, s 773(4): the parent company had provided 'business facilities' to the subsidiaries and on that basis under ICTA 1988, s 770(1) the arm's length price must substitute the actual price charged.

* The arm's length price must be substituted for all the accounting periods from 1989 to 1997. The year-end date was 31 December.

* The basis of costing the arm's length price should be a combination of the borrowing costs of purchasing the shares, trustee fees, management and administrative costs, any other related costs and 'a suitable margin over cost' and that a fair formula should be devised for 'an appropriate apportionment of an aggregate arm's length price between resident and non-resident subsidiaries'.

The company contended that it was not providing a business facility in that it was the employee share trusts that were granting the options and that furthermore the impracticality of ascribing a value to the options made it impossible to make an appropriate adjustment to reflect the value of the options. However, HMRC did not accept this response as a plausible defence and conveyed their position that the arrangements must be considered as a whole and within that context it was clear that the parent company was indeed providing a business facility to its subsidiaries.

Current laws and regulations

Finance Act 1998, Schedule 28AA

36.4 The current application derives from FA 1998, Sch 28AA whose provisions apply automatically, given that it was introduced with the corporation tax self-assessment regime. In contrast, under the old regime of ICTA 1988, s 770 the provision applies only if HMRC issued a direction for it to apply.

Whereas for *section 770* to apply it must be demonstrated that a business facility has been provided, Schedule 28AA applies to a transactior or series of transactions between connected companies where a transaction is defined widely to include arrangements, understandings and mutual practice. Generally speaking, Schedule 28AA is drafted wide enough to catch the grant of options from one company to the employees of anoher company, and applies where an arrangement is made between two persons that differs from the arrangement that would have been made between two independent persons and one of the persons receives an advantage in relation to UK tax.

OECD model tax convention

36.5   Article 9 of the OECD model tax convention is also known as the 'associated enterprises article'. It is the article upon which Schedule 28AA is based. Indeed, Schedule 28AA has to be interpreted in a manner that is consistent with the provisions of Article 9 and the OECD transfer pricing guidelines. The guidelines form part of UK tax law where published before 1 May 1998 or published after that date and designated by treasury order.

It is from Article 9 of the OECD Model Tax Convention that the principle of an arm's length transaction derives as follows:

> When conditions are made or imposed between two associated enterprises in their commercial or financial relations which differ from those which would be made between independent enterprises, then the profits which would, but for these conditions, have accrued to one of the enterprises, but by reason of these conditions, have not so accrued, may be included in the profits of that enterprise and taxed accordingly.

Whatever method a company uses to set inter-company transfer prices they must be consistent with the OECD arm's length principles and benchmarked against the measures set by the OECD TPG.

Tax Bulletin

36.6   The *Tax Bulletin*, which was published on 14 February 2003, sets out principles for transfer pricing following the *Waterloo* case.

The essence of the *Tax Bulletin* is that the principles should apply to future accounting periods and all open periods of the following:

- UK companies with employee share schemes for employees of overseas subsidiaries; and

- UK companies with employees who participate in the employee share schemes of an overseas parent with this provision limited to accounting periods commencing before 1 January 2003.

The reason for the limitation is that under FA 2003, Sch 23 no other statutory deduction is allowed for corporation tax in respect of the cost of providing shares. The interpretation taken by HMRC is that the transfer pricing provisions of Schedule 28AA are overridden by the statutory corporation tax deduction rules of Schedule 23.

HMRC policy and practice

36.7 In the light of the *Waterloo* decision, the position accepted by HMRC as generally prevailing practice is as follows:

Capital exemption

36.8 The understanding of HMRC interpretation of the transfer pricing principles as taken from the *Tax Bulletin* has been that the rules will not apply in circumstances where the company satisfies the exercise of options and always meets its obligations to the employees through the issue of shares directly to the employees (and not through the purchase of existing shares from the market) and employee share trusts are not involved in assisting the company in meeting these obligations. In these circumstances, the payments to the parent by the subsidiary companies would be regarded as capital payments rather than revenue payments. However, the comments made in the HMRC *International Manual* indicate that further clarification is required on the availability of the 'capital exemption'. It is worth noting that HMRC has indicated to practitioners that the capital exemption will be available where the company satisfies its obligations to employees through new issue shares and never satisfies its obligations through existing shares purchased from the market. The opportunity for the capital exemption does, of course, bring into focus the matter of deciding how the shares are to be sourced.

Calculation of the arm's length value

36.9 Methodologies exist for the calculation of the arm's length value of the payment to the parent company as follows:

- through using an option pricing model such as the Black-Scholes or the binomial methods to calculate the value of the options;

- through calculating a finance cost that would be incurred if the options were satisfied by shares purchased on the market, based on the assumption that by purchasing shares in the market and holding those shares in an employee share trust there is a requirement on the part of the company for a hedging policy; and

- the methodology that is based on the so-called 'spread' and often referred to as 'the spread method' is not acceptable to HMRC. It is, incidentally, an acceptable basis in the US although the OECD study of September 2004 is non-committal on the matter. Under the spread method, charges are based on the gain that arises for the employee on the exercise of the option, representing the growth in the value of the shares over the life of the option.

Applicable periods

36.10   The transfer pricing principles will not apply to options that were exercised in accounting periods that ended before 1 January 1997 unless exceptional circumstances prevailed such as circumstances where transfer pricing enquiries of a general nature were open in a company or where enquiries into deductions for share options had been opened anyway or where enquiries had been closed and misleading information had been provided.

Subsidiary company initiative

36.11   Where the subsidiary company is responsible for the grant of the options to its employees, organising the supply of shares on the exercise of the options, and the subsidiary company operates and administers its own employee share scheme and the subsidiary company itself purchases existing shares of the parent company from the market then HMRC considers that the transfer pricing rules will not apply between the parent company and the subsidiary company. This is the approach often referred to as the subsidiary 'doing its own thing' and it does represent a realistic approach to avoiding the transfer pricing rules. However, if in reality it is the parent company rather than the subsidiary company that is at the helm and the leadership of the subsidiary company is an artificial contrivance then the transfer pricing rules will be difficult to avoid.

Finance Act 2004

36.12   The significance of FA 2004 is as follows.

From 1 April 2004 the scope of the transfer pricing rules is extended to transactions between UK resident group companies. Since FA 2004, therefore, the transfer pricing rules are not restricted to transactions across national boundaries.

In circumstances where awards are made or options are granted prior to that date then HMRC takes the view that it is necessary to recognise the transfer pricing cost over a period that spreads across 1 April 2004.

For the UK-based transactions HMRC introduced a two-year period of grace from 1 April 2004 to 31 March 2006 in which penalties will not be pursued for any transfer pricing liabilities that arise during that period.

The key technical principle is that the UK parent company will be deemed to have received taxable income from the UK subsidiary company in relation to the grant of share options to employees of the UK subsidiary company. This principle emanates from the ruling of the European Court of Justice (ECJ) that an exemption from transfer pricing rules for entirely domestic transactions is likely to involve unlawful discrimination under the EC Treaty.

Where there is a payment or adjustment that establishes taxable income in the parent company the question arises as to whether the corresponding expense in the subsidiary company is allowable for corporation tax relief. The difficulty arises through Schedule 23 which prohibits any other relief in respect of the cost of providing shares. However, HMRC has indicated that the transfer pricing payment is not necessarily the same as the Schedule 23 'cost of providing shares'.

UK to UK Transfer Pricing Provisions 2004

36.13 The interaction between FA 2003, Sch 23 and the UK to UK Transfer Pricing Provisions 2004 is interpreted by HMRC as follows.

Where options are granted at market value

36.14 The cost of providing shares is not incurred by the company. Instead, it is incurred by the employee through the payment of the option price. The transfer pricing payment by the subsidiary to the parent represents the cost of hedging that arises from the grant of the option together with the cost of administration rather than the cost of providing shares. This understanding allows the payment by the subsidiary to the parent to be an allowable expense for corporation tax purposes. The taxable income in the parent is offset by the allowable deduction in the subsidiary. Additionally, the subsidiary should be able to claim the Schedule 23 statutory corporation tax relief based upon the gain realised by the employee on exercise.

Where options are granted at a discount and there is no capital exemption

36.15 This would arise in the case of L-TIP awards where the discount may be up to 100% and for Sharesave options where the discount may be up to 20%. In these circumstances, the employee does not incur the full cost of providing shares.

- For the subsidiary, the payment by the subsidiary to the parent must, therefore, include an element to reflect the discount. It will not be possible to claim this element as an allowable expense as it is part of the cost of providing shares.

- For the parent, the receipt by the parent from the subsidiary is taxable income.

  - If the company meets its obligations in satisfying exercises through market share purchases then the parent company qualifies for a corporation tax deduction on the discount as the cost of purchasing and providing shares. The discount is the element of the payment that is not available for a corporation tax deduction by the subsidiary. The final result is that in total all the payment is corporation tax deductible, albeit in two separate components and for different reasons.

— If the company meets its obligations through new issue shares and no capital exemption is available then the discount will not represent an additional cost to the parent. The final result is that the element of the payment from the subsidiary to the parent that is the discount is not corporation tax deductible for either the parent or the subsidiary.

Where there is a mixed use of new issue shares and market purchase shares

36.16 To the extent that the options are MV options, they should not give rise to an additional corporation tax liability.

To the extent that the options are discounted options and satisfied by market share purchases, they should not give rise to an additional corporation tax liability.

To the extent that the options are discounted options and satisfied by new issue shares and the capital exemption is not available, they will give rise to an additional corporation tax liability.

The interaction between Share-Based Payment Accounting and the UK to UK Transfer Pricing Provisions is interpreted by HMRC as follows:

• The corporation tax computation should be adjusted to exclude the Share-Based Payment entries and to include the Transfer Pricing entries.

Small- to medium-sized companies exemption

36.17 The conditions for small-sized companies are less than 50 employees and either turnover or assets not exceeding €10m. The conditions for medium-sized companies are less than 250 employees and either turnover not exceeding €50m or assets not exceeding €43m.

HMRC August 2005 Guidelines

36.18 The August 2005 Guidelines represented a new approach from HMRC on the subject of transfer pricing and sought to accommodate the principles that are embodied in the accounting standards, FRS 20 and IFRS 2, on share-based payment. This use of the accounting standards represented an important development in the transfer pricing debate as it was the first realistic attempt by HMRC to use the share-based payment accounting principles to provide a fair and equitable outcome to the issues that transfer pricing had raised since the *Waterloo* case in 2001.

The August 2005 Guidelines contended that to be consistent with the accounting standards, it was necessary for the receipt by the parent company, in the event of a transfer pricing charge to the subsidiary company, to be credited to the reserves of the parent company.

The implications of this treatment are as follows:

- By-passing the profit and loss account in this way, the credit would not be treated as taxable income. The capital exemption is established as an approach that does not distinguish between new issue shares and existing shares.

- For UK to UK arrangements, where the subsidiary is claiming a corporation tax deduction through Schedule 23, there would be no corresponding deduction in the subsidiary as an additional corporation tax deduction so the overall impact on the corporation tax bill of parent and subsidiary companies combined would be neutral, a position which is clearly acceptable to HMRC. Indeed, the position is so acceptable to HMRC that they have indicated that in these circumstances there is no need to calculate a transfer pricing charge.

- For overseas subsidiary arrangements, depending upon the tax regime of the overseas country, there may be the opportunity for a corporation tax deduction in the subsidiary. Additionally, of course, in UK subsidiary arrangements, where there is no Schedule 23 corporation tax deduction, the spectre of a corporation tax deduction resulting from the transfer pricing charge from the parent reduces the corporation tax intake for HMRC and may not be a position that HMRC is prepared to tolerate.

Arbitrage receipt rules

36.19 The August 2005 Guidelines introduced the concept that the tax arbitrage rules may potentially bring these transactions into their net.

These rules were introduced through F (No 2) Act 2005 and apply where a UK company benefits from a payment and obtains, at the same time: (1) a tax deduction for the payment; and, (2) tax-freedom in relation to income and capital for the benefit. The rules give to HMRC a remedy whereby they can issue a notice to the company that the untaxed amount is treated as taxable income.

Under these rules, the three conditions, identified in FA (No 2) 2005, s 26 that should be examined to determine whether or not they apply to employee share schemes are as follows:

- *Condition 1*: the company's capital value has been increased as a consequence of a qualifying payment.

- *Condition 2*: the payment, in whole or in part, is available as an allowable deduction to the employer somewhere in the world.

- *Condition 3*: for the reason that at least part of the payment is taxable, the company and the employer expected a benefit to arise.

The debate in the autumn of 2005 over the possible application of the arbitrage rules to transfer pricing resulted in guidance issued by HMRC in December 2005, identifying the following conclusions:

- The conditions will not be met, as long as the tax deduction obtained by the company is appropriate to the economic substance and does not exceed the economic value provided.

- As a key general rule of thumb, payments calculated in accordance with the accounting standards, IFRS 2 and FRS 20, would be considered to reflect economic value. There is the potential, therefore, for the arbitrage provisions to apply in circumstances where the payments exceed the expense that has been calculated under IFRS 2 and FRS 20.

- If the employer company is eligible to obtain corporation tax relief under FA 2003, Sch 23 then these rules will not apply.

Chapter 37

Pay-as-you-earn and national insurance contributions

37.1 This chapter considers the changes to the pay-as-you-earn (PAYE) and national insurance contributions (NICs) rules that have been introduced through FA 2003. The chapter explains the extension to the definition of 'readily convertible assets' and the interaction with the Schedule 23 statutory corporation tax deduction. The chapter explains the payment and recovery rules for both PAYE and NICs, and refers to the mechanism for reporting and the special charge provisions for employment-related securities.

The Finance Act 2003 introduced new provisions on PAYE and NICs. In essence, the legislation seeks to redefine and simplify the rules relating to the collection of income tax under PAYE on 'employment-related securities'.

The general principle that the legislation seeks to apply is that PAYE should be applied on the amount on which income tax is most likely to be charged.

Extension of the definition of 'readily convertible assets'

37.2 First and foremost, it is important to understand the basic definition of readily convertible assets which is found is ITE PA 2003, s 702 as follows:

- shares and any other assets that are capable of being sold on a recognised investment exchange, covering the markets established by the London Stock Exchange including the AIM and Tradepoint;

- assets capable of being sold on the New York Stock Exchange;

- assets capable of being sold on a market that is specified in the PAYE Regulations;

- assets which are likely to create rights that enable an amount of money to be produced that is equal to or greater than the expense incurred in the provision of the assets;

- assets for which 'trading arrangements' exist; and

- assets for which 'trading arrangements' are likely to come into existence.

It is important to note that the definition of 'recognised investment exchange' is found in FS MA 2000, s 285 and does not correspond to a recognised stock exchange.

The extension of the definition of readily convertible assets lies in one key principle as follows:

- Although the shares may not be readily convertible assets under the section 702 definition they will nevertheless be treated as readily convertible assets except in circumstances where the employing company is entitled under FA 2003, Sch 23 to corporation tax relief as a consequence of the award of shares to employees.

- The application of this extension brings into PAYE and NICs many circumstances that would not otherwise have income tax accounted for through the PAYE system or be subject to NICs at all, including employee share awards in unquoted foreign parent companies for which the business is not eligible for UK corporation tax relief.

The application of these principles is expressed in summary form as follows:

Situation	Readily convertible assets under section 702	Corpora-tion tax relief under Sched-ule 23	Final status of the shares	Accountabil-ity of employee income tax and NICs (if payable)
1	Non-RCAs	CT relief	Remain non-RCAs	Account for income tax through self-ssessment (no NICs)
2	Non-RCAs	Non-CT relief	Deemed RCAs	Account for income tax through PAYE and NICs
3	RCAs	CT relief	RCAs anyway	Account for income tax through PAYE and NICs

4	RCAs	Non-CT relief	RCAs anyway	Account for income tax through PAYE and NICs

It is interesting to ask the question why the extended definition of readily convertible assets is linked to the Schedule 23 corporation tax relief. When the legislation was being developed the original intention was to classify all securities as readily convertible assets. However, on reflection it was decided that those persons whose securities were not classified as readily convertible securities should not be penalised. It was then determined that the appropriate way to achieve this result was to agree that where the corporation tax relief was available securities that were not currently classified as readily convertible assets should continue not to be classified as readily convertible assets. The view was taken that those persons whose current position should be protected are those persons whose securities through the award of shares or the exercise of options would give to the company the Schedule 23 corporation tax relief.

Payment and the recovery of PAYE tax and NICs on share acquisitions

Payment of PAYE tax

37.3 Where the shares acquired are classified as 'readily convertible assets' then under ITEPA 2003, s 696 the employee's employing company has the responsibility to account for income tax due under PAYE following the usual monthly PAYE accounting payment dates.

The payment should be reported through the tax year-end Inland Revenue Form P35 with the Inland Revenue Form P60 that is issued to the employee incorporating the amounts.

Payment of NICs

37.4 Where the shares are acquired as 'readily convertible assets' a liability arises for Class 1 NICs on the same amount as that on which PAYE is to be accounted for based on the following percentage calculations:

- for the employee, the primary NICs will be calculated at 1% provided the employee's earnings are in that band; and

- for the employing company, the secondary NICs will be calculated at 12.8%.

The NICs will be accountable to HMRC with the PAYE following the usual monthly PAYE accounting payment dates.

Recovery of PAYE tax

37.5 It may be that the tax is borne by the employer rather than the employee in which case the employer must recover the tax from the employee within 90 days after the shares have been provided, otherwise a further liability to income tax arises for the employee under ITEPA 2003, s 222.

The classification of the amount of income tax that is due to be accounted for under PAYE is treated as emoluments of the employee's employment. These emoluments are treated as earnings from the employment for the tax year in which falls the date on which the employer is treated as having provided the shares.

There is no reduction or elimination of the charge in circumstances where the employee makes good the tax after the 90-day time limit has expired.

Recovery of employee's NICs

37.6 There is now no limit on the amount that the employing company can recover each month and the period in which the employee's NICs may be recovered is extended into the following tax year.

The abolition of the limit and the time extension is purposely intended to enable the employing company to recover from the employees the additional 1% uncapped NICs that has been charged on the acquisition of the shares or the exercise of the option.

Reporting of the events to HRMC

37.7 With regard to reporting events to HMRC, in accordance with ITEPA 2003, ss 421J and 421K, the acquisition of the shares must be reported before 7 July in the tax year following the tax year in which the reportable event takes place. The mechanism for the reporting is the HMRC Form 42.

It is important to emphasize that the submission of the completed Form 42 is to report events and is not to be accompanied by payment that, as previously explained, is accountable under the PAYE system.

Special charges on employment-related securities

37.8 Under ITEPA 2003, s 698 PAYE applies where by reason of employment an individual receives an amount that counts as employment income through any one of the following:

- chargeable events in relation to theRSR;
- chargeable events in relation to theCSR;
- charge on acquisition where the MV of the securities is artificially enhanced;

- charge on the discharge of a notional loan where securities have been acquired for less than MV;

- charge in avoidance cases where securities have been acquired for less than MV; and

- chargeable post-acquisition benefit from securities.

Under ITEPA 2003, s 700 PAYE applies where by reason of employment an individual receives an amount that counts as employment income through the following acquisition of securities that relates to a securities option.

Relevant case law

Chilcott, Griffiths and Evolution Group Services Limited v Revenue & Customs Commissioners [2008] UKSPC SPC00727

37.9   This case is of interest in relation to ITEPA 2003, 222 although it arose in relation to the predecessor legislation, ICTA 1988, s 144A. The case illustrates the importance of procedures for recovering PAYE from employee share scheme participants.

The company decided not to apply PAYE when two directors exercised options to acquire shares. The company took the view that the options were not obtained by reason of employment so rather than operate PAYE the directors disclosed the exercises through the self-assessment procedure.

HMRC contended subsequently that the PAYE amount had not been made good to the company by the directors and claimed under ICTA 1988, s 144A that a liability had arisen. The directors' representatives sought to defend their position by presenting a range of arguments, notably that this provision only applied where the motive was tax avoidance and that it amounted to double taxation. In essence, the argument of the defence was that it could not have been the purpose of the section to impose a penalty if there was no evidence of avoidance or evasion of tax. The representation did not convince the Special Commissioner who dismissed the appeal.

Lessons from Chilcott

37.10   The case emphasizes the fact that companies must have procedures in place for the recovery of PAYE income tax that arises on the exercise of share options and that recovery must take place inside the statutory time period of 90 days. As a point of interest in this case, the Special Commissioner suggested that the section should be reviewed and that HMRC should consider the introduction of a graduated penalty linked to the lateness of the reimbursement.

Chapter 38

Corporation tax relief, including deferred tax credits

UK statutory corporation tax deduction

Introduction: the statutory provision

38.1 On 27th November 2002, the government announced the extension of the statutory corporation tax deduction for the cost of providing shares for employee share schemes. This extension became law through FA 2003, Sch 23 and applies to financial periods beginning on or after 1 January 2003.

Basis of the statutory corporation tax deduction

38.2 The basis of the corporation tax deduction is the value of the gain in the hands of the employee. Under the Schedule 23 rules, the gain has the potential to be considerably higher than the initial cost of the purchase of shares by, say, an employee share trust for the reason that the gain represents a market-generated gain.

Previously the cash contribution to the employee share trust provided the basis for the corporation tax deduction. It is anticipated that companies will continue to establish employee share trusts to hedge the purchase cost of the shares and to warehouse the shares until such time when the trust dispenses them to the employees in order to assist the company in meeting its obligations to the employees on, say, the exercise of options. However, the corporation tax deduction will no longer be dependent upon a contribution to an employee share trust or even the existence of an employee share trust. Indeed, it is available under Schedule 23 whether the employee share schemes are serviced through the issue of new shares or the purchase of existing shares from the market.

The rules relating to QUESTs were changed at the same time to remove duplication. Companies that operated QUESTs for savings-related share option schemes received a similar corporation tax deduction under the Schedule 23 rules.

Amount of the statutory corporation tax deduction

38.3 The corporation tax relief is available for the employee's employing company in an amount equal to the MV of the shares, or interest in shares, acquired by an employee by reason of his or her employment less any amount paid by the employee for the shares or the interest in shares provided the statutory conditions are met.

Claim for the corporation tax deduction

38.4 The corporation tax relief is claimed by way of a deduction in computing the profits of the business for the purposes of which the shares are awarded. The claim is made through the submission to HMRC, along with the corporation tax return, of the accounts for the period in which the award of shares was made.

The corporation tax deduction becomes a component of the company's D(1) profit or loss for the year and is treated like any other deductible amount that has contributed to producing profits assessable to corporation tax. The deduction can, therefore, be carried forward into future years.

Conditions for the statutory corporation tax deduction

38.5 The conditions that must be met for the relief to be given are as follows:

(*a*) *The business for the purposes of which the award of shares is made*

- The business, for the purposes of which the award of shares is made, must be carried on by the employing company and be within the charge to corporation tax with respect to the profits of the business.

- If the circumstances are that the award is made partly for the purposes of such a business and partly for the purposes of some other business then the relief is reduced 'to the extent as is just and reasonable'.

(*b*) *The type of shares acquired*

The shares acquired must be:

- ordinary shares;
- fully paid-up; and
- be non-redeemable.

Further, the shares must be:

- in a company that is not under the control of another company under ICTA 1988, s 840; or

- of a class listed on a recognised stock exchange; or

- in a company that is under the control of a company whose shares are listed on a recognised stock exchange.

(c) *Company whose shares are acquired*

The relief is given to a company when shares are awarded to a person by reason of his employment with that company.

The company whose shares are acquired must be:

- either: that company; or

- a company which when the award is made is a parent company of the employing company; or

- a company which when the award is made is the member of a consortium that owns the employing company or its parent company.

(d) *The income tax position of the employee*

The employee must be:

- charged to income tax in respect of the award of the shares; or

- would be charged to income tax were it not for the fact that statutory income tax relief is available through a tax-approved employee share scheme or EMI.

Requirement for deferred tax

38.6   The requirement for deferred tax arises from the time deferral.

The accounting expense arises in an earlier accounting period than the tax deduction arises in the corporation tax computation. This establishes the basis for *the temporary timing difference*.

The technical position is that the temporary timing difference arises from the differences between the carrying amount of the assets and liabilities in the balance sheet and the amount attributed to those same assets and liabilities for corporation tax purposes.

The accounting treatment that arises in relation to share-based payments is analogous to the position that arises in relation to research costs that is the example used to illustrate the principle in IAS 12. For research costs, the carrying amount is nil in the earlier accounting period but the amount is deductible in a future accounting period, generating a deductible temporary timing difference that results in *a deferred tax asset*.

Under IAS 12, the deferred tax asset is recognised for all deductible temporary timing differences to the extent that it is probable that the taxable profit will be available against which the deductible temporary timing difference can be used.

Measurement basis

38.7 The amount of the deferral arises from the measurement basis. The amount of the tax deduction might differ from the amount of the accounting expense. The measurement basis used for accounting purposes might be different from the measurement basis used for tax deduction purposes. In specific terms, the fair value of the option is used for accounting purposes whereas the intrinsic value is used for tax purposes.

Allocation method

38.8 Where the tax deduction received or expected to be received *is less than or equal* to the cumulative expense, the Standard states that the tax benefits received or expected to be received should be recognised as tax income and included in the profit or loss for the period.

Where the tax deduction received, or expected to be received, *is more than* the cumulative expense, the Standard states that the tax benefits received or expected to be received should be recognised directly in equity.

Example 38.1: Worked example

The worked example is based upon IAS 12, Example 5 that has been added as a consequential amendment subsequent to the release of FAS 20.

Consider the following circumstances:

Year	Accounting expense	Number of options at the year-end	Intrinsic value per option
1	188,000	50,000	5
2	185,000	45,000	8
3	190,000	40,000	13
4	0	40,000	17
5	0	40,000	20

The company recognises a deferred tax asset and deferred tax income in years 1 to 4 and current income in year 5. In years 4 and 5, some of the deferred and current tax income is recognised directly in equity for the reason that the estimated and actual tax deduction exceeds the cumulative remuneration expense.

Year 1

Deferred tax asset and deferred tax income = $(50,000 \times 5 \times 1/3 \times 0.40)$ = 33,333

Estimated future tax deduction = $(50,000 \times 5 \times 1/3)$ = <u>83,333</u>

Cumulative remuneration expense = 188,888

Estimated future tax deduction is less than the cumulative remuneration expense so the deferred tax income is all recognised in profit or loss.

Year 2

Deferred tax asset at the year-end = (45,000 × 8 × 2/3 × 0.40) = 96,000

Deferred tax asset at the year-start = 33,333

Deferred income for the year = 96,000 = –33,333 = 62,667

Estimated future tax deduction = (45,000 × 8 × 2/3) = 240,000

Cumulative remuneration expense = (188,000 + 185,000) = 373,000

Estimated future tax deduction is less than the cumulative remuneration expense so the deferred tax income is all recognised in profit or loss.

Year 3

Deferred tax asset at the year-end = (40,000 × 13 × 3/3 × 0.40) = 208,000

Deferred tax asset at the year-start = 96,000

Deferred income for the year = 208,000 – 96,000 = 112,000

Estimated future tax deduction = (40,000 × 13 × 3/3) = 520,000

Cumulative remuneration expense = (188,000 + 185,000 + 190,000) = 563,000

Estimated future tax deduction is less than the cumulative remuneration expense so the deferred tax income is all recognised in profit or loss.

Year 4

Deferred tax asset at the year-end = (40,000 × 17 × 0.40) = 272,000

Deferred tax asset at the year-start = 208,000

Deferred income for the year = 272,000 – 208,000 = 64,000

Estimated future tax deduction = (40,000 × 17) = 680,000

Cumulative remuneration expense = (188,000 + 185,000 + 190,000) = 563,000

Excess tax deduction = 680,000 – 563,000 = 117,000

Excess recognised directly to equity = (117,000 × 0.40) = 46,800

Recognised in profit and loss = 64,000 – 46,800 = 17,200

Year 5

Deferred tax expense

= Reversal of deferred tax asset = 272,000

Amount recognised directly in equity

= Reversal of cumulative deferred tax income recognised directly in equity = 46,800

Amount recognised in profit and loss = 272,000 – 46,800 = 225,200

Current tax income based on intrinsic value of options at exercise date = (40,000 × 20 × 0.40) = <u>320,000</u>

Amount recognised in profit and loss = (563,000 × 0.40) = <u>225,200</u>

Amount recognised directly in equity = 320,000 − 225,200 = <u>94,800</u>

Summary

Year	Accounting expense	Current tax expense (income)	Deferred tax expense (income)	Total tax expense (income)	Equity	Deferred tax asset
		Income statement			Balance sheet	
1	188,000	0	(33,333)	(33,333)	0	33,333
2	185,000	0	(62,667)	(62,667)	0	96,000
3	190,000	0	(112,000)	(112,000)	0	208,000
4	0	0	(17,200)	(17,200)	(46,800)	272,000
5	0	(225,200)	225,200	0	46,800	0
					(94,800)	
Totals	563,000	(225,200)	0	(225,200)	(94,800)	0

Chapter 39

Capital gains tax and stamp duty implications for employee share schemes

Introduction

39.1 This chapter explains the main aspects of CGT legislation that need to be considered for employee share scheme purposes.

Prior to FA 2000, through which the SIP and EMI came on to the statute book, the tax-approved and government-sponsored employee share scheme legislation did not bestow CGT reliefs on the employee participants. The reliefs were limited to income tax reliefs for the employees and corporation tax relief for the employers. While SIP continues to operate its relief from CGT, EMI that embodied its own form of taper relief accumulating from the date of grant, lost that relief with effect from 5 April 2008.

Nevertheless, it has always been possible to combine CGT advantages derived from TCGA 1992 with the operation of the schemes at the point where the shares are sold or transferred. It is the non-share scheme specific TCGA 1992 reliefs that represent the main focus of this chapter.

Taper relief

39.2 With effect from 5 April 2008, taper relief was abolished in favour of the new flat rate capital gains rate of 18%. However, given that the demise of taper relief is comparatively recent, it is important to continue an awareness of its benefits, as calculations involving taper relief, continue to be live with HMRC.

The basic principle that supports the operation of taper relief is that the percentage of the capital gain that is subject to CGT is reduced with the passage of time.

It is important to establish whether the assets for which the capital gain is expected to arise are 'business assets' or 'non-business assets' for the reason that the rates allowed for business assets are more favourable than the rates allowed for non-business assets.

The position that was established through FA 2000 and continued to be operative from 6 April 2000 to 5 April 2008 was as follows:

- The entitlement to taper relief on the disposal of the shares by an individual shareholder was available at business asset rates for any period following the purchase of the shares throughout which the company was a 'qualifying company' in relation to the individual shareholder.

- The company was a 'qualifying company' in relation to the individual shareholder and the shares were classified as 'business assets' provided the following conditions are met:

  — the company must be a trading company or a holding company of a trading group of companies; and one of the following conditions prevails:

    – either: the company is an unquoted company; or

    – the individual shareholder is an employee, full-time or part-time, of the company or an officer of the company or of a company having a 'relevant connection' to the company; or

    – the individual holds at least 5% of the voting rights of the company.

- A 'relevant connection' between companies applied where companies are members of the same group of companies or are associated companies where the businesses can reasonably be taken to be a single composite undertaking.

- An unquoted company was a company whose shares are not listed on a recognised stock exchange and is not a 51% subsidiary of a company that is listed on a recognised stock exchange. Companies whose shares are quoted on the AIM were classified for these purposes as unquoted companies.

The scope of business assets taper relief that applied to shareholdings can be summarised as follows:

- All shareholdings, including all employee shareholdings, in unquoted trading companies or holding companies of trading companies.

- All shareholdings that are held by employees (or officers) in quoted trading companies.

- All shareholdings above 5% that are held by outside investors in quoted trading companies.

Finance Act 2001 extended the scope of business assets taper relief, with effect from 6 April 2000 (not 2001), to include the following:

- All shareholdings that are held by employees (or officers) in non-trading companies or holding companies of non-trading companies provided the individual does not have a material interest in the company or the controlling company.

- A 'material interest' consists of more than 10% of the shares of any class *or* 10% of the voting rights of the company *or* 10% of the rights to profits available on a distribution or 10% of the rights to assets on a winding-up.

At the time taper relief was abolished, the taper relief rates for disposals of 'business assets' was as follows:

Whole calendar years of ownership	Capital gain relieved %	Capital gain taxed %	Effective rate of tax for higher rate taxpayer %	Effective rate of tax for basic rate taxpayer %
1	50	50	20	11
2	75	25	10	5.5

It is very important to emphasise that taper relief applied only to reduce CGT liabilities. It did not in any circumstances reduce any income liability that may arise at the date of exercise of the option or at the date of transfer of the shares.

The application of taper relief to employee share schemes depended upon the *date* when the shares are purchased, or deemed to have been purchased, for the specific purposes of taper relief that is as follows:

- the exercise of the option for:
    — tax-approved discretionary share option scheme;
    — tax-approved all-employee savings-related share option scheme; and
    — tax-unapproved discretionary share option scheme.
- the transfer of the shares from the trust for:
    — tax-unapproved long-term incentive plan.
- The ceasing to be subject to the scheme, usually the transfer from the trust for:
    — tax-approved all-employee SIP.
- The grant of the option for:
    — government-sponsored EMI.

Share identification rules

39.3 In examining the share identification rules it is necessary to distinguish between the position before FA 2008 ('the pre-2008 rules') and the position after FA 2008 ('the post-2008 rules'). By definition, the post-2008 rules now apply. However, there are certain circumstances in which it is necessary to have recourse to the pre-2008 rules.

Post-2008 rules

39.4 The simplification of the CGT regime through FA 2008 made it possible to simply the share identification rules. The regime changes were sweeping and included the withdrawal of taper relief, the withdrawal of indexation allowance and the abolition of the 'kink test' for assets held at 31 March 1982. For the share identification rules, it has, therefore, been possible to introduce a simplification by extending pooling to all shares, regardless of when they were acquired. This means on a practical basis that there is no longer any need to keep records of separate shareholdings acquired at different times. A straightforward pro rata basis will apply in apportioning pool cost to disposals.

The key principle for the post-2008 position is that all shares of the same class in the same company are now pooled together as a single pool with their cost averaged to form a new 'sSection 104 holding' and treated as forming a single asset from 6 April 2008. The section reference is taken from TCGA 1992, s 104. For shares held at 31 March 1982, the acquisition cost of those shares is rebased to their market value at 31 March 1982.

The application of this principle is that disposals are to be matched with acquisitions in the following order:

* shares purchased on the same day as the disposal;

* shares purchased within 30 days following the disposal on the so-called FIFO basis, ie 'first-in, first-out'; and

* shares held in the so-called 'section 104 holding'.

Within the midst of the significant simplification, there is a complication that needs to be identified and fully explained with regard to the composition of the 'section 104 holding'. Suppose that an individual bought and sold shares in the same company before the 2008 rules came into effect and as a consequence of those transactions still owns on 6 April 2008 some of the shares purchased before 6 April 2008. In these circumstances, the individual has to apply the pre-2008 rules to determine which shares he is deemed to own at 6 April 2008. This brings the explanation full circle to a need to fully understand the pre-2008 rules.

Pre-2008 rules

39.5 The pre-2008 share identification rules need to be understood in the context of the 1998 amendments that were made to accommodate the introduction of taper relief:

* the key rule to follow for disposals after April 1998 is the last-in, first out (LIFO) basis.

- the exceptions to the application of LIFO are:

  — where the date of disposal is the same day as the date of purchase; and

  — where shares are purchased within 30 days after the disposal.

- The pooling arrangement was abolished for shares purchased after 5 April 1998. The pooling arrangement is the system that treats shares; of the same class in the same company and held in the same capacity; as a single asset.

- Shares purchased through employee share scheme arrangements follow the normal share identification rules although shares held by trustees should not be pooled for the reason that they are held subject to restrictions in a different capacity.

Under the pre-2008 share identification rules, the order for identifying the shares for disposal purposes within the CGT computation is as follows:

- shares purchased on the same day as the disposal;

- shares purchased within 30 days following the disposal on the so-called LIFO basis;

- shares purchased preceding the disposal but after 5 April 1998 on a LIFO basis;

- shares held in the so-called 'section 104 holding' which is the pool of shares purchased after 5 April 1982 and before 6 April 1998 which is then treated as a single asset; and

- shares held in the so-called '1982 holding' which is the pool of shares held at 5 April 1982.

Same-day share purchases

39.6 The position on same-day share purchases is as follows:

- The rule that requires shares of the same class purchased on the same day by a person acting in the same capacity to be treated as the purchase in a single transaction can create a problem where the resultant base cost is the average cost of all the shares so purchased.

- The problem arises where the base cost of some shares is a higher base cost than the base cost of other shares purchased on the same day. The shares purchased through the exercise of a tax-unapproved discretionary share option will have a higher base cost than the shares purchased through the exercise of a tax-approved discretionary share option, a tax-approved savings-related share option or the government-sponsored EMI. The higher base cost for the shares purchased through the exercise of the tax-unapproved discretionary share option will be the MV of the shares at the date of exercise for the reason that income tax has arisen on the option gain triggered by the exercise.

- The election introduced by FA 2002 and now enshrined in TCGA 1992, s 105A resolves this difficulty by allowing the shares that are purchased under the tax-approved schemes or EMI to be treated as sold *after* the shares purchased under the tax-approved discretionary share option scheme. The legislation applies to shares purchased on the same day on or after 6 April 2002.

- The effect of this election is that the shares purchased under the tax-approved discretionary share option scheme are treated as purchased in a single transaction and the remainder are treated as purchased under a separate single transaction.

- The notice of the election must be made to HMRC on or before the first anniversary of 31 January following the end of the tax year in which the individual makes a disposal of any of these same-day purchased shares.

General exemption limit

39.7   It is often the case that the employee can protect the capital gain through the CGT general exemption limit which for the tax year to 5 April 2010 is £10,100.

Share disposal date

39.8   It is important to recognise that the capital gain is triggered by the sale of the shares. A key planning point is, therefore, to stagger the sales of the shares in order to benefit from the individual CGT general exemption limit in more than one tax year.

Husband and wife transfers

39.9   The key points to be aware of are as follows:

- Once the employee has purchased the shares, the employee may choose to transfer some of the shares to his or her spouse in order to make use of the other spouse's individual general exemption limit on the sale of the shares.

- Assuming that no consideration passes in the transfer between spouses, transfers between husband and wife are not subject to either CGT or stamp duty.

- For taper relief purposes, the transferee inherits the date on which the transferor purchased the shares and the original cost at which the transferor purchased the shares.

Entrepreneurs' relief

39.10   This new relief, entrepreneurs relief, is explicitly a CGT relief. It applies to disposals made on or after 6 April 2008 and has the effect of reducing the rate of CGT from 18% to 10% on the first £1 million of gains (TCGA 1992, s 169N(2)). Similar to the old retirement relief that was phased out with the introduction of taper relief, it operates under TCGA 1992, s 169N(3) as a lifetime allowance. An individual is able to make many claims for the relief but not more than £1 million total which is the lifetime total.

Important point

It is important to emphasize that this relief will be available where the relevant conditions are met for a period of one year ending with the disposal although there is no requirement that the employment is full-time.

The relief applies to the net aggregate gains arising in the disposal of any of the following:

- the whole, or part, of a trading business that is carried on by the individual, either alone or in partnership.

- Assets used in a business that has ceased.

- Shares in a trading company, or holding company of a trading group, provided that the individual owns at least 5% of the voting rights in the company and is an officer or employee of the company.

- Assets used in a partnership or by a company but owned by an individual if the assets disposed of are associated with a disposal of shares or an interest in partnership assets. The individual must make the disposal as part of the withdrawal of the individual from participation in the partnership or the company.

- Certain disposals by trustees of business assets and company shares where a qualifying beneficiary has a qualifying interest in the business/shares.

For employee share scheme purposes, therefore, it is the third item in the list that needs closer examination as follows:

- Under TCGA 1992, s 169S(3) the shares must be in a 'personal company' which means that the employee must have at least 5% of the ordinary share capital and 5% of the voting rights.

- Under TCGA 1992, s 169I(6) the company must be a trading company or the holding company of a trading company and the shareholder must be either an employee or an officer of a company within the group.

The introduction of entrepreneurs relief comes with transitional rules as follows:

- Some individuals may have made a gain prior to 6 April 2008 and have deferred the gain until after 5 April 2008. The relief may be available when the gain becomes chargeable if the sale of shares in a trading company or the sale of an unincorporated business would have met the conditions for the relief if the sale had taken place after 5 April 2008.

- The deferred gains eligible for relief are where:

  — shares in a trading company were disposed of in exchange for loan notes in another company which are qualifying corporate bonds (QCBs).

  — The gains made on shares in a trading company or on the disposal if an unincorporated business were reinvested in enterprise investment scheme (EIS) shares or venture capital trust (VCT) shares.

- If an individual had shares in a trading company which were disposed of in exchange for loan notes in another company which are not QCBs there may be entrepreneurs' relief on the disposal of the loan notes after 5 April 2008. In these circumstances, the loan notes would have to be issued by a trading company in which the individual owns at least 5% of the voting rights in that company and the individual is an employee or officer of that company.

Stamp duty

39.11 Finance Act 2008 contained a provision that established that stamp duty is not payable and certification is not necessary where shares are transferred by way of gift.

The general position is that stamp duty is charged at 0.5% of the amount of the consideration, calculated as 50 pence for every £100 of consideration or part of £100 of the consideration. If the consideration is less than £1,000, an ad valorem duty is payable provided the certification on the reverse of the stock transfer form has been ticked.

Chapter 40

Development of the tax legislation

Introduction

40.1   This chapter is an introduction to the concept of how HMRC will apply punitive income tax charges to employee share schemes unless the scheme is protected by one of the reliefs, either through the tax-approved and government-sponsored schemes or, alternatively, through the general tax legislation. It is, indeed, sometimes the case that a tax-efficient employee share scheme can be constructed from the general tax legislation. However, it is preferable, if at all possible, to structure the scheme using one of the tax-approved schemes or, alternatively enterprise management incentives (EMI) that, even though it does not require tax-approval, is a highly tax-efficient scheme.

Absolute basics of an employee share scheme

40.2   When designing or reviewing a scheme arrangement, it is often helpful to the analysis to appreciate that an employee share scheme will, in broad terms, always fall into one of three categories as follows:

- share gifting scheme;

- share purchase scheme; and

- share option scheme.

Before introducing the plethora of tax reliefs that are available under the tax-approved and government-sponsored legislation, and, indeed, the general legislation, it is important to understand the implications of the UK tax legislation in the event that the scheme is introduced without tax reliefs.

The following examples illustrate the effect for the basic share-gifting scheme, the basic share purchase scheme and the basic share option scheme. There are two examples for the basic share option scheme as follows:

- One for market value (MV) options where the option price is set at the MV of shares at the date of grant of the option.

- One for discounted non-MV where the option price is set at a discount to the MV of shares at the date of grant of the option.

Without any protection from the tax charging provisions, the benefit is subject to an income tax charge in relation to the tax year in which it is received and realized. In the examples, for the share gifting scheme and the share purchase scheme, this is Year 0. For the share option schemes, in the examples, it is Year 3.

Share gifting scheme (without tax reliefs)

40.3

Example 40.1

Suppose that the shares are gifted to an employee from an existing pool of shares when the market value is £10 per share (see Diagram 1).

Diagram 1

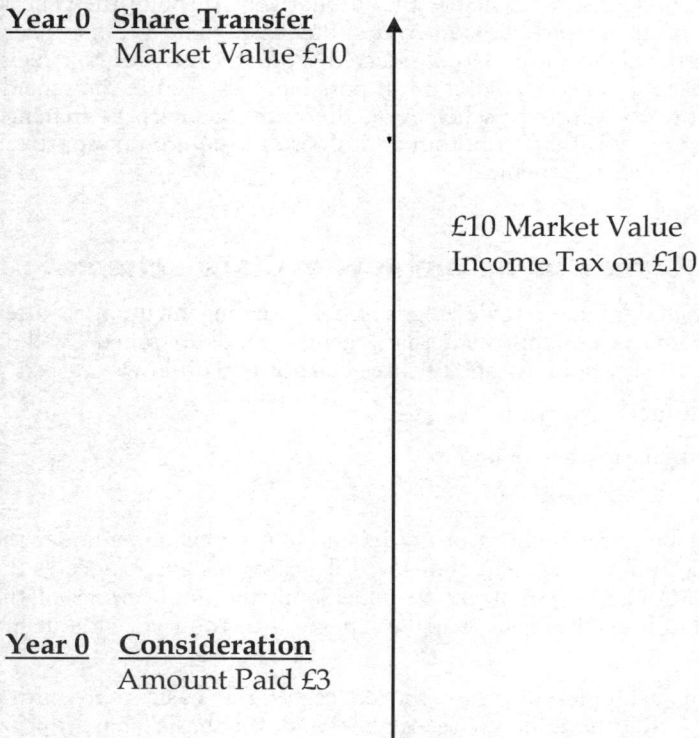

Year 0 Share Transfer
Market Value £10

£10 Market Value
Income Tax on £10

Year 0 Consideration
Amount Paid £3

Share purchase scheme (without tax reliefs)

40.4

Example 40.2

Suppose that the shares are purchased by an employee for £3 per share when the MV is £10 per share (see Diagram 2).

Diagram 2

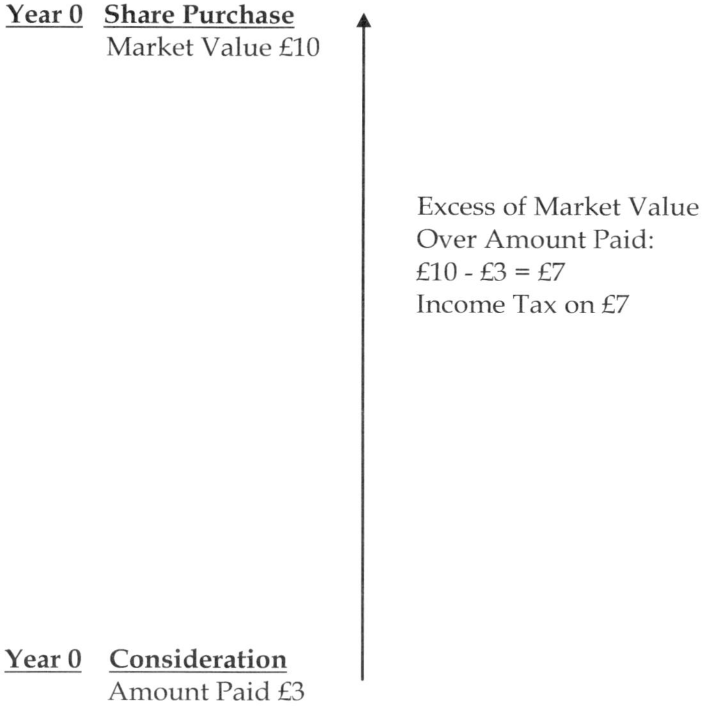

<u>Year 0</u> <u>Share Purchase</u>
Market Value £10

Excess of Market Value
Over Amount Paid:
£10 - £3 = £7
Income Tax on £7

<u>Year 0</u> <u>Consideration</u>
Amount Paid £3

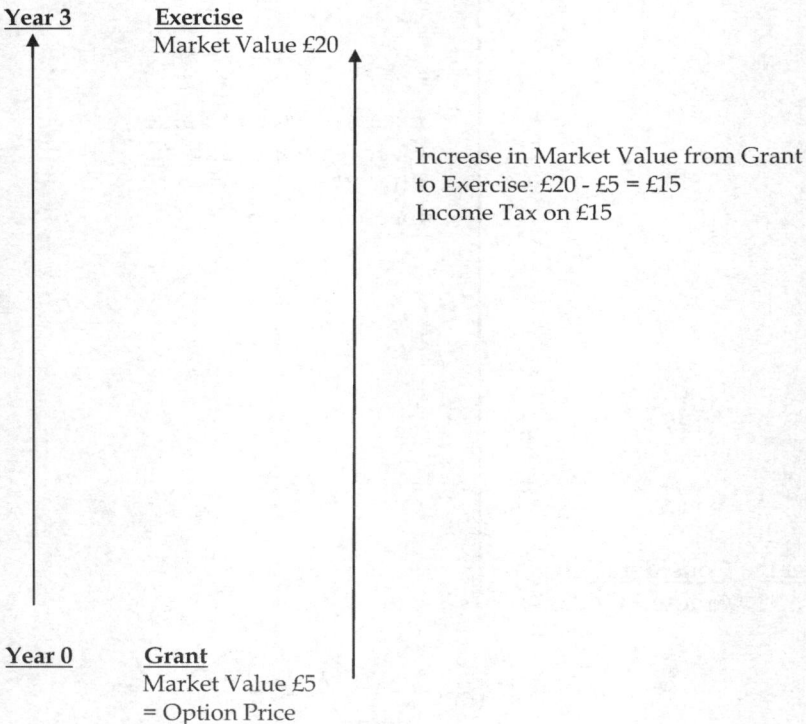

Share option scheme (without tax reliefs)

For market value options

40.5

Example 40.3

Suppose that the option is granted to an employee at an option price of £5 when the MV is £5 and exercised three years later when the market value is £20 (see Diagram 3).

Diagram 3

<u>Year 3</u>   **Exercise**
                Market Value £20

Increase in Market Value from Grant
to Exercise: £20 - £5 = £15
Income Tax on £15

<u>Year 0</u>   **Grant**
                Market Value £5
                = Option Price

Share option scheme (without tax reliefs)

For discounted non-market value options

40.6

Example 40.4

Suppose that the option is granted to an employee at an option price of £1 when the MV is £5 and exercised three years later when the MV is £20 (see Diagram 4).

Diagram 4

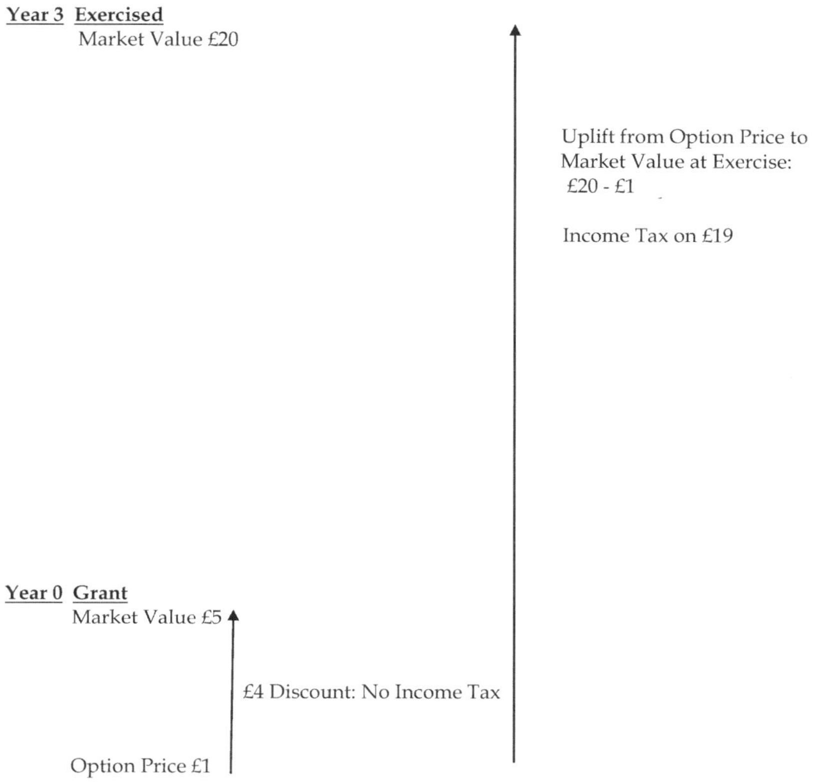

<u>Year 3</u> <u>Exercised</u>
　　　　Market Value £20

Uplift from Option Price to
Market Value at Exercise:
£20 - £1

Income Tax on £19

<u>Year 0</u> <u>Grant</u>
　　　　Market Value £5

£4 Discount: No Income Tax

Option Price £1

Main charging provisions

40.7 Any proposed employee share scheme arrangement should be reviewed to ensure that it does not fall within the charging provisions of ITEPA 2003. The main charging provisions are as follows:

ITEPA 2003, sections 10 and 62: chargeable emoluments (formerlyICTA 1988, section 131)

40.8 A charge to income tax arises in circumstances where an employee or officer of the company receives shares either by issue or transfer at less than the MV of the shares at the date of issue or transfer and the shares are received by virtue of the employment. The charge arises in respect of *any office or employment* for individuals whose emoluments are covered by the cases of Schedule E.

The difference between MV at date of issue or transfer and any consideration paid by the employee is classified as emoluments. The principle that is enshrined in statute is known as 'the rule in *Weight v Salmon*' [1935] All ER 904, a House of Lords case dating back to 1935.

Weight v Salmon

40.9 The facts of this case were that directors of a company were given the privilege of taking unissued shares in the company at par. This was an annual arrangement.

HMRC determined that for the managing director the excess of the MV of the shares over the price that he or she paid for them should be subject to income tax and an assessment was issued accordingly.

The House of Lords heard an appeal but reinforced the view taken by HMRC. The House of Lords determined that the benefit to the managing director of the company was money's worth and was justifiably categorised as emoluments under the part of the definition that covers 'profits whatsoever'. The House of Lords upheld the assessments that had been issued by HMRC.

A case that illustrates the exception to the main rule established in *Weight v Salmon* is the case of *Bridges v Bearsley* a Court of Appeal case that was heard in 1957.

Bridges v Bearsley

40.10 The facts of *Bridges v Bearsley* CA [1957] 2 All ER 281 case were that shares had been transferred to the directors of a company.

The Special Commissioners determined that the shares represented gifts or testimonials. As such, any value attributed to the shares for which payment was not received by the directors, did not constitute remuneration and should not, therefore, be brought into emoluments. The Court of Appeal upheld the decision of the Special Commissioners.

This case showed that in exceptional circumstances an employee could receive a gift not by reason of their employment but by reason of the personal relationship that exists between the transferor of the shares and the transferee. If this is the case then the shares will not represent emoluments arising from the employment.

ITEPA 2003, sections 471–487: gains by directors and employees from share options (formerly ICTA 1988, section 135)

40.11 A charge to income tax arises where an employee realises a gain by the exercise or by the assignment or release of a right to purchase shares and the gain accrues to the employee by virtue of the employment.

The charge arises in respect of a person who is a director or an employee and the gain is brought into charge under Schedule E.

It is the actual gain that provides the basis for the income tax liability.

Sections 192–200: employee shareholdings (formerly ICTA 1988, section 162)

40.12 A charge to income tax arises where an employee purchases shares for less than their current MV at the date of purchase and the benefit from so doing is not otherwise chargeable to income tax.

The charge arises in respect of a person who is employed or about to be employed or a person connected with such a person.

The amount of the undervalue is treated as an interest-free loan on the basis that all or part of the loan has been written-off or waived generating a charge to income tax on the amount of the write-off or the amount of the waiver.

Pre-ITEPA reliefs from the main charging provisions

40.12.1 The reliefs from the charging provisions were found pre-ITEPA 2003 as follows:

Tax-approved legislation, ICTA 1988

40.13 The legislation includes:

- ICTA 1988, s 185: approved share option schemes;
- ICTA 1988, s 186: approved profit-sharing schemes;
- ICTA 1988, s 187: interpretation of sections 185–186 and Schedules 9 and 10;
- ICTA 1988, Sch 9: approved share option schemes and profit-sharing schemes; and
- ICTA 1988, Sch 10: further provisions relating to profit-sharing schemes.

Qualifying employee share trust ('QUEST') legislation, Finance Act 1989

40.14 The following schedules and sections are of relevance:

- Finance Act 1989, s 67: the statutory right to corporation tax relief.
- Finance Act 1989, ss 67–74: the operation of the QUEST arrangement.

Finance Act 2000

40.14.1 The following schedules and sections are of relevance:

- Finance Act 2000, Sch 8: SIPs.
- Finance Act 2000, Sch 14: EMIs.

- Finance Act 2000, s 49: phasing-out provisions for approved profit-sharing schemes where the last date for approval is 5 April 2001 and the last date for appropriations is 31 December 2002.

- Finance Act 2000, s 54: for QUESTs, no rollover relief will be available for disposals made to employee share ownership trusts for disposals made after 5 April 2001.

- Sections 66–67: taper relief for employee shareholdings at business asset rates for holding periods after 5 April 1998 for disposals on or after 6 April 2000 (up to 5 April 2008).

ITEPA reliefs from the main charging provisions

40.15 The reliefs from the charging provisions are now found in ITEPA 2003, Pt 7:

- Chapter 6 and Schedule 2: approved share incentive schemes.
- Chapter 7 and Schedule 3: approved SAYE option schemes.
- Chapter 8 and Schedule 4: approved CSOP schemes.
- Chapter 9 and Schedule 5: EMIs.

Chapter 41

Employment-related securities – Finance Act 2003

Introduction

41.1 This chapter describes the origins of the employment-related securities legislation that is contained within FA 2003 and explains the reason for this key government initiative within the tax rewrite project. The chapter identifies the principles that underpin the legislation and provides an explanation of the concepts that support these principles so that the reader is equipped to apply the principles and concepts to an understanding of the matters that are addressed in subsequent chapters.

Arrival of Finance Act 2003, Schedule 22

41.2 Schedule 22 arrived on the statute book as a set of provisions within FA 2003 as a complete and total rewrite and extension of the income tax and NICs provisions relating to shares held by employees. Schedule 22 of FA 2003 was subsequently consolidated into ITEPA 2003 as Part 7 of that Act.

The original title of FA 2003, Sch 22 is Employee Securities and Options whereas in Part 7 of ITEPA 2003 the same statutory material is titled 'Employment Income: Income and Exemptions Relating to Securities'. The full content of Part 7 covers the tax-approved schemes and EMIs as well as the range of general and unapproved arrangements relating to shares held by employees. The chapters of Part 7 are as follows:

Chapter 1 General

Chapter 2 Restricted Securities

Chapter 3 Convertible Securities

Chapter 3A Securities with Artificially Depressed Market Value

Chapter 3B Securities with Artificially Enhanced Market Value

Chapter 3C Securities Acquired for Less Than Market Value

Chapter 3D Securities Disposed of for More Than Market Value

Chapter 4 Post-Acquisition Benefits from Securities

Chapter 4A Shares in Research Institution Spin-Out Companies

Chapter 5 Securities Options

Chapter 6 Approved Share Incentive Plans

Chapter 7 Approved SAYE Option Schemes

Chapter 8 Approved CSOP Schemes

Chapter 9 Enterprise Management Incentives

Chapter 10 Priority Share Allocations

Chapter 11 Supplementary provisions about Employee Benefit Trusts

The supporting schedules within ITEPA 2003 for Part 7 are as follows:

Schedule 2 Approved Share Incentive Plans

Schedule 3 Approved SAYE Option Schemes

Schedule 4 Approved CSOP Schemes

Schedule 5 Enterprise Management Incentives

Reason for Finance Act 2003, Schedule 22

41.3   The reason why the British Government considers that this legislation is required and for that matter the reason why its predecessor legislation was required is as follows:

> The legislation, through Part 7, seeks to ensure that remuneration in the form of employment-related securities is made subject to income tax with PAYE and NI Cs applied as appropriate. However, it is important to recognise that in the context of opportunities that the legislation offers to the employee and to the employing company, tax planning is still available, albeit within boundaries that are defined and limited by Part 7.

Summary position

Employment-related securities are securities acquired by a person where those securities are made available by reason of the employment of that person or the employment of another person where:

1.   employment includes company directorships including non-executive directorships and includes prospective and future employment; and

2.   securities do not have to be received by the employee for the legislation to apply in that they could be received by a family member or a trust.

Please note the provisions do *not normally* apply where:

> (a) all of the shares of the same class are identically affected by the same event or circumstances;
>
> (b) it is considered that there no tax avoidance; and
>
> (c) for *certain chapters only*, either the company is employee-controlled by that class of shares or the majority of shares are not employment-related securities.

Interaction between Schedule 22 and other taxes legislation

41.4 The interaction with other taxes legislation must be considered as follows:

Income tax

41.5 Notwithstanding the conclusions of Schedule 22, income tax can be imposed through the application of ICTA 1988, s 703, quite independently of the employment-related securities legislation.

National insurance contributions (NICs)

41.6 The legislation has been amended so that in most cases an NIC charge arises where there is a charge to income tax under the employment-related securities legislation.

Capital gains

41.7 The base cost includes the amounts subject to income tax as well as the acquisition cost of the shares. The gain, therefore, that is subject to CGT on a sale of the shares under T CGA 1992, ss 119A and 120, is reduced accordingly. Double taxation is, therefore, normally avoided for gains that are caught by Part 7. However, amounts subject to income tax as a consequence of an artificial increase or reduction in market value cannot benefit from this relief.

Corporation tax

41.8 Finance Act 2003, Sch 23 gives companies automatic corporation tax relief for certain gains on shares made by their employees. These gains include share option gains, gains on restricted and convertible securities, and share gains taxed as income under general principles. Gains arising under ratchet schemes are not deductible. The relief does not extend beyond shares to other types of security.

Key legislative concepts and definitions

41.9 The key concepts and definitions of the employment-related securities legislation that are located in Chapter 1 of Part 7 are as follows.

Definition of securities: section 420

41.10 The term *securities* for purposes of Chapters 1–5 has a much wider meaning that the meaning generally attributed to shares and includes the following:

- stocks and shares in companies;

- debentures, debenture stock, loan stock, bonds, certificates of deposit and instruments that create or acknowledge a debt;

- warrants and instruments that give entitlement for subscription for securities;

- certificates and other instruments that confer rights in respect of securities held by persons other than the persons on whom the rights are conferred and which are transferable without the consent of those persons; typically, ADRs and other forms of certificate of deposit would fall in to this category;

- units in a collective investment scheme;

- options (through FA 2006) and futures (excluding securities options);

- rights under contracts for difference or contracts similar to contracts for differences;

- rights under certain contracts of insurance; and

- alternative finance investment bonds.

Under Section 420(5) the following are not securities for purposes of Chapters 2–5:

- cheques and other bills of exchange, bankers' drafts and letters of credit (other than bills of exchange accepted by a banker);

- money and statements showing balances on a current, deposit or savings account;

- leases and other dispositions of property and heritable securities; and

- rights under a contract of insurance.

Securities options that are dealt with under Chapter 5 'Securities Options'.

The position on securities options requires further amplification as follows:

The securities options that are dealt with in Chapter 5 represent the classic tax-unapproved share option scheme and are defined in section 471(3) as a right or opportunity to acquire a securities option made available:

— either: by a person's employer; or

— by a person connected with a person's employer; and

> — therefore, made available by reason of an employment of that person;
>
>   unless the right or the opportunity is made available to an individual in the normal course of the domestic, family or personal relationships of that person in which case they will not be treated as employment-related securities.

- Where the options do not fall within the Chapter 5 definition, they are subject to income tax at the date of grant on the basis that they represent earnings within ITEPA 2003, s 62. The position that is taken by HMRC is that options that do not fall within the Chapter 5 definition are taxable as convertible securities under ITEPA 2003, Pt 7, Chap 3. In circumstances where there is any element of tax avoidance, the charge to income tax at the date of grant (which will be taken to be the date of acquisition) will be determined by reference to the MV of the securities which could be acquired if the option was exercised immediately. When calculating the tax liability, no credit is given for the amount of any option price that is payable upon the conversion.

- Put options which give a right to sell shares are treated as securities and, therefore, if granted by reason of employment or deemed to be so are treated as convertible securities subject to income tax calculated by reference to the date of grant. Warrants which are normally issued as transferable options to subscribe for shares are similarly treated as convertible securities taxable at the date of grant. An interest in a trading or professional partnership will not be an employment-related security unless the partnership can be demonstrated to be a collective investment scheme.

Meaning of market value: section 421

41.11   The meaning of market value for purposes of Chapters 1–5 has the same meaning as under TCGA 1992, Pt VIII.

Under T CGA 1992, s 272 the determination of MV in relation to any assets means the price which those assets might reasonably be expected to fetch on a sale in the open market. In the MV estimate, no reduction should be made on the assumption that the whole of the assets is placed on the market at one and the same time.

Meaning of consideration: section 421A

41.12   The meaning of *consideration* for purposes of Chapters 1–5 is by reference to the MV of the asset.

If consideration is given for more than one thing then the split between the different elements should be determined on the basis of a just and reasonable apportionment. The consideration does not include the performance of duties in connection with an employment.

Meaning of employment-related securities: section 421B(1) and 421B(3)

41.13 The meaning of employment-related securities applies to Chapters 2–4A and has two definitions under section 421B as follows:

The first definition which is known as the *factual test* is found in section 421B(1) and establishes the position that employment-related securities are securities or an interest in securities that are acquired by a person where the beneficial right or the opportunity to acquire is available:

- either: by reason of his or her employment; or

- by reason of the employment of any other person; and

  under section 421B(2), any reference to employment includes any former and prospective employments.

The second definition which is known as the *deeming provision* is found in section 421B(3) and establishes the position that where a right or an opportunity to acquire securities or an interest in securities is made available:

- either: by a person's employer; or

- by a person connected with a person's employer;

  then the right or the opportunity is to be regarded (deemed) as being made available by reason of the employment of that person, unless; the right or the opportunity is made available to an individual in the normal course of the domestic, family or personal relationships of that person in which case they will not be treated as employment-related securities.

Once the securities or an interest in securities complies with either the factual test or the deeming provision those securities or that interest in securities are employment-related securities for purposes of Chapters 2–4A. For purposes of applying either the factual test or, indeed, the deeming provision, it is very important to be absolutely clear that any reference to employment includes former and prospective employments.

Deeming provision

41.14 The deeming provision establishes the principle that there does not have to be a causal link between the employment and the acquisition of the shares if the individual is a director or an employee of the company that has made the right or the opportunity available. This decoupling of the employment from the acquisition of the shares widens significantly the scope of the charging provisions for employment-related securities. The word 'deeming' emanates from the use of the words in section 421B(3) 'is to be regarded for purposes of subsection (1)'. The effect of the deeming provision is to insert into section 421B(1), therefore, a wider application for purposes of establishing a charge to income tax.

Example 41.1: The grant of the option to a private trust

Suppose that the option is granted by the company to a private trust with independent trustees. However, the option would not have been granted to the private trust were it not for the reason of the individual's employment by the company that has granted the option. In these circumstances, the individual could be subject to income tax under the deeming provision while at the same time, given the independence of the trustees, there is potential for the employee not to receive the actual benefit from the trust.

The same principle applies if the company that has made the right or the opportunity available is connected to the company of which the individual is a director or an employee. The principle does not apply, though, to circumstances where the shares are made available by an unconnected third party.

Example 41.2: The grant of the option by an unconnected third party

Suppose that the option is granted to the employee by a shareholder who neither on his of her own account nor in association with other shareholders controls the company. In these circumstances, the shares are made available by a third party who is not connected with the company and the deeming provision does not apply.

If, of course, the shares are not available by reason of the employment at all then neither the factual test nor the deeming provision apply. The application of this principle requires particular exploration in the case of the founder shareholder who is not an employee or an office-holder at the date of the initial subscription.

Example 41.3: The shares from the founder shareholder

Suppose that the individual is the founder and the controlling shareholder of the company. Furthermore the individual is at the time of the acquisition of the shares neither a director nor an employee of the company. In these circumstances, the shares are made available by the individual himself as the founder shareholder and not by the individual's employer and the deeming provision does not apply. Further support for the position derives from section 421B(8) that states that the term 'employer' must be construed in accordance with the definition of 'employment' in that subsection.

It can be seen that the elasticity of the deeming provision provides the basis for a high capture potential for a charge to income tax. However, HMRC's ESSU does recognise that the application of its logic can in certain circumstances lead to an anomalous result that is not sustainable on the basis of consistency and common sense. It is difficult to provide examples of what constitutes an anomalous result as it will depend on the precise facts of the case. However, in discussions and negotiations with HMRC's ESSU it should be borne in mind that this is a potential outcome.

Meaning of connected persons

4.15   The meaning of connected persons is explained in Income Tax Act 2007 (ITA 2007), s 993 as follows:

An individual is connected with the following:

- the individual's spouse or civil partner;
- any relative of the individual (ie brother, sister, ancestor or lineal descendant);
- any relative of the individual's spouse or civil partner;
- any person with whom he or she is in partnership;
- any relative of any person with whom he or she is in partnership;
- any spouse or civil partner of the aforementioned individuals.;
- any person with whom the individual acts to secure control of a company; or
- any company the individual controls either alone or jointly with connected persons.

As an individual in the capacity as trustee of a settlement with the following:

- any individual settlor of the settlement;
- any person connected with that individual; or
- any body corporate connected with the settlement.

As a company with the following:

- A person who controls the company either alone or with connected persons.
- Any other company under the control of the same person or group of connected persons.

Domestic, family and personal relationship

4.16   The subsection that contains the deeming provision, the clause that is designed to widen the compass of the employment-related securities regime, provides ironically through section 421B(3)(a) and (b) a basis for avoiding the employment-related securities regime altogether where the right or the opportunity is made available to an individual in the normal course of the domestic, family and personal relationships of that person even in circumstances where the individual is an employee of the company whose shares are made available to him or her for acquisition. The most common application of this principle is in relation to family relationships where the argument is presented that shares would have been made available regardless of the family connection. However, the application of the principle is not limited to family members where the domestic and personal relationship is strong, particularly where there are non-business reasons that bind the relationship together and where there is some verifiable longevity to the relationship.

Example 44.4: The shares made available to a long-standing friend

Suppose the 100% shareholder of a company has decided to make available shares in the company to an individual who is a long-standing friend of some 20 years, the two having first become friends when they were working for a previous employer from which they were at the same time made redundant. The friend became an employee of the 100% shareholder's then new company following their respective redundancies. The two individuals share many personal and business confidences together and the families of the two individuals mix socially on a regular basis. In these circumstances, the shares are made available on the basis of domestic, family and personal relationships even though there is no blood relationship between the two individuals.

As a general principle, HMRC's ESSU will not provide a Code of Practice 10 clearance on whether or not the shares have been made available by reason of domestic, family or personal relationships. The decision on whether or not to proceed with this proposition must be on the basis of an evaluation of all relevant factors and usually there will be no one single deciding factor but a combination of factors that provides the basis for the case.

Meaning of employee-controlled: section 421H

41.17 The definition of employee-controlled applies to Chapters 2, 3, 3C and 4 only. The definition does *not* apply to Chapters 3A, 3B, 3D and 5.

A company is employee-controlled by virtue of shares of a class if the following conditions prevail:

- the majority of the company's shares of that class (other than any held by or for the benefit of an associated company) are held by or for the benefit of employees of the company or a company controlled by the company; and

- those employees are together able as holders of the shares to control the company.

For these purposes, an 'employee' includes a person who is to be or has been an employee.

Meaning of offices and office-holders: section 5

41.18 The Income Tax (Earnings and Pensions) Act 2003, s 5 is a section within Part 2 rather than Part 7. However, it is clear that the requirements of section 5 apply to Part 7 from the wording of section 5(1) that states that the provisions of the employment income Parts that apply to employments apply equally to offices, unless otherwise indicated.

The consequences of Section 5 are that the employment-related securities provisions of Part 7 apply to the holder of any office including an executive director, a non-executive director or the company secretary in exactly the same way as if the person, the office-holder, was an employee and the office was an employment. Section 5(3) defines the term 'office' as including any office that has an existence independent of the person who holds that office and may, therefore, be filled by successive holders of the position.

Chapter 42

Restricted securities: Chapter 2

Introduction

42.1 This chapter explores the nature of restricted securities and then goes on to explain the tax treatment that is required by the employment-related securities legislation. These rules relate to restricted securities that are acquired on or after 16 April 2003 by a person by reason of his employment or that of another person.

The principle of restricted securities

42.2 ITEPA Income Tax (Earnings and Pensions) Act 2003, Pt 7, Chap 2 sets out the tax treatment for restricted securities that replaces the tax regime that previously existed for dealing with conditional shares.

> The key principle to recognise when interpreting this legislation is that the restricted securities regime that was introduced through FA 2003 applies to securities that have an actual MV that is less than their *unrestricted* MV. The actual MV is the value taking account of the restrictions and is, therefore, the *restricted* MV of the securities.

When a company introduces a restricted share scheme, the employee takes ownership of the shares from the start of the arrangement. However, the restrictions reduce the value of the shares from what would otherwise be their MV.

Key examples of securities that *are included* in the restricted securities regime are:

Example 42.1

Shares that can be transferred or forfeited in circumstances where the employee would receive less than the MV of the shares on the transfer or the forfeiture.

Example 42.2

Shares that are subject to restrictions on the freedom of the employee to dispose of the shares, whether or not at MV.

Restricted shares are restored to their full value, *the unrestricted MV*, from their *restricted MV*, as a result of one or both of the following:

- the passage of time; and/or

- the achievement of performance conditions.

A restricted securities arrangement provides a clear incentive for the employee to remain with the company and meet the performance conditions as, usually, the employee is obliged on leaving to sell the shares or to forfeit the right to the shares.

The restrictions on the exercise of rights derive from the following:

- The Articles of Association of the company in relation to, for example:

  — voting rights;

  — dividend rights;

  — transfer restrictions; and

  — sale conditions on leaving.

- The terms of a contract between the company and the employee in relation to, for example:

  — transfer restrictions;

  — sale conditions on leaving;

  — agreement to accept/reject instructions on a general offer; and

  — restrictions on voting rights.

The timing of the acquisition of shares could be either of the following:

- Immediate, with full beneficial ownership of the shares through a trust or full legal title if purchased into the employee's own name at the outset.

- Deferred, where the shares are held by trustees of a trust for the duration of the scheme and transferred at the maturity through the exercise of a nil-cost option.

Right at the heart of the determination of whether or not shares are to be treated restricted securities is the distinction between *restrictions* and the share's *inherent characteristics*:

- Under ITEPA 2003, s 423(1)(a) the structural test, restrictions arise through the share being subject to a 'contract, agreement, arrangement or condition' by which the shares are restricted and to be treated as restricted securities.

- In contrast, the absence of particular rights may be an inherent characteristic of the share without having to be subject to a 'contract, agreement, arrangement or condition' in order to deny the exercise of those particular rights. In these circumstances, there is nothing to be restricted as they do not exist in the first place.

In applying this key distinction, it would appear that, in practice, for the Chapter 2 restricted securities regime to apply there would normally be a restriction on the shares compared with other shares in the same class and the restriction would normally reduce the value of the shares compared with the other shares in the same class. Under ITEPA 2003, s 423(1)(b) the depressed market value test, to be restricted securities 'the market value of the employment-related securities is less than it would be but for that provision'.

In determining whether or not the shares are restricted securities, therefore, it is important to apply both the structural test under section 423(1)(a) and the depressed market value test under section 423(1)(b) as both of these features must be in place for the shares to be restricted securities under Chapter 2.

For the restricted securities regime to apply, it is important to recognise the following in relation to the shares:

- there *must* be an identifiable restriction;

- the restriction *must* reduce the value of the shares; and

- they *must* be restricted securities at the time of the acquisition.

There must be no equivocation on any of these three points if the shares are to be treated as restricted securities. Remember, in particular, when applying the structural test and the depressed value test, in tandem as they have to be, that, under Chapter 2, the shares will only be restricted securities if *at the precise time of their acquisition* both of these tests apply. If there is no restriction at the date of acquisition but a restriction is imposed later then the shares are not restricted securities for purposes of Chapter 2.

When understanding the nature of a restriction, it is important to appreciate that restrictions as envisaged by Chapter 2 will typically be of a temporary nature and have the potential to be lifted at some point in the future.

Example 42.3: A class of permanently non-voting shares

Suppose that the shares do not have voting rights and that the non-voting status of the shares is regarded as permanent.

Permanent non-voting status to a class of shares will not be categorised as a restriction. The shares in that class would simply have a value that reflects the fact that the shares do not possess voting rights.

Suppose that although never envisaged at the date of the acquisition of the shares the company in general meeting decide to attach voting rights to these shares.

The question that then arises is how the shares would be viewed under the employment-securities legislation in the event that the restrictions were removed when this removal had never been envisaged. The answer to this apparent conundrum is that it is then necessary to look beyond Chapter 2 to Chapter 4 'Post-Acquisition Benefits from Securities', under which a charge to income tax would arise on the basis that an incremental benefit had as a consequence of the employment.

When structuring the share for purposes of an employee share scheme, a key planning point that emerges at the outset is whether to structure the shares as 'Restricted Securities' under Chapter 2 or 'Convertible Securities' under Chapter 3. As a general rule of thumb, if there appears to be a choice in the structuring of the share then it would normally be preferable for the shares to be categorised under Chapter 2, as 'Restricted Securities'. The preference for the restricted securities regime as opposed to the convertible securities regime is that it offers the opportunity for significant tax planning through the employee and the employer jointly agreeing to make an election under ITE PA 2003, s 425 or s 431. The making of the tax election enables all future gain from the date of the acquisition to be subject to CGT rather than the more punitive income tax regime.

A clinical examination of the statutory provisions

Employment-related securities

42.3 Under ITEPA 2003, s 422 to be treated as restricted securities under Chapter 2, it must be first established that the securities are employment-related securities. If they are then for Chapter 2 to apply they must be either restricted securities or a restricted interest in securities at the time that the securities are acquired.

Restricted securities or an interest in restricted securities

42.4 Under ITEPA 2003, Chap 2, s 423 is explicit about the two tests that must be passed in relation to the securities for the contents of Chapter 2 to apply.

Employment-related securities are classified as restricted securities or an interest in restricted securities if ITEPA 2003, under s 423(1) the following two tests are passed:

Structural test: ITEPA 2003, s 423(1)(a)

The employment-related securities are subject to any contract, agreement, arrangement or condition under which one of the provisions explained below applies.

Depressed market value test: ITEPA 2003, s 423(1)(b)

The market value of the employment-related securities is less than it would be but for that provision.

Provisions within contract, agreement, arrangement or condition

42.5 The provisions, one of which must be contained within the contract, agreement, arrangement or condition for the employment-related securities to be classified as restricted securities or an interest in restricted securities are as follows:

Either: transfer, reversion or forfeiture under ITEPA 2003, s 423(2)

- If certain circumstances arise or, alternatively, certain circumstances do not arise then the holder of the shares or the interest will then be obliged to give up all their beneficial interest in the shares through transfer, reversion of forfeiture and will not then be entitled to receive an amount at least equal to their unrestricted market value at the time.

Or: restriction on freedom to retain or dispose under ITEPA 2003, s 423(3)

- There is a restriction on the freedom of the holder to either retain or dispose of the shares or an interest in the shares or the proceeds of their sale or any other right conferred by them.

Or: disadvantage from disposal or retention under ITEPA 2003, s 423(4)

- The disposal or the retention of the shares or the exercise of the right conferred by them may result in a disadvantage to the holder or, if different, the employee or any person connected with either of them.

Exceptions to the restricted securities regime

42.6 Under ITEPA 2003, s 424 the precise circumstances are set out in which the restricted securities regime does not apply. It is definitively the case that employment-related securities are *not* to be treated as either restricted securities or an interest in restricted securities in any of the following cases:

Non-payment of outstanding calls under ITEPA 2003, s 424(1)(a)

- The employment-related securities are unpaid or partly paid shares that may be forfeited in the event of non-payment of outstanding calls and there is no restriction on the meeting of calls by the person who holds them.

Cessation through misconduct under ITEPA 2003, s 424(1)(b)

- The employment-related securities are to be offered for sale or transfer in the event of the cessation of employment as a result of misconduct.

Timing of the introduction of the new rules

42.7 These Chapter 2 rules that were introduced as new through FA 2003, relate to either restricted securities or an interest in restricted securities that are acquired on or after 16 April 2003 by a person by reason of his or her employment or that of another person.

These new rules replaced and continue to replace the charging regime under ICTA 1988, s 140A and FA 1989, s 78 which continue to apply in modified form to shares or interests in shares that are acquired before 16 April 2003.

Potential difficulties in application

42.8   The position taken by HMRC is that the rules under Chapter 2 are simpler to operate than the predecessor legislation and are fairer to the employees.

In practice, there are potential difficulties that require special attention as follows:

The determination of market value

- The market value has to be determined on the basis of different assumptions and at times when the securities are not necessarily sold at arm's length. This difficulty is compounded by the fact that the definition of 'securities' now operates with a much wider jurisdiction and includes instruments for which it is difficult to establish a market value.

The decision on tax elections

- The decision on whether or not to make a tax election requires very careful thought at the time of the acquisition of the securities or the interest in securities. In practice, both the employee and the employer must be involved in the decision for the reason that as a matter of law the election cannot be made without the support of both employee and employer.

Tax treatment of restricted securities

42.9   The main tax provisions relating to restricted securities or an interest in restricted securities are as follows:

Acquisition of shares

42.10   The first check to make is that the shares are employment-related securities. If as employment-related securities they represent either restricted securities or an interest in restricted securities then these rules on the *acquisition of shares* apply.

The acquisition of shares falls into two categories as follows:

Special rule situation

42.11   The employee will *not* be subject to income tax or NICs at the time the restricted securities are acquired or an interest in restricted securities is acquired in circumstances where any forfeiture or compulsory transfer restrictions cease within the period of five years following the acquisition. The condition is that the forfeiture or compulsory transfer restrictions do not last for more than five years. *This is the special rule where there are forfeiture or compulsory transfer restrictions that do not last for more than five years.*

Important: The tax election under the special rule situation

In the *special rule situation*, the employee may, though, choose through a tax election under ITEPA 2003, s 425 to be subject to income tax on the unrestricted MV at the date of acquisition less any consideration paid for the shares in order to secure CGT treatment for all gain following acquisition.

Where under ITEPA 2003, s 425 there in no tax charge on acquisition, the legislation is explicit through ITEPA 2003, s 425(2) that income tax could still arise in relation to the following:

Acquisition on conversion

- This is covered separately by Chapter 3 'Convertible Securities'.

Acquisition for less than market value

- This is covered separately by Chapter 3C 'Securities Acquired for less than Market Value'.

Acquisition that follows exercise of a securities option

- This is covered separately by Chapter 5 'Securities Options'.

Non-special rule situation

42.12   The employee will be subject to income tax or NICs at the time the restricted securities are acquired or an interest in restricted securities is acquired in circumstances where they are *not* subject to forfeiture or compulsory transfer restrictions but have restrictions, any other type of restriction such as, for example, in relation to dividend rights or voting rights or winding-up rights. In these circumstances, at the time of the acquisition of the shares, they will be subject to income tax and NICs on the difference between the then restricted value and any amount paid for the shares as consideration by the employee.

Important: The tax election under the non-special rule situation

In the *non-special rule situation* the employee may, though, choose through a tax election under ITEPA 2003, s 431 to be subject to income tax on the unrestricted MV at the date of acquisition less any consideration paid for the shares in order to secure CGT treatment for all gain following acquisition.

The administrative features of the elections are as follows:

- it is made by agreement between employer and employee;
- it is irrevocable;
- it follows a form that is approved by HMRC; and
- it must be made in the period up to 14 days after the acquisition or the chargeable event, as appropriate.

Chargeable events

42.13 Again, the first check to make is that the shares are employment-related securities. If as employment-related securities they represent either restricted securities or an interest in restricted securities then these rules on the *chargeable events* apply.

The term 'chargeable' in this context relates to income tax and NICs. It does *not* relate to CGT. Income tax will arise if certain events that are specified in the legislation occur. National insurance contributions will also arise on the occasion of these events if the shares are classified as readily convertible assets in accordance with ITEPA 2003, s 702 and the NIC Regulations.

Under ITEPA 2003, s 427 the legislation states explicitly that income tax will arise in relation to the following:

The ceasing of restrictions under ITEPA 2003, s 427(3)(a)

- The restrictions that cause the employment-related securities to be either restricted securities or an interest in restricted securities are lifted. The ceasing of the restrictions means that the restrictions are lifted.

The variation of restrictions under ITEPA 2003, s 427(3)(b)

- The restrictions that cause the Eemployment-related securities to be either restricted securities or an interest in restricted securities are varied.

The disposal of the shares under ITEPA 2003, s 427(3)(c)

- The disposal for consideration of the employment-related securities at a time when they are still either restricted securities or an interest in restricted securities.

The underlying principle that is applied in the event of a chargeable event is as follows:

- When a chargeable event occurs a charge to income tax arises on such proportion of the unrestricted MV of the shares that has not already been charged to income tax. The income tax charge will arise on the proportion of the value of the shares at acquisition that was *not* subject to income tax.

- If there occurs more than one chargeable event then the untaxed proportion will be reduced on each occasion until it reaches zero. Thereafter, any gain in value of the shares falls wholly within the CGT regime.

- Once there is no untaxed proportion remaining any further gain falls into the CGT regime.

Matrix guide to the restricted securities regime

This matrix guide is designed to assist the understanding of the following:

1. Whether the case is Tthe special rule situation or the non-special rule situation.

2. Which tax election is available in each situation.

Any case involving restricted securities must fall into one (and other one) of the four matrix boxes indicated as follows:

Special rule situation where no election made and no income tax and no NICs on acquisition	Special rule situation where election made (section 425) and income tax and NICs on acquisition on unrestricted MV less amount paid
Non-special rule situation where **no election made** *and* income tax and NICs on acquisition on restricted MV less amount paid	**Non-special rule situation** where **election made (section 431)** *and* income tax and NICs on acquisition on unrestricted MV less amount paid

Remember the reason for a tax election

42.14 All future gain following a tax election falls within the CGT regime.

Four examples: Chargeable events where no tax elections

Example 42.4: One restriction where no consideration paid

Suppose that at the date of acquisition the shares, that are readily convertible assets, have an unrestricted MV of £100. The shares have a three-year sale restriction. The employee receives the shares as a gift. No elections are made.

Suppose also that the shares are sold after the three years when the sale restriction of lifted.

Unrestricted MV at the date of acquisition	£100
Reduction in MV for sale restriction at the date of acquisition	£20
% Reduction in MV for restriction at the date of acquisition	20%
Restricted MV at the date of acquisition	£80
Unrestricted MV after three years	£150

In these circumstances, the income tax treatment is as follows:

- On the acquisition of the shares: 80% of the unrestricted value falls into a charge to income tax and NICs.

- After three years when the sale restriction is lifted: 20% of its unrestricted MV falls into a charge to income tax and NICs.

The taxable income at the date of acquisition

= £80 restricted MV = <u>£80</u>

The taxable income at the lifting of the sale restriction after three years

= £150 unrestricted MV × 20% reduction at date of acquisition = <u>£30</u>

In these circumstances, the CGT treatment is as follows:

- On the sale of the shares, the taxable income amounts represent deductible amounts within the CGT computation.

The capital gain that arises on the sale of the shares

= £150 sales proceeds − £80 taxable income − £30 taxable income = £40

Example 42.5: One restriction where actual consideration paid

Suppose that at the date of acquisition the shares, that are readily convertible assets, have an unrestricted MV of £100. The shares have a three-year sale restriction. The employee pays the restricted value for the shares. No elections are made.

Suppose also that the shares are sold after the three years when the sale restriction of lifted.

Unrestricted MV at the date of acquisition	£100
Reduction in MV for sale restriction at the date of acquisition	£20
% Reduction in MV for restriction at the date of acquisition	20%
Restricted MV at the date of acquisition	£80
Price paid by the employee	£80
Unrestricted MV after three years	£150

In these circumstances, the income tax treatment is as follows:

- On the acquisition of the shares, there is no charge to income tax or NICs. The reason for no charge to income tax or NICs on acquisition is that the price paid for the shares is actual MV.

- After three years when the sale restriction is lifted, 20% of its unrestricted MV falls into a charge to income tax and NICs.

The taxable income at the date of acquisition

= £80 restricted MV – £80 price paid = £0

The taxable income at the lifting of the sale restriction after three years

= £150 unrestricted MV × 20% reduction at date of acquisition = £30

In these circumstances, the CGT treatment is as follows:

- On the sale of the shares, the price paid and the taxable income amounts represent deductible amounts within the CGT computation.

The capital gain that arises on the sale of the shares

= £150 sales proceeds – £80 price paid – £30 taxable income = £40

Example 42.6: One restriction where actual consideration paid and share value fall

This example illustrates the implications of a fall in the value of the shares.

Even if the shares had by the date of sale fallen in value, an income tax liability would still arise and income tax would still be payable. This is for the reason that conceptually once the restrictions are lifted the share in its new state is treated as though it is a different share from its state before the removal of the restrictions.

Suppose that at the date of acquisition the shares, that are readily convertible assets, have an unrestricted MV of £100. The shares have a three-year sale restriction. The employee pays the restricted value for the shares. No elections are made.

Suppose also that the shares are sold after the three years when the sale restriction of lifted.

Unrestricted MV at the date of acquisition	£100
Reduction in MV for sale restriction at the date of acquisition	£20
% reduction in MV for restriction at the date of acquisition	20%
Restricted MV at the date of acquisition	£80
Price paid by the employee	£80
Unrestricted MV after three years	£70

In these circumstances, the income tax treatment is as follows:

- On the acquisition of the shares, there is no charge to income tax or NICs.

- After three years when the sale restriction is lifted, 20% of its unrestricted MV falls into a charge to income tax and NICs.

The taxable income at the date of acquisition

= £80 restricted MV – £80 price paid = £0

The taxable income at the lifting of the sale restriction after three years

= £70 unrestricted market value × 20% reduction at date of acquisition = £14

In these circumstances, the CGT treatment is as follows:

- On the sale of the shares, the price paid and the taxable income amounts represent deductible amounts within the CGT computation.

The capital loss that arises on the sale of the shares

= £70 sales proceeds – £80 price paid – £30 taxable income = – <u>£40</u>

Example 42.7: Two restrictions where no consideration paid

Suppose that at the date of acquisition the shares, that are readily convertible assets, have an unrestricted MV of £100. The shares have a three-year dividend restriction and a five-year sale restriction. The employee receives the shares as a gift. No elections are made.

Suppose also that the shares are sold after the five years when the sale restriction of lifted.

Unrestricted MV at the date of acquisition	£100
Reduction in MV for dividend restriction at the date of acquisition	£20
% Reduction in MV for dividend restriction at the date of acquisition	20%
Reduction in MV for sale restriction at the date of acquisition	£25
% Reduction inMV for sale restriction at the date of acquisition	25%
Restricted MV at the date of acquisition	£55
Total % reduction in MV for sale restriction at the date of acquisition	55%
Unrestricted MV after three years after the chargeable event	£250
Restricted MV after three years after the chargeable event	£187.50
Unrestricted MV after five years	£360

In these circumstances, the income tax treatment is as follows:

- On the acquisition of the shares, 55% of the unrestricted value falls into a charge to income tax and NICs.

- After three years when the dividend restriction is lifted, 20% of its unrestricted MV falls into a charge to income tax and NICs.

- After five years when the sale restriction is lifted, 25% of its unrestricted MV falls into a charge to income tax and NICs.

The taxable income at the date of acquisition

= £55 restricted MV = <u>£55</u>

The taxable income at the lifting of the dividend restriction after three years

= £250 unrestricted market value × (45% – 25%) reduction at date of acquisition

= £250 unrestricted market value × 20% reduction at date of acquisition = <u>£50</u>

The taxable income at the lifting of the sale restriction after five years

= £360 unrestricted market value × 25% reduction at date of acquisition = <u>£90</u>

In these circumstances, the CGT treatment is as follows:

- On the sale of the shares, the taxable income amounts represent deductible amounts within the CGT computation.

The capital gain that arises on the sale of the shares

= £360 sales proceeds − £55 taxable income − £50 taxable income − £90 taxable income = <u>£165</u>

The calculation of the tax charge that arises on the occurrence of a chargeable event is expressed in the terminology of ITEPA 2003, s 428 as follows:

Taxable amount = [UMV × (IUP − PCP − OP)] − CE

where:

UMV = market value immediately after the chargeable event but for any restrictions.

IUP = initial uncharged proportion =

$$\frac{IUMV - DA}{IUMV}$$

where:

IUMV = market value at the date of acquisition if there had been no restrictions; and

DA = the total of any deductible amounts.

OP = outstanding proportion =

$$\frac{UMV - AMV}{UMV}$$

where:

AMV = actual market value immediately after the chargeable event.

CE = expenses incurred by the holder in connection with either cessation or variation of restrictions or disposal of securities.

PCP = previously charged proportion.

The elements that can comprise a deductible amount are as follows:

- any consideration given at the acquisition;

- any earnings in respect of the acquisition;

- any employment income in relation to the securities;

- any employment income in relation to any conversion; and

- any employment income by reason of an acquisition where there is a securities option.

> Where consideration, CD, is less than the actual MV immediately after the chargeable event, AMV, the following formula is applied:

Taxable amount = [UMV × (IUP – PCP – OP)] – CE × CD/AMV

In the above example, the application of the formula *at the lifting of the dividend restriction after three years* would be as follows:

IUMV = market value at the date of acquisition if there had been no restrictions.

= £100

DA = the total of the deductible amounts.

= £55

IUP = initial uncharged proportion =

$$\frac{IUMV - DA}{IUMV}$$

=

$$\frac{£100 - 55}{£100}$$

= 45%

UMV = market value immediately after the chargeable event but for any restrictions = £250

AMV = actual market value immediately after the chargeable event = £200

CE = expenses incurred by the holder in connection with either cessation or variation of restrictions or disposal of securities = Nil

OP = outstanding proportion =

$$\frac{UMV - AMV}{UMV}$$

=

$$\frac{£250 - 187.50}{£250}$$

= 25%

PCP = the aggregate of the result of the application of the formula

= IUP – PCP – OP = 45% – 0% – 25% = 20%

Taxable amount

$$= [UMV \times (IUP - PCP - OP)] - CE$$

$$= [\pounds250 \times (45\% - 0\% - 25\%)] - \pounds0 = \pounds50$$

In the above example, the application of the formula *at the lifting of the sale restriction after five years* would be as follows:

IUMV = market value at the date of acquisition if there had been no restrictions = £100

DA = the total of the deductible amounts = £55

IUP = Initial uncharged proportion =

$$\frac{IUMV - DA}{IUMV}$$

=

$$\frac{\pounds100 - 55}{\pounds100}$$

= 45%

UMV = market value immediately after the chargeable event but for any restrictions = £360

AMV = actual market value immediately after the chargeable event = £360

CE = expenses incurred by the holder in connection with either cessation or variation of restrictions or disposal of securities = Nil

OP = outstanding proportion =

$$\frac{UMV - AMV}{UMV}$$

=

$$\frac{\pounds360 - 360}{\pounds360}$$

= 0%

PCP = the aggregate of the result of the application of the formula

= IUP − PCP − OP

= 45% − 20% − 0% = 25%

Taxable amount

$$= [UMV \times (IUP - PCP - OP)] - CE$$

$$= [\pounds360 \times (45\% - 20\% - 0\%)] - \pounds0 = \pounds90$$

Elections

42.15 The elections that are available disapply fully or partly the restricted securities charges within Chapter 2 and are made in the context of legitimate tax planning by the employee with the co-operation of the employer.

The position that is available for the employee to take is as follows:

- The employee can choose to be taxed under the income tax regime at the time of the acquisition on the difference between the full, unrestricted MV of the shares and any consideration that the employee paid for the shares.

- If the shares are readily convertible assets under ITEPA 2003, s 702 and the NIC Regulations then the difference between the full unrestricted MV of the shares and any consideration that the employee paid for the shares would also attract NICs.

- Any future growth in the value of the shares following their acquisition would be subject to tax under the CGT regime with the CGT triggered at the eventual sale of the shares.

- The tax advantages that arise from making a tax election are as follows:

- The income tax could be charged on a lower full MV at the time the shares are acquired than if income tax was charged on a full MV at a later date, assuming a rising value for the shares.

- The gain that crystallises on the disposal of the shares would be subject to CGT with the full range of exemptions and reliefs available, subject to the circumstances of the employee.

The technical position on the timing of the election is as follows:

- The technical position on the timing of the election is that the employee and the employer can act together to elect:

  — either; at the outset on acquisition; or

  — upon the occurrence of any chargeable event;

    for the income tax charge to be made by reference to the unrestricted MV of the shares.

If no tax election was made in the period of 14 days following the date of acquisition of the shares a further opportunity will arise for the employee to make the tax election within the period of 14 days following any chargeable event that subsequently arises in accordance with ITEPA 2003, s 427.

The difference between the two elections is as follows:

ITEPA 2003, s 425(3) for the special rule situation

- The tax election under ITEPA 2003, s 425(3) is required if there is a desire not to defer the tax charge under the special rule situation where deferral would otherwise arise. This tax election is concerned explicitly with the timing of the tax charge on shares for which there are forfeiture or compulsory transfer restrictions that do not last for more than five years. However, its effect is still to bring all future gain into the CGT regime.

ITEPA 2003, s 431 for the non-special rule situation

- The tax election under ITEPA 2003, s 431 covers any situation concerning restricted securities, risk of forfeiture or any other restrictions except for the precise restriction that is dealt with in the special rule situation. This tax election is required for the income tax charge to be made by reference to the unrestricted value of the shares at the date of acquisition of a chargeable event and allows either full or partial disapplication.

The full range of tax elections that are available for alternative tax treatment under Chapter 2 are as follows:

ITEPA 2003, s 425(3)

- This election is for the disapplication of the exemption from income tax on acquisition for shares where there are forfeiture or compulsory transfer restrictions that do not last for more than five years. This is the disapplication to disapply the special five-year rule. This tax election must be made within 14 days after acquisition.

ITEPA 2003, s 430

- This election is for the charge to income tax to be increased by bringing into charge the whole of any remaining untaxed proportion of the unrestricted MV following the chargeable event, so enabling all subsequent growth to be taxed under the CGT regime. This tax election must be made within 14 days after a chargeable event.

ITEPA 2003, s 431(1)

- This election is for the full disapplication of the restricted securities regime with the effect that income tax is charged on the acquisition of the securities on the full initial unrestricted MV. This tax election must be made within 14 days after acquisition.

ITEPA 2003, s 431(2)

- This election is for the restricted securities regime to apply as if one or more specified restrictions are ignored with the effect that income tax is charged on the acquisition of the securities on the MV of the shares disregarding such restrictions or, if an exemption from the initial charge applies, income tax is charged upon a chargeable event. This tax election must be made within 14 days after acquisition.

It is important to understand the following administrative matters:

- The employee cannot make the election without the support of the employer. The reason is that the election impacts on the employer's corporation tax position and on the employer's liability to employer's NICs.

- The tax election form does not have to be submitted to HMRC by either the employee or the employer. It simply has to be kept with the company records. Most usually the completed form is kept with either the statutory books or the payroll records of the company.

- The period of 14 days was fixed to fit in with the PAYE timetable. The reason for a time limit is to avoid the backdating of tax elections when there is an increase in value. If the time limit is missed, for whatever reason, then no extension is allowed although the occurrence of a chargeable event will give rise to make the tax election.

The key question is to ask whether or not it is always the case that a tax election should be made when the shares are restricted securities. The answer is that a calculation should be performed in each case, taking into account the following:

- What is initial outlay and is it affordable?

- What is the expected growth potential of the shares?

Disposal of securities following the cessation of restrictions

42.16 The disposal of the securities triggers CGT in the normal way. However, care must be taken to construct the CGT computation correctly as follows:

Disposal proceeds:

Less: Any price paid as consideration for the securities

Less: Any amount subject to income tax under the restricted securities regime

---

It is important to recognise that the base cost for CGT purposes accounts for any amount that has already been subject to income tax under the restricted securities regime.

The consideration for the acquisition is taken under TCGA 1992, s 149AA to be the aggregate of the following:

- *Initial purchase consideration:* the actual amount or value given for the securities by the purchaser.

- *Any income taxable amounts:* any amount charged to income tax under the general charging provision on ITEPA 2003, Pt 3, Chap 1 (taxable amounts).

Additionally, if the disposal of the securities is a chargeable event or is the first disposal after a chargeable event then any amount that is counted as employment income is added to the consideration for the acquisition.

Two examples: A section 425 tax election in the special rule situation

Example 44.4: Where consideration is paid for the shares

Suppose that the employee is allowed to purchase 1000 shares by his employing company and that at the date of acquisition the shares, which are readily convertible assets, have an unrestricted market of £5 per share. The acquisition cost of the shares that is taken to be the actual MV, the restricted value of the shares, is £3.50.

The restriction that accounts for the £1.50 discount is that if the employee leaves the company as a bad leaver by reason of resignation or dismissal within five years then he will forfeit the shares. The shares have, therefore, been discounted by 30%.

The company is sold three years later for £15 per share.

Number of shares available for purchase by the employee	1000
Unrestricted MV per share at the date of acquisition	5.00
Reduction in MV for sale restriction at the date of acquisition	£1.50
% Reduction in MV for restriction at the date of acquisition	30%
Restricted MV per share at the date of acquisition	£3.50
Price paid per share for the shares	£3.50
Sale value per share	£15.00

Position without a tax election under section 425

In these circumstances, the income tax treatment is as follows:

- *On the acquisition of the shares, there is no charge to income tax or NICs. The reason for no charge to income tax or NICs on acquisition is that this is the special rule situation.*

- *After three years when the sale restriction is lifted, 30% of its unrestricted MV falls into a charge to income tax and NICs.*

The taxable income at the date of acquisition = £0

The taxable income at the lifting of the sale restriction after three years

= unrestricted MV × reduction at the date of acquisition

= (£15.00 × 1000 shares) × 30% = £4,500

In these circumstances, the CGT treatment is as follows:

- *On the sale of the shares, the price paid and the taxable income amounts represent deductible amounts within the CGT computation.*

The capital gain that arises on the sale of the shares

= £15,000 sales proceeds − £3,500 price paid − £4,500 taxable income = £7,000

The total outlay

= consideration + income tax and NICs paid + CGT paid

= £3,500 + [(40% + 1%) × £4,500] + [18% × £7,000] = £3,500 + £1,845 + £1,260 = £6,605

Position with a tax election under ITEPA 2003, section 425

In these circumstances, the income tax treatment is as follows:

● *On the acquisition of the shares, the difference between the unrestricted MV and the price paid for the shares falls into a charge to income tax or NICs.*

The taxable income at the date of acquisition

= unrestricted MV − price paid

= (1000 shares × £5.00 per share) − (1,000 shares × £3.50 per share)

= £5,000 − £3,500

= £1,500

In these circumstances, the CGT treatment is as follows:

● *On the sale of the shares, the price paid and the taxable income amounts represent deductible amounts within the CGT computation.*

The capital gain that arises on the sale of the shares

= £15,000 sales proceeds − £3,500 price paid − £1,500 taxable income = £10,000

The total outlay

= consideration + income tax and NICs paid + CGT paid

= £3,500 + [(40% + 1%) × £1,500] + [18% × £10,000]

= £3,500 + £615 + £1,800 = £5,915

Summary conclusion

The total outlay without a tax election = £6,605

The total outlay with a tax election = £5,915

On the basis of this assumption about the sale proceeds, the employee and the employer should jointly make an election.

Example 44.5: Where no consideration is paid for the shares

Suppose that the employee is allowed to purchase 1000 shares by his employing company and that at the date of acquisition the shares, which are readily convertible assets, have an unrestricted market of £5 per share. The acquisition cost of the shares is nil.

The restriction is that if the employee leaves the company as a bad leaver by reason of resignation or dismissal within five years then he will forfeit the shares.

The company is sold three years later for £15 per share.

Number of shares available for purchase by the employee	1,000
Unrestricted MV per share at the date of acquisition	£5.00
Reduction in MV for sale restriction at the date of acquisition	£1.50
% Reduction in MV for restriction at the date of acquisition	30%
Restricted MV per share at the date of acquisition	£3.50
Price paid per share for the shares	£0.00
Sale value per share	£15.00

Position without a tax election under section 425

In these circumstances, the income tax treatment is as follows:

- *On the acquisition of the shares, there is no charge to income tax or NICs. The reason for no charge to income tax or NICs on acquisition is that this is the special rule situation.*

- *After three years when the sale restriction is lifted, 30% of its unrestricted MV falls into a charge to income tax and NICs.*

The taxable income at the date of acquisition = £0

The taxable income at the lifting of the sale restriction after three years = unrestricted MV

= (£15.00 × 1,000 shares) = £15,000

In these circumstances, the CGT treatment is as follows:

- *On the sale of the shares, the price paid and the taxable income amounts represent deductible amounts within the CGT computation.*

The capital gain that arises on the sale of the shares

= £15,000 sales proceeds – £0 price paid – £15,000 taxable income = £0

The total outlay = consideration + income tax and NICs paid + CGT paid

= £0 + [(40% + 1%) × £15,000] + £0]

= £0 + £6,150 + £0

= £6,150

Position with a tax election under section 425

In these circumstances, the income tax treatment is as follows:

- *On the acquisition of the shares, the difference between the unrestricted MV and the price paid for the shares falls into a charge to income tax or NICs.*

The taxable income at the date of acquisition

= unrestricted MV – price paid

= (1000 shares × £5.00 per share) – (1000 shares × £0 per share)

= £5000 – £0 = £5000

In these circumstances, the CGT treatment is as follows:

- *On the sale of the shares, the price paid and the taxable income amounts represent deductible amounts within the capital gains tax computation.*

The capital gain that arises on the sale of the shares

= £15,000 sales proceeds − £0 price paid − £5,000 taxable income = £10,000

The total outlay

= consideration + income tax and NICs paid + CGT paid

= £0 + [(40% + 1%) × £5,000] + [18% × £10,000]

= £0 + £2,050 + £1,800 = £3,850

Summary conclusion

The total outlay without a tax election = £6,150

The total outlay with a tax election = £3,850

On the basis of this assumption about the sale proceeds, the employee and the employer should jointly make an election.

Chapter 43

Convertible securities: Chapter 3

Introduction

43.1 This chapter explores the nature of convertible securities and then goes on to explain the tax treatment that is required by the employment-related securities legislation. The legislation has been effective since 1 September 2003 although it applies to all convertible securities that are employment-related securities regardless of the date of acquisition of the securities.

The principle of convertible securities

43.2 Income Tax (Earnings and Pensions) Act 2003, Pt 7, Chap 3 sets out the treatment for convertible securities which are securities that are awarded by a company to its employees with limited rights but with the capacity to convert to ordinary shares on the trigger of certain events. The circumstances in which the company awards this type of securities will typically be those of a venture capital or private equity situation. A typical arrangement will be convertible loan stock or convertible preference shares with a date set in the future at which the right to convert into ordinary shares can be enforced.

Chapter 3 assumes that in circumstances where the company awards to its employees' convertible securities and the employees accept the offer the employees are taking titled acquisition of two assets, namely: (1) the underlying security; and (2) a right to acquire a security at some time in the future. When viewed in this way, the second asset is a form of quasi-option and as with all the chapters within the employment-related securities Part 7 that deal with tax-unapproved schemes Chapter 3 seeks to bring into income tax any increase in value that accrues from the employment.

It is important to recognise that unlike the restricted securities regime that is dealt with through Chapter 2 and embraces the full set of tax elections it is the case that for the convertible securities regime that is dealt with through Chapter 3 there are no tax elections available. The crucial planning point is, therefore, to ensure that in formulating the nature of the shares, if there is a choice between establishing the shares as restricted securities and establishing the shares as convertible securities then the structuring of the shares as restricted securities in accordance with Chapter 2 offers the most tax-efficient approach.

When seeking to determine whether or not the securities are convertible securities it is important to distinguish between: (1) securities whose terms can vary the rights or entitlements of the owner of those securities and, thereby, change the status of the shareholder; and (2) securities which contain provisions which anticipate the owner of the securities holding securities of a different description at some point in the future. The variation of rights and entitlements under the terms of the securities does constitute the characteristics of convertible shares whereas the capacity to convert into securities of a different description does constitute the characteristics of convertible securities.

There has been much discussion with HMRC about 'ratchet arrangements' under which the participation of different ordinary shareholders can vary depending on the performance of the company. Again, these arrangements will not normally constitute the characteristics of convertible securities. Rather, the arrangements will represent the implementation of the terms on which ordinary shareholders have taken title to the securities.

Concept of convertible securities

43.3 The first requirement is to determine whether or not the securities are employment-related securities. This must always be the first port of call. Once it is decided that the securities are employment-related securities then the nature and the structure of the securities must be examined to determine whether or not there are any elements contained within the share that categorize the securities as either convertible securities or an interest in convertible securities.

Income Tax (Earnings and Pensions) Act 2003, s 435, within Pt 7, Chap 3, sets out the jurisdiction of that Chapter 3 which is employment-related securities that are:

- either: convertible securities; or

- an interest in convertible securities;

at the time that the securities are acquired.

Nature of convertible securities

43.4 Income Tax (Earnings and Pensions) Act 2003, s 436 explains that employment-related securities are classified as convertible securities if one of the following three elements prevail:

- the employment-related securities confer on the shareholder an entitlement to convert the securities into securities of a different description. For this purpose, the entitlement can be either immediate or deferred and can be either conditional or unconditional, or;

- the employment-related securities are subject to a contract, an agreement, an arrangement or a condition that authorises or requires the grant of an entitlement to the shareholder in the event of certain circumstances arising or not arising, or;

- the employment-related securities are subject to a contract, an agreement, an arrangement or a condition that provides for conversion into securities of a different description.

Scope of the tax charge for convertible securities

43.5   The scope of the tax charge has widened as a consequence of a more all-embracing definition to include shares that are convertible as follows:

- at the behest of the shareholder;

- at the behest of the issuer; and

- automatically or otherwise in accordance with the terms of the shares.

Important point

The shares are no longer convertible solely at the behest of the shareholder. This is a significant change to the previous legislation under ICTA 1988, s 140D.

The summary position is that Chapter 3 makes gains subject to an income tax charge in the following circumstances:

- gains produced by conversions of shares into another class of securities;

- gains realised when the convertible securities are sold rather than converted; and

- gains that accrue on occasions where shares merely change their description rather than their class.

Tax treatment of convertible securities

43.6   The significance of the legislation is best understood by recognising the following:

- *On the acquisition of the securities:* any income tax charge is now under Chapter 3 by reference to MV of the shares, ignoring the prospect of any conversion in the tax computation, ie treated as though they are not convertible securities. The determination applies to the initial MV that, in practice, may be difficult as it represents the requirement to produce a value that is hypothetical.

- *On the conversion of the securities into securities of a different description*: there is also a new basis under Chapter 3 using conversion gain for calculating the income tax charge that arises on conversion. Under ICTA 1988, s 140D it was based on the full value of the shares into which the originally-acquired shares converted. By contrast under the new rules of ITEPA 2003, Pt 7, Chap 3 it is based purely on the gain on conversion.

The main tax provisions relating to convertible securities are as follows:

Income tax charge on the acquisition of the shares

43.7   Chapter 3, under ITEPA 2003, s 437 is definitive in stating that any charge to tax is to be by reference to the MV of the securities as though they were neither convertible securities nor an interest in convertible securities.

Where convertible securities are subject to an income tax charge on acquisition, the charge will arise as a consequence of either: (1) the general charging provision under ITEPA 2003, s 62 for the acquisition of shares at less than MV; or (2) the provision for the tax charge arising on the exercise of share options under ITEPA 2003, ss 471–484; or (3) the provision for the tax charge under ITEPA 2003, ss 446Q–446W arising under notional loan arrangements; or (4) the provision for the tax charge under ITEPA 2003, s 203 arising on a residual benefit.

The effect of treating the convertible securities on acquisition as though there are not convertible will normally be to reduce the value of the shares for purposes of the income tax charge. However, it is possible to argue a lower value on the conversion into new securities in circumstances where the conversion is into deferred worthless shares.

There is an anti-avoidance provision that came into force effective from 2 December 2004 under which the right to convert will not be ignored for purposes of calculating the MV in circumstances in which it is considered that the main purposes or one of the main purposes of the arrangement is the avoidance of tax or NICs. The anti-avoidance provision will not provide the basis for an override if the MV ignoring the right to convert is greater than the MV incorporating the right to convert.

Income tax charge on the conversion of the shares

43.8   Chapter 3, under ITEPA 2003, s 438 establishes the charge to income tax that is charged on the conversion into new securities triggered by chargeable events.

The chargeable events that are listed under ITEPA 2003, s 439 are as follows:

- The conversion of the securities into securities of a different description in circumstances in which an associated person is entitled to a beneficial interest in the securities *before* the conversion and *after* the conversion.

- The disposal for consideration of any convertible securities by an associated person otherwise than to another associated person.

- The release for consideration of the entitlement to convert the securities into securities of a different description.

- The receipt by an associated person of a benefit in money or money's worth in connection with the entitlement to covert; any benefit received on account for any disability is disregarded for these purposes.

For these purposes, 'an associated person' is as defined in ITEPA 2003, s 421C and is: (1) the person who acquired the securities; (2) the employee (if different); and (3) any 'relevant linked person'. Any 'relevant linked person' means any person who is or has been connected with, or a member of the same household as that of, the person who acquired the securities or the employee. Any 'relevant linked person' excludes: (1) the employer; (2) the person from whom the securities were acquired; (3) the person by whom the right or opportunity to acquire the securities was made available; and (4) the person by whom the shares were issued.

The comparison with the predecessor statutory provisions is as follows:

Under ICTA 1988, section 140D

43.9 The basis of the charge to income tax =

The full MV of the shares into which the originally-acquired shares converted

Less: Any amount paid for the shares

Less: Any amount on which tax was charged in relation to the share acquisition

Under ITEPA 2003, Part 7, Chapter 3

43.10 The basis for the charge to income tax = The gain on conversion =

The MV of the shares acquired on conversion

Less: The MV of the convertible shares at the time (determined as if they were not convertible)

Less: Any additional amount paid on conversion

Suppose the shares are sold without being converted

Then the basis of the charge to income tax =

The consideration received on the sale of the shares

Less: The MV at the time of the sale (ignoring the prospect of any conversion)

Example 43.1: With a right to convert where no consideration paid for the initial acquisition

Suppose that at the date of acquisition an employee receives as a gift from his employer £100 of convertible loan stock with interest at 3%. The employee has a right to convert the convertible loan stock into 100 £1 ordinary shares in three year's time when the value of the loan stock has remained at £100.

	£
3% convertible loan stock, ignoring the prospect of any conversion	100
Value of the loan stock attributable to the conversion right	20
Gross value of the 3% convertible loan stock	120
Nominal value of the ordinary shares into which there is a right to convert	100
Market value of the ordinary shares at the date of acquisition of the loan stock	200
Market value of the ordinary shares after three years at the date of the conversion	1000

In these circumstances, the income tax treatment for the employee is as follows:

- On the acquisition of the shares, the £100 value of the 3% convertible loan stock is subject to income tax with no consideration paid to act as a deduction.

- On conversion after three years, the charge to income tax is calculated on £900.

The MV of the shares acquired on conversion, £1,000.

Less: The MV of the convertible shares at the time, £100 (determined as if they were not convertible).

- The value of the conversion rights is not a deduction on conversion for the reason that it was not subject to income tax on acquisition.

The circumstances in which the charge under ITEPA 2003, s 438 does not apply are stipulated in section 443 as follows:

- the securities are shares or an interest in shares (and not any other form of security such as convertible loan stock) in a company of a given class; and

- all the shares of the given class of shares are convertible securities; and

- the event that affects the employment-related shares also affects all of the other shares of the same class; and

- immediately before the event that would be a chargeable event;

  — either: the company is employee-controlled by virtue of shares of the same class; or

— the majority of the company's shares of the class are not employment-related securities; and

● there is no purposeful attempt at the avoidance of tax and NICs.

Please note: FA 2004 introduced an anti-avoidance clause, effective from 7 May 2004 and subsequently revised with effect from 2 December 2004, stipulating that the exemption will apply:

'unless something which affects the employment-related securities has been done (at or before the time when Section 438 would apply) as part of a scheme or arrangement the main purpose (or one of the main purposes) of which is the avoidance of tax or National Insurance Contributions.'

There is also a disability exclusion under which a benefit received on account of a disability to the employee under the Disability Discrimination Act 1995 (DDA 1995) is treated as outside the employment-related securities legislation.

Chapter 44

Securities with artificially depressed market value: Chapter 3A

Introduction

44.1 This chapter explores the nature of securities with artificially depressed market value and then goes on to explain the tax treatment that is required by the employment-related securities legislation.

The legislation has been effective since 16 April 2003 although it applies to all securities that are employment-related securities regardless of the date of acquisition of the securities. Where, though, Chapter 3A interfaces with Chapter 2 on restricted securities those elements of Chapter 3A do not apply to securities acquired before 16 April 2003. Additionally, in relation to securities that are acquired on or after 16 April 2003; but before 1 September 2003 for purposes of the interface with Chapter 2; they only apply on or after 1 September 2003.

Chapter 3A applies to any conditional interests held at 16 April 2003 in circumstances where the transactions designed to artificially reduce value, the so-called depreciatory transactions, took place on or after 16 April 2003.

The principle that supports Chapter 3A

44.2 Income Tax (Earnings and Pensions) Act 2003, Pt 7, Chap 3A is specifically designed to combat tax avoidance using depreciatory transactions. The purpose, therefore, of Chapter 3A is to reverse the effect of any artificial decrease in the market value of the securities.

HMRC accepts that genuine commercial and market factors may cause the value of shares to be depressed and it is definitely the case that Chapter 3A is not targeted at those genuine situations. However, it is recognised that in certain circumstances a company may take purposeful steps to artificially reduce the market value of the securities at the time of the acquisition by the employees in order to avoid a higher income tax charge arising at the date of acquisition. When the factors that have been artificially engineered to reduce the market value for acquisition are removed or withdrawn, presumably at the behest of the company, then the value of the shares will increase from the artificially reduced level and result in a gain for the employee that is free from income tax.

In ITEPA 2003, s 446A(2) there are two sets of circumstances that are identified by Chapter 3A as initiatives that could be taken by companies for reasons other than genuine commercial reasons as follows:

- Anything done as part of a scheme or arrangement the main purpose or one of the main purposes of which is the avoidance of tax or NICs.

- Any transaction between companies which are members of the same group of companies on terms which are not such as might be expected to be agreed between persons acting at arm's length (other than a payment of group relief); for this reference a group is a company and its 51% subsidiaries.

Section 446A(2) does though make it clear that this list of two sets of circumstances is not exhaustive and, in that context, the provision appears to have a wide compass in terms of its capacity to impose an income tax charge. In practical terms, the decision on the part of HMRC to apply Chapter 3A to date appears to have been limited to circumstances in which HMRC has been able to demonstrate a purposeful attempt at tax avoidance orchestrated by the company.

Income tax charge

44.3 Income Tax (Earnings and Pensions) Act 2003, Chap 3A, s 446B establishes the charge to income tax that is charged when an artificial depression in the market value of the securities is detected. The charge is taken to have arisen on the acquisition date.

- When an employee acquires employment-related securities and their market value has been depressed at least 10% in consequence of anything done 'otherwise than for genuine commercial purposes' within the period of seven years up to the date of acquisition. 'Genuine commercial purposes' excludes purposeful attempts at tax avoidance and manipulation of the value through non-arm's length intra-group trading.

Income Tax (Earnings and Pensions) Act 2003, s 446C sets out the formula for the calculation of the income tax charge as the difference between the following:

- The actual market value of the securities, market value (MV), taking into account the factors that have caused the depression in the market value.

- The value that would have been the higher market value of the securities, fair market value (FMV), had the things not been done to cause the depression in the MV of the shares.

Example 44.1: With depression in market value where actual consideration paid

Suppose that at the date of acquisition an employee purchases shares, which are readily convertible assets, at an artificially depressed MV of £100. HMRC determines that the factors that have caused the depression in the MV are not genuine commercial reasons.

	£
FMV established by HMRC	150
Artificial depression in MV through non-commercial reasons	50
Artificially depressed MV	100
Price paid by the employee	100

On the acquisition of the shares, the amount that is subject to income tax and NICs:

= FMV – MV = £150 – £100 = £50

Example 44.2: With depression in market value where actual consideration paid is less than market value

Suppose that at the date of acquisition an employee purchases shares, which are readily convertible assets, at £120 although the artificially depressed MV is £100. HMRC determines that the factors that have caused the depression in the MV are not genuine commercial reasons.

	£
FMV established by HMRC	150
Artificial depression in MV through non-commercial reasons	50
Artificially depressed MV	100
Price paid by the employee	120

Please note where MV is lower than the consideration paid for the shares MV is deemed to be the amount of the consideration for purposes of the tax computation.

On the acquisition of the shares, the amount that is subject to income tax and NICs:

= FMV – consideration = £150 – £120 = £30

Interaction with restricted securities and convertible securities

44.4 Income Tax (Earnings and Pensions) Act 2003, s 446D clarifies the effects of the interaction as follows:

● If the securities are restricted securities on acquisition then the FMV (but not the MV) is determined for these purposes as though they were not restricted securities. The post-acquisition charges on restricted securities under sections 426–431 do not then apply.

- If the securities are convertible securities then the FMV *and* the MV are determined for these purposes as though they were not convertible securities.

The implications of the securities as restricted securities are as follows:

- If the shares are restricted securities and the employee has suffered an initial charge to income tax by reference to the unrestricted market value of the shares no further charge to income tax will arise subsequently under the restricted securities legislation.

- The charge on acquisition does not apply if the exemption from income tax upon the acquisition of restricted securities applies.

- If an employee acquires sestricted securities the MV of which has not been artificially depressed at the time of acquisition, but which is artificially depressed in any subsequent tax year then a charge to income tax arises at the end of that subsequent year or upon the occurrence of any chargeable event.

Chapter 45

Securities with artificially enhanced market value: Chapter 3B

Introduction

45.1 Chapter 3B explores the nature of securities with artificially enhanced market value (MV) and then goes on to explain the tax treatment that is required by the employment-related securities legislation.

The legislation has been effective since 16 April 2003 although it applies to all securities that are employment-related securities regardless of the date of acquisition of the securities. Where, though, Chapter 3B interfaces with Chapter 2 on restricted securities those elements of Chapter 3B do not apply to securities acquired before 16 April 2003. Additionally, in relation to securities that are acquired on or after 16 April 2003 but before 1 September 2003; for purposes of the interface with Chapter 2; they only apply on or after 1 September 2003.

Share interests acquired before 16 April 2003 are deemed to have been acquired on that date, for purposes of determining the relevant period and the valuation date.

The principle that supports Chapter 3B

45.2 Income Tax (Earnings and Pensions) Act 2003, Pt 7, Chap 3B, is specifically designed to combat tax avoidance where the value of securities is growing artificially rather than through genuine commercial reasons. The purpose, therefore, of Chapter 3B is to subject any artificial increase in the MV of the securities to a charge to income tax.

HMRC accepts that genuine commercial and market factors may cause the value of shares to be increased and it is definitely the case that Chapter 3B is not targeted at those genuine situations. However, it is recognised that in certain circumstances a company may take purposeful steps to artificially enhance the MV of the securities and, indeed, in some circumstances the steps may be more inadvertent than purposeful.

It is thought that the target for HMRC in applying Chapter 3B will be fast-growing businesses where there may be doubt as to whether the reasons for the increase in the share value are artificial or commercial.

In terms of the precise wording of Chapter 3B, the provision to income tax perceived non-commercial artificial increases in share values is highly aggressive. Any company that has been targeted by HMRC could find that its employee shareholders are subjected to an income tax charge on an annual basis in respect of artificial increases of 10% or more per annum in the value of securities. In practice, the manipulation of company values through intra-group trading or off-balance sheet techniques and the introduction of multi-share arrangements where one class can be enhanced at the expense of another class or classes represent the vulnerable practices that could lead to artificial enhancement. Indeed, the company directors may not be aware of the effect that these techniques are having on the share price. It is important, therefore, that vigilance is taken by company directors and their advisers, particularly within the quoted companies which with the quotation on the recognized stock exchanges are open to monitoring by HMRC through the daily publication of the share price.

In Income Tax (Earnings and Pensions) Act 2003, s 446K(2) there are two sets of circumstances that are identified by Chapter 3B as initiatives that could be taken by companies for reasons other than genuine commercial reasons as follows:

- Anything done as part of a scheme or arrangement the main purpose or one of the main purposes of which is the avoidance of tax or NICs.

- Any transaction between companies which are members of the same group of companies on terms which are not such as might be expected to be agreed between persons acting at arm's length (other than a payment of group relief); for this reference a group is a company and its 51% subsidiaries.

Income tax charge

45.3 Under ITEPA 2003, Chap 3B, s 446L, establishes the charge to income tax that is charged when an artificial enhancement in the MV of the securities is detected. The charge is taken to have arisen on the valuation date as defined and explained below.

- When an employee acquires employment-related securities and, at the 'valuation date' in relation to a 'relevant period', their MV has been enhanced by at least 10% in consequence of anything done 'otherwise than for genuine commercial purposes'. 'Genuine commercial purposes' excludes purposeful attempts at tax avoidance and manipulation of the value through non-arm's length intra-group trading.

Under ITEPA 2003, s 446L sets out the formula for the calculation of the income tax charge as the difference between the following:

- The enhanced MV of the securities on the valuation date, initial market value (IMV) where the valuation date is the date on which the relevant period ends.

- The value that would have been the MV of the securities, MV, on the valuation date had such artificial non-commercial increases during the relevant period been disregarded.

Income Tax (Earnings and Pensions) Act 2003, s 446O explains what is meant by 'valuation date' and by 'relevant period' as follows:

- The valuation date in relation to a relevant period is the date on which the relevant period ends.

- The first relevant period, in the year of acquisition of the securities, is the period that begins with the date of acquisition and ends with the following 5 April.

- After the first relevant period, each relevant period begins with 6 April and ends with the following 5 April.

- The last relevant period, in the year of disposal of the securities, is the period that begins with 6 April and ends with the date of disposal or the cessation of the application of the legislation to the company.

- If the securities were acquired before 16 April 2003 then the date of acquisition is treated as 16 April 2003.

Example 45.1: With an artificial enhancement in market value

Suppose that at the valuation date HMRC determines that the shares of an employee, which are readily convertible assets, have been artificially enhanced by £50 to £150 and that the true market value is £100. HMRC determines that the factors that have caused the enhancement in the MV are not genuine commercial reasons.

	£
Enhanced IMV	150
Artificial increase in MV through non-commercial reasons	50
MV established by HMRC	100

On the valuation date at the end of the relevant period, the amount that is subject to income tax and NICs:= IMV − MV = £150 − £100 = £50

Securities that are subject to restrictions during the valuation date

45.4   Under ITEPA 2003, s 446M if the securities are restricted securities on the valuation date and no election has been made to treat the securities as not subject to restrictions or to ignore outstanding restrictions then the amount that is calculated as the overvalue is multiplied by the factor CP:

$$CP = 1 - OP$$

Where: OP =

$$\frac{UMV - AMV}{UMV}$$

UMV = market value immediately after the chargeable event but for the restrictions

AMV = actual market value immediately after the chargeable event

This formula assumes that the chargeable event occurred on the valuation date. The effect of introducing the inverse of the OP formula is to remove the restricted securities element. If the securities are no longer restricted for the reason that an election has been made then the 1-OP formula is not necessary. OP is precisely the amount that would be determined under the restricted securities regime (RSR) for the amount of charge arising on the valuation date in relation to a chargeable event for restricted securities if there were on that date a chargeable event (resulting in no tax charge).

Securities that are subject to restrictions during the relevant period

45.5   Under ITEPA 2003, s 446N if the securities are restricted securities during the relevant period and no election has been made to treat the securities as not subject to restrictions or to ignore outstanding restrictions then a further formula must be applied to the gain that has been calculated for the enhancement in value. For each chargeable event under the RSR, the gain must be reduced by the application of the following formula:

TA − ARTA

Where:

TA = taxable amount determined under the RSR in relation to the chargeable event

ARTA = taxable amount that would have been determined under the RSR in relation to the chargeable event calculated as if any non-commercial increases beginning at the same time as the relevant period and ending immediately before the chargeable event had been disregarded

The application of this formula has the effect of deferring the charge until the restriction has been lifted.

Chapter 46

Securities acquired for less than market value and notional loans: Chapter 3C

46.1 This chapter explores the nature of securities acquired for less than market value (MV) and then goes on to explain the application of this chapter to notional loans.

The legislation for securities acquired for less than MV applies to securities acquired on or after 16 April 2003.

The principle that supports Chapter 3C

46.2 The principle that supports Chapter 3C is that a notional loan is deemed to have been made where there is an undervalue arising on the acquisition of the securities which creates a benefit for the employee arising from the employment that needs to be brought into a charge to income tax. The notional loan, operating as a deemed interest-free loan, is the mechanism that enables the incremental benefits that accrue to the employee to be identified and quantified on the basis of additional value to the employee arising as a consequence of the employment. The notional loan arrangement is the only aspect of the employment-related securities legislation that requires disclosure under the HMRC Form P11D on which the entries are required in Section H entitled 'Interest-free and low interest loans'. It is its status as a deemed loan that requires the company to make this disclosure.

Under ITEPA 2003, s 446S the assumption that underpins the application of the principle is that the employer has advanced an interest-free loan to the employee at the date of the acquisition of the securities. However, if the securities are restricted securities and subject to the special rule under ITEPA 2003, s 425(2) where the nature of the restriction is forfeiture or compulsory transfer restrictions that do not last for more than five years then under ITEPA 2003, s 446Q(4) the notional loan is deemed to have been made on the first occurrence of a chargeable event under the restricted securities regime (RSR).

Under ITEPA 2003, s 446Q the precise circumstances in which the notional loan is deemed to have been made are defined as follows:

- The employment-related securities are acquired without any payment being made by the employee at or before the date of the acquisition.

- The employment-related securities are acquired for a payment on or before the date of acquisition that is less than their MV.

In dealing with these circumstances, any obligation to make a payment or further payment after the date of the acquisition is to be disregarded.

In applying this understanding, it becomes clear that the practical situations in which the income tax charge will arise are as follows:

- The securities are either nil paid or partly paid in relation to their nominal value; the MV is treated as though they are fully paid up.

- The securities are acquired for a consideration that is less than full MV, once any restrictions are taken into account.

- Although the securities have an agreed acquisition price of full MV part or all of the consideration is deferred.

Income tax charge

46.3 The charge to income tax that arises under Chapter 3C on the undervalue will only arise to the extent that the employee is not already subject to income tax under the general charging provision that is established by ITEPA 2003, s 62. It is 'the rule in *Salmon v Weight*' that finds its statutory expression in ITEPA 2003, s 62, based on the case of *Salmon v Weight* [1935] All ER Rep 904. This case established that a charge to income tax arises on the amount of undervalue in circumstances where an employee or officer of the company receives shares either by issue or transfer at less than their MV. The key principle is that where there is a permanent discount on acquisition the charge to income tax will arise under ITEPA 2003, s 62 rather than ITEPA 2003, s 446S.

It is important to recognise that an income tax charge can arise in respect of: (1) ITEPA 2003, s 62; and (2) ITEPA 2003, s 446S in relation to the same transaction. However, this will not constitute a double taxation charge as each statutory section will apply to a different part of the undervalue amount that has arisen at the date of acquisition.

Example 46.1: Illustrating the difference between deferred consideration and discount

The difference between deferred consideration and discount is best illustrated in an example in which both deferred consideration *and* discount arise in the same transaction as follows:

Suppose:

- The MV of the shares at the date of issue = £20.

- The offer price for the shares = £5; representing a 75% discount for employees.

- The amount payable as an initial payment by the employees = £1.

1. Income tax charge under ITEPA 2003, s 62

The immediate liability to income tax arises on the difference between the £20 and the £5 for the reason that this amount represents a discount given by the company on the purchase by the employee of the shares. The discount is a benefit to the employee arising from the employment. The full amount of the discount is subject to income tax in relation to the tax year in which the purchase of the shares takes place.

2. Income tax charge under ITEPA 2003, s 446S

The difference between the £5 and the £1 is the deferred consideration. The employee is treated as having an interest-free loan, the notional loan, equal to the £4 deferred consideration. The annual benefit-in-kind for HMRC P11D purposes is calculated by applying 'the official rate of interest' that is set by the Treasury to the loan amount unless the employee qualifies for one of the exemptions that are available for loans to employees. The official rate of interest was reduced with effect from 1 March 2009 from 6.25% to 4.75%.

Under ITEPA 2003, s 446S it is clear that the notional loan is treated like any other employment-related loan as defined under ITEPA 2003, s 174. It is in this context that there are exceptions from the interest charge as follows:

- Under ITEPA 2003, s 180 the de minimis limit of £5,000 applies; provided the total loans to the employee do not exceed £5,000 at any time during the course of the tax year. In circumstances in which the £5,000 threshold is exceeded then the taxable benefit arises on the interest on the whole loan and is not restricted to the excess over £5,000.

- Under ITEPA 2003 s 178 income tax relief is available against the employee's total income for the relevant tax year for the deemed interest on the notional loan on the basis that the notional loan has arisen from the acquisition of shares in a close company. For the tax relief to be obtained by the employee, the company must be a close company and the borrower must either have a material interest in the company or devote the greater part of his or her time to the actual management or conduct of the company or an associated company.

The context of the notional loan provisions is best understood when it is remembered that the income tax charges that arise under Chapter 3C are in addition to any liability to income tax that arises in respect of the acquisition under any of the following provisions:

- for earnings – under ITEPA 2003, Pt 3, Chap 1;

- for residual liability on taxable benefits under – ITEPA 2003, Pt 3, Chap 10;

- for restricted securities (for a chargeable event arises) under – ITEPA 2003, Pt 7, Chap 2;

- for convertible securities under – ITEPA 2003, Pt 7, Chap 3;

- for securities with artificially depressed MV under – ITEPA 2003, Pt 7, Chap 3A; and

- for securities option – under ITEPA 2003, Pt 7, Chap 5.

Under ITEPA 2003, s 446T there are specified deductible amounts that can be set off against the notional loan as follows:

- Any payment that the employee has made for the securities.

- Any discount amount that has been taxed as earnings under ITEPA 2003, s 62.

- Any amount that counts as employment income at the first chargeable event for restricted securities and there was no charge on acquisition for the reason that the special rule applies for a restriction that is a forfeiture provision or a compulsory transfer provision that does not last more than five years.

- Any amount that counts as employment income on the conversion of convertible securities.

- Any amount that counts as employment income through the exercise of a securities option.

The circumstances in which the charge under ITEPA 2003, s 446S does not apply are stipulated in section 446R as follows:

- the securities are shares or an interest in shares (and not any other form of security such as convertible loan stock) in a company of a given class; and

- all the shares of the given class of shares are acquired for no payment or for a payment that is less than their MV; and

- at the time of the acquisition of the securities;

  — either the company is employee-controlled by virtue of shares of the same class; or

  — the majority of the company's shares of the class are not employment-related securities; and

- there is no purposeful attempt at the avoidance of tax and NICs.

Please note Finance Act 2004 (FA 2004) introduced an anti-avoidance clause, effective from 7 May 2004 and subsequently revised with effect from 2 December 2004, stipulating that the exemption will apply:

unless something which affects the employment-related securities has been done (at or before the time of the acquisition) as part of a scheme or arrangement the main purpose (or one of the main purposes) of which is the avoidance of tax or National Insurance Contributions.

Discharge of the notional loan

46.4   Under ITEPA 2003, s 446U(1) the employee is treated as receiving taxable income equal to the remaining balance of the notional loan if the circumstances in which the notional loan is discharged are any of the following:

- If the employment-related securities are disposed of otherwise than to an associated person.

- If the outstanding or contingent liability to pay for the employment-related securities or an interest in employment-related securities, not fully paid up at the time of acquisition, is released, transferred or adjusted with the consequence of no longer binding any associated person.

- Something that affects the employment-related securities is done as part of a scheme or arrangement the main purpose (or one of the main purposes) of which is the avoidance of tax or NICs.

This last subsection 446U(1)(c) was introduced as an additional anti-avoidance provision through Finance (No 2) Act 2005 (FA (No 2) 2005), s 12, Sch 2 para 14. Section 446UA already existed as anti-avoidance where the initial purchase is through an anti-avoidance scheme in which circumstances the notional loan is discharged immediately.

For these purposes 'an associated person' is as defined in ITEPA 2003, s 421C and is: (1) the person who acquired the securities; (2) the employee (if different); and (3) any 'relevant linked person'.

Any 'relevant linked person' means any person who is or has been connected with, or a member of the same household as that of, the person who acquired the securities or the employee.

Any 'relevant linked person' excludes: (1) the employer; (2) the person from whom the securities were acquired; (3) the person by whom the right or opportunity to acquire the securities was made available; and (4) the person by whom the shares were issued.

Under ITEPA 2003, s 446U(4) the other circumstances in which the notional loan is discharged are the following:

- An associated person makes further payments for the securities equal to the amount that is outstanding.

- The employee dies.

When the difference is deferred consideration it is crucial to ensure that before the shares are sold the employee repays the outstanding amount of the notional loan. If the employee does not repay the loan before the shares are sold then the deferred consideration will be treated as a write-off of the outstanding amount and he will be subject to an income tax and an NIC charge (if the shares are readily convertible assets) on the amount that is written-off. If the sale and repayment of the notional loan both take place as in effect one transaction then HMRC will regard the repayment as taking place in advance of the sale.

Real life case study

Suppose an illustrative situation based on a real life case in which John Brown, an employee of Tangents Plc, is invited to participate in an employee share scheme in which he is requested to make an initial payment of 10p per share at a time when the unrestricted MV is £25 per share.

1. Creation of the notional loan

The implementation of the scheme arrangement has resulted in John Brown having a deemed notional loan with the company. The deemed notional loan has arisen at the time Mr Brown subscribed for shares under the scheme arrangement. The creation of this notional loan is not accidental. Rather it is the purposeful intent of the scheme.

The notional loan equates to the difference between the initial payment of 10p per share and the unrestricted MV of the share multiplied by the number of shares that he has purchased. This amount represents deferred consideration for the purchase of the shares. It is the deferred consideration in which the notional loan consists.

2. Deferred consideration as distinct from discount

From a detailed scrutiny of the documents, it is clear that the difference between the initial payment and the unrestricted MV at the date of issue is deferred consideration rather than discount. This conclusion is substantiated, in particular, from the following statements taken from the company's employee communication document:

Statement 1

The first statement selected from the employee communication document states that:

> the company may make further calls from time to time on the scheme shares up to a maximum of the difference between the unrestricted market value per scheme share (i.e. the price at which the Plan Shares are issued) and the initial payment of 10 pence per scheme share.

Statement 2

The second statement selected from the employee communication document, in which the unrestricted MV per scheme share is assumed to be £25, states that:

---

before the date on which the employee disposes of the shares, the employee must make a payment to the company equal to the difference between the unrestricted market value of £25 and the initial payment of £.010 (i.e. £24.90 per Plan Share).

The outstanding amount is all deferred consideration. It is *not* the case that the shares are issued at a permanent discount to their MV. If they had been issued at a permanent discount to their MV then an income tax charge would arise on the amount of the discount under the rule in *Salmon v Weight* [1935] All ER Rep 904 ((ITEPA 2003, s 62). The fact that none of the difference between the unrestricted MV of £25 and the amount paid of £0.01 represents a permanent discount means that none of difference is subject to a charge to income tax under the taxation of earnings provision in ITEPA 2003, s 62. The difference is all deferred consideration and, therefore, all the difference represents a notional loan under ITEPA 2003, s 446S.

If John Brown is not required to make good the difference between the 10p per share and the unrestricted MV of £25 per share then a Schedule E income tax liability arises. However, the employee communication document anticipates that John Brown will make good this difference before he sells the shares.

Assuming that John Brown has paid off the outstanding amount before sale, when John Brown does actually sell his shares the price that is obtained on sale is £80 per share. The capital gain is, therefore, £55 per share, ie £25–£80.

Chapter 47

Securities disposed of for more than market value: Chapter 3D

Introduction

47.1 This chapter explains the nature of securities disposed for more than market value and then goes on to explain the tax treatment and the relevant case law.

The legislation for securities acquired for more than market value applies to securities disposed of after 16 April 2003, regardless of when the securities were acquired.

The principle that supports Chapter 3D

47.2 The principle that supports Chapter 3D is that the natural price at which the securities can be sold is the price that is achievable in the general market and that in the absence of a general market the market value will be a surrogate value that is established by the recognised share valuation methodologies. Always in applying these methodologies the intention must be to derive a value that is consistent with the Taxation of Chargeable Gains Act 1992 (TCGA 1992), s 272.

The company cannot, therefore, force the introduction of a value that exceeds the market value, actual or surrogate, without consequences for the tax treatment of the proceeds of sale received by the employee. It is in this context that Chapter 3D imposes an income tax charge on any excess value received by the employee on the disposal proceeds over the market value. To the extent that the disposal proceeds do not exceed the market value of the securities at the date of sale the gain will be taxed under the less punitive capital gains tax (CGT) regime.

Chapter 3D is, essentially, aimed at penalising with an income tax charge the 'stop-loss' arrangements that companies sometimes introduce in order to ensure that the employee can recover through a minimum guaranteed sale price the purchase cost despite the fact that it may be the case that the shares have fallen in value in the time period from purchase to sale. In practice, Chapter 3D could apply in any circumstances where the calculation of the sale proceeds is based on a pre-set formula, for example, in the case of an earn-out where the formula may form part of the sale and purchase agreement and the earn-out involves a put/call option arrangement.

Income tax charge

47.3 The charge to income tax that arises under Chapter 3D applies in accordance with ITEPA 2003, s 446X when the following two characteristics prevail:

- The consideration received on the sale of the securities by the employee exceeds the market value of the securities at the date of the disposal.

- An associated person disposes of the securities so that there is no associated person entitled to benefit from the securities.

Under ITEPA 2003, s 446Y the actual charge to income tax is calculated on the basis on the following formula:

> Sales proceeds consideration *less* true MV *less* allowable deductible expenses.
>
> The consequences of the formula are that capital gain is converted into income gain when the company seeks to force a value as the basis for the sale proceeds consideration that is higher than the true market value.

Example 47.1: Illustrating the difference between market value and forced value

Suppose that the MV of a private company's shares at the time of sale using the earnings basis for share valuation, taking into account minority interest, is £15 per share. The earnings basis is considered for this company at this time to be the most appropriate way to achieve a market value for the shares of this company in the absence of a recognised stock exchange. The purchase cost of the shares three years earlier, again calculated on an earnings basis, taking into account minority interest, was £7 per share.

Now the company operates an employee share trust acting as an internal market for the shares. At the time the shares were purchased the company gave a commitment to the employees through a shareholders' agreement that the shares will be sold to the trust three years later on the basis of a pre-set formula. When the company applies that formula three years on at the time of sale the formula values the shares at £20 per share.

- The uplift in the value of the shares from the purchase price of £7 to the MV of £15 will be subject to CGT.

- The additional uplift from the MV of £15 to the forced value of £20 that is calculated on the basis of the shareholders' agreement formula will be subject to income tax.

It is the case that complications can arise in the application of Chapter 3D where a pro rata share valuation, rather than a minority interest share valuation, is used as the basis for the employee sale, typically to an employee share trust. The question that emerges is best illustrated in two contrasting examples that illustrate how HMRC appears to view the matter of sale at pro rata market value by employees in a private company to an employee share trust.

Two examples where sale is at pro rata MV:

Example 47.2: Where purchase is at minority interest market value

Suppose that in a private company at the time the shares are sold the shares have a pro rata whole company MV at sale of £30 per share and a minority interest MV of £20 per share. These values have been determined by applying the recognised share valuation methodologies. The purchase price for the employees was the minority interest MV of £5.

The tax consequences are as follows:

- The uplift in the value of the shares from *the minority interest purchase price* of £5 to *the minority interest sales price* of £20 will be subject to CGT.

- The additional uplift from *the minority interest sales price* of £20 to *the pro rata whole company sales price* of £30 will be subject to income tax.

Example 47.3: Where purchase at pro rata whole company market value

Again suppose that in a private company at the time the shares are sold the shares have a pro rata whole company MV at sale of £30 per share and a minority interest MV of £20 per share. Again these values have been determined by applying the recognised share valuation methodologies. However, in this example, the purchase price for the employees was at *the pro rata whole company market value* of £12.

The tax consequences are as follows:

- The whole uplift in the value of the shares from *the pro rata whole company purchase price* of £12 to *the pro rata whole company sales price* of £30 will all be subject to CGT.

In other words, it appears to be the case that as long as there is a matching between purchase and sale on the use of the pro rata whole company calculation or, alternatively, the use of the minority interest calculation then HMRC takes the view that Chapter 3D will not apply.

There is a further permutation on this theme that is illustrated in a further example in which at the date of acquisition there is no value in the company.

Example 47.4: Where whole company pro rata equals minority interest equals nominal value

Suppose that in a private company the single ordinary class of shares has a nominal value per share of £1 and that at the date of acquisition of the shares by the employees there is no value in the company. The MV is agreed with HMRC as no more than the nominal value, £1 per share. Three years later at the time the shares are sold there is an internal market for the shares. The pro rata whole company MV is £20 per share and the minority interest MV is £15 per share.

In these circumstances, it is not possible at the date of acquisition to distinguish in value between the whole company pro rata MV and the minority interest MV, both of which are £1 per share.

At the date of disposal, therefore, the shares can be sold to the employee share trust by the employee at either minority interest MV or, alternatively, at whole company pro rata MV without any exposure to income tax under Chapter 3D. In essence, this type of situation offers a choice on matching between purchase and sale.

Under ITEPA 2003, s 698 the income tax is accountable by the employer through the PAYE system as the sales proceeds are deemed to be PAYE income. The PAYE system must be applied regardless of whether or not the shares are categorised as 'readily convertible assets' under ITEPA 2003, s 702.

The residence rule that is applicable for Chapter 3D is applied on the basis of the date of the acquisition of the securities. It follows that the income tax charge still applies in circumstances where the employee leaves the UK after acquisition and then sells the securities for a value in excess of MV.

Relevant case law

Gray's Timber Products Limited v Commissioners of Revenue & Customs ([2009] CSIH 11) (Court of Session)

47.4 In *Gray's Timber Products Limited v Commissioners of Revenue & Customs* ([2009] CSIH 11, [2009] STC 889), which was previously known as the *Company A* case, the managing director entered into a subscription agreement with the other shareholders of the holding company of his employing company. The shares belonged to a single class of ordinary shares. The subscription agreement was drawn up with the intention of taking precedence over the articles of association. The terms of the subscription agreement entitled the managing director to a specific share of consideration on the sale of his shares such that although his shareholding represented 5% of the shares he was entitled to 25% of the sale proceeds. The whole of the issued share capital of the company was then sold to an independent third-party acquiring company and on the basis of the subscription agreement the managing director received significantly more per share than any of the other shareholders.

The Court of Session held that by a majority of 2:1 the excess of his consideration over the pro rata MV was subject to pay-as-you-earn (PAYE) and NICs. The Court of Session did not accept the position that the subscription agreement could have precedence over the articles of association. Additionally, the Court of Session noted that the subscription agreement was dated after the date on which the shares were allotted. Furthermore, the Court of Session recognised that although the subscription agreement was binding upon the parties it was not binding upon the purchaser of the company in the event of a sale.

Lessons from the *Gray's Timber Products* case

47.5 The rights that were attached to the managing director's shares appeared to be personal rights linked to the personal circumstances of his employment rather than to the shares that comprised his shareholding. The rights could easily be perceived, therefore, as not being rights that would continue if the ownership of the shares was transferred from the managing director to another party.

The overall structuring of the share arrangement for the managing director was weak and, indeed, a more robust arrangement may have resulted in a different outcome. For example, the inclusion of the rights in the articles of association rather than the subscription agreement would have established a continuity of the rights with successive shareholders regardless of the identity of the shareholder and the creation of a separate class of shares with specific rights as distinct from the other class of shares would have limited to some degree the exposure of the arrangement. However, if this approach had been followed it could be contended that with the enhanced rights the purchase price should be higher to reflect those enhanced rights and that in the absence of the higher purchase price that the shares were purchased below MV with exposure to an earnings charge under ITEPA 2003, s 62 and to a notional loan charge under ITEPA 2003, Pt 7, Chap 3C. Nevertheless, if the rights had been enshrined in the article of association the excess consideration could potentially have been justified on the basis that the excess consideration was inherent in the rights that attach to the shares rather than purely a personal arrangement for the benefit of managing director.

In assessing the relevance of the decision in *Gray's Timber Products* to the share scheme arrangements of companies generally it is important to be aware that there are key factors that need to be considered as follows:

- The share rights together with the transfer provisions should always be included in the articles of association. Even if they are included in the subscription agreement or the shareholders' agreement they should be replicated in the articles of association. As a general principle, if the rights are included in the articles of association then the arrangement should not attract the application of Chapter 3D. The articles of association have continuity over the life of the company and an endurance that is recognised in law regardless of the identity of the shareholders at any point in time.

- The creation of a separate share class for an employee share arrangement with rights that are different from the existing share class/es is a credible approach as long as the employees for whose share scheme the separate class has been established make a genuine investment into the share, and the arrangement is not a substitute for additional remuneration. The key principle to apply is that the rights must be rights inherent in the shares as distinct from personal rights. In other words, the rights must first and foremost attach to the shares rather than to the shareholder.

- The sale by different shareholders of shares from the same class on different terms, indeed terms that could vary significantly, is not necessarily without commercial justification. Some of the shareholders, for example, may offer warranties and indemnities that enhance the price that they can secure for their shares on sale. It may also be the case that in order to release their shares some shareholders demand a premium price and, of course, it is always the case that different percentage holdings may command a higher price.

Chapter 48

Post-acquisition benefits from securities: Chapter 4

Introduction

48.1 This chapter explains what is meant by post-Acquisition benefits from securities as introduced through Finance Act 2003 (FA 2003) in the context of an analytical interpretation of Chapter 4.

The legislation for post-acquisition securities applies in respect of any benefit received on or after 16 April 2003, irrespective of the date of acquisition of the securities that have given rise to the benefit.

The principle that supports Chapter 4

48.2 Her Majesty's Revenue & Customs regards this Chapter 4 as 'the sweep-up chapter' to catch situations where value is put into the hands of employees in connection of their employment and that value is not charged to income tax anywhere else in the legislation. However, meaningful analysis of the legislation leads to a more precise interpretation of the scope of the chapter.

Income tax charge

48.3 The charge to income tax that arises under Chapter 4 applies in accordance with ITEPA 2003, ss 447–448 in the following circumstances:

- Where an employee or associated person receives an additional benefit *in connection with* the ownership of employment-related securities by the employee or another associated person.

- The taxable income is equal to the actual amount received by the employee or associated person or the market value of the benefit.

- The tax year in which the benefit is assessed for a charge to income tax is the tax year in which the benefit is *received* by the employee or associated person. For all practical purposes, it is important, therefore, to identify precisely the date of receipt.

- The charge does not apply to a benefit if it is otherwise chargeable to income tax unless something has been done which affects the employment-related securities as part of a scheme or arrangement the main purpose or one of the main purposes of which is the avoidance of tax or NICs.

In seeking to identify whether or not there is a charge to income tax the following understanding is crucial:

- The words *'in connection with'* substituted the words *'by virtue of'* in Chapter 4 with effect from 2 December 2004 and are intended to establish a wider net for capturing items that can be brought into the charge to income tax. This wider capture potential indicates a resolution from the British Government to apply the principle that any incremental benefit from employment should be income taxed.

- For these purposes, 'an associated person' is as defined in ITEPA 2003, s 421C and is: (1) the person who acquired the securities; (2) the employee (if different); and (3) any 'relevant linked person'. Any 'relevant linked person' means any person who is or has been connected with, or a member of the same household as that of, the person who acquired the securities or the employee. Any 'relevant linked person' excludes: (1) the employer; (2) the person from whom the securities were acquired; (3) the person by whom the right or opportunity to acquire the securities was made available; and (4) the person by whom the shares were issued.

The circumstances in which the charge under ITEPA 2003, s 447 does not apply are stipulated in section 449 as follows:

- the securities are shares or an interest in shares (and not any other form of security such as convertible loan stock) in a company of a given class; and

- a similar benefit is received by all the owners of the other shares of the same class; and

- immediately before the receipt of the benefit;

   — either the company is employee-controlled by virtue of shares of the same class; or

   — the majority of the company's shares of the class are not employment-related securities; and

- there is no purposeful attempt at the avoidance of tax and NICs.

Please note FA 2004 introduced an anti-avoidance clause, effective from 7 May 2004 and subsequently revised with effect from 2 December 2004, stipulating that the exemption will apply:

unless something which affects the employment-related securities has been done as part of a scheme or arrangement the main purpose (or one of the main purposes) of which is the avoidance of tax or National Insurance Contributions.

Absence of a definition of benefit

48.4 There has been considerable debate about the interpretation of Chapter 4 and the extent to which the net is cast to bring certain employee benefit items into the charge to income tax. The debate and, indeed, the active discussion with HMRC, has arisen for the reason that Chapter 4, unfortunately, does not define 'benefit' for purposes of the application of the principle upon which the income tax charge in Chapter 4 is based and, therefore, HMRC, certainly when the legislation was first enacted, assumed that the term 'benefit' had a 'catch-all' meaning and, in consequence, Chapter 4 had a wide jurisdiction.

However, when seeking to apply the provisions of Chapter 4 to the practical situations in companies that may be vulnerable to an income tax charge under Chapter 4, it is important to ask a series of key questions based on recognised distinctions that are accepted in tax and securities law. The need to apply this rigorous set of questioning becomes imperative in the absence of any definition within the legislation whatsoever of 'benefit'. The purpose of the questions is, in essence, to identify the characteristics of the securities and on that basis to assess whether or not Chapter 4 applies.

Is the benefit intrinsic or extrinsic to the securities?

48.5 The question is whether or not the benefit is intrinsic or extrinsic to the securities for which payment has already been made at the date of acquisition and in this respect the following key distinction applies:

- The Chapter 4 charge *would* apply where the employee benefit arises separately and independently from the rights and privileges that are inherent in the securities.

- The Chapter 4 charge *would not* arise where it is the rights and privileges that are inherent in the securities that give rise to the employee benefit.

The application of this distinction is based upon the assumption that if the benefit is inherent in the security and part of 'the bundle of rights' that constitutes the security then the MV of the security at the date of acquisition and the price paid in alignment with that market value will accommodate the value attributable to the benefit. In other words, if it has been paid for once, as part of the payment for the security in the first place, then there is no justification for the benefit to be paid for a second time.

Is the benefit realized or unrealized?

48.6 The question is whether or not the benefit has actually been received and in this respect the following key distinction applies:

- The Chapter 4 charge *would* apply where the employee benefit is *received* in accordance with ITEPA 2003, s 447(3) and, therefore *realized* in the hands of the employee.

- The Chapter 4 charge *would not* apply where the employee benefit is *not received* in accordance with ITEPA 2003, s 447(3) and, therefore *unrealized* in the hands of the employee.

Although there is no definition of 'benefit', ITEPA 2003, s 447(3) is definitive that the benefit must be received to be subject to a charge to tax under Chapter 4. The distinction between realized and unrealized is a recognised principle within UK tax law. For example, exchange gains and losses are only brought into the tax net when they are realized and the same principle apples to the range of accounting provisions that must be realized before they are taxed.

The application of this principle would exclude, therefore, from the jurisdiction of Chapter 4 any increase in the MV of the securities that is generated in the market on the basis of a market awareness of the terms on which the securities were issued in the first place. The contention is quite simply that an increase in the MV of the securities does not constitute a realised gain that can readily or appropriately be described as 'received' for purposes of Chapter 4.

Does the benefit arise from the employment or from the sale of the securities?

48.7 The question is whether the benefit arises from the employment or, alternatively, arises from the sale of the securities and in this respect the following key distinction applies:

- The Chapter 4 charge *would* apply where a received benefit that is separate and independent from the rights and privileges that are inherent in the securities *arises in connection with the employment.*

- The Chapter 4 charge *would not* apply where the benefit, even though it is received and is separate and independent from rights and privileges that are inherent in the securities, *does not arise in connection with the employment* but from something else such as the sale of the securities.

Even where there is a realised gain received as result of the sale of the securities the contention is that the receipt, namely the receipt of the sale proceeds, is by virtue of the sale of the securities where a sale event is distinctly different from the period of ownership of the securities. In other words, the benefit is received but it arises by virtue of the sale of the securities rather than the ownership of the securities or the period of the employment over which that ownership has taken place. The event of the sale as an event in time follows and is distinct from the period of ownership of the securities.

Interaction with the statutory position on dividends

48.8 The interpretation of ITEPA 2003, s 447(4) is that, with regard to dividends, unless they are paid as part of a scheme or arrangement that has as its main purpose or one of its main purposes the avoidance of tax or NICs they would be excluded from the jurisdiction of Chapter 4. The circumstances in which the declaration of dividends could be construed as tax avoidance are where they are introduced in substitute for remuneration (the main salary or the discretionary bonus) attracting a preferential rate of income tax and avoiding both employee's and employer's NICs altogether.

It is definitively the case, of course, that dividends are subject to income tax through statutory provisions outside the scope of Chapter 4. The receipt of dividends is subject to income tax under *Income Tax (Trading and Other Income) Act 2005* (ITTOIA 2005), Pt 4, Chapt 3 entitled 'Dividends Etc. from U.K. Resident Companies Etc.' with ITTOIA 2005, ss 383 and 384 as the main charging provisions. However, despite the existence of these charging provisions for dividends the exclusion from ITEPA 2003, s 447 will not apply if the payment of the dividends is part of a scheme or arrangement the main purpose or one of the main purposes of which is the avoidance of tax or NICs. Previously, under ICTA 1988, s 20(2) it was not possible for dividends to be taxed under any other taxing provision. However, the introduction of ITTOIA 2005 removed that assurance from the legislation. Nevertheless, there remains the assurance courtesy of Taxes Management Act (TMA 1970), s 32 that a double tax charge cannot arise with respect to dividends.

Chapter 49

Alphabet shares

Introduction

49.1 This chapter examines the concept alphabet shares which although not a legal term of art it is a description that is recognised by the HMRC's employee shares and securities unit (ESSU) – in discussion on the application of the employment-related securities legislation. The chapter identifies, in particular, the provisions of Chapter 4, post-acquisition benefits from securities as the main source of tax exposure for this share arrangement.

Types of situation under discussion

49.2 The types of situation that give rise to alphabet share arrangements and which are constantly under discussion with regard to their tax exposure in the light of the employment-related securities legislation are best illustrated in two examples as follows:

Example 49.1: The non-family trading company

Suppose a non-family trading company that has two shareholder directors, each of whom own 50% of the A Shares and with full and equal rights under those A Shares. However, one shareholder director also owns B Shares and the other shareholder director owns C Shares. The B Shares and the C Shares are identical except that they have different dividend rights attached to them. Given the size of the company and the sector in which the company operates both director shareholders receive relatively low salaries and relatively high dividend payments. The salaries are paid on a monthly basis while the dividends are paid on a quarterly basis.

The tax exposure lies in the fact that the dividends appear to be paid as remuneration and by inference a reward for the work contribution from each of the two shareholder directors respectively rather than as a return on their investment in the shares. The exposure is exacerbated by the fact that they each made the same cash investment in the company but receive dividends at different rates.

Example 49.2: The family-owned trading company

Suppose a company that operates as a family-owned trading company with more than 75% of the A Shares controlled by the family. However, each of the family shareholders has a different class of shares, say B Shares, C Shares, D Shares, E Shares, etc, that are identical except that they have different dividend rights attached to them. The salaries are paid on a monthly basis through direct transfer and the dividends also are paid on a monthly basis through direct transfer.

Again, the tax exposure lies in the fact that the dividends could be construed as substitute remuneration and by inference a reward for the work contribution from each of the family members respectively rather than as a return on their investment in the shares. In fact, none of the children paid any amount for their shares so it is difficult to view the dividends as a return on a genuine investment and it is only when the dividend is added to the salary that the monetary return from the business becomes competitive.

Key question

49.3 The question that arises for alphabet share arrangements is whether the income received from the shares as dividends is taxed under the normal treatment that is accorded to dividends or, alternatively, under the normal treatment that is accorded to employment income.

The Chapter 4 section entitled 'The Interaction with the Statutory Position on Dividends' sets out the statutory framework for the taxation of dividends.

If the dividends are to be treated as employment income then the legislation poses a serious and potentially insurmountable problem to the opportunity that has hitherto existed for tax planning on the mix of remuneration and dividends for privately-owned companies. In the first instance, though, the context for this government initiative is best understood from The Ministerial Statement made on 21 June 2005 by the then Paymaster General, Dawn Primarolo, in the Standing Committee on Finance (No.3) Bill 2005 to clarify the scope of the amendment as follows:

Ministerial Statement of 21 June 2005

'These arrangements are devised to deal with the minority of cases where there are complex, contrived arrangements to avoid paying Income Tax and National Insurance on employment rewards. The Government have made clear their intention to close that activity down permanently.

There has been some debate about whether small businesses are caught by the provisions, so I am grateful to have the opportunity to offer small businesses some reassurance.

A change being made to Chapter 4 of the Income Tax (Earnings and Pensions) Act 2003 will remove, where avoidance is involved, the provision that automatically exempts benefits received in connection with securities from a full Income Tax and National Insurance charge, if Income Tax has been paid elsewhere. I am aware, from representations made directly to me and my Department, that professionals have expressed concern about the possible scope of the change. I want to make it clear that this change does not bring all benefits derived from securities into a tax and National Insurance charge. A reference to benefits in the context of the schedule means the employment reward–the passing of

---

value to an employee in return for the employee's labour. Where investors are carrying out their normal investment transaction, this charge will not affect them.

The purpose test introduced in Section 447 of the 2003 Act has been carefully designed to target complex, contrived avoidance arrangements that are used mainly to disguise cash bonuses. If taxpayers use contrived arrangements to get round anti-avoidance legislation–to avoid paying the proper amount of tax and National Insurance–they cannot expect to be excluded from the charge. However, it will be absolutely clear from what I say about the purpose test that this measure will not affect the taxation of those small businesses that do not use contrived schemes to disguise remuneration to avoid tax and National Insurance.'

The page in the *Employment-Related Securities Manual* (ERSM90060 – Post-Acquisition Benefits from Securities – Dividends as Benefits) that sets out The Ministerial Statement of 21 June, 2005 concludes with the following comment from HMRC:

Where an owner-managed company, run as a genuine business, pays dividends out of company profits and there is no contrived scheme to avoid Income Tax or NIC on remuneration or to avoid the IR35 rules, HMRC will not seek to argue that a Chapter 4 benefit has been received by the directors because of the exclusion provided by ITEPA03/S447(4) – see ERSM90200. But see ERSM90210 where the exclusion is removed when avoidance is involved.

It follows that to understand the implications for the owner-managed company it is important to understand what is meant by 'a contrived scheme'. The legislation refers to 'purpose' so the answer appears to be a purposeful attempt to avoid tax and NICs with the emphasis on the purposeful pre-ordained nature of the attempt rather than the level of the complication involved in the scheme or arrangement.

Relevant legislation

49.4   In order to address these matters, it is important to give detailed attention to ITEPA 2003, Pt 7, Chap 4. Part 7 is entitled 'Employment Income: Income and Exemptions Relating to Securities' and concerns the taxation of employment-related securities. Part 7, Chapter 4 is explicitly concerned with the taxation of post-acquisition benefits from securities.

It is the amendments to Chapter 4 through FA (No 2) 2005 that have particular relevance to the treatment of dividends received on alphabet shares. The interpretation of FA (No2) 2005, Sch 2 para 18(3)–(4) is that dividends will be treated as employment income, that is remuneration, if the following criteria is met:

- something has been done on or after 2 December 2004;

- which affects the employment-related securities;

- as part of a scheme or arrangement; and

- the main purpose, or one of the main purposes, of which is the avoidance of tax or NICs.

Direct discussions with the HMRC technical office eESSU during 2006 to 2008 have confirmed that these amendments are designed to challenge the commercial credibility of schemes that operate with alphabet shares.

In interpreting this legislation, the need is to address two key questions as follows:

- What is meant by the wording 'something has been done on or after 2 December 2004?'

- What are the ground rules under which the income will be classified as employment income or, alternatively, as a return on a genuine investment?

'Something has been done on or after 2 December 2004'

49.5 It is curious that the legislation does not give further definition or clarification to this phrase. At first sight, it would appear that schemes involving alphabet shares that were set up before 2 December, 2004 may not fall prey to this legislation. This may be the case if the 'something' was, for example, a change in the rights attached to the shares on or after 2 December 2004 or, say, a reclassification of the shares on or after 2 December 2004. However, the HMRC technical office ESSU is clear that the 'something' is the actual payment of the dividend.

If the 'something' is the payment of the dividend, even though the payment is made on or after 2 December 2004, it could still relate to a structure that was established before 2 December 2004.

This legislation is, of course, only concerned with the tax treatment of income as a benefit of the employment. If, then, employees had title to shares that possessed dividend rights but no dividend was paid then no charge to tax or NICs would be triggered under this legislation. It is the payment of the dividend rather than the existence of dividend rights that appears to constitute the offence.

Justification of genuine investment

49.6 The starting point must be to ask the question as to what are the reasons for different levels of dividend. In the discussions with the HRMC ESSU it is clear that this inquisitive approach characterises their scrutiny of arrangements of this nature.

In particular, it is important to establish whether the dividend income is a reward for work effort and application to work requirements or, alternatively, a reward for investment in the company. If the contention is that the dividend income is a reward for investment in the company then the justification must be on the basis of a genuine investment that possesses the characteristics of a genuine investment and is based on definable commercial factors.

In considering the characteristics of a genuine investment it is important to identify the characteristics that would normally be associated with a genuine investment in the general market for the trading of shares. The key questions that should be asked in determining whether or not the dividend income is a reward for a genuine investment in the shares of the company are as follows:

- Does the investment represent an injection of cash funds?

- Do the shares that constitute the investment carry the full set of rights that are normally associated with a share investment?

- Is there a risk of losing the investment as a consequence of either internal company factors or external market factors?

- Could the investment be easily regarded as part of a portfolio of investments?

- Is there evidence of an expectation of dividend income at the time of the initial investment, say through minutes or agreements?

- Does the payment of the dividends represent part of an active and defined dividend policy that would be attractive to other non-employee investors?

- Does the company actively seek non-employee investors in its shares?

- Can the employment and the investment be regarded as separable and, if necessary, be decoupled?

  — would the employment continue in the event that the investment was withdrawn?

  — would the investment be expected to continue in the event that the employment ended?

Payment of commercial salaries

49.7 As well as determining whether or not the investment that supports the payment of the dividend is genuine it is important to determine whether or not the mix of remuneration and dividends is credible. The dividend return on the investment should reflect the level of the investment. Likewise, the remuneration, in the form of salary and bonuses, should reflect the level of the work effort and application to work requirements. There is statistically researched market data available in the marketplace, that available from recognised remuneration consultancies, that can assist in the determination of market remuneration positions for given job profiles in privately-owned companies as well as in the public quoted companies.

The payment of remuneration, in the form of salaries possibly with bonuses, at market-determined rates, implies that any further payment to the employee/director shareholder may be justified by default as something other than remuneration. The importance for market salaries is in contributing to the credibility of the overall commercial arrangement.

HM Treasury discussion paper

49.8 The HM Treasury Department published in December 2004 a discussion paper entitled *Small Companies, the Self-Employed and the Tax System* in which there are strong and meaningful indications on the approach that the British Government is taking on the tax treatment of business income for small companies and the self-employed. The paper compares and contrasts the position of: (1) the small company; and (2) the unincorporated self-employed business and comes to the following conclusions:

> The issues raised ... may suggest that there are underlying tensions in the tax system. In looking at these tensions the Government will want to ensure that the tax regimes strike the right balance between promoting enterprise and growth and ensuring that everyone pays a fair amount of tax and NICs.

> The current system can offer real benefits to a growing company by enhancing the post-tax return on early year profits. At the same time, to a hard working individual who has chosen to remain self-employed, the rules can in some circumstances appear to be giving an unfair advantage to those who have adopted company form for purely tax reasons. The Government wants to ensure that incentives for growth and enterprise do not come to be seen as unfair to others or unduly costly to the Exchequer.

Earlier on in the discussion paper the Government has made it clear that it does not want the tax system to carry a disproportionate influence on normal commercial decision-making and, particularly in its choice of business structure, whether company or sole trader. In this context, the initiative through FA (No 2) 2005 should be seen as an attempt to standardise the tax treatment of rewards from business involvement and to approximate the tax treatment for those who have chosen the corporate structure more closely to those who have chosen to remain self-employed.

The discussion paper also develops the theme of distinguishing between dividends as a return on the shareholder's investment in the company and earnings as a reward for labour. In the language of economics, it wishes to see genuinely commercial returns being made by the two factors of production of capital and labour. In a separate statement, though, the Paymaster General has said that these new measures should not affect genuine employee share schemes. Beyond the discussion paper, the wider political context must be to maximise the inflow of funds to the UK Exchequer through NICs in order to bolster funding for the public services, particularly the National Health Service (NHS) with which the HM Treasury Department has sought to establish a direct funding link with NICs.

Partly-paid shares as an alternative to alphabet shares

49.9   In a genuine investment situation where commercial salaries are paid it is unlikely that the strictures of FA (No 2) 2005, Sch 2 will apply. However, in considering alternative solutions, the so-called *partly-paid share solution* offers potentially a genuine commercial alternative.

Example 49.3: Partly-paid shares as an alternative to alphabet shares

Suppose that each share has a fully paid up amount of £1. However, the applicant pays only 50p per share on allotment. In these circumstances, the shares are considered to be only partly-paid.

Suppose that the declared dividend policy is to pay dividends pro rata to amounts paid up on the shares. This particular shareholder would only receive half of the full dividend declared on each share.

The principle that underpins the partly-paid share solution is that on allotment only part of the nominal value is paid, leaving the balance on call. This principle can then be extended to a number of individuals with different paid-up amounts.

The justification for the partly-paid share solution is that once the cash funds are paid into the company the risk and the exposure are established. With different paid-up amounts the shareholders have different levels of risk and exposure, and the justification for different levels of dividend has a commercial basis for a genuine investment. If the partly-paid share solution is to be introduced, it should be supported by the words 'pro rata to amounts paid up' on the dividend declarations and on the dividend vouchers. This wording should also be included in the board minutes and in the shareholders minutes.

It should be emphasised that the partly-paid share solution may still be challenged by HMRC. However, if commercial salaries are paid and there is a genuine investment basis for the differential dividends then there is an opportunity for a credible defence.

Other challenges to dividends

49.10   Challenges to dividend payments may come other than from the employment-related securities legislation and, in essence, will fall into one of two categories as follows:

Salary sacrifice

49.11   If there are arrangements introduced to sacrifice salary for an equivalent amount of dividend income then that dividend income would be reclassified anyway as employment income under the principle established through the case of *Heaton v Bell* (HL 1969, 46 TC 211, [1969] 2 All ER 70). However, if the individuals are not guaranteed an alternative payment in the event that legal dividends could not be paid then a salary sacrifice may not have been effected. It is important to note, of course, that HMRC would not necessarily have to demonstrate that the dividends are illegal to apply the principle of *Heaton v Bell* (HL 1969, 46 TC 211, [1969] 2 All ER 70) for salary sacrifice.

Legal dividends

49.12 It is a general rule that at the time that a dividend is recommended or declared the company must have sufficient realised reserves. If it does not have sufficient realised reserves the dividend will be illegal and may be repayable.

It is the responsibility of the directors to ensure that the company has available distributable reserves. There is no standard of information specified for a private company although the directors are required to make a reasonable judgement. Where a company has substantial accumulated distributable reserves the level of information required is arguable less than that for a company that at the previous balance sheet date had minimum or negative reserves. In some cases, proper monthly management accounts or similar reliable accounting information may be required to ensure that interim dividends are properly paid. Contemporaneous board minutes must be prepared to approve the dividend.

Specifically in relation to alphabet shares, it may be possible to contend, although it is arguable, that a share that carries only the right to dividends is in fact not a share at all. If this line of argument succeeds then the dividend cannot be a legal dividend as it is a prerequisite for a dividend to be a legal dividend that it is paid on the basis of a genuine share. If a dividend-only share is sustained as a genuine share then its MV on acquisition would be determined on the basis of the expected flow of the dividend income stream.

Conclusions

49.13 The operation of alphabet shares is open to the charge that it is an artificial contrivance and that in reality the dividend income that is paid on the alphabet shares is de facto employment income subject to income tax and NICs. The recognition of the 'something' in FA (No 2) 2005, Sch 2 as the actual payment of the dividend represents an open challenge to alphabet shares that were created before 2 December 2004 as well as those that were created on or after 2 December 2004.

The shares on which the dividends are paid must constitute a genuine investment. All factors must be considered on balance in order to come to a conclusion on this matter. It will be the case that the payment of commercial salaries will support the contention that amounts paid in excess of the market-rate remuneration are something different in kind, namely dividends, provided they represent a return on a genuine investment. The alternative partly-paid share solution should also be considered, provided it is underpinned by strong commercial justification, and careful structuring of the articles of association.

If the shares have been made available to the individuals through transfer in the normal course of domestic, family or personal relationships then they would not normally be regarded as employment-related securities anyway. In these circumstances the onerous provisions of FA (No 2) 2005, Sch 2 would not apply. The shares would then be regarded as constituting a genuine investment arising from domestic, family or personal relationships.

On all matters involving alphabet shares, the message must be to decide upon a course of action only with great care. This must be the caveat to any advice. This approach with clients is, of course, complicated by the fact that alphabet shares have been so commonly used, particularly with small- and medium-sized companies. However, if there is: (1) genuine investment which could be zero for founder shareholders; (2) commercial salaries in place; and (3) no open substitution of remuneration for dividends then the company should be in a position to defend its position.

Chapter 50

Shares in research institution spin-outs companies: Chapter 4A

Introduction

50.1 This chapter explains what is meant by shares in research institution spin-outs companies and the purpose behind its introduction through FA 2005, Pt 2, Chap 3, s 20.

The legislation is effective for shares or an interest in shares acquired before an agreement for the transfer of intellectual property is made or within 183 days beginning with the date on which such an agreement is made if either: (1) the date of acquisition of the shares or an interest in shares; or (2) the date on which the agreement is made; or (3) both of the aforesaid dates, fall on or after 2 December 2004.

Definitions of Chapter 4A

50.2 The reliefs that are given through Chapter 4A and the whole structure of Chapter 4A are based upon a set of definitions that derive from the main concern which is an uplift in the value of the company's shares arising from the transfer of intellectual property from a research institution to a company.

Although under ITEPA 2003, s 456(2) the Treasury may by order amend the definition of intellectual property, under ITEPA 2003, s 456(1) it has a specific meaning as follows:

Category 1

Any patent, trade mark, registered design, copyright or design right, plant breeders' rights or rights under Plant Varieties Act 1997, s 7.

Category 2

Any right under the law of a country or a territory outside the UK that corresponds to or is similar to a right in Category 1.

Category 3

Any information not protected by a right within Category 1 or Category 2 but having industrial, commercial or other economic value.

Category 4

Any licence or other right in respect of anything within Category 1, Category 2 or Category 3.

Category 5

Any goodwill (having the meaning that it has for accounting purposes) associated with anything within any of Category 1, Category 2, Category 3 or Category 4.

Under ITEPA 2003, s 456(3) the meaning of a *transfer of intellectual property* is defined as including the following:

- sale of the intellectual property;

- grant of a licence or other right; and

- assignment of a licence or other right.

Under ITEPA 2003, s 457 a *research institution* is either one of the following:

- Any institution or other publicly funded institution as defined in Higher Education Act 2004, s 41(2).

- Any institution that carries out research activities, otherwise than for profit, and that is neither controlled nor wholly or mainly funded by a person who carries on activities for profit.

The principle behind Chapter 4A

50.3 Chapter 4A, on the basis of these definitions, seeks to protect employees from a charge to income tax under the employment-related securities legislation in respect of intellectual property that is transferred from a research institution to a company unless the employee together with the employer choose to accept a treatment that does give rise to a charge to income tax.

It is important to recognise that Chapter 4A is concerned solely with the transfers of intellectual property from a research institution to a company and the exemption is applicable solely to the value of the intellectual property that is transferred. There may be other inherent value within the company that is not related to the transfer of the intellectual property. However, the protection from a charge to income tax and, indeed, NICs does not extend to property other than the intellectual property.

The precise circumstances in which a charge to income tax could arise, were it not for the provisions of Chapter 4A, are as follows:

(1) Under ITEPA 2003, Part 7, Chapter 4

The company's employees may have been shareholders from the early days when the company had no value. The company receives a transfer of intellectual property and, as a direct consequence of the transfer the MV of its shares rise in value and, potentially, of course, that rise in value could be substantial. The key question, then, pre-Chapter 4A, was whether or not the transfer triggered a charge to income tax on the employees as a post-acquisition benefit under Chapter 4 arising from ownership of the shares.

(2) Under ITEPA 2003, Part 7, Chapter 2

The company's employees may have restricted securities and the restrictions could be lifted at a time when the employees had no cash funds to pay any income tax liability that arose through a higher value being attributed to the company's shares at the time the restrictions are lifted. An example of when the restrictions are lifted may be when the company is admitted to a recognised stock exchange.

(3) Under ITEPA 2003, Part 7, Chapter 3

The company's employees may have convertible shares and on conversion the exposure to income tax arises on shares that in the interim period since their acquisition have risen in value.

The consequences for the employees, provided advantage is taken of the Chapter 4A tax reliefs, are as follows:

- Any gain that is realized through the sale of their shares, however substantial, is subject to the less punitive CGT regime with all the attendant reliefs and exemptions.

- In the event that the company fails, the employees will not be subject to any taxes whatsoever.

The impetus for the introduction of this legislation through FA 2005 came from lobbying, that in turn had emanated from a concern that the charges that could be imposed though the employment-related securities legislation were deterring the formation of university spin-out companies from research institutions. There was, indeed, evidence of a sharp decline in 2003/04 so it was considered by government that some form of corrective action needed to be taken and what is now Chapter 4A is the legislative response and result!

Income tax exemption and income tax reliefs

50.4   Under ITEPA 2003, s 451(1) the circumstances in which Chapter 4A applies are where all of the following elements prevail:

- An intellectual property agreement is completed for the transfer or transfers of intellectual property from a research institution to a spin-out company.

- An individual acquires shares or an interest in shares in the spin-out company before the intellectual property agreement is made or within 183 days beginning with the date in which it is made.

- The right or opportunity for the individual to acquire the shares or an interest in the shares has arisen by reason of the individual's employment with either the research institution or the spin-out company.

- The individual is involved in research in relation to the intellectual property that is the subject of the intellectual property agreement.

Under ITEPA 2003, s 452(2) the exemptions and reliefs of Chapter 4A are not available if the avoidance of tax or NICs represents the main purpose or one of the main purposes of the arrangements under which the right or the opportunity to acquire the shares or interest in shares is made available.

The tax reliefs that are available are identified in Chapter 4A as:

- Under ITEPA 2003, s 452 tax relief that is available on acquisition.

- Under ITEPA 2003, s 453 tax relief that is available following acquisition.

- Under ITEPA 2003, s 454 a deemed tax election for securities that are treated as restricted securities under ITEPA 2003, Pt 7, Chap 2.

- Under ITEPA 2003, s 455 the disapplication of the tax provisions in relation to securities that are treated as having an artificially enhanced value under ITEPA 2003, Pt 7, Chap 3B.

The precise way in which these tax reliefs operate is explained as follows.

Tax relief that is available on acquisition

50.5 The key determining factor in establishing this tax relief is the market value:

- The tax relief that is available on acquisition is predicated on the basis of the calculation of the MV. For purposes of Chapter 4A, MV specifically disregards the effect on MV of the existence of the intellectual property agreement and any transfer of the intellectual property that has been made under that agreement.

- The effect that this MV calculation will have in many spin-out situations is to reduce dramatically the MV for purposes of Chapter 4A and in the case of a newly formed spin-out company, may quite possibly reduce MV to a negligible position.

The relevant tax purposes to which this MV position will apply are as follows:

- For the earnings charge under ITEPA 2003, s 62 within ITEPA 2003, Pt 3, Chap 1, where a charge to income tax can arise on any discount that is given on MV at the date of acquisition.

- For the convertible securities legislation under ITEPA 2003, Pt 7, Chap 3 where a charge to income tax can arise on a gain resulting from a chargeable event.

- For the notional loan arrangements under ITEPA 2003, Pt 7, Chap 3C where MV needs to be determined for any charge to income tax.

- For any amount that is to be treated as employment income under ITEPA 2003, Pt 7, Chap 5 arising from the exercise of a securities option.

Tax relief that is available following acquisition

50.6 The relief from income tax that applies after the acquisition of the shares is where a post-acquisition event occurs sometime after acquisition and the effect of that event would be to enable the employee to receive value. The amount that is subject to income tax in these circumstances is nil and that, very simply, is the basis of the relief.

The events that are anticipated by this provision are either of the following where they take place after (which may not be immediately after, but sometime after) the acquisition of the shares:

- the signing of the intellectual property agreement; and

- the actual transfer of the intellectual property from the research institution to the spin-out company.

The relief is not available if something has been done at or before the signing of the agreement, or the transfer of the intellectual property that is part of a scheme or arrangement where one of the main purposes is the avoidance of tax or NICs.

Deemed tax election for restricted securities

50.7 The tax election that is available under ITEPA 2003, s 431(1) is deemed to have been made in circumstances; where the shares are restricted securities or the interest in shares is a restricted interest in securities. This provision addresses another of the express concerns of the lobbyists, namely the requirement for a relief for income tax for the employees in circumstances where there is a lifting of restrictions.

The opt-out opportunity from the deemed tax election that is available under ITEPA 2003, s 431(2) would appear to cater for circumstances in which there is already inherent value in the shares quite independently of the intellectual property. The effect of the deemed tax election would be to establish a charge to income tax on the unrestricted MV in circumstances where that value did not disregard inherent value. If it is considered expedient to opt-out from the deeming arrangement then there must be an agreement from both the employee and the employer which is irrevocable, that is made through the HMRC standard form and which must be made within 14 days of the acquisition of the shares.

If the opt-out is put in place for the RSR then the unrestricted MV at the date of acquisition of the shares is calculated disregarding the effect on that value of the intellectual property agreement or any intellectual property transfer that has been made in accordance with the agreement.

The impact of this provision is take the charge to income tax on the value of the intellectual property back to the date of acquisition of the shares at which point the gain was exempt anyway.

Disapplication of the enhanced value provisions

50.8 This disapplication operates very simply by treating the signing of the intellectual property agreement and any intellectual property transfer pursuant to that agreement as genuine commercial arrangements. In other words, these events are not treated as creating an artificial enhancement to the share value.

HMRC Form 42 reporting requirements

50.9 For intellectual property, assuming that the exemption and the reliefs apply, there will never be a charge to income tax or NICs and all gain will be subject to CGT on sale. There is, though, a reporting requirement under the HMRC Form 42: under Section 2, 'Acquisition of securities (including shares)', and under Section 3e, 'Receipt of other benefits from securities'. The requirement is to provide event information, to record that the MV has been affected by a spin-out and to report the receipt of a benefit that, were it not for the provisions of Chapter 4A, would generate an amount that was subject to a charge to income tax.

Chapter 51

Earn-outs

Introduction

51.1   This chapter considers the nature of an earn-out and the potential tax treatment that results from the interaction with the employment-related securities legislation.

The chapter of the employment-related securities legislation that governs the tax treatment of earn-outs will depend upon the nature of the earn-out as follows:

- For earn-outs that are securities options Chapter 5 applies to the exercise of options after 1 September 2003.

- For earn-outs that are restricted securities Chapter 2 applies for restricted securities that are acquired on or after 16 April 2003 that vested from 1 September 2003.

- For earn-outs that are convertible securities Chapter 3 applies effective from 1 September 2003 regardless of the date of acquisition of the securities.

Nature of an earn-out

51.2   An earn-out is part of the consideration for the sale of a business by a vendor. However, it is deferred consideration. It is a recognised common sense approach to organising the transfer of ownership and control from the vendor to the purchaser and is accepted by HMRC as a credible technique effecting a smooth transition.

The sale will typically be for: (1) a cash sum or an issue of securities plus; (2) an earn-out as an additional element of deferred consideration.

The earn-out is commonly regarded as a securities option to purchase shares in an acquiring company. However, in practical business, it may take *any one of a number of forms* as follows:

Securities option under Chapter 5

51.3   A right to receive loan notes (issued by the purchaser) after a certain period has elapsed and dependent on the performance of the newly taken-over business. The loan notes would be redeemable after a certain period or periods of time.

Securities option under Chapter 5

51.4 A right to receive securities in the purchaser or its parent company after a certain period has elapsed, dependent on the performance of the newly taken-over business. These securities may or not have restrictions placed on them.

Restricted securities under Chapter 2

51.5 A right to receive restricted (forfeitable) securities (shares or loan notes) that are issued by the purchaser and which vest after certain performance targets have been reached.

Convertible securities under Chapter 3

51.6 A right to receive convertible securities that are issued by the purchaser and which convert into a more valuable security after certain performance targets have been met.

The practical circumstances in which an earn-out can arise are as follows:

- The vendor and the purchaser may have difficulty in agreeing a fair value for the business at the time of sale. In order to resolve the situation the purchaser chooses to retain a part of the consideration for a period of time over which the performance of the business will be assessed and on the basis of that assessment the final consideration will be agreed. The part retained is the earn-out.

- The purchaser may take the view that he or she wants the vendor to remain in the business, usually as an employee, so he or she makes the payment of part of the consideration conditional upon the vendor in continuing employment for an agreed period of time which is usually not more than one to two years although the precise time period will depend on the circumstances. The conditional element is the earn-out.

Position taken by HMRC

51.7 The summary position that is taken by HMRC is set out in the *HMRC Manual ERSM110910* on Chapter 5 as follows:

- In quoting Dawn Primarolo, the then Paymaster General, during the passage of FA2003 through Parliament, the *HMRC Manual ERSM110910* states:

A point to emphasise here is that the rules introduced by Schedule 22 seek to tax value obtained by reason of employment.

The HMRC guidance juxtaposes two key statements that balance their position.

- *For CGT treatment*

Where an earn-out operates entirely to cover further proceeds of sale, with no element of remuneration then income tax and National Insurance Contributions should not be payable.

- *For income tax treatment*

    Where an earn-out includes an element which passes value to a prospective employee of the acquiring company as reward for services over a performance period then that remuneration element should be within the charge to income tax and National Insurance Contributions.

HMRC accepts that earn-outs are a necessary part of many company sales and has developed through *HMRC Manual ERSM110940* a set of key indicators to determine whether the earn-out is:

1. sale consideration and, therefore, capital gain; or

2. remuneration reward and, therefore, employment income:

Key indicator 1

The content of the sale agreement (sometimes titled *Sale and purchase agreement* (SPA)) as indicated through its terms supports the position that the earn-out is part of valuable consideration given for the securities in the company that has been sold.

Key indicator 2

The value received from the earn-out must reflect the value of the securities given up.

Key indicator 3

If there is an agreement for the vendor to continue to be employed in the business after the business has been sold, the earn-out must not be compensation for the vendor not being fully remunerated for continuing employment with the company. The earn-out must not be a substitute for a competitive salary.

Key indicator 4

If there is an agreement for the vendor to continue to be employed in the business after the business has been sold, the earn-out must not be conditional upon the future employment of the vendor other than for a period that is adjudged necessary to protect the value of the business. For a sense of what is considered to be an appropriate period the company must establish this period on the basis of a reasonable requirement to stay with a view to protecting value.

Key indicator 5

If there is an agreement for the vendor to continue to be employed in the business after the business has been sold, the payment of the earn-out must not be conditional on the achievement of personal performance targets. If there linkage to performance targets at all, and this will often be the case as, in essence, it is why the earn-out has been put in place, then those performance targets must be corporate performance targets rather than personal performance targets.

Key indicator 6

The basis on which remaining employees receive the earn-out is on the same terms as the basis on which the former employees or non-employees receive the earn-out. The former shareholders who continue as employees must not be seen to benefit from their employment status within the company, however temporary or permanent that employment is considered to be.

In addition to the key indicators, HMRC state that the following three factors will be relevant in assessing the earn-out for capital gain or employment income:

Factor 1

The nature and content of the negotiations between the vendor and the purchaser should be evidenced and, in particular, on the matter of determining the level of the earn-out in relation to the value of the consideration given for the securities in the company. In this regard, the records of the negotiations should be kept in order to provide the appropriate evidence of the decision-making that has led to the agreements.

Factor 2

The case for establishing that the earn-out is capital gain rather than employment income could be strengthened by obtaining clearances: (1) under TCGA 1992, s 138; and (2) under ICTA 1988, s 707, that the nature of the transactions is bona fide and the level of the earn-out that is linked to the profitability of the business or other key performance indicators of the business.

Factor 3

The case for establishing that the earn-out is capital gain rather than employment income would be weakened by any evidence that future bonuses had been reclassified or commuted into purchase consideration.

Real life case study

Suppose that ABC Ltd (the company) is to be purchased by XYZ Ltd (the purchaser) and that the transaction is to be governed by the SPA. The purchaser has offered Mr and Mrs ABC ('the vendors') contracts of employment XYZ Ltd.

Sale and purchase agreement

A study of the SPA specifically with regard to the implications for income tax arising from the employment-related securities legislation reveals the following:

- The terms of the SPA allow for 'additional consideration' to arise for the sale of the shares in ABC Ltd to XYZ Ltd.

- The terms of the SPA stipulate that 'any additional consideration' will be payable in the form of loan notes that are to be issued by the Purchaser to Mr and Mrs ABC.

The best interpretation is that 'any additional consideration' represents a deferred consideration earn-out that is linked to the corporate growth and performance of the business as specified in the SPA. There is no indication in the SPA that the earn-out is linked to any personal performance targets for Mr and Mrs ABC.

The earn-out will be in the form of loan notes. Under ITEPA 2003, s 420(1)(b) 'securities' includes 'debentures, debenture stock, *loan stock*, bonds, certificates of deposit and other instruments creating or acknowledging indebtedness [(other than contracts of insurance)],' The definition of 'securities', therefore, includes loan notes that give the potential for the ownership of loan stock at some point in the future.

Advice to Mr & Mrs ABC

In applying the employment-related securities legislation, it is important to recognize that where an earn-out is designed to cover further proceeds of sale and the earn-out does not include any element of remuneration then there should be no charge arising to either income tax or NICs. The reverse of this situation is where the earn-out includes an element that passes value to the prospective employee of the acquiring company as a reward for services over a performance period, in which circumstances a charge will arise to income tax and NICs in relation to the part of the earn-out that falls into this category.

In the case of Mr and Mrs ABC, the earn-out takes the form of a right to acquire securities (loan stock) at some time in the future. This arrangement would constitute the grant of a securities option under ITEPA 2003, s 471(3) if it was made available by reason of an employment. It is clear from the SPA that the purchaser does not have the choice of paying the earn-out in cash or securities. If the purchaser had this choice between cash and securities then it would be undoubtedly the case that the arrangement would not constitute the grant of a securities option for purposes of Chapter 5. Specifically in the case of Mr and Mrs ABC, the provisions of ITEPA 2003, s 471(3) will not give rise to an income tax charge as the right to acquire the securities is considered to be by reason of the sale arrangement rather than by reason of either their former or prospective employment.

The earn-out is, therefore, further consideration for the disposal of their shares in the company rather than value obtained by reason of their former or prospective employment. The value of the securities exchanged for the earn-out will be taken to be equal to the value of the securities acquired under the earn-out itself and no charge to income tax or NICs will arise under Chapter 5 in relation to employment-related securities. It is explicitly the case that these conclusions have no bearing on the rules for calculating CGT.

The key indicators (as explained above) must be addressed, therefore, in order to determine the status of the earn-out as either: (1) sale consideration; and therefore, capital gain; or (2) remuneration reward; and therefore, employment income:

Key indicator 1

The SPA is clear that the earn-out to Mr and Mrs ABC is 'by way of additional consideration' for their shares. The content of the SPA supports, therefore, the position that the earn-out is part of valuable consideration given for the securities in the company that has been sold.

Key indicator 2

The evidence taken from the records of the negotiations including the supporting share valuation calculations indicates that the value received from the earn-out reflects the value of the securities given up.

Key indicator 3

Mr and Mrs ABC are to receive under their new contracts of employment remuneration that is determined at market levels. Independent advice has been received from an independent remuneration consultancy for purposes of determining their salaries.

Key indicator 4

From a detailed examination of the contracts of employment, there does not appear to be any evidence that the contracts of employment are linked to the earn-out given under the SPA. Both Mr and Mrs ABC are expected to stay in the employment of the company for at least 18 months that is adjudged to be a reasonable requirement in order to protect the value of the company.

Key indicator 5

The targets that are set out in the SPA are not personal performance targets and, furthermore, there is no mention whatsoever in the contracts of employment of personal performance targets or, indeed, the earn-out.

Key indicator 6

There are no shareholders other than Mr and Mrs ABC so the comparison with non-employees or former employees is not required.

The conclusion, on the basis of the documents and the evidence available, is that the earn-out arrangement represents sale consideration subject to capital gain rather than any form of employment income.

Chapter 52

Share loan schemes

Introduction

52.1 The chapter explains the opportunity for the share loan scheme that has arisen from the changes that have been introduced through the CA 2006 and involves the purchase of shares by an employee, usually at director or senior executive level, through a loan advanced to him by the company.

Change in the legislation

52.2 The changes in the legislation that facilitate the share loan scheme to directors are orchestrated through CA 2006 as follows:

- Under CA 2006, s 197(1) with effect from 1 October 2007, the general prohibition on loans to directors is abolished and replaced with a shareholder approval for all companies that allow loans, quasi-loans and guarantees to directors and connected persons.

- Under CA 2006, s 197(2)–(4) a written memorandum with the details of the loan must be made available to shareholders before approval is given. Additionally, under CA 2006, s 198 all companies can enter into credit transactions with their directors if shareholder approval has been obtained.

- Under CA 2006, s 213 if shareholder approval is not obtained and there is a breach of the requirements then the transaction is voidable.

There are exemptions available under CA 2006 as follows:

- — under CA 2006, s 207(1) for loans up to £10,000;

- — under CA 2006, s 204(2) for expense accounts up to £50,000; and

- — under CA 2006, s 205 for an advance for defence costs (including regulatory proceedings).

Effect of this change in the legislation

52.3 The effects of this change in the legislation are as follows:

- As a general rule of thumb, the need arises for a loan to be advanced to a director in circumstances where either the director needs to fund the exercise of an option or he or she is required to fund an immediate purchase of shares at MV. These new rules create the opportunity for new deferred payment schemes for directors of public companies, whether executive directors or non-executive directors.

- The new provisions enable the directors of public companies, executive or non-executive, to participate in share loan schemes without the need for an employee benefit trust arrangement.

The full effect of this change is understood when it is appreciated that prior to this change to the legislation on 1 October 2007, under CA 1985, s 330, there was a prohibition on the making of a loan by a company to a director of the company or of its holding company, subject to certain exceptions. Furthermore, there was no 'employees' share scheme' exception for loans to directors to acquire shares. This meant that any loan arrangement to a director had to be from a friendly third party and structured very carefully indeed, in order to avoid an offence.

Appropriateness of share loan scheme

52.4 The share loan scheme arrangement is most appropriate in circumstances where a director is expected to meet share ownership targets soon after joining the company or within a short timescale, say, typically, within one year of joining. Where these targets are set, the company expectation will usually be for the director to acquire at least some of the shares at current market value as a straight purchase, quite apart from any shares that he or she may expect to purchase later through involvement in the company's bona fide employee share schemes. However, it is often the case that the director does not have the readily disposable funds available to make the investment.

This change to the legislation enables the company to provide the funding to the director in the form of a loan so that he or she can make the investment. The director is thereby enabled to become an actual shareholder from the outset of the arrangement with no upfront cost from his or her own resources. There is also for the director the key tax advantages as this structure establishes a position whereby all growth in the value of the shares is captured within the CGT regime rather than the more punitive income tax regime and there is no charge to tax at all at the date of acquisition. The potential downside for the director is that the director is at risk of exposure to loan repayment without available resources in the event of a falling share price.

Structure of the share loan scheme

52.5 The structure of the share loan scheme involves a minimal series of transactions and typically could operate as follows:

- The company lends funds to the director.

- The director applies the funds to subscribing for new issue shares in the company or purchasing the shares at MV in the open market through a stockbroker purchasing them through the recognised stock exchange.

- If the director leaves the company as 'a bad leaver', which in broad terms is usually defined as leaving through resignation or dismissal, then the shares must be offered for sale at the lower of the acquisition cost and the MV at the date of leaving the company.

- On exiting the company, the director sells the shares and the purchase price is deducted from the proceeds of sale in order to make funds available for extinguishing the liability that has been created by the loan. The arrangement is analogous to 'the tail-swallowing technique' with the purchase cost paid for out of the sale proceeds but with a loan period that is longer than a settlement period.

Tax implications of the share loan scheme

52.6 The tax implications are generally advantageous for the director and are as follows:

- There is no income tax or NICs arising on the purchase of the shares for the reason that the director has paid MV for the shares at the date of acquisition. What has happened is that the funding from the company artificially creates the circumstances in which the director has the monies to make a MV purchase. There is, therefore, no exposure to income tax for the director under ITEPA 2003, s 62.

- The growth in the share value following the purchase of the shares is captured by the more tax friendly CGT regime. In other words, the acquisition of the shares is treated as would be an acquisition by any individual in the shares of the company and on the sale of the shares the capital tax annual exemption limit is available in the normal way.

- The benefit of the loan is subject to annual income tax that is collected through the P11D system rather than through PAYE and although employer's NICs are payable there is no exposure to employee's NICs.

Example 52.1

Suppose that the MV of the shares is £10,000 and the director enters into an agreement to pay £10,000 for the shares but with a deferment to pay, say, for example, until there is a change of control.

Suppose that the director has a marginal rate of income tax of 40%.

The annual P11D benefit arising from the employment

= the unpaid price (the loan) × the statutory rate of 4.75%

The income tax charge

= £10,000 × 4.75% × 40% = £189.60

- Where the bad leaver offers the shares for sale at the lower of cost and MV and the share price falls, then the bad leaver makes a capital loss for which there is no income tax relief.

- If the loan is written-off or waived for any reason then the unpaid balance is subject to income tax, which is collected through the PAYE system and NICs are due.

- There is no notional loan under ITEPA 2003, Pt 7, Chap 3C in circumstances where the director makes the acquisition at MV and there is no deferred consideration for the reason that the MV is the agreed purchase price.

- In its 'plain vanilla' form as explained in this chapter, the arrangement does not facilitate statutory corporation tax relief under FA 2003, Sch 23 for the reason that there is, in the technical sense, no gain in the hands of the employee on the acquisition of the shares. However, it is important to note that corporation tax relief will usually be available for any loan write-off or waiver or any bonus that is paid to enable the repayment of the loan.

- For the close company the structure should be implemented in a way that avoids the 25% charge on loans to participators under ICTA 1988, s 419. At the very least the director should not purchase shares from a participator. However, in the case of a close company, careful structuring is required in order to manage the implications of ICTA 1988, s 419 and the director should take quality tax advice at the time of the acquisition.

Wider legal implications of the share loan scheme

52.7 The wider legal implications of the share loan scheme are as follows:

- The loan involvement and any involvement from an employee share trust will constitute financial assistance under CA 2006, ss 678–680 (CA 1985, s 151), although as a bona fide employee share scheme under CA 2006, s 1166 (CA 1985, s 743), there is the employee share schemes exception available under CoA 2006, s 682(2)(c) (CA 1985, s 153(4)(b)).

- Under the prospectus rules, the arrangement may be classified as an offer of shares to the public, depending on the circumstances of the company at the time.

Summary of the corporate advantages

52.8 The corporate advantages of the share loan scheme are summarised as follows:

- The executives have the opportunity to purchase shares at the outset of the arrangement, thereby becoming real shareholders and facilitating 'the identity of interest' immediately with the other shareholders of the company.

- There is for the company a reduced exposure to an accounting charge within the profit and loss account. In essence, the director has purchased shares from funds to which he or she has been given title through the loan advance.

Purchase of shares through bonus monies

52.9   Instead of advancing a loan to the director, the company may decide to make a bonus payment to the director in order to fund his or her purchase of the shares. The bonus payment will be subject to income tax and NICs through the PAYE system in the normal way and, as with the share loan scheme, there is no corporation tax relief under FA 2003, Sch 23. However, there is corporation tax relief for the bonus payment and it may be that the acquisition is being funded when the share price is comparatively low. When a discounted cash flow analysis is performed to test the viability of the bonus funding, it often produces surprisingly favourable results!

Chapter 53

Subsidiary company share schemes

Introduction

53.1 The chapter explains how the provisions of FA 2003 facilitate the introduction of an employee share scheme on a tax-efficient basis using the shares of a company that is a subsidiary of a holding company that is unquoted. The chapter uses a step-by-step approach to explain the practical approach to the introduction of a subsidiary company share scheme, based on the shares of a wholly-owned subsidiary company.

Background

53.2 Prior to FA 2003, the dependent subsidiaries legislation represented a serious impediment on the introduction of a tax-efficient employee share scheme using the shares of a subsidiary company. Even when the dependent subsidiaries legislation was in force there was always the opportunity under the tax-approved savings-related share option scheme, the tax-approved company share option scheme and the tax-approved share incentive scheme, to introduce a tax-approved share scheme into a company that was under the control of a company whose shares are quoted on a recognised stock exchange. There was, though, no such opportunity afforded by the tax-approved legislation for an unquoted company that was under the control of another unquoted company. Furthermore, if caught by the dependent subsidiaries legislation, the scheme participants could only participate in a tax-inefficient scheme with gain subject to income tax.

Courtesy of FA 2003, the dependent subsidiaries legislation is no longer on the statute book. The subsidiary company can, therefore, introduce a tax-unapproved employee share scheme without fear of the punitive charges that the dependent subsidiaries legislation had imposed and, when combined with the tax elections that are available under the restricted securities legislation, the opportunity is available to introduce a highly tax-efficient employee share scheme.

Approach

53.3 The approach to establishing an employee share scheme using the shares of a subsidiary company that is under the 100% control of an unquoted company is as follows:

Step 1: To create a new class of shares

The initial requirement is to create a new class of shares for purposes of the employee share scheme. Typically the existing class of shares will have a nominal value of, say, for example, £1 per share. The new class of shares should have a nominal value of £0.01 per share, or maybe even less, in order to reduce the amount that the employee share scheme participants have to pay per share on the purchase of the shares. Under CA 2006, s 580 (CA 1985, s 100) shares cannot be issued at less than their nominal value so it is important for purposes of reducing the cost outlay by the scheme participants on the acquisition of the shares for the nominal value to be low. The rights of these new shares in the subsidiary company share scheme are normally limited to capital rights only with no dividend rights and no voting rights. These shares will, therefore, be treated as restricted securities under ITEPA 2003, Pt 7, Chap 2.

Step 2: To alter the Articles of Association

The Articles of Association of the subsidiary company must be altered to reflect the creation of this new class of shares and the rights that are attached to the new class of shares. These amendments must be supported by the shareholders' resolution and the directors' minutes together with the submission to Companies House Form 123 to register the increase in the nominal capital.

Step 3: To establish the share value

It is necessary at the outset of the scheme preparation to determine the value of the new shares. If the company is a start-up arrangement then, in these circumstances, it should be possible to demonstrate that the MV of the shares is restricted to the nominal value. Even if the company is trading and making profits, depending on the rights that are attached to the respective classes of shares, and the amendments that have been made to the Articles of Association to reflect these rights, it may be possible to establish the new class of shares as having a MV that is no more than nominal value. It may, indeed, be possible to establish the new class of shares as growth shares, again with a low MV (as explained in Chapter 54 Growth Shares) if the rights of the existing class of shares are sufficiently substantial to attract all current value to them.

Step 4: To grant an employee share option

The employees who have been nominated as share scheme participants should then be granted a share option under a tax-unapproved employee share option scheme with the opportunity for an early exercise. The introduction of a share option scheme at this stage means that the issue of shares to the employees is dependent on their own decision to exercise the option. The shares could be dispensed from an employee share trust if the company has decided to fund a trust with funds to subscribe for the new shares. The option price should be no more than the nominal value of the shares over which the option is granted. The date of exercise of the option represents an income tax point. However, the income tax is calculated by reference to the market value of the shares at the date of exercise that happens to be equal to the low option price. Although the date of exercise is an income tax point, therefore, the income tax arising is nil and the liability to NICs is nil.

Step 5: To make the joint tax election with the company

Immediately following the purchase of the shares each of the share scheme participants, together with the company, should make a joint tax election within the RSR under ITEPA 2003, s 431 for the purchase of the shares to be income taxed at unrestricted MV. Although this election is an administrative matter with minimal bureaucracy, it has the powerful effect of protecting the share scheme participants from future income tax liabilities. The election has to be made within 14 days of the purchase of the shares. Given the negligible value of the shares no charge to income tax will arise. The share purchase, though, must be declared on the HMRC Form 42 However, the importance of the tax election is to ensure that all future gain that attaches to these shares after the date of acquisition will be subject to the CGT regime and definitely not the income tax regime. It is, of course, the use of the tax election that ensures that the treatment of the gain under the provisions of FA 2003 is so very different from the treatment under the pre-FA 2003 dependent subsidiaries legislation. The section 431 tax election form does not have to be filed with HMRC but should be kept in a safe place, typically with the statutory books or sometimes with the payroll records.

Step 6: To secure a post-transaction valuation check

The share valuation, albeit at a negligible value, should be submitted to HMRC through the HMRC Form CG34 for a post-transaction valuation check. The submission should be supported by a share valuation report. The fact that the employee share scheme is neither a tax-approved scheme nor the government-sponsored EMI prevents the company from securing a pre-transaction check. It is, though, best practice, in these circumstances, to secure the agreement of HMRC on the share value as soon as possible after the transaction.

Step 7: To introduce a shareholders' agreement

The ongoing shareholding that the share scheme participants possess (as a consequence of the exercise of their options) should be governed by a shareholders agreement to which share scheme participants and the parent company are the parties. The sale and transfer provisions that are agreed for inclusion in the shareholders' agreement should also be included in the Articles of Association.

Step 8: To arrange for the sale of the shares

When introducing an employee share scheme, it should always be the case at the time of introduction that the company is aware of how value will be delivered to the employees at the maturity of the scheme arrangement. Typically, the sale of the shares would be to an employee share trust in order to secure the CGT treatment for the sale and, indeed, this is safest way to secure the CGT treatment. There is, though, an alternative available, namely for the shares to be sold to the parent company. If this alternative is adopted then the sale would not be treated as a purchase of own shares and should fall within the CGT regime.

Corporation tax deduction

53.4 The corporation tax deduction under FA 2003, Sch 23 is never available under subsidiary company share schemes as under the definition of 'The company whose shares are acquired' in paragraph 6 for awards of shares, and in paragraph 12 for grants of option the company must be independent.

Employee share trust

53.5 The company may choose to introduce the employee share trust at the time the employee share scheme is established and make the contribution of funds to the employee share trust to enable it to subscribe for the new shares. These shares will then be dispensed to the employees in order to satisfy the exercise of the options. The employee share trust will then be available as the market for sale of the shares at the appropriate juncture in the future.

The following diagrams depict the following two scenarios:

- the purchase of shares from the trust following the exercise of the options; and
- the sale of shares to the parent company in the absence of a trust.

Employee share ownership – subsidiary company share scheme

53.4 Please refer to diagrams on the following page.

1. Employee purchase from the employee share trust

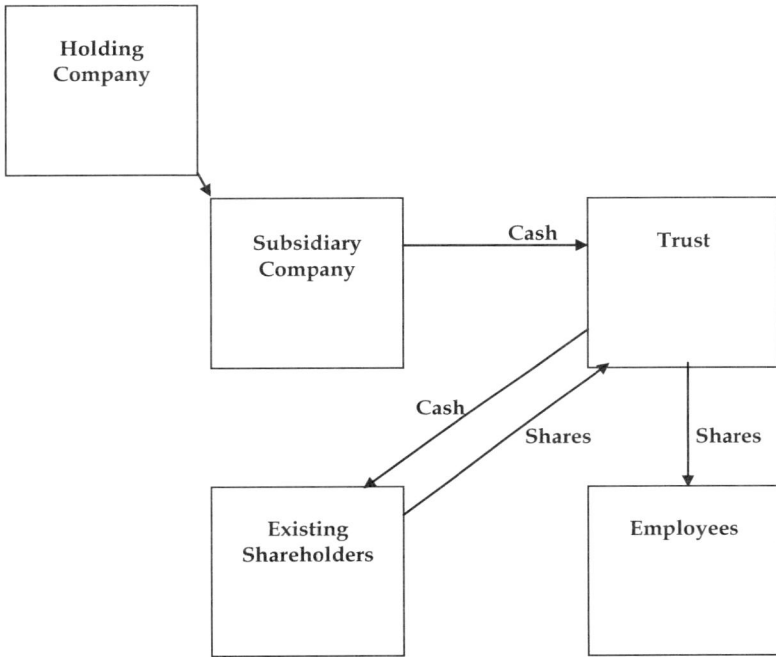

2. Employee sale to holding company as a CGT transaction

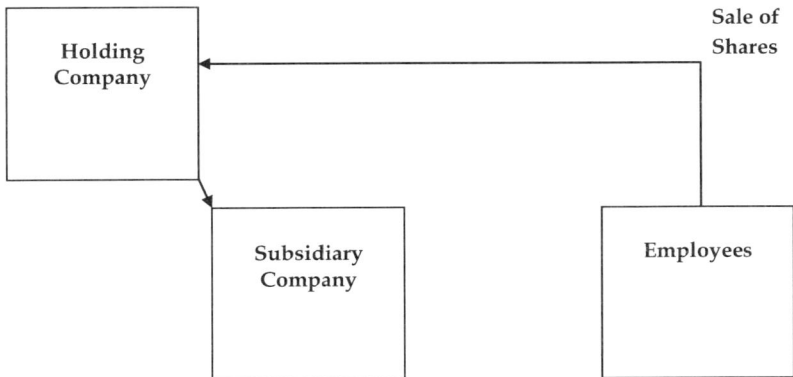

Chapter 54

Growth shares

Introduction

54.1 This chapter explains how growth shares have the potential to provide a powerful incentive to scheme participants and, when combined with value freezing, to establish the whole of the gain within the CGT regime.

The principle behind growth shares

54.2 The principle behind growth shares is that a separate new class of shares is created that has no dividend rights and no voting rights but has full capital rights in the event of a takeover of the company, a sale of trade and assets of the company, the admission of the company to a recognised stock exchange or a winding-up of the company. At the date of creation of this new class of shares their value is no more than their nominal value, say £0.01 or maybe even less. The reason for this low value is that as part of a reclassification of the share capital the other new class of shares that is created is given substantial rights indeed and is classified as a class of preference shares. The rights for the preference shares include full voting rights, full dividend rights and full capital rights. The values attached to the dividend rights and the capital rights are enshrined in the Articles of Association at the date of the reclassification. It is from these rights that it is established that the full value of the company at the date of the reclassification, the value freeze, is attributable to the preference shares. However, the preference shares will never be more than the value attributed to them at the date of the reclassification so that all future growth in the value of the company from the date of the reclassification attaches to the new ordinary shares that are called, therefore, 'the growth shares'.

The creation of growth share represents is a highly flexible approach to an incentive, carrying high levels of tax-efficiency. Ironically, though, both its flexibility and its tax-efficiency derive from the general tax legislation rather than the tax-approved legislation. The growth share approach is not dictated in any way whatsoever by tax-approved legislation; rather it draws upon two elements of the general tax legislation in order to facilitate a high flexibility and tax-efficiency. These two elements of the general legislation that are operative for growth shares when combined with value freezing are: (1) the share reorganisation provisions within TCGA 1992, ss 126–131; and (2) the share valuation provisions within TCGA 1992, s 272.

It is important to be aware that value freezing should not be undertaken unless there are clear non-tax avoidance reasons for freezing the value. An example of a clear non-tax avoidance reason is to protect the value of existing shareholders' wealth.

Objectives of growth shares

54.3 The general objectives of the growth shares is to establish a high motivation tax-efficient share scheme arrangement for the employee scheme participants which are typically the senior executives of the company although the scheme can be extended to the wider employee workforce.

The specific objectives of the growth shares approach are as follows:

- To provide all the incentive and motivational qualities of an employee share scheme with a view to uniting the executive management team and/or employee workforce in contributing to the value of the company through a shareholding in a growth ordinary share capital.

- To enable the executive management team and/or employee workforce to acquire a shareholding in the company that allows each of them to participate in the future capital growth of the company and achieve a realised gain either during the natural life of the company or on exit, typically through a sale to an independent third party acquiring company in the event of a takeover.

- To ensure that the existing shareholders continue to exercise voting control over the decisions of the company and to protect for the existing shareholders the value that the company has created during the life of the company to date, in particular through ensuring that their position is not compromised or undermined in any way through the introduction of the employee share scheme.

The shares of the ultimate holding company are the shares that are typically used for purposes of this share scheme arrangement. However, this share purchase scheme can be linked to the shares of the subsidiary company, if that is so desired.

On the eligibility criteria, the growth share approach is usually introduced as a discretionary arrangement for the participation of executives only. There is no statutory compulsion for the scheme to operate on an all-employee basis although there is no reason why the concepts should not operate equally for an all-employee scheme.

Operation of growth shares

54.4 The operation of the scheme is designed to secure for each of the new participant executives and/or employees a shareholding at the outset in a class of low value ordinary shares that have the potential for significant growth in value over a period of time. Under this arrangement, the names of the scheme participants appear as shareholders in the company on the share register from the inception of the share scheme arrangement for the reason that they are shareholders in their own right. It may, though, be the case that the shares are purchased through the exercise of a share option, typically EMI or the company share option scheme.

The Articles of Association or, alternatively, some other shareholder agreement, should contain covenants that in circumstances where the scheme participants cease to be employees the company can require them to offer their shares for sale to existing shareholders or to a share scheme employee benefit trust, if such a trust exists at the time of the sale.

The advantages for the existing shareholders are as follows:

- The existing shareholders retain 100% of the new preference shares, containing the wealth of the business that has accumulated to date, and a significant proportion of the new ordinary shares. The actual proportion owned by the existing shareholders is a matter of complete flexibility.

- The existing shareholders may choose to hold a proportion of the new ordinary shares. The precise proportions agreed require further discussion. The existing shareholders would then be diluting their actual ordinary shareholding. However, the arrangement offers the opportunity for accelerated growth in the value of the new ordinary shares through a highly motivated group of executives and/or employees, resulting in a higher share value for the new ordinary shares from which existing shareholders *and* executives/employees will benefit.

The advantages for the executives/employees are as follows:

- The executives/employees benefit from any rise in the value of the new ordinary shares, with a high potential upside.

- The executives/employees take minimal risk with the requirement to make a minimal monetary contribution for the purchase of the new ordinary shares.

- The executives/employees are able to use CGT treatment on any gain that accrues following the share reclassification and, indeed, secure the CGT reliefs and exemptions.

Capital tax implications of growth shares

54.5 The capital gains tax implications of growth shares are as follows.

Share reclassification

54.6 The reclassification of the shares is, in essence, a reorganisation of shares and, as a consequence, will *not* trigger a CGT disposal for the existing shareholders. The relevant tax sections are TCGA 1992, ss 126–131. This view is supported by the HMRC *Capital Gains Tax Manual* CG51781, that states as follows:

> *Share reorganisations: alteration of rights: only one class of share*
>
> In strictness TCGA92/S126 (2)(b) would only apply if there was more than one class of share in issue before the reorganisation. You can accept that it will also apply if there is only one class of share before the reorganisation.

Furthermore, value shifting as defined under TCGA 1992, s 29 does not arise. The share reclassification affects all existing shareholders pro rata to their shareholdings and so does not favour one shareholder over another. It follows that the value of any shareholder's entire shareholding in the company will not be diminished by the share reclassification.

The subsequent issue of new ordinary shares to the new share scheme participants for cash, albeit at the low nominal value which is also the MV, should not materially affect the current value of other existing shareholdings. If shares were to be issued to employees at a significant undervalue or otherwise so as to cause a material reduction in the value of the shareholdings of existing shareholders then the position should be re-examined. However, this is not the case in this situation. In practice, under this scheme the value of existing shareholdings would increase rather than diminish for the reason that the scheme has contributed to securing the commitment to the company of key employees.

Share valuation

54.7 The completion of the share reclassification allows the whole value of the company to be attached to the new preference shares. The basis of the whole value is TCGA 1992, s 272(1) as the price that those assets might reasonably be expected to fetch on a sale in the open market.

For all practical purposes, open MV is the best price that could be expected for the shares on a sale in the open market between a hypothetical willing seller and a hypothetical willing buyer on the basis that both are equally informed about the company, its activities and the market within which it operates, and that both the hypothetical willing seller and a hypothetical willing buyer are acting for self-interest and gain.

The information that is available to the parties in a sale for UK tax purposes is outlined in TCGA 1992, s 273(3) which states that:

> there is available to any prospective purchaser of the asset in question all the information which a prudent prospective purchaser of the asset might reasonably require if he were proposing to purchase it from a willing vendor by private treaty and at arm's length.

Income tax implications of growth shares

54.8 The income tax implications of growth shares are as follows.

Restricted securities regime (RSR)

54.9   The tax election under ITEPA 2003, s 431 should be made within 14 days of the acquisition of the shares. Provided the tax election is made and income tax is paid on any excess of the unrestricted MV over the price paid, any future gain will be subject to the CGT regime and definitively not the income tax regime. It could well be argued that the shares are not restricted securities at all and that they represent a class that has a defined set of rights related exclusively to capital and winding-up rights. The fact that this class has neither dividend rights nor voting rights does not mean that these rights are restricted or suppressed; it simply means that they do not have these rights and will never have these rights. Nevertheless, the tax election should be made anyway for protective purposes.

Convertible securities regime

54.10   Convertible securities have a precise definition under ITEPA 2003, s 436 requiring the capacity of the shares to convert into shares of a different description at some point in the future. Under the growth shares approach, the shares will never convert into shares of a different description at any point in the future as their rights are clearly defined in the amended Articles of Association from the date of the reclassification, before the scheme has even been introduced. In this context, it is important not to confuse growth shares with flowering shares that, depending on how the supporting documents are drafted, can blossom on the basis of conversion into shares of a different description at some point in the future.

Post-acquisition benefits from securities regime

54.11   Where the right is inherent in the shares and is intrinsic to the shares from when the shares are first issued, then they have already been paid for as part of the MV price paid at acquisition. This is the case with the growth shares and, therefore, benefits of an increase in value should not be caught under Chapter 4. The view of HMRC is now that Chapter 4 does not apply where the benefit derives from rights inherent in the shares at the date of acquisition.

Enterprise management incentives (EMI)

54.12   Where growth shares are introduced, the share scheme participants sometimes receive their shares through the grant and subsequent exercise of EMI share options. The relevant tax sections are found in ITEPA 2003, Pt 7, Chap 7 and Sch 5.

Summary conclusions

54.13   The growth shares approach can be used to meet a variety of needs. It is presented in this chapter in its standard theme form. However, there are numerous variations on this theme that can be structured in order to meet the needs and requirements of individual company situations.

The implementation of this approach requires professional clearances from experts in various aspects of company law, and tax law, and it is unwise to progress with this approach unless robust professional clearances have been obtained. When considering the implementation it is crucially important to understand fully the current tax status of the existing shareholders who should be encouraged to seek independent advice in relation to their own particular circumstances.

The growth shares approach, properly implemented, provides significant benefits to the existing shareholders and the new executives/employee shareholders. Once the new ordinary shares rise in value, it may be necessary to introduce share option arrangements anyway for the reason that the share value may become too high to request a monetary contribution from any new executives/employees who are invited to take part in the employee share scheme.

Example 54.1: Executive share scheme – the returns on an exit

Consider that the value of the company at the date of the reclassification is £20 million and then, in five years' time, say, the company is sold to an independent third party acquiring the company for £50 million.

These figures indicate the gross amounts that attribute to each of the parties.

Sale to an independent third party acquiring company	£ million
Sale proceeds	50.00
Share of the sale proceeds to preference shareholders	20.00
[The value set at the original share reclassification date = £20 million]	
Share of the sale proceeds to ordinary shareholders	30.00
[£50 million – £20 million = £30 million]	
Share of the sale proceeds to the existing shareholders in total	19.5
[65% × £30 million to the existing shareholders in total]	6.0
Share of the sale proceeds to executive 1	3.0
[20% × £30 million]	1.5
Share of the sale proceeds to executive 2	
[10% × £30 million]	
Share of the sale proceeds to executive 3	
[5% × £30 million]	
Summary of share proceeds split	
Total share of sale proceeds to the existing shareholders in total	39.5
[£20.0m. + £19.5m.]	6.0
Total share of sales proceeds to executive 1 [£6.0m]	3.0
Total share of sales proceeds to executive 2 [£3.0m]	1.5
Total share of sales proceeds to executive 3 [£1.5m]	
Total sale proceeds	**50.00**

Example 54.2: How the general tax legislation assists in developing tax efficiencies

This example is designed to illustrate how the use of share valuation rules coupled with the share reclassification provisions can be used to develop a highly tax-advantageous share purchase scheme using general legislation and case law rather than the tax-approved legislation.

The diagram set out below illustrates the following steps:

1. The original ordinary shares, Ords. 1, of the company have grown steadily in value over many years to a value V1 at time T1.

2. Ords. 1 are reclassified into a combination of new preference shares that now represent the bulk of the accumulated value of the company to date and new ordinary shares, Ords. 2.

3. Ords. 2 are issued at T1 at low value, usually their nominal value.

4. Ords. 2 are subject to negligible income tax at date of issue.

5. Ords. 2 grow as capital assets subject to CGT.

Value post-reclassification represented in preference shares

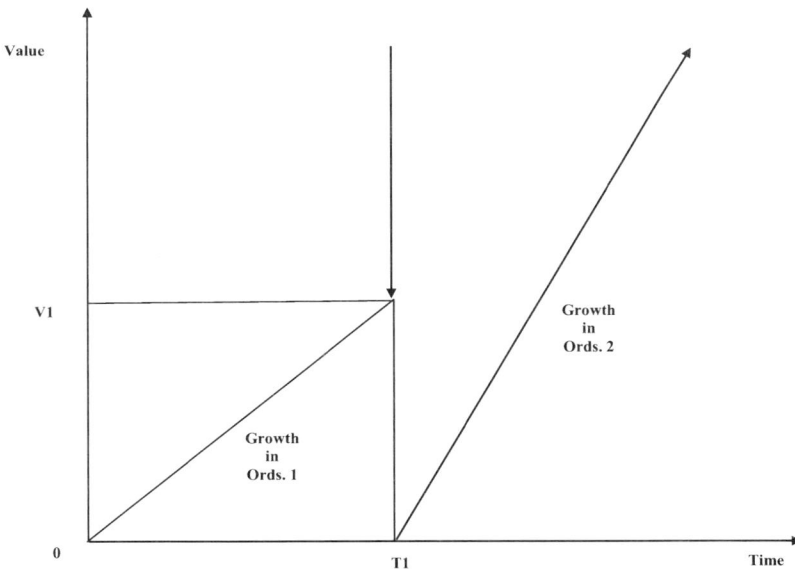

Chapter 55

Flowering shares

Introduction

55.1   This chapter identifies flowering shares as a standalone initiative to establish a class of deferred shares without value freezing and explains the vulnerability of flowering shares to tax charges under ITEPA 2003, Pt 7.

The principle behind flowering shares

55.2   The principle behind flowering shares is that a separate new class of shares is created as a class of deferred ordinary shares with either no rights or limited rights until the happening of a pre-determined event which will typically be linked to the achievement of target profit levels or the success of some corporate business project. Once the rights have been attached to the shares they are considered to have 'flowered' or 'blossomed' and are treated from henceforth as fully-fledged ordinary shares with full rights, ranking pari passu with the other ordinary shares.

The flowering could be the attachment of dividend rights or voting rights or any other form of privilege that can be expressed in the form of share rights. The flowering can adopt a multistage approach and involve a series of successive maturity points for the attachment of the next set of rights.

Objectives of flowering shares

55.3   The objectives of flowering shares are to reward performance and to focus the minds of employees upon targets with the attachment of the rights acting as the reward for achieving those targets. It is not by accident that flowering shares are often referred to as 'performance shares'.

Tax implications of flowering shares

55.4   As a general rule of thumb, flowering shares establish a clear linkage between performance achievement and the attachment of the rights. The questions that arise for HMRC, therefore, are as follows:

- Are the rights restricted from the outset? Are the rights suppressed in some way? Or are rights created afresh at some point in the future without ever being there to be restricted in the first place?

- Do the shares convert into shares of a different class or description? Or do the shares remain as the same class but simply adopt the same characteristics as the main class of ordinary shares?

- Are there any post-acquisition benefits arising from the ownership of the flowering shares? Are the rights that subsequently attach to the shares paid for as part of the acquisition cost of the shares?

- Does the application of one of these regimes automatically exclude the application of the other, in the case of flowering shares?

The answers to these questions are as follows.

Restricted securities regime (RSR)

55.5 It is difficult to sustain the position that flowering shares are restricted securities when the rights that subsequently accrue have never been conferred upon the shares in the first place. It appears to be the case that dividend or voting rights are absent from the shares on a temporary basis and if this is the case then that absence does not constitute a restriction under the definition of restricted securities under ITEPA 2003, s 423. The rights are absent but not because they have been present and are now restricted.

Convertible securities regime

55.6 If shares acquire new rights at various pre-determined junctures, as with flowering shares, then under ITEPA 2003, s 436 it is difficult to refute that they are convertible securities. Under that section, where the shares confer an entitlement to convert into shares of a different description they are convertible securities. Where one day the shares do not have, say, dividend rights and the next day they do have dividend rights, say on the basis of some performance achievement, however that performance achievement is defined, then it must be the case that the shares are now of a different description. This position is based on the fact that a share is 'a bundle of rights', defined on the basis of its rights, so if the rights actually change then the description has changed. By 'description' can only be meant the description in the Articles of Association on the basis of the share rights.

Post-acquisition benefits from securities

55.7 If the price paid for the shares did not accommodate the value attached to the rights that subsequently flower, then the attachment of the rights on flowering, would be a post-acquisition benefit from securities under Chapter 4. This must be the most probable conclusion as it is conceptually difficult to conceive that the employee would pay as part of the acquisition cost for rights that, technically, may never attach to the shares.

Comparison with growth shares

55.8   Flowering shares are not growth shares whose rights are determined at the date of acquisition as capital rights only and there are no other rights that can be restricted and there are no other rights that are ever to be attached. In other words, growth shares will never change 'the bundle of rights' that defines them and their description in the Articles of Association will never change. A growth share will only ever be a 'one rights share' and when those rights deliver value at a capital event the share is not acquiring capital rights at that juncture, as would be the case with flowering shares. The growth share already has those rights and has had those rights ever since the date of acquisition.

Summary conclusions

55.9   The conclusion is that flowering shares are vulnerable to income tax charges under Chapter 3 as convertible securities and under Chapter 4 as post-acquisition benefits from securities. It appears to be the former that HMRC chooses to use as the basis for its strongest challenge. The case under Chapter 2 as restricted securities is somewhat difficult to sustain.

Chapter 56

Ratchet arrangements

Introduction

56.1 This chapter considers the operation of ratchets for management participation in private equity or venture capital investments in the light of the employment-related securities legislation. The chapter goes on to explain the implications of the Memorandum of Understanding (MoU) dated 25 July 2005, representing the agreement between HMRC and the british venture capital association (BVCA) on the subject.

The principle behind ratchet arrangements

56.2 A ratchet is a performance-based reward to management for which they are eligible on the basis of their shareholdings in the company. Through a ratchet arrangement the managers in a company that has venture capital or private equity investment obtain a proportion of the value of the company at the time that the venture capitalist firm exits. The exiting venture capitalist firm takes whatever it has calculated as its internal rate of return and, provided that has been achieved, any additional returns over and above that amount are shared with the managers. The proportion that the managers receive, therefore, is variable and cannot properly be determined until such time as the venture capitalist exits the company.

The conundrum that is posed by the employment-related securities legislation is that the percentage of the value that the managers receive at the time of the exit can be significantly higher than the percentage of their shareholding.

Example 56.1: Scenario for the ratchet arrangement

Suppose that at the time the company was set up, the managers subscribed for 10% of the share capital of the company. However, the managers have the right to receive between 15% and 20% of the value on exit at the time that the venture capitalist chooses to exit the company.

The value can only be determined on exit for the reason that it is calculated on the basis of the company's performance or, alternatively, the venture capitalist's return on the investment. However, it is important to appreciate that the calculation is not on the basis of personal performance from the individual members of the management team.

Tax implications of ratchet arrangements

56.3 The key document for determining the tax implications of a ratchet agreement is the MoU dated 25 July 2005, as it represents the agreement between HMRC and the BVCA on the subject as follows.

Under clause 1.1, the MoU is explicit that this document is concerned with addressing the tax treatment of the shares held by the management, the managers who as employees acquire shares or an interest in shares in a company in which a venture capital or private equity firm invests. To fall within the orbit of the MoU, the shares must be employment-related securities as defined within ITEPA 2003, s 421B.

Under clause 1.2, the MoU explains that the potential exposure to income tax for the managers is under the RSR, ITEPA 2003, Pt 7, Chap 2. Clause 1.2 explains that the MoU sets out the approach that HMRC accepts when determining whether the price paid by the managers for their shares at the date of acquisition is the initial unrestricted MV (where the shares are restricted securities) or MV (where the shares are not restricted securities).

Under clause 4.1, the MoU lists the conditions that must be satisfied for HMRC to accept that no charge to income tax arises either on the acquisition of the shares or at the time the ratchet is operated as follows:

Clause 4.1(a)

The shares for which the managers have subscribed are part of the ordinary share capital of the company.

Clause 4.1(b)

For any leverage that is provided by the venture capitalist as ordinary shareholders in the form of preference share capital it has been made on commercial terms.

Clause 4.1(c)

The managers paid for their shares a price that was not less than the price the venture capitalist paid for its ordinary shares and the shares are of the same class or, alternatively, of another class with substantially the same economic rights.

Clause 4.1(d)

The managers and the venture capitalist acquired their ordinary shares at the same time as each other.

Clause 4.1(e)

The managers do not have any features within their shares that enhance the value of their shares compared with the shares of the venture capitalist.

Clause 4.1(f)

The managers receive remuneration on a fully commercial basis through salaries and bonuses in accordance with their contract of employment.

Under clause 6.2, the MoU lists the conditions that must be satisfied for HMRC to accept that the ratchet arrangements are to be treated as taken into account when determining the unrestricted MV at the date of acquisition of the managers' shares as follows:

Clause 6.2(a)

The ratchet arrangements relate to the performance of the company or to the venture capitalist's return on its investment and definitively not to the personal performance of the managers.

Clause 6.2(b)

The ratchet arrangements for the managers of the company are in existence at the time that the venture capitalist makes its investment in the company through the acquisition of its ordinary shares.

Clause 6.2(c)

The managers must have paid at the date of the acquisition of the shares a price that reflects the maximum economic entitlement of the shares.

The clear practical implications of the MoU are as follows:

- *The key principle that underpins this tax treatment:* If at the date of acquisition of the shares the value is inherent in the shares then no income tax liability should be triggered by any events that happen subsequently. The application of this principle assumes that the price paid for shares at the date of acquisition is for all the value that is intrinsic within the share at that date and that to pay in the event of subsequent events would be to exact a double payment which is not justified.

- For the managers, who are, of course, employees, provided there is full compliance with the conditions of the MoU, HMRC will treat the value at which the managers have acquired their shares as unrestricted MV. Any future gain after the date of acquisition will, therefore, fall into the CGT regime. However, it is always advisable for the managers to make a tax election under ITEPA 2003, s 431 as a protective election. The making of the tax election also has the advantage of being able to assure the purchaser of the business that there are no unidentified tax liabilities.

- For the managers, provided there is full compliance with the conditions of the MoU, there are no obligations on them to report to HMRC.

- For the company, the growth in the value does not provide the basis for a statutory corporation tax deduction under FA 2003, Sch 23. However, there is an advantage for the company in that, provided the MoU applies, there is no liability for the company on employer's NICs.

- For the company, there is a reporting requirement to HMRC through the Form 42 by 6 July of the tax year following the date of acquisition of the shares. This reporting requirement arises for the reason that the shares are employment-related securities as defined in ITEPA 2003, s 421B.

Changed structure of the ratchet arrangement

56.4 The structure of the ratchet arrangement has changed over the years. However, it is important to emphasize that there is now the settled approach that is the *management downwards ratchet* which is the subject of the MoU and which has been fully described above.

To put the current settled approach into context, it is useful to be aware of the two other forms of ratchet that have now been largely abandoned. They are as follows:

- *Management upwards ratchet:* was based on converting a class of convertible ordinary shares, subscribed for by the managers, into shares that would deliver the required percentage of the exit proceeds. This was abandoned as it triggered income tax under the convertible securities regime, ITEPA 2003, Pt 7, Chap 3, on the increase in value that arose on the conversion.

- *Venture capitalist downwards ratchet:* in contrast, this ratchet required the venture capitalist to subscribe for shares which would at some stage in the future be converted downwards into worthless deferred shares so that as a consequence the managers received the specified return in accordance with the ratchet arrangement. Considerable debate ensued between HMRC and practitioners on this approach to ratchets as HMRC took the view that the conversion of the venture capitalist shares created a benefit to the managers that arose as a consequence of their employment. HMRC contended that the incremental value that accrued to the managers was, therefore, employment income and subject to a charge to income tax on the managers. As a consequence, although the practitioner view is to disagree with HMRC on this matter, the approach has largely been abandoned in favour of the management downwards ratchet that has the protection afforded by the MoU.

Summary conclusions

56.5 Ratchets are a recognised part of the venture capitalist activity in the UK and through the MoU the protection is indeed strong. The advice must always be, therefore, to keep to the strictures and the compliance requirements of the MoU and the CGT treatment will be assured.

Chapter 57

Reporting of employment-related securities

Introduction

57.1 This chapter explains the reporting mechanism that was introduced from the tax year 2003/04 for companies to provide HMRC with the details of all reportable events that derive from tax-unapproved arrangements in relation to shares, and other forms of securities that are obtained by reason of employment. This reporting mechanism is the HMRC Form 42 and it has been introduced as a consequence of the revision of employment-related securities that was introduced through FA 2003, Sch 22 the legislation that is now contained in ITEPA 2003, Pt 7.

The practicalities of the reporting

57.2 The legislation relating to these reporting requirements is found in ITEPA 2003, Pt 7, Chap 1 as follows:

- under ITEPA 2003, s 421J for the duty to provide information;

- under ITEPA 2003, s 421K for the reportable events; and

- under ITEPA 2003, s 421L for the persons to whom the duty to provide the information applies.

Where there have been reportable events in a tax year ending 5 April, the rule, with one exception, is that a report must be made to HMRC at the ES SU at 100 Parliament Street in London before 7 July following the end of the tax year. The exception is that in circumstances where the form has been sent to the company on or after 8 June 2009 the company has 30 days from the date of issue to complete the form and make the submission to HMRC.

With effect from 6 April 2007 it is possible for companies to report information provided on Form 42 online provided they are registered for PAYE Online-Internet Service. The website is www.hmrc.gov.uk/online/index.htm The Online Service is also available for the filing of Form 34 (SAYE), Form 35 (CSOP) and Form 39 (SIP). HMRC has made available an Employers CD-Rom that contains an electronic and pdf version of

Form 42 together with detailed guidance on how to complete the form and which includes detailed examples.

The practice that is now adopted by HMRC is to issue notices to file employee share scheme annual returns to companies who they know to have employee share schemes. It is no longer the case that HMRC will issue forms to every company that is registered with them. The duty to provide this information to HMRC lies with the company even in circumstances where HMRC does not issue a notice to file. If the company has chosen to make a paper return then it must print the form from the HMRC website which is www.hmrc.gov.uk/online/index.htm

It must be emphasized that the submission of Form 42 is required solely for the tax-unapproved employee share scheme arrangements. The tax-approved schemes each have their own form, as indicated above, as does the tax-efficient (but not tax-approved) government-sponsored EMI, Form EMI40.

The penalties regime that applies to failure to comply with the reporting requirements under Form 42 derives from TMA 1970, s 98 under which penalty of up to £300 can be imposed for a failure to report events that require reporting under Form 42. Where a penalty is imposed following a failure to respond to a reminder letter HMRC can impose a further penalty not exceeding £60 per day until the return is finally submitted.

Reportable events

57.3 Under ITEPA 2003, s 421K the reportable events are as follows:

Reportable event 1: ITEPA 2003, Pt 7, Chap 1

An acquisition by a person of securities (including by exercise of a securities option) an interest in securities or a securities option:

- by reason of his or her employment; or
- by reason of employment of any other person.

Reportable event 2: ITEPA 2003, Pt 7, Chap 2

An event that is 'a chargeable event' in relation to 'restricted securities' or 'an interest in restricted securities'.

Reportable event 3: ITEPA 2003, Pt 7, Chap 3

An event that is 'a chargeable event' in relation to 'convertible securities' or 'an interest in convertible securities'.

Reportable event 4: ITEPA 2003, Pt 7, Chap 3A

The doing of anything that artificially enhances the MV of the securities.

Reportable event 5: ITEPA 2003, Pt 7, Chap 3C

An event that discharges a notional loan relating to securities and an interest in securities acquired for less than MV.

Reportable event 6: ITEPA 2003, Pt 7, Chap 3D

The disposal of securities, and an interest in securities for more than their MV.

Reportable event 7: ITEPA 2003, Pt 7, Chap 4

The receipt of a benefit from securities or interest in securities, which gives rise to a taxable amount counting as employment income or would give rise to such an amount but for Chapter 4A (shares in research institution spin-out companies).

Reportable event 8: ITEPA 2003, Pt 7, Chap 5

The assignment or the release of a securities option acquired pursuant to a right or the opportunity made available by reason of the employment of the person who acquires the securities option or any other person.

Reportable event 9: ITEPA 2003, Pt 7, Chap 5

The receipt of a benefit in money or money's worth in connection with either failing or undertaking not to acquire securities pursuant to the employment-related securities option, or granting or undertaking to grant to another person a right to acquire securities which are subject to the employment-related securities option.

Exceptions from reporting under Form 42

57.4   The transactions that do not need to be reported on the Form 42 are as follows.

Companies incorporated in the year ended 5 April

57.5   Where a limited company is incorporated in the UK and the initial subscriber shares are acquired:

- directly on incorporation; or

- on transfer from a company formation agent; or

- from another person forming the company, for example, a solicitor or an accountant.

A report is *not* required if *all* of the following conditions are met:

- all the initial subscriber shares are acquired at nominal value; and

- no form of security other than shares is acquired; and

- the shares are not acquired by reason of or in connection with another employment (whether that is the only employment or one of a number of employments); and

- the shares are acquired by a person who is a director or prospective director of the company; or

- someone who has a personal family relationship with the director and the right or opportunity is made available in the normal course of the domestic, family or personal relationship of that person.

Companies incorporated in the year ended 5 April – allotment of further shares

57.6 Where a limited company has been incorporated in the UK and further shares are allotted prior to the commencement of trading or transfer of assets to the company and *all* of the following conditions are met:

- the additional shares are acquired by a person to whom some of the initial subscriber shares have been transferred or the person is a director or prospective director of the company; *and*

- the shares are acquired at nominal value; *and*

- the shares are not acquired by reason of or in connection with another employment (whether that is the only employment or one of a number of employments).

If such shares are allotted following the incorporation of the company it will not be reportable even if the initial subscriber shares (1 above) were acquired before 5 April and the allotment of further shares (2 above) is made after the 5 April.

The majority of newly incorporated companies should meet the above conditions and will *not* have to complete Form 42 in respect of the founder shares.

Company formation shares

57.7 Shares acquired by the company formation agent (initial subscriber shares) on incorporation will *not* be employment-related securities and no report is required.

HMRC tax-approved schemes and government-sponsored EMI schemes

Save-as-you-earn-schemes (SAYE)

57.8 If the employees are granted options and/or exercised options under an HMRC savings-related share option scheme the details should be shown on the Form 34. No entries are required on the Form 42.

Company share option plans (CSOP)

57.9 If the employees are granted options and/or exercised options under an HMRC CSOP the details should be shown on the Form 35. No entries are required on the Form 42.

Share incentive plans (SIP)

57.10 If the employees are awarded shares under an HMRC SIP the details should be shown on the Form 39. No entries are required on the Form 42.

Enterprise management incentives (EMI)

57.11 The limit for options granted under EMI is £120,000 and EMI options up to this limit *must* be reported on Form 40. If options in excess of £120,000 are granted the details of options granted in excess of £120,000 must be included in section 1a of Form 42. Any subsequent exercise/assignment/release of the excess element of the options should also be reported on Form 42 in section 1b or section 1c as appropriate.

Share transfers in normal course of domestic, family or personal relationships

57.12 A report is not normally required where shares are transferred by an individual in the normal course of domestic, family or personal relationships of the person transferring the shares. It will be for the individual making the transfer to determine whether the transfer has been made for purely personal reasons as they are in possession of all the facts relating to the transfer. HMRC may enquire into the reasons for the transfer and where it cannot be agreed that the transfer is for purely personal reasons the matter will be referred to the tax tribunal service.

Flat management companies

57.13 If the company is incorporated in a tax year ended 5 April and unrestricted shares are, or will be, allocated to all residents (including flat owners where the owner leases the flat) at nominal value then this transaction does not need to be reported.

Where on the sale of a flat the resident has to sell their share(s) at nominal value either to the company or to a new resident then no report is required. However, a report would be required if the shares were disposed of for more than nominal value and the transferor or the transferee is an employee (or office holder) in the company.

If the shares acquired by the residents are restricted shares and the transferor or the transferee is an employee (or office holder) in the company, then a report must be made in section 2 on page 7 of Form 42. HMRC does not consider that a requirement to sell the share(s) back to the company or another resident on disposal of the flat makes the share(s) a restricted share and in that case a report is not required.

Members' clubs formed as companies

57.14 If a members' club is incorporated in a tax year ended 5 April and unrestricted shares are allocated to members at nominal value during that tax year then a report is not required.

Shares transferred between members at nominal value during the tax year also do not need to be reported.

However, if the shares are restricted shares and the transferor or the transferee is an employee (or office holder) in the company then a report must be made in section 2 on page 7 of Form 42.

Share for share exchange

57.15 If a person has received shares by reason of employment any additional shares as also treated as received by reason of employment. However, where:

- the employer is a company or part of a group *listed on a recognised stock exchange; and*

- the opportunity to acquire unrestricted shares/securities is made available to all shareholders, including director and employee shareholders, *and*

- the unrestricted shares/securities are acquired independently of the company, for example, through a broker at full MV;

  then a report of those shares acquired by directors and employees is not required.

Rights issue

57.16 A rights issue is a right to acquire securities and, therefore, is an employment-related securities option in relation to employees acquiring those rights. However, if the following conditions apply:

- the employer is a company or part of a group listed on a recognised stock exchange; and

- the opportunity to acquire unrestricted shares/securities is made available to all shareholders, including employee shareholders;

  then a report of such shares/securities acquired by directors and employees is not required.

Bonus shares

57.17 Bonus shares acquired by directors and employees from employing companies will be treated as received by reason of employment. However, if the following conditions apply:

- the employer is a company or part of a group *listed on a recognised stock exchange; and*

- the opportunity to acquire unrestricted shares/securities is made available to all shareholders, including employee shareholders;

  then a report of such shares/securities acquired by directors and employees is not required.

Scrip dividends

57.18 Where HMRC has been given details of the arrangements relating to the scrip dividend by the employer; *and*

- the employer is a company or part of a group *listed on a recognised stock exchange; and*

- the opportunity to acquire unrestricted shares/securities is made available to all shareholders, including employee shareholders;

  then provided HMRC is satisfied with the arrangements and that they meet those conditions, there will be no need to report details of the unrestricted shares/securities acquired by directors and employees through the scrip dividends.

If, following a compliance review, HMRC finds that this is not the case then it will require the company to report the full details.

Dividend reinvestment plans (DRIPs)

57.19 In the case of DRIPs where HMRC has been given details of the arrangements by the employer and where:

- the employer is a company or part of a group *listed on a recognised stock exchange; and*

- the opportunity to acquire shares/securities is made available to all shareholders, including director and employee shareholders; and

- the shares/securities are acquired independently of the company, for example, through a broker at full MV on the open market;

  then provided HMRC is satisfied that the arrangements meet those conditions, there will be no need to report details of the shares/securities acquired by directors and employees through the DRIPs.

If, following a compliance review, HMRC finds that this is not the case then it will require the company to report the full details.

Shares acquired independently by directors and employees

57.20 Where directors and employees acquire shares in their employer and have purchased those shares on the open market, for example, through an independent broker, then if:

- the employer is a company or part of a group *listed on a recognised stock exchange; and*

- the opportunity to acquire unrestricted shares/securities is made available to all shareholders, including director and employee shareholders; *and*

- the unrestricted shares/securities are acquired independently of the company, for example, through a broker at full MV;

then a report of those shares acquired by directors and employees is not required.

The source of the information contained in this section 4 of this chapter is taken from the HMRC document entitled *Employment-Related Securities: A Guide to completing Form 42.*

Position on ex-employees

57.21 The company must be mindful of its responsibility to provide details of reportable event in relation to employment-related securities for any former employee who has left the company in the past seven years. This somewhat demanding requirement derives from ITEPA 2003, s 421B(7) under which the charging provisions of ITEPA 2003, Pt 7, Chaps 2–4 apply for up to seven years after an employee has ceased employment with the company.

Position on overseas employees

57.22 The company must report details of any options granted to employees or office holders who at the date of grant of the options were *any one of the following*:

- resident and ordinarily resident;

- resident but not ordinarily resident;

- not resident but with UK duties; and

- not resident and with no UK duties but at the date of grant there is a reasonable belief that the individual will come to the UK in the near future.

If the individual's residence profile does not fall into any of the above categories then there is no requirement to report grants of option.

Responsibility of the employees

57.23 The filing of the Form 42 by the company does not negate any responsibility on the part of the employee to notify HMRC through the self-assessment procedure.

Chapter 58

Overseas scheme arrangements for overseas employees

Introduction

58.1 This chapter is appreciative of the international nature of the subject of employee share schemes. The chapter explains how the UK tax-approved schemes can be operated for overseas employees before explaining the detailed preparation that is necessary in order to introduce overseas schemes for overseas employees. The chapter is concerned with the circumstances in which an international scheme is introduced that seeks to include employee participants who are resident in different countries and fall under the jurisdiction of the tax regime that prevails in the country of their employing company.

UK approved schemes for overseas employees

58.2 There is no participation exclusion for overseas employees in any of the following UK tax-approved schemes:

- Savings-related share option scheme (SSOS);

- Executive/company share option scheme (E/CSOP); and

- Share incentive plan (SIP).

However, the tax treatment of the overseas employees will be dependent on the residence criteria that apply to those employees as follows:

- At the time they join the scheme through the grant of options or the appropriation of shares.

- During the time of their involvement in the scheme through the interest that they have in the share capital of the company.

At the time they leave the scheme through the exercise of options or the transfer of shares.

For the tax-approved SSOS, the implications for overseas employees are as follows:

- The bonus that is credited at the maturity of the savings arrangement or, alternatively, any interest that is received on the savings may be subject to a tax charge under the tax regime of the country in which the employee is resident.

- The increase in value from the option price that is set at the date of grant to the MV of the shares at the date of exercise may be subject to a tax charge under the tax regime of the country in which the employee is resident.

- The discount on MV at the date of grant which may be given by the company in the calculation of the option price will not usually be subject to a tax charge under the overseas tax regimes although there are certain countries where it is subject to a tax charge.

- Exchange control rules may restrict the transfer of savings monies to the UK savings-carrier that has been nominated to enter into direct savings contracts with the employee participants.

For the tax-approved E/CSOS, the implications for overseas employees are as follows:

- The £30,000 limit on the value of shares available is exactly the same for overseas employees as it is for UK employees.

- The increase in value from the option price that is set at the date of grant to the MV of the shares at the date of exercise may be subject to a tax charge under the tax regime of the country in which the employee is resident.

For the tax-approved SIP, the implications for overseas employees are as follows:

- The scheme/plan can make provision for shares to be awarded to overseas employees. These are employees who would otherwise comply with the eligibility requirements except for the fact that they are not subject to income tax under Schedule E, Case I.

- The scheme/plan can give to the company the right to choose which overseas employees are to be invited to participate.

Overseas schemes for overseas employees

58.3 It has become commonplace for international companies with overseas subsidiaries and branches to establish international schemes for employees throughout the worldwide group.

Where an international company chooses to do this they must continue to be aware and take account of the statutory and institutional environment that governs the operation of the UK schemes.

In particular, full recognition must be given to the requirements of the following:

- the Listing Rules; and

- the institutional investor guidelines (IIGs).

The implications of the Listing Rules are as follows:

- In circumstances where the UK company is basing employee share schemes for its overseas subsidiaries on a UK scheme that is already in existence then it is possible to obtain a general authority without having to request specific approval from a meeting of the shareholders.

The implications of the IIGs are as follows:

- The general principle is that in the calculation of the headroom limits for the availability of shares for employee share scheme purposes the shares that are allocated for overseas employee share schemes must be included.

It is important to recognise also the need to apply the local overseas laws and regulations in relation to the following:

- securities laws;

- exchange controls;

- tax laws, corporate and personal;

- employment laws; and

- data protection laws and regulations.

In this respect it is important to seek the advice of local overseas advisers and to ask for assurances in relation to the following:

- that the information and advice that is provided is fully up-to-date; and

- that the advice is given specifically in relation to the company that is seeking the advice.

In discussions with the local overseas advisers, the company must ensure that it forwards all relevant information in relation to the following:

- the group structure;

- any unusual features that are contained within the shares that are being used for the scheme; and

- comprehensive detail about the proposed scheme, the timing of its implementation and maturity, the number of employees involved and the expected share requirement.

In relation to securities laws, the company should seek advice on the following:

- any local requirement to file a prospectus or listing document;

- any local requirement to provide particular information for the employees;

- any local prohibition on the holding of shares in an overseas holding company;

- any local requirement for the employees to register their shareholding or interest in shares;

- any implications for securities laws arising from the use of an employee benefit trust;

- any restrictions on the transfer of shares within the country; and

- the availability of a local stockbroker to sell shares as necessary.

Any specific investor protections offered by laws or regulations to the employees other than through securities laws.

In relation to exchange controls, the company should seek advice on the following:

- any requirements from the local central bank;

- any restrictions on remitting funds overseas for the purchase of shares in an overseas holding company;

- any obligations for gains on overseas shares to be repatriated to the local country;

- any requirement for depositing share certificates with a local authority;

- any restrictions on savings arrangements for a SSOP; and

- any opportunity to operate a collective arrangement covering a group of employees for the remittance of funds overseas.

In relation to taxation laws, the company should seek advice on the following:

- the tax treatment of employees on the grant of options or the appropriation of shares and the anticipated tax treatment of employees on the eventual date of exercise of options or the transfer of shares;

- any requirement for either the company or the employees to account for social security contributions/social charges and the accounting requirements to the local authorities;

- any opportunity for a corporation tax deduction in the local subsidiary company;

- any requirement for the local subsidiary company to withhold tax and account for employee tax to the local tax authorities;

- any reporting requirements on personal or corporate taxes to the local tax authorities; and

- any tax implications arising from the use of an employee share trust for either the employees or for the local subsidiary company.

In relation to employment laws, the company should seek advice on the following:

- any possibility of establishing employment contractual rights that are exercisable on leaving through employee involvement in an employee share scheme;

- any possibility of establishing precedents by introducing the employee scheme that employees could subsequently claim was a basis for further employee benefits or employee share schemes;

- any requirement to obtain the authority of a works council for the introduction of the employee share scheme;

- any need to consult with a trade union before introducing an employee share scheme;

- any restrictions on the content of employee communication materials that are issued to employees and, indeed, of the content of any verbal communication that is made in order to support the launch of the employee share scheme; and

- any requirement to translate employee communications into the local language.

In relation to data protection laws and regulations, the company should seek advice on the following:

- any authorities or clearances required in order to hold within the company, personal details, usually in the form of computer data, relating specifically to share issues or grants of options over shares to employees;

- any restrictions on transferring personal details to third parties of either the holding company or the employing company, in particular, share registrars, savings-carriers, scheme administrators, trustees of employee share scheme trusts and stockbrokers; and

- any restrictions on transferring personal details into another country.

Chapter 59

Overseas implications for UK interfacing employees

Introduction

59.1 This chapter is appreciative of the international nature of the subject of employee share schemes. It explains the position on UK interfacing employees and then goes on to explain the use of double taxation treaties.

Impact of Finance Act 2008

59.2 To understand the impact of FA 2008 it is important to compare the situation that prevailed up to 5 April 2008 with the situation that now prevails with effect from 6 April 2008 as follows:

Overview of the connection between resident and ordinarily resident

59.3 Up to 5 April 2008, the tax provisions relating to employment-related securities options and certain tax provisions relating to employment-related securities applied only to individuals who were resident and ordinarily resident in the UK at the tax point.

Example 59.1

1. *For securities options:* income tax would arise only if the individual was both resident and ordinarily resident at the time the option was granted.

2. *For restricted securities:* the income tax regime would apply only if the individual was both resident and ordinarily resident at the time the securities were acquired.

With effect from 6 April 2008, the tax provisions relating to employment-related securities options and certain tax provisions relating to employment-related securities now apply to individuals who are resident in the UK at the tax point, regardless of whether or not the individual is at the time ordinarily resident.

Example 59.2

1. *For securities options:* income tax will arise if the individual is resident at the time the option was granted, regardless of whether or not the individual is at the time ordinarily resident.

2. *For restricted securities:* the income tax regime will apply if the individual is resident at the time the securities were acquired, regardless of whether or not the individual is at the time ordinarily resident.

The detailed explanations refer to the Chapters within ITEPA 2003, Pt 7 as follows:

Chapter 2	Restricted Securities
Chapter 3	Convertible Securities
Chapter 3A	Securities with Artificially Depressed Market Value
Chapter 3B	Securities with Artificially Enhanced Market Value
Chapter 3C	Securities Acquired for Less Than Market Value
Chapter 3D	Securities Disposed of for More Than Market Value
Chapter 4	Post-Acquisition Benefits from Securities
Chapter 5	Securities Options

Tax Status of UK resident but not ordinarily resident

59.4 **Up to 5 April 2008**

If the employee was UK-resident *but not ordinarily resident* when he or she received employment-related securities or employment-related securities options then the consequences were as follows:

- No charge to income tax under ITEPA 2003, Pt 7, Chaps 2–4, or 5.

- A charge to income tax under ITEPA 2003, s 62 as the general charging provision, and/or ITEPA 2003, Pt 7, Chaps 3A–3C or 3D, and a charge to income tax under ITEPA 2003, ss 192–200 as the general option gains charging provision.

With effect from 6 April 2008

If the employee is UK-resident *but not ordinarily resident* when he or she receives employment-related securities then the consequences are as follows:

- A charge to income tax arises under ITEPA 2003, Pt 7, Chaps 2–3 and 4.

- A charge to income tax under ITEPA 2003, Pt 7, Chaps 3A–3C or 3D.

If the employee is UK resident *but not ordinarily resident* when he or she is granted employment-related securities options then the consequences are as follows:

- A charge to income tax arises at the date of exercise on the uplift from the option price to the MV at the date of exercise under ITEPA 2003, Pt 7, Chap 5.

Chap-ter	Residence requirement Up to 5 April 2008	Residence requirement With effect from 6 April 2008	Change/ no change
2	Resident and ordinarily resident	Resident	Change
3	Resident and ordinarily resident	Resident	Change
3A	Resident or ordinarily resident, in UK taxable employment	Resident or ordinarily resident, in UK taxable employment	No change
3B	Resident or ordinarily resident, in UK taxable employment	Resident or ordinarily resident, in UK taxable employment	No change
3C	Resident or ordinarily resident, in UK taxable employment	Resident or ordinarily resident, in UK taxable employment	No change
3D	Resident or ordinarily resident, in UK taxable employment	Resident or ordinarily resident, Iin UK taxable employment	No change
4	Resident and ordinarily resident	Resident	Change
5	Resident and ordinarily resident	Resident	Change

Chapter 2: Restricted Securities

Resident but not ordinarily resident at the date of acquisition

59.5 Up to 5 April 2008: The restricted securities regime applied only in circumstances where the employee was both resident *and* ordinarily resident at the date of acquisition. The income tax charge arose, therefore, instead under the general earnings rule in ITEPA 2003, s 62 and was based on the restricted value of the securities at the date of acquisition. Given that no further tax charge arose when the restrictions were lifted, the resident status was irrelevant at the date of lifting.

With effect from 6 April 2008: The restricted securities regime now applies in circumstances where the employee is resident at the date of acquisition, regardless of whether he or she is ordinarily resident. The income tax charge is based on the restricted value of the securities at the date of acquisition and a further charge arises when the restrictions are lifted unless the remittance basis is claimed.

Chapter 3: Convertible Securities

Resident but not ordinarily resident at the date of acquisition

59.6 Up to 5 April 2008: The convertible securities regime applied only in circumstances where the employee was both resident *and* ordinarily resident at the date of acquisition. The income tax charge arose, therefore, instead under the general earnings rule in ITEPA 2003, s 62 and was based on the value of the securities at the date of acquisition. Given that no further tax charge arose when the restrictions were lifted, the resident status was irrelevant at the date of conversion.

With effect from 6 April 2008: The convertible securities regime now applies in circumstances where the employee is resident at the date of acquisition, regardless of whether he or she is ordinarily resident. The income tax charge is based on the value of the convertible securities at the date of acquisition, ignoring the conversion right and a further charge arises when the conversion takes place unless the remittance basis is claimed.

Chapter 3A: Securities with Artificially Depressed Market Value

59.7 Up to 5 April 2008: A charge to income tax arose at the time of an event in circumstances where the employee was resident or ordinarily resident at the date of acquisition, provided the duties of the employment were performed in the UK. If the duties of the employment were not performed in the UK, then any gains will be outside the scope of the Chapter 3A charge unless they were remitted to the UK.

(The position was, therefore, strikingly different from either the RSR or the convertible securities regime (CSR) which required the employee to be both resident *and* ordinarily resident at the date of acquisition.)

With effect from 6 April 2008: The position has not changed and is explained for up to 5 April 2008.

Chapter 3B: Securities with Artificially Enhanced Market Value

59.8 Up to 5 April 2008: A charge to income tax arose at the time of an event in circumstances where the employee was resident *or* ordinarily resident at the date of acquisition, provided the duties of the employment were performed in the UK. If the duties of the employment were not performed in the UK, then any gains will be outside the scope of the Chapter 3B charge unless they were remitted to the UK.

(The position was, therefore, strikingly different from either the RSR or the CSR which required the employee to be both resident *and* ordinarily resident at the date of acquisition.)

With effect from 6 April 2008: The position has not changed and is explained for up to 5 April 2008.

Chapter 3C: Securities Acquired for Less Than Market Value

59.9 **Up to 5 April 2008:** A charge to income tax arose at the time of an acquisition in circumstances where the employee was resident *or* ordinarily resident at the date of acquisition, provided the duties of the employment were performed in the UK. If the duties of the employment were not performed in the UK, then any gains will be outside the scope of the Chapter 3C charge unless they were remitted to the UK.

(The position was, therefore, strikingly different from either the RSR or the CSR which required the employee to be both resident *and* ordinarily resident at the date of acquisition.)

With effect from 6 April 2008: The position has not changed and is explained for up to 5 April 2008.

Chapter 3D: Securities Disposed of for More Than Market Value

59.10 **Up to 5 April 2008:** A charge to income tax arose at the time of a sale in circumstances where the employee was resident *or* ordinarily resident at the date of acquisition, provided the duties of the employment were performed in the UK. If the duties of the employment were not performed in the UK, then any gains will be outside the scope of the Chapter 3D charge unless they were remitted to the UK.

(The position was, therefore, strikingly different from either the RSR or the CSR which required the employee to be both resident *and* ordinarily resident at the date of acquisition.)

With effect from 6 April 2008: The position has not changed and is explained for up to 5 April 2008.

Chapter 4: Post-Acquisition Benefits from Securities

59.11 **Up to 5 April 2008:** The post-acquisition benefits regime applied only in circumstances where the employee was both resident and ordinarily resident. The income tax charge arose, therefore, instead under the general earnings rule in ITEPA 2003, s 62 and was based on the value of the securities at the date of acquisition. Given that no further tax charge arose when the benefit was received, the resident status was irrelevant at the date of receipt.

With effect from 6 April 2008: The post-acquisition benefits regime now applies in circumstances where the employee is resident at the date of receipt, regardless of whether he or she is ordinarily resident. The income tax charge is based on the value of the benefit at the date of receipt unless the remittance basis is claimed.

Chapter 5: Securities Options

59.12 **Up to 5 April 2008:** The securities options regime applied only in circumstances where the employee was both resident *and* ordinarily resident at the date of grant. The income tax charge arose, therefore, instead at the date of exercise under the general option gains taxing rule in ITEPA 2003, ss 192–200 and was based on the uplift in value from the option price to the MV at the date of exercise. Whether or not there was a tax charge at the date of exercise depended on the resident status at the date of grant so the resident status at the date of exercise was irrelevant.

With effect from 6 April 2008: The securities options regime now applies in circumstances where the employee is resident at the date of acquisition, regardless of whether he or she is ordinarily resident. The income tax charge is based on the uplift in value from the option price to the MV at the date of exercise. Whether or not there is a tax charge at the date of exercise depends on the resident status at the date of grant so the resident status at the date of exercise was irrelevant.

Remittance basis and the apportionment rules

59.13 The remittance basis applies to the tax calculations of employees who fall into one or other of the following categories:

- non-UK ordinarily resident; and

- non-UK domiciled.

The remittance basis is applied to foreign source income that triggers a charge to UK income tax to the extent that it is remitted to the UK. For income to be remitted to the UK, it must be the case that money or other property is brought to or received or used in the UK by or for the benefit of the relevant person. Any shares in a UK company are treated by HMRC as UK situs assets and used in the UK for the benefit of the employee. In essence, the foreign source income that arises from shares in a UK company is deemed to have been remitted to the UK. The employee who is non-UK ordinarily resident or non-UK domiciled will not be in a position to avoid the charge to income tax on UK income that has been derived from UK employment-related securities.

The effect of FA 2008 on the remittance basis arises through the application of the new apportionment rules which applies to securities income, identified within ITEPA 2003, Pt 7 on which income tax is charged as follows:

Chapter 2	Restricted Securities
Chapter 3	Convertible Securities
Chapter 3C	Securities Acquired for Less Than Market Value
Chapter 3D	Securities Disposed of for More Than Market Value
Chapter 4	Post-Acquisition Benefits from Securities
Chapter 5	Securities Options

The apportionment rules do *not* apply to the ITEPA 2003 provisions as follows:

Section 62	The General Earnings Provision
Chapter 3A	Securities with Artificially Depressed Market Value
Chapter 3B	Securities with Artificially Enhanced Market Value

The apportionment rules seek to apportion employment-related securities income between the following:

- securities income; and

- foreign securities income.

Certain employees, defined as follows, may have a proportion of their securities income categorized as foreign securities income if part of the so-called 'relevant period' falls within a tax year to which the remittance basis applies:

- An employee who is ordinarily resident in the UK but non-domiciled, and whose employment is with a foreign employer and the duties of which are performed wholly outside the UK.

- An employee who is not ordinarily resident in the UK and some or all of the duties of whose employment are ordinarily resident in the UK and some or all of the duties of whose employment are performed outside the UK.

The 'relevant period' is the period in which the income is earned or to which it most closely relates. The following represents the practical expression of this principle to the Chapters of ITEPA 2003, Pt 7:

Chapter 2	Restricted Securities	The period beginning with the acquisition of the securities and ending on the chargeable event, unless a section 431 tax election has been made in which case the apportionment rules do not apply and the remittance rules apply as they do to general earnings.
Chapter 3	Convertible Securities	The period beginning with the acquisition of the securities and ending on the chargeable event.
Chapter 3C	Securities Acquired for Less Than Market Value	*For the discharge of a notional loan, if the shares were acquired upon the exercise of a share option:* the period beginning on the date of grant and ending on the date on which it first becomes exercisable. *For all other cases:* the tax year in which the notional loan was treated as made or, of the chargeable event occurs in that year, the period beginning with the start of that year and ending with the date on which the chargeable event occurs.
Chapter 3D	Securities Disposed of for More Than Market Value	The period is the tax year in which the disposal occurs.
Chapter 4	Post-Acquisition Benefits from Securities	The period is the tax year in which the benefit is received.
Chapter 5	Securities Options	The period beginning on the grant of the option and ending on the date on which it first becomes exercisable or, if earlier, the date on which a chargeable event occurs.

The application of the apportionment rules is as follows:

- The employment income is treated as accruing evenly over the relevant period.

- The basis for the apportionment of the income is by reference to respective proportions of the employee's UK duties and the employee's non-UK duties.

- For employees who are non-UK domiciled, *the foreign securities income* is that part of the securities income treated as accruing in that part of the relevant period that falls within the tax year in which the remittance basis applies and the duties of the employment fall wholly outside the UK.

- For employees who are UK-domiciled but not UK ordinarily resident, *the foreign securities income* is that part of the securities income treated as accruing in any part of the relevant period that falls within a tax year in which the remittance basis applies, apportioned as between UK duties and non-UK duties on a 'just and reasonable' basis.

The application of the 'just and reasonable' override principle is as follows:

- Where the pro rata calculation produces an amount for foreign securities income that not 'just and reasonable' then either HMRC or the employee can substitute an amount which is 'just and reasonable', such amount being determined having taken into account all the facts of the case.

- The key principle for the apportionment that is explained in the HMRC guidance notes is the application of an even accrual over the relevant period but with the relevant period being the period over which the gain could reasonably be regarded as having been earned.

- The HMRC guidance notes on this point are geared to ensuring that there is a matching between the relevant period and the period over which the gain was earned and gives examples: where shares are awarded to recognise duties in the period preceding the award, where within the relevant period there is a significant period of leave and where the cessation of employment arises during the relevant period.

The PAYE implications of applying the remittance basis are as follows:

- The PAYE system should be applied to the net amount of the employment income *after* the deduction of the foreign source income.

- The application of the PAYE system is predicated upon the employing company having sufficient information to calculate the income that is taxable on a remittance basis.

- If actual amounts are not known then best estimates should be processed through the PAYE system on the UK part of the gain, taking account of the assumption as appropriate that the employee will claim the remittance basis.

- Where best estimates are used and there is an over-payment, the employee can claim the repayment though the self-assessment tax return.

- The apportionment rules relate solely to income tax and do not apply in relation to liabilities for NICs.

The HMRC Form 42 implications of applying the remittance basis are as follows:

- Where the employing company has knowledge that there is a reportable amount that is taxable on a remittance basis then there is a requirement to include in the additional information section of the HMRC Form 42 the employee's name and NI number.

- The employing company in determining the amount to disclose should take into account the effect of the remittance basis in determining the amount on which PAYE was calculated, knowledge of the employee's eligibility to claim and knowledge of the employee's overseas duties.

- Specifically with regard to remittances of foreign securities income, the employing company does not have a reporting obligation.

Use of double taxation treaties

59.14 The application of the double taxation treaties must be interpreted in the light of the statement made by HMRC in *Tax Bulletin 55* that was issued in October 2001 and which was restated in *Tax Bulletin 76* that was issued in April 2005.

The *Tax Bulletin 55* addresses the circumstances as follows:

- The employee is granted a share option in the UK by virtue of his or her employment.

- The employee continued that employment in a country other than the UK for the period between the grant of the option and the exercise of the option.

- The employee is not resident in the UK at the date of exercise.

- The employee has a tax liability in the UK and in the other country on the increase in value from the option price to the MV at the date of exercise.

In these circumstances the UK will give a tax relief on the proportion of the option gain which relates to the period(s) between the date of grant and the date of exercise during which the employee continued the employment in the other country. The period in the other country will in all normal circumstances be calculated on a straightline time apportionment basis.

An alternative method of giving the tax relief in the UK could be to give a tax credit in the UK for the tax that is actually paid in the other country where the employee continued his or her employment between date of grant and date of exercise.

The *Tax Bulletin* 76 introduced a change to the apportionment basis as follows:

- The apportionment must be by reference to workdays spent in the UK and in the other country between the grant of the option and *the vesting of the option* rather than the exercise of the option unless the double tax treaty stipulates another basis which is, for example, the case with the UK/US Double Taxation Treaty which takes the period up to the date of exercise.

Tax Bulletin 55 also addresses the problem that arises in relation to the following circumstances:

- The employee is not subject to income tax in the UK on the option gain.

- The employee is subject to income tax in another country with which the UK has a double tax treaty.

- The employee is subject to UK CGT on the sale of the shares.

- The employee has no relief for the tax suffered in the other country on the option gain.

Tax Bulletin 55 offers a solution by allowing the option gain to be treated as falling within the provisions of the article of the double taxation treaty that deals with employment income. The solution is for HMRC in the UK to allow the tax that has been paid in the other country as a credit against the UK CGT liability. The application of this principle is as follows:

- Where the options are exercised and the shares sold on the same day *the whole gain* is treated as falling within the article that deals with employment income of the double taxation treaty.

- Where there is a delay in the shares being sold after the options have been exercised *part of the gain* is treated as falling within the article that deals with employment income of the double taxation treaty. The tax treatment will depend on the facts of each case and, in particular, the movement in the share price between the date of exercise and the date of sale.

The credit that is given in the UK for tax that is actually paid in the other country cannot exceed the tax that is payable in the UK on the gain. However, the credit can be given for overseas tax paid at the date of grant or at the date of exercise or, indeed, on any other occasion that the overseas charging provisions determined a tax charge to arise.

The interaction between the new remittance rules and the application of the double taxation treaties is as follows:

- The classic case (which is the most usual situation) is that the securities income has been apportioned between UK securities income and foreign securities income and, as a consequence of the application of the apportionment rules, no double taxation has arisen.

- The more unusual case is where there is a mismatch on the calculation of the gain between the apportionment rules and the double taxation treaty rules. The key example is for the UK/US interaction where the remittance rules apportion on the basis of the period from the grant of the option to the exercise of the option whereas the double taxation treaty rules apportion on the basis of the period from the grant of the option to the vesting of the option. The conundrum arises where the double taxation treaty has exempted amounts from UK tax but the remittance rules are only exempt to the extent that there is no remittance to the UK. The matter is resolved through allowing the result arrived at through applying the double taxation treaty rules to supersede the result arrived through applying the remittance rules.

Chapter 60

Employee share schemes in the USA

Introduction

60.1 This chapter explains the employee share schemes that operate in the USA. The reason for the inclusion of the chapter is that the USA is the only other tax jurisdiction that has embraced employee share schemes to a level that can be compared with the UK. It is also one of the two tax jurisdictions, along with France, that Gordon Brown, when Chancellor of the Exchequer, examined in order to develop the FA 2000 employee share schemes, the SIP and EMI.

401K Plan

Operation

60.2 The 401K Plan ('the Plan') is in essence a retirement plan that qualifies for special tax treatment under the 401K provisions in the tax code.

The plan operates with involvement from employee and employer as follows:

- The employee designates funds from pre-tax compensation for investment under the 401K rules. This designation is what the employee voluntarily decides to defer into the Plan. It is usual for the investment to be in four or more investment choices where one of those choices is the shares of the sponsoring company.

- The employer has the opportunity to match the employer contributions and these funds also can be directed into investment into the shares of the sponsoring company. The company contributions can be based on a percentage of what the employees defer or on relative compensation or on a more level formula for all employees whether or not they have chosen to defer.

- The employer cannot require the employees to use their salary deferrals to purchase company shares if the Plan invests more than 10% of its assets in company shares although employees may still choose to invest in company shares.

Tax position for the employee

60.3 The limits for the contributions are as follows:

- The employee deferrals into the Plan are limited to $16,500 for 2009 with an expected annual increase.

- The maximum employer contribution is 25% of eligible pay of each plan participant on an annual basis where eligible pay is limited to $245,000 per employee for 2009 for the purpose of the calculation.

The tax reliefs for the employee are as follows:

- The earnings that arise on the assets that are held by the Plan are not subject to tax for the employee.

- The contributions that the employee makes to the Plan are not subject to tax for the employee.

The position on leaving the company for the employee is as follows:

- In the event of leaving the employee receives a distribution of the benefits.

- If the employee transfers the assets to a retirement plan at another company or to an individual retirement plan which is a tax-sheltered plan under the federal law then any further earnings on the Plan assets are not taxed while they remain in the new plan.

- If the employee does not transfer the assets into a retirement plan then they are taxed at the ordinary income tax rates that prevail at the time together with a 10% penalty.

- When the assets are withdrawn at retirement age they are taxed at the ordinary tax rate of the individual at that time which has the advantage of often being less than the individual's tax rate before retirement.

Tax position for the employer

60.4 The employer receives a tax deduction for contributions that it makes into the Plan up to the maximum of 25% of the eligible employee's pay for pay up to $245,000 for 2009.

Schedules

60.5 Consider the following points:

- In all normal circumstances the shares remain in the Plan until the termination of employment.

- In the event that termination is due to death, retirement or disability employees must receive their distribution not later than one year after the end of the Plan year in which that event arises.

- In the event of termination for any other reason the company can wait until retirement age to make the distribution although that would be unusual given the weight of administration.

Vesting schedules

60.6 Consider the following:

- A vesting schedule is the gradual accumulation of a right to a benefit. Vesting schedules are often used for 401K Plans for employer contributions although they cannot be used for employee contributions for the reason that employees have a right to the income immediately.

- The vesting schedules for employer contributions may vest over six years with 20% vesting in each year after the first year, all at once at the end of three years or at some point before then.

Eligibility

60.7 Eligibility criteria include:

- At least all full-time employees working 1000 hours in any Plan year must be eligible to participate in the Plan subject to certain exceptions.

- The Plan can require at least one year of service before an employee becomes eligible.

Accounting

60.8 The company contributions represent a charge to compensation in the year of contribution.

Employee stock ownership plan (ESOP)

Operation

60.9 The employee stock ownership plan (ESOP) is also a retirement plan that qualifies for special tax treatment.

The key operational features of the ESOP are as follows:

- The company establishes a trust to hold company shares and other investments for the employees until the employee leaves the company.

- It is the company only and not the employee who funds the ESOP by either contributing shares to the ESOP or contributing cash to the ESOP for the purchase of shares or by arranging for the ESOP to borrow money in order to buy shares.

- The shares that are used for the ESOP are either newly-issued shares or existing shares purchased from the market.

- In circumstances where the shares are not purchased through borrowings, the ESOP allocates the shares to individual employee accounts, usually based on relative compensation.

- In circumstances where the purchase of the shares is supported by borrowings, as the loan is repaid the number of shares that is equal to the percentage of the loan repaid in the year is released to the employee accounts.

Tax treatment for the employee

60.10   The tax relief for the employee are as follows:

- The earnings that arise on the assets that are held by the ESOP are not subject to tax for the employee.

The position on leaving the company for the employee is as follows:

- In the event of leaving the employee receives a distribution of the benefits.

- If the employee transfers the assets to a retirement plan at another company or to an individual retirement plan which is a tax-sheltered plan under the federal law then any further earnings on the Plan assets are not taxed while they remain in the new plan.

- If the employee does not transfer the assets into a retirement plan then they are taxed at the ordinary income tax rates that prevail at the time together with a 10% penalty.

- When the assets are withdrawn at retirement age they are taxed at the ordinary tax rate of the individual at that time which has the advantage of often being less than the individual's tax rate before retirement.

Tax treatment of the employer

60.11   Tax treatment considerations include:

- The employer receives a tax deduction for contributions that it makes into the ESOP up to the maximum of 25% of the eligible employee's pay for pay up to $245,000 for 2009.

- In circumstances where the shares are not purchased through borrowings interest paid on the ESOP debt does not count as an employer contribution. Payments on the principal do count as an employer contribution.

- The employer can make tax-deductible dividends to employees if they are used to repay the loan or are passed on directly to the employees or the employees reinvest them in company shares.

Schedules

60.12   Points to bear in mind include:

*   In all normal circumstances the shares remain in the Plan until the termination of employment.

*   In the event that termination is due to death, retirement or disability, employees must receive their distribution to begin not later than one year after the end of the Plan year in which that event arises. Distribution can be in instalments of up to five years.

*   In the event of termination for any other reason the company can wait for up to five years after the end of the plan year in which the employee leaves to start distributions.

Vesting schedules

60.13   A vesting schedule is the gradual accumulation of a right to a benefit. Full vesting must occur over seven years in an ESOP at not less than 20% per year for five years starting after the third year or 100% after five years for vesting that occurs all at the end of the fifth year.

Eligibility

60.14   At least all full-time employees working 1000 hours in any Plan year must be eligible to participate in the Plan subject to certain exceptions. The Plan can require at least one year of service before an employee becomes eligible.

Accounting

60.15   The company contributions represent a charge to compensation in the year of contribution. For loans principal payments are charged as compensation although interest payments are not.

Employee stock purchase plan (ESPP) called section 423 Plan

Operation

60.16   The employee stock purchase plan (ESPP) is *not* a retirement plan. Rather it represents an opportunity for employees to purchase company shares and subsequently make a gain during their employment.

The key operational features of the ESPP are as follows:

*   The employee has an opportunity to purchase company shares, often at a discounted price and usually using accumulated payroll deductions. The ESPP runs over a set period of time, called the offering period, and has specific purchase dates.

- The accumulated payroll deductions are made by the employer, on the basis of an authorisation that the employee gives to the employer to withhold a certain percentage of their paycheck each pay period and accumulate these amounts in a special account.

- There may be specific intervals during the offering period at which the employee may elect to purchase shares with the accumulated funds rather than wait until the end of the offering period.

- The price the employee will pay for the shares may be set at the beginning of the offering period or at the end of the offering period or at some other date or at the lower of the beginning or ending price called a look-back feature. The employer can offer a discount in the calculation of the price. Where a discount is given it is usually at about 15%.

No employee can purchase more than $25,000 worth of shares in any year.

Section 423 preferential tax treatment

60.17   To qualify for preferential tax treatment the ESPP must comply with the requirements that are set out in the *Internal Revenue Service Code*, section 423, as follows:

- There are limitations set on the level of the discount and on the length of the offering period.

- The plans must be open to all full-time employees with at least two years service with some exceptions for highly compensated individuals and 10% owners.

Tax position for the employee

60.18   Provided the applicable schedules are complied with the tax reliefs for the employee are as follows:

- No tax is due until the employee sells the shares when CGT arises on any increase in value during the offering period as well as increases while the shares are held following purchase.

  Note: Income tax is payable on the discount but only when the employee sells the shares.

- The employee benefits under the ESPP are not subject to the alternative minimum tax and employees do not pay FICA or unemployment taxes.

Tax position for the employer

60.19   Provided the applicable schedules are complied with the tax reliefs for the employer are as follows:

- No withholding is required.

Note: No corporate deductions are allowed except in the case of a disqualifying disposition in which case the company can take a deduction that is equal to the amount recognised as ordinary income by the employee.

Schedules

60.20   Requirements include:

- The employee must hold on to the shares for one year after purchase and cannot sell the shares within two years after the beginning of the offering period.

- If the option price is set at 85% or more of the market price at the date of exercise then the offering period may last up to five years.

- If the option price is set at the lesser of 85% at grant or at exercise then the offering period cannot exceed 27 months. This is common practice.

- The employee must remain employed by the company for the entire offering period or until at most three months before purchase.

Eligibility

60.21   Requirements include:

- Only employees of the company are eligible and the company cannot discriminate as to who is eligible so in practice in most cases all full-time employees are eligible.

- Grant values can be based on compensation and the company can establish a maximum that has to be applied to every employee.

- Any employee who owns 5% or more of the company shares is ineligible to participate.

- The company can exclude from the plan highly compensated employees as defined in the IRS, part-time employees defined as those who are working less than 20 hours per week, or less than five months in the year and those who have been employed for less than two years.

- Membership of a trade union is not an acceptable basis for exclusion.

- There are no rules for who must actually participate and any mix of employees can elect not to participate.

Accounting

60.22   The ESPP is considered a non-compensatory plan and, therefore, open to favourable accounting treatment although the position is currently under review through the intention of the IASB to introduce expense accounting for share option schemes.

Restricted stock plan

Operation

60.23 The restricted stock plan (RSP) is an arrangement that provides an employee recipient to acquire a specified number of shares in the company but only when the restrictions to purchase are lifted.

The key operational features of the RSP are as follows:

- The employee is given a right to purchase the shares at a set price or at no cost. If a payment is required for purchase then it is usually the fair MV of the shares at the inception of the plan.

- In private companies the value of the shares is often relatively low at the inception of the plan so this value is used as the basis for the price that the employee will ultimately have to pay for the shares. However, for the publicly-quoted company the price is often set at zero or at a substantial discount as if the price is set at MV the employee may as well buy the shares in the open market without the restrictions.

- The award of a right to purchase shares; is awarded by the company to the employee subject to restrictions or risk of forfeiture. The restrictions may be in the form of a contingency for continued service or personal contribution to the company for a specified period of time ('the vesting period') or the achievement of specified performance conditions.

- During the vesting period, the restricted shares are not transferable and are usually held by the company in an escrow or custodial arrangement.

- If the recipient fails to satisfy the vesting condition the company has the right to repurchase any unvested (unearned) restricted shares at a price that is equal to the initial cost of the shares to the recipient.

Tax position for the employee

60.24 Consider the following:

- There is no taxable event at the grant, the inception of the plan, as the shares are not transferable on the date of purchase or award and are subject to substantial risk of forfeiture.

- As the forfeiture restrictions lapse and the restricted shares vest the difference between the purchase price and the fair MV on the date of vesting is compensation income to the employee and taxed at ordinary income tax rates.

- The employee may elect to close the compensatory element of the transaction and accelerate the time at which compensation income is realised to the inception of the arrangement by filing a section 83(b) election with the Internal Revenue Service.

— If the shares have been purchased at full MV the election has the result of reducing the compensation income to zero. This is the situation in which the employee would typically make the election.

— If the shares have been awarded at zero the election has the result of limiting the base for income tax to the MV of the shares at the date of the inception of the arrangement. This is typically the situation in which the employee would not make the election.

● If the recipient is an employee federal and state withholding obligations for income and employment tax purposes may arise at the time the arrangements vests, or at the inception of the arrangement if a section 83(b) election is made. The relevant withholding taxes include federal income tax, social security (FICA), medicare, state income tax (if applicable), state disability or unemployment (if applicable) and local taxes (if applicable). For employees, under section 6672 of the Internal Revenue Code, a 100% penalty may be imposed for failing to withhold and pay over any taxes. There is no withholding required from a non-employee.

Tax position for the employer

60.25 The company receives a corporate tax deduction for the compensation expense under section 162 of the Internal Revenue Code equal to the amount included as compensation income in the gross income of the employee and generally the company is able to take the benefit of the deduction in the taxable year in which the employee recognises the income.

In the case of restricted shares that are offered to the C EO or one of the four most highly compensated executive officers of a publicly-quoted company the compensation income recognised by the employee is subject to the deduction limit of section 162(m) of the Internal Revenue Code which limits the deductibility of compensation not paid as incentive compensation.

Schedules

60.26 The restricted share purchase by a corporate insider and the award of restricted shares to a corporate insider are reportable events for purposes of section 16(a).

Under the section 16 rules, neither the vesting of a right to receive a security nor the lapse of restrictions relating to a security is subject to section 16.

The Securities Exchange Act (1934) requires that a publicly held company disclose detailed information about the compensation of its executive officers, including compensation under any RSP in its proxy and information statements, periodic reports and other filings.

Eligibility

60.27   The RSP is not subject to statutory eligibility restrictions and can be inclusive of non-employees. Eligibility is at the discretion of the Board of directors.

The RSP usually operates with annual vesting schedules with shares vesting in equal annual instalments over a period of several years.

Stock option plan

60.28   The stock option plan gives an individual the right to buy a certain number of shares in the granting company at a fixed price for a fixed amount of time.

Types of stock option plan

60.29   In the USA, there are two distinct types of compensatory options as follows:

- Incentive stock option (ISO): also referred to as the statutory option or the qualified option, and which may only be granted to employees of the sponsoring company.

- Non-qualified stock option (NSO): also referred to as the non-statutory option, and which may be granted indiscriminately.

The ISO must comply with the US tax regulations that are set out in the Internal Revenue Service Code.

Qualification as an ISO

60.30   To qualify as an ISO *the plan* must have the following character-istics:

- The plan must specify the aggregate number of shares subject to the plan.

- The plan must identify the employees or class of employees eligible to receive options under the plan.

- The plan must have been approved by the company's shareholders; within 12 months before or after the adoption by the Board of directors.

- The plan must not allow options to be granted more than ten years after the plan adoption or approval; whichever is the earlier.

To qualify as an ISO *the option* must have the following characteristics:

- The option cannot be exercised more than ten years after the date of grant.

- The option must be granted to an employee of the company or its subsidiary who maintains continuous employment with the company from the date of grant until no more than three months before the exercise of the option. Certain leaves, not exceeding 90 days, do not interrupt continuous employment.

- The option price must not be less than the fair MV of the underlying shares at the time the option is granted.

- The option may not allow more than $100,000 of the fair MV of the underlying shares, calculated at the time of grant, to become first exercisable in any one calendar year. Any excessive options granted in error automatically lose ISO treatment.

- The option may have no tandem rights other than stock appreciation rights.

- The resultant shares purchased must be held for no less than two years from the date of grant and one year from the date of exercise (the ISO holding periods). These periods can and often overlap.

If these conditions prevail then the final disposition of the shares is considered a 'qualifying disposition' and be eligible for favourable tax treatment.

If share options are held by shareholders who own 10% of more of the company's shares, then to qualify as an ISO the *option* must have the following characteristics:

- The option cannot be exercised more than five years after the date of grant.

- The option price must not be less than 110% of the fair MV of the underlying shares at the time the option is granted.

Tax position for the employee

For the ISO

60.31   At the time the option is exercised, if the employee continues to hold the shares that are purchased as a result of the exercise then no federal personal income tax is assessed.

It is possible that state or local taxes may be assessed on the exercise of options.

If the employee conducts a 'same-day transaction' in which the exercise of a share option is affected with funds received from the sale of the shares purchased then the transaction is considered a disqualifying disposition.

If the shares are sold under a disqualifying disposition then the employee is subject to personal income tax on the *lesser* of *firstly* the spread between the fair MV of the shares at the date of exercise and the sale price and *secondly* the spread between the option price and the fair MV at the date of sale.

For the NSO

60.32 At the time the option is exercised. the employee is subject to personal income tax on the spread between the option price and the fair MV of the shares at the date of exercise.

At the time of the sale of the shares, any further increase in value from the date of exercise is subject to CGT. If the shares have been held for one year or less then the rules for short-term capital gains apply. If the shares have been held for more than one year then the rules for long-term capital gains apply.

Tax position for the employer

For the ISO

60.33 The employing company is entitled to no tax deduction for the grant of the option or for the exercise of the option.

If the ISO is a disqualifying disposition then the employing company is entitled to a tax deduction for the amount of regular income recognised by the employee.

There is no withholding required on the exercise of an ISO.

For the NSO

60.34 The employing company is entitled to a tax deduction for the compensatory value of the NSO that it grants to the extent of the amount of regular income recognised by the employee either at the grant or at the exercise of the share option.

The employer company is obliged to withhold for federal income taxes, state and city taxes and social security and medicare.

Eligibility

60.35 ISO may only be granted to employees of the employing company, its parent company or its subsidiary company.

NSO may be granted indiscriminately.

Appendix A

ABI Guidelines on policies and practices

Section III – Guidance for share-based incentive

Main provisions

Share-based incentives should align the interests of executive directors with that of shareholders and link reward to performance over the longer term. Vesting should therefore be based on performance conditions measured over a period appropriate to the strategic objectives of the company. This will not be less than, and may exceed, three years.

All new share-based incentives or any substantive changes to existing schemes should be subject to prior approval by shareholders by means of a separate and binding resolution. Their operation, rationale and cost should be fully explained so that shareholders can make an informed judgment.

The operation of share incentive schemes should not lead to dilution in excess of the limits acceptable to shareholders.

Executive share options should not be granted at a discount to the prevailing market price.

It is desirable to align the interests of chairmen and independent directors with those of shareholders, for example through payment in shares bought at market prices. However, shareholders consider it inappropriate for chairmen and independent directors to receive incentive awards geared to the share price or corporate performance that would impair their ability to provide impartial oversight and advice.

Shareholders encourage companies to require executive directors and senior executives to build up meaningful shareholdings in the companies for which they work.

Guidance

1. Scope

1.1 This Guidance applies to all share-based schemes whether option-based or involving conditional awards of shares, and including any arrangements whereby the value of an option gain will be paid either in the form of cash or shares (cash or share-settled share appreciation rights respectively).

2. Review and disclosure

2.1 Remuneration Committees should:

- regularly review share incentive schemes to ensure their continued effectiveness, compliance with the current Guidance and contribution to shareholder value;

- provide a statement in the Remuneration Report as to whether a review of the current share incentive schemes has been undertaken both as regards their operation, including how discretion has been exercised, and whether grant levels, performance criteria and vesting schedules which have been previously approved by shareholders remain appropriate to the company's current circumstances and prospects; and

- obtain prior shareholder authorisation for any substantive or exceptional amendments to scheme rules and practice including changes to limits and changes which make it easier to achieve performance targets, and where significant exercise of discretion is proposed by the Remuneration Committee.

2.2 Scheme and individual participation limits must be fully disclosed in share incentive schemes. Disclosure should, inter alia, cover performance conditions and related costs and dilution limits as set out in the relevant sections below. The reasons for selecting the performance conditions and target levels, together with the overall policy for granting conditional share or option awards, should be fully explained to shareholders.

3. Grant policy

Phasing of awards and grants

3.1 The regular phasing of share incentive awards and option grants, generally on an annual basis, is strongly encouraged because:

- it reduces the risk of unanticipated outcomes that arise out of share price volatility and cyclical factors;

- it eliminates the perceived problem that a limit on subsisting options encourages early exercise;

- it allows the adoption of a single performance measurement period; and

- it lessens the possible incidence of 'underwater' options, where the share price falls below the exercise price.

The phased vesting of awards in specific tranches following the minimum three year performance measurement period is not an alternative to phased grants. However, it can help to enhance the linking of vesting of awards to sustained performance and maintain incentivisation.

4. Performance

4.1 The desired alignment of interests is best achieved through the vesting of awards under share incentive schemes being conditional on satisfaction of performance conditions. Performance measures should be fully explained and be clearly linked to the achievement of challenging and stretching financial performance which will lead to enhancement of shareholder value.

Remuneration Committees should satisfy themselves that vesting of awards accord with these objectives.

4.2 Challenging performance conditions should:

- relate to overall corporate performance;

- demonstrate the achievement of a level of financial performance which is demanding and stretching in the context of the prospects for the company and the prevailing economic environment in which it operates;

- be measured relative to an appropriate defined peer group or other relevant benchmark; and

- be disclosed and transparent.

4.3 Threshold vesting amounts should not be significant by comparison to annual base salary. Furthermore, award structures with a marked 'cliff-edge' vesting profile are considered inappropriate, particularly where there may be clustering of performance outcomes around the average.

4.4 The vesting of awards with high potential value should be linked to commensurately higher levels of performance. Full vesting should be dependent upon achievement of significantly greater value creation than that applicable to threshold vesting. Companies should explain clearly how this is achieved, especially when annual grants of options in excess of one times salary, or equivalent long term share incentive awards, are made.

4.5 Sliding scales are a useful way of ensuring that performance conditions are genuinely stretching. They generally provide a better motivator for improving corporate performance than a 'single hurdle'.

4.6 Awards of matching shares arising from annual bonuses payable in the form of shares where these are held for a qualifying period, should be subject to the satisfaction of performance criteria prior to the vesting of the matching element. (see Paragraph 1.3 – Guidance for Base Pay, Bonuses, Pensions and Contracts and Severance)

4.7 Comparator groups used for performance purposes should be both relevant and representative. Where only a small number of companies are used for a comparator group, Remuneration Committees should satisfy themselves that the comparative performance will not result in arbitrary outcomes which are inconsistent with this Guidance. Awards should not vest for less than median performance.

Performance criteria

4.8 Total Shareholder Return (TSR) relative to a relevant index or peer group is one of a number of generally acceptable performance criteria. However, Remuneration Committees should satisfy themselves prior to vesting that the recorded TSR or other criterion is a genuine reflection of the company's underlying financial performance, and explain their reasoning.

4.9 Where TSR is used as a performance criterion and the chosen comparator group includes companies listed in overseas markets, it is essential that TSR be measured on a consistent basis. The standard approach should be for a common currency to be used. Where there are compelling grounds for the calculation to be based on local currency TSR of comparator group companies, then the reasons for choosing this approach should be fully explained.

4.10 The definition of Earnings Per Share (EPS) or any other financial measure should fully reflect the performance of the business on a consistent basis in respect of the measurement period.

4.11 Shareholders need to have sufficient data to judge the appropriate size of the award for any given performance level. They also expect a maximum level of grant to be disclosed.

4.12 The setting of a premium exercise price is not of itself a substitute for the adoption of relative performance conditions in accordance with this Guidance.

Retesting

4.13 It is recognised that any retesting of performance conditions for all share-based incentive schemes is unnecessary and unjustified.

5. Cost and basis of participation

Cost

5.1 The primary information that should be disclosed includes:

- The potential value of awards (see Appendix) due to individual scheme participants on full vesting. This should be expressed by reference to the face value of shares or shares under option at point of grant, and expressed as a multiple of base salary.

- The maximum dilution which may arise through the issue of shares to satisfy entitlements.

5.2 Shareholders also wish to understand the Expected Value (see Appendix) of incentive awards at the outset, bearing in mind the probability of achieving the stipulated performance criteria. Where changes to award levels or structures are being proposed, shareholders wish to have disclosed what changes in Expected Value will result and the reasons why the Remuneration Committee considers this justified.

5.3 There should be prudent and appropriate arrangements that are fully disclosed, governing the acquisition of shares, and financing thereof, to meet contingent obligations under share-based incentive schemes.

5.4 The use of phased grants of share options and restricted shares, and utilisation of both new and purchased shares to satisfy the vesting of awards, requires a comprehensive approach to valuation. Assessment should focus on expected value, which should be disclosed, and it should take account of the performance vesting schedule which is adopted as well as the existence of any 'retesting' and 'replacement option' facilities such as have been prevalent under traditional schemes. Shareholders are helped in this task by disclosure of face value of any share award or option grant as well as of expected value.

Vesting of awards

5.5 Remuneration Committees should consider the use of performance measurement periods of more than 3 years and deferred vesting schedules, in order to motivate the achievement of sustained improvements in financial performance.

5.6 Where LTIP awards are made over whole shares1, a better alignment of interest with shareholders will be achieved if, in respect of those shares that do vest, equivalent value to that which has accrued to shareholders by way of dividends during the period from date of grant also vests in the hands of LTIP recipients. To the extent that the shares conditionally awarded do not vest then nor should any scrip or cash amounts representing the rolled-up dividends.

5.7 Remuneration Committees should ensure that the size of grants made on this basis takes into account reasonable expectations as to the value of the dividend stream on the company's shares over the period to vesting. Where the facility for rolled-up dividends is introduced a smaller initial grant size is required in order to target a similar level of value in the conditional share award.

Performance on grant

5.8 Shareholders expect that future performance should govern the vesting of options or share awards. Performancing at point of grant is generally not considered a suitable alternative.

Change of control provisions

5.9 Scheme rules should state that there will be no automatic waiving of performance conditions either in the event of a change of control or where subsisting options and awards are 'rolled over' in the event of a capital reconstruction, and/or the early termination of the participant's employment. Remuneration Committees should use best endeavours to provide meaningful disclosure that quantifies the aggregate payments arising on a change of control.

5.10 In the event of a change of control, the key determinant of the level of awards vesting should be underlying financial performance. Also, any such early vesting as a consequence of a change of control should be on a time pro-rata basis i.e. taking into account the vesting period that has elapsed at the time of change of control. Remuneration Committees should satisfy themselves that the measured performance provides genuine evidence of underlying financial achievement over any shorter time period. They should explain their reasoning in the Remuneration Report or other relevant documentation sent to shareholders.

Participation

5.11 Participation in share incentive schemes should be restricted to bona-fide employees and executive directors, and be subject to appropriate limits for individual participation which should be disclosed.

5.12 There should be no absolute right of participation in share incentive schemes. Grant policy should be disclosed and consistently applied and, within the limits approved by shareholders, reflect changing commercial and competitive conditions. In the event of declining share price levels it is particularly important to avoid unjustified increases in the actual number of shares or options awarded.

5.13 Participation in more than one share incentive scheme must form part of a well-considered remuneration policy, and should not be part of a multiple arrangement designed to raise the prospects of payout.

6. Pricing and timing

Pricing of options and shares

6.1 The price at which shares are issued under a scheme should not be less than the mid-market price (or similar formula) immediately preceding grant of the shares under the scheme.

6.2 Options granted under executive (discretionary) schemes should not be granted at a discount to the prevailing mid-market price.

6.3 Repricing or surrender and regrant of awards or 'underwater' share options is not appropriate.

Timing of grant

6.4 The rules of a scheme should provide that share or option awards normally be granted only within a 42 day period following the publication of the company's results.

7. Life of schemes and incentive awards

7.1 No awards should be made beyond the life of the scheme approved on adoption by shareholders, which should not exceed 10 years.

7.2 Shares and options should not vest or be exercisable within three years from the date of grant. In addition, options should not be exercisable more than 10 years from the date of grant.

7.3 Options or other conditional share awards are normally granted in respect of the year in question and in expectation of service over the performance measurement period of not less than 3 years.

7.4 Where individuals choose to terminate their employment before the end of the service period, or in the event that employment is terminated for cause, any unvested options or conditional share-based award should normally lapse.

7.5 In other circumstances of cessation of employment (such circumstances may include disability, ill health, redundancy, retirement or analogous reasons for departure of a 'good leaver' nature.), it is to be expected that some portion of the award will vest, to the extent of the service period that has been completed but subject to the achievement of relevant performance criteria. In general the originally stipulated performance measurement period should continue to apply. However, where in the opinion of the Remuneration Committee, early vesting is appropriate, or where it is otherwise necessary (such circumstances may include death and also occasions such as takeover of the company or sale or transfer of the business undertaking where awards are not being rolled over into equivalent awards in the successor entity or new employer), awards should vest by reference to performance criteria achieved over the period to date.

7.6 Where options vest, in the event of death or cessation of employment of the option holder or where a company is taken over (except where arrangements are made for a switch to options of the offeror company), or where they have already vested at the time of such event, they must be exercised (or lapse) within 12 months. Where the performance measurement period applicable to an option extends beyond the point of cessation of employment as provided for by Paragraph 7.5 above, options must be exercised within 12 months of vesting following the end of the performance measurement period.

7.7 Any shares or options that a company may grant in exchange for those released under the schemes of acquired companies should normally be taken into account for the purposes of dilution and individual participation limits determined in accordance with this Guidance.

8. Dilution

8.1 The rules of a scheme must provide that commitments to issue new shares or re-issue treasury shares, when aggregated with awards under all of the company's other schemes, must not exceed 10% of the issued ordinary share capital (adjusted for share issuance and cancellation) in any rolling 10 year period. Remuneration Committees should ensure that appropriate policies regarding flow-rates exist in order to spread the potential issue of new shares over the life of relevant schemes in order to ensure the limit is not breached.

8.2 Commitments to issue new shares or re-issue treasury shares under executive (discretionary) schemes should not exceed 5% of the issued ordinary share capital of the company (adjusted for share issuance and cancellation) in any rolling 10 year period. This may be exceeded where vesting is dependent on the achievement of significantly more stretching performance criteria.

8.3 The implicit dilution commitment should always be provided for at point of grant even where, as in the case of share-settled share appreciation rights, it is recognised that only a proportion of shares may in practice be used.

8.4 For small companies, up to 10% of the ordinary share capital may be utilised for executive (discretionary) schemes, provided that the total market value of the capital utilised for the scheme at the time of grant does not exceed £1,000,000.

9. Joint venture companies and subsidiary companies

9.1 Shareholders generally consider it undesirable for options and other share-based incentives to be granted over the share capital of a joint venture company.

9.2 Discretionary grants over shares of a subsidiary company should only be made in exceptional circumstances. Where companies can justify doing so in terms of contribution to overall value creation, shareholders may consider exceptions subject to the following:

- Participation in subsidiary company schemes is restricted to those whose time is fully allocated to that subsidiary. Parent company directors should not participate in such schemes.

- There is full disclosure of the accounting treatment used when recognising the cost of option or share awards.

- Grants of options or share awards are subject to appropriately challenging performance criteria.

- Dilution limits relating to the subsidiary company should be disclosed in the context of parent company dilution limits.

- The methodology for valuing the subsidiary company shares and in the case of option awards the measurement of volatility of those shares should be disclosed. The party responsible for the valuation process should also be disclosed.

- Any entitlement or obligation to convert subsidiary company shares to parent company shares should be disclosed.

9.3 Shareholders may consider further exceptions where the condition of exercise is subject to flotation or sale of the subsidiary company. In such circumstances, grants should be conditional so that vesting is dependent on a return on investment that exceeds the cost of capital and that the market value of the shares at date of grant is subject to external validation.

9.4 Exceptions will apply in the case of an overseas subsidiary company where required by local legislation, or in circumstances where at least 25% of the ordinary share capital of the subsidiary company is listed and held outside the group.

10. ESOTs and all-employee schemes

Employee share ownership trusts – ESOTs

10.1 ESOTs should not hold more shares at any one time than would be required in practice to match their outstanding liabilities, nor should they be used as an anti-takeover or similar device. Furthermore an ESOT's deed should provide that any unvested shares held in the ESOT shall not be voted at shareholder meetings. The prior approval of shareholders should be obtained before 5% or more of a company's share capital at any one time may be held within ESOTs.

10.2 Where companies have provided for an ESOT to be used to meet scheme requirements, they should disclose the number of shares held by the ESOT in order to assist shareholders with their evaluation of the overall use of shares for remuneration purposes. The company should explain its strategy in this regard.

All-employee schemes

10.3 All-Employee schemes, such as SAYE schemes and Share Incentive Plans (SIPs) – (formerly known as AESOPs), should operate within an appropriate best practice framework. If newly issued shares are utilised, the overall dilution limits for share schemes should be complied with. The Guidance relating to timing of grants (except for pre-determined regular appropriation of shares under SIPs) applies.

Appendix

Potential value of the award

Shareholders are likely to have regard to the potential value of the award assuming full vesting. This should be expressed on the basis that a conditional award is made of shares, or options over shares, with a face value, at current prices, equal to a given percentage of base salary. However the potential value will also be a function of share price at the time of vesting and of illustrative disclosures of potential outcomes may also be helpful. Full vesting of awards of higher potential value should require the achievement of commensurately greater performance.

Expected value

The concept of Expected Value (EV) should be central to assessment of share incentive schemes. Essentially, EV will be the present value of the sum of all the various possible outcomes at vesting or exercise of awards. This will reflect the probabilities of achieving these outcomes and also the future value implicit in these outcomes. The calculation of the EV of share schemes relies on a range of assumptions, and reliance on this concept by Remuneration Committees will require a sufficient measure of disclosure to enable shareholders to make informed judgments about such arrangements.

The nature of performance hurdles governing exercise is also crucial to calculations of EV and it must also be recognised that any facility for 'retesting' will also increase the EV of the award whereas in contrast if the exercise price is set at a premium to the share price at the outset, this will reduce the value of the EV of the instrument.

Shareholders welcome efforts towards ensuring that accounting for share options and other share-based payment awarded under incentive schemes fully reflects the true cost to shareholders.

3 December 2007

Appendix B

HMRC SAYE Option Form 34

Date issued *DD MM YYYY*

PAYE reference number

ESSU scheme reference number

S R S /

SAYE Option Scheme approved under Schedule 3 Income Tax (Earnings and Pensions) Act 2003

You are required by law to send me a form 34 giving me information about the operation of the scheme.

You must make sure that your form 34 reaches me by the date specified in the form 34 notice issued to you. If this form was otherwise issued to you, then you should return the form within three months from the date of issue, shown above.

Penalties may be chargeable where your form 34 is received late or is incomplete or inaccurate.

Explanatory notes are provided to help you complete this form. Please read them before completing this form and signing the declaration. If you have any questions about how to complete this form please contact Employee Shares and Securities Unit at the address aside or phone us on one of the numbers shown.

If there is not enough space in any part of this form, please give further details on supplementary sheets, number and attach them to the completed form when you send it to me.

If there have been no reportable events during the year you can go direct to section 9 and sign the declaration.

You should send the completed form to the address below.

Colin Gibson

Employee Shares & Securities Unit (ESSU)
Room G52
100 Parliament Street
London
SW1A 2BQ

Phone   **020 7147 2853** or **2819**
Fax   **020 7147 2747**

Notes to help you complete this form. Please read these before continuing.

About this form

Paragraph 45 Schedule 3 Income Tax (Earnings and Pensions) Act 2003 enables an officer of HM Revenue & Customs (HMRC) to ask any person to give any information that is considered necessary in relation to the operation of the scheme. This form is provided for that purpose.

Under Paragraph 42(2)(b) Schedule 3 ITEPA 2003, HMRC can withdraw approval of the scheme because of the company's failure to give the information required.

Under Section 98(1) TMA 1970 penalties may be imposed if there is a failure to provide the information requested, or if that information is inaccurate or not provided within the required time limit.

Notes for the company

This form should only be used to return details of options granted or exercised under this scheme. Please do not include on this form details of share options granted or exercised under:

- unapproved schemes or arrangements (complete form 42)
- CSOP Schemes (complete form 35)
- Enterprise Management Incentives (complete form 40).

Cessation of the scheme

If this scheme has ceased and there are no options still outstanding please tick the 'Yes' box in section 8.

Provision of additional scheme information

Normally, you will have notified Employee Share & Securities Unit (ESSU) of any changes under these sections (2, 3, 4 & 6) during the year and we do not require you to provide that information again on this form. The amount of information that you need to provide in other sections has also been reduced. The relevant section notes on the form give further details.

Further help

Further guidance on approved company share option plans in general can be found on our internet web pages, go to **www.hmrc.gov.uk/shareschemes**

1 Options granted

Complete this section if options were granted during the year ended 5 April 2009. You do not need to provide the information in columns 3 – 5, and 9.

Notes

Column 7

Enter the appropriate letter to show how market value was determined:

A   by reference to London Stock Exchange

B   by reference to New York Stock Exchange or any other recognised stock exchange (excluding AIM)

C   by reference to Shares & Assets Valuation.

If none of the above, leave blank.

1	2	3	4	5	6	7	8	9
Company Registration Number (CRN) of company over whose shares options were granted (if non-UK company, leave blank)	Date of grant	Nominal value and class of shares	First date which was used to determine market value	Number of days used to determine market value (see Notes)	Market value used to determine exercise price	How was market value determined?	Exercise price per share	Were applications scaled down? (Yes/No)

2 Exchange of options

Note – You should have already provided ESSU with details of any exchange of options and you do not need to provide those details again.

4 Amendments to scheme rules

Note – You should have already provided ESSU with details of any amendments to scheme rules and you do not need to provide those details again.

5 Options and replacement options exercised and chargeable to Income Tax

You do **not** need to provide the information in columns 14 and 19.

Note – A report is **only** required if the date of exercise was within three years of the date of grant and exercise occurred in one of the following circumstances (relevant event):

1 a change of control resulting from a general offer

2 a change of control resulting from a scheme of arrangement

3 a winding up

4 a sale out of the group of the employing company where the option holder continues to be employed by the same employer.

A report is **not** required if full details have previously been provided to ESSU at the time of the 'relevant event'.

3 Variations of share capital

Note – You should have already provided ESSU with details of any variations of share capital and you do not need to provide those details again.

10	11	12	13	14	15	16	17	18	19
Name of employee	National Insurance number	Employer	PAYE reference	Date of original grant of option	Date shares were acquired	Exercise price per share	Number of shares acquired	Market Value of a share on date shares were acquired	Reason for exercise (see Note – enter 1, 2, 3 or 4)

6 Change in constituent (participating) companies

Note – You should have already provided ESSU with details of any changes to constituent (participating) companies and you do not need to provide those details again.

7 Summary of activity for the year ended 5 April 2009

Note – Columns 20, 25, 29 & 30, only give details of options granted and exercised during this year, you do not need to provide the information in columns 21 – 24, 26 – 28, 31 and 32.

20	21	22	23	24	25	26	27	28	29	30	31	32
Total number of directors and employees to whom options were granted	Total number of contracts where the 7 year bonus is included	Total number of contracts where the 5 year bonus is included	Total number of contracts where the 3 year bonus is included	Total number of contracts where no bonus is included	Number of participants who exercised options (including replacement options)	Number of participants who ceased to take part in the scheme	If shares are listed on any recognised exchange the Market Value on last date options were exercised	Total number of shares for which options were granted (other than replacement options)	Total number of shares issued or transferred on the exercise of options (including replacement options)	Total amount paid by the participants for these shares	The highest monthly savings contributions made during this year for all contracts	Number of participants who paid this amount

8 Cessation of scheme

Note – A scheme has ceased if no options remain and no new options can be granted. Has the scheme ceased? Yes ☐ No ☐

9 Declaration

Note – The Taxes Acts require that the Company Secretary, or the person acting as the Company Secretary, should complete the declaration. If a liquidator has been appointed they should complete the declaration. (S108(1) AND (3) TMA 1970). To the best of my knowledge and belief:
• the information I have given on this Return (and on any supplementary sheets) is correct and complete
• unless otherwise stated the options were granted, exercised and shares were issued or transferred under the terms of the scheme which at the time was approved by HMRC.

Name (use capital letters)

Position in company

Phone

Signature

Date DD MM YYYY

Email

Appendix C

HMRC Company Share Option Form 35

HM Revenue & Customs

Company Share Option Plan

Date issued *DD MM YYYY*

☐☐ ☐☐ ☐☐☐☐

PAYE reference number

☐☐☐ / ☐☐☐☐☐☐☐☐☐☐

ESSU scheme reference number

☒ / ☐☐☐☐☐☐

CSOP Scheme approved under Schedule 4 Income Tax (Earnings and Pensions) Act 2003.

Year ended 5 April 2009

You are required by law to send me a form 35 giving me information about the operation of the scheme.
You must make sure that your form 35 reaches me by the date specified in the form 35 notice issued to you.
If this form was otherwise issued to you, then you should return the form within three months from the date of issue, shown above.

Penalties may be chargeable where your form 35 is received late or is incomplete or inaccurate.

Explanatory notes are provided to help you complete this form. Please read them before completing this form and signing the declaration. If you have any questions about how to complete this form please contact the Employee Shares and Securities Unit at the address aside or phone us on one of the numbers shown.

If there is not enough space in any part of this form, please give further details on supplementary sheets, number and attach them to the completed form when you send it to me.

If there have been no reportable events during the year you can go direct to section 9 and sign the declaration.

You should send the completed form to the address below.

Colin Gibson

Employee Shares & Securities Unit (ESSU)
Room G52
100 Parliament Street
London
SW1A 2BQ

Phone	**020 7147 2853** or **2819**
Fax	**020 7147 2747**

Notes to help you complete this form. Please read these before continuing.

About this form

Paragraph 33 Schedule 4 Income Tax (Earnings and Pensions) Act 2003 enables an officer of HM Revenue & Customs (HMRC) to ask any person to give any information that is considered necessary in relation to the operation of the scheme. This form is provided for that purpose.

Under Paragraph 30(2)(b) Schedule 4 ITEPA 2003, HMRC can withdraw approval of the scheme because of the company's failure to give the information required.

Under Section 98(1) TMA 1970 penalties may be imposed if there is a failure to provide the information requested, or if that information is inaccurate or not provided within the required time limit.

Notes for the company

This form should only be used to return details of options granted or exercised under this scheme. Please do not include on this form details of share options granted or exercised under:

- unapproved schemes or arrangements (complete form 42)
- SAYE Option Schemes (complete form 34)
- Enterprise Management Incentives (complete form 40).

Operation of PAYE and National Insurance contributions (NICs)

The employer is obliged to operate PAYE and NICs on all taxable amounts provided in the form of 'readily convertible assets'. A taxable gain arises when options are exercised within three years, or more than 10 years, from the date of grant. Options exercised in circumstances described in the notes on page 4 (column 27) do not constitute taxable gains.

Readily Convertible Assets (RCAs)

Securities (including shares) are readily convertible assets if:

- the securities can be sold or otherwise realised on a recognised investment exchange, such as the London Stock Exchange, the New York Stock Exchange, or
- trading arrangements are in place in respect of the securities at the time the taxable income is provided, or
- trading arrangements are likely to come into existence in accordance with arrangements or an understanding in place at the time the taxable income is provided.

In all other cases, securities are deemed to be RCAs and subject to PAYE and NICs if securities are not shares for which the company is entitled to a Corporation Tax deduction by reason of Schedule 23 of the Finance Act 2003.

NIC election

Where the employee and his employer have jointly elected that the employee will meet some, or all, of any secondary (employers') NICs due, then the amount paid by the employee should be entered in the column headed NICs election (column 30).

NIC agreement

Where the employee has entered into an agreement with his employer to meet some, or all, of any secondary (employers') NICs due then the amount paid should be entered in the column headed NICs agreement (column 31).

Cessation of the scheme

If this scheme has ceased and there are no options still outstanding please tick the 'Yes' box in Section 7.

Provision of additional scheme information

Normally, you will have notified Employee Share & Securities Unit (ESSU) of any changes under these sections (2, 3, 4 & 8) during the year and we **do not** require you to provide that information again on this form. The amount of information that you need to provide in other sections has also been reduced. The relevant section notes on the form give further details.

Further help

Further guidance on approved company share option plans in general can be found on our internet web pages, go to **www.hmrc.gov.uk/shareschemes**

1 Options granted

Complete this section if options were granted during the year ended 5 April 2009. You do not need to provide the information in columns 3 – 5, 14 and 15.

Notes

Please provide the following details if options were granted during the year ended 5 April 2009.

If options were granted on more than one date during the year, or over more than one class of shares, please photocopy this page before you fill it in, and complete each separate page in the same format as shown below.

If the company is not fully listed on the London Stock Exchange Daily Official List, New York Stock Exchange or other recognised stock exchange (excluding AIM) then prior agreement to the market value of the shares over which options are granted must be obtained from HMRC Shares & Assets Valuation.

Column 7

Enter the appropriate letter to show how market value was determined:

A   by reference to London Stock Exchange

B   by reference to New York Stock Exchange or any other recognised stock exchange (excluding AIM)

C   by reference to Shares & Assets Valuation.

If none of the above, leave blank.

Column 8

If non-UK shares were used enter the exercise price and indicate the currency in which the shares are denominated. For UK shares, leave blank.

Column 9

For UK shares enter the exercise price in pounds sterling.

For non-UK shares you must convert the exercise price shown in column 8 to pounds sterling using the exchange rate applicable at the date of grant.

1	2	3	4	5	6	7	8	9	10	11	12	13	14	15
Company Registration Number (CRN) of company over whose shares options were granted (if non-UK company, leave blank)	Date of grant	Nominal value and class of shares	First date used to determine market value	Number of days used to determine market value	Market value used to determine exercise price	How was market value determined?	Exercise price (if not in sterling state currency used)	Exercise price per share £	Largest value of options granted to one individual	Number of individuals granted the largest value of options	Total number of options granted	Number of individuals granted options	Have any options been granted in excess of £30,000? (Yes/No)	Number of individuals granted options in excess of £30,000

2 Exchange of options

Note – You should have already provided ESSU with details of any exchange of options and you do not need to provide those details again.

3 Variations of share capital

Note – You should have already provided ESSU with details of any variations of share capital and you do not need to provide those details again.

4 Amendments to scheme rules

Note – You should have already provided ESSU with details of any amendments to scheme rules and you do not need to provide those details again.

5 Exercise of options and replacement options

You do not need to provide the information in columns 23 and 24.

Notes

A report is **only** required when options (including replacement options) are exercised:

for reasons that qualify for tax relief (see notes to column 27), or

within 3 years of grant for reasons that **do not** qualify for tax relief (see notes to column 27), or

between 3 and 10 years after the date of grant and exercise has occurred at a time when the scheme is no longer approved, or

more than 10 years after the date of grant.

A report is **not** required when options (including replacement options) are exercised between 3 and 10 years from grant at a time when the scheme

remains approved.

Column 27

To qualify for tax relief an option must be exercised at a time when the scheme is approved and exercise occurs for one of the following reasons:

A Option exercised within 6 months of cessation for injury and less than 3 years from grant.

B Option exercised within 6 months of cessation for disability and less than 3 years from grant.

C Option exercised within 6 months of cessation for redundancy and less than 3 years from grant.

D Option exercised within 6 months of cessation for retirement on or after the age specified in the scheme and less than 3 years from grant.

E Option exercised within 12 months of death and less than 3 years from grant.

Column 28

If you entered 'Yes' in column 27, indicate the reason for exercise from the list, A, B, C, D, or E.

Column 29

If exercise did not qualify for tax relief, enter 'Yes' or 'No' to show whether PAYE was operated. If no tax is due then leave blank.

Column 30 – 33

An entry is only required in these columns if either a NIC election or agreement has been entered into for the employee to meet some or all of the employer's liability to NIC (see notes on page 2).

16 Name of employee	17 National Insurance number	18 Employer	19 PAYE reference	20 Date of original grant of option	21 Date shares were acquired on exercise of options	22 Number of shares acquired	23 Has option been exercised in full? (Yes/No)	24 Number of shares that remain under option from this grant

25 Exercise price per share	26 Market value of a share on the date shares were acquired	27 Does this exercise qualify for tax relief? (Yes/No)	28 Reason why exercise qualifies for tax relief	29 Has PAYE been operated? (Yes/No)	30 Amount of employer's National Insurance contributions (NICs) paid with NICs election	31 Amount of employer's National Insurance contributions (NICs) paid with NICs agreement	32 Date NICs was paid by employee	33 Date NICs was paid over to HM Revenue & Customs

616

6 Summary of activity for the year ended 5 April 2009

Note – You do not need to provide the information in columns 34, 36, 38 – 40, 42 and 43. The only information that you need to provide is that for columns 35, 37 and 41.

34	35	36	37	38	39	40	41	42	43
Number of shares over which options remained at start of the tax year	Number of shares over which options (not including replacement options) were granted during the tax year	Number of directors and employees to whom options (not including replacement options) were granted during the tax year	Number of shares issued or transferred on the exercise of options (including replacement options during the tax year)	Number of shares over which options (including replacement options) lapsed or were cancelled during the tax year	Number of shares over which options were exchanged during the tax year	Number of shares over which options (including replacement options) remained at the end of the tax year	Number of participants who exercised options (including replacement options) during the tax year	Number of directors and employees who held options (including replacement options) at the end of the tax year	If shares are listed on any recognised exchange the market value on last date options were exercised during the year

7 Cessation of scheme

Note
A scheme has ceased if no options remain and no new options can be granted.
Has the scheme ceased?

Yes ☐   No ☐

8 Change in constituent (participating) companies

Note – You should have already provided ESSU with details of any changes to constituent (participating) companies and you do not need to provide those details again.

9 Declaration

Note - The Taxes Acts require that the Company Secretary, or the person acting as the Company Secretary, should complete the declaration. If a liquidator has been appointed they should complete the declaration. (S108(1) and (3) TMA 1970). To the best of my knowledge and belief:

the information I have given on this Return (and on any supplementary sheets) is correct and complete

unless otherwise stated the options were granted, exercised and shares were issued or transferred under the terms of the scheme which at the time was approved by HMRC.

Name *(use capital letters)*

Position in company

Phone

Signature

Date *DD MM YYYY*

Email

Appendix D

HMRC Share Incentive Plan Form 39

HM Revenue & Customs

Date issued *DD MM YYYY*

☐☐ ☐☐ ☐☐☐☐

PAYE reference number

☐☐☐ / ☐☐☐☐☐☐☐☐☐☐

ESSU scheme reference number

A / ☐☐☐☐☐☐

Share Incentive Plan approved under Schedule 2 Income Tax (Earnings and Pensions) Act 2003

Year ended 5 April 2009

You are required by law to send me a form 39 giving me information about the operation of the Share Incentive Plan. You must make sure that your form 39 reaches me by the date specified in the form 39 notice issued to you. If this form was otherwise issued to you, then you should return the form within three months from the date of issue, shown above.

Penalties may be chargeable where your form 39 is received late or is incomplete or inaccurate.

Explanatory notes are provided to help you complete this form. Please read them before completing this form and signing the declaration. If you have any questions about how to complete this form please contact the Employee Shares & Securities Unit at the address aside or phone one of the numbers shown.

If there is not enough space in any part of this form, please give further details on supplementary sheets, number and attach them to the completed form when you send it to me.

You should send the completed form to the address below.

Colin Gibson

Employee Shares & Securities Unit (ESSU)
Room G52
100 Parliament Street
London
SW1A 2BQ
Phone   **020 7147 2853** or **2819**
Fax   **020 7147 2747**

Notes to help you complete this form. Please read these before continuing.

About this form

Paragraph 93 Schedule 2 Income Tax (Earnings and Pensions) Act 2003 enables an officer of HM Revenue & Customs (HMRC) to ask any person to give any information that is considered necessary in relation to the operation of the plan. This form is provided for that purpose.

Under Paragraph 83 Schedule 2 ITEPA 2003, HMRC can withdraw approval of the plan because of the company's failure to give the information required.

Under Section 98(1) TMA 1970 penalties may be imposed if there is a failure to provide the information requested, or if that information is inaccurate or not provided within the required time limit.

Notes for the company

If the company is not fully listed on the London Stock Exhange Daily Official List, New York Stock Exchange or other recognised stock exchange (excluding AIM), prior agreement with HMRC Shares Valuation & Assets is required for the market valuation on awards of shares.

Individual reporting requirements

Even though awards and withdrawals of shares under the plan are included on this form, the individual must still declare the transaction on his or her personal Tax Return where taxable income arises.

Further help

Further guidance on how to complete this Return and on Share Incentive Plans in general can be found on our internet web pages at **www.hmrc.gov.uk/shareschemes**

1 Shares awarded

Share Incentive Plan

Complete one row for each date on which shares were awarded or bought for employees and for each type of award or acquisition

Notes

Column 1 Date of award for free shares and matching shares

The award date is the date on which shares are appropriated to employees by the trustees.

Column 1 Date of acquisition for partnership shares

The acquisition date is a date, set by the trustees, which must be within 30 days of:

in a plan with no accumulation period, the last date on which the partnership share money to be applied in acquiring shares was deducted, and

in a plan with an accumulation period, the end of the accumulation period.

Column 1 Date of acquisition for dividend shares

The acquisition date is a date, set by the trustees, which must be within 30 days of the date the trustees receive the dividend to be reinvested.

Column 2 Description of shares

Give the class and denomination of share and the name of the company.

Column 3 Type of award

You must enter in this column one of the following letters A–F which describe the type of award or acquisition.

A   Free shares *without reference to performance*

These are shares awarded without any reference to performance criteria (disregard columns 9 to 15).

B   Free shares *with method 1* performance criteria

a) at least 20% of the award of shares must be without reference to performance

b) the remaining shares must be awarded by reference to performance, and

c) the highest number of shares within (b) awarded to an individual must not be more than four times the highest number of shares within (a) awarded to an individual (disregard columns 9 to 12).

C   Free shares *with method 2* performance criteria

a) some or all of the shares must be awarded by reference to performance, and

b) the awards of shares to members of the same performance unit must be on the same terms (that is varied only in accordance with level of pay, length of service or hours worked) (disregard columns 9 to 15).

D   Partnership shares

These are shares bought for employees under the plan during the year. If on any date shares are bought of more than one class or denomination then complete a separate row (disregard column 9 and columns 12 to 15).

E   Matching shares

These are shares awarded to employees for whom partnership shares are also acquired under the plan during the year. If on any date shares are awarded of more than one class or denomination then complete a separate row (disregard columns 7 to 11 and columns 13 to 15).

F   Dividend shares

These are shares bought for employees with dividends arising on plan shares. If on any date shares are bought of more than one class or denomination then complete a separate row (disregard columns 7, 8 and 10 to 15).

Column 9 Dividend shares

Dividend reinvestment cannot be more than £1,500 for each participant. Any provision for dividend reinvestment outside the plan should not be included on this Return.

Page 3

1 Shares awarded continued

1	2	3	4	5	6	7	8	9	10	11	12	13	14	15
Date of award or acquisition	Description of shares	Type of award	Market value per share on acquisition or award date	Total value of shares awarded/ acquired or dividends reinvested	Number of participants in this award or acquisition	For award types A, B, C and D (see box 3) the largest value of shares awarded to/ acquired by any one participant	For award types A, B, C and D (see box 3) the number of the participants awarded/ acquiring largest value	For award type F the largest value of dividends reinvested by any one participant	For award type D the length of any accumulation period	For award type D indicate if share applications scaled down (Yes/No)	For award type E the ratio of matching shares to partnership shares (for example 2:1)	For award type B the % of shares awarded without reference to performance conditions	For award type B the value of the highest performance award made to an individual	For award type B the value of the highest non-performance award made to an individual

2 Shares ceasing to be subject to the plan

Notes

If free, matching or partnership shares ceased to be part of the plan before the third anniversary of the award then provide details in this section by completing columns 16 to 21. You should also complete column 25 if tax arises as a consequence of the event, otherwise leave blank.

If free or matching shares ceased to be part of the plan on or after the third anniversary and less than five years after the award then provide details in columns 16 to 19, 22 and 23. You should also complete column 25 if tax arises as a consequence of the event, otherwise leave blank.

If partnership shares ceased to be part of the plan on or after the third anniversary and less than 5 years after the award then provide details in columns 16 to 19, 22 and 24. You should also complete column 25 if tax arises as a consequence of the event, otherwise leave blank.

If there is more than one class or denomination of share in respect of any of the events then complete a separate row for each.

Free shares or matching shares that were forfeited, or dividend shares ceasing to be subject to the plan, should **not** be included in this section.

Column 25 If tax arises

A charge to Income Tax arises on the date on which the shares cease to be subject to the plan unless the participant has ceased employment by reason of:

- injury, disability or redundancy
- a transfer of employment to which the Transfer of Undertakings Regulations (TUPE) apply
- a company reorganisation under which the employer company loses its associated status
- retirement on or after the age specified in the plan or death.

16	17	18	19	20	21	22	23	24	25
Name of employee	National Insurance number	Employer	PAYE reference	Date shares ceased to be subject to the plan if **within 3 years** of date of award	Free shares, matching shares and partnership shares: Total market value on date in column 20	Date shares ceased to be subject to the plan if **between** 3 and 5 years of date of award	Free shares and matching shares: Total market value on date in column 22 or if less on the award date	Partnership shares: Total market value on date in column 22 or if **less** the amount of partnership share money used to buy them	If tax arises, has PAYE/NICs been operated? Enter 'Yes' if PAYE has been operated, enter 'No' if tax is due but PAYE has not been operated. If no tax is due, leave blank

Page 5

3 Capital reorganisations and/or reconstruction

Notes

Column 27 Nature of the event

If the company has been subject to a capital reorganisation and/or reconstruction, enter one of the following letters A to G to indicate the nature of the event.

A Bonus issue

B Rights issue

C Alterations of rights attaching to a share class

D Conversion of securities including exchanges

E Company amalgamations and takeovers

F Reduction or reorganisation of share capital

G Other, please enter the nature of the reorganisation on page 8

26	27
Date of the event	Nature of the event

4 Summary of forfeiture in the event of cessation of employment within 3 years of award

Notes

Column 28

If the answer to this is Yes then an entry is required in column 30.

Column 29

If the answer to this is Yes then an entry is required in column 31.

28	29	30	31
Do awards made under the plan provide for forfeiture of free shares on leaving employment? (Yes/No)	Do awards made under the plan provide for forfeiture of matching shares on leaving employment? (Yes/No)	Where free shares are forfeited the total initial or adjusted value of free shares forfeited in the year	Where matching shares are forfeited the total initial or adjusted value of matching shares forfeited in the year

5 Withdrawal of partnership shares within 3 years of award

Note

Column 32

If the answer to this is Yes then an entry is required in column 33.

32	33
On withdrawal of partnership shares do awards made under the plan provide for forfeiture of matching shares? (Yes/No)	What was the total initial or adjusted value of matching shares forfeited in the year?

6 Market value and details of shares remaining

Notes

Column 34 The exchange

Enter one of the following letters A to E if the plan shares are listed on an exchange or F if the shares are not listed.

A London Stock Exchange Official List

B AIM

C New York Stock Exchange

D NASDAQ

E Any other exchange

F Not listed

Column 35 Share price

Enter the share price at 5 April 2009 if one of the letters A-E is entered in column 34. If not listed on any exchange then leave blank.

34	35	36
Exchange where listed	Share price at 5 April 2009	The number of shares remaining in the plan more than 5 years after award

7 Declaration

Note: The Taxes Acts require that the Company Secretary, or the person acting as the Company Secretary, should complete the declaration. If a liquidator has been appointed they should complete the declaration (S108(1) and (3) TMA 1970).

To the best of my knowledge and belief:

the information I have given on this Return (and on any supplementary sheets) is correct and complete

throughout the year (or that part of it in which plan shares were awarded or held in the plan) the plan shares satisfied the requirements of Paragraph 25 Schedule 2 ITEPA 2003. References to plan shares are to the shares that have been awarded or acquired by participants in accordance with the plan

no alterations have been made to any key features of the plan which have not been approved by HMRC. A feature of the plan is a 'key feature' if it relates to a provision that is necessary in order to meet the requirements of Schedule 2 ITEPA 2003.

Name *(use capital letters)*

Signature

Position in company

Date *DD MM YYYY*

Phone

Email

Additional information

Appendix E

HMRC Enterprise Management Incentives Form EMI 40

HM Revenue & Customs

Enterprise Management Incentives

Date issued *DD MM YYYY*

☐☐ ☐☐ ☐☐☐☐

Reference

EMI /

Enterprise Management Incentives (EMI) annual return year ended 5 April 2009
Schedule 5 Income Tax (Earnings and Pensions) Act 2003 (ITEPA 2003)

Please complete and return this form to me at the address given below.

You must send the return to me before 7 July 2009. Penalties may be charged if the return is not received on time, or is not complete or accurate.

If there is not enough room for all the entries on any page, please give details on supplementary sheets (photocopies are acceptable) and number them. Supplementary sheets should be in the same format as the return.

If there has been no activity during this year, there is no need to complete sections 1 to 6 on this form. You can go straight to section 7.

If you need help filling in this form please phone **029 2032 7400** quoting the reference shown above.

Stephen P C Hopkins

HM Revenue & Customs
Small Company Enterprise Centre
CRI
Ty Glas
Llanishen
Cardiff
CF14 5ZG

Notes to help you complete this return

AMV (Actual Market Value)

AMV (Actual Market Value) is the market value of a share after taking into account any restrictions or the risk of forfeiture as set out in the company's Articles of Association. Restrictions on the transfer of shares as contained in the Articles may be treated as restrictions for this purpose.

If the shares are subject to restrictions or the risk of forfeiture, there will be two market values, AMV and UMV (see below). AMV will be the lower of the two values.

UMV (Unrestricted Market Value)

UMV (Unrestricted Market Value) is the market value of a share ignoring any restrictions or the risk of forfeiture. See the notes above on AMV for information on restrictions.

If the shares are subject to restrictions or the risk of forfeiture, there will be two market values, AMV and UMV. UMV will be the higher of the two values.

Election under Section 431(1) of Income Tax (Earnings and Pensions) Act 2003

This applies where shares are acquired that are subject to restrictions. Please see the notes on AMV for information on restrictions. The effect of the election is that, when calculating the amount subject to Income Tax, the shares are treated as if they are not restricted shares.

1 Adjustment of options

Adjustment of options, following a variation in the share capital of the company whose shares are under option.

Complete this section if options have been adjusted to reflect a change in the company's share capital.

1	2	3	4	5	6	7	8	9	10
Unique option reference allocated by HMRC, for example 1A, 2A	Name of option holder *(surname, initials)*	Date option adjusted	Original number of shares under the option	Original price payable for a share under the option	Adjusted number of shares under the option	Adjusted price payable for a share under the option	AMV of a share at date of grant	Changed description of shares *(if applicable)*	Is the adjustment a disqualifying event? *(Yes/No)*
				£		£	£		
				£		£	£		
				£		£	£		
				£		£	£		
				£		£	£		
				£		£	£		
				£		£	£		
				£		£	£		
				£		£	£		
				£		£	£		
				£		£	£		

Notes to help you complete this section

Column 8

For information on AMV see page 2.

Column 10

A variation in the share capital of the company is a disqualifying event if it involves the creation, variation or removal of a right or restriction to which the shares are subject and this alteration is not done for commercial reasons or is done to increase the value of the shares. If the variation in the share capital is a disqualifying event, you will also need to complete section 4.

2 Replacement of options – company reorganisation

Complete this section if during this year another company obtained control of the company and the option holder released his options in return for an equivalent new option in the acquiring company. Do not enter this release of options in section 3.

1	2	3	4	5	6
Unique option reference allocated by HMRC, for example 1A, 2A	Name of option holder (surname, initials)	Date of grant of old option	Date of grant of new option	AMV of a share under old option at the date of release	Name and registered number of the company whose shares are the subject of the new option
				£	
				£	
				£	
				£	
				£	
				£	
				£	

Notes to help you complete this section

Columns 1 and 2

If all shares under option were exchanged for new shares, do not enter individual details; write 'all' in these columns.

Column 5

For information on AMV see page 2.

3 Options released or lapsed

Complete this section if during this year options have been released or lapsed (including when this occurred after a disqualifying event).

1	2	3	4	5	6	7
Unique option reference allocated by HMRC, for example 1A, 2A	Name of option holder (surname, initials)	National insurance number of option holder	Date of release or lapse of option	Number of shares in respect of which options can no longer be exercised	If money or value was received by the option holder for the release or otherwise, in connection with the option, enter the amount of money or value received	Was this amount subject to PAYE and NIC? (Yes/No)

4 Disqualifying events

Complete this page if a disqualifying event occurred in this year unless the option has been released or lapsed in this year. Where the option has been released or lapsed, enter the details in section 3 on page 4.

1	2	3	4	5	6		7
Unique option reference allocated by HMRC, for example 1A, 2A	Name of option holder *(surname, initials)*	Nature of disqualifying event *(enter A to H)*	Date of disqualifying event	Can the options still be exercised? *(Yes/No)*	At date of disqualifying event		Has this market value been agreed with HM Revenue & Customs? *(Yes/No)*
					AMV of a share (£)	UMV of a share (£)	

Notes to help you complete this section

Columns 1 and 2

If all the options suffered the same disqualifying event, do not enter individual details: write 'all' in these columns.

Column 3

Enter the appropriate letter for the type of disqualifying event:

A - the company has come under the control of another company

B - the company has ceased to meet the trading activities requirement

C - the option holder has ceased to be an employee of the company or of a qualifying subsidiary or has ceased to work there for 25 hours per week or 75% of working time

D - the terms of the option have been varied causing the value of the shares to be increased or the option no longer to be a qualifying option

E - the share capital has been varied and you have entered 'Yes' in section 1 column 10

F - the shares were converted into a different class of shares and this conversion did not happen to the whole class of shares

G - the option holder has been granted an option under an HMRC approved CSOP resulting in him or her holding EMI and CSOP options over shares with a UMV in excess of £100,000

H - the company has not started carrying on a qualifying trade within two years of the grant of the option or preparations to carry on a qualifying trade have ceased.

Column 6

For information on AMV and UMV see page 2.

5 Non-taxable exercise of options

Complete this section if during the year options (or replacement options) have been exercised and the price paid to acquire a share was not less than the market value of a share on the date the option was granted and there was no disqualifying event or the option was exercised within 40 days of the date of a disqualifying event.

There is no Income Tax payable on these exercises.

For information on AMV see page 2.

1 Unique option reference allocated by HMRC, for example 1A, 2A	2 Name of option holder (surname, initials)	3 Date of exercise	4 Number of shares acquired	5 AMV of a share at date of exercise	6 Total amount paid to acquire these shares
				£	£
				£	£
				£	£
				£	£
				£	£
				£	£
				£	£
				£	£
				£	£
				£	£
				£	£
				£	£
				£	£
				£	£
				£	£
				£	£
				£	£
				£	£
				£	£
				£	£

Page 6

6 Taxable exercise of options

Complete this section if during the year options (or replacement options) have been exercised more than 40 days after a disqualifying event and/or the price paid to acquire a share was less than the market value of a share on the date the option was granted. Include any options exercised where the disqualifying event was in the previous year(s). Income Tax is payable on such exercises (PAYE and NIC where the shares are Readily Convertible Assets).

1	2	3	4	5	6	7	8	9	10	11	12
Unique option reference allocated by HMRC, for example 1A, 2A	Name of option holder (surname, initials)	AMV of share at date of grant (£)	Exercise price paid to acquire a share (£)	Number of shares acquired	Date of exercise of option	Date of disqualifying event	AMV of a share at date of exercise (£)	UMV of a share at date of exercise (£)	Has an election been made under S431(1)? (Yes/No)	What amount was subjected to PAYE deductions? (£)	Was employer's NIC paid by election or agreement? (Yes/No)

Notes to help you complete this section

Columns 3 and 8
For information on AMV see page 2

Column 9
For information on UMV see page 2

Column 10
For information on elections under Section 431(1) see page 2

7 Nil Return

If there has been no activity during the year, please tick this box. ☐

8 Summary of EMI options

This section must be completed if there has been any activity during the year. There is no need to complete it if the box in section 7 is ticked.

Number of people holding options at 6 April 2008

☐☐☐☐☐

Number of people granted options during this year (this may include people also shown in the box above)

☐☐☐☐☐

Number of people who ceased to hold any options in this year on assignment, release, lapse or exercise of options (as shown on pages 4, 6 and 7)

☐☐☐☐☐

Number of people holding options at 5 April 2009

☐☐☐☐

Unrestricted market value of all options (taken at date of grant) still in existence at 5 April 2009

[ ]

9 Change of details

If the company has changed its name enter details below

[ ]

If the company has changed the address of its registered office, phone or fax number, please enter the new details below

New company address

[ ]

Postcode

☐☐☐☐ ☐☐☐☐

New phone number

[ ]

New fax number

[ ]

Old company name

[ ]

Old company address

[ ]

10 Certificate

I confirm that all disqualifying events have been included in this Return.

I certify that to the best of my knowledge and belief this is a complete and accurate Return.

Name *in capitals*

[ ]

Position in company

[ ]

Phone number

[ ]

Email address

[ ]

Fax number

[ ]

Signature

[ ]

Date *DD MM YYYY*

☐☐ ☐☐ ☐☐☐☐

Appendix F

HMRC Employment Related Securities Form 42

HM Revenue & Customs

Employment-related securities

Date of issue *DD MM YYYY*

☐☐ ☐☐ ☐☐☐☐

PAYE reference number

☐☐☐ / ☐☐☐☐☐☐☐☐☐☐

ESSU scheme reference number

U / ☐☐☐☐☐☐☐

Employment-related securities and options reportable events under Section 421J Income Tax (Earnings and Pensions) Act 2003

This notification is to advise you that you are required by law to send me a form 42 giving me information in relation to reportable events under Section 421J Income Tax (Earnings and Pensions) Act 2003.

You must make sure that your form 42 reaches me by 6 July 2009. If this form has been sent to you on or after 8 June 2009 you have 30 days from the date of issue, shown above, to complete it and send it to me.

Penalties may be chargeable where your form 42 is received late or is incomplete or inaccurate. Explanatory notes are provided to help you complete this form. Please read them before completing the form and signing the declaration. If you have any questions about how to complete this form please contact the Employee Shares & Securities Unit at the address aside or phone us on one of the numbers shown.

If there is not enough space in any part of this form, please give further details on supplementary sheets, number and attach them to the completed form when you send it to me.

You should send the completed form to the address below.

Colin Gibson

Employee Shares & Securities Unit (ESSU)
Room G52
100 Parliament Street
London
SW1A 2BQ

Phone	**020 7147 2843** or **2841**
Fax	**020 7147 2747**

About this form

You must provide me with details of reportable events. You can do this by using this form. If you prefer, you may use your own form, spreadsheet or letter but it must give the same details and in the same format as our own form. Detailed guidance on reportable events and how to complete form 42 is available at **www.hmrc.gov.uk/shareschemes**

Approved Share Plans/Option Schemes

Do **not** include details of options granted from HM Revenue & Customs approved Company Share Option Scheme (CSOP), Save As You Earn Option Schemes (SAYE Option Scheme) and shares acquired from approved Share Incentive Plans.

Enterprise Management Incentives (EMI)

Do **not** include details of EMI options granted up to £120,000. You must include in section 1 EMI options granted in excess of £120,000.

No reportable events

If there are no reportable events, go to page 12, complete sections 5 and 6, and return the form to me.

Companies incorporated in year ended 5 April 2009

Where a limited company is incorporated in the UK in the year ended 5 April 2009 a report of the acquisition of the initial subscriber shares (also called founder shares) by the directors or prospective directors is not required if certain conditions are fulfilled. Details of the conditions to be met are in form 42 guidance at **www.hmrc.gov.uk/shareschemes**

The majority of newly UK incorporated companies should meet the conditions and will be relieved of the requirement to complete this form.

If other transactions in shares or securities have occurred then a report is required.

Reportable events

If there are reportable events to disclose, the index below will help you identify which sections of the form you need to complete and will direct you to the appropriate page. You only need to complete those pages where there is a reportable event. Please tick the box shown opposite the reportable events for which you are giving details. Then complete and sign the declaration on page 12 and return the form to me.

Page	Reportable events	✓
	Section 1 Securities options (including share options) You must complete this section if employees were granted or exercised options (including consideration received for giving up the option)	
4	1a Summary of grants of securities options	☐
5	1b Acquisition of securities in connection with (including exercise of) securities options	☐
6	1c Assignment and release of securities options	☐
7	**Section 2 Acquisition of securities (including shares)** You must complete this section if securities were acquired by employees	☐
	Section 3 Events occurring after the acquisition of securities You must complete this section if taxable events occurred after the employee has acquired the securities	
8	3a Restricted securities (including shares)	☐
8	3b Variation of restrictions for shares acquired before 16 April 2003	☐
9	3c Conversion of securities on or after 6 April 2008	☐
9	3d Discharge of notional loans	☐
10	3e Receipt of other benefits from securities	☐
10	3f Securities sold for more than market value	☐
11	3g Artificial enhancement of market value	☐
12	Additional information – where you know that any part of the securities income reported is taxable on the remittance basis, please give the name and National Insurance number of the affected employee.	☐

1 Employment-related securities (including shares) and options

'Employment-related' securities and securities options are those acquired by reason of employment, or deemed to be so acquired because the opportunity to acquire them is made available to employees by an employer or a person connected with an employer. Securities include:

- shares in any body corporate (wherever incorporated) or in any unincorporated body constituted under the law of a country or territory outside the United Kingdom
- debentures, loans, bonds, certificates of deposit and other instruments creating or acknowledging indebtedness (other than contracts of insurance)
- options and futures.

More information is given in form 42 guidance at **www.hmrc.gov.uk/shareschemes**

2 Operation of PAYE and NICs

PAYE and NICs must be operated on all taxable amounts provided in the form of 'Readily Convertible Assets'.

Readily Convertible Assets (RCAs)

Securities (including shares) are readily convertible assets if:

- the securities can be sold or otherwise realised on a recognised investment exchange, such as the London Stock Exchange, the New York Stock Exchange, etc, or
- trading arrangements are in place in respect of the securities at the time the taxable income is provided. or
- trading arrangements are likely to come into existence in accordance with arrangements or an understanding in place at the time the taxable income is provided.

In all other cases, securities are deemed to be RCAs and subject to PAYE and NICs if securities are not shares for which the company is entitled to a Corporation Tax deduction by reason of Schedule 23 to the Finance Act 2003.

NICs agreement. Where the employee has entered into an agreement with their employer to meet some or all of any secondary NICs due then the amount paid by the employee should be entered in the column headed NICs agreement.
NICs election. Where the employee and his employer have jointly elected that the employee will meet some, or all, of any secondary NICs due then the amount paid by the employee should be entered in the column headed NICs election.

3 Non-resident or not ordinarily resident employees

- Do not complete section 1 or section 2 if the employee was non-resident at the date of option grant or securities award, and the grant or award was not in respect of prospective or former employment.
- Do not complete sections 3a, 3b, 3c, 3e and 3f if the employee was not resident (or for awards before 6 April 2008 not ordinarily resident) at the date of securities award, and the award was not in respect of employment including future or former employment when the employee was resident.

4 Remittance basis from 6 April 2008

The remittance basis may apply where an individual who acquires securities on or after 6 April 2008 (except those acquired pursuant to a securities option granted before that date) is resident but either not ordinarily resident or not domiciled in the UK. Where the employee has had both UK and non-UK duties during the 'relevant period' (broadly, the period, in which the income was earned), the income derived from the securities may be apportioned. The part relating to non-UK duties is chargeable to tax when remitted to the UK. Where you know that any part of the income you are reporting is taxable on this basis list the employee's name and National Insurance number in Additional information (Page 12).

5 Artificial adjustment of market value arising from non-commercial actions

Sections 2 and 3g apply to artificial increases and reductions in the market value of securities arising from non-commercial actions. Non-commercial actions include anything done:

- other than for a genuine commercial purpose
- as part of a scheme or arrangement designed to avoid tax or NICs
- between companies in a group of companies on terms other than would be expected from persons acting at arm's length.

6 Market value (MV) (where required)

The market value to be shown is the best available value at the time of the particular transaction. Where the value you enter on this form differs from that on which PAYE and NICs was operated, you should attach a note to this form explaining the difference. If, after the submission of this form, you determine that a different value is more appropriate, then that revised value should be used in your Corporation Tax computation and by employees in their Self Assessment Tax Returns. There is no need to send in a revised form 42. Provided that the valuation reported on this form is the best available at the time of the transaction, then if a different value is subsequently agreed, we will not regard the form as incorrect.

7 Market value (MV) to be used when calculating 'chargeable amount' (section 2)

- for security Type A – the MV (see note above)
- for security Types B, C & D (where an election has been completed) – the MV ignoring the value of any restrictions that have been disregarded
- for security Type C & D (where **no** election completed) the MV taking into account the value of any restrictions (the actual or restricted MV)
- for security Type E – the MV ignoring the value of the right to convert
- for security Type F – the MV ignoring the effect of the artificial reduction.

8 Restricted securities

Securities (or an interest in securities) are restricted securities if their market value is less than it would otherwise be because:

- there is a restriction on the rights relating to the securities, including restrictions on the rights to retain or dispose of the securities
- there is a provision under which a disadvantage may arise from the exercise of rights related to the securities, including disadvantages arising from the retention or disposal of the securities
- there will be a transfer, reversion or forfeiture of the securities, if certain circumstances arise or do not arise.

The securities are not restricted because of a provision under which they must be sold or transferred should employment end by reason of misconduct.

Page 3

637

Section 1 Securities options (including share options)

Complete one row for each grant of options.

1a Grant of securities options

You must complete this section if employment-related securities options were granted during the tax year ended 5 April 2009. Any EMI options granted in excess of £120,000 during the tax year ended 5 April 2009 should be shown in this section.

Non-resident employees

Do not include within this section grants to employees who were non-resident at the date of grant and those employees who do not have any UK duties and who are unlikely to come to the UK.

	1a.01 Date of grant	1a.02 Description of securities	1a.03 Total number of securities over which options have been granted	1a.04 Acquisition price for each security	1a.05 Number of employees granted options
1					
2					
3					
4					
5					
6					

Section 1b Acquisition of securities in connection with (including exercise of) securities options

You must complete this section where securities including shares (with or without restrictions) were acquired in connection with an employment-related securities option during the tax year ended 5 April 2009. You do not need to complete section 2 in addition to this section for shares acquired by the exercise of an option.

Column 1b.06 Non-residents

If an employee was not both resident and ordinarily resident when the option was granted before 6 April 2008, or was not resident when the option was granted after that date, enter 'Yes' here. See section 3d to provide details of the discharge of notional loans.

Column 1b.07 Date securities acquired

This is the date an employee or a person connected with the employee acquires a beneficial interest in the securities connected to the option. In most cases, this will be the date of exercise rather than the date that the securities are transferred or an ownership certificate is issued.

Column 1b.08 Elections

If an election has **not** been made to disregard restrictions leave this column blank. Enter '1' if an election has been made to disregard all restrictions. Enter '2' if an election has been made leaving some restrictions outstanding.

Column 1b.10 Market value (see note 6 on page 3)

If the securities do not carry any restrictions, enter the market value here. Where no election has been made and the securities carry restrictions (including personal restrictions) enter the restricted market value.

If '1' is in column 1b.08, enter the unrestricted market value.

If '2' is in column 1b.08, enter the market value of the securities taking into account restrictions still attached to the securities.

If the market value of these securities has been artificially reduced (see note 5 on page 3) by more than 10% in a period of 7 years ending on the date of acquisition, complete this section entering the reduced market value and also complete section 2 (security Type F, column 2.08).

Column 1b.11 Deductible amounts

The total consideration paid for the grant of the option and for the acquisition of the securities (including the exercise price) together with expenses incurred in connection with the acquisition of the securities. Do not include any expenses in connection with the sale or disposal of the securities.

Column 1b.12

Tax will be due in respect of the acquisition unless the employee was non-resident at grant (see note column 1b.06). PAYE/NICs should be operated if the securities acquired are Readily Convertible Assets (RCAs) at the time of acquisition (see note 2 page 3). Enter 'Yes' if PAYE has been operated, enter 'No' if PAYE has **not** been operated. If **no** tax is due then leave blank.

Column 1b.13 – 1b.16

An entry is only required in these columns if either a NICs election or agreement has been entered into for the employee to meet some or all the employer's liability to NICs (see note 2 page 3).

1b.01	1b.02	1b.03	1b.04	1b.05	1b.06	1b.07	1b.08	1b.09	1b.10	1b.11	1b.12	1b.13	1b.14	1b.15	1b.16
Employee name	National Insurance number	Employer	PAYE reference	Description	Enter 'Yes' if not resident at grant (see note above). If No leave blank	Date securities acquired (see note above)	Elections (see note above)	Number of securities acquired	Total market value of securities acquired (see note above)	Deductible amounts (including Exercise Price) (see note above)	If tax arises, has PAYE/NICs been operated (Yes/No)? (see note above)	NICs election (amount paid)	NICs agreement (amount paid)	Date paid by employee	Date NICs paid over to HMRC

Section 1c Assignment and release of securities options

You must complete this section if a chargeable event has arisen during the tax year ended 5 April 2009.

Chargeable events are:

the assignment or release of the securities options for consideration (unless the consideration received is another securities option), or

the receipt of a benefit in money, or money's worth, in connection with the securities option (other than the acquisition of securities shown in section 1b).

Do not complete this section if options lapse for nil consideration.

Column 1c.08

If the consideration received is in the form of securities the market value of which has been artificially reduced (see note 5 on page 3) by more than 10% in the 7 year period ending on the date the consideration is received, enter the consideration received ignoring the effect of the artificial reduction.

Column 1c.09

Tax will arise on the occasion of a chargeable event (see note above). Enter 'Yes' if PAYE has been operated, enter 'No' if PAYE has **not** been operated.

Columns 1c.10 – 1c.13

An entry is only required in these columns if either a NICs election or agreement has been entered into for the employee to meet some or all the employer's liability to NICs (see note 2 page 3).

1c.01	1c.02	1c.03	1c.04	1c.05	1c.06	1c.07	1c.08	1c.09	1c.10	1c.11	1c.12	1c.13
Employee name	National Insurance number	Employer	PAYE reference	Description	Date of chargeable event	Number of securities affected	Total amount of consideration or money's worth (see note above)	If tax arises, has PAYE/NICs been operated (Yes/No)? (see note above)	NICs election (amount paid)	NICs agreement (amount paid)	Date NICs paid by employee	Date NICs paid over to HMRC
a	b	c										
ncvj	jcnk	kjcdn	vbh	hjbsd	01/05/09	5	15.00	Yes	12.00	14.00	03/05/09	05/05/09
		jncdskj	jncdskj	jckdnkjd	02/05/09	6	16.00	Yes	14.00	16.00	11/05/09	12/05/09

Section 2 Acquisition of securities (including shares)

You must complete this section if securities were acquired during the tax year ended 5 April 2009. You do not have to complete this section for any securities that have already been reported in section 1b unless the securities have an artificially reduced market value (security Type F).

Column 2.08 Type of security. You must enter in this column one of the following letters A – G which describes the type of security acquired. Options that are part of a scheme or arrangement to avoid tax and/or NICs should be indicated as Type F and enter y in column 2.09. For restricted securities also see note 8 on page 3.

A   Unrestricted securities (disregard columns 2.09 and 2.10).

B   Restricted securities with a forfeiture provision lasting 5 years or less (disregard column 2.09).

C   Restricted securities with a forfeiture provision lasting more than 5 years (disregard column 2.09).

D   Restricted securities without a forfeiture provision (disregard column 2.09).

E   Convertible securities (disregard columns 2.09 and 2.10).

F   Securities with an artificially reduced market value (see note 5 on page 3 and disregard column 2.10).

G   Research Institute Spin Out Company (complete columns 2.01 to 2.08 and 2.11).

Column 2.09 Artificial reduction of market value (see note 5 on page 3)
For security Type F you must enter:

x to signify by reason of a non-commercial transaction

y to signify by reason of a scheme or arrangement designed to avoid tax or National Insurance contributions

z to signify by reason of inter-company transaction on a non arms length transaction. This also applies to completion of 3a.10, 3c.10, 3e.11 and 3f.10 where relevant.

Column 2.10 Elections
For security types B, C and D if there has been an election to disregard restrictions you must enter:

1 if an election has been made to disregard all restrictions

2 if an election has been made leaving some restrictions outstanding

3 if in the case of a restricted security with a forfeiture restriction you have elected with the employee for tax to arise on acquisition.

The effect of an election is to ignore some or all of the restrictions in determining the market value.

Column 2.11 Amount paid
If the price paid for the securities is less than the market value (see notes 6 and 7 on page 3) then a charge to Income Tax will arise on the acquisition of the securities. If a charge to Income Tax arises you should enter the total price paid in column 2.11 and also complete column 2.12. When calculating any amount chargeable to tax you should take into account any elections entered into and/or artificial reductions in the MV. If the price paid for the securities is at least equal to the MV then no entry is required in column 2.11 or column 2.12.

Column 2.12
PAYE/NICs should be operated if the securities acquired are Readily Convertible Assets (RCAs) at the time of acquisition (see note 2 page 3). Enter 'Yes' if PAYE has been operated, enter 'No' if PAYE has not been operated. If no tax is due then leave blank.

2.01	2.02	2.03	2.04	2.05	2.06	2.07	2.08	2.09	2.10	2.11	2.12
Employee name	National Insurance number	Employer	PAYE reference	Description	Date securities acquired	Number of securities	Type of security (see note above)	Nature of artificial reduction (see note above)	Elections (see note above)	Amount paid (see note above)	If tax arises, has PAYE/NICs been operated (Yes/No)? (see note above)

Section 3 Events occurring after the acquisition of securities

This section provides for details of taxable events arising after securities have been acquired and is in addition to any tax paid when the securities were acquired.

3a. Restricted securities (including shares)

You must complete this section if a chargeable event arises during the tax year ended 5 April 2009. Securities are restricted securities if their market value is less than it would otherwise be as a result of certain restrictions relating to transfer, reversion or forfeiture relating to the securities (see note 8 on page 3).

Chargeable events arise if:

the securities cease to be subject to forfeiture (conditional)

any restriction relating to the securities is removed or varied by any means, including the passage of time

the securities are sold to a non-associated person while still restricted.

Do not complete this section if the exceptions detailed at Section 429 ITEPA 2003 apply, or a Section 431(1) ITEPA 2003 election to ignore all restrictions has been entered into.

Column 3a.09 Chargeable amount
Shares acquired after 15 April 2003

The chargeable amount is calculated by the application of a formula. An electronic calculator to help you determine this amount is available from the address shown on the front of this form. A manual worksheet is also available from the same contact point or

from www.hmrc.gov.uk/shareschemes

If the shares are convertible, ignore the right to convert in arriving at the market value.

Conditional interests in shares acquired before 16 April 2003
The chargeable amount is the total market value less any deductible amount. Deductible amount is:

payments made to acquire the shares

amounts subject to Income Tax in respect of the acquisition of the shares.

Column 3a.11
Tax will arise on the occasion of a chargeable event (see note above). Enter 'Yes' if PAYE has been operated, enter 'No' if PAYE has not been operated.

Columns 3a.12 – 3a.15
An entry is only required in these columns if either a NICs election or agreement has been entered into for the employee to meet some or all of the employer's liability to NICs (see note 2 on page 3).

3a.01	3a.02	3a.03	3a.04	3a.05	3a.06	3a.07	3a.08	3a.09	3a.10	3a.11	3a.12	3a.13	3a.14	3a.15
Employee name	National Insurance number	Employer	PAYE reference	Description	Date securities originally acquired	Number of securities	Date of chargeable event	Total chargeable amount	Nature of artificial reduction (see note for 2.09 on Page 7)	Has PAYE/NICs been operated (Yes/No)?	NICs election (amount paid)	NICs agreement (amount paid)	Date NICs paid by employee	Date NICs paid over to HMRC

3b. Variation of restrictions for shares acquired before 16 April 2003

You must complete this section to provide details of chargeable events in the tax year ended 5 April 2009 if the value of shares acquired before 16 April 2003 is increased by an alteration in the rights or any restrictions attached to them or to other shares in the company.

Do not complete this section in connection with the variation if:

all of the shares of the same class are similarly restricted, **and**

the majority of the shares are held by persons other than employees or directors, **or**

employees or directors control the company by virtue of their holdings of that class of shares, **or**

the company is a subsidiary and has only one class of shares.

3b.01	3b.02	3b.03	3b.04	3b.05	3b.06	3b.07	3b.08	3b.09
Employee name	National Insurance number	Employer	PAYE reference	Date securities originally acquired	Date of variation	Total MV of shares directly before variation	Total MV of shares directly after variation	Number of shares

Page 8

3c. Conversion of securities on or after 6 April 2008

You must complete this section if an employee has acquired employment-related securities that carry an immediate or potential entitlement to be converted into securities of a different description and a chargeable event occurs on or after 6 April 2008.

Do not complete this section if:

all the shares of the same class are convertible securities, **and**

all the shares of the same class are affected by an event similar to the chargeable event, and either immediately before the chargeable event

- employees hold the majority of the company's shares of that class and as a consequence can control the company, **or**

- associated companies, employees and their relations do not hold the majority of the company's shares of the same class as those shares acquired, **and**

the avoidance of tax and NICs was not the main purpose, or one of the main purposes, of the arrangements under which the right or opportunity to acquire the employment-related securities was made available.

3c.09 Chargeable events are (enter a, b, c or d)

a the conversion of securities into securities of a different description

b the disposal of the securities whilst they carry the entitlement to convert

c the release of the entitlement to convert

d the receipt of money or money's worth in connection with the entitlement to convert.

3c.11 The chargeable amount is

AG – CE, where

AG is the amount of any gain realised on the occurrence of the chargeable event, and

CE is the amount of any consideration given for the entitlement to convert the employment-related securities in which they are an interest together with the amount of any expenses incurred by the holder of the employment-related securities in connection with the conversion, disposal, release or receipt.

Column 3c.12

Tax will arise on the occasion of a chargeable event (see note above). Enter 'Yes' if PAYE has been operated, enter 'No' if PAYE has **not** been operated.

Columns 3c.13 – 3c.16

An entry is only required in these columns if either a NICs election or agreement has been entered into for the employee to meet some or all of the employer's liability to NICs (see note 2 on page 3).

3c.01	3c.02	3c.03	3c.04	3c.05	3c.06	3c.07	3c.08	3c.09	3c.10	3c.11	3c.12	3c.13	3c.14	3c.15	3c.16
Employee name	National Insurance number	Employer	PAYE reference	Description	Date securities originally acquired	Number of securities	Date of chargeable event	Nature of chargeable event (see note above)	Nature of artificial reduction (see note for 2.09 on Page 7)	Total chargeable amount (see above)	Has PAYE/NICs been operated (Yes/No)?	NICs election (amount paid)	NICs agreement (amount paid)	Date NICs paid by employee	Date NICs paid over to HMRC

3d. Discharge of notional loans

You must complete this section where the employment-related securities were acquired on or after 16 April 2003 and a notional loan (see section 1b) is treated as discharged (creating a taxable amount) when the employment-related securities are disposed of other than to a connected person or an outstanding liability to pay for the securities is released.

Tax will arise on the occasion of a notional loan being discharged (see note above). Enter 'Yes' if PAYE has been operated, enter 'No' if PAYE has **not** been operated.

3d.01	3d.02	3d.03	3d.04	3d.05	3d.06	3d.07	3d.08
Employee name	National Insurance number	Employer	PAYE reference	Number of securities	Date of discharge	Amount of notional loan outstanding immediately before discharge	Has PAYE/NICs been operated (Yes/No)?

3e. Receipt of other benefits from securities

You must complete this section if an employee, or a person connected with an employee, has received a benefit on or after 6 April 2008, not otherwise chargeable to Income Tax, in connection with employment-related securities. The 'not otherwise chargeable exemption does not apply in cases involving avoidance of tax or National Insurance contributions.

If the shares acquired are in a spin out company, enter 'spin out relief' in column 3e.09 and leave the remaining columns blank.

Column 3e.12

Tax will arise on the occasion of a benefit being provided (see note above). Enter 'Yes' if PAYE has been operated, enter 'No' if PAYE has **not** been operated.

3e.01	3e.02	3e.03	3e.04	3e.05	3e.06	3e.07	3e.08	3e.09	3e.10	3e.11	3e.12
Employee name	National Insurance number	Employer	PAYE reference	Description	Date securities originally acquired	Number of securities	Date benefit received	Nature of benefit received	Amount or **MV** of the benefit	Nature of artificial reduction (see note for 2.09 on Page 7)	Has PAYE/ NICs been operated (Yes/No)?

3f. Securities sold for more than market value

You must complete this section if the employee, or a person connected with the employee, has disposed of employment-related securities on or after 6 April 2008 for more than their market value, at the time of disposal. In this case the consideration received on disposal of the employment-related securities, less their market value and expenses incurred at the time of disposal, is employment income of the employee.

Column 3f.12

Tax will arise on the occasion of securities being disposed of for more than their MV (see note above). Enter 'Yes' if PAYE has been operated, enter 'No' if PAYE has **not** been operated.

3f.01	3f.02	3f.03	3f.04	3f.05	3f.06	3f.07	3f.08	3f.09	3f.10	3f.11	3f.12
Employee name	National Insurance number	Employer	PAYE reference	Description	Number of securities	Date of disposal	Consideration received on disposal	Total **MV** of securities on disposal (see note 6 on Page 3)	Nature of artificial reduction (see note for 2.09 on Page 7)	Expenses incurred on disposal	Has PAYE/ NICs been operated (Yes/No)?

Page 10

3g. Artificial enhancement of market value

You must complete this section if the market value of an employee's employment-related securities is increased by more than 10% in a relevant period by non-commercial actions (see note 5 on page 3) and the date of the taxable event is on or after 6 April 2008 regardless of when the securities were acquired.

The relevant period runs from the date the securities are acquired to the earlier of the date of disposal or 5 April 2009. The date of the taxable event will be 5 April 2009 or the date the securities were disposed of if earlier.

Sections 3g.09 and 3g.10 Unrestricted market value (UMV)

This is the market value of the securities ignoring the effect of the restrictions, any artificial reduction, or in relation to convertible securities the MV excluding the right to convert.

Column 3g.11

Tax will arise on the occasion of a taxable event (see note above). Enter 'Yes' if PAYE has been operated, enter 'No' if PAYE has not been operated.

3g.01	3g.02	3g.03	3g.04	3g.05	3g.06	3g.07	3g.08	3g.09	3g.10	3g.11
Employee name	National Insurance number	Employer	PAYE reference	Description of securities originally acquired	Date of original acquisition	Number of securities	Date of taxable event	Total **UMV** on 5 April 2009 or, if earlier, the date of disposal (see note above)	Total **UMV**, ignoring effect of artificial increase on date of taxable event (see note above)	Has PAYE/NICs been operated (Yes/No)?

Section 4 Participating companies

If only one company is issuing employment-related securities to its employees, there is no need to complete this section. However, if this form is completed to cover a group of companies or organisations, please enter details below of the companies for whom the return applies.

4.01	4.02	4.03	4.04
PAYE reference	Corporation Tax reference	Company registration number	ESSU reference number (if any)

645

Additional information

Section 5 Nil return

If the scheme/plan was registered with the ESSU and there is no reportable event during the tax year, please enter 1 in the box.

Section 6 Declaration

Note The Taxes Acts require that the Company Secretary or the person acting as the Company Secretary should complete the declaration.

If a liquidator has been appointed they should complete the declaration. (S108(1) and (3) TMA 1970).

To the best of my knowledge and belief the information I have given on this return (and on any supplementary sheets) is correct and complete.

Name (use capital letters)

Signature

Position in company

Name of company

Date DD MM YYYY

Phone

Email

Page 12

Appendix G

Further reading

1. HMRC Enterprise Management Incentives Form EMI 1:

   http://www.hmrc.gov.uk/shareschemes/emi/emi1.rtf

2. HMRC Restricted Securities Joint Election under Section 431 ITEPA 2003:

   http://www.hmrc.gov.uk/shareschemes/s431-2-pe.rtf

3. HMRC Restricted Securities Joint Election under Section 425(3) ITEPA 2003:

   http://www.hmrc.gov.uk/shareschemes/s425-2-pe.rtf

4. HMRC Restricted Securities Joint Election under Section 430 ITEPA 2003:

   http://www.hmrc.gov.uk/shareschemes/s430-2-pe.rtf

5. Memorandum of Understanding between the BVCA and Inland Revenue on the income tax treatment of Venture Capital and Private Equity Limited Partnerships and Carried Interest:

   http://admin.bvca.co.uk/library/documents/PDF_1.pdf

6. UITF Abstract 25: National Insurance Contributions on Share Option Gains

7. UITF Abstract 32: Employee Benefit Trusts and Other Intermediate Payment Arrangements

8. UITF Abstract 38: Accounting for ESOP Trusts

Index